SAT
Red Math

Version 3.0

C2 Education is a registered trademark of C2 Educational Center, Inc.

This publication is designed to provide accurate and authoritative information in regard to the subject matter covered. It is sold with the understanding that the publisher is not engaged in rendering legal, accounting, or other professional service. If legal advice or other expert assistance is required, the services of a competent professional should be sought.

© 2019 by Reetiforp, LLC. All rights reserved. Except as permitted under the United States Copyright Act of 1976, no part of this publication may be reproduced or distributed in any form or by any means, or stored in a data base or retrieval system, without the prior written permission of the publisher.

Printed in the United States of America
International Standard Book Number:

Published by Reetiforp, LLC Publishing, a division of Reetiforp, LLC Reetiforp

Published books are available at special quantity discounts to use for sales promotions, employee premiums, or educational purposes. Please report any errors or corrections to curriculum@c2educate.com. To order more workbooks, log in to your C2 center's Emprint account. Further instructions can be found on the C2 Smart Cloud.

Copyright © 2019 C2 Education. All rights reserved. SAT® is a registered trademark of the College Board, which was not involved in the production of, and does not endorse, this product. ACT® is a registered trademark of ACT, Inc., which was not involved in the production of, and does not endorse, this product. PSAT/NMSQT® is a trademark jointly owned by the College Board and the National Merit Scholarship Corporation, which were not involved in the production of, and do not endorse, this product. None of the trademark holders are affiliated with C2 Education or this website.

Letter to Students and Parents

To Students and Parents

C2 Education's Redesigned SAT workbooks focus on curriculum that will help students build key foundation skills and learn problem-solving methods to tackle the new SAT that was released in 2016. We strongly recommend that students use these workbooks aligned with instructions and guidance from our tutors at a C2 Education center.

This book contains a number of exercises designed to guide the student through a careful, progressive process that will build layers of understanding and present problems with an increasing degree of difficulty. Each colored (belt) level will confront a variety of topics within the realms of Writing, Essay, Reading, and Math; some topics may re-appear in other workbooks of different difficulties while some topics may only appear once. The ultimate goal of C2 Education's workbooks is to cover the academic content in a comprehensive manner with sufficient practice sets and homework review.

Students will obtain the greatest benefit and improvement from these workbooks by following the workbooks from Lesson 1 to the end. Each lesson will contain the following:

- A pre-assessment designed to help our C2 tutors gauge the student's understanding prior to the lesson
- Instructional text and information focused on methodology and problem-solving thought processes
- Practice problems about the concepts presented and any connecting concepts from other lessons
- Test-like practice problems geared to emulate the real exam
- Homework problems to review academic information covered in class and the workbook

We wish you the best of luck in your academic endeavors and we hope that our workbooks will provide you with strong improvements, facilitated understanding, and expanded problem-solving skills. Thank you for being a part of the C2 family; we hope that you enjoy your time learning with us!

- C2 Education's Curriculum Team

SAT Red Math Table of Contents

Lesson 1A: Review of Arithmetic and Algebraic Concepts 9

Lesson 1B: Advanced Multi-Step Unit Conversions 21

Lesson 2A: Understanding and Analyzing Systems of Equations 35

Lesson 2B: Functions 49

Lesson 3A: Practice Sections 67

Lesson 3B: Exponential Functions 79

Lesson 4A: Rational Functions 93

Lesson 4B: Linear, Quadratic, and Exponential Models 105

Lesson 5A: Advanced Right Triangles and Trigonometry 121

Lesson 5B: Practice Sections 139

Lesson 6A: Advanced Circles 149

Lesson 6B: Graphs of Circles and Parabolas 163

Lesson 7A: Advanced Geometry 177

Lesson 7B: Advanced Volume 193

Lesson 8A: Practice Sections 207

Lesson 8B: Advanced Statistics 219

Lesson 9A: Advanced Scatterplots 235

Lesson 9B: Two-Way Tables - Probabilities and Frequencies 257

Lesson 10A: Practice Sections 273

Lesson 10B: Practice Sections 283

Lesson 11A: Review of Arithmetic and Algebraic Concepts 293

Lesson 11B: Advanced Multi-Step Unit Conversions 303

Lesson 12A: Understanding and Analyzing Systems of Equations 315

Lesson 12B: Functions 325

Lesson 13A: Practice Sections 337

Lesson 13B: Exponential Functions 347

Lesson 14A: Rational Functions 357

Lesson 14B: Linear, Quadratic, and Exponential Models 367

Lesson 15A: Advanced Right Triangles and Trigonometry 377

Lesson 15B: Practice Sections 387

Lesson 16A: Advanced Circles 397

Lesson 16B: Graphs of Circles and Parabolas 407

Lesson 17A: Advanced Geometry 417

Lesson 17B: Advanced Volume 429

Lesson 18A: Practice Sections 439

Lesson 18B: Advanced Statistics 451

Lesson 19A: Advanced Scatterplots 461

Lesson 19B: Two-Way Tables - Probabilities and Frequencies 477

Lesson 20A: Practice Sections 487

Lesson 20B: Practice Sections 497

Contributors 507

SAT Red Math
Lesson 1A: Review of Arithmetic and Algebraic Concepts

RED MATH LESSON 1A: REVIEW OF ARITHMETIC AND ALGEBRAIC CONCEPTS
Getting Your Feet Wet

Directions: The problems below are intended as a short diagnostic exam.

$$T = 2\pi \sqrt{\frac{L}{g}}$$

1. The period of a pendulum, T, can be modeled by the equation above, where L is the length of the pendulum in meters and g is the acceleration due to gravity in meters per second squared. How would the period of a pendulum be affected by changing the surrounding environment from Earth ($g = 9.8$ m/s²) to the moon ($g = 1.6$ m/s²)?
   A) The period of a pendulum on the moon would be approximately six times that of its period on Earth.
   B) The period of a pendulum on the moon would be approximately one-sixth that of its period on Earth.
   C) The period of a pendulum on the moon would be approximately five-halves that of its period on Earth.
   D) The period of a pendulum on the moon would be approximately two-fifths that of its period on Earth.

2. A projectile following the path $s(t) = -4.9t^2 + 114.66t$ is launched straight upwards from ground level at an initial time of 0 seconds. After how many seconds did the projectile reach its peak height?
   A) 5.85 seconds
   B) 11.7 seconds
   C) 23.4 seconds
   D) 670.76 seconds

3. Colorimetry is a technique for determining the concentration of colored substances by measuring how much light they absorb; absorbance and concentration have a linear relationship. A solution with a 1.50×10^{-6} molar concentration of β-carotene (a plant pigment) has an absorbance of 0.201, while 2.70×10^{-6} molar has an absorbance of 0.361. Anthraquinone (a dye derived from coal tar) has an absorbance of 0.148 at a concentration of 3.25×10^{-6} molar, while 6.45×10^{-6} molar gives an absorbance of 0.292. At what concentration do the two substances have the same absorbance?
   A) 0 molar
   B) 8.49×10^{-9} molar
   C) 3.84×10^{-1} molar
   D) They will never have the same absorbance.

Version 3.0

Unauthorized copying or reuse of any part of this page is illegal.

SAT Red Math
Lesson 1A: Review of Arithmetic and Algebraic Concepts

RED MATH LESSON 1A: REVIEW OF ARITHMETIC AND ALGEBRAIC CONCEPTS

Wading In

Directions: Read the explanation for each problem type mentioned below. Pay special attention to the methods and techniques used to solve the sample problems. Then, do the practice exercises that follow; use the appropriate method to solve each problem.

TOPIC OVERVIEW: REVIEW

This lesson will focus on many different arithmetic and algebraic concepts found in our Blue Level material. However, these problems will be a little trickier than those found in Blue Level. Read each question carefully, and we'll work through them together.

SAMPLE PROBLEM 1: REVIEW

$$T = 2\pi\sqrt{\frac{L}{g}}$$

The period of a pendulum, *T*, can be modeled by the equation above, where *L* is the length of the pendulum in meters and *g* is the acceleration due to gravity in meters per second squared. How would the period of a pendulum be affected by changing the surrounding environment from Earth ($g = 9.8$ m/s^2) to the moon ($g = 1.6$ m/s^2)?

A) The period of a pendulum on the moon would be approximately six times that of its period on Earth.
B) The period of a pendulum on the moon would be approximately one-sixth that of its period on Earth.
C) The period of a pendulum on the moon would be approximately five-halves that of its period on Earth.
D) The period of a pendulum on the moon would be approximately two-fifths that of its period on Earth.

Although many questions on the SAT seem very conceptual, they can be solved quickly even when the underlying concept isn't immediately obvious. For a question like this, let's set up both equations for *T* using the two different values of *g*:

$$T = 2\pi\sqrt{\frac{L}{g}} \qquad\qquad T = 2\pi\sqrt{\frac{L}{g}}$$

$$T = 2\pi\sqrt{\frac{L}{9.8}} \qquad\qquad T = 2\pi\sqrt{\frac{L}{1.6}}$$

At this point, we can plug in whichever value of *L* we'd like, as the length of the pendulum does not change in the two situations. Then we can just compare the two values of *T*.

$$T = 2\pi\sqrt{\frac{L}{9.8}} \qquad\qquad T = 2\pi\sqrt{\frac{L}{1.6}}$$

$$T = 2\pi\sqrt{\frac{100}{9.8}} \qquad\qquad T = 2\pi\sqrt{\frac{100}{1.6}}$$

$$T = 2\pi\sqrt{\frac{100}{9.8}} \qquad T = 2\pi\sqrt{\frac{100}{1.6}}$$
$$T = 20.07 \qquad T = 49.67$$

So, our second value of T is approximately 2.5 times the first value of T. This ratio will hold true for any value of L. Our answer must be **C**.

SAMPLE PROBLEM 2: REVIEW

A projectile following the path $s(t) = -4.9t^2 + 114.66t$ is launched straight upwards from ground level at an initial time of 0 seconds. After how many seconds did the projectile reach its peak height?
  A) 5.85 seconds
  B) 11.7 seconds
  C) 23.4 seconds
  D) 670.76 seconds

Typically, the fastest method of solving questions involving quadratic functions like this involves graphing the function in a graphing calculator.

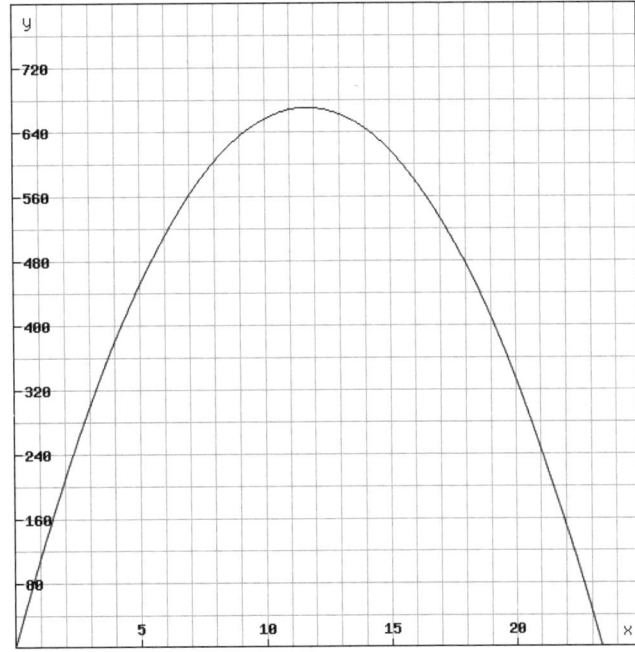

Since the function is quadratic, its highest (or lowest) point will always occur exactly between the two x-intercepts. Our intercepts appear when $x = 0$ and $x \approx 23$, so our maximum point must be exactly between them, at approximately 11.5. Thus, our answer is **B**.

If we're not allowed to use our calculators on a question like this, we still have other options. Most Algebra courses teach a method of finding the x-coordinate of the vertex of a quadratic with the formula $y = Ax^2 + Bx + C$ via the expression $-\frac{B}{2A}$. Using this expression, we get a more exact answer, $x = 11.7$.

SAT Red Math
Lesson 1A: Review of Arithmetic and Algebraic Concepts

SAMPLE PROBLEM 3: REVIEW

Colorimetry is a technique for determining the concentration of colored substances by measuring how much light they absorb; absorbance and concentration have a linear relationship. A solution with a 1.50×10^{-6} molar concentration of β-carotene (a plant pigment) has an absorbance of 0.201, while 2.70×10^{-6} molar has an absorbance of 0.361. Anthraquinone (a dye derived from coal tar) has an absorbance of 0.148 at a concentration of 3.25×10^{-6} molar, while 6.45×10^{-6} molar gives an absorbance of 0.292. At what concentration do the two substances have the same absorbance?

    A) 0 molar
    B) 8.49×10^{-9} molar
    C) 3.84×10^{-1} molar
    D) They will never have the same absorbance.

Since the relationship between absorbance and concentration is linear, we should be able to come up with the equation of a line for each chemical compound:

β-carotene: $(1.50 \times 10^{-6}, 0.201)$ and $(2.70 \times 10^{-6}, 0.361)$
Anthraquinone: $(3.25 \times 10^{-6}, 0.148)$ and $(6.45 \times 10^{-6}, 0.292)$

Next, we should come up with equations to both lines:

β-carotene: $y = 1.3333 \times 10^5 x + 0.001$
Anthraquinone: $y = 4500x + 0.00175$

The point where these two lines meet can be found by setting the two equations equal to each other:

$$1.3333 \times 10^5 x + 0.001 = 4500x + 0.00175$$

Solving, we get $x = 8.49 \times 10^{-9}$. Our answer is **B**.

WRAP-UP

The questions in the following lessons will cover a variety of topics that we have reviewed in much more detail in both our Yellow and Blue Math Workbooks. Please refer back to those books for extra practice if you find any of these types of questions particularly challenging. Good Luck!

RED MATH LESSON 1A: REVIEW OF ARITHMETIC AND ALGEBRAIC CONCEPTS
Learning to Swim

Directions: Answer each question below.

PRACTICE SET 1 (CALCULATOR)

1. In physics, acceleration due to gravity is given by the equation $g = \frac{GM}{r^2}$, where G is the gravitational constant $6.67 \times 10^{-11} \frac{N \cdot m^2}{kg^2}$, M is mass, and r is distance. If the acceleration due to gravity of an object increases by a factor of 10, by what factor does the distance change?

2. The growth and decay of one organism in a lab experiment is mapped by the equation $f(t) = 1.025t^2 - 2.45t + 3.68$, and the growth and decay of a second organism in the same experiment is mapped by the equation $f(t) = -0.685t^2 + 3.7t + 11.04$. At what time will the two organisms exist in equal quantities if t is measured in hours and the experiment begins at 8:45 AM? Round to the nearest minute.

3. Mike's US credit card company charges him a fee of 2.7% on all purchases made in Canada. The fee is not processed in Canada, but appears when he checks his statement in the United States. If Mike was charged $153 in Canada, and was charged $141.56 on his statement in the United States, how many US dollars are equivalent to one Canadian dollar?

4. If $f(x) = \sqrt[3]{x^2} + 3x$, $g(x) = \frac{x^2}{2} + 4x + 15$, and $h(x) = -4x^2 + \sqrt{x} + 2$, then what is the value of $f\left(g\left(h\left(\frac{3}{2}\right)\right)\right)$ when rounded to the nearest tenth?

5. If $|x + 6| = 2x + 3$, what is the value of x^2?

RED MATH LESSON 1A: REVIEW OF ARITHMETIC AND ALGEBRAIC CONCEPTS
Diving into the Deep End

Directions: Answer each question below.

PRACTICE SET 2 (CALCULATOR)

6. The value of an investment is compounded annually at 7.5%. At the end of how many years will the investment have at least doubled in value?
   A) 9
   B) 10
   C) 11
   D) 16

7. The volume of a sphere is given by $V = \frac{4}{3}\pi r^3$. If a sphere with radius 3 cm is melted down with no change in volume and reformed into a cube, what will the length of one of the sides of the cube be?
   A) 4.84 cm
   B) 6.97 cm
   C) 10.6 cm
   D) 12.6 cm

$$x^2 = a^2 + 2b^2$$
$$y^2 = a^2 - b^2$$

8. Using the equations above what is a in terms of x and y?
   A) $\frac{(x+y)}{3}$
   B) $\pm\sqrt{\frac{x^2+2y^2}{3}}$
   C) $\pm\sqrt{\frac{2x^2-y^2}{3}}$
   D) $\frac{(x^2+y^2)}{2}$

9. According to Einstein's Special Theory of Relativity, an object's mass m is related to its rest mass m_0 and velocity v by the equation

$$m = \frac{m_0}{\sqrt{1-\frac{v^2}{c^2}}}$$

   where c is the velocity of light (3×10^8 meters/second). By what percentage is the mass of a rocket increased over its rest mass when it is travelling at one tenth of the speed of light?
   A) 0.5%
   B) 1%
   C) 2%
   D) 10%

10. If $x^{-\frac{2}{5}} = 2a^{-2}$ and $y^{\frac{2}{5}} = 3b^2$, what is $(xy)^{\frac{1}{5}}$ in terms of a and b?
    A) $\pm\frac{2a}{3b}$
    B) $\pm ab\sqrt{\frac{3}{2}}$
    C) $\pm\sqrt{\frac{3a}{2b}}$
    D) $\pm\frac{2a^2}{3b^2}$

$$\frac{m^2+n^2}{m+n} + \frac{m^2-n^2}{m-n} + \frac{2mn}{m+n}$$

11. Simplify the above expression.
    A) $2(m+n)$
    B) $2m$
    C) $\frac{m+n}{m-n}$
    D) $m^2 + n^2$

12. A curve is given parametrically by the equations

$$x = 2\sqrt{t}$$
$$y = 3t - 4$$

What is the slope of the line joining the point where $x = 4$ to the point where $y = 5$?
A) 0
B) 0.536
C) 5.60
D) 9.33

$$\frac{1}{a+x} + \frac{1}{b+x} = \frac{1}{c+x}$$

13. The equation above is equivalent to which of the following quadratic equations?
A) $ax^2 + bx + c = 0$
B) $x^2 + 2cx + bc + ac - ab = 0$
C) $2x^2 + (b + c - a)x + b(c + a) = 0$
D) $\frac{x^2}{a^2} + \frac{b^2}{c^2} = \frac{b+c}{a+c}$

14. Jamie fits a straight line to a set of data points by eye. She measures the slope and intercept using a ruler and determines the equation of the fitted line to be
$$y = 3.64x + 0.8$$

She then realizes that it makes more sense physically for the fitted line to go through the origin, and draws the line from the origin to the point on her original line where $x = 5$. What is the slope of her new line that passes through the origin?

$$x^2 = \frac{6x}{5-x}$$

15. What is the sum of the roots of the above equation?

PRACTICE SET 3 (CALCULATOR)

16. The dimensions of a triangle are changed by increasing the base by a factor of x^2 and by increasing the height by a factor of $2x^3$. Which of these expressions could be used to find the percent increase in the area of the triangle?
A) $100(b + x^2)(h + 2x^3)$
B) $2x^5 - 1$
C) $100(2x^5 - 1)$
D) $(b + x^2)(h + 2x^3) - 1$

For questions 17 and 18 use the following equations:

$$f(x) = x^2 + 3$$
$$g(x) = \sqrt{x - 6}$$
$$h(x) = \sqrt[3]{x + 9}$$
$$i(x) = x^3$$

17. Which of the following expressions has a domain of all real numbers?
A) $g(h(x))$
B) $h(g(x))$
C) $g(i(x))$
D) $h(f(x))$

18. Of the following choices, what produces a linear equation?
A) $f(i(x))$
B) $i(f(x))$
C) $h(i(x))$
D) $i(h(x))$

For questions 19 and 20 use the following equations:

$$h_1(t) = -4.9t^2 + 11.16t$$
$$h_2(t) = -1.86t^2 + 11.16t$$

19. A projectile's height in meters is modeled by the equation $h_1(t)$, which contains Earth's gravitational pull. The projectile's height can also be modeled by $h_2(t)$ if it contains Mars's gravitational pull. If the initial time for both equations is at $t = 0$, what is the difference between the time the projectile reaches the ground in $h_1(t)$ and the time it reaches the ground in $h_2(t)$?
    A) 2.28 seconds
    B) 3.04 seconds
    C) 3.72 seconds
    D) 6 seconds

20. What is the difference between the maximum height of $h_2(t)$ and the maximum height of $h_1(t)$?
    A) 6.35 meters
    B) 10.39 meters
    C) 11.16 meters
    D) 16.74 meters

$$P_1 + \rho g h_1 + \frac{1}{2}\rho v_1^2 = P_2 + \rho g h_2 + \frac{1}{2}\rho v_2^2$$

21. Using the equation above what is the expression for $h_1 - h_2$ in terms of all other variables in the equation?
    A) $\frac{P_1 - P_2 + \frac{1}{2}\rho(v_1^2 - v_2^2)}{\rho g}$
    B) $\frac{P_2 - P_1 + \frac{1}{2}\rho(v_2^2 - v_1^2)}{\rho g}$
    C) $\frac{P_2 - P_1 + \rho(v_2^2 - v_1^2)}{2\rho g}$
    D) $\frac{P_1 - P_2 + \rho(v_1^2 - v_2^2)}{2\rho g}$

22. If a cylinder has height h and radius r, which of the following would NOT result in a doubling of the cylinder's volume?
    A) Doubling the radius.
    B) Doubling the height.
    C) Increasing the radius by a factor of $\sqrt{2}$.
    D) Doubling the radius and halving the height.

23. Kyu is running through an airport to catch a plane. There is a motorized walkway halfway to the plane that will carry him the rest of the way to its entrance. He reckons that he will be able to run at 10 mph for half the total distance, and will have to walk at 3 mph over the other half. What strategy will get him to the plane the fastest?
    A) Walk to the walkway, then run on it.
    B) Run to the walkway, then walk on it.
    C) Walk and run equal distances both on and off the motorized walkway.
    D) It doesn't matter; all of the above methods will take the same amount of time.

24. The path of a ball that is thrown vertically upwards, starting with a time of 0 seconds, is $h(t) = -4.9t^2 + 20.2t$. If $h(t)$ represents the height of the ball in meters, what is the maximum height, to the nearest tenth of a meter, that the ball reaches?

25. If $1 + \frac{1}{d} + \frac{1}{d^2} + \frac{1}{d^3} = 1$, what is the value of $d^2 + d + 1$?

RED MATH LESSON 1A: REVIEW OF ARITHMETIC AND ALGEBRAIC CONCEPTS
Race to the Finish

Directions: Answer each question below.

HOMEWORK SET (CALCULATOR)

1. Given the functions $f(x) = 2x - 5$, $g(x) = x^4$, and $h(x) = \sqrt{x}$, which of these compositions produces a quadratic function over the domain $(0, \infty)$?
   A) $g(f(x))$
   B) $f(g(x))$
   C) $h(f(x))$
   D) $g(h(x))$

2. An engineer designing new cube-shaped packaging for a product is interested in studying how the ratio of the volume to the surface area scales at different sizes. If she quadruples the lengths of the edges, how will the ratio change?
   A) It will stay the same.
   B) It will be multiplied by a factor of 4.
   C) It will be multiplied by a factor of 16.
   D) It will be multiplied by a factor of 64.

3. Abhi, a computer scientist, develops four different programs to solve a problem. Listed below are the equations for the time, T, that each program will take, given different inputs, x. If the input can range from 0 to 20 and Abhi wants to minimize the maximum amount of time that each program could take, which method should he pick?
   A) Program 1: $T(x) = 5x + 3$
   B) Program 2: $T(x) = -x^2 + 20x$
   C) Program 3: $T(x) = -10x + 200$
   D) Program 4: $T(x) = 2^x$

4. The curvature of a surface, K, is computed using the equation $K = \frac{eg - f^2}{EG - F^2}$, where $e, g, f, E, G,$ and F are variables known as the coefficients of the fundamental forms. Which of the following operations will leave the curvature of a surface unchanged?
   A) Multiply $e, f, E,$ and F by 2.
   B) Divide e by $\frac{1}{2}$ and multiply E by 2.
   C) Divide f and F by 2, multiply g and G by 2.
   D) Multiply g and G by 4, multiply f and F by 2.

5. Rajiv measures the amount of power used by a computer as it boots. After 1 second, he finds that the computer is using 1 watt of power. After 2 seconds, the computer is using 8 watts of power. After 3 seconds, the computer is using 27 watts of power, and the data continues to follow this pattern. If Rajiv wants to transform this data to be linear, what operation should he perform?
   A) Square the number of seconds.
   B) Take the cube root of the wattage.
   C) Multiply the number of seconds by 3.
   D) Divide the wattage by 3.

6. Coulomb's Law is given by $F = \frac{kq_1q_2}{r^2}$ where q_1 and q_2 are the charges of the particles, r is the distance between the particles, and k is Coulomb's constant. If the charge of each of the particles is doubled, and the distance is increased by a factor of 2, what is the effect on the force between them?
   A) The force is doubled.
   B) The force is reduced by a factor of 2.
   C) The force is reduced by a factor of 4.
   D) The force remains the same.

Version 3.0

SAT Red Math
Lesson 1A: Review of Arithmetic and Algebraic Concepts

$$3x^5y - 24x^3y^3 + 48xy^5$$

7. Factor the polynomial above.
   A) $3xy(x+2y)^3(x-2y)$
   B) $3xy(x+2y)^2(x-2y)^2$
   C) $3xy(x+2y)(x-2y)^3$
   D) $3xy(x-2y)^4$

8. As summer approaches, Joe needs to fill his swimming pool with water. If his pool is in the shape of a rectangular prism with length l ft, width w ft, and depth d ft, and his hose can release water at a rate of r in^3/sec, then how many minutes would it take to fill his pool?
   A) $\dfrac{5r}{lwd}$
   B) $\dfrac{lwd}{60r}$
   C) $\dfrac{lwd}{5r}$
   D) $\dfrac{144lwd}{5r}$

9. The Ideal Gas Law formula is represented by the following equation:

   $$PV = nRT$$

   where $P, V, n,$ and T are the pressure, volume, amount of substance, and temperature, respectively, of a system. (R is constant.)

   For a given system, which of the following does NOT result in doubling the pressure?
   A) Halving V, halving n, and doubling T
   B) Halving V, doubling n, and halving T
   C) Doubling V, doubling n, and doubling T
   D) Doubling V, halving n, and halving T

$$2x + y = 4$$
$$kx + \frac{5}{2}y = l$$

10. For the system of equations above, for what values of k and l does the system yield infinitely many solutions?
    A) $k = \dfrac{4}{5}$ and $l = \dfrac{8}{5}$
    B) $k = \dfrac{4}{5}$ and $l = -10$
    C) $k = -5$ and $l = \dfrac{8}{5}$
    D) $k = 5$ and $l = 10$

11. At Sally's donut shop, it costs her $0.20 to make each donut and $0.75 to make each éclair. If she sells d donuts and e éclairs each hour and charges p_d dollars per donut and p_e dollars per éclair, then which of the following represents her profit margin during an 8-hour work day? [Note: Profit margin is defined as profit divided by revenue.]
    A) $1 - \dfrac{0.2d + 0.75e}{p_d d + p_e e}$
    B) $1 - \dfrac{0.2d - 0.75e}{p_d d + p_e e}$
    C) $8 - \dfrac{1.6d + 6e}{p_d d + p_e e}$
    D) $8 - \dfrac{1.6d - 6e}{p_d d + p_e e}$

$$r(x) = \frac{3}{2}x + 7$$
$$s(x) = -\frac{1}{2}x + 3$$

12. Using the equations above, which of the following is NOT a solution to the inequality $\frac{1}{2}r(x) \leq s(x-4)$?
    A) $x = -4$
    B) $x = -2$
    C) $x = 0$
    D) $x = 2$

SAT Red Math | 19
Lesson 1A: Review of Arithmetic and Algebraic Concepts

Use the following information for questions 13 through 15:

Over a 24-hour period, the temperature (T in Celsius) as a function of time (t in hours) is given by the following quadratic equation:

$$T(t) = -\frac{1}{6}(t^2 - 24t + 63)$$

Assume that time starts ($t = 0$) at 2 AM.

13. Which of the following is the best approximation for the temperature at 9:30 AM?
    A) 8.9°C
    B) 10.1°C
    C) 11.3°C
    D) 12.5°C

14. When is the temperature zero degrees Celsius?
    A) 3 AM and 9 PM
    B) 5 AM and 11 PM
    C) 10:30 AM
    D) 12:30 PM

15. The formula to convert degrees Celsius (C) to degrees Fahrenheit (F) is given by the following equation:

$$F = \frac{9}{5}C + 32$$

    What is the maximum temperature (in Fahrenheit) over the 24-hour period?
    A) 13.1°F
    B) 32°F
    C) 56.3°F
    D) 63°F

16. If $f(x) = 3x^5$ and $g(x) = 2x^{-4}$, what is $g(f(x))$?
    A) $20x$
    B) $\frac{162}{x}$
    C) $\frac{162}{x^{20}}$
    D) $\frac{2}{81x^{20}}$

$$h(x) = (kx - 1)(lx + 2)^2(mx - 3)^3(nx + 4)^4$$

17. For the function $h(x)$ above, k, l, m, and n are constants. What is the greatest number of distinct zeroes that can exist for the function $h(x)$?

$$2x = 4 + Ay$$
$$4y = \frac{1}{2}Ax - 4$$

18. Which value of A will make the above system of equations have infinitely many solutions?

19. Larry plans to invest an amount of money, m, into a project with an expected return of $E(m) = 0.5m^2 - 10$. He will then take the return from that project and invest it into a second project with an expected return of $R(m) = (m + 10)^3$. If Larry invests double the amount that he's planning to, by what factor will his expected return after both projects be multiplied?

20. Victoria's Footwear Factory makes pairs of sneakers, which take 2 laces, 2 soles, and 4 leather strips. It also makes pairs of Velcro shoes, which take 2 soles and 2 leather strips. Finally, it makes special "foot socks" using 5 leather strips for every 2 socks manufactured. If the factory has 400 laces, 1600 soles, and 3000 leather strips on hand and uses all of them, how many foot socks will it produce?

Version 3.0

SAT Red Math
Lesson 1B: Advanced Multi-Step Unit Conversions

RED MATH LESSON 1B: ADVANCED MULTI-STEP UNIT CONVERSIONS
Getting Your Feet Wet

Directions: The problems below are intended as a short diagnostic exam.

1. A local coffee shop sells coffee beans in two sized bags: 8 ounces for $7.95 or 1 pound for $15.78. Additionally, the shop sells disposable cups in packs of 10 for $4.63 or 15 for $6.42.

   Clay needs to buy coffee and disposable cups for a school fundraiser; he buys 6 pounds of coffee and 180 disposable cups.

   Part 1: How much money, in dollars, did Clay save by buying the larger sizes of both coffee and disposable cups instead of the smaller sizes of each? (16 ounces = 1 pound)

   Part 2: Two tablespoons of ground coffee beans will make approximately 6 ounces of coffee, and each ounce of coffee beans is equivalent to 5 tablespoons of ground beans. If each cup holds 4 ounces of coffee, how many more cups should be purchased so that all of the coffee can be given out?

SAT Red Math
Lesson 1B: Advanced Multi-Step Unit Conversions

RED MATH LESSON 1B: ADVANCED MULTI-STEP UNIT CONVERSIONS
Wading In

Directions: Read the explanation for each problem type mentioned below. Pay special attention to the methods and techniques used to solve the sample problems. Then, do the practice exercises that follow; use the appropriate method to solve each problem.

TOPIC OVERVIEW: MULTI-STEP UNIT CONVERSIONS

In previous lessons, we focused mainly on questions that featured straight unit conversions: We were given a number or measurement in a specific unit and asked to convert to another unit. Unfortunately, the SAT will include these unit conversion in other questions, especially those that focus on concepts like rates. Let's look at one of these:

SAMPLE PROBLEM 1: MULTI-STEP UNIT CONVERSIONS

A local coffee shop sells coffee beans in two sized bags: 8 ounces for $7.95 or 1 pound for $15.78. Additionally, the shop sells disposable cups in packs of 10 for $4.63 or 15 for $6.42.

Clay needs to buy coffee and disposable cups for a school fundraiser; he buys 6 pounds of coffee and 180 disposable cups.

Part 1: How much money, in dollars, did Clay save by buying the larger sizes of both coffee and disposable cups instead of the smaller sizes of each? (16 ounces = 1 pound)

Part 2: Two tablespoons of ground coffee beans will make approximately 6 ounces of coffee, and each ounce of coffee beans is equivalent to 5 tablespoons of ground beans. If each cup holds 4 ounces of coffee, how many more cups should be purchased so that all of the coffee can be given out?

Each SAT will feature one "Extended Thinking" question—these questions will require you to solve a multi-step problem, providing grid-in answers for each part. To solve questions like these, we must always analyze the question first.

We know that the coffee shop has two different prices for coffee—8-ounce bags for $7.95 and 1-pound bags for $15.78. Since Clay needs 6 pounds of coffee, let's figure out how much it costs him to buy 6 pounds via each method:

$$\frac{6 \text{ pounds of coffee}}{1} \times \frac{\$15.78}{1 \text{ pound of coffee}} = \$94.68$$

$$\frac{6 \text{ pounds of coffee}}{1} \times \frac{16 \text{ ounces of coffee}}{1 \text{ pound of coffee}} \times \frac{\$7.95}{8 \text{ ounces of coffee}} = \$95.40$$

SAT Red Math
Lesson 1B: Advanced Multi-Step Unit Conversions

Next, let's do the math to figure out how much Clay will spend on cups:

$$\frac{180 \text{ cups}}{1} \times \frac{\$6.42}{15 \text{ cups}} = \$77.04$$

$$\frac{180 \text{ cups}}{1} \times \frac{\$4.63}{10 \text{ cups}} = \$83.34$$

So, if Clay buys both the large sizes of coffee and cups, he will spend $94.68 + $77.04 = $171.72. When he buys the smaller size of each, he spends $95.40 + $83.34 = $178.74. So the answer to **Part 1**, the difference in price between the two, is **$7.02**.

For **Part 2**, we should start by figuring out how many cups of coffee we can make with our current amount of coffee beans:

$$6 \text{ pounds of beans} \times \frac{16 \text{ oz of beans}}{1 \text{ pound of beans}} \times \frac{5 \text{ tbsp of ground beans}}{1 \text{ oz of beans}} \times$$

$$\frac{6 \text{ oz of coffee}}{2 \text{ tbsp of ground beans}} \times \frac{1 \text{ cup}}{4 \text{ oz of coffee}} =$$

So, we get 360 cups of coffee. Since Clay originally purchased 180 cups, we need **180** more cups.

WRAP-UP

Questions involving unit conversions will show up frequently on the SAT, so get used to solving them. Always analyze the units of any given situation, as units are one of the easiest places to make a simple mistake. For the following problem sets use the unit conversions provided below. Good Luck!

SAT Red Math
Lesson 1B: Advanced Multi-Step Unit Conversions

Metric Conversions:

Prefix	Symbol	Factor
Giga	G	10^9
Mega	M	10^6
Kilo	k	10^3
Hecto	h	100
Deca	da	10
Deci	d	0.1
Centi	c	0.01
Milli	m	0.001

Distance Conversions:

Inch (in)		2.540 cm
Foot (ft)	12 in	0.305 m
Yard (yd)	3 ft	0.914 m
Mile (mi)	5280 ft	1.609 km

Area Conversions:

Acre	43,560 ft²	4046.9 m²

Weight Conversions:

Ounce (oz)		28.349 g
Pound (lb)	16 oz	453.59 g
Ton	2000 lb	907.185 kg

Volume Conversions:

Teaspoon (tsp)		4.927 mL
Tablespoon (tbsp)	3 tsp	14.781 mL
Fluid Ounce (fl oz)	2 tbsp	29.563 mL
Cup (cp)	8 fl oz	0.237 L
Pint (pt)	2 cup	0.473 L
Quart (qt)	2 pint	0.946 L
Gallon (gal)	4 quart	3.784 L
	1 cm³	1 mL

Temperature Conversions:

$$F = \frac{9}{5}C + 32$$

Time Conversions:

Second (sec)	
Minute (min)	60 secs
Hour (hr)	60 mins
Day	24 hrs
Week	7 days
Year	52 weeks

SAT Red Math
Lesson 1B: Advanced Multi-Step Unit Conversions

RED MATH LESSON 1B: ADVANCED MULTI-STEP UNIT CONVERSIONS
Learning to Swim

Directions: Answer each question below.

PRACTICE SET 1 (CALCULATOR)

1. One gallon of gasoline costs $3.09 in Alexandria, VA. It costs €1.35 per liter in Maastricht, the Netherlands. If $1 is about 0.79 euros, which town has more expensive gasoline? By how much is it more expensive, in US$ per gallon? Round to the nearest cent.

2. Mr. Dinkins wants to cover his 3-acre yard with a special insect-resistant grass that he can only order from a company in Japan. The company only sells full bags of grass seed, and each bag of seed costs 1,500 yen and can cover 1,000 square meters of land. Shipping is an additional flat rate of 4,500 yen. If one dollar equals 107.27 yen, how much should Mr. Dinkins expect to spend, in US dollars rounded to the nearest cent, on his yard?

3. A hotel in Indonesia will let an American tourist pay for a room in US$ at the daily foreign exchange rate of his check-out time, but will charge him a 6% convenience fee. The hotel room one particular tourist booked cost 350,000 Rupiahs per night. When the tourist looks at his credit card statement back in the States, he sees that he was charged $90.86 total for staying 3 nights in his room. What was the daily foreign exchange rate used by the bank during check out time, in Indonesian Rupiahs per US dollar? Round your answer to the nearest whole number.

4. Mary's dog Lola needs to eat exactly 8 cups of food per day. Mary normally feeds her dog only dry food, but because of Lola's recent health problems, Mary is going to start mixing in one container of Swiss-formulated vitamin concentrate with Lola's daily dry dog food intake. Each cup of dry dog food weighs 180 grams per cup. Each vitamin concentrate container weighs 100 grams. If the total amount of food Lola eats needs to stay exactly the same, how many pounds of dry dog food does Lola consume in thirty days? Round to the nearest tenth of a pound.

5. Lisa wants to send a delivery package before the post office closes. The post office is 2.3 miles away, and will be closing in 25 minutes. Lisa is able to run in a straight path to the post office. How fast must she run, in feet per second, to arrive exactly when the post office is closing? Round to the nearest tenth.

Version 3.0

SAT Red Math
Lesson 1B: Advanced Multi-Step Unit Conversions

RED MATH LESSON 1B: ADVANCED MULTI-STEP UNIT CONVERSIONS
Diving into the Deep End

Directions: Answer each question below.

PRACTICE SET 2 (CALCULATOR)

6. The drug company DoWell, Inc. states that an advanced antibiotic it manufactures should be administered so that the amount taken per day does not exceed 2.0 mg per kilogram of body weight. What is the maximum daily dose, to the nearest milligram, for someone who weighs 145 pounds?
   A) 30 mg
   B) 66 mg
   C) 132 mg
   D) 638 mg

7. In medieval Poland, some farmers measured their fields in "morgens." Historians have determined that a morgen is approximately 2500 square meters. Approximately how many square feet are in one-tenth of a morgen? Round your answer to the nearest square foot.
   A) 230
   B) 2687
   C) 4556
   D) 26870

8. The densest naturally occurring element is Osmium. A 6 inch × 4 inch × 2 inch bar weighs approximately 17.8 kg. What is the density of Osmium in grams per cubic centimeter? Round your answer to the nearest tenth of a gram per cubic centimeter.
   A) $22.6 \frac{g}{cm^3}$
   B) $145 \frac{g}{cm^3}$
   C) $370.8 \frac{g}{cm^3}$
   D) $22,600 \frac{g}{cm^3}$

9. The maximum acceptable level for a certain pollutant in soil is 15.0 parts per million or 15.0 grams pollutant per 1 million grams of soil. What is the maximum amount of milligrams of pollutant allowable in 10.0 pounds of soil?
   A) 0.068
   B) 4.2
   C) 41.8
   D) 68.0

10. If Anderson can write x lines of computer code in one minute, how many lines of code can he write in n work days if each work day is z hours?
    A) $\frac{60z}{nx}$
    B) $\frac{480x}{nz}$
    C) $60nxz$
    D) $144nxz$

11. Alesia needs 80 square yards of cloth to make curtains for the windows of her new house. The store that supplies the cloth, however, only sells the cloth in square meters. If a square meter of cloth costs $5.15, how much will Alesia need to spend on fabric for her curtains?
    A) $114.77
    B) $147.02
    C) $344.18
    D) $376.62

Version 3.0

Lesson 1B: Advanced Multi-Step Unit Conversions

12. One barn is equal to $1.0 \times 10^{-28} m^2$. When a barn is multiplied by a megaparsec (a very large unit of length used for measuring the distances between galaxies), the result is a human-scaled unit of volume. Convert a barn megaparsec to teaspoons. (A parsec is 3.036×10^{16} meters, 1 cubic meter = 264.172 gallons)
    A) 0.62
    B) 1.4
    C) 2.7
    D) 4.8

13. Coffee beans have a density of 35 pounds per cubic foot. Each coffee bean has a mass of 0.15 grams, and it takes 70 coffee beans to produce 1 cup of coffee. Which of the following most closely approximates the volume of coffee beans, in cubic feet, that is required to produce 1 quart of coffee? (Density is mass divided by volume.)
    A) 0.001
    B) 0.003
    C) 0.092
    D) 2.6

14. Rashid is eating at a restaurant with a relative in Germany. At the end of the meal, he discovers he has forgotten to convert his U.S. dollars to euros. The restaurant agrees to exchange his 40 dollars at the current exchange rate of $1.32 dollars per euro. The meal costs 17 euros. Rashid decides to take the change he receives (in euros) and convert it into Turkish lira for a future trip. The exchange rate is 2.88 Turkish lira per euro. How many Turkish lira does Rashid obtain from the change he received at the restaurant? Round your answer to the nearest lira.

15. Madison goes to a hardware store to buy paint for a house remodeling project. The sales clerk at the store tells her that each gallon of the paint she wishes to use covers about 300 square feet of wall. The paint is sold in 4 liter cans and the project requires 370 square meters of walls to be painted. What is the smallest number of cans of paint Madison must buy to complete the remodeling job?

Practice Set 3 (Calculator)

16. How much would a brick of gold 10 inches by 3 inches by 2 inches be worth? The density of gold is $19,320 \frac{kg}{m^3}$, and gold costs $1219.40 per ounce.
    A) $ 235,588.08
    B) $ 818,695.87
    C) $ 85,978,717.91
    D) $ 1,263,807,543.40

17. On Esther's latest business trip, she started out with US$ 1,000 cash. She changed the money into Brazilian real, and then spent 800 real. She then went to South Korea, changed her money to won, and spent 230,000 won. Her next stop was Israel, where she spent 1500 sheqel (after changing her money first, of course). Her last stop was in Hungary, where she changed her money to forint, withdrew 100,000 forint from her bank, and spent 47,000 forint. After returning to the US, she decided to trade her remaining forint in for some cryptocoin. How much cryptocoin was she able to get? (US$ 1 = 2.38 real; 1 won = 0.0022 real; 1 won = 0.0035 sheqel; 1 forint = 0.015 sheqel; and 1 forint = 0.000012 cryptocoin)
    A) 0.02 cryptocoin
    B) 0.8 cryptocoin
    C) 28 cryptocoin
    D) 107 cryptocoin

18. If a battleship is travelling 40 knots, how fast is it going in $\frac{m}{s}$? (1 knot is approximately 1.15 miles per hour)
    A) 3.2
    B) 10.8
    C) 20.6
    D) 40

SAT Red Math
Lesson 1B: Advanced Multi-Step Unit Conversions

19. Most countries use the International System of Units. In contrast, the humorous Furlong/Firkin/Fortnight system of units of measurement draws attention by being extremely old fashioned and off-beat. How fast is a furlong per fortnight in cm/min? (1 furlong = 660 feet, 1 fortnight = 2 weeks)
    A) 0.00017 cm/min
    B) 0.034 cm/min
    C) 0.29 cm/min
    D) 1 cm/min

20. A lightyear is the distance light travels in a year. Convert that to miles. (Light travels with a speed of $3 \times 10^8 \frac{m}{s}$.)
    A) 3.27×10^4
    B) 5.88×10^{12}
    C) 8.29×10^{13}
    D) 9.72×10^{22}

21. It takes 10.2 electron volts (eV) of energy to excite the electron in one hydrogen atom. How many moles of hydrogen atoms could be excited by the energy in one medium apple? One medium apple has 95 Calories. 1 Calorie = 4186 Joules, 1 eV = 1.6×10^{-19} Joules, and 1 mole = 6.022×10^{23} atoms.
    A) 0.4
    B) 0.7
    C) 1.2
    D) 3.5

22. Chris wants to buy duct tape for a class project. The project requires 14 feet of duct tape, and Chris currently does not have any. If the price of duct tape is $0.50 per 20 centimeters, how much money, to the nearest cent, must he spend to purchase the necessary amount of duct tape? (Assume that it is possible to purchase any length of duct tape)
    A) $0.89
    B) $4.20
    C) $10.67
    D) $213.36

23. Driving to work and back takes Wendy a total of 30 minutes at an average speed of 42 miles per hour. Wendy's car can travel 40 miles for each gallon of gasoline, and the local gas station charges $3.00 per gallon of gas. If driving to and from work comprises the entirety of Wendy's driving and Wendy works 5 days a week, how much money to the nearest cent will she spend on average on gas every week? (Assume that she makes one round-trip to and from her workplace per day.)
    A) $1.58
    B) $3.68
    C) $7.88
    D) $11.03

24. Julie wants to keep her vacation relaxing, so she only wants to drive 4 days a week. If she drives 6 hours a day at an average of 55 mph, what is her expected length of time in weeks to drive the 5069 km from Seattle, Washington to Portland, Maine? Round to the nearest tenth of a week.

25. What is the difference in weight in ounces between 10 cubic feet of salt water (density of 1030 $\frac{kg}{m^3}$) and 10 cubic feet of fresh water (density 1000 $\frac{kg}{m^3}$)? Round to the nearest whole number.

RED MATH LESSON 1B: ADVANCED MULTI-STEP UNIT CONVERSIONS
Race to the Finish

Directions: Answer each question below.

HOMEWORK SET (CALCULATOR)

1. Dave is planning to cook a dish using a recipe, but he must first take a trip to the grocery store. The ingredients that he needs to buy are sugar, milk, and table salt, as he currently has none of these. The recipe calls for 22 ounces of sugar, 1 quart of milk, and 3 pinches of table salt. At the grocery store, sugar is sold in 1 pound units for $4.00 per unit; milk is sold in 1 gallon units for $3.50 per unit; and table salt is sold in 750 milligram units for $0.50 per unit. Items must be bought in whole unit amounts at the store. If Dave wants to buy enough of each of the above items to follow the recipe, what is the least amount of money he can spend? (Assume 1 pinch of table salt is equivalent to 500 milligrams.)
   A) $7.38
   B) $9.88
   C) $10.00
   D) $12.50

2. A certain cube has a surface area of 54 cm². Five of the cubes have a combined mass of 540 g. What is the density of one cube, in g/cm³?
   A) $\frac{\sqrt{6}}{9}$
   B) 4
   C) 10
   D) 20

3. Florence's Fabrics offers fabrics in two different widths, 45" and 60". A 1-yard length of each of the types of cloth, 45"-wide cotton and 60"-wide cotton, costs $5.50 and $6.00, respectively. What is the positive difference in unit price for the two options, in cents per square inch? Round your answer to the nearest hundredth.
   A) 0.06
   B) 0.4
   C) 0.74
   D) 2.22

4. Daisy's car has a fuel economy of 25 miles per gallon (mpg) for city driving and 32 mpg for highway driving. On a road trip, she drove a total of 50 miles in cities and 600 miles on highways. If she purchased gas for $4.10 per gallon, what was the average cost per mile of her trip, in dollars? Round your answer to the nearest hundredth.
   A) 0.13
   B) 0.15
   C) 6.95
   D) 7.64

5. A certain ceiling hook can support a maximum of 200 pounds of weight. An interior designer wants to use a chain that weighs 3 pounds per foot to hang a chandelier from the ceiling hook. Which of the following functions f models the maximum chandelier weight that can be supported for a chain that is x inches long?
   A) $f(x) = 200 - 3x$
   B) $f(x) = \frac{200 - 3x}{12}$
   C) $f(x) = 200 - \frac{1}{4}x$
   D) $f(x) = 200 - 36x$

6. On a certain street the parking meters take both coins and debit cards. Parking costs a flat rate at all hours, with an additional fee charged for using a debit card. Shelly paid $5.60 to park for 3.5 hours, which included a $0.35 fee for using her debit card. How many minutes would a customer paying with change get for a quarter?
   A) $\frac{1}{6}$
   B) $\frac{2}{3}$
   C) 10
   D) 40

Version 3.0

SAT Red Math
Lesson 1B: Advanced Multi-Step Unit Conversions

7. For a physics lab, Corazon found that an object weighing m kilograms took t minutes to fall d centimeters through a viscous fluid. She finds the net force F that pulled it down using the formula $F = \frac{md}{t^2}$, giving her a force in units of $\frac{\text{kg·cm}}{\text{min}^2}$. In order to convert this force to Newtons, a unit of force equivalent to $\frac{\text{kg·m}}{\text{sec}^2}$, what does she need to do now?
   A) Multiply by 6000
   B) Divide by 6000
   C) Multiply by 360,000
   D) Divide by 360,000

8. The motor on a toy car turns the wheels one complete revolution every 3 seconds. If the diameter of the wheels is 3 cm, how many meters would the car travel in 3 minutes and 45 seconds? Round your answer to the nearest hundredth.
   A) 2.25
   B) 6.50
   C) 7.07
   D) 14.14

9. Janelle is adding music to her phone. She sees that a song that is 3 minutes and 30 seconds long takes up 4.9 megabytes (MB) of memory on the device. If the device already has 2 hours and 15 minutes of music, which of the following functions f models the total memory, in MB, required when she adds t more minutes of music to the device, provided that there is a linear relationship between the length of a song and the amount of memory it uses?
   A) $f(t) = 30 + 1.4t$
   B) $f(t) = 96 + 0.71t$
   C) $f(t) = 189 + 1.4t$
   D) $f(t) = 200 + 1.48t$

10. A common type of shipping container used to transport goods on ships, trucks, and trains is 8' 6" tall, 8' wide, and 20' long. When empty, the container weighs 4,850 lbs. If the density of water is 62.4 lb/ft³, what is the maximum weight that can be carried inside a sealed container so that the container's density is at most the same as that of water? Round your answer to the nearest pound.
    A) 80,014
    B) 81,012
    C) 84,864
    D) 85,862

11. One type of photovoltaic solar panel uses silicon crystals. The cylindrical crystals are sliced into wafers, and most manufacturers further cut the circular wafers into the largest square inscribed in the circle. If a wafer with a diameter of 30 cm can receive at most 70.7 watts (W) of power from the sun, what is the maximum amount of power a square wafer made from the same circle can receive? Assume that there is a linear relationship between the area of the wafer and the amount of power it can receive. Round your answer to the nearest tenth of a watt.
    A) 11.3
    B) 27.8
    C) 45
    D) 90

12. Cletus covers an acre of his flat land with an inch-thick layer of cement. Assuming the density of the cement is $3.15 \frac{\text{g}}{\text{cm}^3}$, how much cement, in kilograms, did Cletus put on his land?
    A) 26,791.98
    B) 32,378.90
    C) 267,919.81
    D) 323,788.98

13. An electric company charges 15 cents per kilowatt-hour of electrical energy used. A family that is currently on contract with this company is trying to decipher their most recent bill. During the previous billing period of 31 days, a portion of the family's electricity consumption came from light bulb usage. In their house, there are 10 light bulbs that each run at 60 watts, and each one is turned on for an average of 75 minutes per day. How much does the family pay each billing period to run their light bulbs? (1 kilowatt-hour equals a 1 kilowatt power source doing 1 hour of work)
    A) $3.49
    B) $23.25
    C) $209.25
    D) $3487.50

14. A cylindrical tube with one closed end is filled to its limit with water. The tube has a radius of 52 millimeters and a length of 100 inches. What is the approximate mass of water in the tube in kilograms? (Density is mass divided by volume; water has a density of 1 gram per milliliter)
    A) 6.9 kilograms
    B) 8.5 kilograms
    C) 21.6 kilograms
    D) 2200 kilograms

15. At the beginning of a hiking trail, there is a map that is scaled 1:10,000, meaning 1 unit on the map corresponds to 10,000 equivalent units on the actual trail. A hiker wants to determine how long the trail is, and thus proceeds to measure the trail on the map. She finds that the trail is 32 inches on the map. What is the length of the actual trail in miles? Round to the nearest hundredth of a mile.
    A) 0.16 mile
    B) 5.05 miles
    C) 15.15 miles
    D) 60.61 miles

16. A painter is planning to paint all four vertical walls of a room with red paint. The room is shaped like a rectangular prism: the base (floor) is a rectangle with a length of 16 feet and a width of 12 feet, and the height (ceiling) of the room is 10 feet from the ground. The painter plans to paint each wall such that the final thickness of the painted layer will be 1 millimeter. At the local supply store, red paint comes in 3 liter cans priced at $26.00 per can. If the painter can only buy whole cans, what is the least amount of money the painter can spend? (Assume that the painter begins with zero paint and the room has no doors or windows. Ignore the effect of paint drying.)
    A) $451
    B) $468
    C) $1353
    D) $4853

SAT Red Math
Lesson 1B: Advanced Multi-Step Unit Conversions

17. Visible light is perceived by humans as the colors red, red-orange, orange, yellow, green, blue, indigo, and violet. The frequency of light corresponding to each of these colors is about 1.075 times the frequency of the previous color in the list. Light also obeys the relationship $\lambda = \frac{3 \times 10^{17}}{f}$, where λ is the wavelength of the light in nanometers and f is the frequency in hertz. If the wavelength of red light is 680 nanometers, what is the wavelength of violet light in nanometers? Round your answer to the nearest whole nanometer.

18. Using information from the previous question, at what wavelength does the wavelength of light in nanometers equal the frequency in terahertz? Round your answer to the nearest whole nanometer. (Note: 1 Terahertz = 10^{12} Hertz)

19. A light-year is the distance traveled by a photon through a vacuum in a 365-day year. If a photon can travel through vacuum at 186,000 miles per second, how far, in quadrillions of miles, is it from the Sun to Alpha Centauri, which is 4 light-years away? Round your answer to the nearest tenth. (Note: 1 quadrillion miles = 10^{12} miles)

20. Using information from the previous question, a photon can travel 75% as fast underwater as it can in vacuum. A photon is fired into the Sun end of a water-filled tube which stretches from the Sun to Alpha Centauri. Another photon is fired from Alpha Centauri toward the Sun through the vacuum of space. How many days, to the nearest day, does it take for the photons to pass one another?

SAT Red Math
Lesson 2A: Understanding and Analyzing Systems of Equations

RED MATH LESSON 2A: UNDERSTANDING AND ANALYZING SYSTEMS OF EQUATIONS

Getting Your Feet Wet

Directions: The problems below are intended as a short diagnostic exam.

$$y^2 + 5 = x^2$$
$$|x| = y + 1$$

1. If (x, y) is a solution to the above system of equations, which of the following is a possible value of $y - x$?
   A) −5
   B) 0
   C) 1
   D) 5

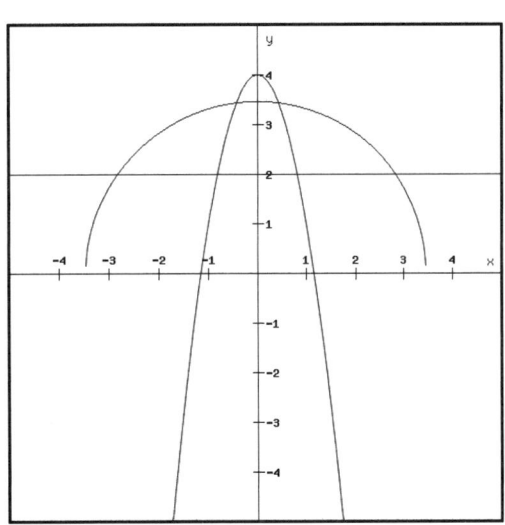

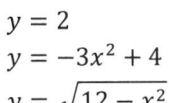

$y = 2$
$y = -3x^2 + 4$
$y = \sqrt{12 - x^2}$

2. A system of three equations and their graphs in the xy-plane are shown above. How many solutions does the system have?
   A) Zero
   B) Two
   C) Four
   D) Six

3. A run-bike duathlon is a competition in which athletes run a certain distance then bike to the finish line. At his first competition, Mike ran at a constant rate of 6 miles per hour then biked at a constant rate of 10 miles per hour, reaching the finish line in 2 hours. The following year at the same duathlon, Mike was able to increase his constant run rate and bike rate to 9 and 15 miles per hour, respectively, allowing him to finish in 1 hour and 20 minutes. Which of the following systems of equations could be solved to find x, the running distance, and y, the biking distance (in miles) of the run bike duathlon?

A) $6x + 10y = 2$
$9x + 15y = \frac{4}{3}$

B) $\frac{x}{6} + \frac{y}{10} = 2$
$\frac{x}{9} + \frac{y}{15} = \frac{4}{3}$

C) $\frac{x}{6} + \frac{y}{10} = 2$
$\frac{x}{9} + \frac{y}{15} = 1.2$

D) $6x + 10y = 2$
$9x + 15y = 1.2$

RED MATH LESSON 2A: UNDERSTANDING AND ANALYZING SYSTEMS OF EQUATIONS
Wading In

Directions: Read the explanation for each problem type mentioned below. Pay special attention to the methods and techniques used to solve the sample problems. Then, do the practice exercises that follow; use the appropriate method to solve each problem.

TOPIC OVERVIEW: SYSTEMS OF EQUATIONS

There are many things the SAT can do to make solving a system of equations more difficult. Let's look at a question that involves purely algebraic methods before delving into new territory:

SAMPLE PROBLEM 1: SYSTEMS OF EQUATIONS

$$y^2 + 5 = x^2$$
$$|x| = y + 1$$

If (x, y) is a solution to the above system of equations, which of the following is a possible value of $y - x$?

- A) −5
- B) 0
- C) 1
- D) 5

Remember that absolute value bars represent the distance something is from 0. So, to get rid of the absolute value bars, set your expression equal to two different things: one positive and one negative:

$$x = y + 1 \qquad x = -y - 1$$

Now all we have to do is plug both equations into the top equation and solve for y.

$$y^2 + 5 = x^2$$

$$y^2 + 5 = (y+1)^2 \qquad\qquad y^2 + 5 = (-y-1)^2$$
$$y^2 + 5 = y^2 + 2y + 1 \qquad\qquad y^2 + 5 = y^2 + 2y + 1$$

Since both of these expressions are the same, there's no real need to solve both:

$$y^2 + 5 = y^2 + 2y + 1$$
$$4 = 2y$$
$$2 = y$$

Now that we have a value for y, we can plug it into either of our two equations to find possible values of x:

$$y^2 + 5 = x^2$$
$$2^2 + 5 = x^2$$
$$9 = x^2$$
$$x = \pm 3$$

So, our possible values of $y - x$ are 5 and −1. Our answer must be **D**.

SAMPLE PROBLEM 2: SYSTEMS OF EQUATIONS

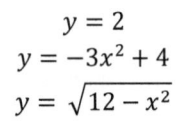

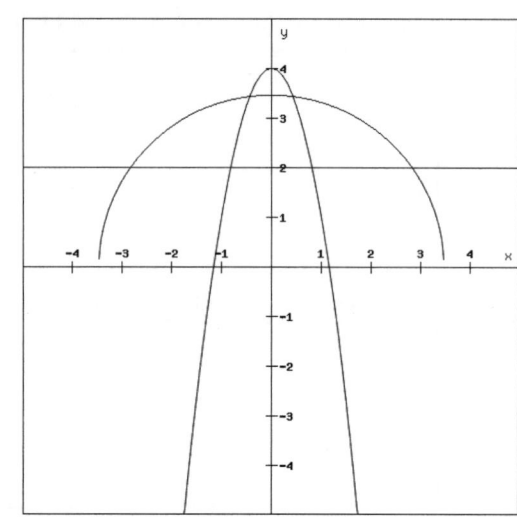

$y = 2$
$y = -3x^2 + 4$
$y = \sqrt{12 - x^2}$

A system of three equations and their graphs in the xy-plane are shown above. How many solutions does the system have?

A) Zero
B) Two
C) Four
D) Six

The graphical solution to a system of equations is the point at which all three curves meet. In the above case, the three curves do not intersect anywhere. Thus, our answer is **A**, zero solutions.

Lesson 2A: Understanding and Analyzing Systems of Equations

SAMPLE PROBLEM 3: SYSTEMS OF EQUATIONS

A run-bike duathlon is a competition in which athletes run a certain distance then bike to the finish line. At his first competition, Mike ran at a constant rate of 6 miles per hour then biked at a constant rate of 10 miles per hour, reaching the finish line in 2 hours. The following year at the same duathlon, Mike was able to increase his constant run rate and bike rate to 9 and 15 miles per hour, respectively, allowing him to finish in one hour and 20 minutes. Which of the following systems of equations could be solved to find x, the running distance, and y, the biking distance (in miles) of the run bike duathlon?

A) $6x + 10y = 2$
$9x + 15y = \frac{4}{3}$

B) $\frac{x}{6} + \frac{y}{10} = 2$
$\frac{x}{9} + \frac{y}{15} = \frac{4}{3}$

C) $\frac{x}{6} + \frac{y}{10} = 2$
$\frac{x}{9} + \frac{y}{15} = 1.2$

D) $6x + 10y = 2$
$9x + 15y = 1.2$

Setting up the equations to word problems involving rates can be very tricky. First of all, remember that $distance = rate \times time$. However, notice that we aren't given the distances necessary; instead, we are given rates and a total time. So, let's rearrange our formula to solve for time: $time = \frac{distance}{rate}$. Let's try to set up an equation for each year to give us total time.

$$Time_{First\ year} = Time_{Biking} + Time_{Running}$$
$$Time_{Second\ year} = Time_{Biking} + Time_{Running}$$

$$Time_{First\ year} = \frac{distance_{biking}}{rate_{biking}} + \frac{distance_{running}}{rate_{running}}$$
$$Time_{Second\ year} = \frac{distance_{biking}}{rate_{biking}} + \frac{distance_{running}}{rate_{tunning}}$$

$$2 = \frac{x}{6} + \frac{y}{10}$$
$$\frac{4}{3} = \frac{x}{9} + \frac{y}{15}$$

So, our answer must be **B**.

WRAP-UP

The SAT will present systems of equations in a variety of ways, so it's important to get as much practice as possible with them. Work through the next set of problems to master the concepts presented. Good Luck!

SAT Red Math
Lesson 2A: Understanding and Analyzing Systems of Equations

RED MATH LESSON 2A: UNDERSTANDING AND ANALYZING SYSTEMS OF EQUATIONS
Learning to Swim

Directions: Answer each question below.

PRACTICE SET 1 (NO CALCULATOR)

$$x^2 - 3y^2 = 0$$
$$2x^2 + 4y = 2$$

1. Using the system of equations above, what is the product of the two possible values of $x^2 y$?

$$x = \sqrt{y^2 + 2y}$$
$$y + \sqrt{x^2 + 2} = 3$$

2. What ordered pair satisfies the system of equations above?

$$x^2 - 3y^2 = 1$$
$$5y = 3x - 1$$

3. Using the system of equations above, what is the largest possible value of $y^2 - 2x$, where (x, y) is a solution to the system?

$$x^2 = y + 2x$$
$$5y - x = 12$$

4. Using the system of equations above, if $x \geq 0$ and $y \geq 0$, what is the value of $\frac{x}{y}$, where (x, y) is a solution to the system?

$$xy = 2$$
$$x^2 = 3 + y^2$$

5. Using the system of equations above, what is the value of $|xy|$? (Assume x and y are both real)

Red Math Lesson 2A: Understanding and Analyzing Systems of Equations
Diving into the Deep End

Directions: Answer each question below.

Practice Set 2 (No Calculator)

$$y = x - 1$$
$$y = -x^2 + 3x + 2$$

6. Which of the following lists both real solutions to the system of equations above?
   A) $(-2, -3)$ and $(1, 2)$
   B) $(-2, -1)$ and $(2, 3)$
   C) $(-1, -2)$ and $(3, 2)$
   D) $(2, 1)$ and $(3, 2)$

$$y = \sqrt{12 - x}$$
$$y = -x$$

7. Using the system of equations above, what is a possible value of $\sqrt{y}$?
   A) 0
   B) $\sqrt{3}$
   C) 2
   D) 3

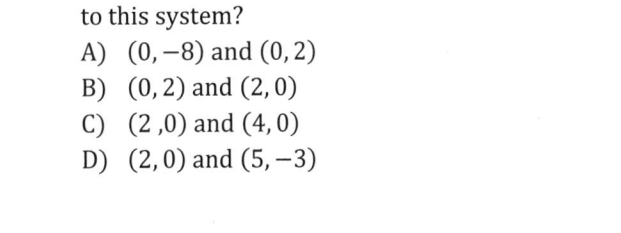

$$7p - 2q + r = 14$$
$$3p = 2q - 2r$$
$$p + r = -4$$

8. Using the system of equations above, what is the value of q?
   A) -6
   B) -3
   C) 2
   D) 3

9. The graph above shows a system of equations with one linear and one quadratic equation in the xy-coordinate plane. What are the solutions to this system?
   A) $(0, -8)$ and $(0, 2)$
   B) $(0, 2)$ and $(2, 0)$
   C) $(2, 0)$ and $(4, 0)$
   D) $(2, 0)$ and $(5, -3)$

10. If $y = 4x - 7$ and $2x^2 - 4y = 14$, at which of the following points do the graphs of the equations intersect in the xy-coordinate plane?
    A) $(0, 4)$
    B) $(3, 1)$
    C) $(7, 14)$
    D) $(7, 21)$

11. At which two points in the xy-coordinate plane does the line $y = x + 3$ intersect the circle $(x - 2)^2 + y^2 = 25$?
    A) $(-3, -6)$ and $(2, 5)$
    B) $(-3, 0)$ and $(2, 5)$
    C) $(-2, 1)$ and $(3, 6)$
    D) $(-1, 4)$ and $(6, 3)$

12. A skyscraper will be built on two adjacent, square-shaped lots. The combined area of the lots is 16,900 square meters. The side length of Lot A is 20 meters more than twice the side length of Lot B. What is the side length of Lot B?
    A) 50 meters
    B) 66 meters
    C) 112 meters
    D) 120 meters

$$m^2 + n^2 = 20$$
$$m - 2 = n$$

13. Using the system of equations above, what is a possible value for m?
    A) -4
    B) -2
    C) 0
    D) 2

$$s = \frac{1}{3}r + 60$$
$$s = \left(\frac{r}{10}\right)^2 + 44$$

14. A medical researcher identifies two models to estimate the relationship between a person's resting heart rate, r, and that person's systolic blood pressure, s. The equations for the two models are shown above. If $r \geq 0$ and $s \geq 0$, what resting heart rate results in the same systolic blood pressure for both models?

$$2a = -c - 1$$
$$3b - 4a = 9$$
$$2b + 7 = c$$

15. Using the system of equations above, what is the value of c?

Practice Set 3 (No Calculator)

$$y = 3x^2 - 5x + 20$$
$$y = 2x^2 - 3x + 35$$

16. What is the distance between the two points of intersection of the above system of equations?
    A) -3
    B) 5
    C) 8
    D) $8\sqrt{2}$

$$x^2 + y^2 = 144$$
$$x^2 - 4x + y^2 = 0$$

17. Find the x-coordinate of the point of intersection of the above system.
    A) -36
    B) 2
    C) 36
    D) No solution

$$by = 2ax + 20$$
$$ay = 5ax - 3b$$

18. If a and b are constants such that the unique solution (x, y) to the above system is $(6, 28)$, what is the value of a^b?
    A) 2
    B) 3
    C) 6
    D) 9

$$4y = -3x + 11$$
$$3y = 4x - 23$$
$$7y = x + 13$$

19. What is the solution to the above system of equations?
    A) $(1, 2)$
    B) $(5, -1)$
    C) $(8, 3)$
    D) No solution

SAT Red Math

Lesson 2A: Understanding and Analyzing Systems of Equations

20. In the previous problem, what is the area of the region bounded by the three equations?
    A) $\frac{25}{2}$
    B) $\frac{25\sqrt{2}}{2}$
    C) 25
    D) $25\sqrt{2}$

$$-2x - 4y - 2z = -4$$
$$x + 2y + z = 2$$

21. Which equation, when added to the above system, will yield an infinite number of solutions?
    A) $x - y + 2z = 4$
    B) $2x + 5y + z = 4$
    C) $2x - 2y + 4z = 8$
    D) $2x + 4y + 2z = 4$

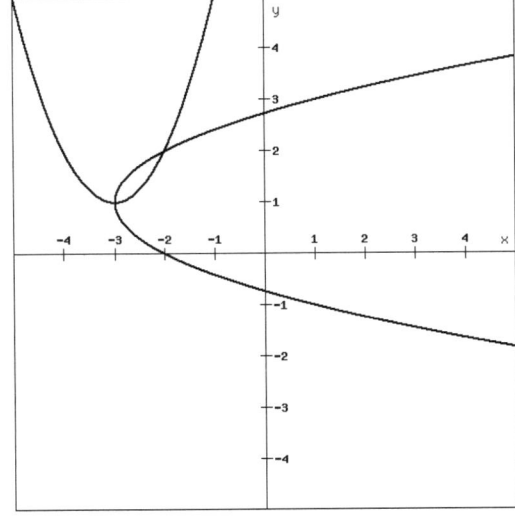

	S	M	L	Revenue
Day 1	20	40	30	$2400
Day 2	30	50	60	$3950
Day 3	60	100	90	$5360
Day 4	40	60	50	?

23. Miranda runs a flower shop where she sells flower bouquets in three sizes: small, medium, and large. The table above shows her sales and revenues for four days. Day 3 was a holiday, so there was a 20% discount on all three sizes. What is her revenue for Day 4? (Assume no taxes)
    A) $3120
    B) $3600
    C) $3900
    D) $4050

22. Which of the following systems best represents the graph above?
    A) $y = (x + 3)^2 + 1$
       $x = (y - 1)^2 - 3$
    B) $x = (y + 3)^2 + 1$
       $y = (x - 1)^2 - 3$
    C) $y = (x + 1)^2 + 3$
       $x = (y - 3)^2 - 1$
    D) $y = 2(x + 3)^2 + 1$
       $x = 3(y - 1)^2 - 3$

$$a + b + 2c = 3$$
$$2a + b + 3c = 7$$
$$2a + 4b - 2c = -20$$

24. In the above system of equations, what is the value of $+b + c$?

$$15 = 9x + 3by$$
$$a = 3x - 6y$$

25. If the above system has an infinite number of solutions, then what is the absolute value of the sum of a and b?

SAT Red Math
Lesson 2A: Understanding and Analyzing Systems of Equations

HW

RED MATH LESSON 2A: UNDERSTANDING AND ANALYZING SYSTEMS OF EQUATIONS
Race to the Finish

Directions: Answer each question below.

HOMEWORK SET (CALCULATOR)

$$6x - y + 4z = 5$$
$$2x - 3y + 5z = 4$$
$$3x + y - 2z = 3$$

1. Using the above system of equations, what is the value of $x + y - z$?
   A) $\frac{-67}{31}$
   B) $\frac{-4}{31}$
   C) $\frac{34}{31}$
   D) 12

$$4x + y - 2z = 9$$
$$2x + 5y - z = -9$$
$$-x - 2y + 2z = 9$$

2. Which of the following is a solution to the system of equations above?
   A) $(0, \frac{-9}{7}, -4)$
   B) $(5, -3, 4)$
   C) $(7, 3, 11)$
   D) No solution

$$9y^2 + 54y + 4x^2 - 32x = -109$$
$$y = \frac{2x - 11}{3}$$

3. What are the two solutions to the system of equations above?
   A) $(1, -3), (5, -\frac{1}{3})$
   B) $(1, -3), (4, -1)$
   C) $(2, -\frac{7}{3}), (5, -\frac{1}{3})$
   D) $(2, -\frac{7}{3}), (4, -1)$

4. A study is comparing two types of bacteria. If 20 grams of bacterium A, which doubles every 10 min, and 320 grams of bacterium B, which doubles every 30 min, are placed in Petri dishes, how long (minutes) will it take for there to be an equal amount of each type of bacteria?
   A) 30
   B) 45
   C) 60
   D) 75

$$\frac{x^2}{4} - \frac{y^2}{16} = 1$$
$$(x - 1)^2 + y^2 = 24$$

5. Which of the following is a solution to the system of equations above?
   A) $(3, 4.47), (-2.6, 3.32)$
   B) $(3, \pm 4.47), (-2.6, \pm 3.32)$
   C) $(5, 9.17), (2, 0)$
   D) $(5, \pm 9.17), (2, 0)$

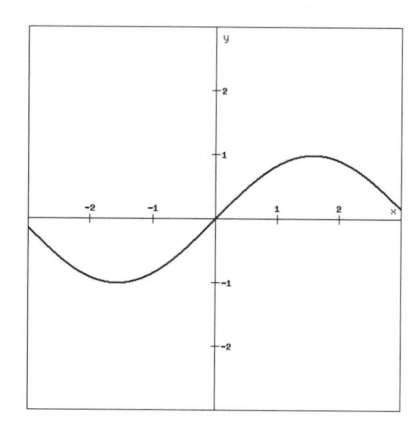

6. How many times does the function $f(x) = \frac{1}{2}x$ intersect $\sin x$?
   A) 1
   B) 2
   C) 3
   D) 4

SAT Red Math
Lesson 2A: Understanding and Analyzing Systems of Equations

7. Which one of the following equations intersects $\frac{x^2}{25} + \frac{y^2}{25} = 1$ at the points $(4, -3)$ and $(-4, 3)$?
   A) $y = \frac{3}{4}x$
   B) $y = -\frac{3}{4}x$
   C) $y = \frac{4}{3}x$
   D) $y = -\frac{4}{3}x$

8. $50,000 was invested in short term bonds, long term bonds, and a savings account. In one year $2775 in interest was earned. The savings account earns 1.5% annually, short term bonds earn 5% annually, and long term bonds earn 8% annually. If the amount invested in long term bonds is half the amount invested in short term bonds, how much money was invested in long term bonds?
   A) $5,000
   B) $10,000
   C) $15,000
   D) $20,000

$$|x - y| = 1$$
$$x^2 + 3y = 7$$

9. Using the system of equations above, which of the following is NOT a possible value of x?
   A) -4
   B) -3
   C) 1
   D) 2

$$2x^2 - 3y = 11$$
$$y = 2x - 5$$

10. Using the system of equations above, what is a possible value of $x - y$, where (x, y) is a solution to the system of equations?
    A) 0
    B) 1
    C) 2
    D) 3

$$y = \sqrt{x + 5}$$
$$x = 3y - 7$$

11. Using the system of equations above, what is a possible value of $\sqrt{y}$?
    A) -2
    B) 1
    C) 2
    D) 3

$$\frac{x}{5} + y^2 = 3$$
$$y^2 = 2x + 14$$

12. Using the system of equations above, what is a possible value of $x + y$?
    A) -3
    B) -1
    C) 1
    D) 3

$$x^3 + y^3 = 72$$
$$y = 2x$$

13. Using the system of equations above, what is a possible real value of $y - x$?
    A) 0
    B) 1
    C) 2
    D) 3

$$y = 2x^2 - 16x + 33$$
$$y = |x - 5|$$

14. Using the system of equations above, what is a possible value of y^2?
    A) 0
    B) 1
    C) 2
    D) 3

46 | SAT Red Math
Lesson 2A: Understanding and Analyzing Systems of Equations

HW

$$\frac{x}{3} + y^2 = 2$$
$$y^2 = 2x + 16$$

15. Using the system of equations above, y could equal
    A) -2
    B) -1
    C) 0
    D) 1

$$y = 2x^2$$
$$2x^3 + 3y = 8x$$

16. Using the system of equations above, what is NOT a possible value of y?
    A) 0
    B) 2
    C) 16
    D) 32

$$(x+3)^2 + (y-2)^2 = 50$$
$$y = x - 5$$

17. Using the system of equations above, what is the value of x?

$$2y^2 - x^2 = 272$$
$$y = 3x$$

18. Using the system of equations above, what is the value of x^2?

$$x^2 + y^2 = 104$$
$$y = -5x$$

19. Using the system of equations above, what is the value of $|x|$?

$$(y-1)^2 = 4 + x$$
$$x + 2y = -2$$

20. Using the system of equations above, what is the value of y^2?

RED MATH LESSON 2B: FUNCTIONS
Getting Your Feet Wet

Directions: The problems below are intended as a short diagnostic exam.

1. If w is greater than 0, which of the following could be the graph of $\left(\frac{y}{x}\right)^2 = y\left(x - \frac{w}{x^2}\right)$ in the xy-coordinate plane?

A)

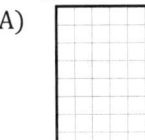

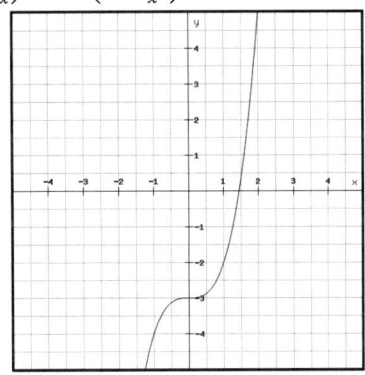

B)

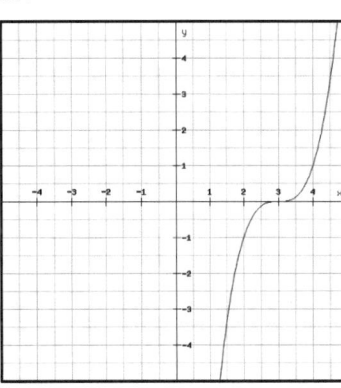

C)

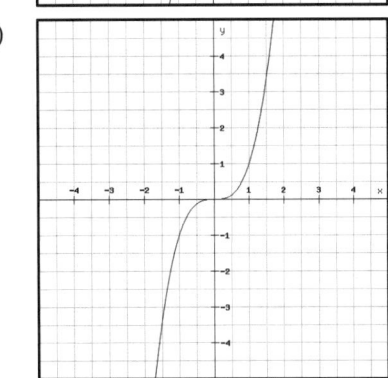

D)

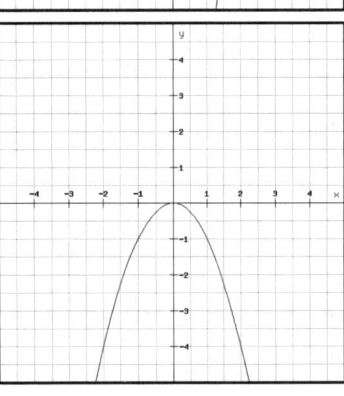

2. The graph of $f(x)$ is shown above. Which of the functions listed is the equation of the graph of $f(x)$?

A) $x^4 + 4x^3 - x^2 + 6x - 2$
B) $x^4 + 4x^3 + x^2 - 6x$
C) $x^4 + 4x^3 - x^2 - 4x + 2$
D) $x^4 + 4x^3 + x^2 + 4x + 6$

RED MATH LESSON 2B: FUNCTIONS
Wading In

Directions: Read the explanation for each problem type mentioned below. Pay special attention to the methods and techniques used to solve the sample problems. Then, do the practice exercises that follow; use the appropriate method to solve each problem.

TOPIC OVERVIEW: FUNCTIONS

Many of the questions on the SAT that involve the graphs of functions will involve parent functions and their transformations. Below are the major parent functions tested on the SAT and their graphs:

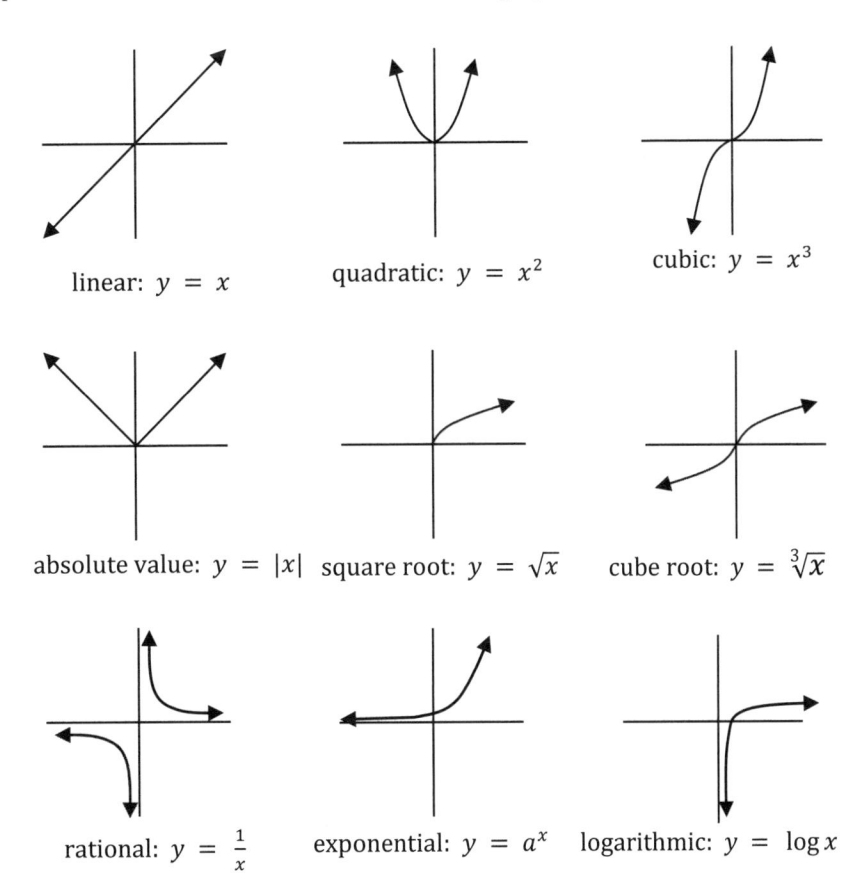

linear: $y = x$ quadratic: $y = x^2$ cubic: $y = x^3$

absolute value: $y = |x|$ square root: $y = \sqrt{x}$ cube root: $y = \sqrt[3]{x}$

rational: $y = \frac{1}{x}$ exponential: $y = a^x$ logarithmic: $y = \log x$

We have the ability to change the shapes of graphs using transformations. Look below for a review of the common function transformations tested on the SAT.

Translation	Function notation	Example ($b = 3$)
Up b units	$f(x) + b$	$x^2 + 3$
Down b units	$f(x) - b$	$\log x - 3$
Left b units	$f(x + b)$	2^{x+3}
Right b units	$f(x - b)$	$\dfrac{1}{x - 3}$

SAT Red Math
Lesson 2B: Functions

Reflection	Function notation	Example
Over the x-axis	$-f(x)$	$-x^2$
Over the y-axis	$f(-x)$	$\sqrt{-x}$

Stretch or Compression	Function notation	Example ($b = 3$)
Horizontal stretch by a factor of b	$f\left(\dfrac{x}{b}\right)$	$\left(\dfrac{x}{3}\right)^2$
Horizontal compression by a factor of b	$f(bx)$	$\ln 3x$
Vertical stretch by a factor of b	$bf(x)$	$3 * e^x$
Vertical compression by a factor of b	$\dfrac{1}{b}f(x)$	$\dfrac{1}{3}x$

Let's try a question involving some of these transformations:

SAMPLE PROBLEM 1: FUNCTIONS

If w is greater than 0, which of the following could be the graph of $\left(\dfrac{y}{x}\right)^2 = y\left(x - \dfrac{w}{x^2}\right)$ in the xy-coordinate plane?

A)

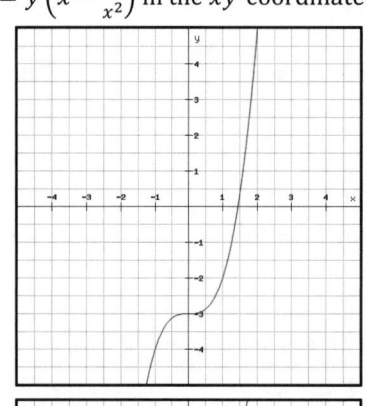

B)

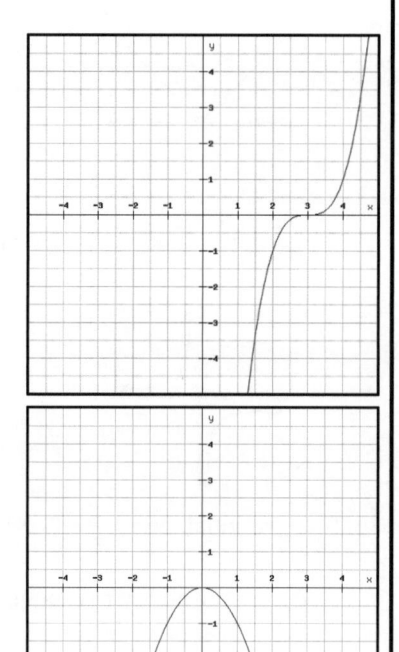

C)

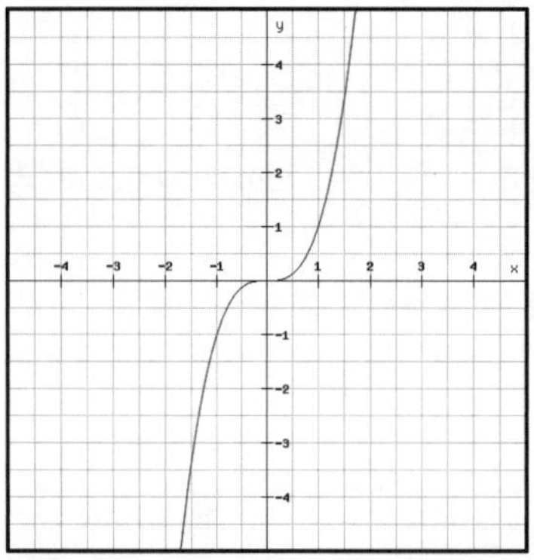

D)

Initially, this expression seems next to impossible to solve, as we have three different variables. Let's start out by solving for y to make things a little easier:

$$\left(\frac{y}{x}\right)^2 = y\left(x - \frac{w}{x^2}\right)$$
$$\frac{y^2}{x^2} = y\left(x - \frac{w}{x^2}\right)$$
$$\frac{y^2}{x^2} = y\left(\frac{x^3}{x^2} - \frac{w}{x^2}\right)$$
$$\frac{y^2}{y} = x^2\left(\frac{x^3}{x^2} - \frac{w}{x^2}\right)$$
$$y = x^3 - w$$

So, our graph should just be a graph of the cubic function shifted down w units. The only thing we know about w is that it's positive. So, we should shift the graph down some number of units (note that if the equation were $y = x^3 + w$, we would be shifting the graph up w units instead). Thus, our answer must be **A**.

Let's try another problem dealing with the graphs of functions. When we're provided with the graph of a function or a function from which we're expected to match the graph, the two most important things to look at are the y-intercept and the zeros of the function. Let's see how we would use this information to solve a problem:

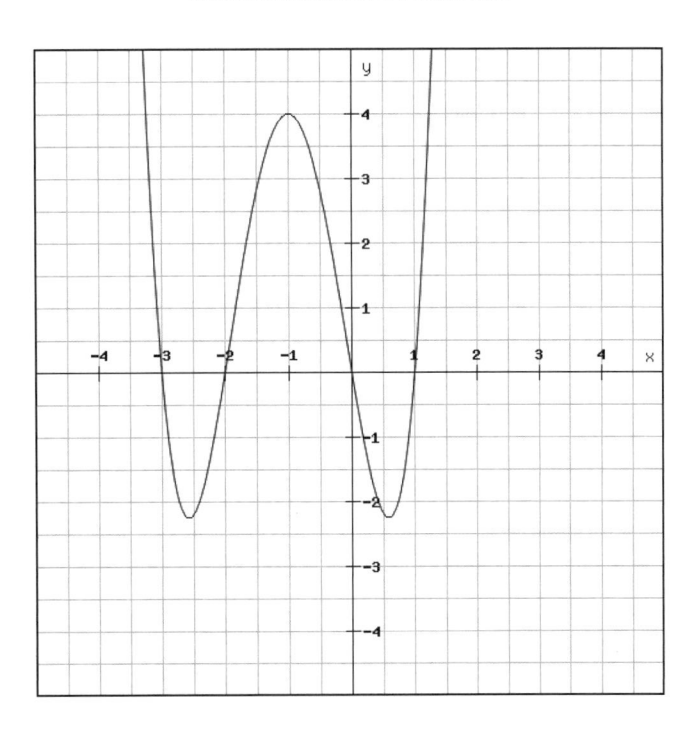

SAMPLE PROBLEM 2: FUNCTIONS

The graph of $f(x)$ is shown above. Which of the functions listed is the equation of the graph of $f(x)$?

A) $x^4 + 4x^3 - x^2 + 6x - 2$
B) $x^4 + 4x^3 + x^2 - 6x$
C) $x^4 + 4x^3 - x^2 - 4x + 2$
D) $x^4 + 4x^3 + x^2 + 4x + 6$

With a graphing calculator, figuring out the answer to this question is trivial: simply graph each of the answer choices and figure out which one best represents the image shown above. However, without that option, we have to resort to looking at zeros and intercepts. To solve it via intercepts, we must realize that the graph has intercepts at $x = -3, x = -2, x = 0$, and $x = 1$. So, we know that the equation of the graph must be $f(x) = a(x+3)(x+2)(x)(x-1)$ where a is the coefficient of x^4. As all the answer choices have 1 for this coefficient, we can set $a = 1$ and FOIL out this expression to give us **B**.

However, we can solve this question even more quickly by looking at the graph's y-intercept: $y = 0$! Since the graph of a polynomial has its y-intercept equal to the value of its constant term when expressed in standard form, we must simply choose the polynomial whose constant term is zero. Only **B** is missing a constant term.

WRAP-UP

The majority of function questions on the SAT will prevent us from using our calculators, so knowing all of the tricks and tips dealing with transformations, zeros, and y-intercepts will be tantamount. Review those tips and tricks frequently, and good luck!

RED MATH LESSON 2B: FUNCTIONS
Learning to Swim

Directions: Answer each question below.

1. The function $f(x)$ has range $[-3, 12]$. $g(x) = 4f(x+1)$ and $h(x) = g(2x) + 10$. What is the range of $h(x)$?

$$j(t) = 4t^2 + 6t + 8$$
$$k(t) = 5t^2 + 4t + 5$$
$$l(t) = j(t) - k(t)$$

2. Using the equations above, what is the maximum value of $l(t)$?

$$y \geq 0$$
$$x \geq -4$$
$$x^2 + y^2 + 8x \leq 0$$

3. Find the area of the region in the xy-plane that is enclosed by the above inequalities.

$$f(x) = (x-p)(x+q)(x-r)(x+s)(x-t)$$

4. Using the equation above let $p, q, r, s,$ and t be real numbers with $p < q < r < s < t < 0$. What is the product of the y-intercept of the graph of f and its greatest x-intercept (in terms of $p, q, r, s,$ and t)?

$$f(x) = 5\sin(x - \pi)$$

5. The function f above has domain $\frac{\pi}{2} \leq x \leq c$. If the inverse of f is also a function, what is the maximum value of c?

RED MATH LESSON 2B: FUNCTIONS
Diving into the Deep End

Directions: Answer each question below.

PRACTICE SET 2 (NO CALCULATOR)

6. Which of the following scenarios could be best-represented by an exponential function?
   A) The amount of water in a pool which is being filled by a hose
   B) The number of players eliminated each round of a ping pong tournament, when half of the players are eliminated each round
   C) The steady melting of snow on a warm winter day versus time
   D) The temperature of a house versus the position of the sun

Use the following information for questions 7 and 8:

The Heavyside function is used in engineering analysis to model sudden changes in events. The Heavyside function returns either the integer 1 or 0 for values of t as defined:

$$H(t - c) = \begin{cases} 0 \text{ if } t < c \\ 1 \text{ if } t \geq c \end{cases}$$

7. The temperature in a cold furnace starts at 20 degrees Celsius at time $t = 0$ minutes. After 5 minutes a fire is lit causing the temperature (T) to increase by 2 degrees Celsius every minute. The fire is put out after 1 hour and the furnace then starts to cool by the surrounding air. Which of the following functions, $T(t)$, best models the temperature of the furnace for the first 30 minutes?
   A) $T(t) = (2t) \cdot H(t - 5)$
   B) $T(t) = (2t + 20) \cdot H(t - 5)$
   C) $T(t) = 20 + (2(t - 5) \cdot H(t - 5))$
   D) $T(t) = 2t + (20 \cdot H(t - 5))$

$$V(t) = 120 \sin(t) \left(1 - H(t - 5) + H(t - 10)\right)$$

8. The voltage in a circuit is modeled by the function above. Which of the graphs below best represents this function?

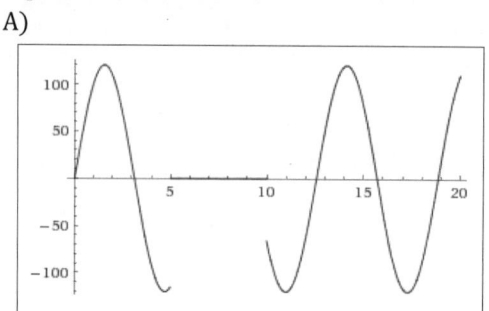

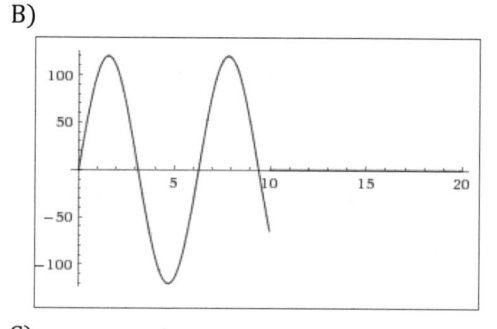

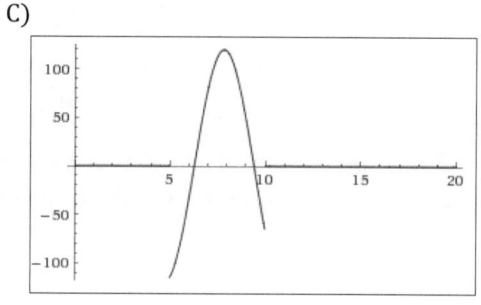

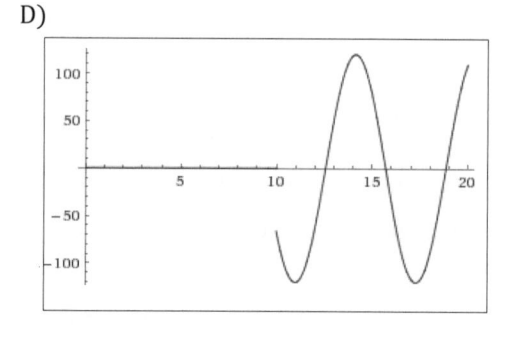

   A)

   B)

   C)

   D)

9. The graph of the function $f(x) = x^2 - 5x + 8$ is to be reflected across the y-axis and then translated down one unit. What function best describes the resulting graph?
   A) $f(x) = -x^2 + 5x - 9$
   B) $f(x) = -x^2 - 5x - 9$
   C) $f(x) = x^2 + 5x + 7$
   D) $f(x) = x^2 - 5x + 7$

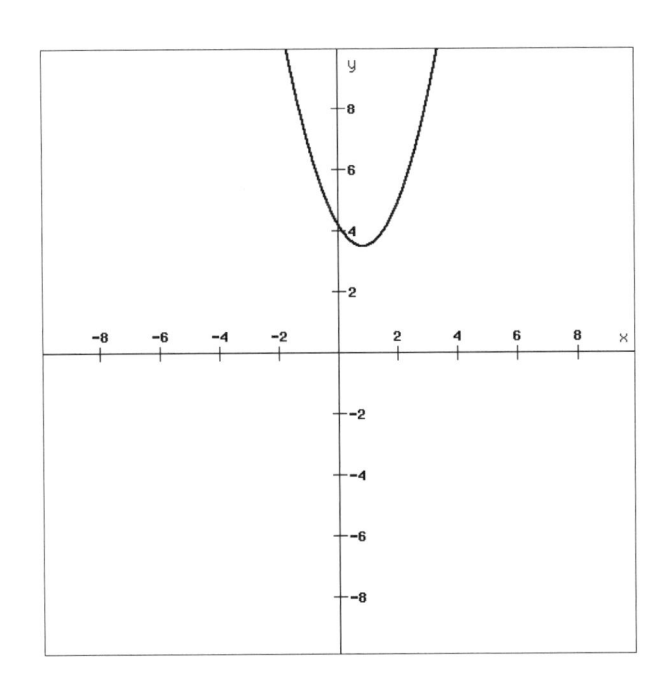

10. The figure above is represented by the function $f(x) = x^2 + bx + c$, where b and c are constants. Which of the following must be true for the function?
   A) $b > c$
   B) $b < 2c$
   C) $b = c^2$
   D) $bc > 4$

11. Which of the following must always be true for functions $f(x) = dx^2$ and $g(x) = jx$ provided that $x \neq 0$? Assume $a, b, c, d,$ and j represent integer constants.
   A) $f(g(x)) = g(f(x))$
   B) $g(af(x)) = af(x)g(x)$
   C) $g(bg(x)) = \frac{b}{x}(g(x))^2$
   D) $cf(g(x)) = cf(x)g(x)$

12. The graph of the function $f(x) = x^2 + 4x$ is to be reflected about the y-axis resulting in a graph described by the function $h(x) = ax^2 + bx$, where a and b are integer constants. A horizontal translation is then done to the graph of $h(x)$ resulting in a graph described by $g(x) = a(x+c)^2 + b(x+c)$, where c is also an integer constant. What are the values of $a, b,$ and c if $g(x)$ is equal to $f(x)$?
   A) $a = 1, b = -4, c = 4$
   B) $a = -1, b = 4, c = 4$
   C) $a = 1, b = 4, c = -4$
   D) $a = 1, b = -4, c = -4$

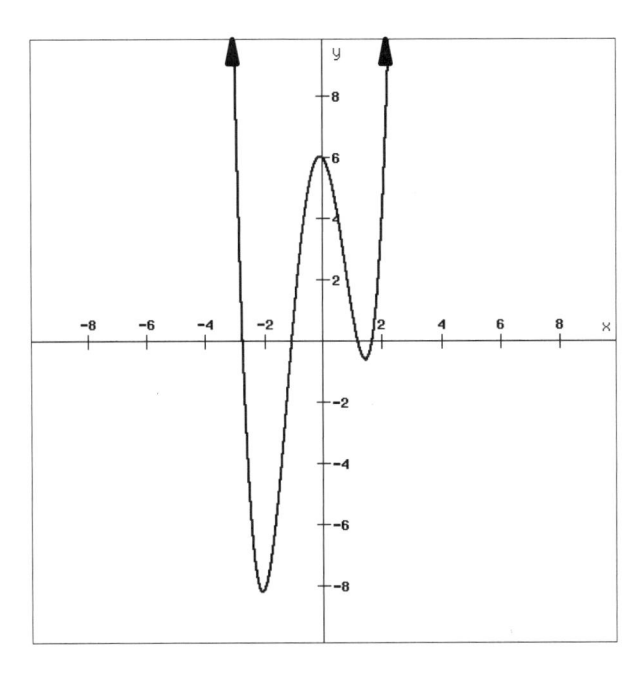

13. Which of the following could express the function shown above, provided that $a, b, c, d, e,$ and $f \neq 0$?
   A) $ax^2 + bx + c$
   B) $ax^3 + bx^2 + cx + d$
   C) $ax^4 + bx^3 + cx^2 + dx + e$
   D) $ax^5 + bx^4 + cx^3 + dx^2 + ex + f$

14. A rectangle has a perimeter of 24. The function that gives the rectangle's area in terms of its width is:
    A) Logarithmic
    B) Exponential
    C) Linear
    D) Quadratic

15. The population of a town doubles every 5 years. Knowing this, the post office modeled the number of postal workers needed to fulfil the town's needs as a function of postal workers (W) versus town population (p). The function used by the post office is $W(p) = 20(1.06^{p/10000})$. If the town initially had 9574 people, how many postal workers are needed after 10 years?

PRACTICE SET 3 (CALCULATOR)

16. Chemists use the pH scale to measure hydrogen ion concentration; when that concentration is divided by ten, the pH goes up by one. The pH as a function of hydrogen ion concentration is:
    A) Logarithmic
    B) Exponential
    C) Quadratic
    D) Cubic

17. A cubic function has roots −3, −1, and 2, and passes through the point (1, −16). Which equation represents this function?
    A) $P(x) = (x + 3)(x + 1)(x - 2)$
    B) $P(x) = (x - 3)(x - 1)(x + 2)$
    C) $P(x) = (x - 3)(x - 1)(x + 2) - 16$
    D) $P(x) = 2(x + 3)(x + 1)(x - 2)$

The exponential decay of a substance can be described by the formula:

$$N(t) = N_0 \left(\frac{1}{2}\right)^{\frac{t}{T}}$$

N_0 is the initial quantity of the substance that will decay,
$N(t)$ is the quantity that has not yet decayed after a certain amount of time,
T is the half-life of the substance, and
t is the time, in years.

18. The most common isotope of uranium is U-238, which decays to a characteristic isotope of lead, Pb-206, with a half-life of 4.468×10^9 years. Assuming that Pb-206 accumulates in rocks only as a result of this process, what formula gives the age of a rock whose U-238:Pb-206 ratio is 3:5?
    A) $\ln\frac{3}{5} = \frac{\ln 0.5}{4.468 \times 10^9} t$
    B) $\ln\frac{3}{8} = \frac{\ln 0.5}{4.468 \times 10^9} t$
    C) $\ln\frac{3}{5} = t \ln\frac{0.5}{4.468 \times 10^9}$
    D) $\ln\frac{3}{8} = \ln\frac{0.5t}{4.468 \times 10^9}$

19. Cylindrical aluminum beverage cans are made in two pieces before the top piece is added; the piece that forms the sides is 0.012 inches thick, while the bottom is 25% thicker. If the height to radius ratio is 4:1, which of the following gives the volume of aluminum required for this entire part of the can as a function of radius?

A) $V(r) = 0.012\pi \left[(2r)\left(\frac{1}{4}r\right) + 1.25r^2\right]$
B) $V(r) = 0.012\pi[(2r)(4r) + 0.25r^2]$
C) $V(r) = 0.012\pi[(2r)(4r) + 1.25r^2]$
D) $V(r) = 0.012\pi[2rh + 1.25r^2]$

20. If $f(x) = \frac{x^2+7}{x}$ and $g(x) = x$, which of the following represents $f(x) + g(x)$?

A) $2x^2 + 7$
B) $x^2 + 7$
C) $\frac{2x^2+7}{x}$
D) $\frac{x^2+x+7}{x}$

21. The population of bacteria in a petri dish triples every 20 hours. What is the hourly growth rate k (expressed as a percentage)?

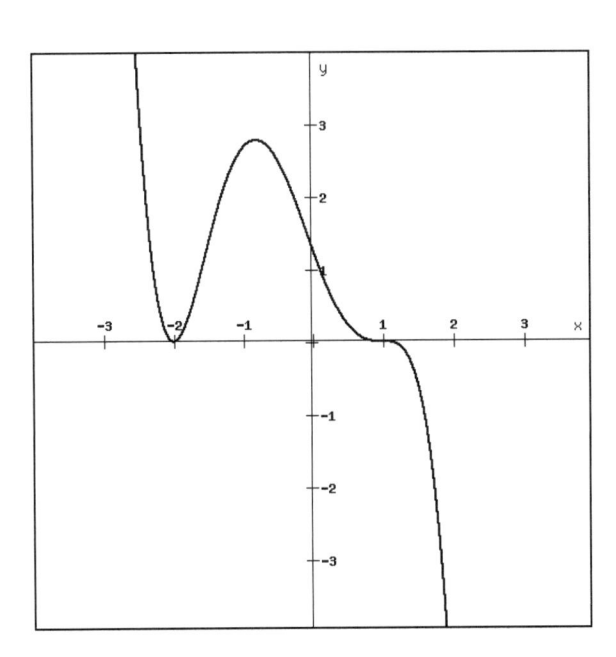

A) 4.65%
B) 5.65%
C) 6.65%
D) 7.65%

22. Which of the following is a possible equation for the function graphed above?

A) $q(x) = \frac{1}{3}(x+2)^2(x-1)^3$
B) $q(x) = \frac{1}{3}(x+2)^2(x-1)$
C) $q(x) = -\frac{1}{3}(x+2)^2(x-1)^3$
D) $q(x) = -\frac{1}{3}(x-2)(x+1)$

SAT Red Math
Lesson 2B: Functions

For questions 23 through 25 use the following information:

Compound interest can be calculated using the formula:

$$A = P\left(1 + \frac{r}{n}\right)^{nt}$$

Where P is the principal amount,
r is the annual rate of interest in decimal form,
t is the number of years the amount is deposited for,
A is the amount of money accumulated after n years,
and
n is the number of times the interest is compounded per year.

Continuously compounded interest can be calculated using the formula:

$$A = Pe^{rt}$$

P is the principal amount,
r is the annual rate of interest in decimal form,
t is the number of years the amount is deposited for,
and
A is the amount of money accumulated after n years.

23. Jill will be investing $1100. Which of the following functions can she use to determine the advantage of an investment that pays 5% interest compounded continuously over an investment that pays 6% compounded monthly?
    A) $A(t) = 1100(e^{0.05t} - 1.005^{12t})$
    B) $A(t) = 1100(e^{1.05t} - 1.06^{t})$
    C) $A(t) = 1100(e^{1.05t} - 1.06^{12t})$
    D) $A(t) = 1100(e^{0.05t} - 1.06^{t})$

24. If Cory invests $10,000 in an account that earns 7.1% interest continuously and Trevor invests $10,000 in an account that earns 6.5% interest quarterly, what will be the positive difference in the value of their investments at the end of two and a half years? Round to the nearest dollar.

25. On the first day of the year 2000, Julian invested $10,000 at a continuously compounded rate of 9.3%. On the first day of 2004, he withdrew the interest earned from the first investment and reinvested it in in an account earning an annual rate of 8.5% compounded monthly. How much money did he make in the period beginning exactly halfway through the year 2002 and ending exactly halfway through the year 2008? Round to the nearest dollar.

Red Math Lesson 2B: Functions
Race to the Finish

Directions: Answer each question below.

Homework Set (No Calculator)

$$f(x) = x^2$$
$$g(x) = 2x + 1$$

1. If $f(x)$ and $g(x)$ are defined as above, and $f(a + 1) = g(a)$, what is the value of a?
   A) -2
   B) 0
   C) 2
   D) 3

2. Sales of a single on the GoodListen website increased by roughly 50% each day during a marketing campaign. If there were 2,592 sales on the 5th day, about how many sales were there on the first day?
   A) 81
   B) 341
   C) 512
   D) 864

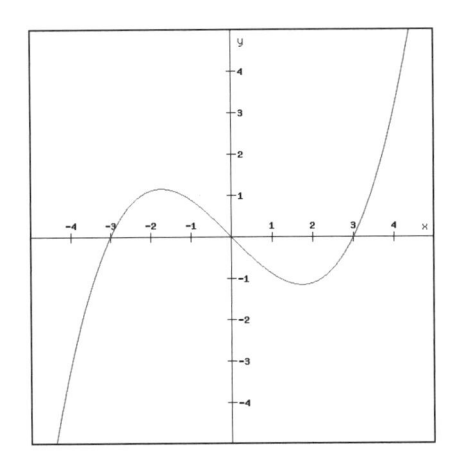

3. If $f(x)$ is the function depicted by the above graph, which of the following is true for all x?
   A) $f(x) = f(x + 3)$
   B) $f(x) = f(-x)$
   C) $f(x) = -f(x)$
   D) $f(x) = -f(-x)$

4. If $a = 10^{10}$, for which function f is $f(a)$ the greatest?
   A) $f(x) = \frac{1}{1000} 2^x - 10^{10}$
   B) $f(x) = 2x^{10} + 100x$
   C) $f(x) = 1{,}000{,}000 x^2 + 10^{10}$
   D) $f(x) = 10^{10} x + 10^{20}$

5. For which of the following relations can y not be described as a function of x?
   A) $x^2 + y = 6$
   B) $2x + 3y = 6$
   C) $y^2 + x = 6$
   D) $\sqrt{y} + x = 6$

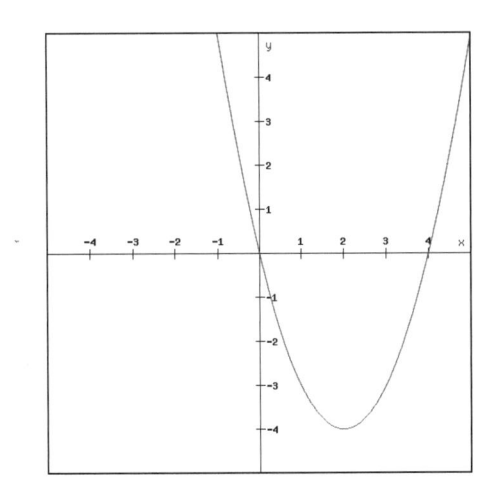

6. Which of the following functions generates the above graph?
   A) $f(x) = x^2 + 4x$
   B) $f(x) = x^2 - 4x$
   C) $f(x) = 4x - x^2$
   D) $f(x) = x^2 + 2x$

SAT Red Math
Lesson 2B: Functions

7. If $t(x)$ gives the tax-included price of a purchase costing x dollars and $s(x)$ gives the shipping-included price of an x dollar purchase, which of the following gives the total price of an x-dollar item that is purchased on sale for 30% off, given that shipping charges are not legally taxable?
   A) $s(0.7t(x))$
   B) $t(s(0.7x))$
   C) $t(s(0.3x))$
   D) $s(t(0.7x))$

8. If $f(f(x)) = 6x + f(x)$, which of the following could be true?
   A) $f(x) = 2x$
   B) $f(x) = 3x$
   C) $f(x) = 2^x$
   D) $f(x) = x^2$

$$P = 10{,}000(1 + S)^6$$

9. A banker uses the function above to calculate the value of an investment that uses compound interest. What does S represent in the function?
   A) The number of times the interest is compounded
   B) The interest rate of the investment
   C) The value of the first interest payment
   D) The value of the investment after 6 interest payments

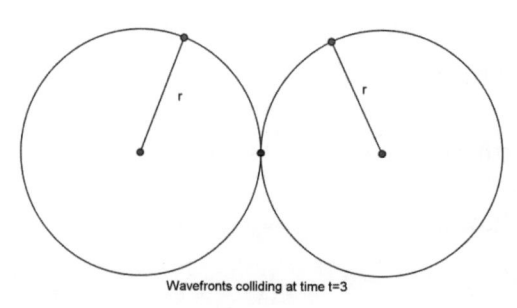

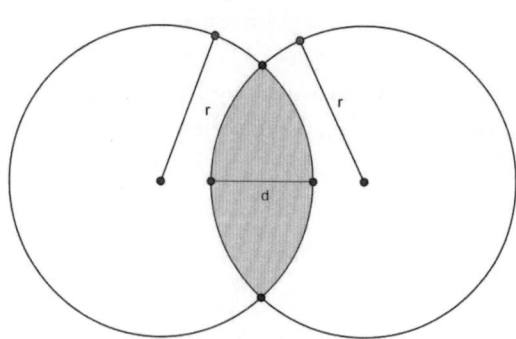

10. Two rocks are simultaneously thrown into a pond, creating circular waves on impact, the radius of each after t seconds being given by $r(t)$. Three seconds later, the circular wavefronts meet and begin to overlap. The function $A(d)$ gives the area of the shaded region given the length of the segment d. For $t > 3$, which expression gives the area of the overlap t seconds after the rocks hit?
    A) $A(2r(t) - 2r(3))$
    B) $A(2r(t-3))$
    C) $2A(r(t-3))$
    D) $2A(r(t) - r(3))$

11. A polynomial function graphed in the xy-coordinate plane crosses the x-axis at $x = 3$, $x = 2$, and $x = 1$. Which of the following expressions is a factor of that polynomial?
    A) $x^2 - 5x + 6$
    B) $x^2 - 2x - 3$
    C) $x^2 + 3x + 2$
    D) $x^2 + 5x + 6$

12. Which of the following could be a function with zeroes at $x = \{-2, 1, 5\}$?

A)

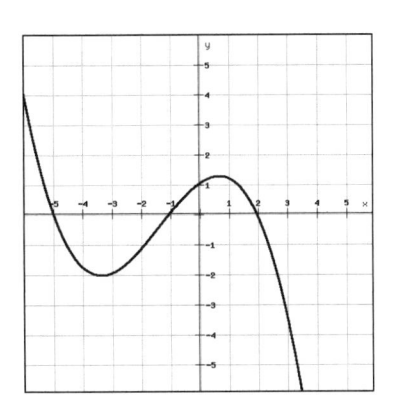

B)

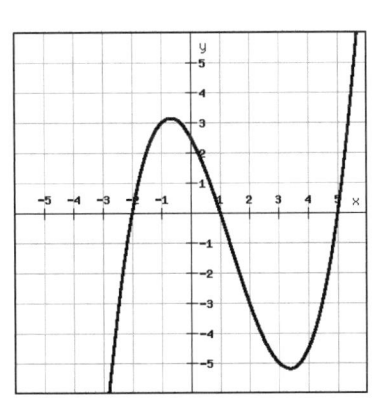

C)

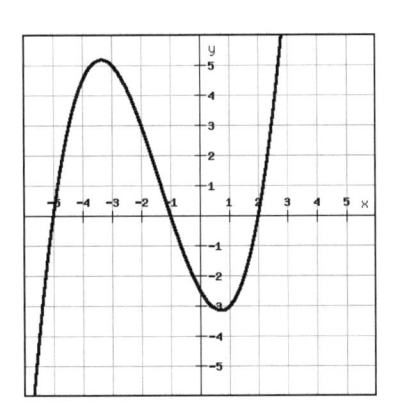

D)

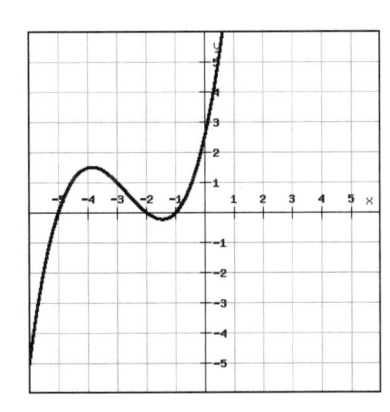

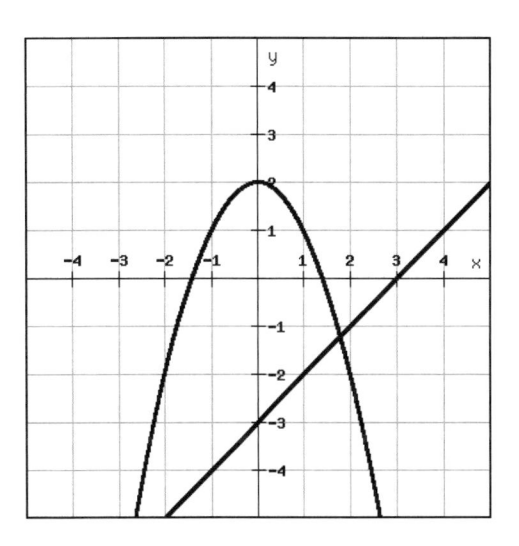

13. The figure above shows the graphs of the quadratic function $f(x)$ and the linear function $g(x)$. What is $f(g(x))$?
A) $f(g(x)) = -x^2 + 5$
B) $f(g(x)) = -x^2 + 6x - 7$
C) $f(g(x)) = x^2 - 2x + 1$
D) $f(g(x)) = x^2 - 6x + 11$

$$N = 150 \cdot 2^t$$

14. The function above shows the population among a newly introduced squirrel species after t years. What does 2 represent in the function?
A) The population increases by 2 squirrels per year
B) The starting population was 2 squirrels.
C) The population doubles every year.
D) The population doubles every t years.

15. A function $f(x)$ has zeroes at $x = -7$, $x = -3$, and $x = 0$. If $g(x)$ is the function that results when $f(x)$ is reflected across the x-axis, then moved 2 units to the left, what are the zeroes of $g(x)$?
A) $x = -9$, $x = -5$, and $x = -2$
B) $x = -5$, $x = -1$, and $x = 2$
C) $x = -2$, $x = 1$, and $x = 5$
D) $x = 2$, $x = 5$, and $x = 9$

$$-t^2 + 8t + 5$$

16. Marta throws a baseball and measures its height until it hits the ground. The height (in feet) is given by the function $h(t)$ above, where t is the number of seconds since the ball was thrown. What does the 5 represent in the function?
    A) The ball's height, in feet, when Marta threw it.
    B) The ball's peak height, in feet.
    C) The amount of time, in seconds, that the ball was in the air.
    D) The horizontal distance, in feet, that the ball traveled.

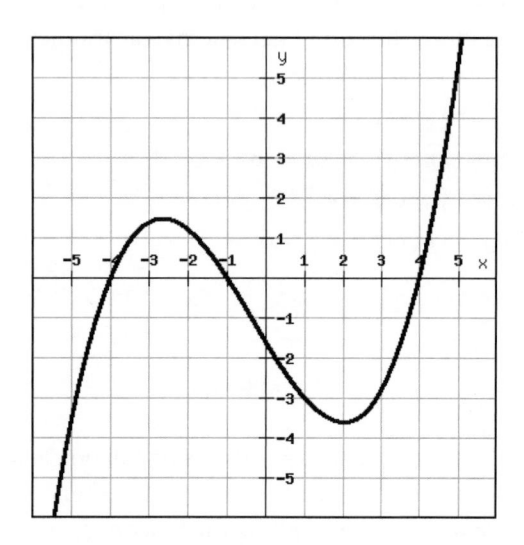

17. The function graphed above has zeroes at all of the following EXCEPT
    A) $x = -4$.
    B) $x = -1$.
    C) $x = 1$.
    D) $x = 4$.

18. Which of the following represents $\frac{f(x)}{g(x)}$ for all values of $x \neq -3$ if $f(x) = 3x^3 + 9x^2$ and $g(x) = x + 3$?
    A) $3x + 3$
    B) x^3
    C) $3x^2$
    D) $3x^2 + 1$

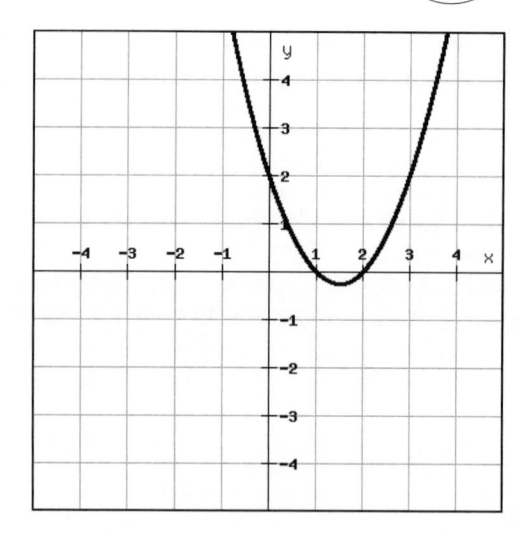

19. The graph above shows $f(x)$. Which of the following is equal to $f(-x)$?
    A) $-x^2 - 3x + 2$
    B) $-x^2 + 3x - 2$
    C) $x^2 + 3x + 2$
    D) $x^2 - 3x - 2$

20. Given that $f(x) = x + 1$ and $g(x) = (x + 2)(x - 3)$, which of the following lists all the zeroes of the function $g(f(x))$?
    A) -3 and 2
    B) -2 and 3
    C) -1 and 4
    D) $1, -2$, and 3

RED MATH LESSON 3A: PRACTICE SECTIONS
Learning to Swim

Directions: Answer each question below.

PRACTICE SET 1 (CALCULATOR)

1. A new machine at a factory can produce 120,000 units. Every year the productivity decreases so that the machine can produce only 97% of the units that it produced in the previous year. The factory will keep the machine in operation as long as it produces at least 85,000 units in one year. How many years will a new machine remain in operation?

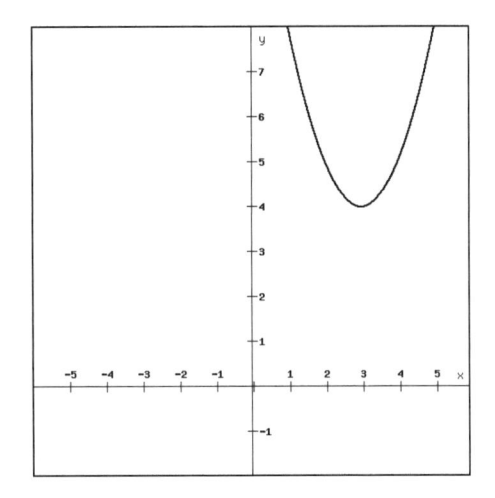

2. The graph for $y = (x - 3)^2 + 4$ is shown above. If a circle with the equation $(x - 3)^2 + (y - 7)^2 = r^2$ is added to the graph, at what value of r would the parabola and the circle intersect at three points?

3. A quadratic function $y = ax^2 + bx + c$ has a y-intercept at $(0, 5)$ and only one x-intercept. What is the value of $\frac{b^2}{a}$?

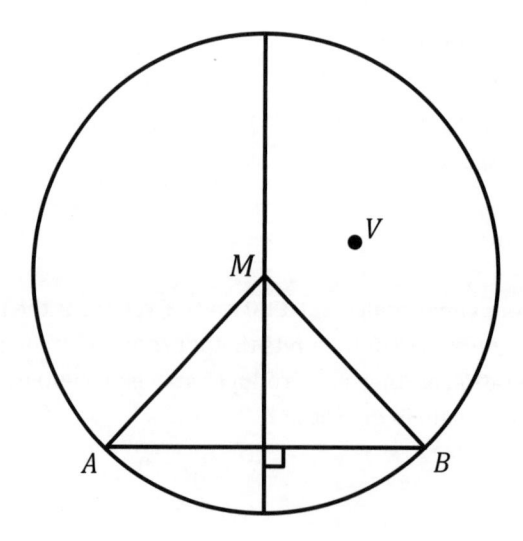

4. In the figure above, M is the center of the circle. The length of chord $\overline{AB}$ is $\frac{6}{\sqrt{\pi}}$, and $\angle AMB = 120°$. What is the area of the section of the circle that contains Point V?

5. The volume of a cone can be found by the equation $V = \frac{1}{3}\pi r^2 h$. If the volumes of two cones are equal, but the radius of Cone A is 3 times the radius of Cone B, what is the height of Cone A in terms of the height of Cone B, h?

Red Math Lesson 3A: Practice Sections
Diving into the Deep End

Directions: Answer each question below.

Practice Set 2 (No Calculator)

6. If $z^3=27$ and $(xy+z)^3 = -1$, which of the following could not be a possible value of x?
   A) $x = -4$
   B) $x = -1$
   C) $x = 0$
   D) $x = 7$

	Yes	No	Total
Crescent Lake	36	24	60
Oak Hill	28	12	40
Total	64	36	100

7. A survey was conducted in which 100 residents from two neighborhoods of a town were asked if they supported funding for a new park. The results of the survey are summarized above. Given that a resident is from the Oak Hill neighborhood, what is the probability that he or she supports the funding?
   A) 0.28
   B) 0.40
   C) 0.64
   D) 0.70

8. Which of the following functions has a horizontal asymptote at $y = 1$ and a vertical asymptote at $x = -3$?
   A) $y = \frac{x+2}{x+3}$
   B) $y = \frac{x^2+2x-3}{x+3}$
   C) $y = \frac{x-1}{x-3}$
   D) $y = \frac{x+3}{x-5}$

Total Students Enrolled at Hamilton Middle School

	Grade 6	Grade 7	Grade 8	
Male	84	75	64	223
Female	60	80	56	196
	144	155	120	419

Makeup of the Hamilton Middle School Track Team

	Grade 6	Grade 7	Grade 8	
Male	0.14	0.18	0.18	0.50
Female	0.12	0.22	0.16	0.50
	0.26	0.40	0.34	1

Use the tables above for questions 9 and 10.

9. The tables above give information about the student enrollment and the makeup of the track team at Hamilton Middle School. The second table, for example, shows that 12% of the members of the track team are females in grade 6. If there are 50 students on the track team, which of the following groups has the highest percentage of students participating in the track team?
   A) 6th Grade Males
   B) 7th Grade Females
   C) 8th Grade Females
   D) 8th Graders

10. Assuming the tables on the previous page are representative of all middle school students in the United States and there are 10 million students attending middle schools in the United States, of which 500,000 students are on track teams, approximately what percentage of females in the 6th grade are on a track team in the United States?
    A) 4%
    B) 5%
    C) 6%
    D) 7%

11. Force $= \frac{Gm_1 m_2}{r^2}$ is an equation that can be used to model the gravitational force between two objects. Assuming G is constant, if m_1 is decreased by half and r is doubled, how can m_2 be changed to maintain a constant gravitational force?
    A) Multiply m_2 by 8
    B) Multiply m_2 by 4
    C) Divide m_2 by 2
    D) Divide m_2 by 4

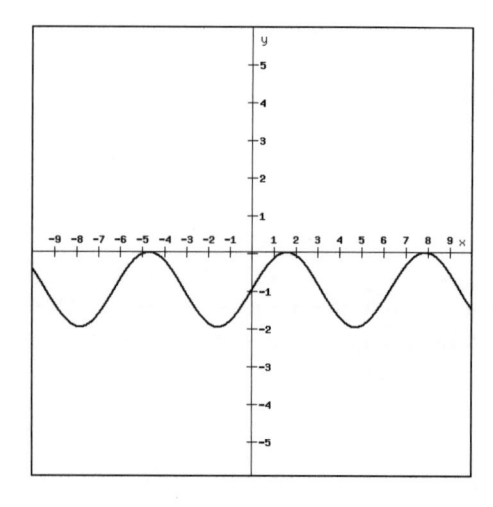

12. The graph of $f(x) = \sin x - 1$ is shown above. Which of the following equations is equivalent to $f(-x)$?
    A) $f(x) = \cos\left(x - \frac{\pi}{4}\right) - 1$
    B) $f(x) = -\sin x + 1$
    C) $f(x) = \cos\left(x + \frac{\pi}{2}\right) - 1$
    D) $f(x) = \cos x - 1$

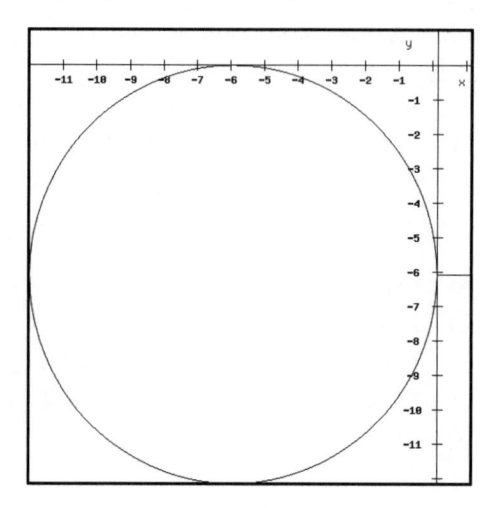

13. The graph above shows the circle with the equation $(x + 6)^2 + (y + 6)^2 = 36$. Point D is located at $(-6, 0)$, and point E is located at $(0, -6)$. Which of the following is a point F on the circle such that the difference in length between the arcs is $\widehat{EF} - \widehat{DF} = \pi$?
    A) $(-4, -4 + 4\sqrt{2})$
    B) $(-6 - 2\sqrt{5}, -10)$
    C) $(-6 - 2\sqrt{6}, -6 - 2\sqrt{3})$
    D) $(-6 - 3\sqrt{3}, -9)$

14. James sold a total of 400 tickets for his high school's theater production. Adult tickets cost $8.00, student tickets cost $5.00, and senior tickets cost $6.00. If James sold $2675 worth of tickets, and he sold 50 more student tickets than senior tickets, how many adult tickets did James sell?

PRACTICE SET 3 (CALCULATOR)

16. Gary is planning to save for his retirement and hopes to save at least $400,000. He currently has $170,000 saved in his retirement account. The amount of money in his account increases by 7% each year. How many years will it take for Gary to reach his goal?
    A) 8
    B) 13
    C) 16
    D) 18

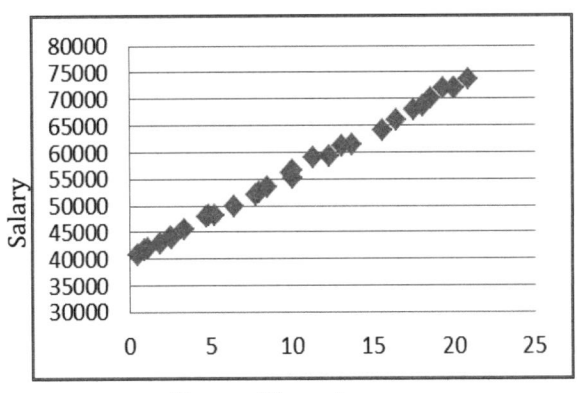

15. Joanna has recently been hired to Company A, whose employees' salaries and years' experience are shown in the plot above. Joanna had considered another job at Company B that had the same starting salary but had an average salary growth rate only about half of that of her new job. If she works at Company A for five years, about how much higher will her annual salary be than if she had worked at Company B for five years? Round to the nearest thousand dollars.

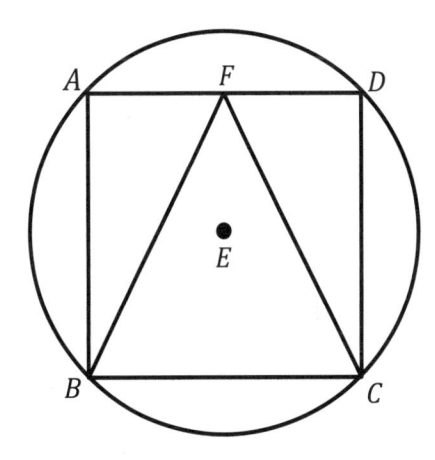

17. If the radius of the circle in the image above is 10, and $\overline{AD}$ is bisected by point F, what is the area of the portion of square $ABCD$ not covered by triangle BFC?
    A) 25
    B) 50
    C) 100
    D) 150

18. Which of the following equations has vertical asymptotes at $x = 4$ and $x = -5$?
    A) $y = \frac{(x-4)(x+5)}{x}$
    B) $y = \frac{x-1}{(x+4)(x+5)}$
    C) $y = \frac{3}{(x-4)(x+5)}$
    D) $y = \frac{5x}{(x-4)+(x+5)}$

19. Which of these situations best maps onto a quadratic equation?
    A) The height of a tennis ball which has been thrown into the air at a 70° angle.
    B) The cost of a cab ride involving an initial flat fee and subsequent charge per quarter mile.
    C) The amount of carbon-14 in a fossil, given the half-life of carbon-14.
    D) The relationship between the number of diners at a party and the size of each piece of cake.

20. Which of the following is a factor of the polynomial function $f(x) = 4x^3 - 2x^2 + x - 8$?
    A) $(x - 1)$
    B) $(x - 2)$
    C) $(x - 3)$
    D) None of the above

21. What is the center of the circle with the equation $x^2 + y^2 - 4x + 6y - 12 = 0$?
    A) $(-2, 3)$
    B) $(0, 0)$
    C) $(2, -3)$
    D) $(4, -6)$

22. A survey polling 3500 professional musicians discovered that those polled attended an average of 5 concerts a month. Which of the following statements is a reasonable assumption given this information?
    A) Professional musicians attend more concerts than amateur musicians
    B) Professional musicians attend at least one concert a week
    C) Most people attend 5 concerts a month
    D) Professional musicians attend an average of 60 concerts a year

$$x^3 + 2x^2 - 5x - 6$$

23. Which of the following is a factor of the polynomial above?
    A) $x - 1$
    B) $x + 2$
    C) $x + 3$
    D) $x - 4$

24. A circle with an area of 64π is enlarged to have a new area of 125.44π. What is the percent increase of the circle's radius?

25. An airplane is 2 km directly above an air control tower. If the plane intends to land at a position on the runway 4 miles north from the air control tower, at what angle, in degrees, is the plane descending? (One km is approximately 0.621 miles)

RED MATH LESSON 3A: PRACTICE SECTIONS
Race to the Finish

Directions: Answer each question below.

HOMEWORK SET (NO CALCULATOR)

$$f(x) = x^4 + 3x^2$$
$$g(x) = x^4 + 3x^2 - 2.7$$
$$h(x) = (x - 6.4)^4 + 3(x - 6.4)^2$$

Use the above equations for questions 1 and 2.

1. What is the relation between the domain and range of $f(x)$ and $g(x)$?
   A) The domain of $f(x)$ and $g(x)$ are equivalent, and the range of $f(x)$ and $g(x)$ are equivalent as well.
   B) The range is the same for $f(x)$ and $g(x)$, but the domain begins 2.7 units lower in $g(x)$ then it does for $f(x)$.
   C) The domain is the same for $f(x)$ and $g(x)$, but the range begins 2.7 units lower in $g(x)$ then it does for $f(x)$.
   D) Both the domain and range begin 2.7 units lower in $g(x)$ then they do for $f(x)$.

2. What is the relation between the domain and range of $f(x)$ and $h(x)$?
   A) The domain of $f(x)$ and $h(x)$ are equivalent, and the range of $f(x)$ and $h(x)$ are equivalent as well.
   B) The domain is the same for $f(x)$ and $h(x)$, but the range begins 6.4 units lower in $h(x)$ then it does for $f(x)$.
   C) The range is the same for $f(x)$ and $h(x)$, but the domain begins 6.4 units to the right in $h(x)$, as opposed to $f(x)$, whose domain starts at $x = 0$.
   D) The range is the same for $f(x)$ and $h(x)$, but the domain begins 6.4 units to the left in $h(x)$, as opposed to $f(x)$, whose domain starts at $x = 0$.

$$(x - 3)^2 + y^2 = 40$$
$$y - 4 = 2x$$

3. Which of the following is a solution to the system of equations above?
   A) $(-3, 2)$
   B) $(-1, 6)$
   C) $(3, -2)$
   D) $(1, 6)$

4. A car dealership pays its salespeople a 3% commission on the sale price of any cars it sells. The dealer wishes to make a profit equal to at least 10% of the price it paid the manufacturer for the car. To achieve this, the sale price must exceed what percent of the manufacturer's price, to the nearest tenth of a percent?
   A) 113.0%
   B) 113.3%
   C) 113.4%
   D) 114.4%

13 Pesos to 1 Dollar
15 Pesos to 1 Euro

5. A currency exchange offers the exchange rates listed above. In addition, the exchange charges a fee equal to 2% of the amount exchanged. If a person exchanges $30,000 to pesos and then exchanges the remaining amount after the fee into euros, how much will remain, to the nearest euro?
   A) 24,970 euros
   B) 27,050 euros
   C) 28,812 euros
   D) 33,245 euros

$$\frac{2}{3}(x-4) = \frac{7}{6}(y+3)$$
$$y = \frac{8}{14}x + \frac{k}{7}$$

6. For what value of k will the above system of equations have an infinite number of solutions?
   A) -74
   B) -37
   C) 35
   D) 37

7. When graphed in the xy-coordinate plane, the function $f(x) = \frac{1}{2}x^3 + 5x^2 - \frac{9}{2}x - 45$ crosses the x-axis at $x =$
   A) $-5, \frac{9}{2},$ and 5
   B) $-3, -\frac{9}{2},$ and 3
   C) $-10, -3,$ and 3
   D) $-\frac{5}{2}, 3,$ and 5

8. If $f(x) = (x-2)^2$ and $g(x) = 2x + 1$, what is the result when $g(f(x))$ is reflected across the y-axis?
   A) $h(x) = -2(x-2)^2 - 1$
   B) $h(x) = -(2x-1)^2 - 1$
   C) $h(x) = (2x+1)^2 + 1$
   D) $h(x) = 2(x+2)^2 + 1$

9. When ordering an oversized sub sandwich for a party, each adult needs at least 6 inches of sandwich and each child needs at least 4 inches of sandwich. If the sandwich can be no more than 10 feet long, and at least 30 people will be at the party, which system of equations represents this scenario?
   A) $a + c \geq 120$
   $\frac{1}{6}a + \frac{1}{4}c \leq 30$
   B) $6a + 4c \leq 10$
   $a + c \geq 30$
   C) $6a + 4c \leq 120$
   $a + c \geq 30$
   D) $10(a + c) \leq 120$
   $a + c \geq 30$

$$3a - 2b + c = 6$$
$$a + 2b - c = -4$$
$$4a + 2c = 8$$

10. In the system of equations above, what is the value of b?
    A) -3
    B) $-\frac{3}{4}$
    C) $-\frac{1}{4}$
    D) $\frac{1}{2}$

11. A block of oak wood is a cube with side length 30 centimeters. A smaller cube with side length 20 centimeters is carved out of the larger cube. If oak has a density of 650 kilograms per cubic meter, what is the mass of the remaining block of wood?
    A) 12.35 kg
    B) 32.50 kg
    C) 65.00 kg
    D) 123.5 kg

12. Which of the following matches the graph in the xy-coordinate plane shown above?

   A) $f(x) = -\frac{1}{3}(x-2)^2 + 1$
   B) $f(x) = -\frac{1}{3}(x-1)^2 + 2$
   C) $f(x) = -\frac{1}{3}(x+1)^2 + 2$
   D) $f(x) = -\frac{1}{3}(x+2)^2 + 1$

13. The actual population of a town is 12,560, of whom 75% are eligible voters, 60% of which are expected to actually vote. Based on these estimations, the number of expected votes cast in an election is most likely closest to:

   A) 5,652
   B) 7,065
   C) 7,536
   D) 9,420

14. Let $f(q)$ be defined by $f(q) = \frac{50-q^2}{|q|}$. Which of the following numbers is not in the domain of $f(q)$?

   A) 0
   B) 5
   C) $5\sqrt{2}$
   D) 50

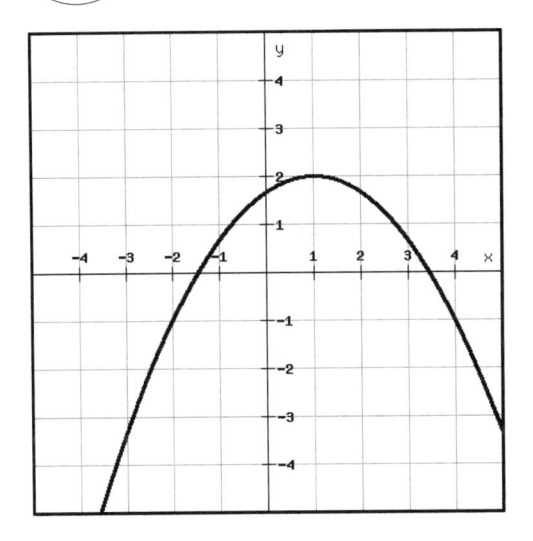

15. The value of a car depreciates (decreases) by an estimated 15% per year. Which of the following expressions is equal to the estimated value of a car originally purchased new for $18,500 after it has been owned for 7 years?

   A) $18500 \cdot 0.15^7$
   B) $18500 \cdot 0.85^7$
   C) $(18500 \cdot 0.85)^7$
   D) $18500(1 - 0.15 \cdot 7)$

16. If x is an angle in radians such that $0 \leq x < 2\pi$, $\sin x = -\cos x$, and $\sec x > 0$, what is the value of x?

   A) $\frac{\pi}{4}$
   B) π
   C) $\frac{5\pi}{4}$
   D) $\frac{7\pi}{4}$

17. Rose plans to open a small craft shop and sell hand-knit clothing. She can make an initial investment of no more than $1,500 in yarn. The yarn required for a sweater costs $50, while that required for a scarf costs $15. Rose intends to invest at least 200 hours into knitting. A sweater takes 6 hours to make, while a scarf takes 4. What is the greatest number of items she can knit within her budget and minimum time commitment?

$$y + 6 = m(x + 2)$$

18. The graph of the above function will NOT pass through the origin or the fourth quadrant, provided that m is greater than what number?

20. By varying the price of the sandwiches sold at a food truck, the truck's owner finds that for each dollar the price rises, the number of sandwiches sold each day decreases linearly by 10%. If the truck sells $500 of sandwiches in a day for $d each and $560 of sandwiches in a day for $(d + 2) each, what is d?

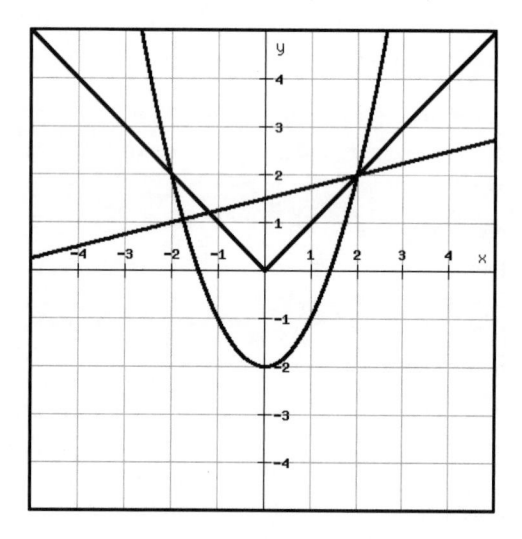

19. The figure above shows the graphs of the functions $y = |x|$, $y = x^2 - 2$, and $y = \frac{1}{4}x + \frac{3}{2}$. How many real solutions are there for this system of equations?

RED MATH LESSON 3B: EXPONENTIAL FUNCTIONS
Getting Your Feet Wet

Directions: The problems below are intended as a short diagnostic exam.

1. How long, to the nearest year, will it take the amount of money in a savings account to double when its interest is being compounded continuously at a rate of 3.3% per year?

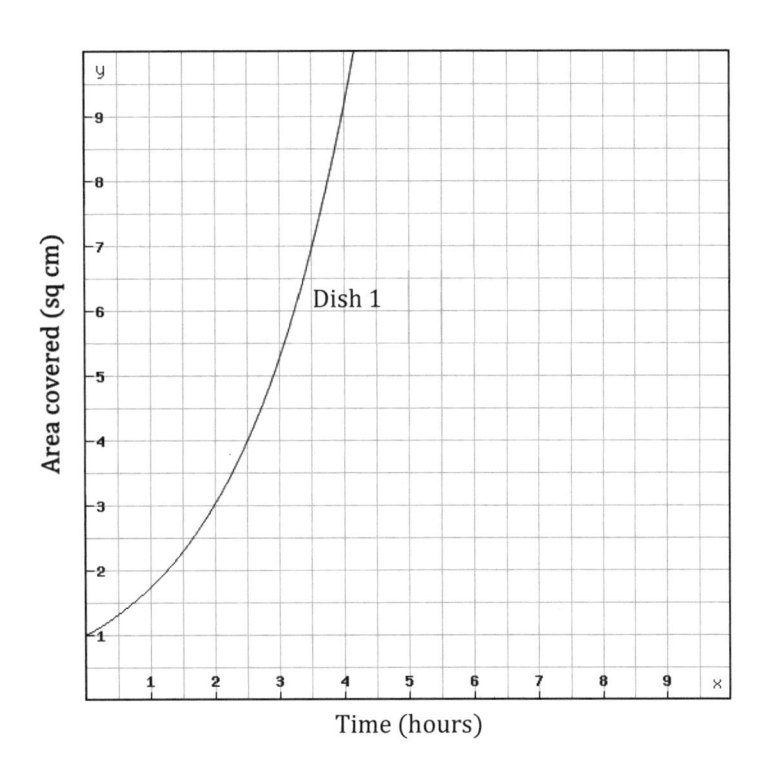

2. A biologist places two different colonies of bacteria into two different petri dishes, each of which has an area of 10 square centimeters. After the initial placement of the bacteria ($t = 0$), the biologist measures and records the area covered by the bacteria in the dish every 15 minutes. The data for the first dish was fit by a smooth curve, as shown above. The data for the second dish was found to fit the curve modeled by the function $A(t) = 2 \times 2^{0.5t}$, where $A(t)$ represents the area covered by the bacteria after t hours. Which of the following is a correct statement about the data above?
    A) At time $t = 0$, more of Dish 1 was covered by bacteria than Dish 2.
    B) At time $t = 1$, more of Dish 1 was covered by bacteria than Dish 2.
    C) The bacteria in Dish 2 took a greater amount of time to cover 100% of the dish than the bacteria in Dish 1 did.
    D) The bacteria in Dish 1 took a greater amount of time to cover 100% of the dish than the bacteria in Dish 2 did.

RED MATH LESSON 3B: EXPONENTIAL FUNCTIONS
Wading In

Directions: Read the explanation for each problem type mentioned below. Pay special attention to the methods and techniques used to solve the sample problems. Then, do the practice exercises that follow; use the appropriate method to solve each problem.

TOPIC OVERVIEW: MODELING EXPONENTIAL FUNCTIONS

Many of the questions on the SAT involving exponential functions will be word problems that require us to interpret, model, and solve exponential expressions. Many of these situations can be modeled using the continuous growth formula, $A = Pe^{kt}$, where A is the ending amount, P is the initial amount, r is the rate of growth or decay (which is always expressed as a decimal, not a percent), and t is the time, expressed in the same unit as the rate of growth or decay. Let's try one of these questions together:

SAMPLE PROBLEM 1: MODELING EXPONENTIAL FUNCTIONS

How long, to the nearest year, will it take the amount of money in a savings account to double when its interest is being compounded continuously at a rate of 3.3% per year?

Since interest is being compounded continuously, we should set up the equation $A = Pe^{kt}$. We do not actually have the values for A or P; we just want to know how long it'll take for P to double. So, we can manipulate our equation so that the ratio of A to P is 2 to 1:

$$A = Pe^{rt}$$
$$\frac{A}{P} = e^{rt}$$
$$2 = e^{rt}$$

Now we can plug in our interest rate, 3.3%, or 0.033, into r and solve for t:

$$2 = e^{rt}$$
$$2 = e^{0.033t}$$
$$\ln 2 = \ln e^{0.033t}$$
$$0.693 = 0.033t$$
$$21 = t$$

Thus, our answer is **21** years. Note that the continuous growth formula can be used for situations besides interest; however, the SAT will typically provide the formula for these situations. On the other hand, situations that involve a repeated rate of growth or decay, like a population doubling every 10 years or the number of viruses in a host decreasing by 10% an hour, will require us to model the situation on our own.

SAT Red Math
Lesson 3B: Exponential Functions

SAMPLE PROBLEM 2: MODELING EXPONENTIAL FUNCTIONS

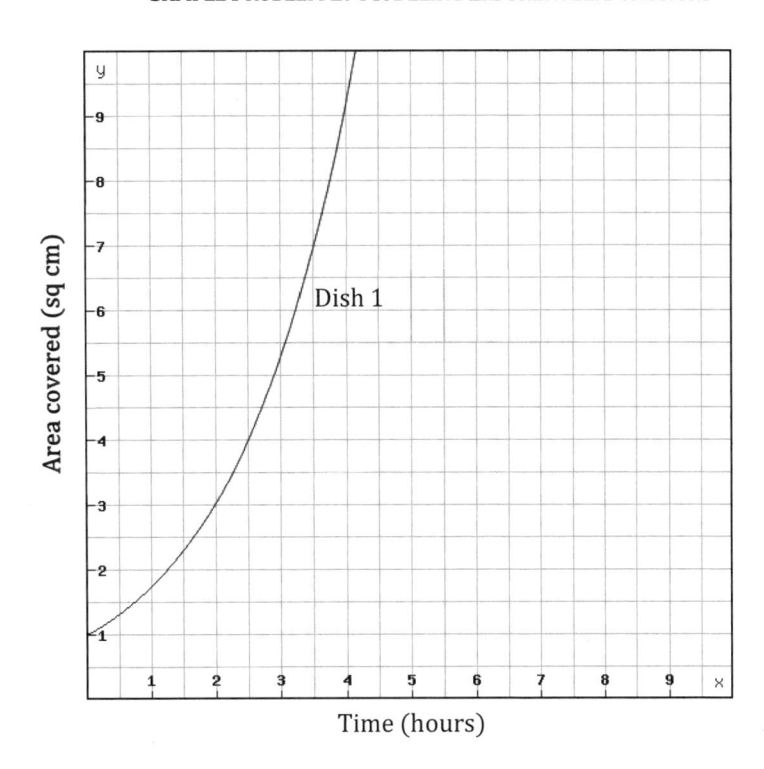

[Graph showing "Dish 1" curve with Area covered (sq cm) on y-axis and Time (hours) on x-axis]

A biologist places two different colonies of bacteria into two different petri dishes, each of which has an area of 10 square centimeters. After the initial placement of the bacteria ($t = 0$), the biologist measures and records the area covered by the bacteria in the dish every 15 minutes. The data for the first dish were fit by a smooth curve, as shown above. The data for the second dish was found to fit the curve modeled by the function $A(t) = 2 \times 2^{0.5t}$, where $A(t)$ represents the area covered by the bacteria after t hours. Which of the following is a correct statement about the data above?

A) At time $t = 0$, more of Dish 1 was covered by bacteria than Dish 2.
B) At time $t = 1$, more of Dish 1 was covered by bacteria than Dish 2.
C) The bacteria in Dish 2 took a greater amount of time to cover 100% of the dish than the bacteria in Dish 1 did.
D) The bacteria in Dish 1 took a greater amount of time to cover 100% of the dish than the bacteria in Dish 2 did.

Since we probably will not be able to precisely graph the data for Dish 2, we need to analyze three things: Dish 2's population at $t = 0$, at $t = 1$, and the amount of time it takes Dish 2 to cover the dish completely. The first two steps are easy: we'll just plug 0 and 1 in for t and solve.

$$A(0) = 2 \times 2^{0.5(0)} = 2$$

Since only 1 square cm of Dish 1 is covered at $t = 0$, we can cross out answer choice **A**.

$$A(1) = 2 \times 2^{0.5(1)} = 2\sqrt{2} \approx 2.828$$

An area of approximately 1.7 square cm of Dish 1 is covered at $t = 1$, so we can cross out answer choice **B**.

Now let's figure out when the bacteria covers Dish 2 completely. In this case, $A(t) = 10$.

$$A(t) = 2 \times 2^{0.5t}$$
$$10 = 2 \times 2^{0.5t}$$
$$5 = 2^{0.5t}$$
$$\log_2 5 = 0.5t$$
$$4.64 = t$$

Since the bacteria in Dish 1 only took around 4.2 hours to cover the dish completely, our answer must be **C** and cannot be **D**.

WRAP-UP

Constant practice is the only way to improve when it comes to exponential functions. Try the next few practice sets using what we've just learned. Good Luck!

SAT Red Math
Lesson 3B: Exponential Functions

RED MATH LESSON 3B: EXPONENTIAL FUNCTIONS

Learning to Swim

Directions: Answer each question below.

PRACTICE SET 1 (CALCULATOR)

1. Jane is studying the growth of a population of bacteria. Jane is hoping to have 1,073,600 bacteria after 20 hours. If Jane begins her experiment with a single bacterium, and the number of bacteria double every hour, by how many bacteria will Jane be short of her goal?

2. In Jane's new experiment, she is comparing two bacteria populations. One population begins with 50 bacteria and doubles every 2.5 hours. The second population begins with 100 bacteria and doubles every 4.5 hours. At what time will the two populations be equal if Jane begins her experiment at 1:00 pm?

3. The formula for half-life decay is $N = N_o \left(\frac{1}{2}\right)^{t/h}$, where N is the remaining quantity, N_o is the original quantity, t is time, and h is half-life, in years. The half-life of carbon-14 is 5730 years. If 0.0378 grams of carbon-14 remain, and Steve knows that his sample originally contained 1 gram of carbon-14, how many years have passed since Steve's sample was formed? Round to the nearest year.

4. If Steve were measuring the remaining quantity of an original substance with a half-life of 6285 years and a mass of 1 gram, how many grams of that substance would remain after the amount of time obtained in the previous question?

$$\log_7 xy^2 + \log_7 yz = \log_\pi 1 + \log_7 x^3 z + 1$$

5. Given the equation above, what is the value of $\frac{y^3}{x^2}$?

SAT Red Math
Lesson 3B: Exponential Functions

RED MATH LESSON 3B: EXPONENTIAL FUNCTIONS
Diving into the Deep End

Directions: Answer each question below.

PRACTICE SET 2 (CALCULATOR)

Days Rented (t)	Additional Fee (f)
1	5.00
2	6.50
3	8.45

Use the table above for questions 6 and 7.

6. A car rental company charges $25 a day for a customer to rent a car. The company also charges an additional rental fee f, which is based on the number of days the customer rents the car. If the above chart represents the price of the additional rental fee for t days, and if f is determined exponentially, what would be the total fee for someone who rents a car for 5 days using this company?
   A) $14.28
   B) $45.23
   C) $139.28
   D) $170.23

7. Which of the following appropriately models the total rental fee in terms of t?
   A) $\frac{50}{13}(1.3^t)$
   B) $25t + \frac{50}{13}(1.3^t)$
   C) $\frac{1250}{13}t(1.3^t)$
   D) $25t + 5(1.5^t)$

8. If $f(x) = \ln(5x + 1)$, which of the following changes will NOT cause $f(x)$ to have a domain of $(0, \infty)$?
   A) Subtract 1 from the terms inside the natural logarithmic function.
   B) Shift $f(x)$ to the right $\frac{1}{5}$ of a unit.
   C) Multiply each of the inside terms of $f(x)$ by $\frac{1}{5}$, then, subtract by $\frac{1}{5}$.
   D) Multiply $f(x)$ by a factor of $\frac{1}{5}$.

$f(x) = 3\log_2(x^2 + 5x) + 4\log_2(x^2 - 8) - \log_2(x^2 - 8)^2$

9. What of the following is equivalent to $f(x)$ above?
   A) $f(x) = \log_2[(x^2 + 5x)^2(x^2 - 8)^3]$
   B) $f(x) = \log_2[(x^2 + 5x)^3(x^2 - 8)^2]$
   C) $f(x) = \log_2[(x^2 + 5x)^5(x^2 - 8)^2]$
   D) $f(x) = \log_2[(x^2 + 5x)^2(x^2 - 8)^5]$

10. Which of the following is equivalent to $k(x) = e^{2x} - 5e^x + 6$?
    A) $\ln 2x - \ln 5x + \ln 6$
    B) $(e^x - 6)(e^x - 1)$
    C) $2x - 5x + \ln 6$
    D) $(e^x - 3)(e^x - 2)$

11. What function $d(x)$ has a domain of all real numbers and a range of $(2.4, \infty)$?
    A) $d(x) = e^{5.8x} + 2.4$
    B) $d(x) = e^{5.8x+2.4}$
    C) $d(x) = \ln(2.4x - 5.76)$
    D) $d(x) = \ln(2.4x) + 5.76$

$$c(t) = e^{\frac{1}{2}t+3}$$
$$s(t) = e^{2t-6}$$

14. There are two brands of medicine that Janice prescribes to people who have colds. The function $c(t)$ above models how many affected cells the first medicine, Cold-Bgone, attacks in a day after taking the recommended dose for t days. The function $s(t)$ models the same for the second medicine, Soothe-Me. If one person takes Cold-Bgone and another takes Soothe-Me at the same time, after how many days would the number of affected cells that have been attacked on a given day be the same in both patients?

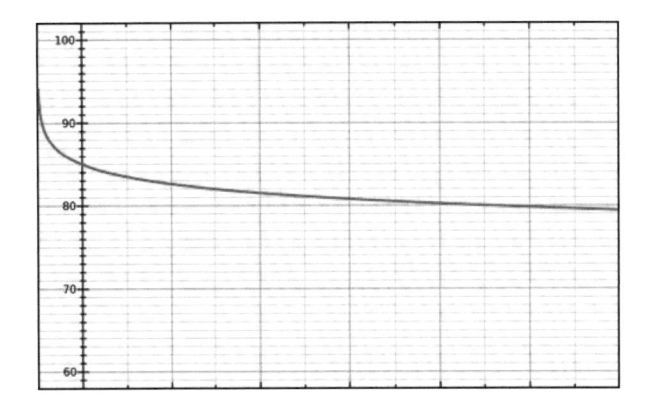

12. Dr. Monroe has conducted an experiment that analyzes memory. He did this by giving a test to his participants and then retesting them each month to see how much they remembered. Dr. Monroe discovered that the average score during the beginning of the experiment was 85%, and after 9 months, the average was an 80%. The graph above shows this, with the x-axis representing the number of months t after the first test, and the y-axis representing the average percent test score $a(t)$. Which of the following functions models a as a function of t?
    A) $a(t) = 85 - 5\ln(t + 1)$
    B) $a(t) = 85 - 5\log_{10}(t + 1)$
    C) $a(t) = 90 - 5\ln(t + 1)$
    D) $a(t) = 90 - 5\log_{10}(t + 1)$

15. Using the functions $c(t)$ and $s(t)$ above, which of the following best describes the relationship between the two medicines?
    A) $c(t)$ has a lower growth rate than $s(t)$ does, so Soothe-Me will eventually attack more diseased cells than Cold-Bgone will, despite not doing so initially.
    B) $s(t)$ has a lower starting point ($t = 0$) than that of $c(t)$, so Cold-Bgone will attack more diseased cells than Soothe-Me will, regardless of the value of t.
    C) $s(t)$ has a lower growth rate than $c(t)$ does, so Cold-Bgone will eventually attack more diseased cells than Soothe-Me will, despite not doing so initially.
    D) There is not enough information given to consider any relationship.

13. The average heart rate in beats per minute of Sal's track students, who jog at a steady and constant pace for t minutes, can be modeled by the equation $r(t) = 100e^{0.02t}$. If the average student maximum heart rate is 200 beats/min, and if Sal does not want them to reach this maximum and strain themselves, what is the longest time Sal should advise his students they run for daily? (Round to the nearest tenth of a minute)

SAT Red Math
Lesson 3B: Exponential Functions

PRACTICE SET 3 (CALCULATOR)

16. Element A has a half-life of 15 days and decays into Element B. So, after 15 days, the mass of Element A is reduced by half, and all of the "decayed" matter becomes Element B. A sample begins with 40 g of Element A. Which of the following correctly models the amount of Element B on day t?

    A) $40\left(\frac{1}{2}\right)^{\frac{t}{15}}$

    B) $40\left(1 - \left(\frac{1}{2}\right)^{\frac{t}{15}}\right)$

    C) $40(2)^{\frac{t}{15}}$

    D) $40\left(1 - (2)^{\frac{t}{15}}\right)$

17. A biologist isolates a culture of 10 bacteria on January 1, 2014. These bacteria double in population every four months. Another biologist isolates a culture of 2 bacteria in May 1, 2014. This second group of bacteria triple in population every three months. During which month will the second culture have twice the population as the first culture?

    A) May 2015
    B) June 2015
    C) July 2015
    D) August 2015

18. If $10^{ax+b} = c$, what is x in terms of a, b and c?

    A) $x = \frac{\frac{c}{10} - b}{a}$

    B) $x = \frac{\log c - b}{a}$

    C) $x = \frac{c - b}{10a}$

    D) $x = \frac{c - 10^b}{a}$

$$g(x) = Ae^{-\frac{x^2}{2\sigma^2}}$$

19. A Gaussian function has the form above, where A and σ are constants. What is the ratio of $g(0)$ to $g(2\sigma)$?

    A) e^{-2}
    B) e^{-1}
    C) e
    D) e^2

$$10^{2x} - 11(10^x) + 10 = 0$$

20. Find the solution set for the equation above.

    A) $x = \{1\}$
    B) $x = \{0,1\}$
    C) $x = \{0\}$
    D) $x = \{\emptyset\}$

21. If $e^{i\vartheta} = \cos(\vartheta) + i\sin(\vartheta)$, where $i^2 = -1$, what is the value of $e^{i\pi} + 1$?

    A) 0
    B) 1
    C) e
    D) π

22. If the value of an investment doubles every 10 years, how long will it take for the investment to increase in value one thousand fold?

    A) 100 years
    B) 1,000 years
    C) 10,000 years
    D) 1,000,000 years

23. If $10^x + 10^{-x} = 10\frac{1}{10}$, what is a possible value of x?

    A) 1
    B) 2
    C) 10
    D) 10π

24. If $e^x + e^{-x} = 2$, what is the value of $e^{2x} + e^{-2x}$?

$$B = 10^{-0.4(m - m_0)}$$

25. The magnitude of a star m and its brightness B are related by the equation above, where m_0 is a constant. What is the ratio of the brightness of a star of magnitude 1.0 to that of a star of magnitude 6.0?

RED MATH LESSON 3B: EXPONENTIAL FUNCTIONS
Race to the Finish

Directions: Answer each question below.

HOMEWORK SET (CALCULATOR)

$$\left(\frac{25}{49}\right)^{d-6} = \left(\frac{7}{5}\right)^{d+3f}$$
$$(2^d)^4 = \left(\frac{1}{16}\right)^{-f}$$

1. Solve the above system of equations.
   A) $d = -6, f = -6$
   B) $d = 2, f = 2$
   C) $d = 3, f = -3$
   D) No solution

$$2\log(2x - 1) = \log(2x + 1) + \log(x + 1)$$

2. For what value(s) of x is the above equation true?
   A) $x = 0$
   B) $x = \frac{7}{2}$
   C) $x = 0$ or $\frac{7}{2}$
   D) No solution

$$f(x) = \ln e^x + \log_3 \frac{x-1}{9} + \log_5\left(\frac{2}{x} + x - 2\right) - \frac{\log_7(18x)}{\log_7 6}$$

3. What is the value of $f(2)$ using the function above?
   A) -2
   B) -1
   C) 1
   D) 2

$$g(x) = \log_{10}[\log_{10}(x^2 - 2x + 1)]$$

4. The domain of the function above includes all real values of x such that:
   A) $x < 0$ or $x > 2$
   B) $0 < x < 2$
   C) $x < 1$
   D) $x \neq 1$

$$3^{6z^3}\left(\frac{1}{3}\right)^{7z^2} = \left(\frac{1}{9}\right)^z$$

5. Which answer choice is NOT a solution to the equation above?
   A) $z = 0$
   B) $z = \frac{1}{3}$
   C) $z = \frac{1}{2}$
   D) $z = \frac{2}{3}$

6. A hedge fund manager promises Chloe annual returns of $r_1\%$ on an investment. In reality, he is recklessly losing Chloe's money at an annual rate of $r_2\%$. After how many years will the actual value of Chloe's account be half of the expected value of her account?
   A) $\dfrac{\log 2}{\log\left(\frac{100+r_1}{100-r_2}\right)}$
   B) $\dfrac{\log 2}{\log\left(\frac{100-r_1}{100+r_2}\right)}$
   C) $\dfrac{-\log 2}{\log\left(\frac{100+r_1}{100-r_2}\right)}$
   D) $\dfrac{\log 2}{\log\left(\frac{100+r_1}{100+r_2}\right)}$

$$A(t) = A_0 e^{rt}$$

7. Cesium-137 is a radioactive isotope that decays exponentially according to the equation above, where A_0, r, and t are the initial amount in grams, a constant, and time in years, respectively. After 3 years, a 30-gram sample decays to 28 grams. To the nearest whole year, how long does it take for a different sample to reduce to 25% of its original amount?
   A) 15 years
   B) 30 years
   C) 45 years
   D) 60 years

$$h(x) = b \log_{10}(x + c) + d$$

8. If b is any real number, $c < 0$, and $d \geq 0$, then which of the following CANNOT be the graph for the equation above?

A)

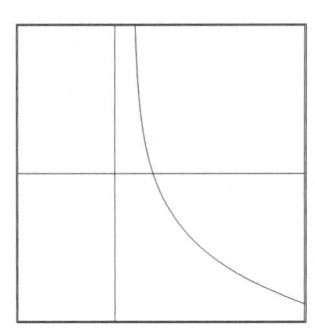

B)

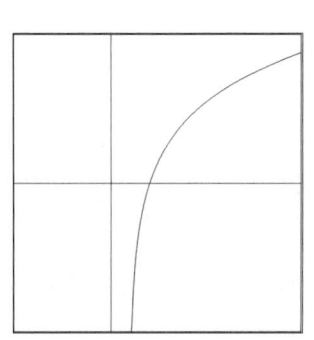

C)

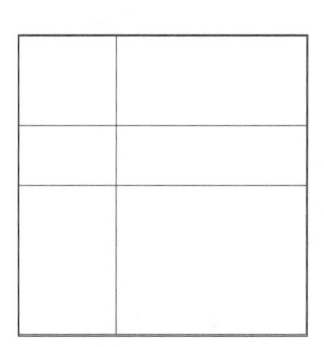

D)

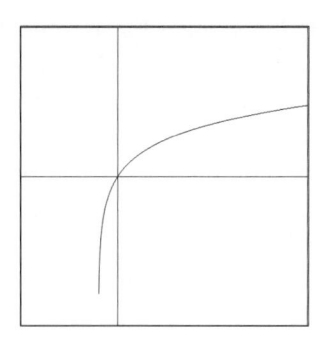

$$\log_a \left(\frac{\sqrt[3]{b}}{\sqrt{b}} \div \frac{\sqrt[3]{c}}{\sqrt{c}} \right)$$

9. If $\log_a b = 4$ and $\log_a c = -5$, then what is the value of the expression above?

A) $\frac{-3}{2}$
B) $\frac{-1}{6}$
C) 0
D) $\frac{1}{6}$

$$7 \log_2 u - \frac{\log_2 v}{5} + \log_4 (uv)^2$$

10. Rewrite the above expression as a single logarithm.

A) $\log_2 \left(\frac{u^5}{\sqrt[5]{v^{11}}} \right)$
B) $\log_2 \left(\frac{u^7}{\sqrt[5]{v}} \right)$
C) $\log_2 \left(u^9 \sqrt[5]{v^9} \right)$
D) $\log_2 \left(u^8 \sqrt[5]{v^4} \right)$

11. For which of the following scenarios is an exponential model not appropriate?
   A) The amount of electricity used by a small town when the electricity needed increases by a fixed wattage for every new resident.
   B) The yearly incidence of lung cancer following a successful campaign which reduces the rate of lung cancer development by half.
   C) The number of cells when a group of cells splits into two new cells every hour.
   D) The interest earned from an investment compounds upon itself monthly.

SAT Red Math — Lesson 3B: Exponential Functions

12. A biologist observes the growth rate of two samples of bacteria. Both samples have the same initial amount of bacteria. In Sample A, the amount of bacteria doubles every hour. In Sample B, the amount of bacteria triples every hour. Which statement correctly describes how the logarithm of the ratio of the population of Sample A to Sample B changes over time?
    A) The logarithm of the ratio stays at a constant $\frac{2}{3}$.
    B) The logarithm of the ratio follows a linear model with a coefficient of $\log\left(\frac{2}{3}\right)$.
    C) The logarithm of the ratio follows a linear model with a coefficient of $\frac{\log(2)}{\log(3)}$.
    D) The logarithm of the ratio decreases exponentially with a base of $\frac{2}{3}$.

13. The concentration of moss in a pond decreases by 25% per month. After approximately how many months can you expect to have a concentration of moss that is 25% of the original concentration?
    A) 1 month
    B) 3 months
    C) 5 months
    D) Impossible to tell without knowing the original concentration.

$$4(\log_7 10)(\log_{10} 7^6) = \log_x 169^{12}$$

14. Which value of x satisfies the above equation?
    A) 7
    B) 10
    C) 13
    D) 16

Use the following data for questions 15 and 16.

Year	# of New Customers
1	32
2	48
3	72
4	108
5	162
6	243
7	365

15. If the pattern presented in the data above holds true, approximately how many new customers would the store owner expect to have in the twentieth year after opening her business?
    A) 8000
    B) 40,000
    C) 70,000
    D) 106,000

16. The store owner charts the percent increase in total customers from the previous year for years 1 through 5. If she were to graph this data, what model would best fit it?
    A) A constant function.
    B) An increasing linear function.
    C) A quadratic function.
    D) An exponential function.

17. What is the sum of the solutions of the equation $\log\sqrt{4 - 2t + t^2} = \log(t + 2)$?

SAT Red Math
Lesson 3B: Exponential Functions

18. What is the product of the real solutions of the equation $(\log_3 x)^2 - \log_3\left(\frac{1}{x^2}\right) - 8 = 0$?

19. Tim puts $5000 into a savings account that accrues a monthly compounded annual interest of 5% for 10 years. He then takes all of the money out of the savings account and invests it in a business which, unfortunately, loses 20% of his investment. If Tim takes his remaining money and puts it back in the original savings account, how many full months must he leave it in before he has more money than when he took it out to invest?

20. You are deciding between two savings accounts in which to deposit $10,000 for five years. Bank A offers a 2.5% yearly interest rate compounded continuously but will charge a $500 fee to take the money out of the account. Bank B offers the same interest rate, but compounded monthly, and will not charge an early removal fee. After the fee is assessed, Bank A's return will be approximately what percent of Bank B's return? Round to the nearest percent.

C2 education
be smarter.

Red Math Lesson 4A: Rational Functions
Getting Your Feet Wet

Directions: The problems below are intended as a short diagnostic exam.

1. If the expression $\frac{8x^2-6}{2x-2}$ is written in the equivalent form $C + \frac{1}{x-1}$, what is C in terms of x?
   A) $2x + 2$
   B) $4x + 3$
   C) $4x + 4$
   D) $8x + 8$

$$f(x) = \frac{3x^2+8x+4}{6x^3+7x^2+2x}$$

2. What is the domain of the above function?
   A) All real values of x except 0 and $-\frac{1}{2}$.
   B) All real values of x except $-\frac{2}{3}$ and -2.
   C) All real values of x except 0, $-\frac{1}{2}$, and $-\frac{2}{3}$.
   D) All real values of x.

RED MATH LESSON 4A: RATIONAL FUNCTIONS
Wading In

Directions: Read the explanation for each problem type mentioned below. Pay special attention to the methods and techniques used to solve the sample problems. Then, do the practice exercises that follow; use the appropriate method to solve each problem.

TOPIC OVERVIEW: RATIONAL FUNCTIONS

In Blue Math Lesson 6A, we were introduced to many of the basic operations on rational functions, such as adding, subtracting, multiplying, and synthetic division. We will discuss synthetic division in a little more detail, then talk about the graphs of rational function in full, including their holes and asymptotes.

We will most often need to use synthetic division (or polynomial long division) on questions that involve decomposition of fractions. These questions involve taking an expression such as $\frac{9x^2}{3x+3}$ and turning it into something like $3x - 3 + \frac{9}{3x+3}$. Let's try one of these questions below:

SAMPLE PROBLEM 1: RATIONAL FUNCTIONS

If the expression $\frac{8x^2-6}{2x-2}$ is written in the equivalent form $C + \frac{1}{x-1}$, what is C in terms of x?

A) $2x + 2$
B) $4x + 3$
C) $4x + 4$
D) $8x + 8$

Since we're decomposing a rational function into smaller terms, we know we need to use synthetic or polynomial long division. First, let's simplify our expression by pulling a 2 out of both the numerator and the denominator:

$$\frac{8x^2-6}{2x-2} = \frac{4x^2-3}{x-1}$$

Now we can use synthetic division (if you need a refresher course on synthetic division, please read back over Blue Math Lesson 6A):

$$\begin{array}{c|ccc} 1 & 4 & 0 & -3 \\ & \downarrow & & \\ \hline & 4 & & \end{array}$$

$$\begin{array}{c|ccc} 1 & 4 & 0 & -3 \\ \times & & 4 & \\ \hline & 4 & & \end{array}$$

SAT Red Math
Lesson 4A: Rational Functions

$$\begin{array}{c|ccc} 1 & 4 & 0 & -3 \\ & & 4 & \\ \hline & 4 & 4 & \end{array}$$

$$\begin{array}{c|ccc} 1 & 4 & 0 & -3 \\ & & 4 & 4 \\ \hline & 4 & 4 & \end{array}$$

$$\begin{array}{c|ccc} 1 & 4 & 0 & -3 \\ & & 4 & 4 \\ \hline & 4 & 4 & 1 \end{array}$$

Thus, $\frac{8x^2-6}{2x-2}$ is equivalent to $4x + 4 + \frac{1}{x-1}$. Our answer must be **C**.

TOPIC OVERVIEW: THE DOMAIN AND RANGE OF RATIONAL FUNCTIONS

The graphs of rational functions will only be rarely tested on the SAT. We do, however, need to be very aware of discontinuities, or values excluded from the domain of a rational function. To find these excluded values, set the denominator of the rational function equal to 0, then solve. Those values of x will not appear in the domain of your function. Let's look at an example:

SAMPLE PROBLEM 2: THE DOMAIN AND RANGE OF RATIONAL FUNCTIONS

$$f(x) = \frac{3x^2+8x+4}{6x^3+7x^2+2x}$$

What is the domain of the above function?

A) All real values of x except 0 and $-\frac{1}{2}$.
B) All real values of x except $-\frac{2}{3}$ and -2.
C) All real values of x except 0, $-\frac{1}{2}$, and $-\frac{2}{3}$.
D) All real values of x.

To find the domain of a rational function, simply set the denominator equal to 0, factor and solve:

$$6x^3 + 7x^2 + 2x = 0$$
$$x(3x+2)(2x+1) = 0$$

$x = 0$ $3x + 2 = 0$ $2x + 1 = 0$
$x = 0$ $x = -\frac{2}{3}$ $x = -\frac{1}{2}$

So, our answer is **C**.

Topic Overview: Asymptotes and Holes

Sometimes, we may be asked to find whether or not a rational function has any asymptotes or holes. Horizontal and slant asymptotes are easier to find if the polynomials that make up the numerator and denominator are in expanded, rather than factored, form. Let's look for some general patterns here:

$$f(x) = \frac{Ax^n + Bx^{n-1} + \cdots}{Fx^m + Gx^{m-1} + \cdots}$$

For rational function $f(x)$ above, use the following rules to determine horizontal and slant asymptotes:

- If $n < m$, then the line $y = 0$ is the horizontal asymptote.
- If $n = m$, then the line $y = \frac{A}{F}$ is the horizontal asymptote.
- If $n > m$, then there is no horizontal asymptote. However, if $n = m + 1$, then there will be a slant asymptote which can be found by dividing the denominator of the rational function into its numerator. The quotient, $y = mx + b$, is the equation of the slant asymptote (disregard the remainder).

On the other hand, vertical asymptotes are easier to determine if the numerator and denominator of the function are in factored form:

$$g(x) = \frac{(x-a) \times (x-b) \times \cdots}{(x-c) \times (x-d) \times \cdots}$$

As we learned in our discussion of the domain and range of rational functions, any value of x that would cause the denominator of the function to equal 0 is a discontinuity. If the term that causes this discontinuity can be cancelled out with a term on the top, then the discontinuity is a hole. If the discontinuity cannot be cancelled out, then the discontinuity is a vertical asymptote. So, the function $h(x)$ below has a hole at $x = 4$ and a vertical asymptote at $x = 2$.

$$h(x) = \frac{x(x-4)}{(x-2)(x-4)}$$

Wrap-Up

Rational functions will not show up too often on the SAT, and when they do, they will always be considered one of the harder question types. Familiarize yourself with the topic over the next few practice sets. Good Luck!

RED MATH LESSON 4A: RATIONAL FUNCTIONS
Learning to Swim

Directions: Answer each question below.

PRACTICE SET 1 (NO CALCULATOR)

$$f(x) = \frac{x^2+5x+6}{(x-1)(x-2)(x-3)(x-4)}$$

1. The function above has how many vertical asymptotes?

$$g(x) = \frac{5x^2-7x+100}{3x^2-200x+1}$$

2. To what value does the above function approach as x becomes large and negative?

$$y(x) = \frac{3x-7}{4x^3-3x^2+2x-1}$$

Use the function above for questions 3 and 4.

3. The above function crosses the x-axis at what value when graphed in the coordinate plane?

4. The above function crosses the y-axis at what value when graphed in the coordinate plane?

$$y = \frac{10x^3-\frac{1}{2}x^2+3x-7}{x^2-10x+21}$$

5. Which values of x are not present in the domain for the equation above?

SAT Red Math
Lesson 4A: Rational Functions

RED MATH LESSON 4A: RATIONAL FUNCTIONS
Diving into the Deep End

Directions: Answer each question below.

PRACTICE SET 2 (NO CALCULATOR)

6. If $f(x) = \frac{x^2+2x}{x+6}$, and $g(x) = \frac{2x+6}{x+3}$, what is $f(x) + g(x)$?
   A) $\frac{x^2+5x+6}{x+6}$
   B) $\frac{x^2+4x+12}{x+6}$
   C) $\frac{3x^2+4x+12}{x+6}$
   D) $\frac{3x^2+20x+36}{x+6}$

7. All of the following contain a horizontal asymptote EXCEPT for which function?
   A) $\frac{x^2+3}{2x^2-4}$
   B) $\frac{x+3}{2x^2-4}$
   C) $\frac{x^2+x+3}{2x^2-4}$
   D) $\frac{x^2+3}{2x-4}$

8. For the function $h(x) = \frac{3x^3-6x+8}{x+2}$, what is the value of the remainder after polynomial long division is done?
   A) -4
   B) 4
   C) 16
   D) 20

9. What is the positive difference between the x-value of the smallest zero of the function $f(x) = \frac{x^3-25x}{x-5}$, and the x-position of the vertical asymptote of the function $g(x) = \frac{9x^2-3x+7}{x^3+8}$?
   A) 0
   B) 2
   C) 3
   D) 5

10. The equation $\frac{x}{x-7} = \frac{63}{x^2-5x-14}$ is true for which of the following values of x?
    A) $x = -9, 7$
    B) $x = -7, 9$
    C) $x = -9$
    D) $x = 7$

11. If $f(x) = \frac{x+2}{x+9}$ and $g(x) = \frac{3x^2+36x+81}{x+3}$ and $x \neq -9$ or -3, then $f(x)g(x) =$
    A) $\frac{3x+6}{(x+9)(x+3)}$
    B) $\frac{x^2+12x+27}{(x+9)(x+3)}$
    C) $\frac{3x+6}{x+3}$
    D) $3x+6$

12. Which of the following functions contains a vertical asymptote of $x = 7$ and a horizontal asymptote of $y = \frac{3}{2}$?
    A) $\frac{\sqrt[3]{x^2-11x+12}}{x-7}$
    B) $\frac{3x^2+6x-5}{2x^3-7}$
    C) $\frac{3x-13}{2x-14}$
    D) $\frac{3x^2-8x+15}{2x^2-14}$

Lesson 4A: Rational Functions

13. For the function $f(x) = \frac{x^3-8x^2+15x}{4x-20}$, which function $g(x)$ makes the statement $f(x) - g(x) = 0$ true for all $x \neq 5$?
    A) $g(x) = \frac{1}{4(x-3)}$
    B) $g(x) = \frac{x-3}{4}$
    C) $g(x) = \frac{x^2-3x}{4}$
    D) $g(x) = \frac{x^2-3x}{4(x-5)}$

14. The graph of which of the following functions contains a hole?
    A) $f(x) = \frac{x^2-7x+6}{x^2-10x+28}$
    B) $f(x) = \frac{x^2+9x+20}{x^2-10x+28}$
    C) $f(x) = \frac{x^2-7x+6}{x^2+2x-8}$
    D) $f(x) = \frac{x^2+9x+20}{x^2+2x-8}$

15. Which of the following equations has a range of all real numbers except $y = 1$?
    A) $f(x) = \frac{3x^3-x^2-10x-8}{2x^3+10x^2+17x-28}$
    B) $f(x) = \frac{2x^3+6x^2+11x+6}{3x^3+10x^2+17x-28}$
    C) $f(x) = \frac{-x^3-x^2-10x-8}{x^3-x^2-17x-15}$
    D) $f(x) = \frac{2x^3+6x^2+11x+6}{2x^3-6x^2+11x-6}$

Practice Set 3 (No Calculator)

16. Assuming $x \neq 2$ or -2, $\frac{x^2-3x+2}{x^2-4} \cdot \frac{x+2}{x^2+4x+4} =$
    A) $\frac{(x-1)(x-2)}{(x+2)^2}$
    B) $\frac{(x-1)(x-2)}{x+2}$
    C) $\frac{x-1}{(x+2)^2}$
    D) $\frac{x-1}{x+2}$

17. What is $\frac{x+2}{x-5} + \frac{x-1}{x+3}$?
    A) $\frac{2x+1}{x^2-2x-15}$
    B) $\frac{11x+1}{x^2-2x-15}$
    C) $\frac{2x^2-x+1}{x^2-2x-15}$
    D) $\frac{2x^2-x+11}{x^2-2x-15}$

18. If $\frac{x}{2x+3} = \frac{1}{x-2} + C$, what is C in terms of x?
    A) $\frac{x-1}{x+2}$
    B) $\frac{-x-5}{2x^2-x-6}$
    C) $\frac{x^2-4x+3}{2x^2-x-6}$
    D) $\frac{x^2-4x-3}{2x^2-x-6}$

19. How many distinct real solutions exist for the equation $\frac{x^2-8x+16}{x-2} \cdot \frac{x^2-4}{x-4} = 0$?
    A) 0
    B) 1
    C) 2
    D) 3

SAT Red Math
Lesson 4A: Rational Functions

20. Which of the following expressions is a factor of both the numerator and the denominator of the expression $\frac{x^3+3x^2-x-3}{x^2+5x+6}$?

    A) $x + 3$
    B) $x + 1$
    C) $x - 1$
    D) $x - 3$

21. Assuming $z \neq 3$ or -3, $\frac{z^2-z-12}{z^2-6z+9} \div \frac{z^2-9}{z-4} =$

    A) $\frac{(z+3)^2}{z-3}$
    B) $\frac{z-4}{(z-3)^2}$
    C) $\frac{(z-4)^2}{(z-3)^2}$
    D) $\frac{(z-4)^2}{(z-3)^3}$

22. For all $x \neq -5$, which of the following expressions is equivalent to the expression $\frac{x^5+5x^4-5x^3-25x^2+4x+20}{x+5}$?

    A) $x^5 - 5x^3 + 4x$
    B) $x^4 - 5x^2 + 4$
    C) $x^4 + 4x^3 - 5x^2 - 25x + 4$
    D) $x^4 + x^3 - 5x^2 - 5x + 4$

23. For all $x \neq 2$, which of the following expressions is equivalent to the expression $\frac{3x^4-2x^2+8}{x-2}$?

    A) $3x^3 - 6x^2 - 14x + 28 + \frac{48}{x-2}$
    B) $3x^3 + 6x^2 + 10x - 20 + \frac{32}{x-2}$
    C) $3x^3 + 6x^2 + 10x + 20 + \frac{32}{x-2}$
    D) $3x^3 + 6x^2 + 10x + 20 + \frac{48}{x-2}$

24. What is the range of the function $f(x) = \frac{3x^2+10x+3}{x+3}$?

    A) All real values of y except -8
    B) All real values of y except -3
    C) All real values of y greater than -8
    D) All real values of y less than -3

25. A rational function graphed in the xy-coordinate plane has an asymptote at $x = -1$ and intercepts at $y = 6$ and $x = -3$. Which of the following could be the function?

    A) $f(x) = \frac{x^3+3x^2+2x+6}{x-1}$
    B) $f(x) = \frac{x^3+6x^2+x+6}{x-1}$
    C) $f(x) = \frac{x^3+3x^2+2x+6}{x+1}$
    D) $f(x) = \frac{x^3+6x^2+x+6}{x+1}$

Red Math Lesson 4A: Rational Functions
Race to the Finish

Directions: Answer each question below.

Homework Set (No Calculator)

1. Which of these combinations of asymptotes is it not possible for a rational function to have?
   A) A horizontal asymptote at $y = 0$, and a vertical asymptote at $x = -1$.
   B) Two horizontal asymptotes at $y = -1$ and $y = 2$.
   C) No horizontal asymptotes and no vertical asymptotes.
   D) No horizontal asymptotes and vertical asymptotes at:
   $x = \{0, 1, 2, 3, 4, 5, 6, 7, 8, 9, 10\}$

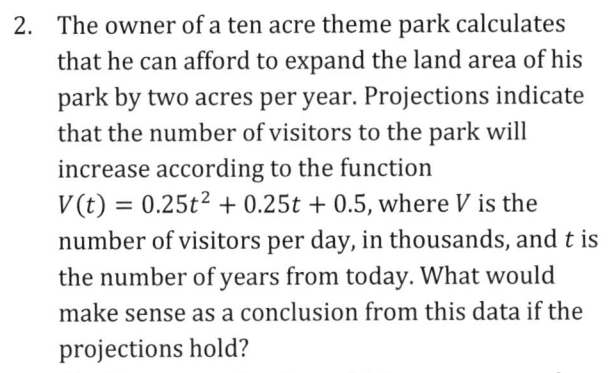

2. The owner of a ten acre theme park calculates that he can afford to expand the land area of his park by two acres per year. Projections indicate that the number of visitors to the park will increase according to the function $V(t) = 0.25t^2 + 0.25t + 0.5$, where V is the number of visitors per day, in thousands, and t is the number of years from today. What would make sense as a conclusion from this data if the projections hold?
   A) The current land acquisition strategy makes sense. It will preserve the density of visitors/acre in the park, preventing overcrowding.
   B) The owner plans to purchase too much land per year. Over the long term, the number of customers cannot support this increase in area.
   C) If the owner does not find a way to purchase more land immediately, the density of visitors in the park will begin ramping up next year.
   D) The owner will need to find a way to purchase more land if he wants to maintain the current density of visitors; the additional land will be sufficient to maintain the current visitor density in the short term, but the density will increase in the long term."

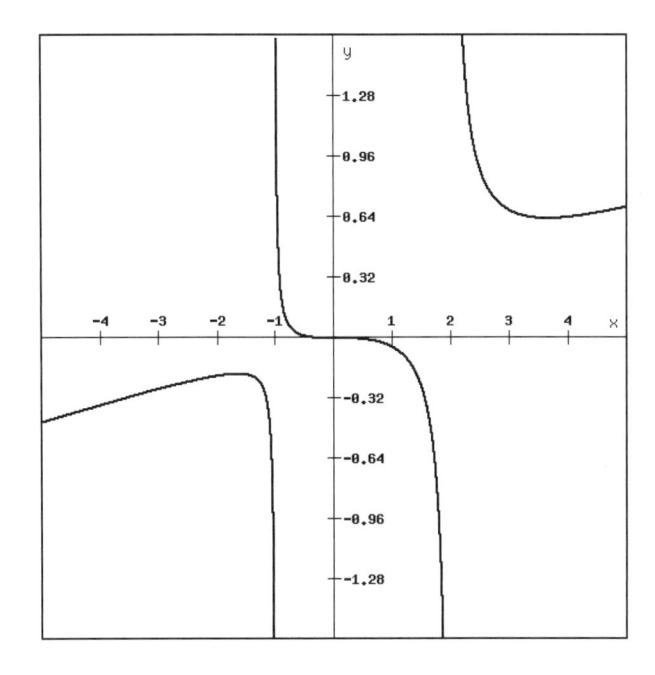

Use the above graph for questions 3 and 4.

3. Which of the following rational functions could be represented by the graph?
   A) A linear function divided by a quadratic function.
   B) The ratio of two quadratic functions.
   C) A cubic function divided by a quadratic function.
   D) The ratio of two cubic functions.

4. Which of the following most accurately represents the domain of the graph?
   A) $(-\infty, -1) \cup (-1, 2) \cup (2, \infty)$
   B) $(-\infty, -1] \cup [-1, 2] \cup [2, \infty]$
   C) $[-1.6, 1.6]$
   D) All real numbers.

SAT Red Math
Lesson 4A: Rational Functions

5. If you divide a cubic polynomial by a quadratic polynomial, what form(s) can the remainder take?
   A) Only constant.
   B) Only quadratic.
   C) Both linear and quadratic.
   D) Both constant and linear.

$$f(x) = \frac{5x}{x-3} + \frac{3x}{x-2}$$

6. What of the following types of asymptotic behavior will the function above display?
   A) A horizontal asymptote at $y = 0$.
   B) A horizontal asymptote at $y = 5$.
   C) A horizontal asymptote at $y = 8$.
   D) A slant asymptote of $y = 3x$.

7. The graph of which of the following functions has a hole at $x = -1$?
   A) $\frac{x^3+2x+17}{x^2-1}$
   B) $\frac{x^4+7x^3+5x^2-31x-30}{x^3+1}$
   C) $\frac{1}{x+1}$
   D) $\frac{x^2+2x+1}{x^2+1}$

8. Clayton takes x hours to quality check a shipment of 400 boxes. Michael takes 4 more hours to check a shipment of 300 boxes than it takes Clayton to check a shipment of 400 boxes. Which of the following expressions represents the number of boxes per hour that they could check together?
   A) $\frac{700}{2x+4}$
   B) $\frac{700x}{x^2+4x}$
   C) $\frac{700x+1600}{x(x+4)}$
   D) $700(2x+4)$

9. A certain model of car costs $16,500 to buy. The depreciation of the value of the car, D, given t years after its purchase can be modeled by $D(t) = \frac{800t-200}{0.05t+100}$. Approximately what percentage of the car's original value will it be worth in the long run (asymptotically)? Note: the car's value is equal to its original value minus its depreciation.
   A) 1%
   B) 3%
   C) 5%
   D) 10%

$$f(x) = x^3 - 2x^2 - 4x + 8$$
$$g(x) = x^3 - 4x^2 + 4x$$

10. Find the greatest common factor of the two functions above.
    A) $x^2 - 4$
    B) -4
    C) $x^2 - 4x + 4$
    D) $x + 2$

11. Identify the domain and range of the following function: $f(x) = \frac{3}{x+5} - 2$
    A) Domain = all real numbers except for 5, Range = all real numbers except for -2.
    B) Domain = all real numbers except for -5, Range = all real numbers except for 2.
    C) Domain = all real numbers except for -5, Range = all real numbers except for -2.
    D) Domain = all real numbers except for -5, Range = all real numbers.

12. Solve: $\frac{16}{x(x-4)} + \frac{8}{x} = \frac{4}{x-4}$
    A) $-4, 0$
    B) $4, 0$
    C) 4
    D) No solution

$$f(x) = \frac{x^3+5}{x^2}$$

13. Identify the horizontal and vertical asymptotes of the graph of the function above.
    A) Horizontal: $y = 0$, Vertical: $x = -5$
    B) Horizontal: $y = 0$, Vertical: $x = 0$
    C) Horizontal: none, Vertical: $x = 0$
    D) Horizontal: $y = 0$, Vertical: none

14. The graph of which of the following rational functions has vertical asymptotes at both $x = -2$ and $x = 5$?
    A) $f(x) = \frac{x-5}{(x+2)(x-5)}$
    B) $f(x) = \frac{x+5}{(x+2)(x-5)}$
    C) $f(x) = \frac{x+5}{(x-2)(x+5)}$
    D) $f(x) = \frac{x-5}{(x-2)(x+5)}$

$$\frac{x^2+2x-8}{x+3} \div \frac{x-2}{x+3} \times \frac{x}{x+4}$$

15. For all $x \neq -3$ or 2, the above expression is equivalent to which of the following?
    A) x
    B) $-x$
    C) $\frac{x(x+2)(x-4)}{(x-2)(x+4)}$
    D) $-x(x+2)(x-4)$

$$f(x) = \frac{x^3-9x}{x^2-2x-3}$$

Questions 16 and 17 refer to the above function.

16. What are the discontinuities, if any, of $f(x)$?
    A) There are vertical asymptotes at $x = -1$ and $x = 3$.
    B) There are no discontinuities.
    C) There are discontinuities when $x = -1$ and $x = 3$, and the one at $x = 3$ is removable (a hole).
    D) There are removable discontinuities (holes) when $x = -1$ or $x = 3$.

17. What are the vertical and/or horizontal asymptotes, if any, of $f(x)$?
    A) There are neither vertical nor horizontal asymptotes.
    B) The vertical asymptotes are $x = -1$ and $x = 3$, and the horizontal asymptote is $y = 0$.
    C) The vertical asymptote is $x = -1$, and the horizontal asymptote is $y = 0$.
    D) The vertical asymptote is $x = -1$, and there is no horizontal asymptote.

$$\frac{x^3-5x^2+2x+8}{x^2+3x+2} \times \frac{x}{x-2} \div \frac{x-4}{x^3+9x^2+14x}$$

18. Which of the following is equivalent to the expression above for all values of x for which it is defined?
    A) $x^3 + 3x^2$
    B) $x^3 - 4x^2$
    C) $x^3 + 7x^2$
    D) $2x^3 - 14x^2$

$$f(x) = 2x^3 + 8x^2 - 40x - 96$$
$$g(x) = 3x^3 + 24x^2 + 12x - 144$$

19. Which of the following is a factor of both of the above functions?
    A) $x + 4$
    B) $x - 4$
    C) $x + 6$
    D) $x - 6$

20. What are the horizontal and vertical asymptotes for the function $f(x) = \frac{7}{x^2+9}$?
    A) Horizontal: $y = 3$ and $y = -3$, Vertical: none
    B) Horizontal: $y = 3$ and $y = -3$, Vertical: $x = 7$
    C) Horizontal: none, Vertical: $x = 0$
    D) Horizontal: $y = 0$, Vertical: none

RED MATH LESSON 4B: LINEAR, QUADRATIC, AND EXPONENTIAL MODELS
Getting Your Feet Wet

Directions: The problems below are intended as a short diagnostic exam.

1. Pickling, a process that removes rust from steel before processing, treats steel with hydrochloric acid (HCl). If a factory has a tank that contains 20 L of HCl and dispenses HCl at a rate of 500 mL per hour, how many liters of HCl will be left in the tank after t minutes of pickling? (Note: a liter, L, contains 1000 milliliters, mL)

   A) $20 - \frac{t}{2}$
   B) $20 - \frac{t}{120}$
   C) $20t - \frac{t}{120}$
   D) $20 + \frac{t}{120}$

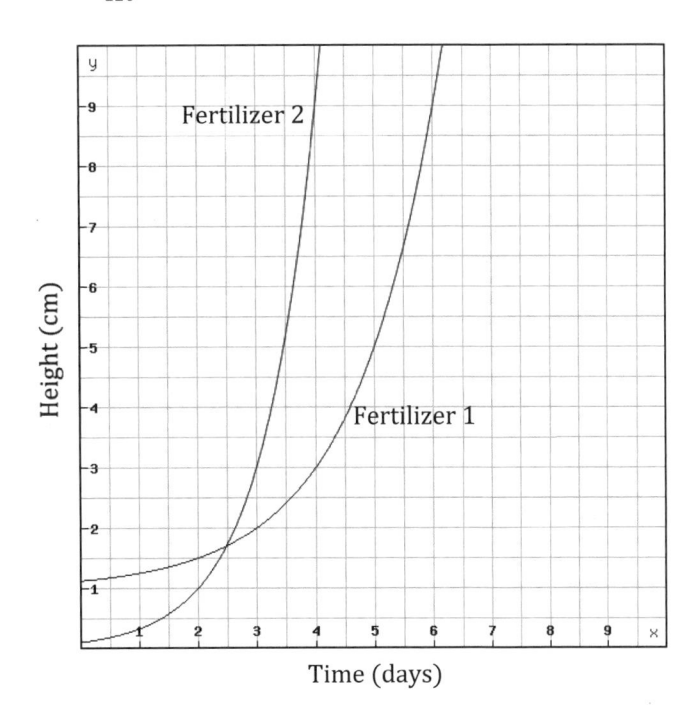

2. A botanist records the heights, in cm, of two different pea plants, each of which was treated with a different fertilizer, twice daily. The data for each plant were fit by a smooth curve, as shown above. Which of the following is a correct statement about the data above?

   A) After 6 days, the plant treated with Fertilizer 1 is nearly twice as tall as the one treated with Fertilizer 2.
   B) Initially, the plant treated with Fertilizer 2 was 1 cm taller than the one treated with Fertilizer 1.
   C) The rate of growth of the plant treated with Fertilizer 2 is three times the rate of growth of the plant treated with Fertilizer 1.
   D) After two and a half days, the plants were approximately the same height.

SAT Red Math
Lesson 4B: Linear, Quadratic, and Exponential Models

RED MATH LESSON 4B: LINEAR, QUADRATIC, AND EXPONENTIAL MODELS
Wading In

Directions: Read the explanation for each problem type mentioned below. Pay special attention to the methods and techniques used to solve the sample problems. Then, do the practice exercises that follow; use the appropriate method to solve each problem.

TOPIC OVERVIEW: MODELING

Modeling is one of the most important skilled that we learn in high school mathematics, as it allows us to use what we learn in the classroom to analyze real-world situations in order to increase our understanding and improve our decision making. In real life, we will generally use technology to create these models, but it's important to understand the mathematics behind the models first.

To model a real-world situation, start by:

1. Identifying the variables—what changes in the situation?
2. Formulating a model based on the data given or situation described.
3. Analyzing the model to draw any required conclusions.
4. Validating the conclusions.

Let's look at a question together to get a feel for how these problems work:

SAMPLE PROBLEM 1: MODELING

Pickling, a process that removes rust from steel before processing, treats steel with hydrochloric acid (HCl). If a factory has a tank that contains 20 L of HCl and dispenses HCl at a rate of 500 mL per hour, how many liters of HCl will be left in the tank after t minutes of pickling? (Note: a liter, L, contains 1000 milliliters, mL)

A) $20 - \frac{t}{2}$

B) $20 - \frac{t}{120}$

C) $20t - \frac{t}{120}$

D) $20 + \frac{t}{120}$

Let's go through each step together:

1. **Identifying the variables—what changes in the situation?**

   For this problem, we're given one variable, t, which represents the number of minutes that pickling has taken place for. We also know

SAT Red Math
Lesson 4B: Linear, Quadratic, and Exponential Models

that our total amount of HCl, let's call it h, is based on an initial amount, 20 L, that is being slowly used up.

2. **Formulating a model based on the data given or situation described.**

   Now we have to think about the situation. We know that we started with 20 L of HCl. Every hour, 500 mL of HCl leaves the tank. However, our unit for t is minutes. So, let's use our unit conversion rules we learned in Red Math Lesson 1B to figure out how many liters we lose per minute:

   $$\frac{500 \text{ mL}}{1 \text{ hour}} \times \frac{1 \text{ L}}{1000 \text{ mL}} \times \frac{1 \text{ hour}}{60 \text{ minutes}} = \frac{1}{120} \frac{\text{L}}{\text{min}}$$

   So, after t minutes, $t \text{ min} \times \frac{1}{120} \frac{\text{L}}{\text{min}} = \frac{t}{120}$ L of HCL have been used. To find h, we need to take that value and subtract it from 20. So, our answer is $20 - \frac{t}{120}$.

3. **Analyzing the model to draw any required conclusions.**

   Since this question only asks us for a function to model the amount of HCl remaining, we do not have any conclusions to make. We will try a question with a conclusion soon.

4. **Validating the conclusions.**

   Again, there are no conclusions to validate. Our answer must be **B**.

Let's try another sample problem on the next page; this one will require us to make a conclusion.

SAMPLE PROBLEM 2: MODELING

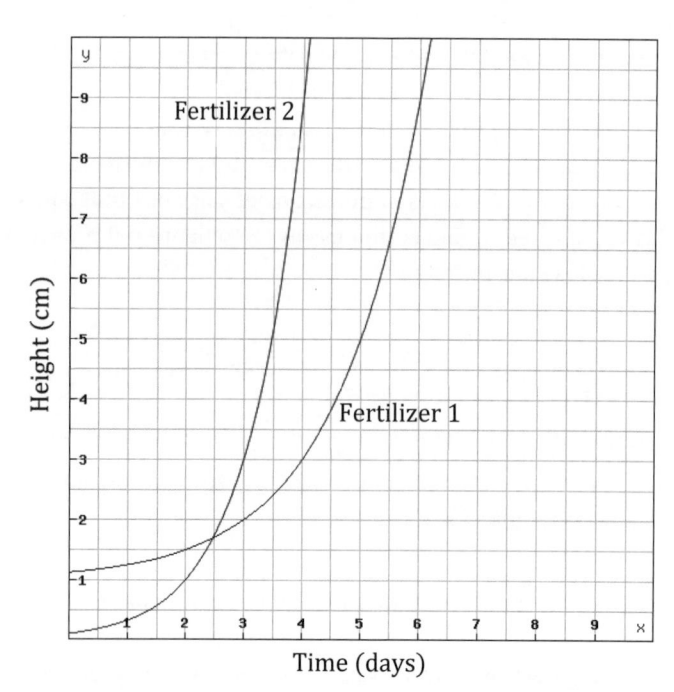

A botanist records the heights, in cm, of two different pea plants, each of which was treated with a different fertilizer, twice daily. The data for each plant were fit by a smooth curve, as shown above. Which of the following is a correct statement about the data above?

A) After 6 days, the plant treated with Fertilizer 1 is nearly twice as tall as the one treated with Fertilizer 2.
B) Initially, the plant treated with Fertilizer 2 was 1 cm taller than the one treated with Fertilizer 1.
C) The rate of growth of the plant treated with Fertilizer 2 is three times the rate of growth of the plant treated with Fertilizer 1.
D) After two and a half days, the plants were approximately the same height.

Again, let's go through each step together:

1. **Identifying the variables—what changes in the situation?**

   For this situation, we're comparing the time, in days, represented on the *x*-axis of the graph above, and the height of two different pea plants on the *y*-axis.

2. **Formulating a model based on the data given or situation described.**

   We see that the initial height of the plant treated with Fertilizer 1 is initially 1 cm taller than the plant treated with Fertilizer 2, that the two plants are the same height after approximately 2.5 days, and that the plant treated with Fertilizer 2 seems to be increasing its height at a much faster rate. It doesn't appear that we have to come up with any equations for the data shown, though it certainly wouldn't hurt to do so if we have time.

3. **Analyzing the model to draw any required conclusions.**

    We will never have to come to a conclusion on our own on the SAT; instead, we have to analyze the conclusions provided to us. Focus on proving three of these conclusions wrong; this is generally much easier than proving that one of them is correct. Let's look at each:
    A. After 6 days, the plant treated with Fertilizer 1 is 9 cm tall, but the height of the plant treated with Fertilizer 2 is so great that it is not even chartable in the window of our graph. This cannot be the answer.
    B. In step 2, we already determined that the plant treated with Fertilizer 1 was initially taller, so this cannot be the answer.
    C. On the surface, this seems like it could be true, as the plant treated with Fertilizer 2 does increase its height at a much greater rate. But, let's look at the heights of both plants after 3 days and 4 days: The plant treated with Fertilizer 1 goes from 2 cm to 3 cm, while the plant treated with Fertilizer 2 goes from 3 cm to 9 cm. This is clearly not the answer.
    D. This must be the answer, because we proved everything else wrong. A quick look at the graphs proves it to be the case.

4. **Validating the conclusions.**

    We can validate our answer by looking at the graph above. Both plants are approximately 1.7 cm tall after 2.5 days.

So, our answer must be **D**.

WRAP-UP

Whenever we have to model a situation on the SAT, always remember these four steps:

1. **Identifying the variables—what changes in the situation?**
2. **Formulating a model based on the data given or situation described.**
3. **Analyzing the model to draw any required conclusions.**
4. **Validating the conclusions.**

The next few questions will largely deal with real-world situations, so be sure to analyze each of them thoroughly; it will take a lot of practice to be able to finish these problems within the time limits provided by the SAT. Good Luck!

Red Math Lesson 4B: Linear, Quadratic, and Exponential Models

Learning to Swim

Directions: Answer each question below.

Practice Set 1 (Calculator)

1. Kelsey deposits $5,000 in an investment account that yields 6% interest compounded semiannually. What will be her balance, to the nearest cent, after 5 years? Is that a better account than one that yields 3% interest compounded quarterly?

2. Diamond engagement rings actually depreciate in value at a rate of 8% per year, adjusting for inflation, which is a general price increase of consumer goods. If inflation increases at a rate of 3% per year, and Carlos purchased a $15,000 princess-cut, diamond engagement ring for his fiancée in 2012, by what percent will the ring have depreciated in value after 10 years, rounded to the nearest tenth?

3. A wildlife park in Sulawesi, Indonesia, has been particularly fervent in trying to breed the anoas, which are extremely endangered water buffaloes. Unfortunately, their efforts, while having resulted in many successful births, still have not been able to counteract the continuous decrease in the anoa population. If the anoa population in that park has been falling at about 0.5% annually and there are 100 anoas left in 2014, how many anoas (rounded to the nearest whole number) did the park start out with when it opened in 1993?

SAT Red Math
Lesson 4B: Linear, Quadratic, and Exponential Models

Use the following information for questions 4 and 5.

SegNu is a company that claims to have revolutionized the Segway design so that it is much safer to use by city commuters. The company will spend $800,000 on overhead costs like marketing, machinery, and wages, and $125 to make each SegNu. Based on other similar products, the company expects its sales of SegNu units to follow the linear Units Sales model: $80{,}000 - 100p$, where p is the price of each SegNu.

Total Sales = Unit Sales × Price
Costs = Overhead + Cost per scooter × Unit Sales
Profit = Total Sales – Costs

4. What is the best price for each SegNu if the company would like to maximize its profit?

5. If SegNu sells at its maximized price, what would be the company's expected profit?

SAT Red Math
Lesson 4B: Linear, Quadratic, and Exponential Models

RED MATH LESSON 4B: LINEAR, QUADRATIC, AND EXPONENTIAL MODELS
Diving into the Deep End

Directions: Answer each question below.

PRACTICE SET 2 (CALCULATOR)

6. Chandra's parents contributed $10,000 dollars towards her college expenses as a graduation present. They obtained the money by investing for three years in a special college IRA fund which paid interest at 9% per year, compounded semi-annually. Assuming that the value of the investment was $10,000 at the end of three years, by what percent did the value of their investment increase?
   A) 14.12%
   B) 25.28%
   C) 30.23%
   D) 67.71%

$$P(t) = \frac{300}{\left[0.05 + \left(\frac{300}{n_0} - 0.05\right)e^{-0.55t}\right]}$$

7. A field biologist determines that a population of mole rats varies according to the model above, where n_0 denotes the initial mole rat population. Two mole rat populations, Group A, which starts with 500 individuals, and Group B, which starts with 2000 individuals, are observed over a 20 year period. Their populations change approximately as the logistical growth model predicts. At the end of the observational period, what is the approximate ratio of the population of Group A to that of group B?
   A) 1 : 400
   B) 1 : 20
   C) 1 : 4
   D) 1 : 1

8. Ticket sales for a concert sell according to the equation $t = -0.2d^2 + 12t + 11$, where t is the number of tickets sold on day number d. On which day are the most tickets sold?
   A) Day 1
   B) Day 12
   C) Day 20
   D) Day 30

9. The population of the United States on January 1, 2014 was approximately 317,500,000 and approximately 315,100,000 on January 1, 2013. Assuming the linear growth rate in 2013 continues, what would be the expected population of the United States at the beginning of 2025? Round your answer to the nearest hundred thousand.
   A) 343,900,000
   B) 353,600,000
   C) 742,000,000
   D) 848,200,000

Year (t)	Profit (× 10^6)
1	0
2	3
3	10
4	21
5	36
6	55

10. A financial analyst is attempting to model a function, $P(t)$, for the profits realized by an internet start-up company in 6 successive years. The company's profits are represented by the data in the table above. What function BEST models the company's profits (in millions of dollars)?
    A) $P(t) = t^2 - 2t + 1$
    B) $P(t) = 2t^2 - 3t + 1$
    C) $P(t) = 3t^2 - 2t + 1$
    D) $P(t) = \left(\frac{10}{3}\right)b^{0.3t}$

11. Atmospheric pressure decreases exponentially as altitude increases. The pressure at sea level (where the altitude is 0) is 1013 kPa, and the pressure at 2 km is 784.5 kPa. Which of the following equations best models this situation? P is pressure in kPa, and a is altitude in km.
    A) $P = 1013 \times 0.77^a$
    B) $P = 114.25a + 1013$
    C) $P = 1013 \times 0.88^a$
    D) $P = 1013 \times 1.88^a$

12. A lab technician who compares the old and new manufacturing systems for computer chips notes that the old manufacturing technique produces approximately 4 chips every 30 minutes, whereas the new technique produces chips according to an exponential function in the form $N(t) = ar^t$, where $r > 0$ and t represents time in hours. Furthermore, the technician finds that both techniques produce the same amount of chips at thirty minutes and at an hour into the manufacturing process. Which of the following pairs of functions for the old manufacturing technique, $O(t)$, and the new technique, $N(t)$, could produce the results the lab technician recorded?
    A) $N(t) = 4 \times 2^t$ and $O(t) = 2t$
    B) $N(t) = 2 \times 4^t$ and $O(t) = 8t$
    C) $N(t) = 4 \times 2^{t+1}$ and $O(t) = 4t$
    D) $N(t) = 2 \times 4^t$ and $O(t) = 16t$

13. The Peach Computer Company project sales figures for its new laptop in China with the function $P(t) = 3^t$ where t is the time in months. Peach expects the sales of the same laptop in the United States to be defined by the function $P(t) = 3t^3 - 3t^2 + t + 5$. If Peach begins selling its laptop on March 1, 2015 in the two countries, during which month can the sales of laptops in China be expected to exceed those in the United States?
    A) April 2015
    B) September 2015
    C) October 2015
    D) August 2015

14. An entomologist studies the birth and death rates of a population of Californian Figeater beetles. She estimates the current population size to be approximately 3,000. Over the course of a month, she records 500 births and 200 deaths in the beetle population. The entomologist wishes to predict the Figeater's future population growth with a model in which net population growth rate is the difference between the birth rate (births divided by the starting population) and the death rate (deaths divided by the starting population). Assuming that the beetle population grows exponentially, what would a population of 3000 Figeater beetles grow to in half a year, to the nearest whole beetle?

15. New cars lose, on average, 50 percent of their value in the first three years after they are purchased. The 2010 Vegan Hybrid's value, however, decreases at a rate of 13.4% per year instead. If the 2010 Vegan Hybrid purchased at the beginning of 2010 has a value of $25,000 at the beginning of 2013, what was the percent decrease in its value from 2010 to 2013? Round to the nearest tenth of a percent.

Practice Set 3 (Calculator)

16. A sum of $500 is placed in a mutual fund at the beginning of the year. Interest is compounded at a rate of 2% monthly. If A represents the amount in the fund after m years, which of the following functions correctly models this situation?

   A) $A = 500 \times 2^{\frac{m}{12}}$
   B) $A = 500 + 2^{12m}$
   C) $A = 500 \times 1.02^{\frac{m}{12}}$
   D) $A = 500 \times \left(1 + \frac{0.02}{12}\right)^{12m}$

Year	Number of Stores
1986	25
1987	40
1988	60
1989	90
1990	133
1991	201
1992	302
1993	453
1994	680

18. The table above shows the number of new stores in a coffee shop chain that opened during the years 1986 through 1994. Which of the following types of functions BEST models the data?

   A) Linear
   B) Quadratic
   C) Exponential
   D) Logarithmic

Species	Brain weight (g)	Gestation time (days)
Cat	25.6	63
Donkey	419	365
Gray seal	325	310
Rabbit	12.1	31
Red fox	50.4	52
Sheep	175	151

17. The table above shows the brain weights in grams and gestation time in days of several animal species. If the data were presented as a scatter plot, the most logical curve of best fit would be given by what sort of function?

   A) Linear
   B) Quadratic
   C) Exponential
   D) There is no apparent relationship between brain weight and gestation time, so it does not make sense to try to fit a curve.

19. A sum of $500 is placed in an account at the beginning of the year. Each month, $20 is added to the account, and no other deposits or withdrawals are made. If A stands for the amount in the account after m months, which of the following functions models the amount added to the account after m months?

   A) $A - (500 \times 20^m)$
   B) $A - (m^2 + 20m + 500)$
   C) $A - (500 + 20m)$
   D) $A - (500 \times -20^m)$

20. A sum of $500 is placed in a mutual fund at the beginning of the year. Each month, a 2% fee is taken from the account. If A stands for the amount in the fund after m months, which of the following functions correctly models this situation?

   A) $A = 500 \times -2^m$
   B) $A = 500 - 2^m$
   C) $A = m^2 - 2m + 500$
   D) $A = 500 \times 0.98^m$

21. Which of the following is the best type of model for the height of a projectile as a function of time when it is shot up into the air and acted upon by gravity?
    A) Linear
    B) Quadratic
    C) Cubic
    D) Exponential

Population	Revenue
40,000	$600,000
45,000	$700,000
50,000	$800,000

22. An economist wishes to model the revenue of a pizza parlor chain that has branches in several different cities and has collected the above data. Which of the following types of functions would most appropriately model this trend?
    A) Linear
    B) Quadratic
    C) Exponential
    D) None of the above

23. Kim is jogging at a constant speed of v meters per second along a straight track. If she is 5 meters from the starting line at time $t = 0$ seconds, which of the following most accurately models her distance x from the starting line at time t (in seconds)?
    A) $x = 5$
    B) $x = vt$
    C) $x = vt^2$
    D) $x = vt + 5$

24. Global human population growth can be modeled exponentially by the equation $y = a \times b^x$, where y represents the population and x represents the number of years that have passed since 1800. If the human population was 1 billion in 1800 and 7 billion in 2012, in what year would the population exceed 8 billion?

25. Using the information provided in problem 24, if global human population growth were instead modeled linearly, in what year would the population exceed 8 billion?

SAT Red Math
Lesson 4B: Linear, Quadratic, and Exponential Models

Red Math Lesson 4B: Linear, Quadratic, and Exponential Models
Race to the Finish

Directions: Answer each question below.

Homework Set (Calculator)

1. In the human body, cell division occurs such that each cell self-replicates and becomes 2 cells after each replication cycle. Therefore, after each cycle, the total number of cells is doubled. Which of the following best models the number of cells C there will be after r replication cycles starting with an initial population of C_0 cells?
   A) $C = 2C_0$
   B) $C = C_0 r^2$
   C) $C = C_0 2^r$
   D) $C = C_0 e^r$

2. An astrophysicist wants to model the expansion of the universe using an exponential growth function. If the universe is always expanding, which of the following equations is NOT an appropriate model for such a trend? Assume S is current size, S_0 is initial size, t is time (years), and $t > 0$.
   A) $S = S_0 2^{5t}$
   B) $S = S_0 10^{5t}$
   C) $S = S_0 e^{-5t}$
   D) $S = S_0 e^{5t}$

3. When an object is in free fall, it is subject to gravitational acceleration. The height of such an object is given by the function $y = y_0 - v_0 t - \frac{1}{2}gt^2$, where y is current height (meters), y_0 is initial height (meters), v_0 is positive initial vertical speed (meters per second), g is $9.8 \frac{m}{s^2}$, and t is time (seconds). How much time does it take for a diver that begins at rest to descend to the pool from a 10 meter diving board? Assume the diver falls straight down and does not jump at the beginning of the dive. Round to 2 decimal places.
   A) 1.43 seconds
   B) 2.04 seconds
   C) 4.47 seconds
   D) 20 seconds

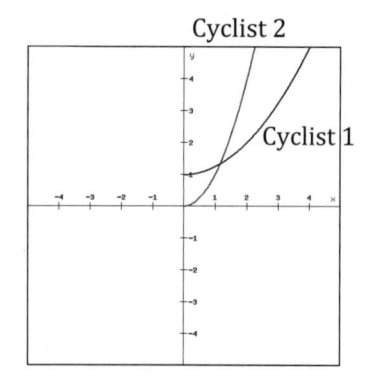

4. The graph above shows the trajectories of two cyclists that begin at rest and accelerate along the same track. The vertical axis represents distance from the track starting line in meters, and the horizontal axis represents time in seconds. Which of the following is a true statement regarding the two trajectories?
   A) During the first 2 seconds, cyclist 1 is moving at a faster average speed than cyclist 2.
   B) The trajectories can both be modeled using a linear function.
   C) At time $t = 0$, cyclist 1 is positioned 1 meter ahead of cyclist 2.
   D) During the entirety of the first 4 seconds, cyclist 1 is positioned ahead of cyclist 2.

5. A bank offers its customers an interest rate of 4% that is compounded annually. Which of the following functions best models the total amount C, in dollars in one of its savings accounts that initially contains C_0 dollars after the interest has been allowed to compound for t years.
   A) $C = C_0 + 1.04t$
   B) $C = C_0 + 1.04t^2$
   C) $C = C_0 (0.04)^t$
   D) $C = C_0 (1.04)^t$

6. The radioactive decay of carbon-14 can be modeled using the exponential decay function $C = C_0 e^{-kt}$, where C is the current mass in grams, C_0 is the initial mass in grams, k is a constant in years^{-1} and t is the elapsed time in years. The half-life of a radioactive element is the time it takes for half of the initial amount to decay. If the half-life of carbon-14 is 6000 years, what is the value of k used in carbon-14's decay model?

   A) $k = \dfrac{\ln\left(\frac{1}{2}\right)}{6000}$

   B) $k = \dfrac{e^{\frac{1}{2}}}{-6000}$

   C) $k = \dfrac{\ln\left(\frac{1}{2}\right)}{-6000}$

   D) $k = \dfrac{\ln(2)}{-6000}$

7. A bank offers its customers an interest rate of 7% that is compounded continuously. Which of the following functions best models the amount of money C, in dollars, that will be in one of its savings accounts that initially contained C_0 dollars after t years have passed?

   A) $C = C_0 + 1.07t$
   B) $C = C_0 + 1.0t^2$
   C) $C = C_0 e^{0.07t}$
   D) $C = C_0 (1.07)^t$

8. Population growth can be modeled using exponential growth. If the population of a country increases by 1.5% annually, what is the ratio of that country's current population to its population 5 years ago? Assume P is current population and P_0 is population 5 years ago. Round to three decimal places.

   A) $\dfrac{P}{P_0} = 0.928$
   B) $\dfrac{P}{P_0} = 1.015$
   C) $\dfrac{P}{P_0} = 1.077$
   D) $\dfrac{P}{P_0} = 7.594$

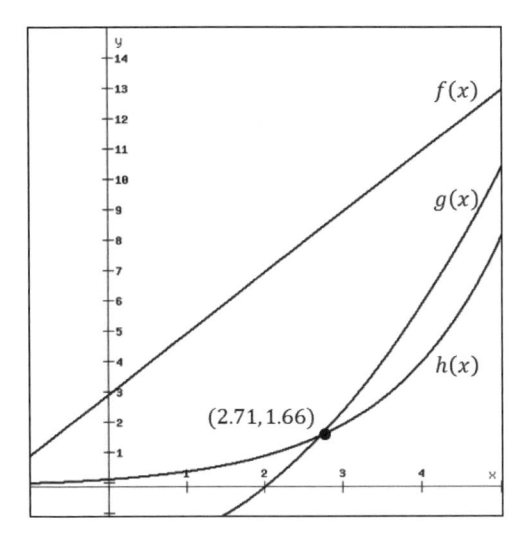

$f(x) = 2x + 3$

$g(x) = \dfrac{1}{2}x^2 - 2$

$h(x) = \dfrac{1}{4}e^{\frac{7}{10}x}$

Use the above information for questions 9 and 10.

9. Assume $c - b = b - a$, and $c > b > a > 0$. If the ratio of $h(b)$ to $h(a)$ is e^π, then what is the ratio of $h(c)$ to $h(b)$?

   A) 1
   B) $e^{\frac{1}{2}\pi}$
   C) e^π
   D) $e^{2\pi}$

10. Which of the following statements is true?
    A) For all positive values of x, $f(x) > g(x)$.
    B) For values of $x > 2.71$, $g(x) > h(x)$.
    C) When $x = 2^{100}$, $f(x) > g(x) > h(x)$.
    D) When $x = 2^{100}$, $h(x) > g(x) > f(x)$.

11. If $f(t)$ represents the number of plants in a population of wildflowers at time t, then which of the following functions does NOT show population growth over time?

    A) $f(t) = \left(-\dfrac{1}{2}t\right)^2 + \dfrac{2}{3}$
    B) $f(t) = \dfrac{4}{5}(-4 - t)^2 - 10$
    C) $f(t) = -e^{-t+2} + 10$
    D) $f(t) = -e^{t-5} + 4$

118 SAT Red Math
Lesson 4B: Linear, Quadratic, and Exponential Models

x	2	3	5	6
$f(x)$	0.5	1.5	13.5	40.5

12. What relationship is most likely being modeled by the data above?
   A) Growth of a microbial population over time.
   B) Area of a regular polygon as its perimeter increases.
   C) Distance traveled by a runner over time.
   D) Speed of a falling object as distance traveled increases.

Stem Length (cm)	1	2	3	4	5	6	7
Petal Area (cm²)	0.5	9	2	8	31	4	19

Use the above information for questions 13 and 14.

13. To test the effectiveness of a new fertilizer, Michael records the stem length and petal area of a flower over time. If $f(x)$ models petal area as a function of stem length according to the above table, then $f(x)$ is most likely a(n):
   A) Exponential model
   B) Linear model
   C) Quadratic model
   D) None of the above

14. If the measurements in the table were taken every 5 days, which of the following statements is true?
   A) The stem length shows exponential growth over the time period.
   B) The stem length shows linear growth over the time period.
   C) The petal area shows exponential growth over the time period.
   D) The petal area shows linear growth over the time period.

15. Samantha throws a ball in the air and it bounces twice as it hits the ground, then comes to a complete stop. Each time the ball bounces it travels half the horizontal distance that it travelled the previous time. If the ball comes to a rest after travelling 21 feet horizontally, how many feet had it travelled horizontally when it reached its maximum height?
   A) 3
   B) 6
   C) 7
   D) 12

16. Chris wants to enlarge an image that he took using his camera. He wants the final area to be 337.5 inches squared. If the width of the image is $\frac{3}{2}$ times the height, what will be the width of the image after the enlargement? Assume the enlargement is done such that the height-to-width ratio is retained. Round to the nearest inch.
   A) 15 inches
   B) 23 inches
   C) 28 inches
   D) 45 inches

17. The formulas for continuous and annual compounded interest are $A = Pe^{rt}$ and $A = P(1 + r)^t$ respectively, where A is the current amount of money, P is the principal, or initial amount of money, r is the annual interest rate, and t is the number of years interest is allowed to compound. At what interest rate, to the nearest tenth of a percentage, will the two methods of compounding interest accumulate to the same amount?

18. If a ball is thrown into the air, its height over time will follow a quadratic model. When a certain ball is thrown from a height of 1.2 meters, its height is 6.3 meters after 1 second and 1.6 meters after 2 seconds. How many seconds is the ball in the air before hitting the ground? Round your answer to the nearest hundredth.

19. A professor is building a supercomputer for her science lab. In order to run her and her students' simulations, she needs at least 576 Gibibytes (GB) of RAM. The tower that she's using has space for 72 memory cards. If 2^x represents the size of an individual memory card in Bytes, what is the minimum value of x that will meet her requirements? Round your answer to the nearest whole number.

Note: One Gibibyte is equivalent to 2^{30} Bytes.

20. A scientist is studying a type of bacteria that produces by binary fission: the original cell is divided into two new daughter cells. She counts 3 bacteria in the petri dish at time $t = 0$ and continues to record the population every 10 minutes. There are 12 bacteria after 40 minutes and 96 bacteria after 1 hour and 40 minutes. If this growth model continues, how many bacteria will there be after 3 hours? Round your answer to the nearest whole number.

SAT Red Math
Lesson 5A: Advanced Right Triangles and Trigonometry

RED MATH LESSON 5A: ADVANCED RIGHT TRIANGLES AND TRIGONOMETRY
Getting Your Feet Wet

Directions: The problems below are intended as a short diagnostic exam.

1. If $\cos\theta = -\frac{3}{5}$ and $\tan\theta = \frac{4}{3}$, what is the value of $\sin(-\theta)$?

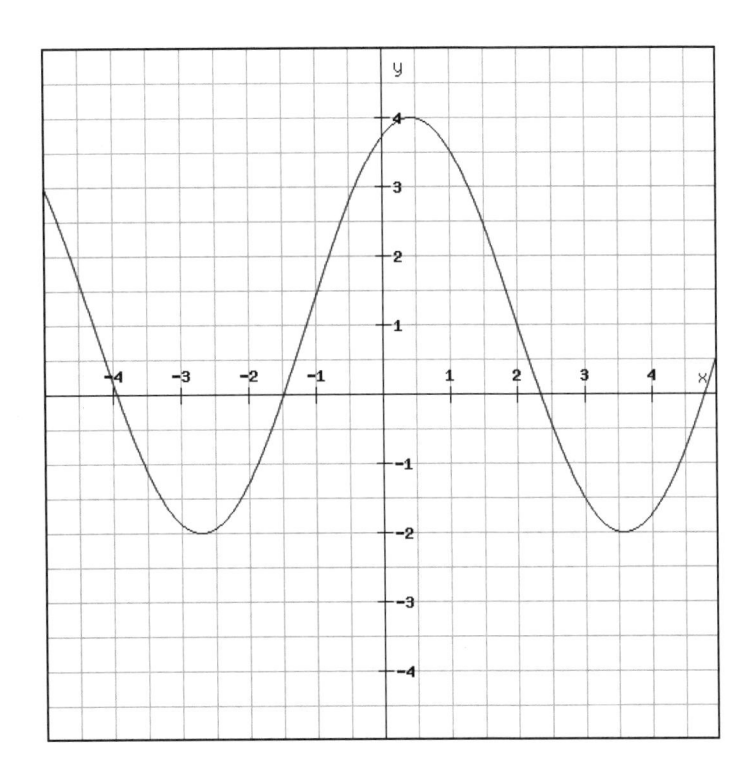

2. Which of the following functions best models the above graph?
   A) $3\sin(-x - 2) + 1$
   B) $-3\sin(x - 2) + 1$
   C) $3\cos(x - 2) + 1$
   D) $3\cos(-x - 2) + 1$

SAT Red Math
Lesson 5A: Advanced Right Triangles and Trigonometry

RED MATH LESSON 5A: ADVANCED RIGHT TRIANGLES AND TRIGONOMETRY
Wading In

Directions: Read the explanation for each problem type mentioned below. Pay special attention to the methods and techniques used to solve the sample problems. Then, do the practice exercises that follow; use the appropriate method to solve each problem.

TOPIC OVERVIEW: OTHER TRIGONOMETRIC FUNCTIONS

There are three more trigonometric functions besides sine, cosine, and tangent: cosecant, secant, and cotangent. Let's look below for the ratios of these new trigonometric functions, as well as a quick review of all of the rest:

$$\sin x = \frac{\text{opposite}}{\text{hypotenuse}} \qquad \cos x = \frac{\text{adjacent}}{\text{hypotenuse}}$$

$$\csc x = \frac{\text{hypotenuse}}{\text{opposite}} = \frac{1}{\sin x} \qquad \sec x = \frac{\text{hypotenuse}}{\text{adjacent}} = \frac{1}{\cos x}$$

$$\tan x = \frac{\text{opposite}}{\text{adjacent}} = \frac{\sin x}{\cos x} \qquad \cot x = \frac{\text{adjacent}}{\text{opposite}} = \frac{\cos x}{\sin x} = \frac{1}{\tan x}$$

Note that unlike the domains of sine and cosine, the domains of the other four functions contain some excluded values. For example, $\sec x$ is undefined when $\cos x = 0$, and $\cot x$ is undefined whenever either $\sin x = 0$ or $\tan x = 0$.

TOPIC OVERVIEW: TRIGONOMETRIC RELATIONSHIPS

The most important trigonometric identity that the SAT assesses is the relationship between sine and cosine of complementary angles. In essence, $\sin x = \cos\left(\frac{\pi}{2} - x\right)$ and $\cos x = \sin\left(\frac{\pi}{2} - x\right)$. The SAT will frequently test these two rules in the section in which we're not allowed to use our calculators, so we must commit these to memory. We'll list a few more trigonometric relationships which may show up on the SAT below:

$$\sin(-x) = -\sin x \qquad \cos(-x) = \cos x \qquad \tan(-x) = -\tan x$$
$$\csc(-x) = -\csc x \qquad \sec(-x) = \sec x \qquad \cot(-x) = -\cot x$$

So, sine, tangent, cosecant, and cotangent are all odd functions ($f(-x) = -f(x)$), while cosine and secant are both even functions ($f(x) = f(-x)$). Odd functions are symmetric when rotated 180° about the origin, while even functions are symmetric about the y-axis.

SAT Red Math
Lesson 5A: Advanced Right Triangles and Trigonometry

TOPIC OVERVIEW: THE UNIT CIRCLE

The unit circle is a circle with radius of length 1 that can be used as an easy way to see relationships between the different trigonometric functions. While it is not required that we memorize the unit circle for the SAT (though it can save us a lot of time if we do), most precalculus and trigonometry teachers will require us to memorize this for their classes. Try to find the pattern that exists among the values; don't just memorize each piece of information on the chart. Note that in each ordered pair below, the x-value represents $\cos\theta$, while the y-value represents $\sin\theta$.

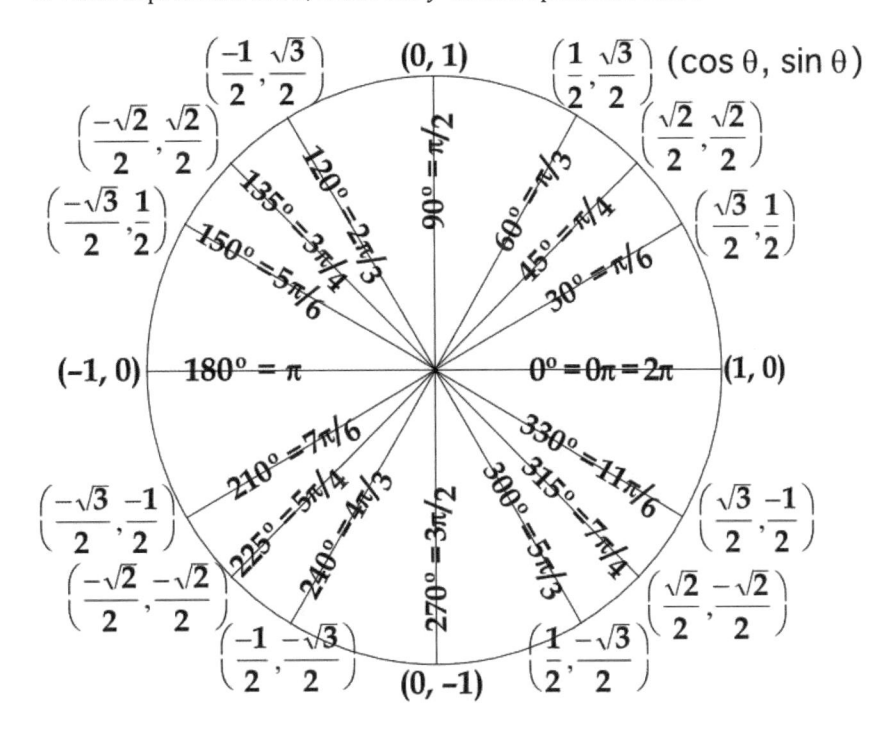

Reminder: On the SAT, angle measurements can appear in both degrees and radians. 1 radian $= \frac{180}{\pi}°$ and $1° = \frac{\pi}{180}$ radians.

The coordinate plane above can be a big help for many trigonometric problems. We can easily figure out whether the sine or cosine of a given angle is positive or negative, and from there we can extrapolate the signs of the other four trigonometric functions. The graphic on the next page may help with this concept:

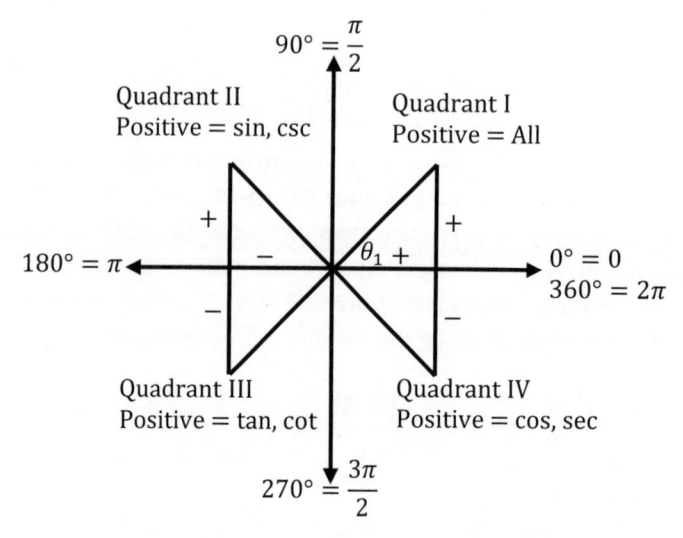

SAT Red Math
Lesson 5A: Advanced Right Triangles and Trigonometry

$90° = \frac{\pi}{2}$

Quadrant II
Positive = sin, csc

Quadrant I
Positive = All

$180° = \pi$

θ_1

$0° = 0$
$360° = 2\pi$

Quadrant III
Positive = tan, cot

Quadrant IV
Positive = cos, sec

$270° = \frac{3\pi}{2}$

Let's look at a sample problem to show how we can use this information:

SAMPLE PROBLEM 1: THE UNIT CIRCLE

If $\cos\theta = -\frac{3}{5}$ and $\tan\theta = \frac{4}{3}$, what is the value of $\sin(-\theta)$?

To start a question like this, let's first figure out what quadrant our angle is in. Since cosine is negative and tangent is positive, we must be in Quadrant III. Let's draw a picture similar to the one on the previous page:

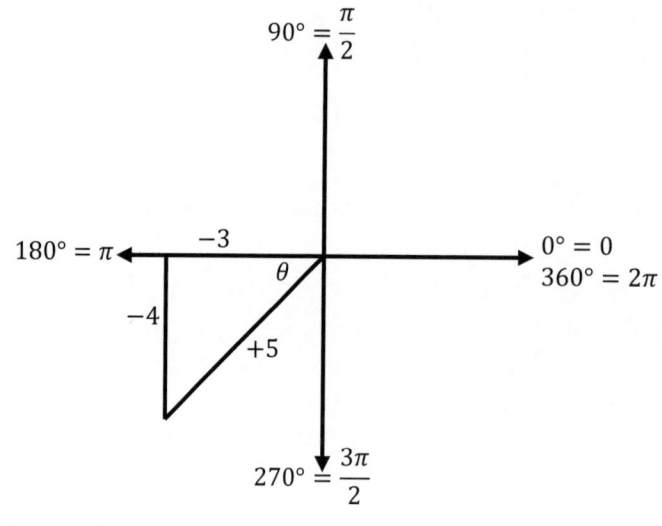

$90° = \frac{\pi}{2}$

$180° = \pi$ -3 θ $0° = 0$
$360° = 2\pi$

-4

$+5$

$270° = \frac{3\pi}{2}$

Now that we know what our triangle looks like, we know that $\sin\theta = -\frac{4}{5}$. By our identities, we know that $\sin(-x) = -\sin x$, so $\sin(-\theta) = \frac{4}{5}$.

SAT Red Math
Lesson 5A: Advanced Right Triangles and Trigonometry

TOPIC OVERVIEW: GRAPHS OF TRIGONOMETRIC FUNCTIONS

Like every other function, trigonometric functions can also be graphed.
Look at the graphs of sine, cosine, and tangent:

$$f(x) = \sin(x)$$

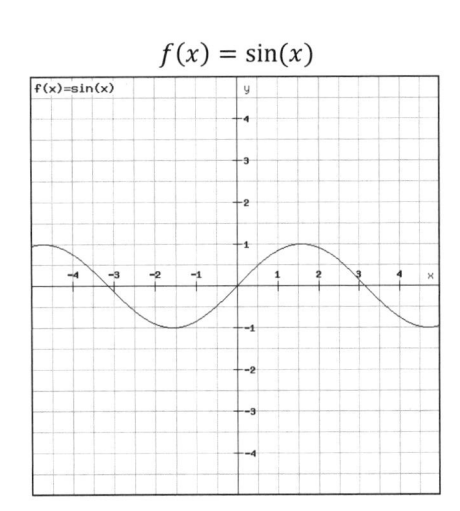

$$f(x) = \cos(x)$$

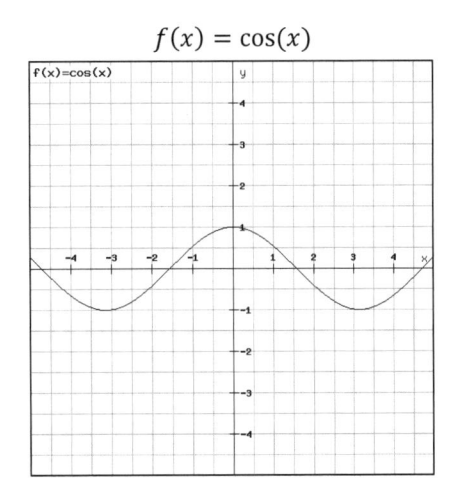

$$f(x) = \tan(x)$$

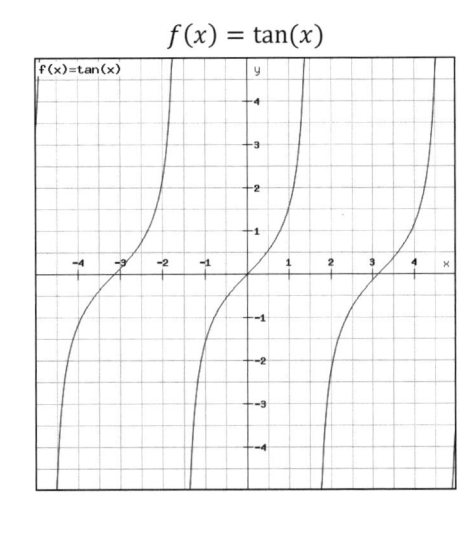

The graphs of trigonometric functions can also be altered by a variety of transformations. The general form of a trigonometric function's graph is:

$$f(x) = A\sin(B(x - C)) + D$$

- A affects the **amplitude**, or distance from the **center line** (typically the x-axis) of the function to the topmost (or bottommost) point of the function. Normally, the amplitude of a sine or cosine function is 1. The tangent function does not have an amplitude, and the effects of A on the graph of tangent functions will not usually be tested on the SAT.
- If the value of A is negative, then the graph of the trigonometric function will be flipped across the x-axis.
- B affects the **period** of the graph. The period is the length, in the x direction, of how long it takes the function to make a complete circuit. The period of a sine or cosine function is always $\frac{2\pi}{|B|}$, while the period of a tangent function is $\frac{\pi}{|B|}$.
- C affects the **phase shift**, or horizontal shift of the graph. A trigonometric function will be shifted C units to the right.
- D affects the **vertical shift** of the function. If D is positive, the center line of the function will be shifted up D units; if D is negative, the opposite will happen.

Let's look at a question that tests these rules:

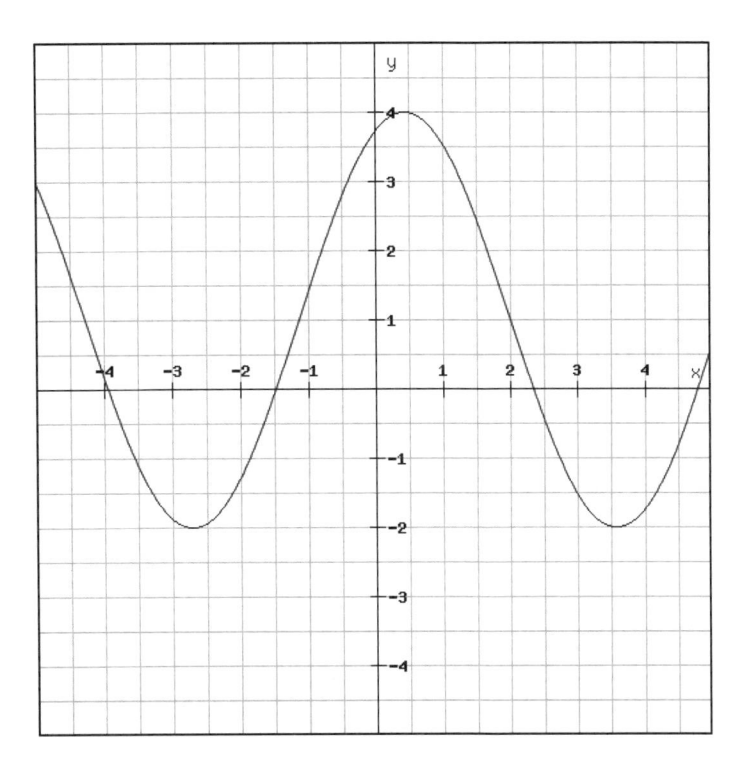

SAMPLE PROBLEM 2: GRAPHS OF TRIGONOMETRIC FUNCTIONS

Which of the following functions best models the above graph?
A) $3\sin(-x - 2) + 1$
B) $-3\sin(x - 2) + 1$
C) $3\cos(x - 2) + 1$
D) $-3\cos(-x - 2) - 1$

The answer is **B**. The graph of sin x was flipped over the x-axis, has an amplitude of 3, and the graph was moved up one unit and to the right 2 units.

WRAP-UP

Memorize the material covered in this lesson as quickly as possible, as knowledge of all of these rules will significantly reduce the amount of time required to solve questions involving trigonometric functions on the SAT. Good Luck!

128 | SAT Red Math
Lesson 5A: Advanced Right Triangles and Trigonometry

RED MATH LESSON 5A: ADVANCED RIGHT TRIANGLES AND TRIGONOMETRY
Learning to Swim

Directions: Answer each question below.

PRACTICE SET 1 (CALCULATOR)

1. Sasha is competing in an orienteering contest. She walks across a flat plain, intending to travel from the first marker, Alpha, to the second marker, Beta, which are exactly 4 miles apart. After walking 1.8 miles, Sasha realizes she is 6° off-course. To the nearest tenth of a mile, how far from Marker Beta is Sasha when she realizes her error?

2. An airline pilot plots the course a plane is currently traveling. The plane is 300 miles due west of its destination. If it continues on its current course it will travel 325 miles and end up 125 miles due south of its destination. To the nearest degree, how many degrees is the plane off course?

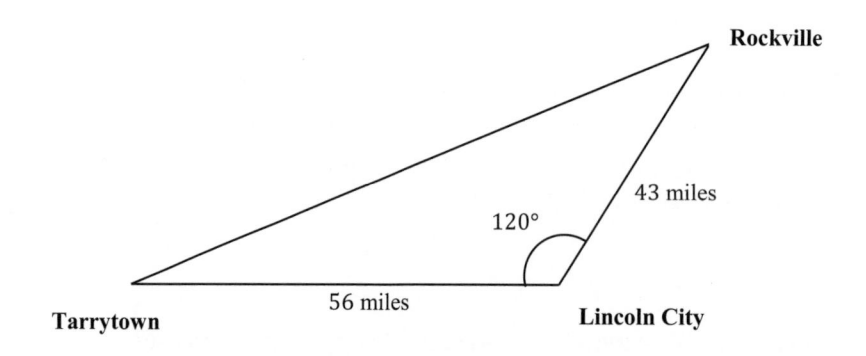

3. A highway engineer determines that there are two routes that might be built to connect Rockville and Tarrytown. The direct route is a straight line between the two cities, but the cost of building the road will be $30 dollars per foot because the ground is swampy. The indirect route would go 43 miles from Rockville to Lincoln City and then 56 miles to Tarrytown. The angle between the road from Rockville to Lincoln City and the road from Lincoln City to Tarrytown form an angle of 120 degrees as indicated in the figure above. The cost of building the indirect route would be $20 per foot. What would be the difference in cost between the indirect route and the direct route, rounded to the nearest hundred thousand dollars?

SAT Red Math | 129
Lesson 5A: Advanced Right Triangles and Trigonometry

$$A = \sqrt{s(s-a)(s-b)(s-c)}$$
$$s = \frac{a+b+c}{2}$$

4. Joshua is creating a triangular horticultural display using straight landscape timbers which measure 19 feet, 23 feet, and 27 feet. He lays them down to form a triangular shape. What is the area of the display to the nearest square foot? (Heron's formula is above, with the area of the triangle as A and the lengths of the sides a, b, and c respectively)

5. To verify the height of Mount Everest, an international survey group makes the following observations: At a location some distance south of the peak, the surveyors find that the angle from level ground to the peak is 42 degrees. When the surveyors hike to a location 0.854 miles due south of the site of the first measurement, they observe that the angle between level ground and the peak is 34 degrees. Both measurements were taken at 16,900 feet above sea level. Given the surveyors data, what height is Mt. Everest to the nearest hundred feet?

Version 3.0

SAT Red Math
Lesson 5A: Advanced Right Triangles and Trigonometry

RED MATH LESSON 5A: ADVANCED RIGHT TRIANGLES AND TRIGONOMETRY
Diving into the Deep End

Directions: Answer each question below.

PRACTICE SET 2 (NO CALCULATOR)

6. Solve $\sin x = \frac{-\sqrt{3}}{2}$ over the interval $0 \leq x < 2\pi$.
   A) $\frac{4\pi}{3}$ only
   B) $\frac{\pi}{3}$ and $\frac{2\pi}{3}$
   C) $\frac{4\pi}{3}$ and $\frac{5\pi}{3}$
   D) $\frac{\pi}{3}$ only

7. If $\sin 38° = 0.6157$, then what is x if $\cos x = 0.6157$?
   A) 38°
   B) 52°
   C) 60°
   D) 90°

8. What is $\tan\left(\frac{23\pi}{6}\right)$?
   A) $-\frac{\sqrt{3}}{3}$
   B) $\frac{\sqrt{2}}{2}$
   C) 1
   D) $-\sqrt{3}$

9. If $\sec x = \frac{13}{5}$, and $\frac{3\pi}{2} < x < 2\pi$, what is $\tan x$?
   A) $-\frac{12}{5}$
   B) $-\frac{5}{13}$
   C) $\frac{5}{13}$
   D) $\frac{12}{5}$

10. What is the period of the graph of $y = 3\sin(4x - \pi) + 2$?
    A) $\frac{\pi}{4}$
    B) $\frac{\pi}{2}$
    C) 2π
    D) 4π

11. Which of the following angles makes the equation $2\sin x - \sqrt{3} = 0$ true?
    A) $x = 30°$
    B) $x = 60°$
    C) $x = 150°$
    D) $x = 240°$

12. If $\cos(x) = 0.5$, which of the following is a possible value for $\cot(x)$?
    A) $-\sqrt{3}$
    B) $-\frac{\sqrt{3}}{3}$
    C) $\sqrt{3}$
    D) 2

13. Consider the two functions $f(x) = 2\cos x$ and $g(x) = 4\cos 2x - 3$. Graphing the two functions would show differences in which of the following characteristics?
    A) Period only
    B) Period and amplitude only
    C) Period, amplitude, and vertical shift only
    D) Period, amplitude, vertical shift, and horizontal shift

14. If the secant of an angle that lies in Quadrant I equals $\sqrt{2}$, what is the tangent of the angle? Round to the nearest hundredth.

15. If $\tan \beta = \frac{3}{4}$ and $\frac{\pi}{2} < \beta < \frac{3\pi}{2}$, what is $\csc(\beta + 3\pi)$?

PRACTICE SET 3 (CALCULATOR)

16. A boat crosses a 100 ft wide river at an angle. If the boat actually travels 115 ft, what is the measure of θ, the angle that the direction of the boat can make with the shore?
    A) 35°
    B) 52°
    C) 60°
    D) 83°

17. If $\cos(x) = 0.6$, and $0 \leq x \leq \frac{\pi}{2}$, what is $\cot\left(\frac{\pi}{2} - x\right)$?
    A) $-\frac{4}{3}$
    B) $\frac{2}{3}$
    C) $\frac{3}{4}$
    D) $\frac{4}{3}$

18. If $0 \leq 3x \leq \frac{\pi}{2}$, and $\sin(3x) = \cos(2x)$, what is the value of x?
    A) $-\frac{\pi}{10}$
    B) $\frac{\pi}{10}$
    C) $\frac{\pi}{6}$
    D) $\frac{\pi}{4}$

19. What is the value of $\sec(46°) - \csc(44°)$?
    A) 0
    B) $\tan(2°)$
    C) $\frac{1}{\cos(46°)+\sin(44°)}$
    D) 1

20. What is the value of $\sin^{-1}\left(\cos\left(-\frac{\pi}{3}\right)\right)$?

   A) $-\frac{\pi}{3}$
   B) 0
   C) $\frac{\pi}{6}$
   D) $\frac{\pi}{3}$

23. If $\tan\theta = \frac{5}{12}$ and $\frac{\pi}{2} < \theta < \frac{3\pi}{2}$, what is $\cos(-\theta)$?

   A) $-\frac{5}{13}$
   B) $-\frac{12}{13}$
   C) $\frac{5}{13}$
   D) $\frac{12}{13}$

$$\cos x = -a$$
$$\sin x = a$$

21. In the equations above, x is the radian measure of an angle for $0 < x < 2\pi$, and $a > 0$. If $\cos y = -a$ and $\sin y = -a$, which of the following could be the value of y?

   A) $\pi - x$
   B) $\pi + x$
   C) $2\pi - x$
   D) $2\pi + x$

24. In construction projects, a triangle with side lengths of 6", 8", and 10" is often used to check that an angle measures 90°. What is the degree measure of the smallest angle in that triangle? Round your answer to the nearest tenth of a degree.

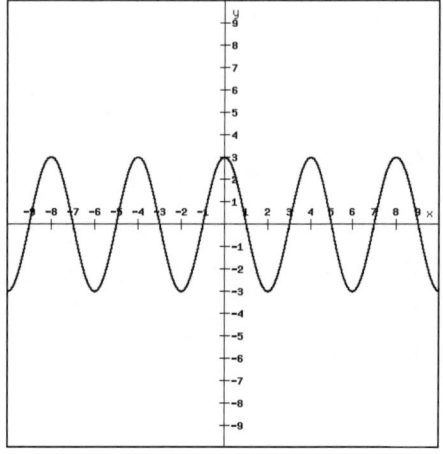

$$\frac{\sin A}{a} = \frac{\sin B}{b} = \frac{\sin C}{c}$$

25. The Law of Sines, given above, states that in any triangle, the ratio between the sine of an angle and its opposite side is constant. (A denotes an angle and a denotes a side.) A roof is being designed as an isosceles triangle with a base of 15 meters. One side of the roof has an angle of elevation of 40°. What is the distance in meters from the peak of the roof to the base, measured along the face of the roof? Round your answer to the nearest tenth of a meter.

22. Which of the following functions does NOT represent the graph above?

   A) $y = 3\cos\left(\frac{\pi}{2}x\right)$
   B) $y = -3\cos\left(\pi - \frac{\pi}{2}x\right)$
   C) $y = 3\sin\left(\frac{\pi}{2} - \frac{\pi}{2}x\right)$
   D) $y = -3\sin\left(\frac{\pi}{2} + \frac{\pi}{2}x\right)$

RED MATH LESSON 5A: ADVANCED RIGHT TRIANGLES AND TRIGONOMETRY
Race to the Finish

Directions: Answer each question below.

HOMEWORK SET (CALCULATOR)

1. The angle of depression from a hot air balloon to its landing site is 17°. If the hot air balloon is 4500 m above the earth's surface, how far is it from the landing site (as measured on the ground from the point directly below the balloon)?
   A) 1.376 km
   B) 4.706 km
   C) 14.719 km
   D) 14719 km

2. If $\cos\theta = \frac{1}{2}$ and $0 > \theta > -\pi$, what is $\cot\theta$?
   A) $-\frac{\sqrt{3}}{3}$
   B) $\frac{\sqrt{3}}{3}$
   C) $-\sqrt{3}$
   D) $\sqrt{3}$

3. If $\sin\theta = -0.9$, which of the following is NOT equivalent to -0.9?
   A) $\cos\left(\frac{\pi}{2} - \theta\right)$
   B) $-\sin(-\theta)$
   C) $\frac{1}{\csc\theta}$
   D) $\sin(\theta - \pi)$

4. If $\sec\theta = \frac{-17}{15}$ and $0 < \theta < \pi$, what is $\sin(-\theta)$?
   A) $-\frac{8}{17}$
   B) $-\frac{15}{17}$
   C) $\frac{8}{17}$
   D) $\frac{15}{17}$

$$\cot\theta = -a$$
$$\sec\theta = a$$

5. In the equations above, $a > 0$. Which of the following would NOT be found in Quadrant I?
   A) $-\theta$
   B) $2\pi - \theta$
   C) $2\pi + \theta$
   D) $4\pi - \theta$

6. If $\sin\left(\frac{x}{2}\right) = \frac{1}{2}$ and $0 \leq x \leq \frac{\pi}{2}$, then what is $\cos 2x$?
   A) $\frac{-1}{2}$
   B) $\frac{1}{2}$
   C) $\sqrt{3}$
   D) 1

7. If $\sin x < \sin 2x$, then which of the following regions contains a possible value of x?

   i. $0 \leq x < \frac{\pi}{2}$
   ii. $\frac{\pi}{2} \leq x < \pi$
   iii. $\pi \leq x < \frac{3\pi}{2}$

   A) I only
   B) I and II
   C) I and III
   D) I, II and III

8. Triangle $\triangle ABC$ is a right triangle, in which $\angle A < \angle C < \angle B$. $\overline{BD}$ is an altitude. If $\overline{AC} = 10$ and $\overline{BD} = 4$ then what is the length of $\overline{BC}$?
   A) 2
   B) $2\sqrt{5}$
   C) $5\sqrt{2}$
   D) Not enough information to determine.

9. Which of the following curves is a graph of the function $y = \cos 4x - 2$?

A)

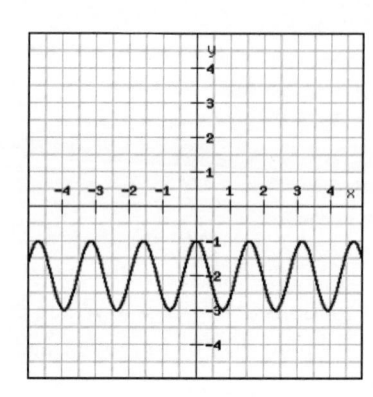

B)

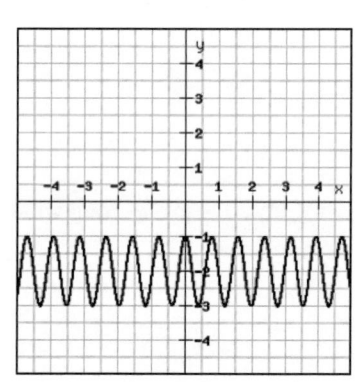

C)

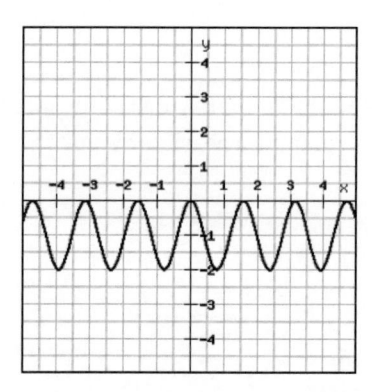

D)

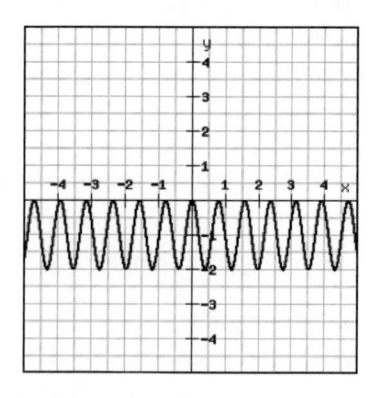

10. Which of the following could never be true?
A) $\cos x = 1.5 - \sin x$
B) $\sin x = \sin^2 x$
C) $\sin x = \sin x^2$
D) $\sin x = \cos(-x)$

11. If $2\cos^2 x + \cos x - 1 = 0$, then which of the following is not a possible value of $\sin x$?
A) $\frac{-\sqrt{3}}{2}$
B) 0
C) $\frac{1}{2}$
D) $\frac{\sqrt{3}}{2}$

12. If $\sin x = b$ and $\sin w = 1 - b$, then which of the following could not be a value of w?
A) π
B) $x - \frac{\pi}{2}$
C) $x + \frac{\pi}{2}$
D) $x + \pi$

13. Two people are watching a helicopter from the same house. One person is on the upstairs porch looking up at a 40° angle of elevation, and the other person is 20 feet directly below on the first floor porch looking up at a 70° angle of elevation. What must the horizontal distance be between the house and the helicopter?
   A) 10.5 feet
   B) 38.2 feet
   C) 47.2 feet
   D) 67.4 feet

14. If $\sin\left(\frac{\pi}{2} - x\right) = b$ and $\cos x = 1 - b$, what is a possible value of b?
   A) -1
   B) $\frac{1}{2}$
   C) 0
   D) 1

$$\cos x = -a$$
$$\sin x = a$$

15. In the equations above, x is the radian measure of an angle for $0 < x < 2\pi$. Additionally, $\cos y = -a$ and $\sin y = -a$. If $a > 0$, which of the following could be the value of $y - x$?
   A) $\frac{\pi}{2}$
   B) π
   C) $\frac{3\pi}{4}$
   D) 3π

16. Which of the following graphs best represents the function $y = \sin 5x - \cos\left(\frac{\pi}{2} - 5x\right) + 1$?

   A) 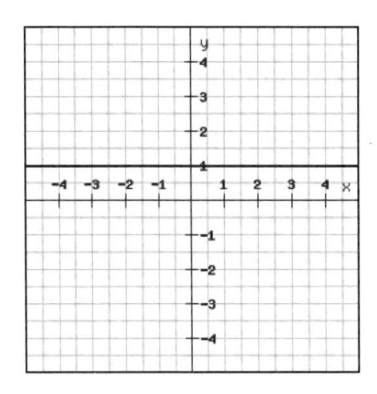
   B) 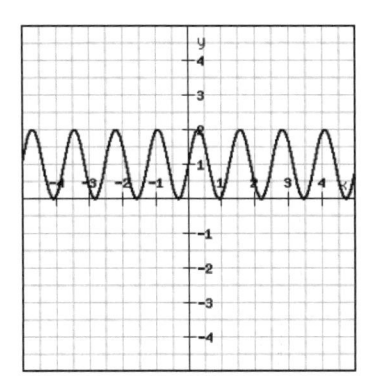
   C) 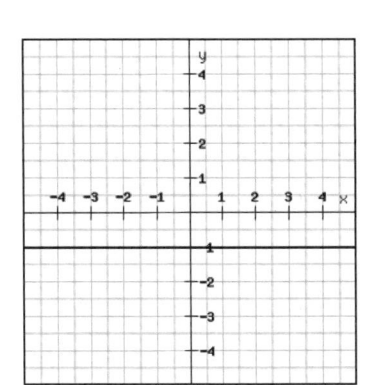
   D)

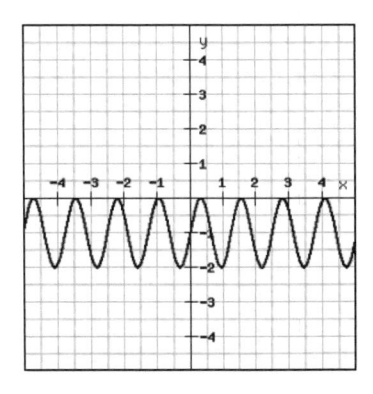

17. What is the smallest positive value of x at which the graph of $y = \sin\left(\frac{\pi}{3}x\right) + \frac{1}{2}$ crosses the x-axis?

18. If $\sin x = \frac{-\sqrt{3}}{2}$ and $\tan x < 0$, what is the value of $\sec x$?

$$\frac{\sin A}{a} = \frac{\sin B}{b} = \frac{\sin C}{c}$$

19. A surveyor is attempting to find the distance from city A to city B, but city B is in a country he can't enter. He forms a triangle using another city C that he has access to, and determines that the angle at city C between A and B is 27°, and the angle at city A between B and C is 79°. If the distance between city A and C is 19.30 miles, what is the distance in miles between city A and B? Round to the nearest hundredth of a mile.

20. If $\sin\left(\theta + \frac{\pi}{2}\right) = \frac{-\sqrt{2}}{2}$, what is the value of $\cos(\theta + \pi)$? Round to the nearest hundredth.

RED MATH LESSON 5B: PRACTICE SECTIONS
Learning to Swim

Directions: Answer each question below.

PRACTICE SET 1 (NO CALCULATOR)

$$f(x) = 3x^3 + 4x^2 - 6x + 15$$
$$g(x) = 2x^3 + 8x^2 + 13x + 29$$

1. If the functions $f(x)$ and $g(x)$ above are equal, what are the values of x?

2. How many times do the graphs of $(x + 2)^2 + (y - 4)^2 = 25$ and $x = (y + 1)^2 - 2$ intersect?

3. What is the surface area of a cube with side length 4?

4. For what values of x is $x^2 - 6 > 2x$ true?

5. If $f(x) = 2x^2 - 1$ and $g(x) = \sqrt{1 + x}$, then for what values of x is $f(g(x)) = g(f(x))$?

RED MATH LESSON 5B: PRACTICE SECTIONS
Diving into the Deep End

Directions: Answer each question below.

PRACTICE SET 2 (NO CALCULATOR)

6. Simplify: $\frac{x^2-6x-7}{x^2-5x+6} \div \frac{x^2-2x-3}{x^2-9x+14}$

   A) $\frac{x^2-14x+49}{x^2-6x+9}$

   B) $\frac{x^2-14x+49}{x^2-4x+4}$

   C) $\frac{x^2+2x+1}{x^2-6x+9}$

   D) $\frac{x^2+2x+1}{x^2-4x+4}$

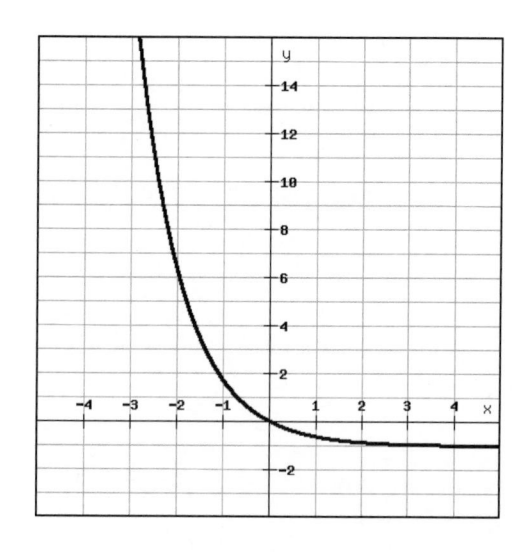

7. Which of the following functions matches the graph in the xy-coordinate plane above?

   A) $f(x) = -e^{-x}$
   B) $f(x) = -e^{x}$
   C) $f(x) = e^{-x} - 1$
   D) $f(x) = e^{x} - 1$

8. If $\sec\theta = \sqrt{2}$ and $0 < \theta < \pi$, what is θ?

   A) $\frac{\pi}{4}$
   B) $\frac{\pi}{3}$
   C) $\frac{2\pi}{3}$
   D) $\frac{3\pi}{4}$

9. A fungus increases in volume by 50% every 3 days. If the fungus has a volume of 10 cubic centimeters today, which function can be used to find the fungus' volume d days from today?

   A) $v(d) = 15^{d/3}$
   B) $v(d) = 3 \cdot 1.5^{d/10}$
   C) $v(d) = 10 \cdot 0.5^{d}$
   D) $v(d) = 10 \cdot 1.5^{d/3}$

10. What is the domain of the function $f(x) = \log(x+1) - 3$?

    A) All real values of x
    B) All real values of x greater than -3
    C) All real values of x greater than -2
    D) All real values of x greater than -1

11. If $x \neq 3$ or 2, what is $\frac{x+2}{x-3} - \frac{x+1}{x-2}$?

    A) $\frac{-4x-1}{x^2-5x+6}$
    B) $\frac{-2x-8}{x^2-5x+6}$
    C) $\frac{-4}{x^2-5x+6}$
    D) $\frac{2x-1}{x^2-5x+6}$

12. Which of the following functions, when graphed in the xy-coordinate plane, passes through $(2, 2)$ and has a range of all real values of y greater than 1?

    A) $f(x) = 5^{x-2}$
    B) $f(x) = 5^{x-2} + 1$
    C) $f(x) = 5^{x+2}$
    D) $f(x) = 5^{x+2} + 1$

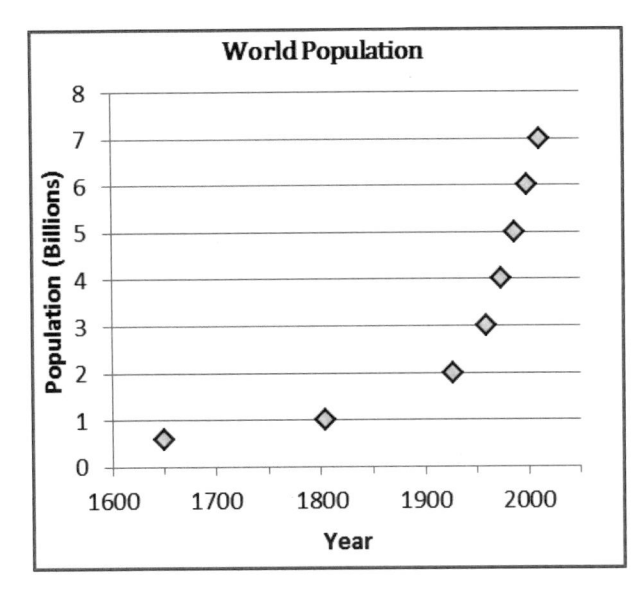

PRACTICE SET 3 (CALCULATOR)

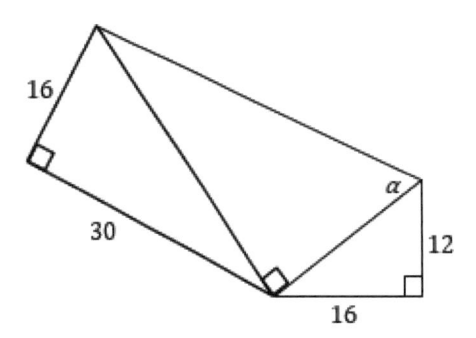

13. The graph above shows the world's population at different points from 1800 onward. The trend in this data can best be described as:
    A) Linear
    B) Exponential
    C) Quadratic
    D) Logarithmic

16. What is tan α?
    A) $\frac{10}{17}$
    B) $\frac{3}{4}$
    C) $\frac{17}{10}$
    D) $\frac{17}{9}$

17. What is the remainder when $x^5 - 4x^3 + x$ is divided by $x^2 + 1$?
    A) $x + 5$
    B) $2x$
    C) $4x$
    D) $6x$

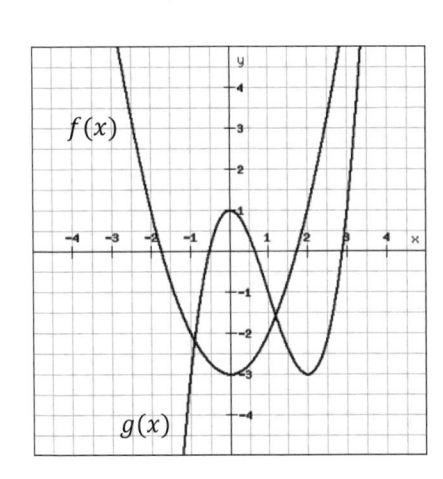

$$f(x) = 0.5x^4 - 3.5x^3 + 2.5x^2 + 15.5x - 15$$

14. What is the sum of the zeroes of the equation above?

$$f \circ h(x) = h \circ f(x)$$

15. If $f(x) = \sqrt{x-1}$ and $h(x) = x^4 + 1$, then for what value of x is the above statement true?

18. What is the value of $g(f(-2))$ using the graph above?
    A) -3
    B) -2
    C) -1
    D) 1

19. Ten years ago, John's parents put money into a savings account for his college fund, which is annually compounded at a 5% interest rate. Five years after setting up the account, his parents withdrew $5,000 due to a financial emergency. The remaining amount was untouched for another five years. If the account has $60,000 after the ten years, then approximately how much money was initially put into the account?
    A) $36,835
    B) $39,904
    C) $40,752
    D) $41,835

20. If $2^{3y-3} = \dfrac{8^{4x^2}}{4^{9x}}$ and $(3^{4y})(9^{10x}) = 3^{12x^2+28}$, then what could be the value(s) of x?
    A) -2
    B) 3
    C) -2 or 3
    D) All real numbers

21. A pizza restaurant's profit is a function of P, the price of one pizza, and Q, the quantity of pizzas sold. The profit and quantity sold are modeled by the equations below. To maximize profit, what price should the restaurant charge for one pizza?

    $$\text{profit} = PQ - 5Q$$
    $$Q = 900 - 50P$$

    A) $5
    B) $11.5
    C) $18
    D) $23

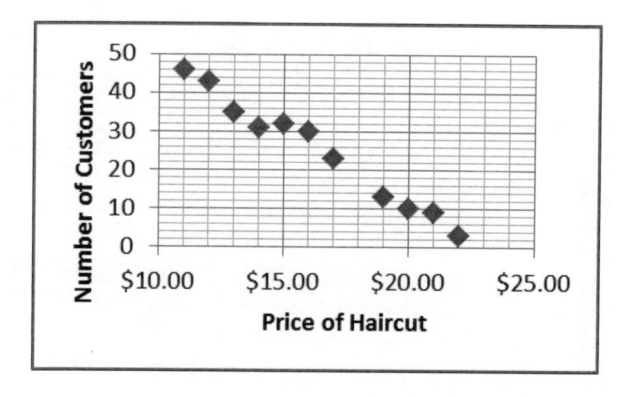

Use the scatterplot above for questions 22 and 23.

22. The scatterplot above shows the prices for haircuts in Los Angeles barber shops and their daily average number of customers. According to the data above, if a barber shop wants to decrease its current price of $18 by 15%, what would be the expected increase in the number of customers?
    A) 4
    B) 10
    C) 57
    D) 58

23. The scatterplot from the previous problem does not show a data point which has been omitted because it was an outlier. If including the outlier would increase the slope of the linear model, which of the following points could be that outlier?
    A) ($13.50, 20)
    B) ($17, 18)
    C) ($19.50, 5)
    D) ($20.50, 30)

24. If a rectangle with a width to length ratio of 3:5 has its perimeter doubled without changing that ratio, then by what percent will its area increase?

	B&W	Color	Total
#360	400	500	$140
#361	700	600	$171
#362	500	500	$135

25. A printing office charges two different prices for black and white (B&W) and color copies. The table above shows three printing orders and the total cost of each order. A 10% discount was applied to orders of 1000 copies or more. How much more expensive, in cents, is one color copy compared to one B&W copy?

SAT Red Math
Lesson 5B: Practice Sections

RED MATH LESSON 5B: PRACTICE SECTIONS
Race to the Finish

Directions: Answer each question below.

HOMEWORK SET (CALCULATOR)

$$g(x) = 5x^2 + 3bx + 10$$
$$h(x) = 4x^2 + 2bx + 6$$

1. For what value(s) of b will the two functions above have only one point of intersection?
   A) -4
   B) 4
   C) ± 4
   D) All real numbers

$$f(x) = \sqrt{x-2} + 1$$
$$g(x) = f^{-1}(x-2) + 3$$

2. Given the two functions above, what is the range of $g(x)$?
   A) $(-\infty, -5]$
   B) $[2, \infty)$
   C) $[5, \infty)$
   D) $[7, \infty)$

3. A college professor conducts a survey of his students and finds an approximately linear relationship between the time spent studying for a final exam and the resulting score. On average, for 3 additional hours spent studying, a student will score 2 points higher on the final. Which of the following models DOES NOT reflect this relationship?
   A) $\frac{y}{2} = \frac{x}{3} + 10$
   B) $3y = 2x + 60$
   C) $4y = 3x + 260$
   D) $6y = 4x + 420$

4. James uses a garden hose to fill an empty pool which has a rectangular base that is 10 feet by 20 feet. The garden hose has a constant rate of 34 GPM (gallons per minute). He starts filling the pool at noon. When he comes back to check at 1:28 pm, the pool was exactly one-fourth full. If James only wants to fill the pool up to 1 foot from the top, at approximately what time should he come back to turn off the hose?
   (1 ft^3 $\approx$ 7.48 gallons)
   A) 3:40 pm
   B) 4:24 pm
   C) 5:08 pm
   D) 5:52 pm

$$g(x) = 2x^2 + 5x$$
$$h(x) = 2x + 14$$

5. Given the equations above, what is the domain of $f(x) = \sqrt{g(x) - h(x)}$?
   A) $(-3.5, 2)$
   B) $[-3.5, 2]$
   C) $(-\infty, -3.5) \cup (2, \infty)$
   D) $(-\infty, -3.5] \cup [2, \infty)$

6. Tony invests $5000 in a savings account, which is annually compounded at a 4% interest rate. For the next two years, he'll deposit x dollars into the same account at the beginning of each year. If his savings account will have $7745.92 by the end of the third year, what is the value of x rounded to the nearest dollar?
   A) $943
   B) $981
   C) $1000
   D) $1886

$$x^2 + y^2 \leq 25$$
$$y \geq |x|$$

7. What is the area of the region bounded by the two inequalities above?
   A) 6.25π
   B) 12.5π
   C) 18.75π
   D) 25π

$$C = 4 + 2.25(m-3) + 0.20t$$

8. The cost C in dollars of a taxi ride of length m miles lasting t minutes is given by the equation above. What does the 1 in the term $2.25(m-3)$ represent?
   A) The number of miles that are exempt from any per-mile fee
   B) The number of minutes that are exempt from any per-minute fee
   C) The per-mile fee, in dollars per mile
   D) The flat fee that applies to any ride of any length

9. A zoo has room in its African hoofed animal paddock for up to 8 animals, which can be giraffes or zebras. A giraffe costs $120,000 to acquire initially and $30,000 per year to care for. A zebra costs $50,000 to acquire and $16,000 per year to care for. The zoo's five-year budget for the African hoofed animal exhibit is $950,000. Which of the following represents the set of constraint inequalities for this scenario?
   A) $G + Z \leq 8$
      $150G + 66Z \leq 190$
   B) $G + Z \leq 8$
      $150G + 66Z \leq 950$
   C) $G + Z \leq 8$
      $270G + 130Z \leq 950$
   D) $120G + 50Z \leq 950$
      $150G + 80Z \leq 190$

Use the following information to answer Questions 10 and 11.

Housing affordability is perceived as a crisis in certain U.S. cities with very high rents, but a more accurate picture of the affordability of housing is obtained by comparing the median rent in a city to the median family income in that same city. This comparison was done for 22 cities, and the results are shown in the scatter plot below, with a few of the largest cities identified by name.

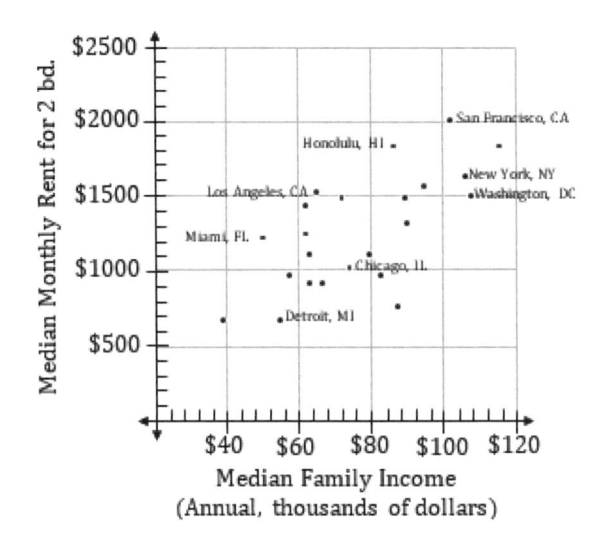

10. If a best-fit line is drawn to fit the data above and its equation is $y = 12.5x + 500$, what does the coefficient 12.5 represent?
    A) The approximate increase, in dollars, in the median income for each $1000 increase in the median rent
    B) The approximate increase, in dollars, in the median rent for each $1000 increase in the median income
    C) The predicted median rent, in dollars, for a city with a median income of $0
    D) The predicted median income, in thousands of dollars, for a city with a median rent of $0

146 SAT Red Math
Lesson 5B: Practice Sections

HW

11. If the affordability of a city is measured by the ratio of its median monthly rent to its median family income, which of the following cities is the LEAST affordable, according to the scatter plot?
    A) Detroit
    B) Miami
    C) San Francisco
    D) Washington, DC

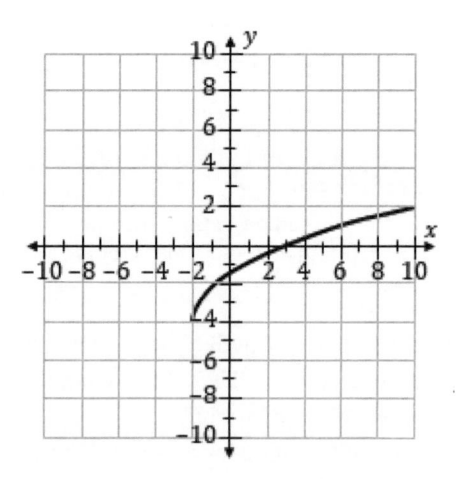

Category	Intend to Vote	Actual Voters	Number Surveyed
Men <29	12	7	23
Women <29	20	16	31
Men 30-55	30	27	40
Women 30-55	38	26	45
Men >55	30	27	35
Women >55	20	17	26

13. A survey was conducted in a small town several weeks before an election. 200 randomly selected residents of voting age were called and asked whether they planned to vote. After the election, the same people were called and asked whether they had, in fact, voted. The results are above. Which of the following must be an accurate statement, according to the data?
    A) Of those surveyed, the highest percentage rates of both intended voting and actual voting occurred among men older than 55.
    B) Among the categories surveyed, the group of women aged 30 to 55 contained the greatest percentage of people who said they intended to vote and yet did not vote.
    C) There are more women aged 30 to 55 living in this town than there are men.
    D) Of those people who responded that they intended to vote, 25% did not cast votes.

12. The above graph is described by which of the following equations?
    A) $y = 3\sqrt{x+2} - 4$
    B) $y = \sqrt{3x-2} - 4$
    C) $y = \sqrt{3(x-2)} + 4$
    D) $y = \sqrt{3(x+2)} - 4$

14. In a set of 20 test scores, the median is equal to the (unique) mode. If a 21st number, equal to the mean of the original 20 scores, is inserted into the set, which of the following might change?
    A) The mean
    B) The median
    C) The range
    D) None of the above

15. Let $z_1 = 3 - i$ and $z_2 = 4 + 7i$, where $i^2 = -1$. If $az_1 + bz_2$ is a real number for real integer coefficients a and b, which of the following MUST be true?
    A) $b = 7a$
    B) $a - b = 7$
    C) $a = 7$
    D) $\frac{a}{b} = 7$

$$y = x^2 - 6x + 7$$
$$y = k$$

16. If the above system of equations has exactly one solution, what is the value of k?
    A) -2
    B) 3
    C) 7
    D) 9

17. Sarah has been selling homemade bracelets for a month. In the second month, she reduced her price by 20% and tripled her sales compared to the first month; as a result, her profit doubled. If she originally sold one bracelet for $10, then how much does it cost her to make one bracelet? (profit = total revenue − total cost)

18. A circle in the xy-plane has a diameter with endpoints $(-2, -4)$ and $(6, 2)$. If the point $(-1, a)$ lies on the circle and $a > 0$, what is the value of a?

19. A digital photograph measures 8×10 inches. In an uncompressed file format, a single pixel requires 3 Bytes of memory to record (one for each of the primary colors: red, green, and blue). The *resolution* of an image refers to the number of pixels required to span 1 inch in either width or height. If Sean must attach this photo to an email and his attachment may be no larger than 15 MB, what is the highest resolution at which he can send the image, in pixels per inch? (Note: 1 MB = 1024 KB, and 1 KB = 1024 Bytes.)

20. A teacher wishes to divide his 29 students into groups of 3 and groups of 4, with no extra students remaining. He also needs to have a total of 8 groups. How many of the students will be in groups of 3?

RED MATH LESSON 6A: ADVANCED CIRCLES
Getting Your Feet Wet

Directions: The problems below are intended as a short diagnostic exam.

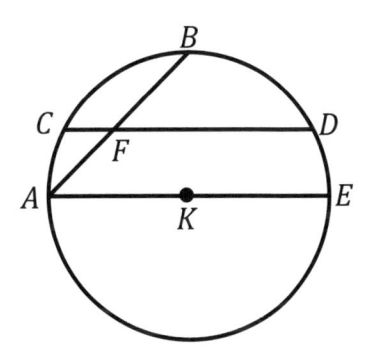

1. Circle K above has a diameter of $10\sqrt{2}$ and Chord $\overline{CD}$ bisects Chord $\overline{AB}$. If $\angle AKB$ is a right angle, which of the following are possible values of $\overline{CF}$ and $\overline{FD}$?
   A) 2, 12
   B) 2.5, 10
   C) 3, 8
   D) 3.5, 7.5

RED MATH LESSON 6A: ADVANCED CIRCLES
Wading In

Directions: Read the explanation for each problem type mentioned below. Pay special attention to the methods and techniques used to solve the sample problems. Then, do the practice exercises that follow; use the appropriate method to solve each problem.

TOPIC OVERVIEW: SECTOR AREA AND ARC LENGTH

A **sector** of a circle is a very specific piece of a circle that resembles a slice of pizza. The pointed end of the pizza is known as the **central angle**—this angle will always be between 0 and 360 degrees. The crust of the slice of pizza is called the **arc** of a circle.

Finding the area of a sector of a circle is easy if we calculate it in the same way we would find the area of a slice of pizza. If one slice of pizza is one-eighth of the pizza, then its area must be one-eighth the area of the entire pizza. There always exists a ratio between the central angle of the sector and the whole circle, 360°. This ratio is equivalent to the ratio of the area of the sector to the area of the circle. The same steps can be applied to find the length of an arc: the ratio of the arc length to the entire circumference is equivalent to the ratio of the central angle to 360°. This can be summed up in the formula below:

$$\frac{\text{central angle}}{360°} = \frac{\text{sector area}}{\text{area of circle}} = \frac{\text{arc length}}{\text{circumference of circle}}$$

Since we covered many problems like these in the Blue Math workbook, we will not go over any here. Review those lessons as necessary.

TOPIC OVERVIEW: OTHER PROPERTIES OF CIRCLES

Many other properties of circles may be tested on the SAT. Let's look at a few of these:

- **Inscribed Angles:** The measure of an inscribed angle is half the measure of its intercepted arc. Similarly, any intercepted arc is twice the measure of any inscribed angle whose sides pass through the endpoints of the arc.

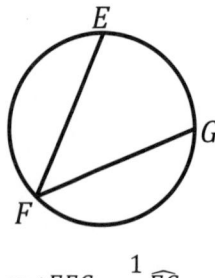

$$m\angle EFG = \frac{1}{2}\widehat{EG}$$

SAT Red Math
Lesson 6A: Advanced Circles

- **Tangent Lines:** If a radius of a circle is drawn to a point of tangency, that radius is perpendicular to the tangent line containing that point of tangency.

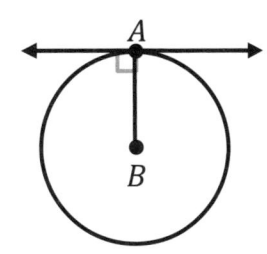

- **Diameters and Chords:** If a diameter is perpendicular to a chord, then it bisects the chord and its arcs. Similarly, if a diameter bisects a chord and its arcs, then it is perpendicular to the chord.

- **Intersecting Chords:** If two chords intersect inside a circle, then the product of the lengths of the two segments of one chord equals the product of the lengths of the segments of the other chord.

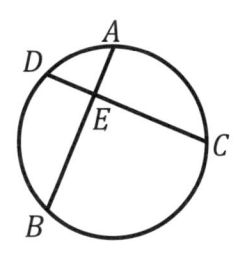

$$\overline{DE} \times \overline{EC} = \overline{AE} \times \overline{EB}$$

Let's try a few sample questions that deal with the information we've just reviewed:

SAMPLE PROBLEM 1: OTHER PROPERTIES OF CIRCLES

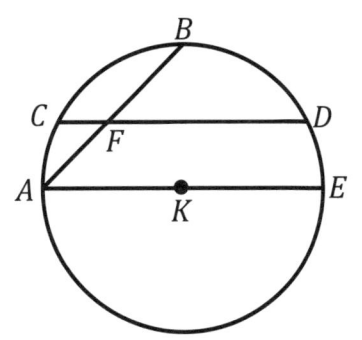

Circle K above has a diameter of $10\sqrt{2}$ and Chord $\overline{CD}$ bisects Chord $\overline{AB}$. If $\angle AKB$ is a right angle, which of the following are possible values of $\overline{CF}$ and $\overline{FD}$?

A) 2, 12
B) 2.5, 10
C) 3, 8
D) 3.5, 7.5

We're given a lot of information for this problem, so let's start by synthesizing what we know so that we can add anything relevant to the provided image. Since we know that ∠AKB is a right angle, let's draw in radius $\overline{BK}$. We can mark that angle as a right angle, and since both legs are the same length (they're both radii), we know it's a 45-45-90 triangle. Thus, the length of $\overline{AB}$ must be 10. Let's add these details, in gray, to our image on the next page:

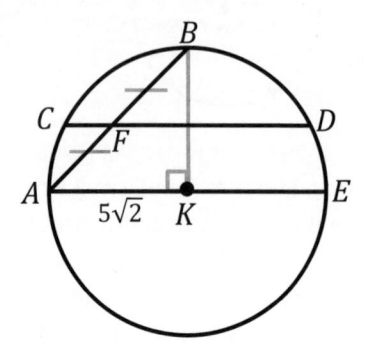

Since Chord $\overline{AB}$ measures 10 units, Segments $\overline{AF}$ and $\overline{FB}$ must both measure 5 units. We also see that Chords $\overline{AB}$ and $\overline{CD}$ intersect each other, so the products of their segments must be equivalent. The product of the lengths of $\overline{AB}$ and $\overline{CD}$ is 25, so answer choice **B** works.

WRAP-UP

Circles will show up much less frequently on the new version of the SAT than the old version, but memorizing these relationships will help solve the few circle questions that do show up much more easily. Keep practicing with these questions until everything comes naturally. Good Luck!

Red Math Lesson 6A: Advanced Circles
Learning to Swim

Directions: Answer each question below.

Practice Set 1 (No Calculator)

1. Alex's Pizza Company offers two sizes for its pizzas, small and large. The small pizza has a circumference of 24π cm and is divided into 4 pieces. The large pizza has a circumference of 40π cm and is cut into 8 pieces. What is the difference in area, in cm², between a slice of the large pizza and a slice of the small pizza?

2. Chloe gets a new tricycle with back wheels that each have 24 spokes. When she rides her tricycle, the back wheels spin at a rate of 100 revolutions per minute. Over the course of an hour of riding, she travels a total of $72,000\pi$ inches. What is the radius, in inches, of the back tricycle wheels?

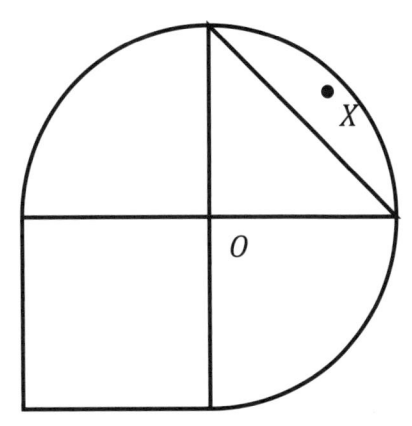

3. In Circle O above, the square and isosceles right triangle intersect at the center, O and have vertices on edge of the circle. If the area of the square is 64 what is the area of the smallest region of the circle that contains Point X?

4. Square $ABCD$ has an area of 200 and is inscribed in a circle. What is the arc length between Point A and Point B on the square?

5. A dartboard is made up of a small circle (the bull's-eye) contained within the larger circle of the whole board. The larger circle is divided into 20 equally sized sections numbered 1 to 20. Hitting a section earns the number of points that section is numbered (i.e. hitting section 10 earns 10 points), while hitting the bull's-eye earns 25 points. If the bull's-eye has a diameter of 20 cm and the entire board has a circumference of 72π cm, what portion of the board is worth at least 16 points?

Red Math Lesson 6A: Advanced Circles
Diving into the Deep End

Directions: Answer each question below.

Practice Set 2 (Calculator)

6. Simon is hosting a pizza party and orders two pizzas from Illumi's Pizza: one large and one medium. The large has a diameter of 18 inches and is sliced into 10 pieces. The medium has a circumference of 16π inches and is sliced into 8 pieces. If Simon ate two slices from the medium pizza and one slice from the large, what was the total area (in square inches) of the slices of pizza that Simon ate?
   A) 8.1π
   B) 24.1π
   C) 48.4π
   D) 96.4π

7. On a circular cricket field, the batter stands at the center of the field. The batter attempts to bat the ball in any direction and have it land without being caught. Jennifer's team is playing defense and decides to place four players at four points along the boundary of the field so that they make a square. If the area of the field is 784π square yards, what is the exact distance between any two adjacent defenders who make up the corners of the square?
   A) 28 yards
   B) $28\sqrt{2}$ yards
   C) 56 yards
   D) $56\sqrt{2}$ yards

8. A target is created with four concentric circles that make up rings. The radius of the smallest circle is 3, the radius of the next largest circle is 7, the radius of the second largest circle is 12, and the radius of the last circle is 20. Ann throws a ball at the target. What percent of the target is made up of either the inner circle or outer ring?
   A) 36
   B) 60
   C) 66.25
   D) 81.75

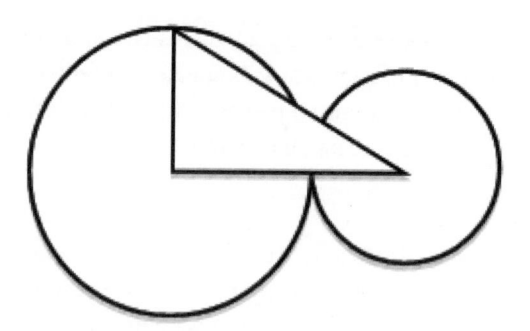

9. In the figure above, the two circles are tangent to one another. The right triangle has end points at the center points of the two circles as well as a third end point on the edge of the large circle. If the area of the larger circle is 256π and the circumference of the smaller circle is 20π, what is the length of the hypotenuse of the triangle?
   A) $2\sqrt{89}$
   B) $4\sqrt{41}$
   C) $2\sqrt{233}$
   D) 20

10. A circular dartboard has a bull's-eye and 20 equally sized sectors that sit outside the bull's-eye. The area of the bull's-eye makes up 1/100th of the area of the total dartboard. If the bull's-eye has a 2-inch diameter, what is the area of any of the non-bull's-eye sectors?
    A) 4.95π square inches
    B) 5π square inches
    C) 19.8π square inches
    D) 20π square inches

11. A pie has 8 equally sized slices, each with an area of 84.5π square inches. What is the arc length of the crust along the edge of 3 slices of pie?
    A) 18π inches
    B) 19.5π inches
    C) 31.6875π inches
    D) 253.5π inches

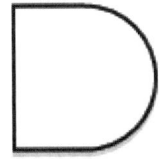

12. The shape above is a rectangle attached to a semicircle. The short side of the rectangle has a length of 7. If the semi-circle has an arc length of 12π, what is the area of the entire shape?
    A) $84 + 36\pi$
    B) $84 + 72\pi$
    C) $168 + 72\pi$
    D) $168 + 144\pi$

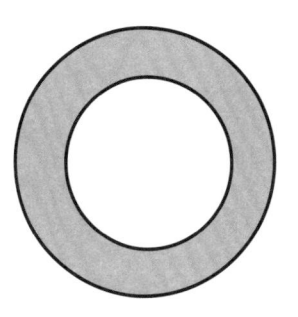

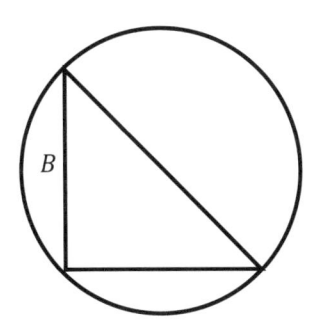

13. An isosceles right triangle is inscribed in a circle as illustrated above. The triangle runs through the center point of the circle. If the lengths of the two legs of the triangle are $16\sqrt{2}$, what is the area of Sector B?
    A) $64\pi - 128$
    B) $128\pi - 128$
    C) $128\pi - 256$
    D) $256\pi - 256$

14. The shaded area of the image above has an area that is 8π more than the area of the inner circle. If the inner circle has a diameter that is 12 less than the diameter of the outer circle, what is the radius of the inner circle?

15. A coin can be assigned a value of cents per square inches (CPSI), which is obtained by dividing the value of the coin (in cents) by the total area of the face of one side of the coin and rounding the answer to the nearest tenth. If a dime (10 cents) has a diameter of 0.7 inches and a quarter (25 cents) has a radius of 0.5 inches, what is the result obtained when a quarter's CPSI is subtracted by a dime's CPSI? Round to the nearest tenth.

SAT Red Math
Lesson 6A: Advanced Circles

PRACTICE SET 3 (CALCULATOR)

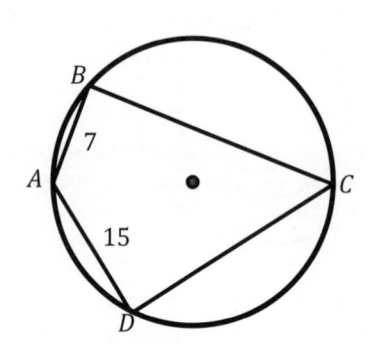

16. The above circle has an area of 156.5π. If $\overline{AC}$ is the diameter, what is the area of the inscribed quadrilateral?
    A) 234
    B) 237.5
    C) 271.5
    D) 275

17. Line $\overline{CG}$ and line $\overline{FE}$ are tangent to both circles. The area of circle B is 25 square units. If the measurement of $\overline{FD}$ is equal to 1.5 and the measurement of $\overline{DG}$ is equal to 3.75, what is the area of the sector enclosed by central angle $\angle CAF$, to the nearest tenth, assuming that $m\angle CAF$ is less than 180°?
    A) 0.7
    B) 1.5
    C) 4.0
    D) 9.3

18. A circle with radius 12 is centered at the origin in the coordinate plane. Which of the following is the equation of a tangent line that goes through point $(0, 13)$?
    A) $y = \frac{144}{13}x + 13$
    B) $y = \frac{5}{12}x + 13$
    C) $y = \frac{36}{15}(x - 13)$
    D) $y = \frac{15}{36}(x - 13)$

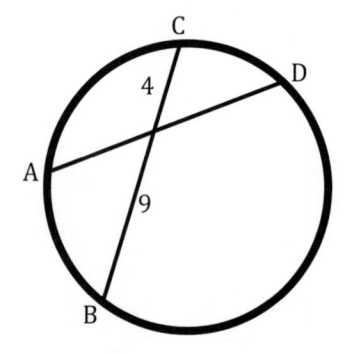

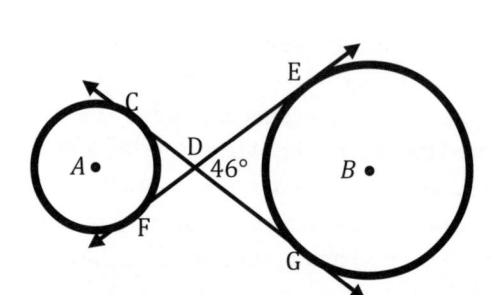

19. If $\overline{CB}$ bisects $\overline{AD}$, what is the length of segment $\overline{AD}$?
    A) 12
    B) 6
    C) 3
    D) 2

20. If a circle with an area of 6.25π is inscribed in an equilateral triangle, what is the area of the triangle, to the nearest tenth?
    A) 8.1
    B) 16.2
    C) 32.5
    D) 65

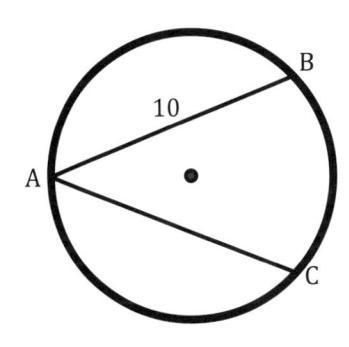

SAT Red Math
Lesson 6A: Advanced Circles
157

21. If $m\angle BAC$ equals 60°, and $\overline{AB}$ is congruent to $\overline{AC}$, what is the circumference of the circle?
   A) 18.1
   B) 31.4
   C) 36.3
   D) 62.8

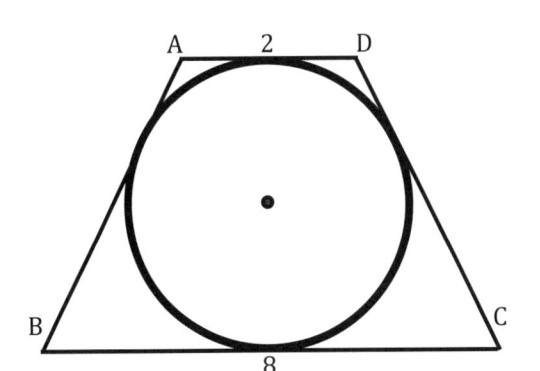

22. If the circumference of the above circle is 4π, what is the area of the trapezoid that circumscribes it?
   A) 8
   B) 10
   C) 20
   D) 32

23. Joana is riding her bike at a constant speed. If the front tire of her bike has a diameter of 26" and has a lateral cut that touches the ground 3% of the time, what is the length of the cut?
   A) 2.5 inches
   B) 4.9 inches
   C) 24.5 inches
   D) 49.0 inches

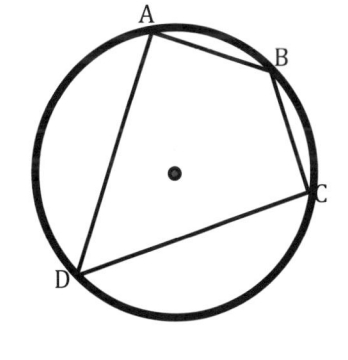

24. Segment $\overline{AB}$ is congruent to segment $\overline{BC}$; $m\angle ADC$ is equal to 80°. If the area of the circle is $\frac{324}{\pi}$, what is the length of minor arc $\widehat{AB}$?

25. If a 72° angle inscribed in a circle results in a minor arc of length 2, what is the area of the circle, to the nearest whole number?

Version 3.0

RED MATH LESSON 6A: ADVANCED CIRCLES
Race to the Finish

Directions: Answer each question below.

HOMEWORK SET (CALCULATOR)

1. What is the area of a circle inscribed in an equilateral triangle of side length 5?
   A) $\frac{25\pi}{12}$
   B) $\frac{25\pi}{3}$
   C) 50π
   D) 100π

2. An equiangular hexagon with a side length of 4 is inscribed in a circle. What is the positive difference between the circumference of the circle and the perimeter of the hexagon?
   A) $16\pi - 24$
   B) $12\sqrt{3} - 4\pi$
   C) $8\pi - 12\sqrt{3}$
   D) $8\pi - 24$

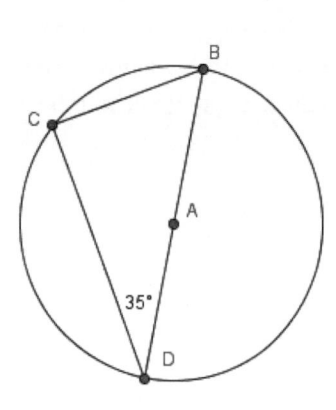

3. What is the length of minor arc $\overset{\frown}{CD}$ given that the radius of circle A is 18?
   A) 8π
   B) 9π
   C) 11π
   D) 15π

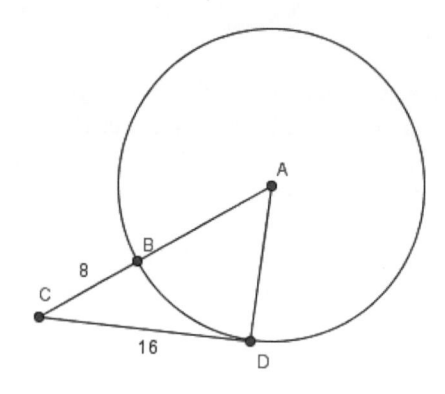

4. What is the area of Circle A if line segment $\overline{CD}$ is tangent to the circle?
   A) 64π
   B) 120π
   C) 144π
   D) 192π

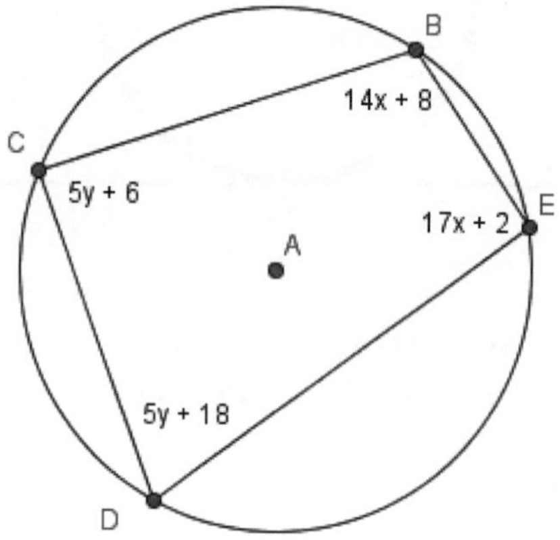

5. Given the angle measures in degrees for circle A above, what is the product of x and y?
   A) 21
   B) 30
   C) 72
   D) 84

SAT Red Math
Lesson 6A: Advanced Circles
159

6. The distance between the Earth and Sun is approximately 150,000,000 kilometers or 150 gigameters. How long is the arc, in gigameters, traveled by Earth after one month? Assume that the Earth revolves around the Sun in a trajectory that is perfectly circular and that each month is of equal length.
   A) 25π
   B) 30π
   C) 50π
   D) 65π

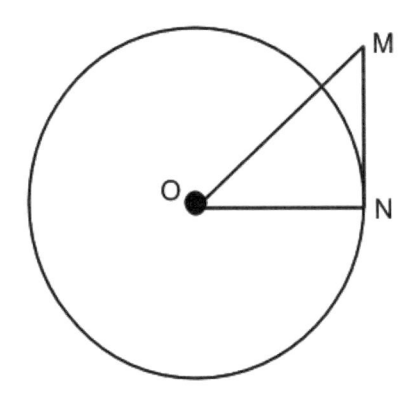

7. Side $\overline{MN}$ of isosceles triangle $\triangle MNO$ is tangent to Circle O at Point N. If Triangle $\triangle MNO$ has area 8π, what is the area of Circle O?
   A) 16π
   B) $8\pi^2$
   C) $16\pi^2$
   D) 64π

8. A semicircular wooden board has been marked to be cut into 6 pieces. These pieces are congruent sectors, each of arc length $\frac{3\pi}{2}$ feet. What is the perimeter of the intact board (in feet)?
   A) 9π
   B) $9\pi + 9$
   C) $9\pi + 18$
   D) 18π

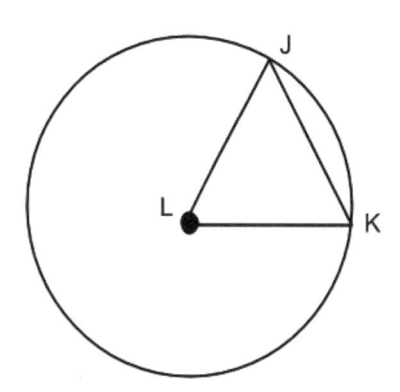

9. Equilateral triangle $\triangle JKL$ has vertices J and K on Circle L. If minor arc $\widehat{JK}$ has length 4π, what is the area of Circle L?
   A) 24π
   B) 36π
   C) 64π
   D) 144π

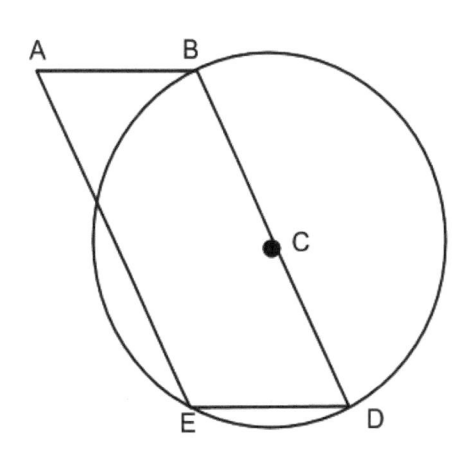

10. Side $\overline{BD}$ of parallelogram $ABDE$ is a diameter of Circle C. $m\angle EAB = 60°$, $\overline{ED} = 3$, and the area of $ABDE$ is $9\sqrt{3}$. What is the radius of Circle C?
    A) $\sqrt{3}$
    B) 3
    C) 6
    D) 9

Version 3.0

SAT Red Math
Lesson 6A: Advanced Circles

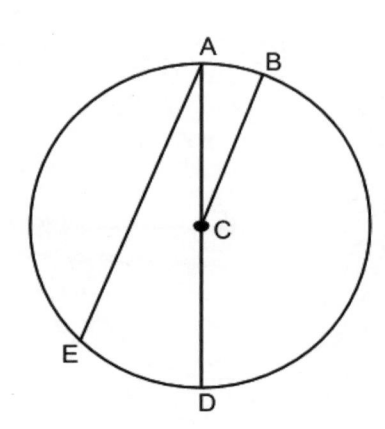

11. In Circle C above, $m\angle EAC = 30°$, Chord $\overline{EA}$ is parallel to radius $\overline{CB}$, and minor arc $\widehat{AB}$ has length π. What is the circumference of Circle C?

A) 6π
B) 12π
C) 24π
D) 36π

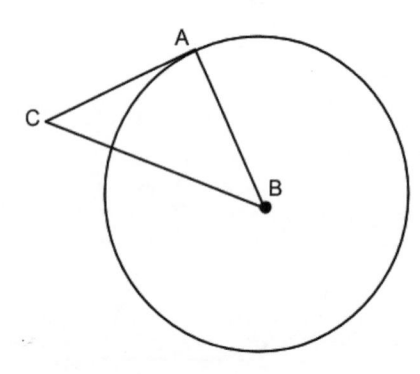

12. Segment $\overline{CA}$ is tangent to Circle B at Point A and has length $2\sqrt{2}$. The length of $\overline{BC}$ is 4. What is the area of the sector defined by $\angle ABC$?

A) $\frac{\pi}{2}$
B) π
C) 2π
D) $2\sqrt{2}\pi$

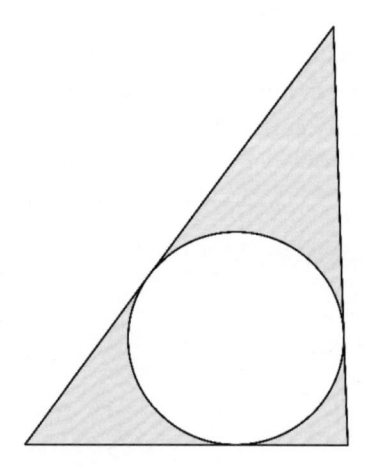

13. A circle of circumference 8π is inscribed in a triangle of height 5π. The ratio of the circle's diameter to the length of the triangle's base is 2:3. What is the area of the shaded region?

A) 4π
B) 6π
C) 14π
D) 16π

14. A circle is inscribed in a square piece of paper of perimeter $4x$. A square is cut from each corner of the paper to create four flaps that can be folded up to form an open box. The squares must not cut away any of the circle. What is the maximum width of one of these squares, in terms of x?

A) $\frac{2x - x\sqrt{2}}{4}$
B) $\frac{x\sqrt{2}}{2}$
C) $\frac{x^2 - x\sqrt{2}}{4}$
D) $\frac{x\sqrt{2} - x}{2}$

15. A circular pizza is cut into 5 pieces with central angles in the ratio 1:2:2:3:4. If the largest piece has area 12π square inches, what is the diameter of the pizza (in inches)?

A) 9
B) 12
C) 18
D) 24

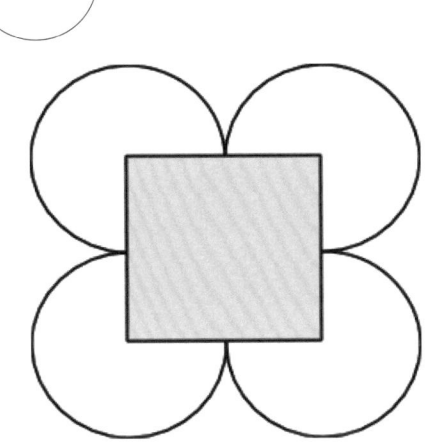

SAT Red Math
Lesson 6A: Advanced Circles

16. The shaded figure above has its vertices on the centers of 4 congruent circles. If the visible arcs have a combined length of $3\sqrt{3}\pi$, what is the area of the shaded region?

   A) $\sqrt{3}$
   B) 3
   C) $\sqrt{3}\pi^2$
   D) $3\pi^2$

17. What is the perimeter of a dodecagon that has a side length equal to half the radius of a semi-circle with area 98π?

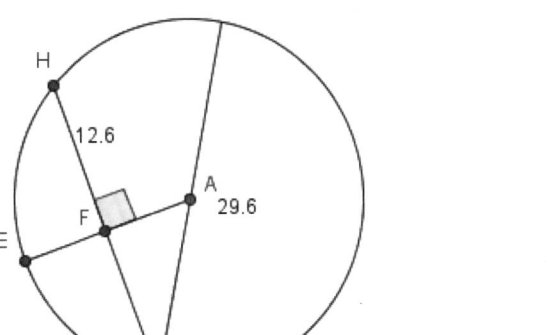

18. For Circle A above, what is the length of segment $\overline{EF}$ given the diameter and length of $\overline{FH}$? (Round your answer to the nearest tenth)

19. A pizza was cut up into equal slices and shared by Jack, Mary, and Bob. Jack had three times as many slices as Mary, and Bob had twice as many slices as Mary. Mary never eats the crust of her pizza. If the outside edge of the crust of Mary's pizza measures 6.28 inches, what is the diameter of the pizza? (Round your answer to the nearest tenth of an inch)

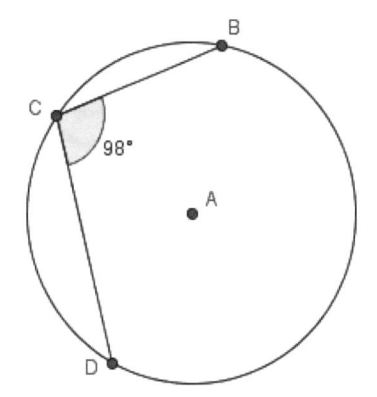

20. The length of minor arc $\widehat{BC}$ is $\frac{5\pi}{2}$ and the radius of Circle A is 6. What is the length of minor arc $\widehat{CD}$ to the nearest tenth?

Red Math Lesson 6B: Graphs of Circles and Parabolas
Getting Your Feet Wet

Directions: The problems below are intended as a short diagnostic exam.

$$x^2 + y^2 - 8x + 14y + 48 = 0$$

1. What is the center and radius of the circle graphed in the xy-plane via the equation above?
   A) $(4, -7), \sqrt{17}$
   B) $(-4, 7), \sqrt{17}$
   C) $(4, -7), 17$
   D) $(-4, 7), 17$

$$(x-2)^2 + \left(y - \frac{3}{2}\right)^2 = 9$$

2. The vertex of which of the following parabolas lies on the same point as the center of the circle above?
   A) $x = -5\left(x + \frac{3}{2}\right)^2 - 2$
   B) $x = -5\left(x - \frac{3}{2}\right)^2 + 2$
   C) $x = -5\left(y + \frac{3}{2}\right)^2 - 2$
   D) $x = -5\left(y - \frac{3}{2}\right)^2 + 2$

RED MATH LESSON 6B: GRAPHS OF CIRCLES AND PARABOLAS
Wading In

Directions: Read the explanation for each problem type mentioned below. Pay special attention to the methods and techniques used to solve the sample problems. Then, do the practice exercises that follow; use the appropriate method to solve each problem.

> **Directions:** Read the explanation for each problem type mentioned below. Pay special attention to the methods and techniques used to solve the sample problems. Then, do the practice exercises that follow; use the appropriate method to solve each problem.
>
> ### TOPIC OVERVIEW: CIRCLES
>
> The graphs of two conic sections will show up frequently on the SAT—circles and parabolas. The standard form of the graph of a circle in the xy-coordinate plane is:
>
> $$(x - h)^2 + (y - k)^2 = r^2$$
>
> where (h, k) is the center of the circle and r is the length of its radius.
>
> Frequently, however, we will be given the equation of a circle in a much different format; we have to use completing the square to obtain the equation of the circle in standard form. Let's try a question to see how this is done.
>
> ---
> **SAMPLE PROBLEM 1: CIRCLES**
>
> $$x^2 + y^2 - 8x + 14y + 48 = 0$$
>
> What is the center and radius of the circle graphed in the xy-plane via the equation above?
> A) $(4, -7), \sqrt{17}$
> B) $(-4, 7), \sqrt{17}$
> C) $(4, -7), 17$
> D) $(-4, 7), 17$
>
> ---
>
> To complete the square, we should always start by organizing our equation so that the x-terms are together on one side of the equation, the y-terms are together on the same side of the equation, and the number is on the other side of the equation:
>
> $$x^2 + y^2 - 8x + 14y + 48 = 0$$
> $$x^2 - 8x + y^2 + 14y = -48$$

Next, we need to add a number to each side of the equation to make the x-terms form a perfect square. To do this to an expression such as $Ax^2 + Bx$, add the number $\left(\frac{B}{2}\right)^2$ to each side of the equation, then simplify and factor:

$$x^2 - 8x$$
$$x^2 - 8x + \left(-\frac{8}{2}\right)^2$$
$$x^2 - 8x + 16$$
$$(x-4)^2$$

Now, our equation looks like this:

$$x^2 - 8x + y^2 + 14y = -48$$
$$x^2 - 8x + 16 + y^2 + 14y = -48 + 16$$
$$(x-4)^2 + y^2 + 14y = -32$$

Do the same thing with the y-terms now:

$$(x-4)^2 + y^2 + 14y = -32$$
$$(x-4)^2 + y^2 + 14y + 49 = -32 + 49$$
$$(x-4)^2 + (y+7)^2 = 17$$

We see that the center of our circle is at the point $(4, -7)$ and its radius is $\sqrt{17}$. Our answer must be **A**.

TOPIC OVERVIEW: PARABOLAS

The graph of a parabola can also be written in vertex form:

$$y = a(x-h)^2 + k$$

where (h, k) is the vertex of the parabola. If $a > 1$, then the graph of the parabola is compressed horizontally by a factor of a. If $0 < a < 1$, then the parabola is stretched horizontally by a factor of a. If a is positive, then the graph of the parabola opens upwards, while a negative a value causes the parabola to open downwards. Most Algebra 2 and Trigonometry classes discuss the directrix and focus of a parabola, but the SAT will not require us to know these terms.

There is also a shortcut to find the vertex of a parabola: If the parabola is in the form $y = ax^2 + bx + c$, then the x-coordinate of the vertex of the parabola can be found at $x = -\frac{b}{2a}$. Alternatively, the x-coordinate of a parabola will always be halfway between its two zeroes.

SAT Red Math
Lesson 6B: Graphs of Circles and Parabolas

Additionally, parabolas can also open sideways. The vertex form of these parabolas is nearly identical:

$$x = a(y - k)^2 + h$$

where (h, k) is the vertex of the parabola. If $a > 1$, then the graph of the parabola is compressed vertically by a factor of a. If $0 < a < 1$, then the parabola is stretched vertically by a factor of a. If a is positive, then the graph of the parabola opens to the right, while a negative a value causes the parabola to open to the left.

Let's try a sample question dealing with parabolas:

SAMPLE PROBLEM 2: PARABOLAS

$$(x - 2)^2 + \left(y - \frac{3}{2}\right)^2 = 9$$

The vertex of which of the following parabolas lies on the same point as the center of the circle above?

A) $y = -5(x + 2)^2 - \frac{3}{2}$

B) $y = -5(x + 2)^2 + \frac{3}{2}$

C) $x = -5\left(y + \frac{3}{2}\right)^2 - 2$

D) $x = -5\left(y - \frac{3}{2}\right)^2 + 2$

We know that the circle has its center at the point $\left(2, \frac{3}{2}\right)$. So, the equation of the parabola must also have its vertex at the point $\left(2, \frac{3}{2}\right)$. Since $h = 2$ and $k = \frac{3}{2}$, our answer must be **D**. The vertex of the equation in answer choice A is $\left(-2, -\frac{3}{2}\right)$, while the vertex of B is $\left(-2, \frac{3}{2}\right)$. The vertex of answer choice C is the same as A, $\left(-2, -\frac{3}{2}\right)$.

WRAP-UP

Many of the questions involving circles and parabolas on the new SAT will involve their graphs, so memorizing the equations presented in this lesson is mandatory. Additionally, the SAT will test our ability to see when circles and parabolas intersect the graphs of other functions. The ability to quickly sketch a graph while working through these situations will help us narrow down our choices quickly and effectively. Good Luck!

RED MATH LESSON 6B: GRAPHS OF CIRCLES AND PARABOLAS
Learning to Swim

Directions: Answer each question below.

PRACTICE SET 1 (NO CALCULATOR)

1. What is the equation of a circle that has a center at $(-3, 4)$ and a radius of 4?

2. Write the following equation in vertex form. $8x = y^2 - 4y + 20$

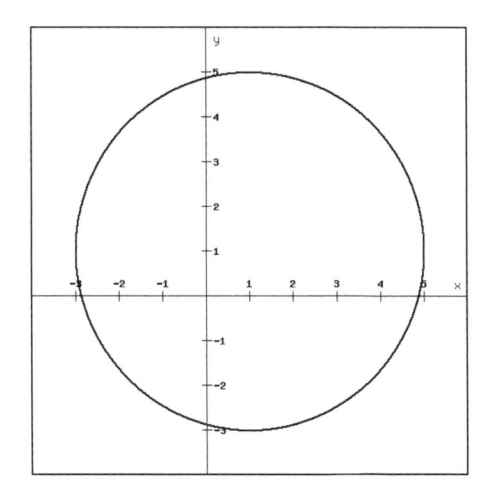

3. If the circle shown above is shifted 3 units left and 1 unit up, what would be the equation of the resulting graph?

$$2y + 10x = x^2 + 19$$

4. What is the vertex of the above parabola?

5. A circle is defined by the equation: $y^2 + x^2 + 2x = 4y + 3$. If the circumference of the circle is tripled, what is the area of the resulting circle?

SAT Red Math
Lesson 6B: Graphs of Circles and Parabolas

RED MATH LESSON 6B: GRAPHS OF CIRCLES AND PARABOLAS
Diving into the Deep End

Directions: Answer each question below.

PRACTICE SET 2 (NO CALCULATOR)

6. The graph of $x = ay^2 + by + c$ is symmetrical about the line $y = -\frac{1}{8}$. What is the ratio of a to b?
   A) $1:4$
   B) $1:2$
   C) $2:1$
   D) $4:1$

7. The graph of $y = 2x^2 + 6x - q$ intersects the graph of $y = 1 - 2x$ at exactly one point. What is the value of q?
   A) -9
   B) -1
   C) 1
   D) 9

$$(x+4)^2 + (y-4)^2 = 9$$

8. Circle C is given by the equation above. Circle C^* is the reflection of C across the x-axis, which is then shifted 3 units to the right and dilated by a factor of 2. Which of the following is the equation for Circle C^*?
   A) $(x+7)^2 + (y-4)^2 = 36$
   B) $(x+1)^2 + (y-4)^2 = 18$
   C) $(x+1)^2 + (y+4)^2 = 36$
   D) $(x+1)^2 + (y+4)^2 = 18$

$$\tfrac{1}{4}(x^2 + y^2) = 3x + 2y - 12$$

9. What is the center of the circle given by the equation above?
   A) $(-12, -8)$
   B) $(-2\sqrt{3}, -2\sqrt{2})$
   C) $(\tfrac{3}{2}, \tfrac{1}{2})$
   D) $(6, 4)$

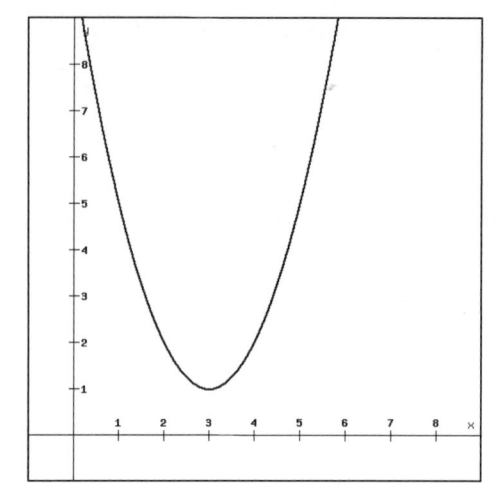

10. The graph above shows $f(x)$. Which of the following equations corresponds to $g(x) = f(x+2) - 4$?
    A) $g(x) = (x-5)^2 - 3$
    B) $g(x) = (x-1)^2 - 3$
    C) $g(x) = (x-7)^2 + 3$
    D) $g(x) = (x+1)^2 - 1$

11. An archway sits atop a doorframe. The arch's shape is described by the graph of $y = -\tfrac{1}{4}x^2 + x + c$, where x is the horizontal distance in feet from where the left side of the arch meets the top of the doorframe, and y is the height in feet of the arch above the floor, and c is the height of the doorframe where it meets the arch. If a 6-foot-tall person must be able to walk through the center of the arched doorway with at least 1 foot of clearance above his/her head, what is the minimum possible value of c?
    A) 7
    B) $6\tfrac{1}{4}$
    C) $6\tfrac{1}{16}$
    D) 6

SAT Red Math
Lesson 6B: Graphs of Circles and Parabolas
169

12. Polygon $ABCD$ has endpoints of $(0,0), (8,0), (8,8),$ and $(0,8)$. A circle with an equation $(x-h)^2 + (y-k)^2 = r^2$ is inscribed in the polygon. What is the sum of $h, k,$ and r?
    A) 4
    B) 12
    C) 16
    D) 24

13. The graph of $y = k(x-1)^2 + 3$, with $k \neq 0$, has both its vertex and its y-intercept on a circle with center $(4, 7)$. Which of the following is a possible value of k?
    A) 3
    B) 4
    C) 7
    D) 10

$$x^2 + y^2 - 2x + 4y = 20$$

14. What is the diameter of the circle given by the equation above?

$$x^2 + y^2 + 6x - 12y = 55$$

15. At how many points does the function above intersect the line $y = \frac{3}{4}x - \frac{17}{4}$?

Practice Set 3 (No Calculator)

16. A circle is represented by the equation $(x-h)^2 + (y-11)^2 = 121$. What is a possible coordinate of the endpoint of a diameter that is perpendicular to the diameter with an endpoint of $(15, 0)$?
    A) $(-7, 11)$
    B) $(4, 11)$
    C) $(26, 15)$
    D) $(26, -11)$

17. A circle with the equation $x^2 + y^2 - 2x + 6y - 90 = 0$ is reflected about the y-axis. What are the coordinates of the center of the circle after reflection?
    A) $(-1, -3)$
    B) $(-2, 6)$
    C) $(1, -9)$
    D) $(1, 3)$

18. A circle with the equation $(x-h)^2 + (y-k)^2 = r^2$ passes through the following points: $(12, -2), (15, -5),$ and $(8, -12)$. What is the value of r?
    A) $\sqrt{13}$
    B) $\sqrt{29}$
    C) $\sqrt{48}$
    D) $\sqrt{64}$

Version 3.0

SAT Red Math
Lesson 6B: Graphs of Circles and Parabolas

19. A circle represented by the equation $(x - h)^2 + (y - k)^2 = r^2$ has a center that lies in the fourth quadrant. If the circle is tangent to the lines $y = -10, x = -1, y = -18$ what is the sum of h and k?
    A) 18
    B) 15
    C) −8
    D) −11

20. The diameter of a circle has endpoints with the coordinates $(-4, 15)$ and $(-14, 7)$. If the circle is translated up 5 units, what is the equation for the circle after the translation?
    A) $(x + 9)^2 + (y - 11)^2 = 25$
    B) $(x + 9)^2 + (y - 16)^2 = 41$
    C) $(x + 9)^2 + (y - 16)^2 = 164$
    D) $(x + 14)^2 + (y - 9)^2 = 164$

21. A circle represented by the equation $(x - 2)^2 + (y - 3)^2 = 1$ is reflected about the origin. What is a possible coordinate for the point of intersection between the reflection and the line $y = x$?
    A) $(1, 1)$
    B) $(0, 0)$
    C) $(-1, -1)$
    D) $(-2, -2)$

22. Which of the following is the equation of a parabola with its vertex at $\left(-\frac{1}{2}, 8\right)$?
    A) $y = x^2 + \frac{1}{2}x + 8$
    B) $y = x^2 + x + \frac{17}{4}$
    C) $y = 2x^2 + 2x + \frac{17}{2}$
    D) $y = 2x^2 + 2x + 8$

23. The equation for a certain parabola is $0 = y^2 - 16y - 4x + 84$. If the parabola is to be reflected about the origin, what would be the resulting equation in vertex form?
    A) $-4(x + 5) = (y + 8)^2$
    B) $-4(x - 5) = (y - 8)^2$
    C) $4(x - 5) = (y - 8)^2$
    D) $4(x + 5) = (y + 8)^2$

$$x^2 + 12x + y^2 + 6y + 29 = 0$$

24. The circle described by the equation above is reflected about the line $y = -x$, the radius is increased by 6 and the circle is shifted down 5 units. (a, b) is the point of intersection between the new circle and the line $y = -\frac{4}{3}x - \frac{35}{3}$. What is the product of a and b?

$$y - 8 = (x + 1)^2$$
$$(x + 1)^2 + (y - 2)^2 = 36$$

25. If (a, b) is the point of intersection between the two graphs above, what is $a + b$?

Red Math Lesson 6B: Graphs of Circles and Parabolas
Race to the Finish

Directions: Answer each question below.

Homework Set (No Calculator)

1. What is the minimum value of the function $f(x) = \frac{1}{3}x^2 + 4x + 14$?
    A) -6
    B) $-\frac{2}{3}$
    C) 2
    D) 50

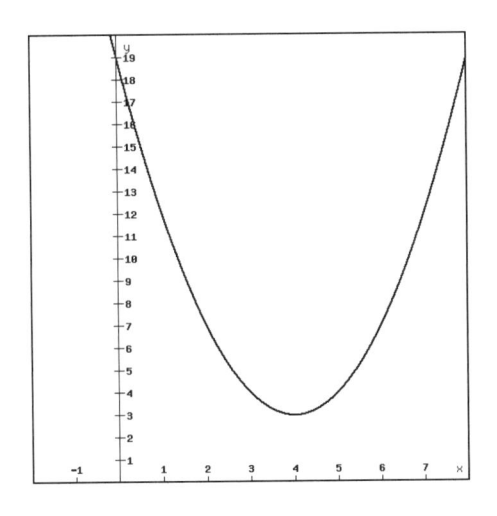

2. The equation of the parabola graphed above is:
    A) $y = x^2 + 19$
    B) $y = x^2 - 8x + 19$
    C) $y = x^2 - 8x - 13$
    D) $y = x^2 + 8x + 13$

$$9x^2 + 9y^2 - 72x + 144y = -716$$

3. The length of the radius of the circle described by the equation above is:
    A) $\frac{4}{9}$
    B) $\frac{2}{3}$
    C) $\frac{26}{3}$
    D) $8\sqrt{10}$

4. A diameter of a circle has endpoints $(-9, -3)$ and $(3, 1)$. What is the equation of the circle?
    A) $(x - 6)^2 + (y - 2)^2 = 4$
    B) $(x + 6)^2 + (y + 2)^2 = 6$
    C) $(x - 3)^2 + (y - 1)^2 = 144$
    D) $(x + 3)^2 + (y + 1)^2 = 40$

5. At how many points do the graphs of $x = \frac{1}{4}(y - 1)^2 - 4$ and $y = 3(x - 1)^2 + 2$ intersect?
    A) 0
    B) 1
    C) 2
    D) 4

6. The circles described by $x^2 + y^2 = 25$ and $(x - 10)^2 + (y + 5)^2 = 100$ intersect at $(q, 3)$. Which if the following is a possible value of q?
    A) -4
    B) $-5 + \sqrt{51}$
    C) 4
    D) 16

7. The parabola $y = x^2 - 2x + 4$ intersects the circle $(x - 8)^2 + (y - k)^2 = 169$ at a point whose x-coordinate is two units to the right of the x-coordinate of the vertex of the parabola. Which of the following is a possible value of k?
    A) $3 - 2\sqrt{42}$
    B) -5
    C) -1
    D) $3 + 2\sqrt{30}$

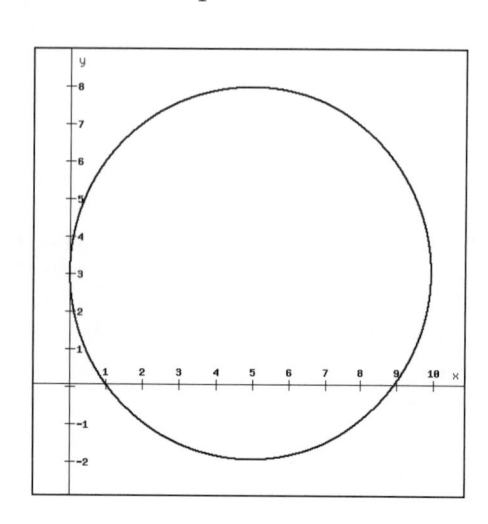

172 SAT Red Math
Lesson 6B: Graphs of Circles and Parabolas

HW

8. Which of the following is the equation of the circle graphed above?
   A) $x^2 - 10x + y^2 - 6y = -9$
   B) $x^2 - 10x + y^2 - 6y = 25$
   C) $(x - 1)^2 + y^2 = 25$
   D) $y = (x - 1)(x - 9)$

9. A self-published author finds that the price and sales of her eBooks have a linear relationship; for every $3 she raises the price of her eBooks, she sells 10,000 fewer copies per year. If the price is $20, she can sell 30,000 copies in a year. At what price should she offer the eBooks to maximize her revenue? (Revenue is total money brought in by sales, and depends on both the number of units sold and on the price per unit.)
   A) $14.50
   B) $15.00
   C) $18.17
   D) $20

10. The graphs of $x^2 + 2x + y^2 = 97$ and $x^2 - 6x + y^2 = 0$ intersect at how many points?
    A) 0
    B) 1
    C) 2
    D) 4

11. Which of the following is the graph of $x^2 + y^2 + 2x - 8y - 8 = 0$?
    A) 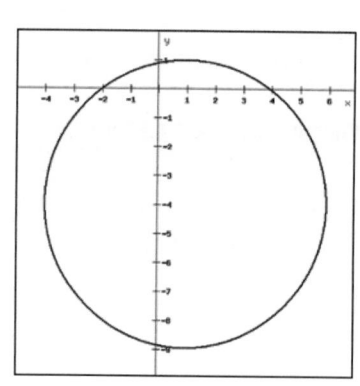
    B) 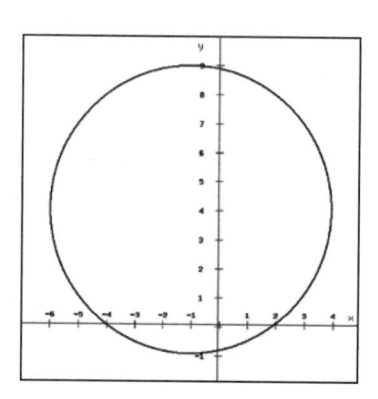
    C) 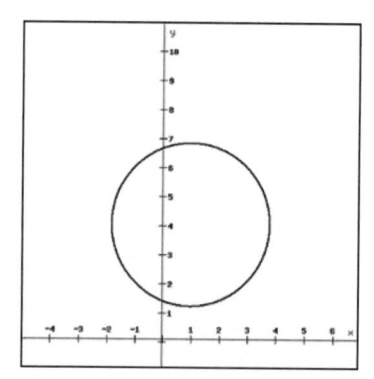
    D)

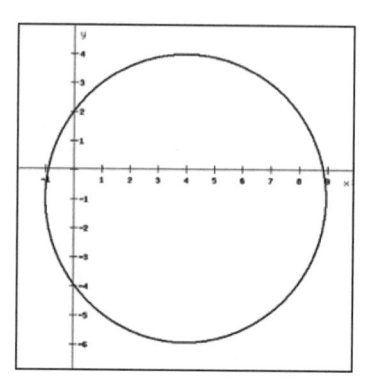

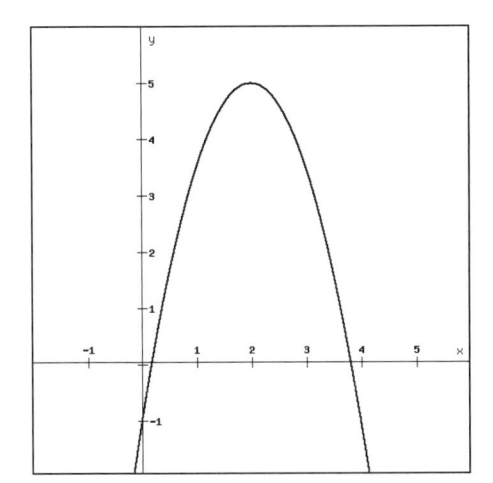

SAT Red Math — Lesson 6B: Graphs of Circles and Parabolas

173

12. The equation of the parabola graphed above is:
    A) $y = -x^2 + 4x + 1$
    B) $y = -x^2 - 4x + 9$
    C) $y = -\frac{3}{2}x^2 + 6x - 1$
    D) $y = -\frac{3}{2}x^2 + 6x + 11$

13. The graph of $y = (x - 3)^2 - 2$ intersects a line passing through the origin with slope 2 at (c, d). What is a possible value of d?
    A) -10
    B) 7
    C) 14
    D) There is no real solution.

14. A circle centered at $(-5, 2)$ intersects the y-axis at 14. The coordinates of one of its intersections with the line $y = 4 - x$ are:
    A) $(-7, 11)$
    B) $(7, -3)$
    C) $(14, -10)$
    D) $(\frac{70}{3}, -\frac{58}{3})$

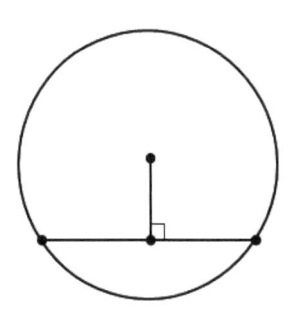

15. A circle intersects the x-axis at 10 and -20. The segment drawn from the center of the circle to the x-axis, as shown above, is 8 units long. Which of the following is the equation of the circle?
    A) $x^2 + (y - 17)^2 = 289$
    B) $(x + 5)^2 + (y - 8)^2 = 289$
    C) $(x + 5)^2 + y^2 = 225$
    D) $(x - 5)^2 + (y + 8)^2 = 225$

16. A parabola intersects the x-axis at -2 and 8. What is the y-coordinate of its vertex?
    A) -25
    B) -16
    C) 3
    D) It cannot be determined from the information provided.

174 — SAT Red Math — Lesson 6B: Graphs of Circles and Parabolas — HW

17. A parabola intersects the x-axis at 3 and 9. What is the x-coordinate of its vertex?

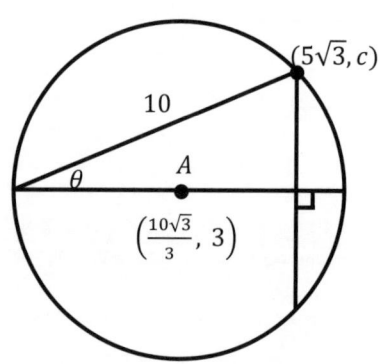

19. If $\cot\theta = \sqrt{3}$, what is the value of c, which lies on Circle A above? Round to the nearest tenth.

18. A parabola with the equation $x = -a(y-k)^2 + h$ and the vertex $(3, 4)$ passes through the point $(1, 9)$. What is the value of a?

20. $$x^2 + y^2 + 20x - 24y = -19$$
How many times does the function above intersect the line $y = \frac{4}{3}x + \frac{4}{3}$?

Red Math Lesson 7A: Advanced Geometry
Getting Your Feet Wet

Directions: The problems below are intended as a short diagnostic exam.

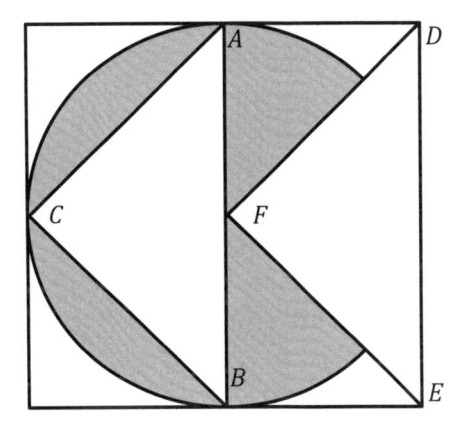

1. AB is the diameter of the circle inscribed in the square above, and $\triangle ABC$ and $\triangle DEF$ are congruent isosceles triangles. Find the area of the shaded portion of the figure above if the area of the square is 100 square meters.

   A) $\dfrac{75\pi - 200}{4}$

   B) $\dfrac{75\pi - 100}{8}$

   C) $25\pi - 50$

   D) $\dfrac{75\pi - 100}{4}$

SAT Red Math
Lesson 7A: Advanced Geometry

RED MATH LESSON 7A: ADVANCED GEOMETRY
Wading In

Directions: Read the explanation for each problem type mentioned below. Pay special attention to the methods and techniques used to solve the sample problems. Then, do the practice exercises that follow; use the appropriate method to solve each problem.

TOPIC OVERVIEW: ADVANCED GEOMETRY

Many of the geometry questions on the SAT require knowledge of only one figure, be it a circle, a rectangle, or a triangle. Sometimes, however, the SAT challenges us with problems that draw from all of our knowledge. Solving these questions may require algebra, trigonometry, or even knowledge of more than one geometric figure. As always, if the test makers do not provide us with an image, we should draw one first. Then, we can fill out any information we can surmise from the problem and our knowledge of mathematics. Let's look at a sample problem to see how to approach these.

SAMPLE PROBLEM 1: ADVANCED GEOMETRY

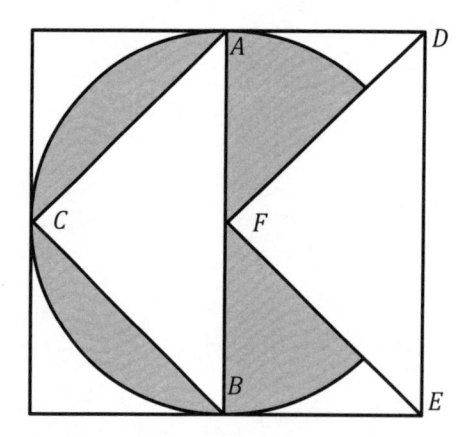

AB is a diameter of the circle inscribed in the square above, and $\triangle ABC$ and $\triangle DEF$ are congruent isosceles triangles. Find the area of the shaded portion of the figure above if the area of the square is 100 square meters.

A) $\dfrac{75\pi - 200}{4}$

B) $\dfrac{75\pi - 100}{8}$

C) $25\pi - 50$

D) $\dfrac{75\pi - 100}{4}$

Let's start by adding the information we learned from the problem to our image. Since the area of the square is 100 square meters, its side length must be 10 m. Since AB is a diameter of the circle, we know that angle C must be a right angle. This makes both triangles right isosceles triangles, which means we can easily figure out their side lengths if necessary:

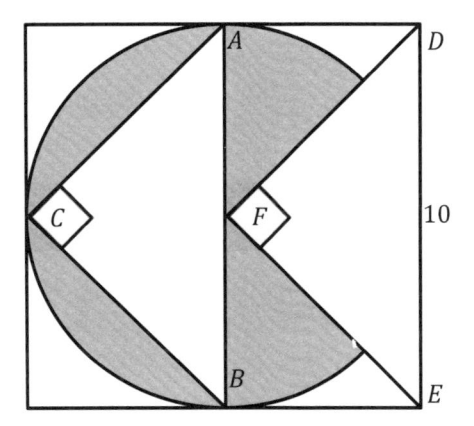

At this point, we can break the circle up into two halves: the part on the left side of diameter AB and the part on the right side of the diameter. Let's find the area of the left side first:

This figure is a half circle, so its area is $\frac{1}{2}\pi r^2$. Its area is $\frac{25}{2}\pi$. To find the area of the shaded portion, we must subtract the white triangle. Since it has a hypotenuse of 10, its legs must measure $5\sqrt{2}$ each, so its area is 25. To find the area of the shaded portion of the left side, we must simply subtract:

$$\frac{25}{2}\pi - 25$$

Finding the area of the shaded portion of the right side is simpler. Since we know that the central angle included in the triangle is 90 degrees, the combined central angles of the combined wedges must also be 90 degrees. Thus, the area of the shaded portion is:

$$\frac{1}{4}(25\pi) = \frac{25}{4}\pi$$

Adding the shaded portions of both sides together, we get **D**.

WRAP-UP

When tackling advanced geometry problems, always remember to draw an image if one is not given and to include as much information as possible when an image is given. Keep practicing until solving these questions becomes second nature. Good luck!

RED MATH LESSON 7A: ADVANCED GEOMETRY
Learning to Swim

Directions: Answer each question below.

PRACTICE SET 1 (CALCULATOR)

1. An equilateral triangle is inscribed in a circle, which is inscribed in another equilateral triangle. What is the ratio of the area of the smaller triangle to the area of the larger one?

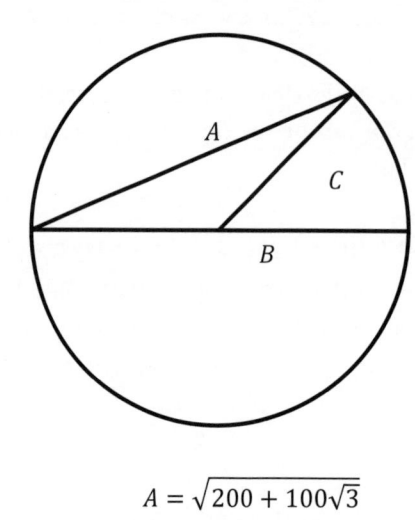

$$A = \sqrt{200 + 100\sqrt{3}}$$

2. B, the diameter of the circle above, has a length of 20. What is the area of sector C?

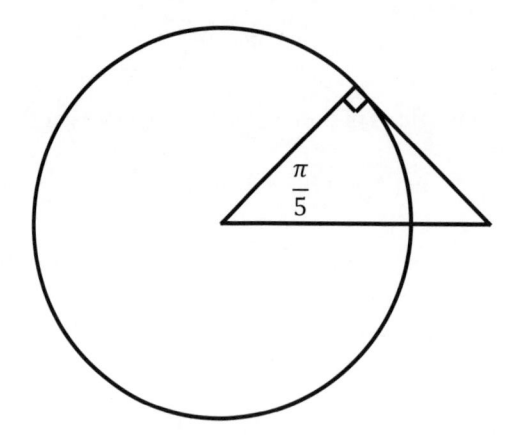

3. In the interior of the above figure, the area of the circle outside the triangle is 5. What is the area of the triangle? Give an exact answer, leaving any trigonometric functions unevaluated.

Use the following information for questions 4 and 5:

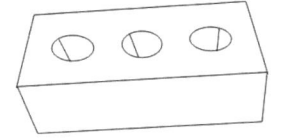

Big Brick Company wants to design a brick that is twice as long as it is wide and $\frac{3}{4}$ as tall as it is wide. Three identical cylindrical mortar holes oriented along its height will be removed such that the volume is $\frac{5}{6}$ of that of a solid brick.

4. What should the radius of each hole be in terms of the length, l, of the brick?

5. If Big Brick Company uses a clay that weighs 2 grams for every cubic centimeter, how many grams will a 25 cm long brick (of the above design) weigh?

RED MATH LESSON 7A: ADVANCED GEOMETRY
Diving into the Deep End

Directions: Answer each question below.

PRACTICE SET 2 (NO CALCULATOR)

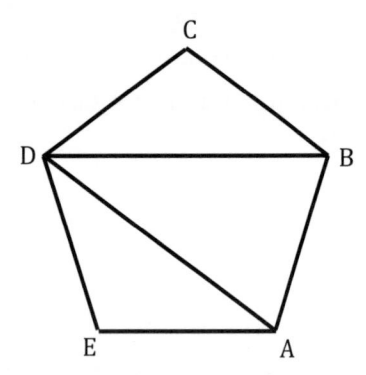

6. The regular pentagon shown above has a side length of 5, what is the area of $\triangle ABD$?
   A) 12.4
   B) 14.3
   C) 18.9
   D) 19.2

7. A pendulum swings thorough an arc of 2 radians. If the arc length is 37.5 in, what is the length of the pendulum?
   A) 18.75 in
   B) 37.5 in
   C) 56.25 in
   D) 75 in

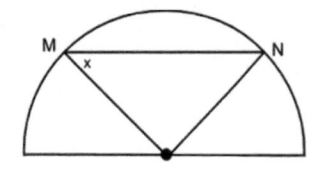

8. In the semicircle above, the length of chord $\overline{MN}$ is $4\sqrt{3}$ and the radian measure of angle x is $\frac{\pi}{6}$. What is the length of arc $\widehat{MN}$?
   A) $\frac{2\pi}{3}$
   B) $\frac{5\pi}{3}$
   C) $\frac{8\pi}{3}$
   D) $\frac{10\pi}{3}$

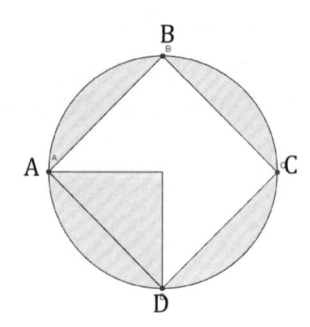

9. In the above figure, square $ABCD$ is inscribed in a circle and $AB = 35$. What is the area of the shaded region?
   A) $35\sqrt{2}\pi$
   B) $\frac{1225}{2}(\pi - 1)$
   C) $\frac{1225}{4}(2\pi - 3)$
   D) $\frac{1225}{8}(5\pi - 8)$

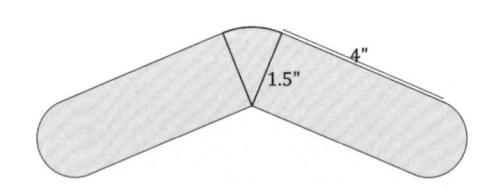

10. The above boomerang is formed by attaching two rectangles to a circular sector of central angle $\frac{\pi}{4}$, then capping the other end of each rectangle with a semicircle. What is the exact area of the boomerang in square inches?
    A) $12 + \frac{9\pi}{16}$
    B) $12 + \frac{27\pi}{32}$
    C) $12 + \frac{45\pi}{32}$
    D) $12 + \frac{81\pi}{32}$

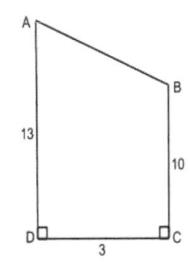

SAT Red Math
Lesson 7A: Advanced Geometry

Practice Set 3 (Calculator)

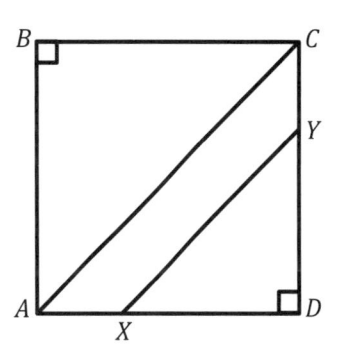

11. What is the area of the trapezoid above?
    A) 30
    B) 34.5
    C) 39
    D) 54

12. What is the surface area of a tetrahedron with side length 2 feet? (A tetrahedron is a three-dimensional object with four equilateral triangles for sides)
    A) $2\sqrt{3}$ ft²
    B) $4\sqrt{3}$ ft²
    C) $6\sqrt{3}$ ft²
    D) $8\sqrt{3}$ ft²

13. How tall is a tetrahedron with side length 2 when it's sitting on one face?
    A) $\sqrt{\frac{2}{3}}$
    B) $2\sqrt{\frac{2}{3}}$
    C) $\frac{3}{2}$
    D) 2

14. A cube with side length $\sqrt{3}$ is inscribed in a sphere, which is then inscribed in another cube. What is the volume of the larger cube?

15. A regular hexagon is inscribed in a circle of radius 2. If the area of the hexagon can be represented as $x\sqrt{3}$, what is the value of x?

16. In the figure above, the triangles ADC and XDY are similar and the ratio of AX to XD is 2:3. If $XY = 18\sqrt{2}$, what is the area of square $ABCD$?
    A) 144
    B) 324
    C) 576
    D) 900

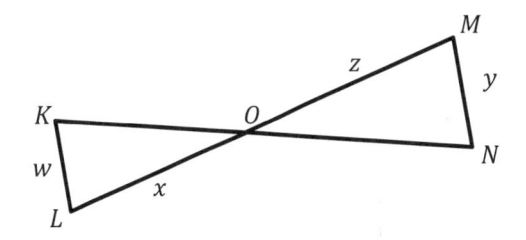

17. In the figure above, segments $\overline{KL}$ and $\overline{MN}$ are parallel. What is z in terms of w, x, and y?
    A) $\frac{xy}{w}$
    B) $\frac{xw}{y}$
    C) $\frac{wy}{x}$
    D) $\frac{w}{xy}$

18. The angle of a sector in Circle O is $\frac{4}{9}\pi$ radians, and the area of that sector is 18π. What is the diameter of Circle O?
    A) 8
    B) 9
    C) 16
    D) 18

184 | SAT Red Math
Lesson 7A: Advanced Geometry

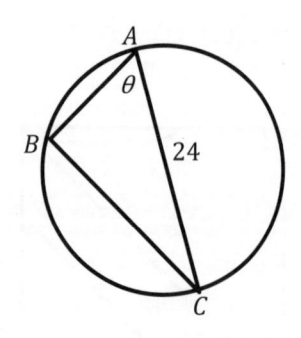

19. In the figure above, $\overline{AC}$ is a diameter of the circle. If $\cos \theta = \frac{1}{2}$, what is the length of minor arc $\widehat{BC}$?

    A) 8π
    B) 9π
    C) 12π
    D) 16π

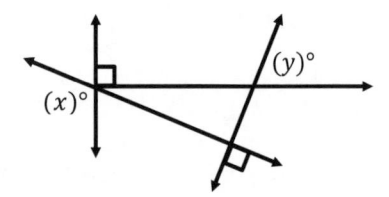

20. In the figure above, what is x in terms of y?

    A) $y + 90$
    B) $2y$
    C) $180 - y$
    D) y

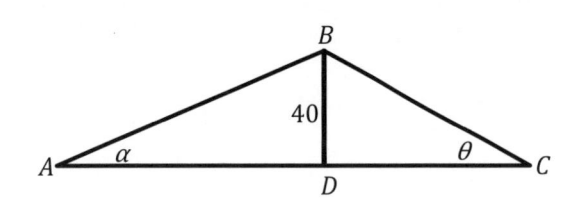

21. In the figure above, $\sin \alpha = \frac{5}{13}$ and $\sin \theta = \frac{8}{17}$. What is AC?

    A) 160
    B) 171
    C) 189
    D) 200

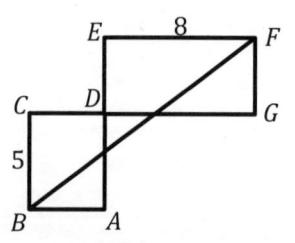

22. In the figure above, rectangles $ABCD$ and $DEFG$ share a vertex and $\overline{CD} \cong \overline{DE}$. If $BF = 15$, what is CD?

    A) 3
    B) 4
    C) 5
    D) 6

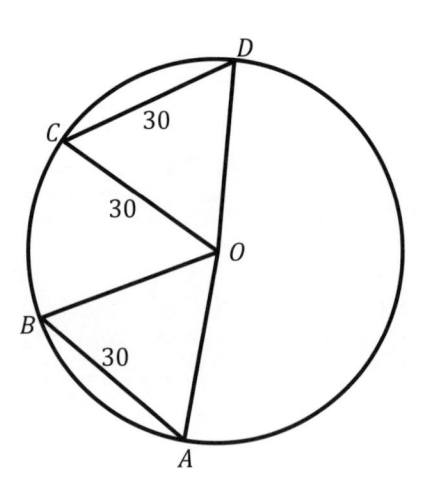

23. In the figure above, what is the sum of the lengths of minor arc $\widehat{BC}$ and major arc $\widehat{DA}$ in Circle O?

    A) 20π
    B) 30π
    C) 40π
    D) 60π

Use the following image for questions 24 and 25.

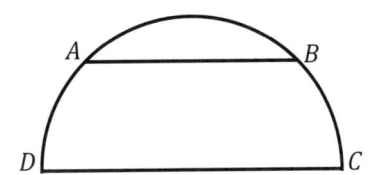

25. The area of the portion of the semicircle bounded by the chord and the diameter can be written as $a\pi + b\sqrt{3}$. What is the sum of $a + b$?

24. Chord $\overline{AB}$ above is parallel to the diameter $\overline{CD}$ of the semicircle above. If the length of $\overline{AB}$ is $\frac{1}{2}$ the length of $\overline{CD}$, and the radius of the circle has a length of 6, what is the distance between the chord and the diameter? Round to the nearest tenth of a unit.

RED MATH LESSON 7A: ADVANCED GEOMETRY
Race to the Finish

Directions: Answer each question below.

HOMEWORK SET (CALCULATOR)

Use the following information for questions 1 and 2.

1. The shaded areas represent the leftover metal that is wasted in the process of cutting a stop sign out of a sheet of metal. Let the length of each side of the octagon be x inches. What is the total amount of wasted metal in square inches, in terms of x?

   A) $\frac{(1-x)^2}{4}$
   B) $(1-x)^2$
   C) $\frac{x^2\sqrt{2}}{2}$
   D) x^2

2. If the side length of the entire square sheet of metal is 30 inches, what is the shaded area in square inches?
   A) 100
   B) 200
   C) $900 - 200\sqrt{3}$
   D) $2700 - 1800\sqrt{2}$

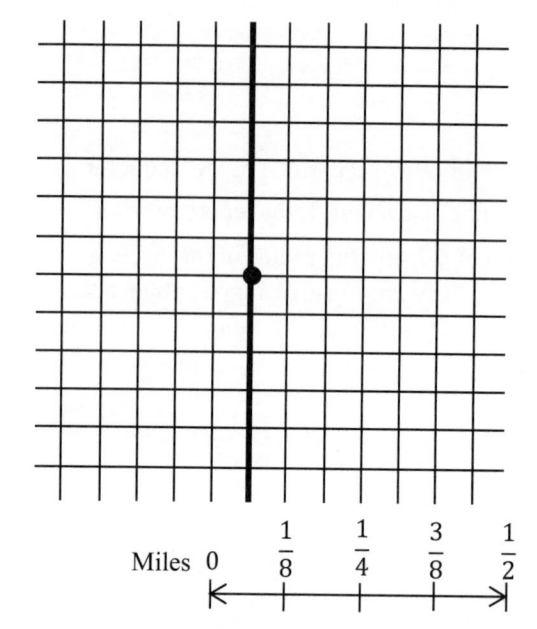

3. A city is divided into blocks by a grid of parallel north-south and east-west streets, evenly spaced $\frac{1}{16}$ of a mile apart. The bold line on the map above represents a major road, and the black dot is a subway station. If residents can only walk along the streets (no cutting through blocks on the diagonal), what is the area in square miles of the smallest quadrilateral that contains all intersections within a quarter-mile walk of the subway station?

   A) $\frac{1}{16}$ mi²
   B) $\frac{1}{8}$ mi²
   C) $\frac{1}{4}$ mi²
   D) $\frac{\sqrt{2}}{2}$ mi²

SAT Red Math | 187
Lesson 7A: Advanced Geometry

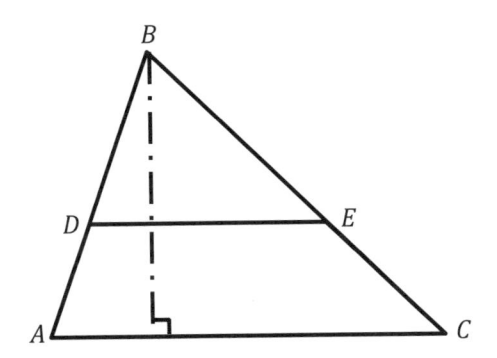

4. In $\triangle ABC$ above, $\overline{AC} = 68\sqrt{2}$, $\overline{BE} = 60$, $\overline{EC} = 36$, $m\angle ACB = 45°$, and $\overline{DE}$ is parallel to $\overline{AC}$. What is the length of segment $\overline{AD}$?
   A) $15\sqrt{2}$
   B) $\frac{39\sqrt{2}}{2}$
   C) 36
   D) $\frac{52\sqrt{2}}{2}$

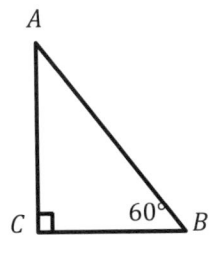

5. In $\triangle ABC$ above, if a segment is drawn from vertex C to the midpoint M of hypotenuse $\overline{AB}$ (not shown), what is the measure of $\angle AMC$?
   A) $30°$
   B) $60°$
   C) $120°$
   D) $150°$

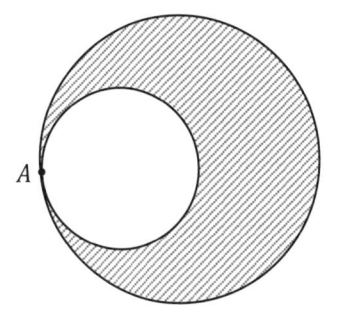

6. Two circles are internally tangent at point A as shown above, such that the shaded crescent-shaped region has exactly 8 times the area of the smaller circle. If the radius of the smaller circle is r, what is the radius of the larger circle, in terms of r?
   A) $\sqrt{3}r$
   B) $2\sqrt{2}r$
   C) $3r$
   D) $9r$

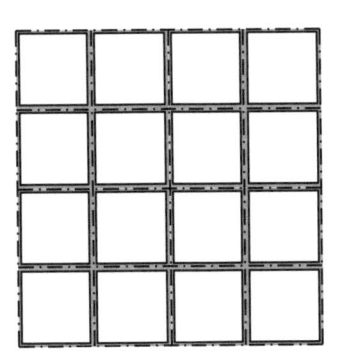

7. A tile floor is laid out in a repeated square pattern, shown by the dashed lines in the figure above. The identical dashed squares have side length 33 cm. The tiles themselves (white squares) have side length 30 cm and are centered within the dashed squares. What fraction of the total area depicted above is occupied by the white tiles?
   A) $\frac{1}{11}$
   B) $\frac{100}{121}$
   C) $\frac{10}{11}$
   D) $\frac{120}{121}$

188 | SAT Red Math
Lesson 7A: Advanced Geometry

HW

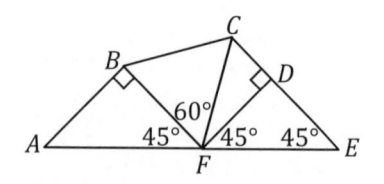

8. In the figure shown above, with angle measures indicated, $BC \cong CF$. If $\overline{AF} = 2$, what is the length of $\overline{AE}$?
   A) $\sqrt{2} + \sqrt{6}$
   B) $2 + \sqrt{2}$
   C) $2 + \sqrt{3}$
   D) 4

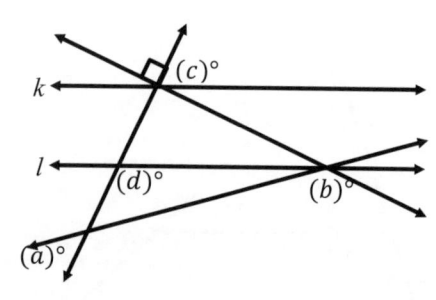

10. In the figure above, lines k and l are parallel. Which of the following must equal 90?
    A) $a + c$
    B) $b - a$
    C) $b - c$
    D) $d - a$

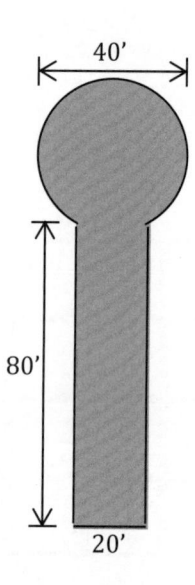

11. In the figure above, sectors QOP and SOR have equal areas. What is $m\angle ROS$ in degrees?
    A) $30°$
    B) $40°$
    C) $45°$
    D) $50°$

9. A cul-de-sac is a dead-end street with a circular area at the end allowing cars to easily turn around. The cul-de-sac depicted above, with the given measurements in feet, is being repaved. If asphalt costs $3.20 per square foot, what will be the total cost of the asphalt needed to pave this street, to the nearest dollar?
   A) $2,820
   B) $9,025
   C) $9,141
   D) $9,695

12. Another sector has a radius of 12 and the same area as sectors QOP and SOR in the previous question. What is the measure of the sector's angle in radians?
    A) $\frac{\pi}{8}$
    B) $\frac{\pi}{6}$
    C) $\frac{\pi}{4}$
    D) $\frac{\pi}{2}$

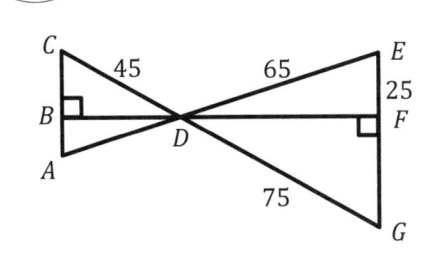

SAT Red Math | 189
Lesson 7A: Advanced Geometry

13. In the figure above, what is AC?
    A) 27
    B) 39
    C) 42
    D) 45

14. In the figure from the previous question, what is the tangent of $\angle CDB$?
    A) $\frac{7}{12}$
    B) $\frac{3}{5}$
    C) $\frac{3}{4}$
    D) $\frac{4}{3}$

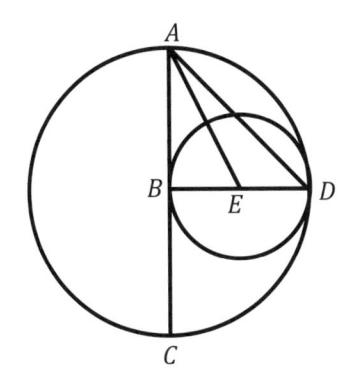

15. In the figure above, $\overline{BD}$ is a radius of Circle B and a diameter of Circle E. What is $m\angle EAD$?
    A) 18.43°
    B) 22.5°
    C) 30°
    D) 45°

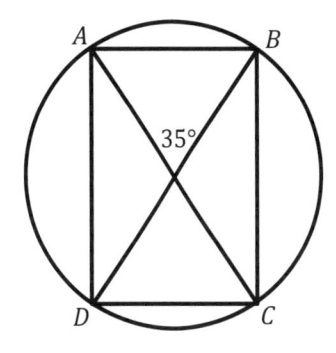

16. In the figure above, minor arc $\widehat{BC}$ is 58π units long. What is the length of diameter $\overline{BD}$?
    A) 94
    B) 116
    C) 144
    D) 172

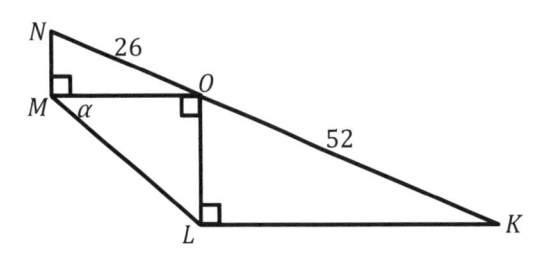

17. In the figure above, $\tan \alpha = \frac{5}{6}$. What is KL?

18. In the figure for the previous question, what is the sine of $\angle NOM$?

19. A cube with side length 1 is inscribed in a sphere. What is the volume the sphere? Round to the nearest tenth.

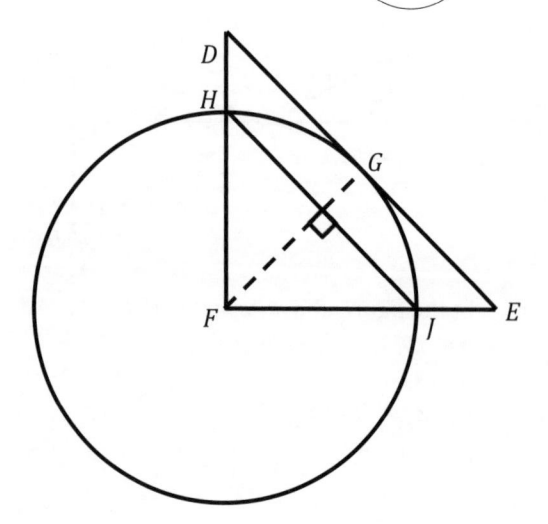

20. Line segment $\overline{DE}$ is tangent to ray $\overline{FG}$ of Circle F above at point G. Chord $\overline{HJ}$ is parallel to line segment $\overline{DE}$. What is the ratio of the area of $\triangle HFJ$ to the area of $\triangle DFE$?

RED MATH LESSON 7B: ADVANCED
VOLUME
Getting Your Feet Wet

Directions: The problems below are intended as a short diagnostic exam.

1. The cup in the image above is a piece of a cone, and both of its circular bases make right angles with its height. If the height of the cup is 5 inches, the diameter of the top of the cup is 8 inches, and the diameter of the bottom of the cup is 4 inches, what is the volume of the cup?
    A) $\frac{80\pi}{3}$
    B) $\frac{140\pi}{3}$
    C) $\frac{240\pi}{3}$
    D) $\frac{560\pi}{3}$

SAT Red Math
Lesson 7B: Advanced Geometry

RED MATH LESSON 7B: ADVANCED VOLUME
Wading In

Directions: Read the explanation for each problem type mentioned below. Pay special attention to the methods and techniques used to solve the sample problems. Then, do the practice exercises that follow; use the appropriate method to solve each problem.

TOPIC OVERVIEW: ADVANCED VOLUME

As we learned in the last lesson, the SAT makers can increase the difficulty of geometry problems by involving multiple figures or non-geometric concepts. This holds true for volume problems, too. Let's look at a sample problem dealing with tougher concepts in three-dimensional figures:

SAMPLE PROBLEM 1: ADVANCED VOLUME

The cup in the image above is a piece of a cone, and both of its circular bases make right angles with its height. If the height of the cup is 5 inches, the diameter of the top of the cup is 8 inches, and the diameter of the bottom of the cup is 4 inches, what is the volume of the cup, in cubic inches?

A) $\frac{80\pi}{3}$
B) $\frac{140\pi}{3}$
C) $\frac{240\pi}{3}$
D) $\frac{560\pi}{3}$

Since we know that the cup above is a piece of a cone, let's draw the entire cone first, then fill in the information that we know:

SAT Red Math — Lesson 7B: Advanced Geometry

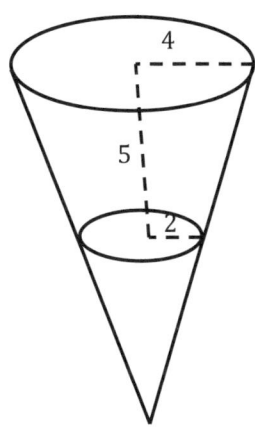

Now that we've taken care of that, let's analyze our image. We don't have a good way to find the volume of the piece of the cone given; however, we know that the larger cone must be proportional to the smaller cone. So, let's find the volume of the larger cone, then subtract from that the volume of the smaller one. First, though, we must find the height of the smaller cone. So let's set up a ratio:

$$\frac{4}{5+x} = \frac{2}{x}$$

Solving this proportion, we see that the height of the smaller cone must be 5. Now we can find the volume of the cup portion relatively easily by subtracting the volume of the smaller cone from that of the larger one:

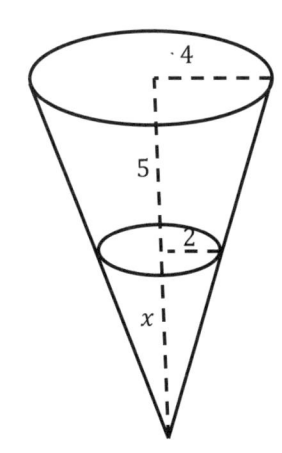

$$V_{cup} = \frac{\pi r_{large}^2 h_{large}}{3} - \frac{\pi r_{small}^2 h_{small}}{3}$$

$$V_{cup} = \frac{\pi (4^2)(10)}{3} - \frac{\pi (2^2)(5)}{3}$$

$$V_{cup} = \frac{160\pi}{3} - \frac{20\pi}{3} = \frac{140\pi}{3}$$

Thus, our answer must be **B**.

WRAP-UP

As with the last section, it's imperative that we draw a picture and fill in all of our information before tackling any volume problems. Good Luck!

SAT Red Math
Lesson 7B: Advanced Geometry

RED MATH LESSON 7B: ADVANCED VOLUME
Learning to Swim

Directions: Answer each question below.

PRACTICE SET 1 (NO CALCULATOR)

1. When a cylindrical bucket with diameter d is half-filled with water and placed on a scale, the scale reads a mass of m kilograms. When an irregular solid object is dropped into the bucket, it sinks to the bottom and is completely submerged. The scale now gives a reading of M kilograms and the level of water in the bucket appears to be h millimeters higher. In terms of d, h, m, and M, what is the density of the object?

2. Two cubes, Cube A and Cube B, have side lengths in the ratio $r:s$.
   a. What is the ratio of their volumes, in terms of r and s?
   b. What is the ratio of their surface areas?

3. A cylinder's height is twice the diameter of its base. Its volume is V. Write an equation for the cylinder's radius r in terms of V.

4. A cube's surface area in square centimeters is equal to its volume in cubic centimeters. What is its side length in centimeters?

5. The lampshade depicted above consists of the bottom portion of a cone. The larger (bottom) base is a circle of radius 6". The top is a circle of radius 3". The height is 8". What is the volume of this lampshade in cubic inches?

RED MATH LESSON 7B: ADVANCED VOLUME
Diving into the Deep End

Directions: Answer each question below.

PRACTICE SET 2 (CALCULATOR)

6. What is the volume of the largest cylinder that can fit inside a rectangular box with interior dimensions of 6 inches by 12 inches by 12 inches?
   A) 216π in^3
   B) 288π in^3
   C) 432π in^3
   D) 864π in^3

7. Today, the Great Pyramid of Giza stands 139 meters tall with a square base of side length 230 meters. However, it is estimated to have originally stood 147 meters high with a side length of 235 meters. Approximately how much greater was the pyramid's original volume, compared to its current volume?
   A) 210,000 m^3
   B) 250,000 m^3
   C) 630,000 m^3
   D) 760,000 m^3

8. A rectangular aquarium is 18 inches long, 10 inches wide, and 10 inches high. It contains 300 spherical decorative stones, each with a radius of 0.5 inches. What volume of water must be added to fill the aquarium?
   A) $1800 - 150\pi$ in^3
   B) $600 - 100\pi$ in^3
   C) $1800 - 50\pi$ in^3
   D) $600 - 12.5\pi$ in^3

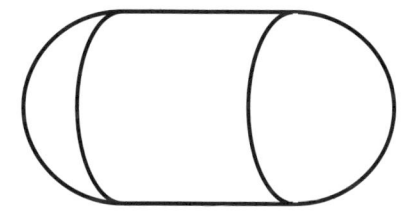

9. The figure above shows an enlarged view of a pill. The pill has a cylindrical body with radius 6 mm and width 12 mm. Each end is closed with a hemisphere. What is the volume of the pill?
   A) 504π mm^3
   B) 648π mm^3
   C) 720π mm^3
   D) 1152π mm^3

10. Michelle is shopping for tents; she wants to choose the tent with the largest volume from among 4 comparatively priced tents. Which tent should she choose?
    A) An 8-foot-long prism with a triangular cross section of height 6 feet and base 5 feet
    B) A 6-foot-long prism with a rectangular cross section of height 5 feet and width 5 feet
    C) A hemisphere with radius 4 feet
    D) A pyramid with a square base of side length 8 feet and a height of 6 feet

SAT Red Math
Lesson 7B: Advanced Geometry

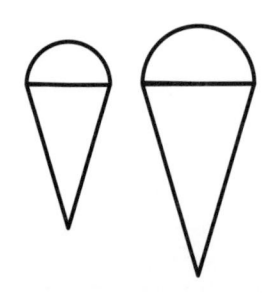

11. An ice cream shop offers two sizes of waffle cone. The small cone has a radius of 4.5 cm and a height of 15 cm. The large cone has a radius of 6 cm and a height of 20 cm. Each cone comes filled with ice cream, plus an additional amount that forms a hemisphere on top of the cone, as shown above. What is the ratio of the volume of ice cream that comes with a large cone to the volume that comes with a small cone?
   A) 64:45
   B) 5:3
   C) 16:9
   D) 64:27

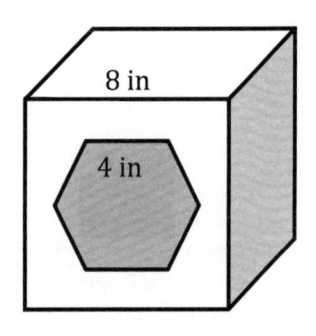

12. The figure above shows an 8-inch wood cube with a hole drilled through it. The hole is a regular hexagon with side length 4 inches. What is the volume of the remaining wood?
   A) $64 - 24\sqrt{3}$ in^3
   B) 128 in^3
   C) $512 - 192\sqrt{3}$ in^3
   D) $512 - 24\sqrt{3}$ in^3

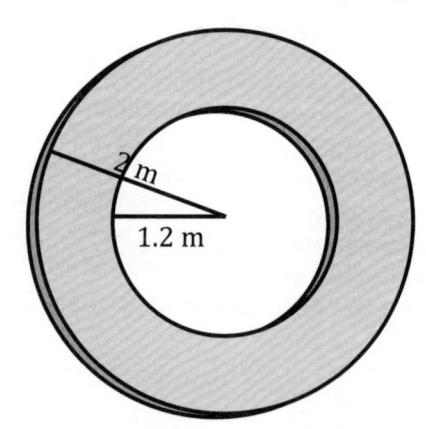

Questions 13 and 14 use the following diagram:

13. A slab of marble 5 centimeters thick is cut into a 2-meter-radius circle for use as a countertop. Then, a 1.2-meter-radius circle is cut out of the middle of the countertop, leaving a ring shape as shown above. What is the volume of the remaining marble in the countertop?
   A) $12,800\pi$ cm^3
   B) $72,000\pi$ cm^3
   C) $128,000\pi$ cm^3
   D) $200,000\pi$ cm^3

14. The circular hole in the countertop is filled with the same volume of wood. The wood has a density of 0.56 grams per cubic centimeter, and the marble has a density of 2.56 grams per cubic centimeter. What is the mass of the countertop, to the nearest kilogram?

15. A water cooler comes with conical cups with a radius of 5 cm and a height of 12 cm. How many cups full of water will it take to fill a cylindrical pitcher with a height of 24 cm and a radius of 10 cm?

Practice Set 3 (Calculator)

16. A pencil is 6 inches long. The tip is a cone of height 0.5 inches, while the remainder of the pencil is a cylinder. If the pencil's volume is $\frac{17\pi}{192}$ cubic inches, what is its diameter?
    A) 0.125 in
    B) 0.25 in
    C) 0.32 in
    D) 0.375 in

17. A rectangular swimming pool is to have a slanted floor, so that it is 10 feet deep at its west end and 3 feet deep at its east end. The pool covers 600 ft² of ground. What volume of water, in cubic feet, can it hold?
    A) 3900
    B) 4200
    C) 4800
    D) 7800

18. Boyle's Law states that if a fixed amount of a gas is held at a constant temperature, the product of its pressure and volume will always be equal; that is, $PV = k$ for some constant k. Thus, decreasing the volume of the gas's container will increase its pressure, and vice versa. If scientists wish to quadruple the pressure of a gas in a cylindrical container, they could transfer it to another cylindrical container with:
    A) the same height and twice the radius.
    B) half the height and half the radius.
    C) the same height and one-fourth the radius.
    D) the same height and half the radius.

19. A sphere in three-dimensional coordinate space is centered at the origin, the point with coordinates $(x, y, z) = (0, 0, 0)$, and it has diameter 10. Which of the following is closest to the volume of the portion of this sphere's interior for which $x \geq 0$, $y \geq 0$, and $z \geq 0$?
    A) 65
    B) 98
    C) 131
    D) It cannot be determined from the given information.

20. A soft-drink company is considering different can designs for a new product, which the company has decided to sell in 500 mL cans (1 mL = 1 cm³). The cost of the aluminum to manufacture a soda can is directly proportional to the can's surface area. If the company wishes to minimize this cost, which of the following can designs should it use?
    A) A cylinder with volume 500 mL and radius 5 cm
    B) A cylinder with volume 500 mL and radius 3 cm
    C) A cube with volume 500 mL
    D) A rectangular prism with volume 500 mL and a square base with side length 5 cm

21. The density of liquid water is 1.0 g/cm³. To measure the density of ice, Betsy drops an ice cube of dimensions 2 cm × 2 cm × 2 cm into a rectangular container 4 cm wide × 5 cm long, and waits for the ice to melt. When it has melted, the water level has risen by exactly 0.364 cm. What was the density of the ice cube?
    A) 0.636 g/cm³
    B) 0.728 g/cm³
    C) 0.910 g/cm³
    D) 7.280 g/cm³

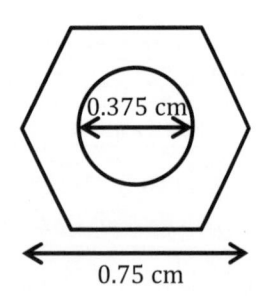

22. A metallic nut in the shape of a regular hexagon has a diameter of 0.75 cm as shown above (top-down view). In its center is a circular hole of diameter 0.375 cm. If the nut is 0.375 cm thick, and assuming it has no rounded edges, which of the following is closest to the volume of metal that it contains, in cubic centimeters?
A) 0.096
B) 0.117
C) 0.151
D) 0.233

23. A sphere with volume $36(\pi)^{-\frac{1}{2}}$ has the same surface area as a cube with what side length?
A) $\sqrt{6}$
B) $\sqrt{\frac{6}{\pi}}$
C) $\frac{3\sqrt{\pi}}{\pi}$
D) $\frac{6\sqrt{\pi}}{\pi}$

24. The cost of copper is $6.61 per kg. The density of copper is 8.933 g/cm³. A penny has diameter 19.05 mm and thickness 1.52 mm. If a penny were made of pure copper (note: this is no longer the case), what would be the value of the copper, to the nearest hundredth of a cent? Assume that the penny is a perfect right cylinder.

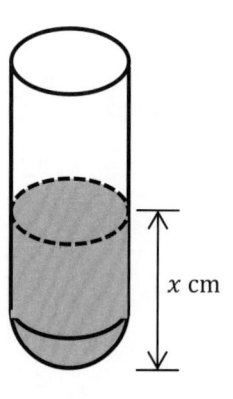

25. Mercury, a heavy metal that takes the form of a very thick liquid, has a density of 13.534 g/cm³. A test tube of diameter 1.2 cm is a cylinder with a hemispherical base, as shown above. If 100 grams of mercury are poured into this test tube, what will be the level of the mercury's surface above the tube's base? Round to the nearest hundredth of a centimeter.

RED MATH LESSON 7B: ADVANCED VOLUME
Race to the Finish

Directions: Answer each question below.

HOMEWORK SET (CALCULATOR)

1. A delivery truck has a rectangular cargo area that is 7.5 feet wide, 9 feet long, and 6 feet high. It is hauling cubic boxes that measure 18 inches on a side. How many of these boxes can fit into the truck's cargo area?
   A) 22
   B) 45
   C) 60
   D) 120

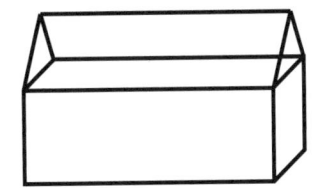

2. The figure above shows a house, which consists of a triangular prism on top of a rectangular prism. The total height of the house is 16 feet; the house is 32 feet long and 12 feet wide. The house's volume is 4800 cubic feet. What is the height of the triangular part of the house?
   A) 7 feet
   B) 8 feet
   C) 9 feet
   D) 10 feet

3. A spherical balloon is filled with water until it has a radius of 15 centimeters. The water is then poured out into a cylindrical can with a radius of 10 centimeters. What height does the water reach in the can?
   A) 10 cm
   B) 15 cm
   C) 30 cm
   D) 45 cm

4. The figure above shows a pyramid with a square base. The pyramid is 10 units high and has a volume of 120 units. If a prism has a base that is an equilateral triangle with the same side length as the base of the pyramid, and the prism is 8 units high, what is the volume of that prism?
   A) $36\sqrt{3}$ units
   B) $72\sqrt{3}$ units
   C) $108\sqrt{3}$ units
   D) $144\sqrt{3}$ units

5. A mailbox is shaped like a rectangular prism with a half-cylinder attached to its top. The half-cylinder has a radius of 5 inches; the prism is 8 inches high and as wide as the half-cylinder. The combined shape is 18 inches long. What is the mailbox's volume?
   A) $720 + 225\pi$ in^3
   B) $720 + 450\pi$ in^3
   C) $1440 + 225\pi$ in^3
   D) $1440 + 450\pi$ in^3

6. A cylindrical silo with radius 8 feet is filled to a height of 6 feet with grain. On top of this, there is a cone of grain that rises an additional 3 feet. What is the total volume of grain in the silo?
   A) 324π ft^3
   B) 396π ft^3
   C) 448π ft^3
   D) 496π ft^3

202 SAT Red Math
Lesson 7B: Advanced Geometry

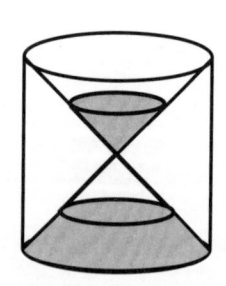

HW

7. The figure above shows an hourglass, which consists of two cones with radius 27 cm and height 27 cm, one inverted over the other. The bottom cone is filled with sand to a height of 12 cm and the top cone is filled to a height of 12 cm. The sand is flat in both cones. What is the total volume of sand in the hourglass?
   A) 4608π cm³
   B) 5527π cm³
   C) 6012π cm³
   D) 6561π cm³

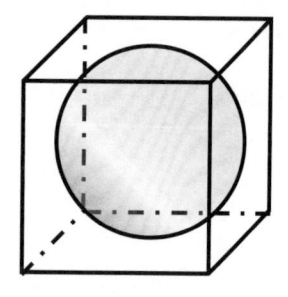

8. A sphere is inscribed in a cube so that it touches all six faces. What percent of the volume of the cube is NOT within the sphere, to the nearest whole percent?
   A) 21%
   B) 38%
   C) 48%
   D) 52%

9. A cone with a circular base of radius 5 and height 12 has the same volume as a cylinder with:
   A) radius 5 and height 4.
   B) radius 15 and height 12.
   C) radius 5 and height 36.
   D) radius 10 and height 2.

10. A spherical ping-pong ball is made of plastic with a uniform thickness of n millimeters. The inside of the ball is hollow. If the ball is to have a diameter of 3 cm (measured from outside), what volume of plastic in cubic centimeters is required to make it, in terms of n?
    A) $\frac{9}{2}\pi - \frac{4}{3}\pi\left(\frac{3}{2} - \frac{n}{10}\right)^3$
    B) $36\pi - \frac{4}{3}\pi\left(3 - \frac{n}{10}\right)^3$
    C) $\frac{9}{2}\pi - \frac{4}{3}\pi\left(\frac{3}{2} - \frac{n}{5}\right)^3$
    D) $36\pi - \frac{4}{3}\pi\left(\frac{3}{2} - n\right)^3$

11. The radius of the planet Jupiter is 11 times that of Earth. Jupiter's average density is 24% of Earth's average density. Jupiter's mass is approximately how many times Earth's mass?
    A) 46
    B) 319
    C) 504
    D) It cannot be determined from the given information

12. Gold has a market price of $40 per gram and a density of 19.30 g/cm³. A gold bar is dropped into a cylindrical bucket of water with diameter 30 cm, and fully submerged. This causes the water level to rise from 10.2 cm to 10.5 cm, as measured on a vertical ruler painted on the inside of the bucket. What is the value of the gold bar, to the nearest dollar?
    A) $2,700
    B) $8,482
    C) $52,110
    D) $163,708

Version 3.0

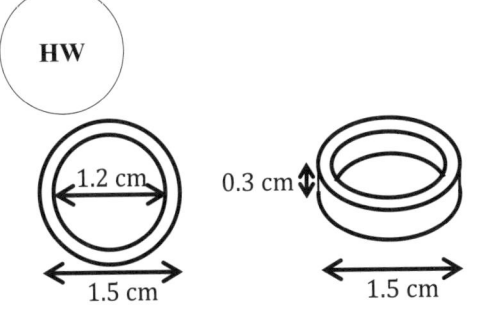

SAT Red Math
Lesson 7B: Advanced Geometry

13. A 100% pure platinum ring is a cylinder of height 0.3 cm with a hole in the middle. It has an inner diameter of 1.2 cm and an outer diameter of 1.5 cm. Its mass is 4.08 grams. What is the density of platinum, to the nearest tenth of a gram per cm³?
    A) 0.8
    B) 5.3
    C) 21.4
    D) 46.8

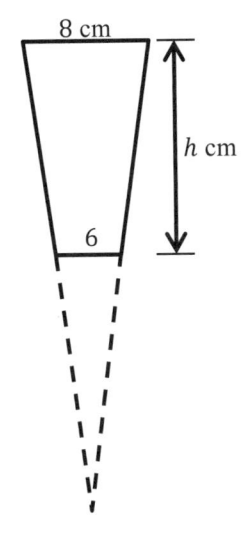

14. A drinking glass has a circular base of diameter 6 cm, a circular rim of diameter 8 cm, and a volume of 500 cm³. Its shape can be described as the result of removing a smaller cone of diameter 6 cm from a larger cone of diameter 8 cm, as shown above. Which of the following is closest to the glass's height h?
    A) 12.9 cm
    B) 22.5 cm
    C) 29.8 cm
    D) 51.6 cm

15. An orange wedge with central angle $\frac{\pi}{4}$ is cut from a spherical orange with a diameter of 4.5 inches. What is the volume of the wedge?
    A) $\frac{\pi}{3} 2.25^3$ in³
    B) $\frac{\pi}{8} 2.25^3$ in³
    C) $\frac{\pi}{6} 4.5^3$ in³
    D) $\frac{\pi}{6} 2.25^3$ in³

16. A pill is two hemispheres attached to the end of a cylinder and the radius of all three is 0.5 cm. If the pill can hold 2 cm³ of medicinal power, what is the pill's length?
    A) $\frac{8}{\pi} - \frac{2}{3}$
    B) $\frac{8}{\pi} - \frac{1}{2}$
    C) $\frac{8}{\pi}$
    D) $\frac{8}{\pi} + \frac{1}{3}$

17. What is the volume of the largest square pyramid that can fit into a cone with a volume of 48π cubic inches and a height of 9 inches? Round to the nearest cubic inch.

SAT Red Math
Lesson 7B: Advanced Geometry

HW

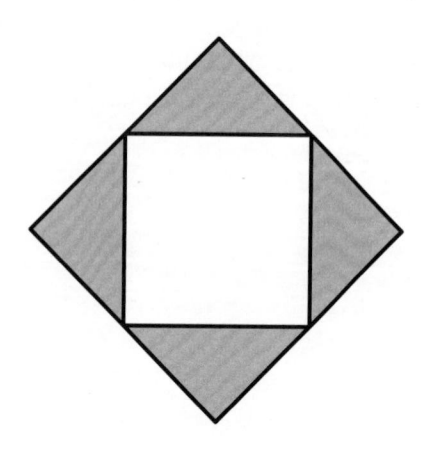

18. The figure above shows a top view of a two-layer cake. The bottom layer (in gray) has a 16-inch square base and is 3 inches high. The top layer touches the midpoints of each of the bottom layer's sides; it is 4 inches high. What is the total volume of the cake in cubic inches?

19. Using information from the previous question, the cake's layers have different densities. The bottom layer has a density of 6 g/in³ and the top layer has a density of 5 g/in³. What is the mass of the cake, to the nearest tenth of a kilogram?

20. The walls and bottom of a rectangular swimming pool are to be painted blue. The pool is 4 feet deep at the shallow end, 11 feet deep at the deep end, 24 feet long from the shallow end to the deep end, and its bottom is a uniformly sloping plane. If the total painted area is 1080 square feet, what is the width of the pool to the nearest foot?

Red Math Lesson 8A: Practice Sections
Learning to Swim

Directions: Answer each question below.

Practice Set 1 (No Calculator)

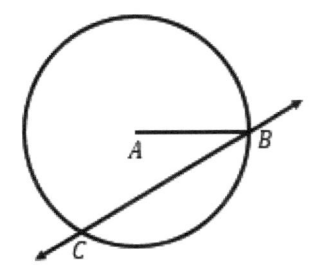

1. In the figure above, the length of radius $\overline{AB} = 10\sqrt{3}$, and $m\angle ABC = 30°$. What is the length of chord $\overline{BC}$?

2. What is the equation of a circle in the xy-coordinate plane that is centered at $(-2, 3)$ and that passes through $(4, -5)$?

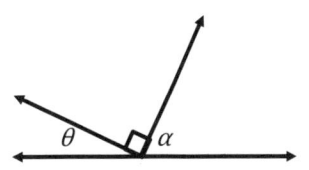

3. If $\sin \theta = 0.4$ in the figure above, what is $\cos \alpha$?

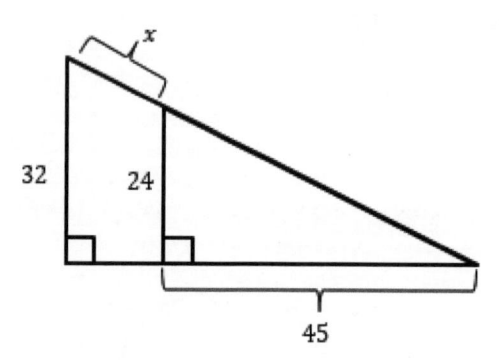

4. Using the figure above, what is the value of x?

5. A pyramid has a square base with side length 20 meters and a height of 15 meters. The top 6 meters of the pyramid are then removed. What is the volume of the remaining solid in cubic meters?

RED MATH LESSON 8A: PRACTICE SECTIONS
Diving into the Deep End

Directions: Answer each question below.

PRACTICE SET 2 (CALCULATOR)

6. A pod of blue whales migrates 6000 miles south each fall along the western coast of North America. The whales' speed is increased by that of the powerful California Current, which also flows from north to south. They make the journey in 30 days. The return trip northbound in the spring takes 75 days because the whales are swimming against the current, although the current itself is only half as fast as in the fall. What would be the whales' travel speed with no current, in miles per day?
   A) 80
   B) 120
   C) 125
   D) 200

7. Which of the following statements is true of the graph of $y = \frac{x^2+3x-4}{x^2+6x+8}$?
   A) It has a vertical asymptote at $= -2$.
   B) It has a vertical asymptote at $x = -4$.
   C) It passes through the point $(-1,0)$.
   D) All of the above

8. Data centers containing the servers used by many of the largest internet media companies require a large amount of electricity to operate. Cooling alone costs an average of $3.50 per square foot per year. At this rate, which of the following is closest to the cost of cooling a warehouse-sized data center measuring 300 × 250 yards for one week?
   A) $5,000
   B) $6,500
   C) $15,000
   D) $45,000

$$y = 3 - x^2$$
$$y = \frac{2}{9}x^2 - 9$$
$$x^2 + (y+3)^2 = 36$$

9. How many solutions exist to the system of equations above?
   A) 0
   B) 2
   C) 8
   D) It cannot be determined from the given information.

10. If θ is an angle in radians such that $0 \leq \theta < 2\pi$, and $\cos\theta + \sqrt{3}\sin\theta = 0$, which of the following could be the value of θ?
    A) $\frac{7\pi}{6}$
    B) $\frac{4\pi}{3}$
    C) $\frac{5\pi}{3}$
    D) $\frac{11\pi}{6}$

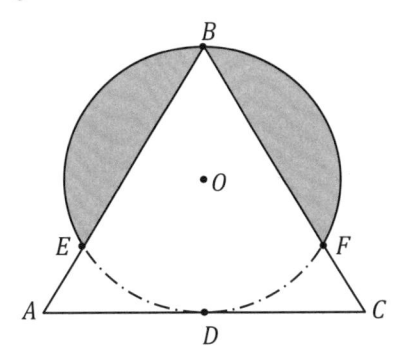

11. Circle O depicted above has radius 6, and equilateral triangle ABC intersects the circle at its vertex B and at the midpoint of its base, D. What is the area (shaded) that lies inside the circle but outside the triangle?
    A) $12\pi - 9\sqrt{3}$
    B) $24\pi - 18\sqrt{3}$
    C) $24\pi - 36\sqrt{3}$
    D) $24\pi - 48$

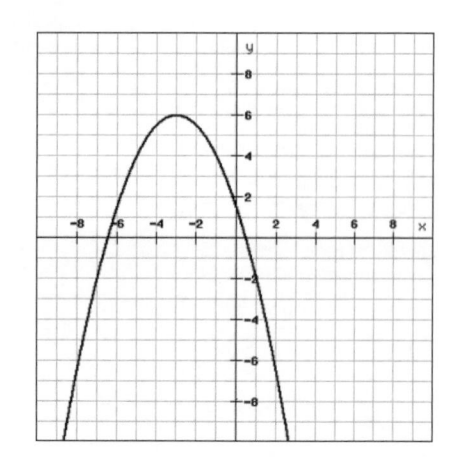

SAT Red Math
Lesson 8A: Practice Sections

PRACTICE SET 3 (NO CALCULATOR)

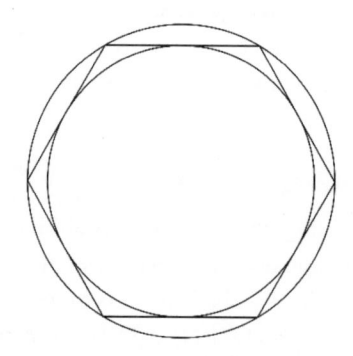

12. Which of the following represents the graph above?

    A) $y + 6 = -\frac{1}{2}(x + 3)^2$
    B) $y + 6 = -\frac{1}{2}(x - 3)^2$
    C) $y - 6 = -(x - 3)^2$
    D) $y - 6 = -\frac{1}{2}(x + 3)^2$

13. Eight years ago, Yolanda invested money in the stock market. The money she invested increased each year by 5% of its previous amount and is currently worth $6000. Which of the following expresses the original amount of money Yolanda invested in the stock market?

    A) $\frac{(6000)(1.05)}{8}$
    B) $(6000)(1 - (8)(0.05))$
    C) $\frac{6000}{1.05^8}$
    D) $(6000)(0.95^8)$

$$\sqrt{x - 1} = x - 7$$

14. What is the product of all solutions to the equation above?

15. The amount of a heart medication active in a patient's system decreases by 10% each hour after the dose is administered. To be effective, at least 60% of the original dose must be present. Approximately how many hours after the original dose does the patient need to take the drug again?

16. In the figure above, a circle is inscribed in a regular hexagon, which is inscribed in a circle of radius 4. What is the area of the inner circle?

    A) 4π
    B) 8π
    C) 9π
    D) 12π

17. If $\sin x = -\cos y$, and $0 < x < \frac{\pi}{4}$, which of the following ranges could contain y?

    A) $\frac{\pi}{4} < y < \frac{3\pi}{4}$
    B) $0 < y < \frac{\pi}{4}$
    C) $\pi < y < \frac{5\pi}{4}$
    D) $\frac{7\pi}{4} < y < 2\pi$

18. If $f(x) = 2x^2 + x - 5$ and $f(-x) = \frac{f(x)}{2}$, what is a possible value for x?

    A) $-\frac{5}{2}$
    B) -1
    C) 0
    D) 2

Soil	Heights
X	10 11 11 12 13 14 16 17 17 17 18 19
Y	7 9 10 11 12 12 16 18 19 22 23 24
Z	10 10 10 11 11 12 14 14 14 14 14 14

19. A plant biologist conducted an experiment in which she measured the heights of plants under different soil conditions. Above are the three sets of data. Which of the following statements about the data is true?
    A) The mean height of Soil Z is the highest.
    B) The mode height of Soil Z is equal to the median of Soil Y.
    C) The median heights of Soil X and Soil Z are equal.
    D) The histograms of all three sets of data would skew to the right.

20. Marvin can finish a task in x minutes. Henry takes twice as long as Marvin to finish the same task. Jerry takes three times as long as Marvin to finish the same task. When they work together, they finish the task in Y minutes. Which of the following equations can be used to model this scenario?
    A) $\frac{1}{x} + \frac{2}{x} + \frac{3}{x} = \frac{1}{Y}$
    B) $\frac{1}{x} + \frac{1}{2x} + \frac{1}{3x} = \frac{1}{Y}$
    C) $\frac{1}{x} + \frac{2}{x} + \frac{3}{x} = Y$
    D) $\frac{1}{x} + \frac{1}{2x} + \frac{1}{3x} = Y$

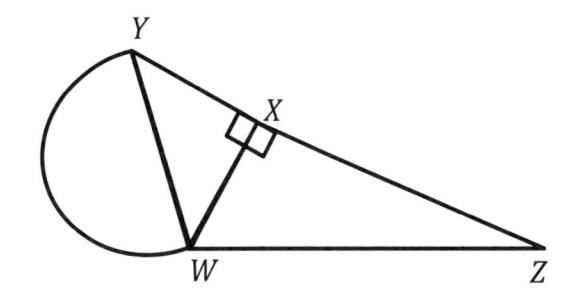

21. In the figure above, $\overline{XZ} = 10\sqrt{3}$, $\angle XZW = 30°$, and $\angle WYX = 45°$. What is the area of the semicircle?
    A) 10π
    B) $10\pi\sqrt{2}$
    C) 25π
    D) 50π

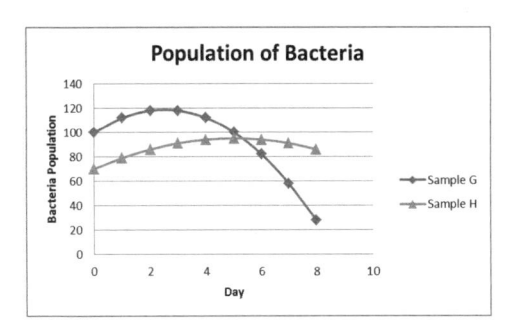

$$g(x) = -3x^2 + 15x + 100$$
$$h(x) = -x^2 + 10x + 70$$

22. A microbiologist conducts an experiment in which he measures the population size of two samples of bacteria. The populations of samples G and H are modeled by the functions $g(x)$ and $h(x)$ above. Which of the following statements is true?
    A) After day 3, both samples immediately decreased in population.
    B) Sample H increased and decreased at a faster rate than Sample G
    C) Both samples had a population of about 75 at the same time.
    D) The population of both samples combined was higher on day 3 than on day 5.

Package	Initial Cost	Price per Ticket
J	200	0
K	75	10
L	40	15

23. The cost of admission to an amusement park is $25. The amusement park also offers three packages that allow customers to pay a reduced ticket price after paying for the initial cost of the package. Which of the following is a true statement?
    A) Package L is the best choice for 8 visits.
    B) Package J is the best choice for 11 or more visits.
    C) For 7 visits, two packages have an equal value.
    D) If someone plans to visit fewer than 6 times, all of the packages would be more expensive than buying $25 per visit.

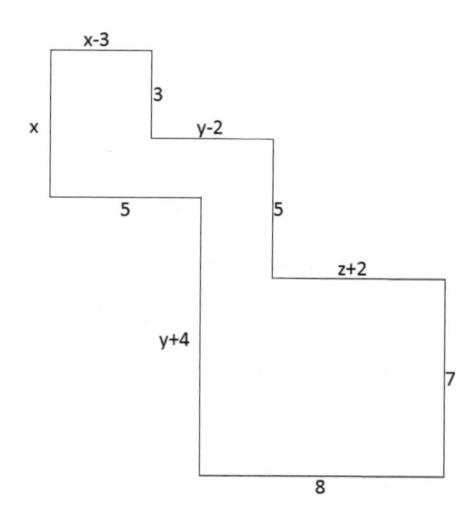

24. The equation $R = \frac{V}{I}$ can be used to model the relationship between electrical resistance (R), voltage (V), and current (I). The equation $P = I^2 R$ shows the relationship between power (P), current (I), and electrical resistance (R). If $P = 16$, and $V = 2$, what is the value of I?

25. In the figure above, all line segments are perpendicular to each other. What is the perimeter of the figure?

RED MATH LESSON 8A: PRACTICE SECTIONS
Race to the Finish

Directions: Answer each question below.

HOMEWORK SET (CALCULATOR)

1. Becky deposits $27,500 in a bank account that compounds continuously at an annual rate of 1.07%. How much money will be in the account in exactly 20 years?
    A) $27,994.82
    B) $33,385.05
    C) $34,062.12
    D) $35,859.25

2. Marcus is growing cherry tomatoes and wants to maximize the number of tomatoes he can pick each day. He knows that the best fertilizer for growing the greatest number of tomatoes is one that has a nitrogen(N)-phosphorous(P)-potasium(K) ratio of 5:7:6. Unfortunately, Marcus has two fertilizers: Brand A with an $N:P:K$ ratio of 1:1:1 and Brand B with an $N:P:K$ ratio of 1:5:3. If Marcus wants 12 cups of fertilizer in total for his tomatoes, what ratio of Brand A fertilizer to Brand B fertilizer would allow him to maximize the number of tomatoes he can pick each day?
    A) 9:1
    B) 3:1
    C) 2:5
    D) 5:2

3. NASA's *Cassini* spacecraft was sent to take readings of gravity variations on Saturn's moon Enceladus to check for an ocean of water. *Cassini* can transmit readings at a rate of 2.7 megabits per second. If each reading is 13 gigabits in size, and the storage drive can only upload readings for 10 hours a day, how many full readings can be uploaded by the end of the 2nd day? Assume that 1 gigabit = 1024 megabits.
    A) 6
    B) 7
    C) 8
    D) 14

4. At the local ice rink, the current Zamboni can smooth the ice in 6 minutes. The latest Zamboni model can smooth the ice in 2 minutes less time. The ice is smoothed two times every hour, and the rink is open for 8 hours each day of the week. Over an entire week, how much time is saved by using BOTH Zambonis instead of the original?
    A) 3.73 hrs
    B) 4.72 hrs
    C) 5.73 hrs
    D) 6.72 hrs

5. The Gross Domestic Product (GDP) per capita of a nation can be calculated by dividing the overall Gross Domestic Product by the population of that nation. Similarly, Percent Participation in the Labor Force can be calculated by dividing the number of workers (Labor Force) by the total population. If from one year to the next, the GDP of a nation increases by 4.1%, the number of workers (Labor Force) increases by 3.6%, and Percent Participation in the Labor Force increases by 7.1%, what are the percent changes in population and GDP per capita?
   A) Percent change in population of −3.3% with a +7.6% change in GDP per capita
   B) Percent change in population of +3.5% with a −7.6% change in GDP per capita
   C) Percent change in population of −3.3% with a +7.9% change in GDP per capita
   D) Percent change in population of +3.5% with a −7.9% change in GDP per capita

6. From 1990 to 2000, Hooverville's population increased by 5% each year. From 2000 to 2010, the population increased 10% each year. What is the total percent increase in Hooverville's population from 1990 to 2010?
   A) 150%
   B) 300%
   C) 322.5%
   D) 422.5%

7. How many distinct real roots does the function $f(x) = 12x^4 + 3x^2$ have?
   A) 1
   B) 2
   C) 3
   D) 4

$$\frac{-4}{y-3} + 1 = \frac{-10}{y^2+y-12}$$

8. Solve the above equation.
   A) $y = -3$ or $y = -6$
   B) $y = -3$ or $y = 6$
   C) $y = 3$ or $y = -6$
   D) $y = 3$ or $y = 6$

9. A circle is divided into 7 unequal sectors. The first two are equal in size, but each successive sector thereafter is twice as large as the previous one. If the sector that is double the area of each of the first two sectors has an area of 200, what is the diameter of the circle?
   A) $\frac{80}{\sqrt{\pi}}$
   B) $\frac{80}{\pi}$
   C) $\frac{160}{\sqrt{\pi}}$
   D) $\frac{160}{\pi}$

10. In the Cartesian coordinate system, the line segment made from connecting the points $(-6, -5)$ and $(0, 3)$ is the diagonal of a square. What is the coordinate of the square's vertex that is located in Quadrant IV?
    A) $(-1, 4)$
    B) $(1, -4)$
    C) $(-7, 2)$
    D) $(7, -2)$

11. Factory A can sell each unit of Product C for a profit of $5 and each unit of Product D for a profit of $6. Factory B can sell each unit of Product C for a profit of $4, but actually loses $8 for each unit of Product D it produces. Assuming Factory A must earn a profit of $5,400 to remain in production, Factory B can lose no more than $800 to do the same, and both factories must produce the same number of Product C and the same number of product D, what is the minimum amount of each product independently considered that could be produced at each factory, while keeping both open?
    A) 1080 units of Product C, 0 of Product D
    B) 0 units of Product C, 900 of Product D
    C) 600 units of Product C, 0 of Product D
    D) 600 units of Product C, 400 of Product D

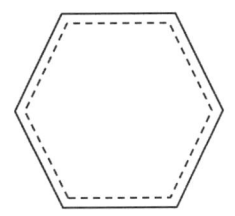

12. Alice is sewing a patch onto her son's letterman jacket. The patch is in the shape of a regular hexagon (as shown above) with sides equal to 4 cm. If the thread is 2 mm away from the edge of the patch, as represented by the dashed lines, then how much thread is needed to sew the patch? [Assume amount of thread needed is equal to the perimeter of the dashed hexagon.]
    A) $24 - 8\sqrt{3}$ cm
    B) 12 cm
    C) $24 - 0.8\sqrt{3}$ cm
    D) 22.8 cm

$$\frac{9k+3x}{6} = \frac{1}{2} + \frac{2x}{4}$$

13. If the equation above is true for all values of x, what is the value of k?
    A) $\frac{1}{4}$
    B) $\frac{1}{3}$
    C) $\frac{1}{2}$
    D) $\frac{2}{3}$

14. Jim is climbing a mountain. He starts at a base camp directly south of the peak and begins climbing directly north. Each meter he walks north leads to 0.5 meter increase in elevation. For every meter he heads north at a fixed elevation, the temperature decreases by 0.01 of a degree and for every meter his elevation increases at a fixed latitude, the temperature decreases by 0.12 of a degree. If it is 47.65 degrees at base camp, what is the temperature (t) at Jim's location as a function of the distance north (n) he has travelled?
    A) $t = 47.65 - 0.01n - 0.12(-0.5n)$
    B) $t = 47.65 - 0.01n + 0.12(-0.5n)$
    C) $t = 47.65 - 0.01n + 0.12(0.5n)$
    D) $t = 47.65 + 0.01n + 0.12(-0.5n)$

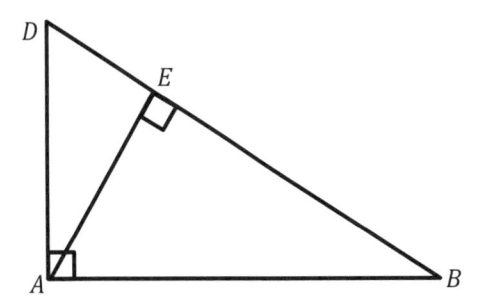

15. Which of the following is NOT an expression for $(DB)^2$?
    A) $(EB)^2 + 2(AE)^2 + (DE)^2$
    B) $(AD)^2 + (AB)^2$
    C) $\frac{(EA)^2}{(EB)^2}$
    D) $\frac{(AD)^4}{(DE)^2}$

16. James will receive $589,023 in 10 years. If the annual interest rate of 8.32% is compounded monthly, what is the present value of this lump sum payment?
    A) $256,329.90
    B) $257,066.87
    C) $331,956.13
    D) $1,353,522.00

$$\frac{x^4-2x^3-7x^2+8x+12}{x^3-x^2-6x}=0$$

17. How many solutions does the above equation have?

18. If $e^{i\theta} = \cos\theta + i\sin\theta$ for all θ expressed in radians, what is the value of $3e^{i\frac{\pi}{6}} \cdot 5e^{i\frac{11\pi}{6}}$?

19. If $4 - \frac{1}{4}x^2 > mx + b$ implies $-4 < x < 1$, what is the value of m?

20. If the expression $\frac{x^2+6x+9}{x+2}$ is rewritten in the equivalent form $x + 4 + \frac{J}{x+2}$, what is the value of J?

SAT Red Math
Lesson 8B: Advanced Statistics

RED MATH LESSON 8B: ADVANCED STATISTICS
Getting Your Feet Wet

Directions: The problems below are intended as a short diagnostic exam.

1. A random sample stratified by income is conducted in Seattle. Of the 1,000 people sampled, 500 have an income over $60,000/year and 500 have an income under $60,000/year. During the sample, 260 people with an income over $60,000/year said their favorite sports team is the Seattle Electric Eels, while 310 people with an income under $60,000/year said their favorite sports team is the Seattle Electric Eels. If Seattle has a population of 700,000 people and 40% of Seattle's population has an income over $60,000/year, how many people who live in Seattle would be expected to say the Seattle Electric Eels are their favorite sports team?
   A) 392,000
   B) 406,000
   C) 420,000
   D) 434,000

	DS 1	DS 2
Data	60, 61, 61, 61, 61, 62, 62, 62, 62, 62, 63, 63, 63, 63, 63, 64, 64, 64, 64, 64, 64, 65, 65, 66, 66, 66, 66, 66, 67, 67, 67, 67, 68, 68, 68, 68, 68, 68, 68, 69, 69, 69, 70, 70, 70, 70, 71, 71, 72, 73	58, 59, 59, 59, 59, 61, 61, 62, 64, 64, 65, 66, 66, 67, 68, 69, 69, 69, 69, 69, 69, 72, 72, 73, 73, 74, 74, 74, 74, 75
#	$n = 50$	$n = 30$
Standard Deviation	$\sigma = 3.33$	$\sigma = 5.46$
Mean	$\mu = 65.82$	$\mu = 67.1$

2. Using the data above, which of the following conclusions is most justified?
   A) DS 1 has less width and more measurement error than DS 2
   B) DS 2 has less width and more measurement error than DS 1
   C) DS 1 will have confidence intervals with greater range than DS 2
   D) DS 2 will have confidence intervals with greater range than DS 1

3. Which of the following is least likely to cause an increase in measurement error?
   A) An increase in standard deviation and an increase in the number of outliers
   B) An increase in standard deviation and a decrease in sample size
   C) An increase in sample size and an increase in standard deviation
   D) An increase in sample size and a decrease in standard deviation

RED MATH LESSON 8B: ADVANCED STATISTICS
Wading In

Directions: Read the explanation for each problem type mentioned below. Pay special attention to the methods and techniques used to solve the sample problems. Then, do the practice exercises that follow; use the appropriate method to solve each problem.

TOPIC OVERVIEW: ESTIMATION WITH POPULATION PARAMETERS

A population parameter question will always involve comparing the proportion of one set of data to another, usually a random sample within the total population. A simple example would be to say that of 1000 people randomly sampled who live in Los Angeles, 250 reported that their favorite flavor of ice cream is Mint Chocolate Chip. If there are 4 million people living in Los Angeles, approximately how many would be expected to report that their favorite ice cream flavor is Mint Chocolate Chip?

It's important to make sure that the sample is representative of the greater population. In this case, the sample is said to be random; random samples are assumed to be representative. The problem also may state outright that the sample is representative of the overall population. If it isn't established that the sample is representative, then no conclusions can be drawn about the greater population.

After determining that the sample is representative, the problem becomes a straightforward ratio question. $\frac{250}{1000}$ (4 million) = 1 million, so approximately 1 million people living in Los Angeles would be expected to report that their favorite flavor of ice cream is Mint Chocolate Chip.

Let's try a more complicated example:

SAMPLE PROBLEM 1: ESTIMATION WITH POPULATION PARAMETERS

A random sample stratified by income is conducted in Seattle. Of the 1,000 people sampled, 500 have an income over $60,000/year and 500 have an income under $60,000/year. During the sample, 260 people with an income over $60,000/year said their favorite sports team is the Seattle Electric Eels, while 310 people with an income under $60,000/year said their favorite sports team is the Seattle Electric Eels. If Seattle has a population of 700,000 people and 40% of Seattle's population has an income over $60,000/year, how many people who live in Seattle would be expected to say the Seattle Electric Eels are their favorite sports team?

A) 392,000
B) 406,000
C) 420,000
D) 434,000

$\frac{260}{500} = 52\%$ of people with income over \$60k/year support the SEE

$\frac{310}{500} = 62\%$ of people with income under \$60k/year support the SEE

$$700,000\big(0.4(0.52) + 0.6(0.62)\big) = 406,000$$

So our answer is **B**.

TOPIC OVERVIEW: STANDARD DEVIATION AND CONFIDENCE INTERVALS

The standard deviation of a data set is a measure of how spread apart the data is from the mean. Fortunately, the SAT will never make us calculate a standard deviation, but we do need to understand how standard deviations work. First, an increase in standard deviation will increase the width of graphed data, and if the standard deviation decreases, then so will the graph's width. This is why it's called a measure of spread; the greater the standard deviation, the more spread apart the data is. The second important thing to know is that a standard deviation exists in the same units as the data itself, so if you have data of people's heights in inches, then the standard deviation will also be measured in inches.

The last important thing deals with another topic: confidence intervals. Statistics can't make precise predictions, but confidence intervals allow statisticians to make reliable statements within a certain range. As an example, a statistician may say "based on the available data, we are 95% confident that a man selected at random will be between 5'4" and 6'2" tall." Confidence intervals always exist as a range instead of a single point, and they have a degree of confidence based on the strength of the data being analyzed. As the sample size gets bigger, the range of the confidence interval gets smaller. As with standard deviation, the SAT will never ask us to calculate a confidence interval, but questions may appear to test the general understanding of what a confidence interval is.

The last thing we need to know about standard deviations is that they're positively correlated with the range of confidence intervals; a larger standard deviation will result in a larger confidence interval range, and a smaller standard deviation will cause a smaller confidence interval range.

One last note: confidence intervals are not probabilities! A confidence interval allows us to make a reliable statement with confidence, but that does not mean any probabilities are involved. If, for example, a random person is selected, the probability of his height being between 5'4" and 6'2" is either 0 or 1, depending on how tall that person actually is. When we say we are 95% confident about that person's height, this is not stating anything about probability.

Let's try a problem to make sure we understand:

SAT Red Math
Lesson 8B: Advanced Statistics

> **SAMPLE PROBLEM 2: STANDARD DEVIATION AND CONFIDENCE INTERVALS**
>
> | | DS 1 | DS 2 |
> |-----------|------|------|
> | Data | 60, 61, 61, 61, 61, 62, 62, 62, 62, 62, 63, 63, 63, 63, 63, 64, 64, 64, 64, 64, 64, 65, 65, 66, 66, 66, 66, 66, 67, 67, 67, 67, 68, 68, 68, 68, 68, 68, 69, 69, 69, 70, 70, 70, 70, 71, 71, 72, 73 | 58, 59, 59, 59, 59, 61, 61, 62, 64, 64, 65, 66, 66, 67, 68, 69, 69, 69, 69, 69, 69, 72, 72, 73, 73, 74, 74, 74, 74, 75 |
> | # | $n = 50$ | $n = 30$ |
> | Std. Dev. | $\sigma = 3.33$ | $\sigma = 5.46$ |
> | Mean | $\mu = 65.82$ | $\mu = 67.1$ |
>
> Using the data above, which of the following conclusions is most justified?
> A) DS 1 has less width and more measurement error than DS 2
> B) DS 2 has less width and more measurement error than DS 1
> C) DS 1 will have confidence intervals with greater range than DS 2
> D) DS 2 will have confidence intervals with greater range than DS 1

Answer choices **A** and **B** compare width and measurement error. Standard deviation is positively correlated with width and positively correlated with statistical measurement error, so neither of these answer choices are particularly well supported.

Answer choices **C** and **D** compare sample size, standard deviation, and the range of confidence intervals. The range of confidence intervals are negatively correlated with sample size, and positively correlated with standard deviation. DS 1 has a smaller standard deviation and larger sample size than DS 2, both of which indicate the range of its confidence intervals will be smaller.

Our answer is **D**.

TOPIC OVERVIEW: MEASUREMENT ERROR

Measurement error has two different but related meanings. The first is statistical measurement error, which is the difference between a data point and the mean of the overall data set. The second is practical measurement error, which refers to errors made while collecting data, either from improper use of instruments or from observer bias. Like some earlier topics, the SAT will never ask us to calculate measurement error, but questions may be asked to test our general understanding of the topic.

The statistical measurement error of a data set can be increased either from having data more spread out or from having more outliers. Statistical measurement error will also tend to decrease as the sample size increases.

Questions about statistical measurement error will tend to be theoretical rather than practical, simply testing general knowledge of the topic.
On the other hand questions about practical measurement error will have to do with the methods of data collection. Outliers in data collection also increase practical measurement error. The other two main sources of practical measurement error are flawed data collection methods and observer bias. There are many ways a measurement can be flawed: imprecise instruments, reading functional instruments incorrectly, or even inputting data incorrectly. Observer bias happens when the party collecting data influences the conclusions that can be drawn from that data, such as a drug company paying more attention to positive drug trials than negative ones.

Both of these topics are closely related as both kinds of measurement error make the conclusions that can be drawn from data analysis less valid. Statisticians strive to minimize measurement error, and the process of minimizing measurement error is what the SAT is likely to test.

Let's try a problem to familiarize ourselves with the concept:

SAMPLE PROBLEM 3: MEASUREMENT ERROR

Which of the following is least likely to cause an increase in measurement error?

A) An increase in standard deviation and an increase in the number of outliers
B) An increase in standard deviation and a decrease in sample size
C) An increase in sample size and an increase in standard deviation
D) An increase in sample size and a decrease in standard deviation

---

This question is tricky—it asks which is least likely to lead to an increase in measurement error, not which could lead to an increase in measurement error.

Answer choice **A** posits an increase in standard deviation and an increase in the number of outliers, both of which are likely to increase measurement error. Answer choice **B** posits an increase in standard deviation and a decrease in sample size, both of which are likely to cause an increase in measurement error. Answer choice **C** posits an increase in sample size and an increase in standard deviation; the increase in sample size is likely to decrease measurement error, but an increase in standard deviation is likely to increase it. Answer choice **C** is more correct than **A** or **B**.

Answer choice **D** however posits an increase in sample size and a decrease in standard deviation, both of which are likely to decrease measurement error. Our answer is **D**.

SAT Red Math
Lesson 8B: Advanced Statistics

WRAP-UP

There are a wide variety of statistics questions that could be tested on the SAT, but most of them are likely to test basic knowledge such as the definitions and relationships of various concepts. Study the definitions, remember the relationships, and practice plenty of problems and the problems should become manageable. Good Luck!

RED MATH LESSON 8B: ADVANCED STATISTICS
Learning to Swim

Directions: Answer each question below.

PRACTICE SET 1 (CALCULATOR)

	Age ≥ 35	Age < 35
% Income ≥ $70,000/year	55	15
Mean Annual 401k Contribution	$6,200	$500

For questions 1 and 2 use the above table. A random sample was taken among the population of employed adults in Chicago.

1. The population of working adults in Chicago is 1.8 million, 55% of which are 35 or older. How many people can be expected to have an income greater than or equal to $70,000/year in Chicago?

2. The working population of the United States is 192 million. Assuming 40% of them are over 35 and the mean annual 401k contributions in Chicago are representative of the country as a whole, what is the expected mean annual 401k contribution of working adults in the United States?

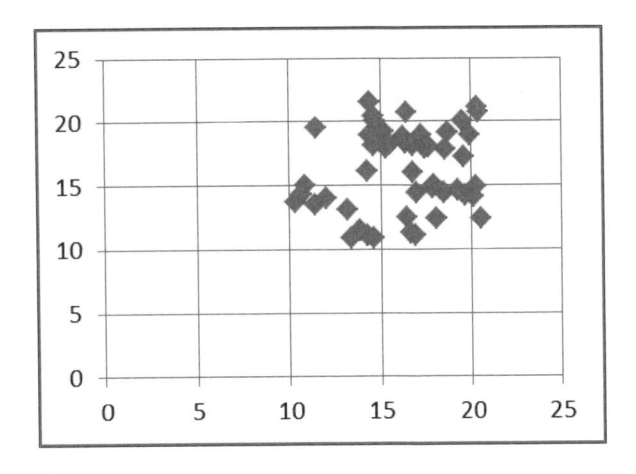

3. If the point (5, 25) was added to the above data set, what would happen to the data set's standard deviation, confidence interval range, and measurement error?

4. If outliers are added to a data set, what happens to the data sets confidence interval ranges? Why?

5. If a data set's measurement error decreases when ten new observations are added, what can be expected to happen to the data set's standard deviation?

RED MATH LESSON 8B: ADVANCED STATISTICS
Diving into the Deep End

Directions: Answer each question below.

PRACTICE SET 2 (CALCULATOR)

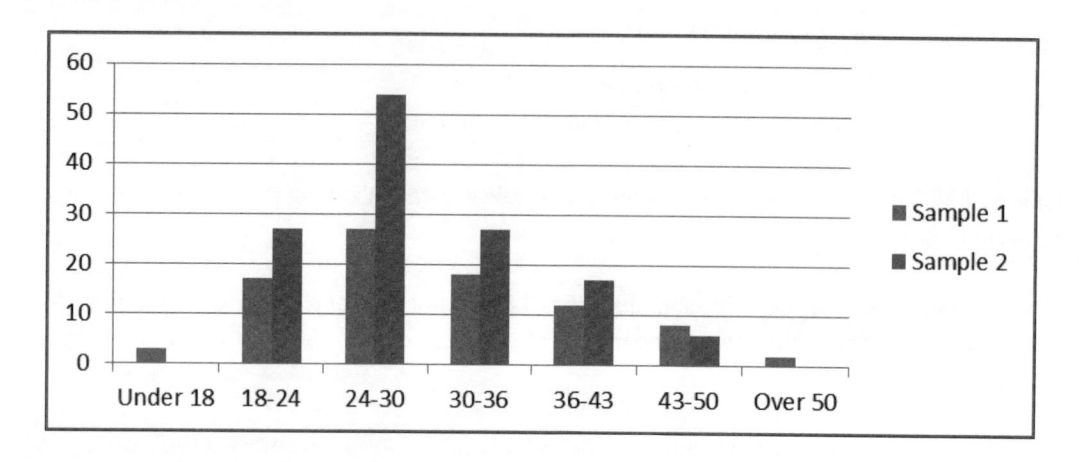

Use the above graph of two samples of people with varied ages for questions 6 through 9.

6. What conclusions can be drawn about the standard deviations of the two samples?
   A) Sample 1's standard deviation is bigger
   B) Sample 2's standard deviation is bigger
   C) Their standard deviations are equal
   D) Not enough information to determine

7. What conclusions can be drawn about the sample size of the two samples?
   A) Sample 1's sample size is bigger
   B) Sample 2's sample size is bigger
   C) Their sample sizes are equal
   D) Not enough information to determine

8. Which of the following is the most appropriate measure of center for a data set that includes both samples?
   A) Mean
   B) Median
   C) Mode
   D) Not enough information to determine

9. If the two data samples compile the ages of citizens in New York, what is the expected average age of a citizen of New York?
   A) 24-30
   B) 30-36
   C) 36-43
   D) Not enough information to determine

	Votes Received	Margin of Error
Candidate A	310	±3%
Candidate B	152	±5%
Candidate C	300	±2%

10. The above data shows the preliminary results of an election poll. Based on the information above, which candidate is likely to win?
    A) Candidate A
    B) Candidate B
    C) Candidate C
    D) It is impossible to determine

	Data set 1	Data set 2
Mean	85.4	90.4
Median	84	92
Range	59	61
Standard Deviation	$\sigma = 9.4$	$\sigma = 5.1$

Use the above information for problems 11 and 12

11. Assuming the sample size for both data sets is the same, which of the following conclusions is best supported?
    A) Data set 1 has a higher mode
    B) Data set 2 has a higher mode
    C) Data set 1 has higher measurement error
    D) Data set 2 has higher measurement error

12. If these two sets of data were collected analyzing the same variables, which of the following conclusions is NOT supported?
    A) Data set 1 is more likely to be flawed because it has a higher standard deviation
    B) More observations need to be recorded to clarify why the analysis is so different
    C) Data set 1 is less likely to make accurate predictions because it has a higher standard deviation
    D) Data set 1 is less likely to be flawed because it has a smaller range

13. A scientist is trying to ascertain the surface temperature of a lake over the course of four seasons. Which of the following is NOT likely to increase measurement error?
    A) Taking readings in different places around the lake and using a weighted average
    B) Taking readings at different times of day and using a weighted average
    C) Taking readings at different lakes and using a weighted average
    D) Allowing each reading to be taken by a different researcher and taking a weighted average.

14. Brown, black, and polar bears are the only three species of bear native to Alaska. In a random sample it was found that 24 brown bears ate 384 fish, 11 black bears ate 231 fish, and 6 polar bears ate 144 fish in a single day. If forest rangers estimate that there are 30,000 brown bears, 100,000 black bears and 5,000 polar bears in Alaska, how many fish (in millions) are expected to be eaten by bears in Alaska tomorrow? Round to the nearest hundredth of a million.

> 33, 44, 46, 50, 51, 51, 53, 56, 58,
> 58, 58, 59, 59, 59, 60, 60, 60, 62,
> 62, 62, 62, 63, 63, 64, 65, 65, 67,
> 67, 70, 72, 73, 74, 85, 89

15. The data above has a mean of 61.176, a standard deviation of 10.6583 and a sample size of 34. If five new observations are added with the values {90, 91, 92, 93, 94}, how much does the mean increase? Round to the nearest hundredth.

SAT Red Math
Lesson 8B: Advanced Statistics

PRACTICE SET 3 (CALCULATOR)

16. Which of the following situations would NOT be likely to contaminate conclusions with observer bias?
    A) A forest ranger analyzing data about how much forest rangers should be paid.
    B) A senator analyzing data about the effects of fracking for possible legislation, when this senator receives campaign contributions from companies who engage in fracking.
    C) An oceanographer analyzing data about the surface temperatures of oceans.
    D) A drug company analyzing the effectiveness of drug trials for the company's own drugs.

17. A melittologist is collecting data about how many flowers a certain species of worker bee visits in a day. He has currently collected ten observations: 70, 103, 110, 95, 123, 101, 0, 88, 118, and 131. His colleague has another data set with 15 observations; the mean of his colleague's data set is 112.7. If he removes the outlier from his data set, what is the mean of the two data sets combined?
    A) 103.30
    B) 105.18
    C) 108.52
    D) 109.56

18. Which of the following is NOT true?
    A) An increase in graph width will tend to increase confidence interval ranges.
    B) Standard deviations exist in the units of the data being studied.
    C) Confidence intervals allow statisticians to make probabilistic predictions.
    D) Confidence interval ranges tend to decrease when sample size increases.

19. Which of the following graphs contains a left skew and a mode of 7?
    A) 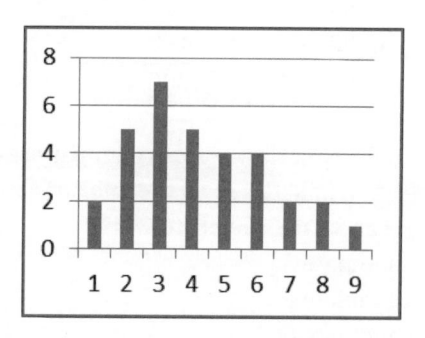
    B) 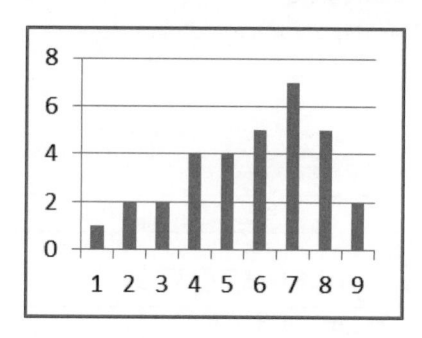
    C) 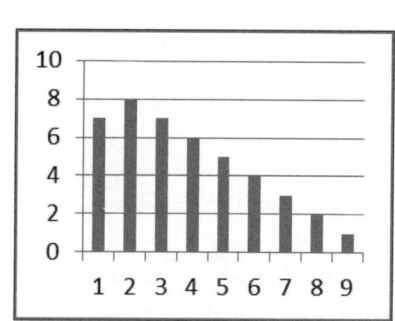
    D)

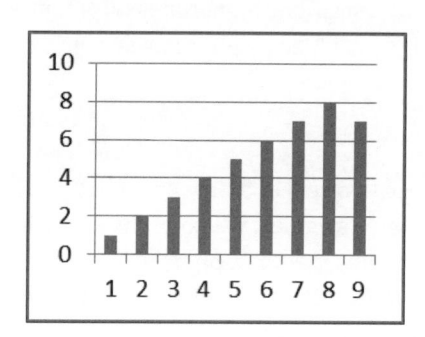

SAT Red Math
Lesson 8B: Advanced Statistics

20. Which of the following would be most appropriate sampling method if you wanted to know the most popular brand of frozen pizza in a particular city?
    A) Look at the sales figures of various brands of frozen pizzas from local supermarkets.
    B) Send out a flier asking which brand was most preferred to random addresses.
    C) Ask customers coming out of supermarkets what brand of frozen pizza they prefer.
    D) Figure out which company spends the most money on advertising.

	Widow's Peak	Detached Earlobes	Both	Total
Men ≥ 35	24	61	17	200
Men < 35	51	99	23	300
Women ≥ 35	82	28	29	225
Women < 35	103	38	36	275

Use the data above for questions 23 and 24. The table shows the results of a stratified random sample of the citizens of Arkansas.

23. If the population of Arkansas is 3 million, 61% of of its citizens are 35 years or older, and 50% of either age demographic is male, how many people can be expected to have detached earlobes in Arkansas?
    A) 976,000
    B) 980,000
    C) 984,000
    D) 988,000

	Sample A	Sample B
μ	102.1	103.4
σ	13.4	28.0
Sample Size	100	100

Questions 21 and 22 use the table above. Assume that both samples were measuring the same property of the same population.

21. Which of the following observations is most supported given samples A and B?
    A) Sample B has less measurement error
    B) Sample B has a higher median
    C) Sample B has smaller confidence interval ranges
    D) Sample B has larger confidence interval ranges

24. It is assumed that the data is representative of the population of Little Rock. What percentage of the population is either male with a widow's peak or detached earlobes (but not both) or a woman with both a widow's peak and detached earlobes? Round to the nearest whole percent.

22. Which of the following conclusions is most supported about samples A and B?
    A) An error was likely made gathering data, and more data is required to draw valid conclusions
    B) The data in sample A was collected incorrectly and should be thrown out
    C) The data in sample B was collected incorrectly and should be thrown out
    D) The data will allow valid conclusions if it's combined into one data set with sample size 200

25. A sociologist has collected data on 15,671 people and determined that the median height is 65 inches. Six people are added to the sample size with heights of 71, 59, 57, 49, 65 and 69 inches. What is the new median height in inches?

RED MATH LESSON 8B: ADVANCED STATISTICS
Race to the Finish

Directions: Answer each question below.

HOMEWORK SET (CALCULATOR)

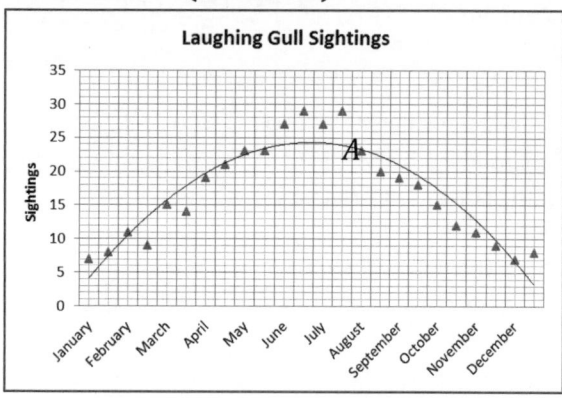

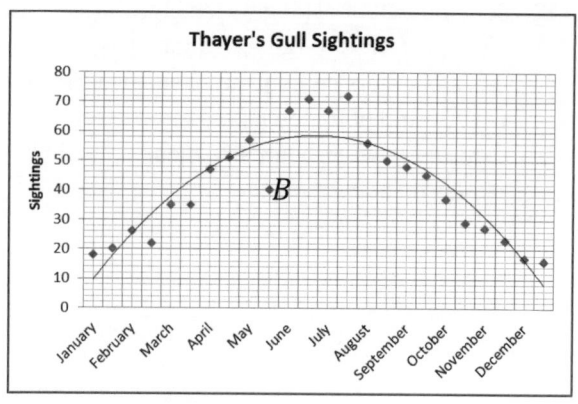

Questions 1 through 4 refer to the graphs above, which record information about Laughing Gull and Thayer's Gull sightings in the Kisatchie National Forest in Louisiana over the course of two years.

1. Which measure of center is most appropriate for these two graphs?
   A) Median for both
   B) Median for Laughing Gull, mean for Thayer's Gull
   C) Mean for Laughing Gull, median for Thayer's Gull
   D) Mean for both

2. Which of the following conclusions about the data is most supported?
   A) The data was collected on the same day in each month.
   B) The data sheds some light on when the gulls leave the Kisatchie National Forest
   C) Data analysis would allow a statistician to determine the total population of gulls in the Kisatchie National Forest
   D) The sample of Thayer's Gulls has a much higher measurement error than the sample of Laughing Gulls

3. Which of the following would NOT decrease the measurement error in corresponding data sets?
   A) Remove the data point labeled A from the data set of Laughing Gull Sightings.
   B) Remove the data point labeled B from the data set of Thayer's Gull Sightings.
   C) Increase the sample size of both data sets to include another year of observations.
   D) Resample the data over the course of the next two years with a totally unbiased observer.

4. Which of the following conclusions is best supported by these data sets?
   A) There are approximately 2.5 times as many Thayer's Gulls as Laughing Gulls in the Kisatchie National Forest
   B) The confidence intervals bounding the expected number of Thayer's Gulls would be narrower than those bounding the expected number of Laughing Gulls
   C) The standard deviation of the number of sightings for the two bird species are identical
   D) The data is invalid to draw conclusions from because there was too much measurement error present

Annual Income	< $30,000	$30,000 – $100,000	> $100,000
PhDs	0%	80%	20%
Master's	15%	77%	8%
Bachelor's	29%	78%	3%

Questions 5 and 6 refer to the table above, which contains a representative sample of the income distribution by highest level of education in Houston, Texas. Assume that all people with PhDs also have a master's degree, and all people with a master's degree also have a bachelor's.

5. In a sample of 100 citizens of Houston, 9 have PhDs, 31 have master's degrees and 79 have bachelor's degrees. Assuming all those who make more than $100,000 per year have at least one of those degrees, how many people can be assumed to make over $100,000/year? Round to the nearest integer.
   A) 4
   B) 5
   C) 6
   D) 7

6. Which of these conclusions is best supported by the table above?
   A) A sample of people with bachelor's degrees has lower measurement error than a sample of people with master's degrees.
   B) A sample of people with PhDs should use a different measure of center than a sample of people with bachelor's degrees.
   C) A sample of people with bachelor's degrees will have smaller confidence interval ranges than a sample of people with PhDs
   D) A sample of people with PhDs will have a lower standard deviation than a sample of people with bachelor's degrees

7. Which of the following is NOT expected to happen if an outlier is added to a data set?
   A) Measurement error increases
   B) Confidence interval ranges decrease
   C) Standard deviation increases
   D) Mean increases

8. A campaign manager wants to predict how the residents of New York will react to a new bill proposed in the state senate. Which of the following study designs is most likely to provide reliable results for the campaign manager?
   A) Surveying a group of 1,200 randomly selected US residents
   B) Mailing a questionnaire to each of 300 randomly selected residents of New York
   C) Surveying a group of 500 randomly selected residents of New York
   D) Interviewing a group of students randomly selected from a high school in New York

9. Which of the following is most likely to happen when the standard deviation of a data set increases?
   A) Measurement error decreases
   B) Range increases
   C) Mean increases
   D) Confidence interval ranges increase

10. Which of the following would be most appropriate to determine the distribution of occupations in a city?
    A) Collect the occupations of people who work in office buildings
    B) Hand out surveys asking people about their occupations outside a polling booth
    C) Check the census's occupation data for people with random social security numbers
    D) Send a survey to random homes and record the results when they are returned

Age	12, 14, 15, 15, 17, 18, 19, 21, 25, 27, 31, 40, 42, 60, 71

Height (in feet)	21, 28, 31, 34, 36, 39, 41, 42, 43, 43, 44, 45, 46, 47, 47, 48, 51, 51, 52, 54, 54

Questions 11 through 12 refer to the data above about the ages of a group of people in San Jose.

11. If the population of San Jose is 1 million, how many people are expected to be older than 40?
    A) 200,000
    B) 266,667
    C) 350,000
    D) Not enough information to determine

12. Which of the following is the most likely cause of measurement error in this sample, if the goal is to draw conclusions about San Jose as a whole?
    A) Not taking a representative sample
    B) Not taking a voluntary sample
    C) Not taking a stratified random sample
    D) Having a biased observer collect and analyze the data

13. Which of the following would most likely result in a decrease in measurement error?
    A) Increasing the median
    B) Increasing the confidence interval ranges
    C) Increasing the standard deviation
    D) Increasing the sample size

Questions 14 through 16 refer to the data above about the height of buckeye trees in Ohio.

14. Which of the following is the most accurate description of this data?
    A) The data is left-skewed.
    B) The data is right-skewed.
    C) The mean is the most appropriate measure of center for this data.
    D) The standard deviation is the most appropriate measure of center for this data.

15. Which of the following would be most likely to happen if more data points were added to the sample?
    A) The range of confidence intervals would increase.
    B) The range of confidence intervals would decrease.
    C) The range of the data set would increase.
    D) The range of the data set would decrease.

16. If the average height of a buckeye tree in Ohio were 40 feet, which of the following would be the most valid conclusion to draw based on the data?
    A) The samples were taken in a forest where the trees are mostly younger than average.
    B) The samples were taken in a forest where the trees are mostly older than average.
    C) The samples were taken in a forest where the trees are mostly taller than average.
    D) The samples were taken in a forest where the trees are mostly shorter than average.

SAT Red Math
Lesson 8B: Advanced Statistics

	Rock Dove	Inca Dove	Mourning Dove
Sample Size	103	34	89
Mean Age (years)	2.1	3.4	2.9

19. A random sample of doves were caught and studied in the Nebraska National Forest. If the sample is assumed to be representative, what is the mean age of the populations of Rock, Inca, and Mourning Doves in the Nebraska National Forest? Round to the nearest hundredth of a year.

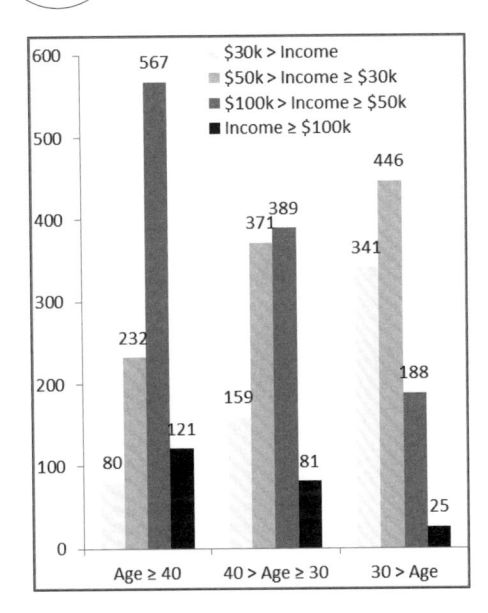

Question 17 uses the graph above. A stratified random sample was taken of the annual incomes of people in downtown Atlanta.

$\{0, 6, 13, 36, 38, 41, 45\}$

17. Downtown Atlanta's actual working population is 450,000, 34.25% of which are under 30, 43.89% of which are between 30 and 40, and 21.86% of which are over 40. How many people in downtown Atlanta are expected to have an income over $50k/year in thousands? Round to the nearest thousand people.

20. Another survey of the Nebraska National Forest found the above data about the population of the Canada Thistle (an invasive plant species) in various regions of the forest. Due to data corruption three of the data points were lost, but the surveyor had written down that the range of the data set was 56, the mode was 45, and the mean was 31.4. What is the median of the data set?

	Votes Received	Margin of Error
Candidate D	1850	±5%

18. The above data shows the preliminary results of an election poll. The margin of error provided is at the 90% confidence level. Based on the information above, what is the difference between the highest and lowest number of people expected to vote for Candidate D?

C2 education
be smarter.

RED MATH LESSON 9A: ADVANCED SCATTERPLOTS
Getting Your Feet Wet

Directions: The problems below are intended as a short diagnostic exam.

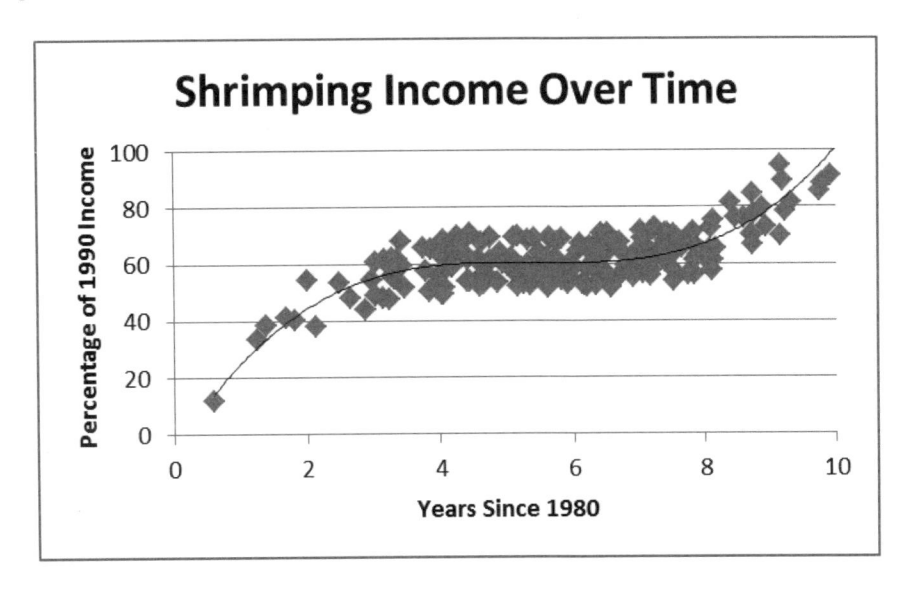

Shrimping Income Over Time

For questions 1 and 2 use the scatterplot above.

In 1990 a statistician collected the above income information from local shrimping businesses to analyze the financial effect of hurricanes in 1983, 1985, and 1986.

1. Which of the following best resembles the curve of best fit?
   A) $y = 0.4292x^3 + 6.957x^2 + 37.322x - 6.72$
   B) $y = 0.4292x^3 - 6.957x^2 + 37.322x - 6.72$
   C) $y = -0.4292x^3 + 6.957x^2 + 37.322x - 6.72$
   D) $y = -0.4292x^3 - 6.957x^2 + 37.322x - 6.72$

2. At the beginning of 1990, a local shrimp business reported annual earnings of $130,650. How much can the business expect to make at the beginning of 1991?
   A) $174,143
   B) $177,684
   C) $181,604
   D) $185,523

Lesson 9A: Advanced Scatterplots

Average Weekly Workload for People with Graduate Degrees

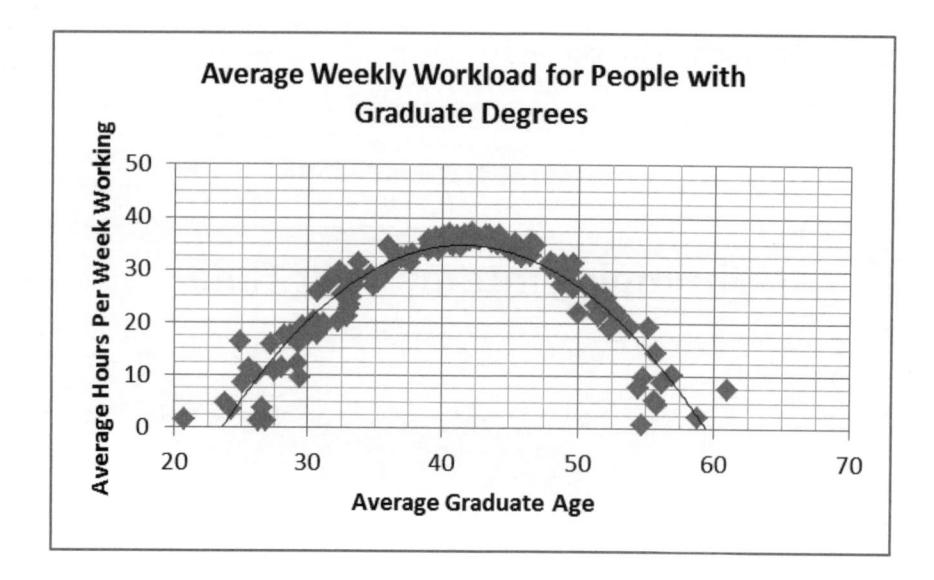

Use the scatterplot above for questions 3 and 4.

3. The scatterplot above shows information that was collected about different graduating classes of graduate students. Based on this information, which of the following conclusions is not supported?
   A) These students started working in their mid-twenties on average, around the time most people finish graduate school.
   B) These students did not start reaching their peak hours worked per week until roughly the age of forty, probably because graduate students often stay in school to obtain more education.
   C) These students started working less or retiring around their mid-forties, probably because these students had higher than average income and were able to retire earlier.
   D) These students never work past the age of 60, because people with graduate degrees make enough money to retire by then.

4. How many more hours per week will a group of graduates with an average age of 30 be expected to work in ten years' time?
   A) 5 hours
   B) 10 hours
   C) 15 hours
   D) 20 hours

Red Math Lesson 9A: Advanced Scatterplots
Wading In

Directions: Read the explanation for each problem type mentioned below. Pay special attention to the methods and techniques used to solve the sample problems. Then, do the practice exercises that follow; use the appropriate method to solve each problem.

Topic Overview: Polynomial Scatterplots

The majority of the scatterplots on the SAT will contain lines or curves of best fit that are polynomials, generally linear, quadratic, or cubic functions. Since obtaining the best line or curve of fit by hand can be extremely tedious, our best option to find these lines or curves of best fit is to plug in a few likely points into our possible answer choices, then eliminate the ones that don't quite fit. Let's try an example:

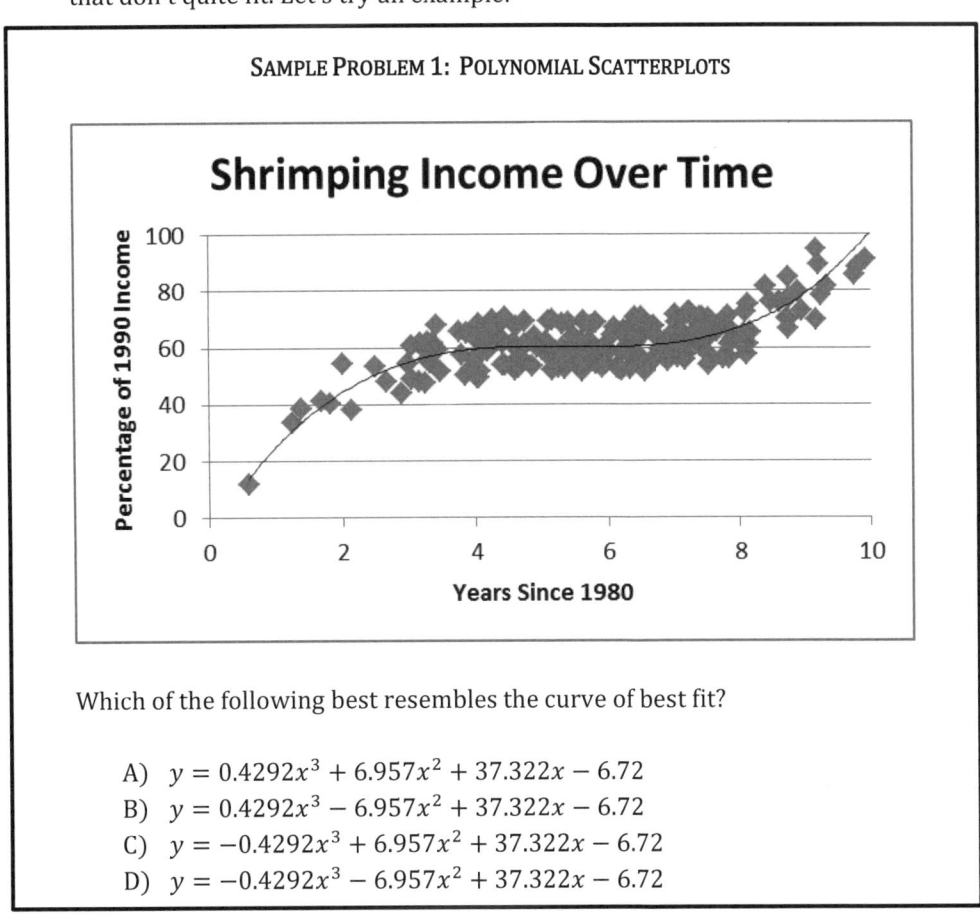

Sample Problem 1: Polynomial Scatterplots

Shrimping Income Over Time

(Scatterplot: x-axis "Years Since 1980" from 0 to 10; y-axis "Percentage of 1990 Income" from 0 to 100)

Which of the following best resembles the curve of best fit?

A) $y = 0.4292x^3 + 6.957x^2 + 37.322x - 6.72$
B) $y = 0.4292x^3 - 6.957x^2 + 37.322x - 6.72$
C) $y = -0.4292x^3 + 6.957x^2 + 37.322x - 6.72$
D) $y = -0.4292x^3 - 6.957x^2 + 37.322x - 6.72$

Since the curve of best fit in the above image is a cubic function that increases from left to right, we know the x^3 coefficient is positive. So, we really only have to plug numbers into answer choices **A** and **B**.

Because the y-axis is percent of 1990 income and the x-axis is years since 1980, we know the point $(10, 100)$ must exist on the curve of best fit. To find out whether **A** or **B** is the correct answer we plug 10 into the equations and see if we get 100 out.

$$0.4292(10^3) + 6.957(10^2) + 37.322(10) - 6.72 = 1491.4$$

So, answer choice **A** cannot be correct. If we were running short on time, we could have attempted to estimate the value of y at $x = 10$ by noticing that the first three terms of the polynomial were positive. Since 10^3 is 1000, answer choice A has to be at least 492 ($0.492x^3$), which is far greater than 100.

Now let's try answer choice **B**.

$$0.4292(10^3) - 6.957(10^2) + 37.322(10) - 6.72 = 100$$

Because the point (10, 100) exists, answer choice **B** is very likely correct. Let's check a second point just to be sure. Plugging in $x = 4$ should make y roughly 60.

$$0.4292(4^3) - 6.957(4^2) + 37.322(4) - 6.72 = 58.7248$$

Answer choice **B** is correct. We could have assumed this by eliminating the other three answer choices, but we should always verify our answers as long as we have enough time.

SAMPLE PROBLEM 2: POLYNOMIAL SCATTERPLOTS

At the beginning of 1990, a local shrimp business reported annual earnings of $130,650. How much can the business expect to be making at the beginning of 1991?
  A) $174,143
  B) $177,684
  C) $181,604
  D) $185,523

Because we found the curve of best fit in the previous question, we can simply plug in $x = 11$ to find the percentage of 1990 income and then multiply this by the business's 1990 earnings.

$$0.4292(11^3) - 6.957(11^2) + 37.322(11) - 6.72 = 133.29$$

$$\$130{,}650 \times 1.3329 = \$174{,}143.4$$

Answer choice **A** is correct.

SAT Red Math
Lesson 9A: Advanced Scatterplots

Topic Overview: Drawing Conclusions From Scatterplots

Sometimes, we have to do more than just find a curve of best fit of the data of a scatterplot. We have to analyze the situation given and draw conclusions from that data. Let's look at a new set of data and a few questions dealing with this analysis:

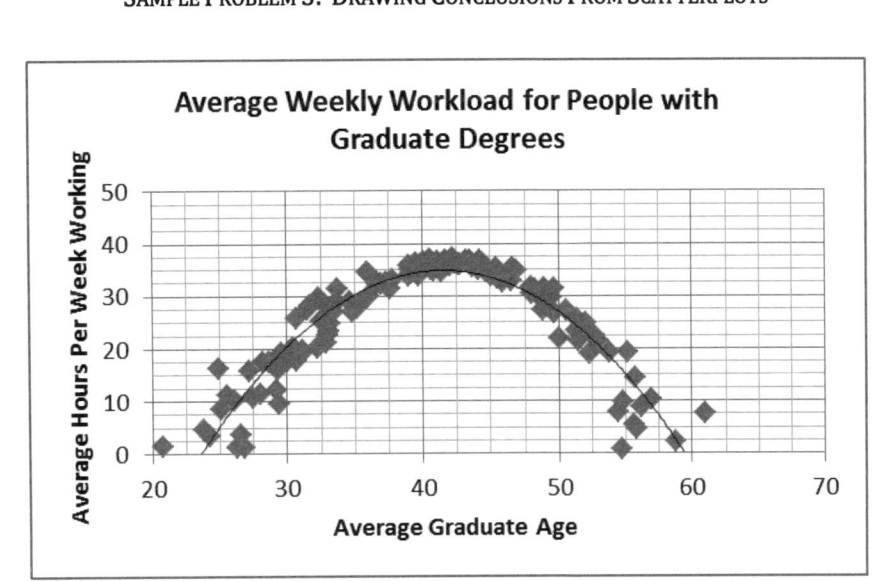

Sample Problem 3: Drawing Conclusions From Scatterplots

Average Weekly Workload for People with Graduate Degrees

(Scatterplot: x-axis "Average Graduate Age" from 20 to 70; y-axis "Average Hours Per Week Working" from 0 to 50. Data forms an inverted parabola peaking around age 40 at roughly 38 hours.)

The scatterplot above shows information that was collected about different graduating classes of graduate students. Based on this information, which of the following conclusions is not supported?

A) These students started working in their mid-twenties on average, around the time most people finish graduate school.

B) These students did not start reaching their peak hours worked per week until roughly the age of forty, probably because graduate students often stay in school to obtain more education.

C) These students started working less or retiring around their mid-forties, probably because these students had higher than average income and were able to retire earlier.

D) These students never work past the age of 60, because people with graduate degrees make enough money to retire by then.

Each answer to this question has a statement and a justification. If any of the statements is wrong, then we've found the correct answer choice. Otherwise we need to consider the justifications and figure out which one is not supported.

Answer choice **D** states that students will never work past the age of 60, but there is an outlier on the scatterplot with an average student age of approximately 61. So, **D** must be the correct answer.

SAT Red Math
Lesson 9A: Advanced Scatterplots

As an aside, absolute statements in statistics questions are usually incorrect. Statistics are not capable of making an absolute statement about anything, so if an answer choice to a statistics-based question contains absolute words like 'always' or 'never', it is very likely wrong.

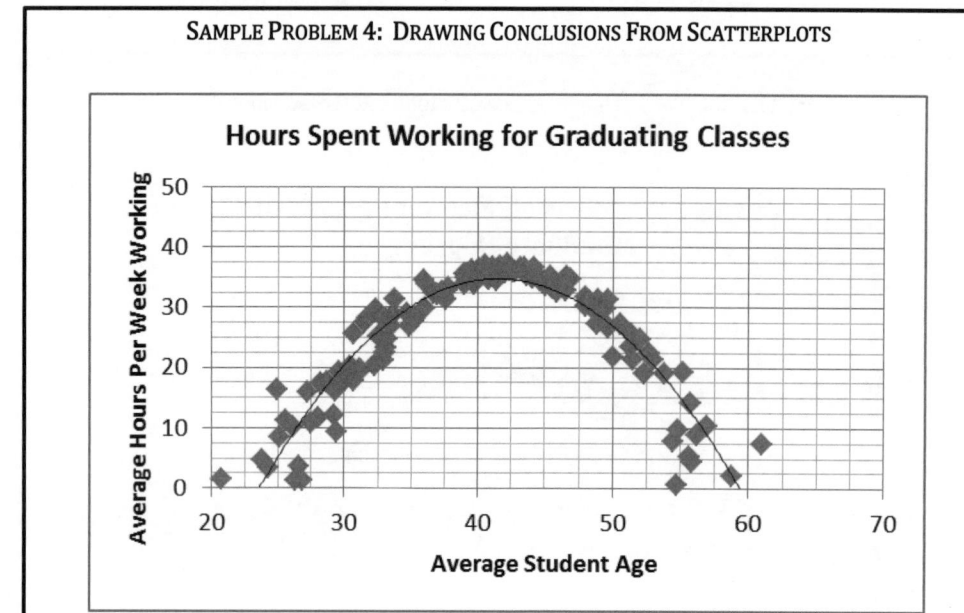

SAMPLE PROBLEM 4: DRAWING CONCLUSIONS FROM SCATTERPLOTS

Hours Spent Working for Graduating Classes

(Scatterplot: x-axis "Average Student Age" from 20 to 70; y-axis "Average Hours Per Week Working" from 0 to 50; data forms an inverted parabola peaking near age 40 at about 35 hours.)

How many more hours per week will a group of graduates with an average age of 30 be expected to work in ten years' time?
- A) 5 hours
- B) 10 hours
- C) 15 hours
- D) 20 hours

This is an interpolation question, so we need to identify two points on the scatterplot to answer the question. At age 30 the curve of best fit indicates an average of 20 hours worked per week, so (30, 20) is our first point. In ten years' time, the work load of these students would be around 35 hours, so the other point is approximately (40, 35) according to the curve of best fit. The difference in the y coordinates is 15, so **C** is the correct answer choice.

TOPIC OVERVIEW: EXPONENTIAL SCATTERPLOTS

There are two other types of functions that may come up in scatterplots on the SAT: positive and negative exponential functions. Like the curves of best fit of many polynomial functions, these curves of best fit are too complicated for us to use anything more than guess-and-check to determine their curves of best fit. Instead, we should focus on knowing the general patterns of each type of exponential function.

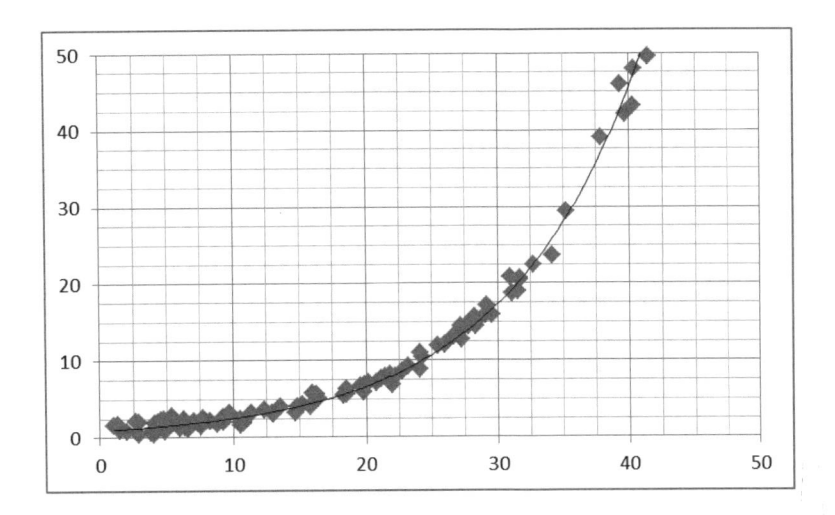

The above is a scatterplot of a positive exponential function, with the curve of best fit close to 1.1^x. Exponential functions are named after the fact that the variable is an exponent.

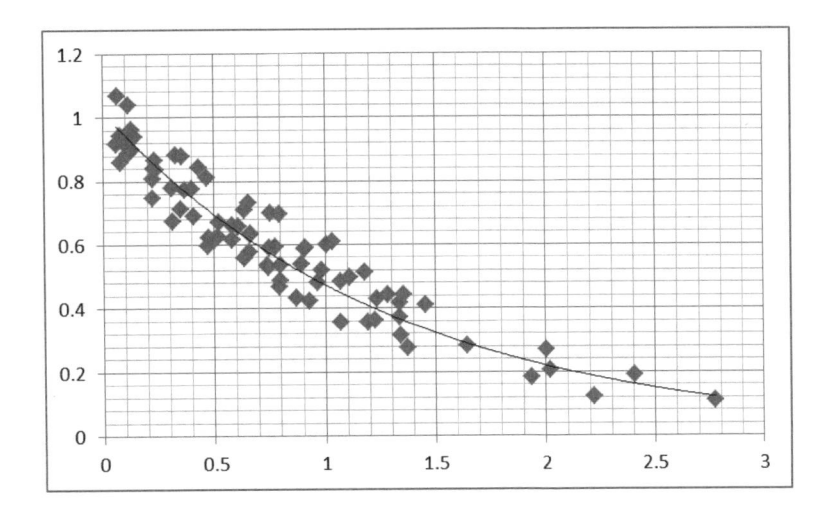

The above is a scatter of a negative exponential function, for example 1.1^{-x}. Both positive and negative exponential functions have similar curves, and like cubic functions you can tell whether they are positive or negative by whether they increase or decrease respectively.

WRAP-UP

The more advanced scatterplot questions may seem intimidating at first, but the SAT should compensate for complex curves of best fit by asking easier questions. Just solve the problems step-by-step in the same way simpler scatterplots were solved. Remember to check your answers when interpolating/extrapolating and the problems should be manageable. Good Luck!

RED MATH LESSON 9A: ADVANCED SCATTERPLOTS
Learning to Swim

Directions: Answer each question below.

PRACTICE SET 1 (CALCULATOR)

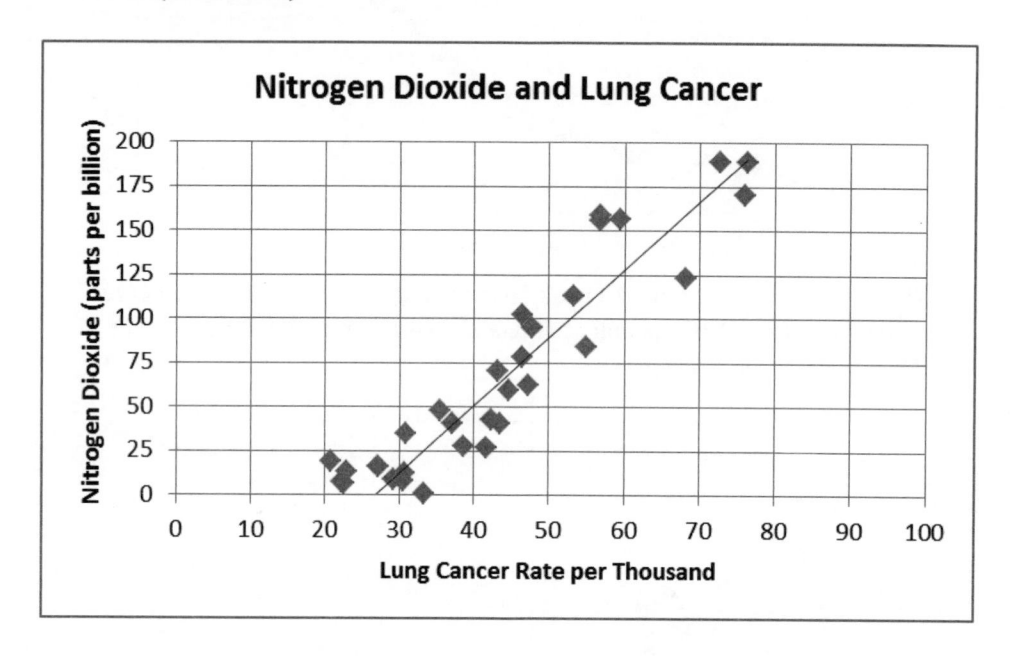

Nitrogen Dioxide and Lung Cancer

For questions 1 through 3, use the above scatterplot about the rates of nitrogen dioxide air pollution and lung cancer rates per thousand people in various cities.

1. Estimate the curve of best fit.

2. Assuming this sample is representative of the greater population, what nitrogen dioxide concentration (in parts per billion) would be expected for a city in which 2 out of a hundred people get lung cancer?

3. How many more incidences of lung cancer per thousand people would be expected in a city with a nitrogen dioxide level of 300 parts per billion over a city with 75 parts per billion nitrogen dioxide?

Automobile Buying Habits

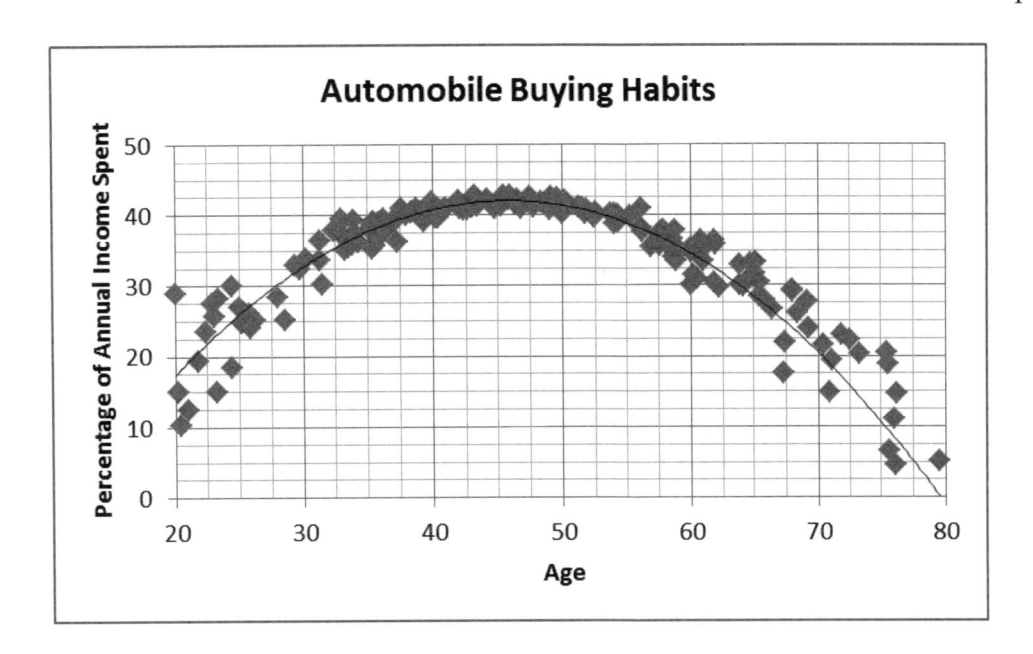

For questions 4 and 5, use the above scatterplot with information about how much people spend on automobiles as a percentage of their annual income.

The curve of best fit is $y = -0.0369x^2 + 3.3782x - 35.434$.

4. What are the x-intercepts of the curve of best fit?

5. If a person spends 41.875% of her annual income on automobiles, what age is she expected to be?

Red Math Lesson 9A: Advanced Scatterplots
Diving into the Deep End

Directions: Answer each question below.

PRACTICE SET 2 (CALCULATOR)

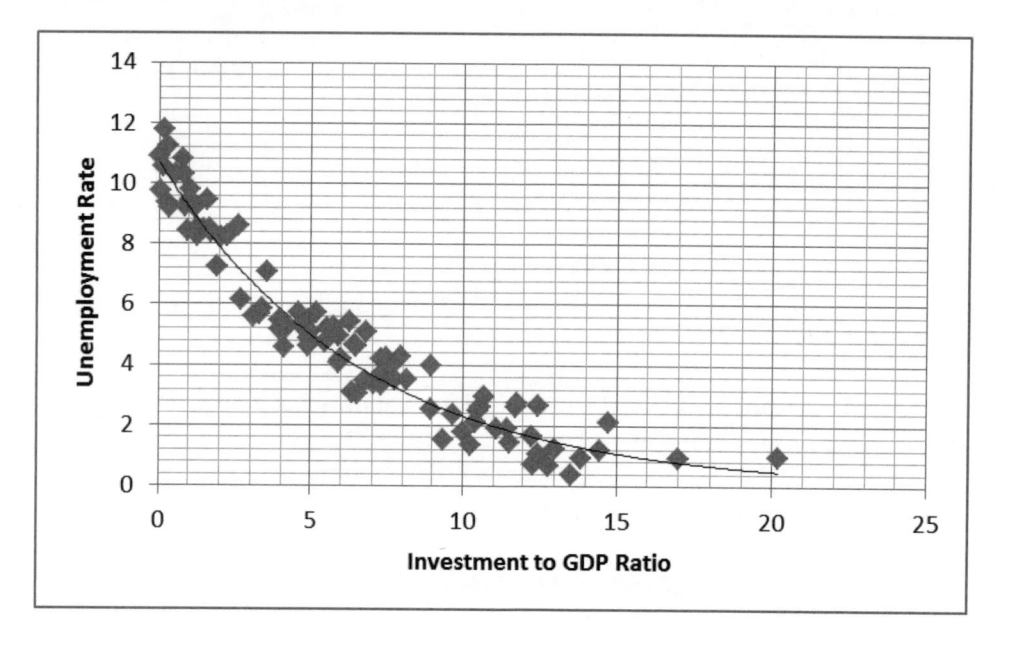

For questions 6 through 8, use the above scatterplot of the unemployment rate and investment to GDP ratio of various countries.

6. Which of the following best resembles the curve of best fit?
   A) $y = 10.724e^{0.153x}$
   B) $y = 10.724e^{-0.153x}$
   C) $y = 10.724e^{1.53x}$
   D) $y = 10.724e^{-1.53x}$

7. If a country's unemployment rate increased over the course of three years from 4% to 8%, what would be the expected decrease in the Investment to GDP Ratio?
   A) 1.1289
   B) 1.8803
   C) 2.6618
   D) 4.5304

8. What conclusions can be drawn from the scatterplot above about the relationship between a country's unemployment rate and its GDP?
   A) A country with a higher unemployment rate is likely to have a higher GDP.
   B) A country with a higher unemployment rate is likely to have a lower GDP.
   C) There is no correlation between the unemployment rate of a country and its GDP.
   D) There is not enough information to determine the relationship between a country's unemployment rate and its GDP.

9. An auto company wants to determine how long it will take to stop its 2017 Model M car from various speeds. Which of the following data collection methods would best allow the company to accomplish this?
   A) Use the data from the 2016 Model M, since it's the same make of car.
   B) Take the car onto a test strip of land and record how long it takes to stop the car at 10 mph intervals.
   C) Take the car onto a test strip of land and record many trials to test how long it takes to stop at various speeds.
   D) Use the data from the 2017 Model N which it tested earlier in the month.

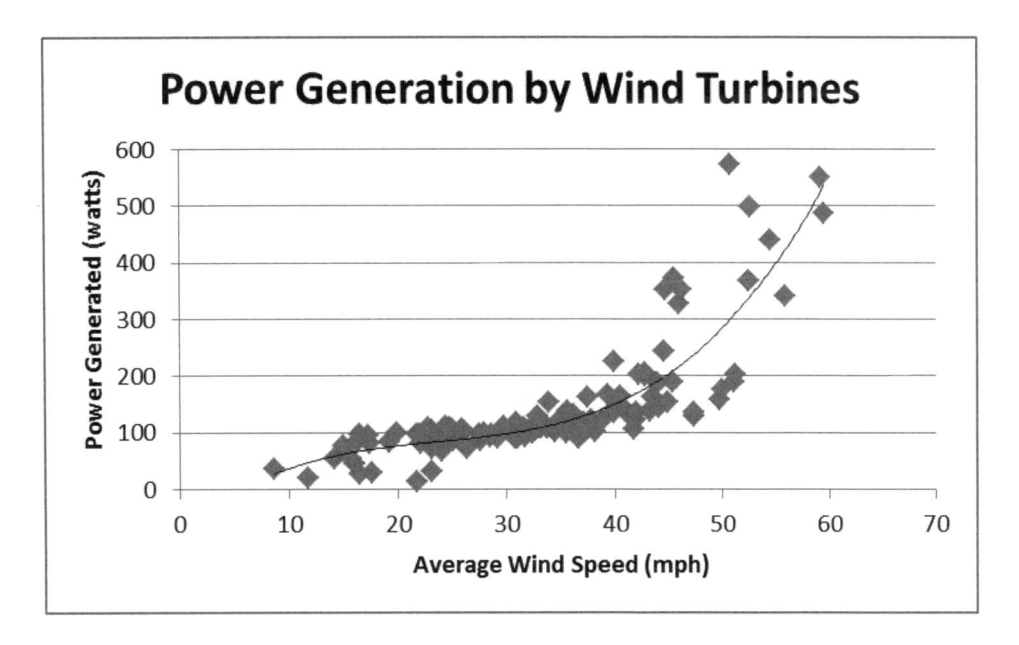

Power Generation by Wind Turbines

For questions 10 through 12, use the scatterplot above.

10. Which of the following best resembles the curve of best fit?
    A) $y = 0.0048x^3 - 0.4077x^2 + 16.016x + 55.30$
    B) $y = 0.0084x^3 - 0.4077x^2 + 25.201x - 70.85$
    C) $y = 0.0048x^3 - 0.5977x^2 + 25.201x + 55.30$
    D) $y = 0.0084x^3 - 0.5977x^2 + 16.016x - 71.85$

11. Which of the following conclusions is not supported by the scatterplot?
    A) It is more cost efficient to build a wind turbine on a mountain that experiences typical wind speeds around 50 mph than to build one on a hill that experiences typical wind speeds below 30 mph, even if the costs of building on the mountain would be twice as high.
    B) It is never worthwhile to build a wind turbine that experiences wind speeds below 10 mph.
    C) Wind turbines have a difficult time generating more power between wind speeds of 20 and 30 mph.
    D) Power generation increases greatly when the wind speed exceeds 50 mph.

12. How much more power would a wind turbine be expected to generate if the region's wind speed increased from 42 to 48 mph?
    A) 3.667 watts
    B) 51.157 watts
    C) 79.972 watts
    D) 237.682 watts

SAT Red Math
Lesson 9A: Advanced Scatterplots

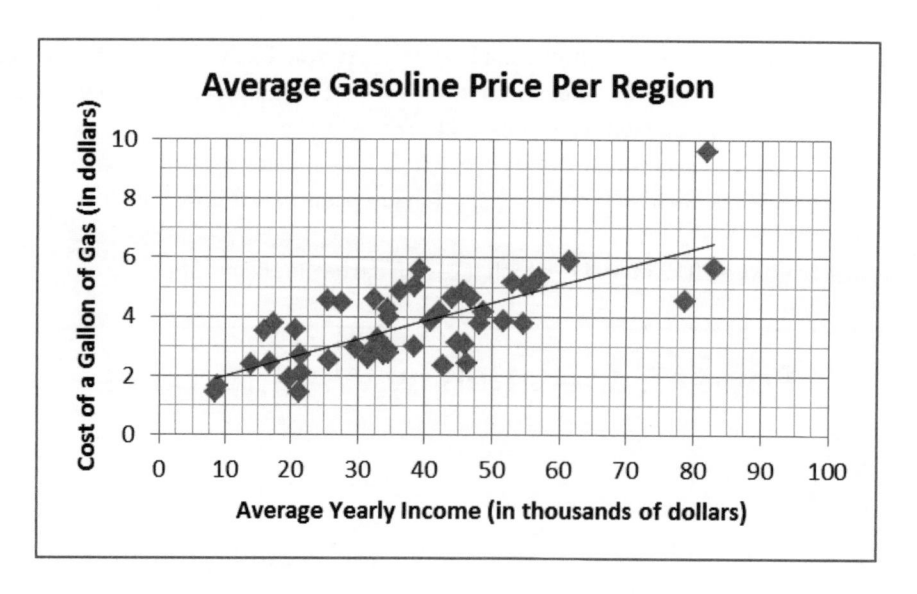

Average Gasoline Price Per Region

(Scatterplot: Cost of a Gallon of Gas (in dollars) vs. Average Yearly Income (in thousands of dollars))

For questions 13 through 15, use the above scatterplot.

13. Which of the following best resembles the line of best fit?
    A) $y = 0.0611x + 1.409$
    B) $y = -0.0611x + 1.409$
    C) $y = 0.054x + 1.016$
    D) $y = -0.054x + 1.016$

14. If a gallon of gas costs $6 in Turkey, what would you expect the average yearly income in Turkey to be in thousands of dollars? Round to the nearest tenth.

15. If the average yearly income in France increased from $40,135 to $61,057 over a ten-year period, how much would you expect the price of a gallon of gas to have increased in the same period? Round to the nearest hundredth.

PRACTICE SET 3 (CALCULATOR)

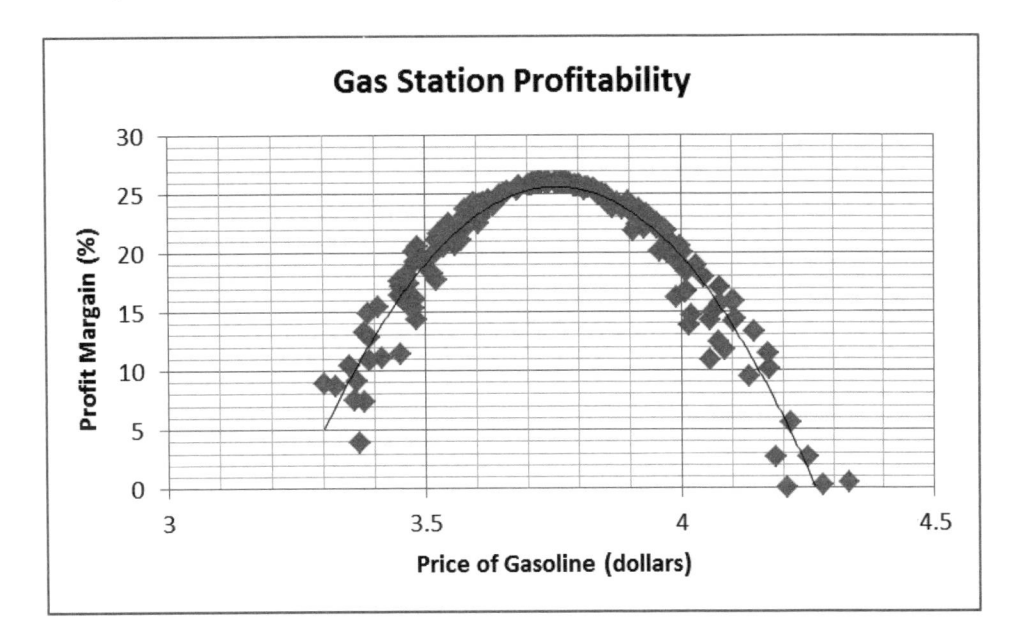

Gas Station Profitability

For questions 16 through 18, use the scatterplot above detailing the profit margin for local gas stations according to how much they charge for a gallon of gasoline.

16. Which of the following best resembles the curve of best fit?
    A) $y = 66.996x^2 + 732.67x + 1380.9$
    B) $y = -66.996x^2 - 748.83x + 1380.9$
    C) $y = 99.669x^2 - 732.67x - 1380.9$
    D) $y = -99.669x^2 + 748.83x - 1380.9$

17. According to the curve of best fit, at what price will the profit margin be maximized?
    A) $3.643 per gallon
    B) $3.757 per gallon
    C) $3.871 per gallon
    D) $3.985 per gallon

18. If a local gas station raises its price per gallon of gas from $3.30 to $3.60, what will be the expected difference in profit margin?
    A) 13.486%
    B) 18.334%
    C) 358.483%
    D) 363.331%

SAT Red Math
Lesson 9A: Advanced Scatterplots

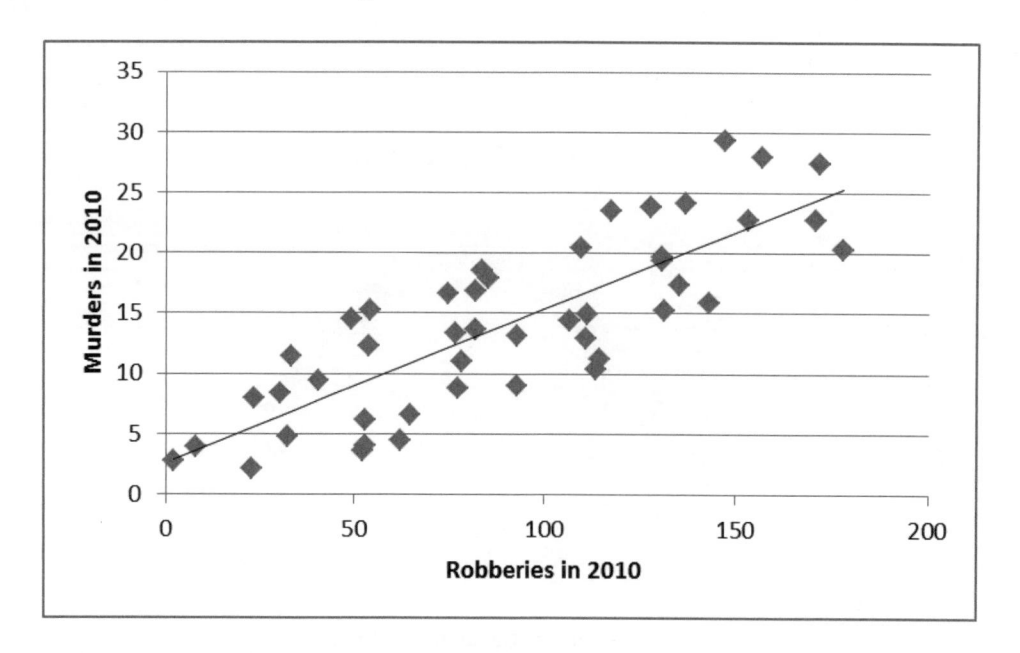

For questions 19 through 21, use the above scatterplot which compares the rates of robbery and murder in a number of cities in 2010.

19. Which of the following best resembles the line of best fit?
    A) $y = 0.1279x + 2.5971$
    B) $y = 0.2421x + 2.5971$
    C) $y = -0.1279x + 4.5779$
    D) $y = -0.2421x + 4.5779$

20. If a larger city had 416 murders in 2010, what would be the expected number of robberies?
    A) 1,700
    B) 1,708
    C) 3,217
    D) 3,232

21. Two neighboring cities had 2,150 and 5,617 robberies in 2010 respectively. What is the expected difference in the number of murders between the two cities in 2010?
    A) 440
    B) 443
    C) 446
    D) 449

SAT Red Math — Lesson 9A: Advanced Scatterplots

22. If a curve of best fit yields points $(2, 10)$, $(4, 20)$, $(6, 40)$, $(8, 80)$, and $(10, 160)$, which of the following is the correct shape of the curve of best fit?
    A) Quadratic
    B) Cubic
    C) Exponential
    D) Logarithmic

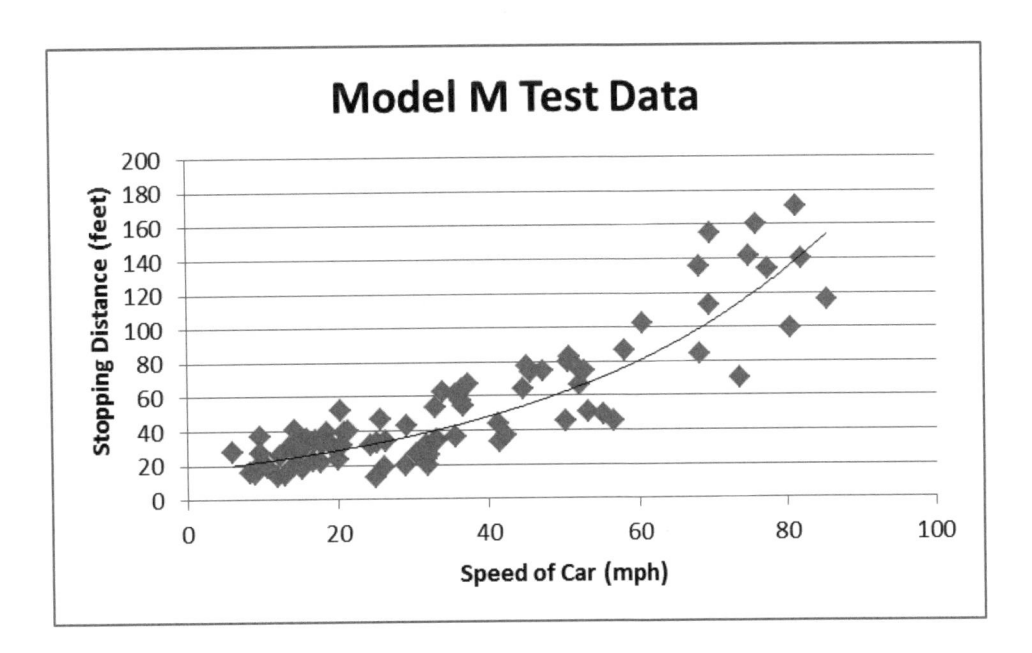

Model M Test Data

(Scatterplot: Stopping Distance (feet) vs. Speed of Car (mph))

For questions 23 through 25 use the above information about an auto manufacturer's tests on its 2017 Model M car.

23. Which of the following best resembles the curve of best fit?
    A) $y = 17.097e^{0.0258x}$
    B) $y = 26.508e^{0.0258x}$
    C) $y = 17.097e^{0.258x}$
    D) $y = 26.508e^{0.258x}$

24. If a 2017 Model M took 200 feet to come to a complete stop, how fast would it be expected to be traveling, in miles per hour? Round your answer to the nearest tenth.

25. Two 2017 Model M's were driving on a course and started stopping at the same time. One was traveling at 82.5 miles per hour and the other was traveling at 66.7 miles per hour. What is the difference in the amount of feet it took them to stop? Round to the nearest tenth.

RED MATH LESSON 9A: ADVANCED SCATTERPLOTS
Race to the Finish

Directions: Answer each question below.

HOMEWORK SET (CALCULATOR)

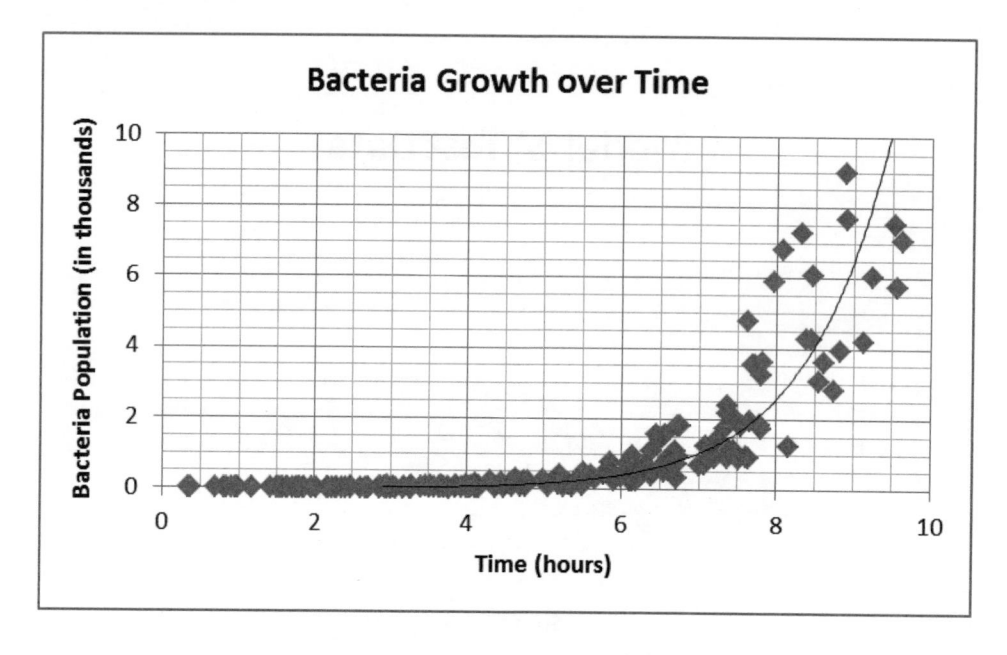

Bacteria Growth over Time

For questions 1 through 3, use the scatterplot above. A group of scientists wanted to predict how a particular bacterial culture may behave in the future, so they recorded how much the bacteria reproduced over time.

1. Which of the following best resembles the curve of best fit?
   A) $-0.0016e^{0.09231x}$
   B) $0.0016e^{0.9231x}$
   C) $-0.016e^{0.09231x}$
   D) $0.016e^{0.9231x}$

2. What is the predicted bacteria population percentage increase from hour 5 to hour 7?
   A) 333.57%
   B) 433.57%
   C) 533.57%
   D) 633.57%

3. If a scientist finds a bacterial culture with a population of 8.1 thousand, how long has it been reproducing?
   A) 8.6 hours
   B) 8.8 hours
   C) 9.0 hours
   D) 9.2 hours

New Hampshire Lake Treatment

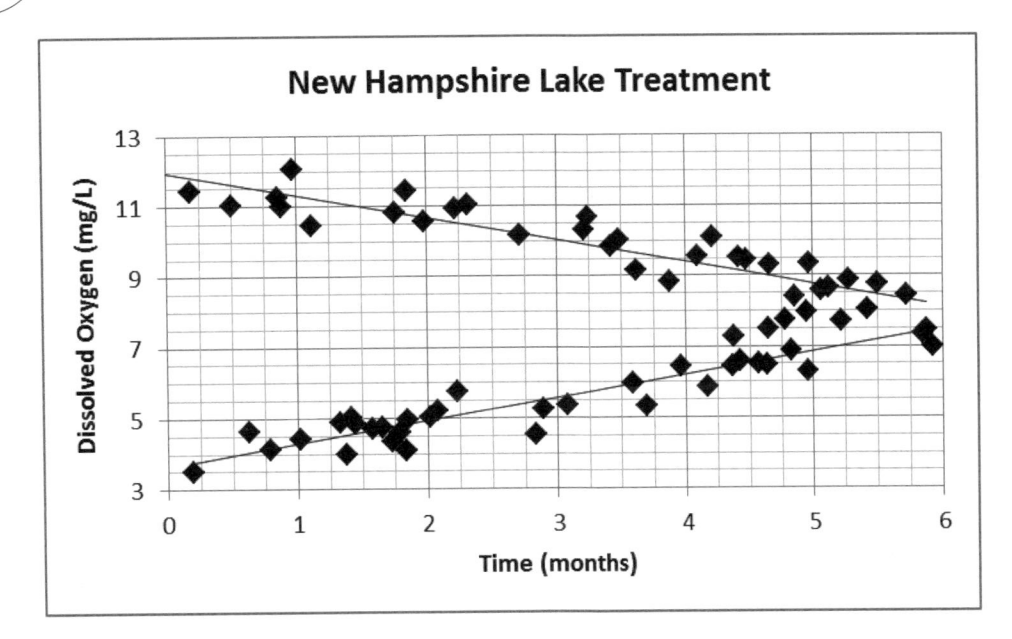

For questions 4 through 7, use the scatterplot above. A group of chemists apply a treatment plan to a number of lakes in New Hampshire to try and normalize their dissolved oxygen levels.

4. Which of the following best explains why there are two lines of best fit?
   A) Some of the lakes are larger than others, and thus have different chemistries.
   B) Some of the lakes are infected with a microbe which changes those lakes' chemistries.
   C) Some of the lakes have more fish than the other lakes.
   D) One of the scientists who sampled the lakes had compromised sampling instruments.

5. Which of the following best resembles the lines of best fit?
   A) $y = -0.6443x + 4.6474, y = 0.6337x + 10.936$
   B) $y = -0.6443x + 3.6474, y = 0.6337x + 11.936$
   C) $y = 0.6443x + 4.6474, y = -0.6337x + 10.936$
   D) $y = 0.6443x + 3.6474, y = -0.6337x + 11.936$

6. If a lake had a dissolved oxygen level below 5 mg/L one month into this treatment plan, what would be the expected increase in dissolved oxygen over the next three months?
   A) 1.2674 mg/L
   B) 1.2886 mg/L
   C) 1.9011 mg/L
   D) 1.9329 mg/L

7. If a lake had a dissolved oxygen level of 11.4 mg/L, what is the estimated duration the lake has been receiving treatment?
   A) 0.7322 months
   B) 0.8458 months
   C) 8.6432 months
   D) 10.4805 months

Engine Emissions

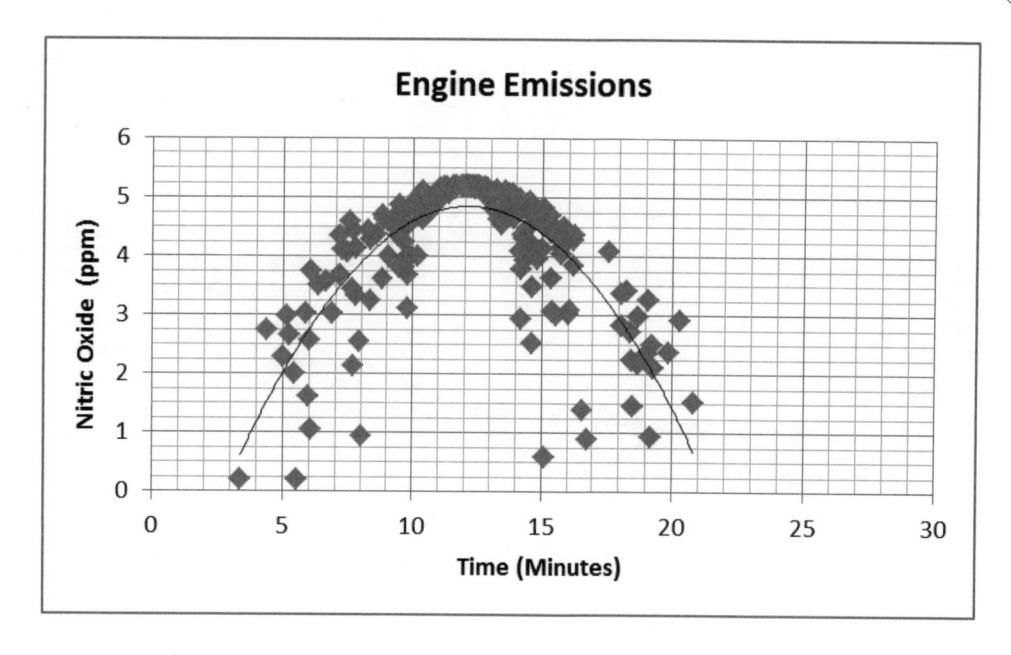

For questions 8 through 10, use the above scatterplot with data about the nitric oxide emissions of a certain engine over time.

8. Which of the following best resembles the curve of best fit?
   A) $y = 0.0555x^2 + 1.3482x - 3.3339$
   B) $y = -0.0555x^2 + 1.3482x - 3.3339$
   C) $y = 0.0555x^2 - 1.3482x - 3.3339$
   D) $y = -0.0555x^2 - 1.3482x - 3.3339$

9. Which of the following best explains why the curve of best fit predicts 0 nitric oxide emissions at 2 minutes?
   A) The measuring device was far enough away from the engine to not detect emissions for 2 minutes
   B) The engine doesn't produce any pollutants for the first 2 minutes it runs
   C) The data was recorded inaccurately; every data point is recorded 2 minutes too late
   D) The nitric oxide recorded actually came from a source other than the engine

10. If the recorded nitric oxide level is 4.854 ppm, how long is the engine expected to have been running?
    A) 12.05 minutes
    B) 12.15 minutes
    C) 12.25 minutes
    D) 12.35 minutes

Eruptive Products of Volcanic Eruption

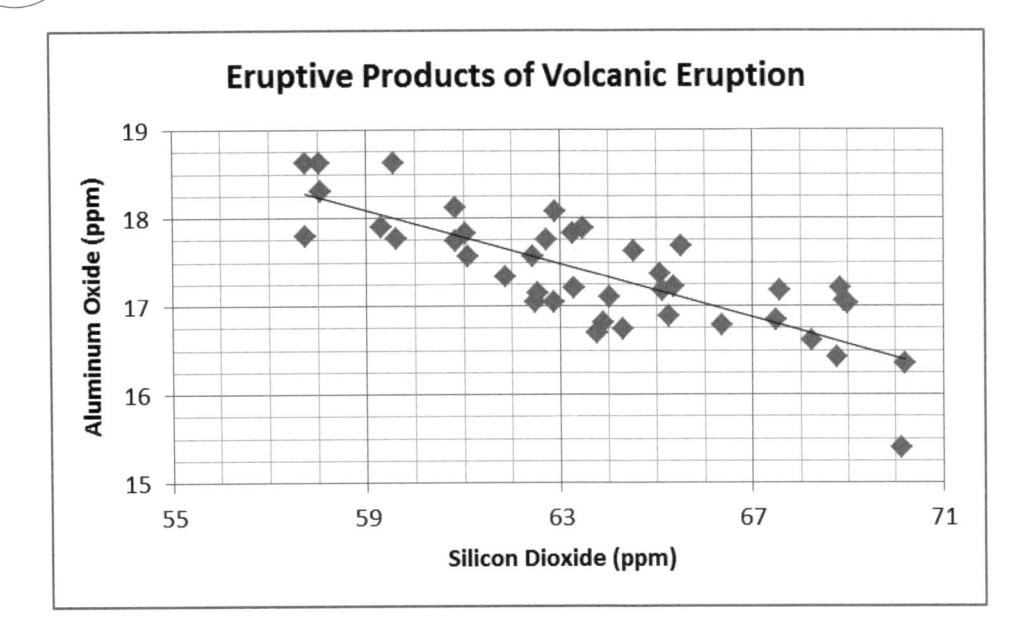

For questions 11 through 13, use the above scatterplot with data about the chemical composition of material found after volcanic eruptions.

11. Which of the following best resembles the line of best fit?
    A) $y = -0.1514x + 27.017$
    B) $y = -0.1514x + 37.017$
    C) $y = -0.1914x + 27.017$
    D) $y = -0.1914x + 37.017$

12. There have been two recent volcanic eruptions in the Russian tundra. The second eruption had 6.8 ppm less silicon dioxide, but the researchers were unable to measure the aluminum oxide levels with their available instruments. How much more aluminum oxide would be expected in the material found around the second eruption?
    A) 1.0295 ppm
    B) 1.1655 ppm
    C) 1.3015 ppm
    D) 1.4375 ppm

13. The Russian researchers acquired new equipment and found that in a third volcanic eruption there was an aluminum oxide concentration of 23.4 ppm. What is the expected silicon dioxide concentration?
    A) 22.94 ppm
    B) 23.89 ppm
    C) 32.94 ppm
    D) 33.79 ppm

SAT Red Math
Lesson 9A: Advanced Scatterplots

New Hampshire Lake Treatment

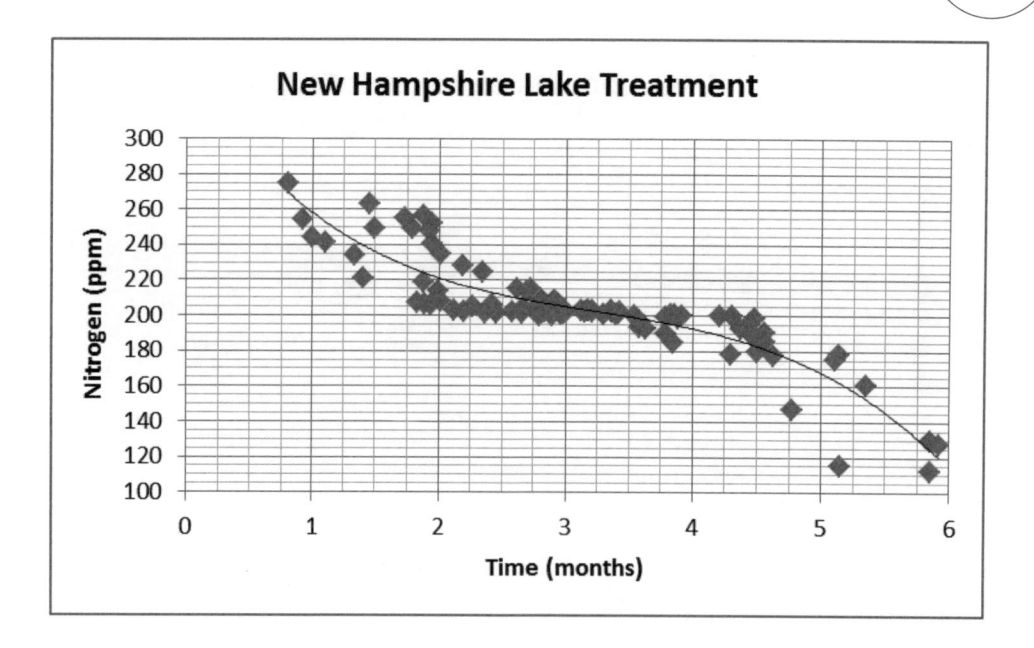

For questions 14 through 16, use the above scatterplot. A group of chemists apply a treatment plan to a number of lakes in New Hampshire to try and normalize their dissolved oxygen levels, and unexpectedly this treatment also changes the nitrogen concentration of the lakes.

The curve of best fit is $y = -2.7401x^3 + 26.658x^2 - 97.521x + 331.56$.

14. If the above scatterplot refers to the same lake treatment as the scatterplot from problems 4 through 7, which of the following best explains why the nitrogen content remains relatively consistent through all the lakes studied while the dissolved oxygen content doesn't?
    A) The variable that affected the dissolved oxygen content had little effect on the nitrogen content.
    B) Only lakes with a certain number of fish had their nitrogen content reported.
    C) The variable that affected the dissolved oxygen content caused an increase in nitrogen content.
    D) Only lakes at a certain elevation or higher had their nitrogen content reported.

15. If the ideal nitrogen content for biodiversity is $180 \leq n \leq 220$ ppm, in which month is the lake treatment expected to push the lakes' nitrogen level below ideal levels for biodiversity?

16. If a further treatment is applied to keep the lakes' nitrogen content at a constant level starting at the beginning of month 3, what is the expected difference in nitrogen content between the beginning of months 1 and 6? Round answer to the nearest tenth.

First Year University Students

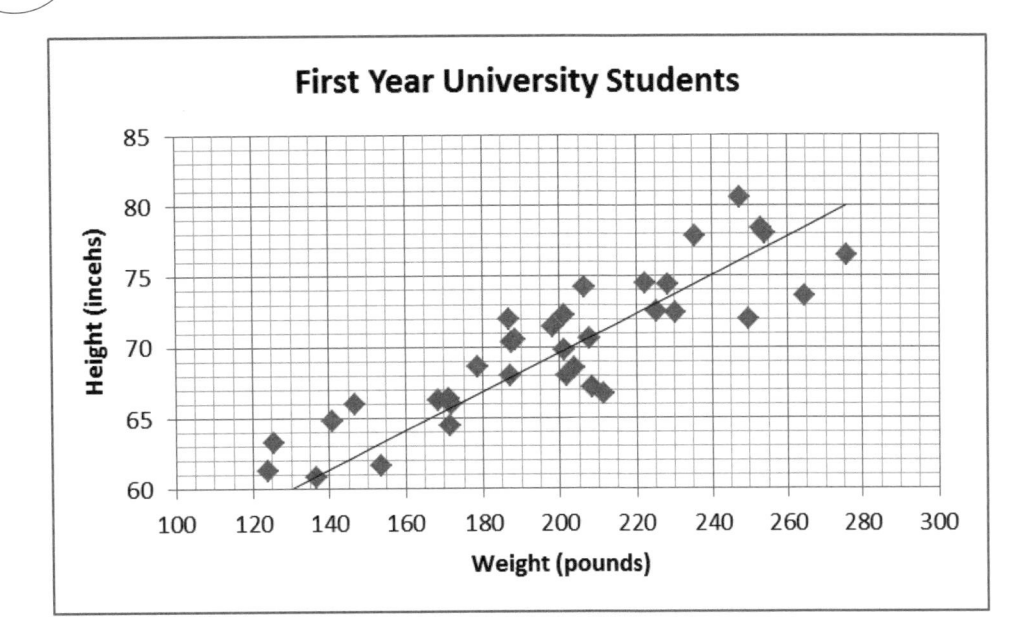

For questions 17 through 20, use the scatterplot above.

17. Which of the following best resembles the line of best fit?
    A) $y = 0.1373x + 42.14$
    B) $y = 0.1373x + 52.32$
    C) $y = 0.1661x + 42.14$
    D) $y = 0.1661x + 52.32$

18. Which of the following students would most be considered an outlier in this data set?
    A) A student that is 55 inches tall and 100 lbs.
    B) A student that is 65 inches tall and 140 lbs.
    C) A student that is 75 inches tall and 280 lbs.
    D) A student that is 90 inches tall and 260 lbs.

19. If two new students have a combined height of 150 inches, what is their expected combined weight? Round to the nearest pound.

20. If a new student is 100 lbs. heavier than another new student, what is the expected difference in their heights, in inches? Round to the nearest tenth of an inch.

RED MATH LESSON 9B: TWO-WAY TABLES – PROBABILITIES AND FREQUENCIES
Getting Your Feet Wet

Directions: The problems below are intended as a short diagnostic exam.

Reported Voting by Yearly Income

	Voted	Did Not Vote	No Response	Total
$0 - $20,000	34,726	37,757	10,198	82,681
$20,000 - $50,000	33,869	19,273	8,869	62,011
$50,000 - $100,000	33,486	4,831	3,023	41,340
$100,000 and over	15,503	3,149	2,018	20,670
Total	117,584	65,010	24,108	206,702

A survey was conducted among a randomly chosen sample of voting-eligible U.S. citizens about U.S. voter participation in the November 2008 presidential election. The table above displays a summary of the survey results.

1. According to the above data, the people of which yearly income are least likely to vote?
   A) $0 - $20,000
   B) $20,000 - $50,000
   C) $50,000 - $100,000
   D) $100,000 and over

2. What percentage of people who did not respond to the survey earned at least $50,000 per year?
   A) 8.37%
   B) 12.54%
   C) 20.91%
   D) 79.09%

3. Of the people who made between $20,000 and $50,000 in yearly income and reported voting, 1,000 were selected to do a follow-up survey in which they were asked which candidate they voted for. There were 456 people in the follow-up survey who voted for Candidate D, 245 people who voted for Candidate R, and the rest voted for someone else. If this ratio holds approximately true among everyone who voted in the survey, approximately how many people in the survey voted for Candidate D?
   A) 28,277
   B) 28,808
   C) 35,157
   D) 53,618

RED MATH LESSON 9B: TWO-WAY TABLES – PROBABILITIES AND FREQUENCIES
Wading In

Directions: Read the explanation for each problem type mentioned below. Pay special attention to the methods and techniques used to solve the sample problems. Then, do the practice exercises that follow; use the appropriate method to solve each problem.

TOPIC OVERVIEW: TWO-WAY TABLES

A two-way table is a means of presenting data that allows us to easily examine the relationship between two different categorical variables. Look at the example of a two-way frequency table below:

Reported Voting by Yearly Income

	Voted	Did Not Vote	No Response	Total
$0 - $20,000	34,726	37,757	10,198	82,681
$20,000 - $50,000	33,869	19,273	8,869	62,011
$50,000 - $100,000	33,486	4,831	3,023	41,340
$100,000 and over	15,503	3,149	2,018	20,670
Total	117,584	65,010	24,108	206,702

A survey was conducted among a randomly chosen sample of voting-eligible U.S. citizens about U.S. voter participation in the November 2008 presidential election. The table above displays a summary of the survey results.

For this table, our two categorical variables are **whether or not the person voted** and **yearly income**. All of the values for yearly income are listed in the horizontal rows, while all of the values for voting preference are listed in the vertical columns. Each box in the table gives us a specific number—the number of people in a certain income range and whether or not they voted. Most of the questions associated with a two-way table will involve calculating probabilities or will ask us to compare different segments of the population based on the information gathered above. Let's try a question based on the above data:

SAT Red Math
Lesson 9B: Two-Way Tables – Probabilities and Frequencies

> **SAMPLE PROBLEM 1: TWO-WAY TABLES**
>
> According to the above data, the people of which yearly income are least likely to vote?
> A) $0 - $20,000
> B) $20,000 - $50,000
> C) $50,000 - $100,000
> D) $100,000 and over

The first question is relatively straightforward. All we need to do is divide the number of people who voted in each economic group by the total number of people surveyed in that group. The group that makes less than $20,000 yearly, choice **A**, wins in a landslide.

Let's try another question:

> **SAMPLE PROBLEM 2: TWO-WAY TABLES**
>
> What percentage of people who did not respond to the survey earned at least $50,000 per year?
> A) 8.37%
> B) 12.54%
> C) 20.91%
> D) 79.09%

For this question, our answer is **C**. We need to figure out how many people earned more than $50,000 a year and did not respond to the survey. Then, we will divide that sum by the number of people who did not respond to the survey:

$$\frac{2018+3023}{24108} = 20.91\%$$

We will try one more question based on the previous information:

SAT Red Math
Lesson 9B: Two-Way Tables – Probabilities and Frequencies

> **SAMPLE PROBLEM 3: TWO-WAY TABLES**
>
> Of the people who earned between $20,000 and $50,000 in yearly income and reported voting, 1,000 were selected to do a follow-up survey in which they were asked which candidate they voted for. There were 456 people in the follow-up survey who voted for Candidate D, 245 people who voted for Candidate R, and the rest voted for someone else. If this ratio holds approximately true among everyone who voted in the survey, approximately how many people in the survey voted for Candidate D?
>   A) 28,277
>   B) 28,808
>   C) 35,157
>   D) 53,618

We know that 456 of the 1000 voters in the follow-up survey voted for Candidate D. Since this ratio holds true for all the voters, we simply have to take 45.6% of 117,584. Our answer is **D**.

WRAP-UP

Two-way tables may seem confusing at first, but practice with the questions provided in the next sections will help immensely. Always be sure to read the information given in the blurb before or after the table. Good Luck!

SAT Red Math 261
Lesson 9B: Two-Way Tables – Probabilities and Frequencies

RED MATH LESSON 9B: TWO-WAY TABLES – PROBABILITIES AND FREQUENCIES
Learning to Swim

Directions: Answer each question below.

PRACTICE SET 1 (CALCULATOR)

	Spanish	French	Chinese	Total
Grade 9	0.08	0.11	0.10	0.29
Grade 10	0.06	0.08	0.09	0.23
Grade 11	0.05	0.07	0.11	0.23
Grade 12	0.10	0.09	0.06	0.25
Total	0.29	0.35	0.36	1

Use the table above for questions 1 and 2.

1. Given that a student is in the 12th grade, what is the probability that he or she takes French?

2. Among students in the 11th grade, there are 48 more students taking Chinese than Spanish. How many students in the high school take Spanish?

	A	B	C	D	Total
People 20 years old and under	32	36	20	20	108
21- to 40-year-olds	36	76	24	12	148
41- to 60-year-olds	40	36	20	8	104
People 61 years old and over	12	12	8	8	40
Total	120	160	72	48	400

Use the table above for questions 3 through 5. The table above shows the results of a survey conducted by a restaurant researching the popularity of four new dishes that it has added to its menu. The restaurant gave samples to randomly selected individuals.

3. Let X be the probability that a person is 61 years old or over given that he or she selected dish C. Let Y be the probability that a person selected dish C given that he or she is 61 years old or over. What is the value of $\frac{X}{Y}$?

4. What is the probability that a person is between 41 and 60 years old or selected dish B?

5. The restaurant decides to conduct the survey with 100 new people and without including dish D. If the distribution of ages and preferences remains the same, and the people who would have chosen D instead chose A, B, or C in the same proportion as people did originally, how many people in the new survey would be expected to select dish A? (Round to the nearest whole number.)

Version 3.0

SAT Red Math
Lesson 9B: Two-Way Tables – Probabilities and Frequencies

RED MATH LESSON 9B: TWO-WAY TABLES – PROBABILITIES AND FREQUENCIES
Diving into the Deep End

Directions: Answer each question below.

PRACTICE SET 2 (CALCULATOR)

	Myers	Suzuki	Lopez	Total
County A	129	312	59	500
County B	43	179	278	500
County C	78	209	213	500
Total	250	700	550	1500

Questions 6 and 7 use the table above. A congressional district consists of three counties. A company conducted a poll of 500 likely voters from each county and recorded the candidate preference of each respondent, as shown in the table.

6. Which event described below has the lowest expected probability?
   A) A respondent who prefers Suzuki is chosen at random, and that person lives in County A.
   B) A respondent who lives in County A is chosen at random, and that person prefers Suzuki.
   C) A respondent who prefers Lopez is chosen at random, and that person lives in County B.
   D) A respondent who lives in County B is chosen at random, and that person prefers Lopez.

7. The three counties do not have equal numbers of likely voters. If the same total number of people had been surveyed, but the poll had used a weighted sample instead, the sample would have included 298 people from County A, 669 from County B, and 533 from County C. Based on this information and the table above, if 30,000 people vote in the election, approximately how many will vote for Myers?
   A) 4350
   B) 5000
   C) 5650
   D) 6300

	Forest	Plains	Desert	Total
Georgia	34,000	23,000	1,000	58,000
Kansas	11,000	69,000	2,000	82,000
Nevada	8,000	44,000	58,000	110,000
Texas	52,000	115,000	94,000	261,000
Total	105,000	251,000	155,000	511,000

Questions 8 through 10 use the table above, which shows the results of a geographic survey on how many square miles of each state is forest (plants above 10 feet tall), plains (plants below 10 feet tall), or desert (no significant plant life).

8. If a point is chosen at random in each state, which would be most likely?
   A) The point in Nevada would not have significant plant life.
   B) The point in Nevada would have significant plant life.
   C) The point in Georgia would be in forest.
   D) The point in Texas would be in plains.

9. If the data for Kansas are removed from the table, what would happen to the probability of a randomly chosen point from among the given states being in plains?
   A) It would decline by about 13 percentage points.
   B) It would decline by about 7 percentage points.
   C) It would decline by about 1 percentage point.
   D) It would increase by about 9 percentage points.

Lesson 9B: Two-Way Tables – Probabilities and Frequencies

10. A randomly chosen 1 square mile plot of land from the state of Texas was found to be desert. What is the probability that that plot of land is adjacent to a plot of 1 square mile plot of land that is made up of forest or plains?
    A) 0.09
    B) 0.36
    C) 0.64
    D) It is impossible to determine from the information given.

	Short-Period	Long-Period	Total
Small	68	12	80
Medium	44	23	67
Large	21	15	36
Total	133	50	183

Questions 11 through 13 use the table above with information about observed comets size and orbital period.

11. A short-period comet and a long-period comet are chosen at random from the observations. Which is least likely?
    A) The long-period comet is small.
    B) The short-period comet is medium-sized.
    C) The long-period comet is large.
    D) The short-period comet is large.

12. If the data above is considered representative of all comets in the solar system, and scientists have discovered 4,000 comets in the solar system, approximately how many of these comets are medium-sized with short periods?
    A) 500
    B) 960
    C) 1320
    D) 1460

13. Given that a randomly selected comet has a long period, what is the probability that that comet is large-sized?
    A) 0.08
    B) 0.20
    C) 0.30
    D) 0.42

	Voted for A	Voted for B	Voted on Neither	Total
Male	153	63	18	234
Female	47	82	122	251
Total	200	145	140	485

Questions 14 and 15 use the table above. A survey was conducted among a randomly chosen sample of Washington voters about whether or not they voted on two resolutions, A and B. The table below displays a summary of the survey results.

14. Given that a Washington voter voted on neither resolution, what is the expected probability that the voter is female? Round to the nearest whole percent.

15. Given that the above sample is representative of Washington voters as a whole, and the fact that there are approximately 3.9 million active, registered voters in the state of Washington, approximately how many million people would be expected to vote on Resolution A or B? Round to the nearest tenth of a million.

SAT Red Math
Lesson 9B: Two-Way Tables – Probabilities and Frequencies

PRACTICE SET 3 (CALCULATOR)

	Sciences	Arts	Business	Total
Male	622	442	357	1421
Female	451	497	436	1384
Total	1073	939	793	2805

Questions 16 through 18 refer to the above table which shows the numbers of male and female students majoring in each of three areas at a college.

16. Which of the following probabilities is highest?
    A) A sciences major chosen at random is female.
    B) An arts major chosen at random is female.
    C) A business major chosen at random is female.
    D) A female student chosen at random is an arts major.

17. A survey gathers the opinions of 500 male students who participated in the above survey. Of these, 225 say they are in favor of a proposal to build a new student center. Approximately how many male students from the original survey are expected to be in favor of the proposal?
    A) 110
    B) 480
    C) 640
    D) 1260

18. Of the students of the college, 15% major in a field of study besides Sciences, Arts, or Business. If the male-to-female ratio of the table above is roughly indicative of the college as a whole, approximately how many males major in another field of study?
    A) 213
    B) 244
    C) 250
    D) 494

	Full Leaves	Partial Leaves	No Leaves	Total
Oak	56	16	44	116
Elm	36	40	21	97
Cottonwood	4	12	34	50
Aspen	109	63	40	212
Total	209	131	139	475

Questions 19 through 21 refer to the table above, which shows the results of a survey a scientist took of randomly selected individuals of four species of deciduous trees in a West Virginian forest at one point in mid-autumn.

19. Ten trees are chosen at random from each of the four species. About how many of the chosen trees would be expected to have full leaves?
    A) 11
    B) 15
    C) 18
    D) 20

20. Which of the following expected probabilities is highest?
    A) A tree with no leaves chosen at random is an oak.
    B) A tree with no leaves chosen at random is a cottonwood.
    C) A tree with full leaves chosen at random is an aspen.
    D) A tree with partial leaves chosen at random is an aspen.

21. Further study has determined that approximately 50% of the elm trees with partial leaves and 80% of the elm trees with no leaves were infected with emerald ash borers, a type of beetle. None of the elm trees with full leaves were found to be infected. If the forest contains approximately 180,000 elm trees, how many would be expected to be infested with the emerald ash borer?
    A) 25,000
    B) 65,000
    C) 68,000
    D) 112,000

SAT Red Math
Lesson 9B: Two-Way Tables – Probabilities and Frequencies

	Candidate A	Candidate B	Did Not Vote	No Response	Total
District 1	1123	124	82	100	1429
District 2	852	354	53	163	1422
District 3	345	843	46	43	1277
District 4	725	4235	72	212	5244
Total	3045	5556	253	518	9372

Questions 22 through 25 refer to the table above. A survey was conducted among a randomly chosen sample of South Carolina voters from four different districts about candidate selection in the 2014 congressional elections.

22. According to the table, which district obtained the highest percentage of people voting for a single candidate?
    A) District 1
    B) District 2
    C) District 3
    D) District 4

23. Of the voters in District 4 who gave a response and reported voting, 500 people were selected at random to do a follow-up survey in which they were asked who they expected to win the election, regardless of whom they voted for. Of the 500 people, 389 chose Candidate A. Using the data from both the follow-up survey and the initial survey, which of the following is most likely to be an accurate statement?
    A) Of the 200,000 registered voters in District 4, at least 147,173 would predict Candidate A to win the election.
    B) Of the 2,600,000 registered voters in South Carolina, approximately 2,000,000 would predict Candidate A to win the election.
    C) Of the 200,000 registered voters in District 4, approximately 155,000 would predict Candidate B to win the election.
    D) Of the 450,000 registered voters in Districts 1, 2, 3, and 4, approximately 350,000 would predict Candidate A to win the election.

24. Provided that a voter in the initial survey voted for Candidate B, what is the probability that that voter was from District 2 or 3? Round to the nearest whole percent.

25. Each of the voters who did not respond to the survey voted in the election, but did not want to reveal his or her vote. Within each district, these voters maintained the same ratio of votes for Candidate A to votes for Candidate B as found in the initial survey. Approximately how many people surveyed, to the nearest ten people, voted for Candidate A in all?

Version 3.0

SAT Red Math
Lesson 9B: Two-Way Tables – Probabilities and Frequencies

RED MATH LESSON 9B: TWO-WAY TABLES – PROBABILITIES AND FREQUENCIES
Race to the Finish

Directions: Answer each question below.

HOMEWORK SET (CALCULATOR)

	Stay in State	Leave the State	Total
Snow Boarders	60	45	105
Skiers	30	70	100
Total	90	115	205

Use the table above for questions 1 through 3.

1. At the beginning of each snow season, hordes of snowboarders and skiers flock to the slopes both in and out of state. Using the data in the table above, given that the person is a snow boarder, what is the probability that he/she will stay in state?
   A) 0.43
   B) 0.44
   C) 0.57
   D) 0.67

2. What is the probability that a randomly selected person on the slopes is a skier from out of state?
   A) 0.34
   B) 0.39
   C) 0.56
   D) 0.61

	Stay in State	Leave the State	Total
Snow boarders	a	b	0.51
Skiers	0.15	0.34	d
Total	c	0.56	1.00

3. Using the data in the table above, fill out the probabilities above:
   A) $a = 0.67, b = 0.39, c = 0.44, d = 0.50$
   B) $a = 0.29, b = 0.22, c = 0.44, d = 0.49$
   C) $a = 0.67, b = 0.33, c = 1.00, d = 0.49$
   D) $a = 0.57, b = 0.30, c = 0.44, d = 0.49$

	Intend to take part	Do not intend to take part
Water	13	5
Soda	2	11
No Preference	6	12

Use the table above and the information below for questions 4 through 6.

Eric is planning a work picnic and needs to determine how much water and soda to bring. He emails his coworkers to ask which beverage they prefer and if they plan to play in the company softball game. A small portion of Eric's coworkers responded to his email, of which a randomly-selected sample is shown above.

4. What is the probability that someone from Eric's company both intends to play softball and drink soda? Round to the nearest percent.
   A) 2%
   B) 4%
   C) 10%
   D) 15%

5. Of the people who responded to Eric's email, 56 do not intend to take part in the company softball game. If only 14% of Eric's coworkers responded to the email, how many coworkers does Eric have?
   A) 14
   B) 98
   C) 114
   D) 700

6. Using the data from the sample on the previous page, which of the following is most likely to be an accurate statement?

   A) Eric's coworkers who play softball are more likely than those who don't play softball to prefer water to soda.
   B) Eric's coworkers largely have no preference about what they drink.
   C) People who do not play sports prefer soda more than people who do play sports do.
   D) People who play softball will generally drink water if given the option.

	Boys	Girls
Engineering	7	5
Medicine	6	12
Liberal Arts	4	10
Other	3	3

Use the table above for questions 7 through 9. Jessica is a senior getting ready for college and she is trying to decide what major to choose. She decides to ask a random sample of 50 her classmates who she knows plan to attend college what they plan to be major in.

7. If a random student chosen from Jessica's class is intending to major in something other than engineering, medicine, or liberal arts, is it more likely that he or she will be a boy or a girl and why?
   A) Boy, because 15% of boys choose a major defined as other.
   B) Girl, because 15% of girls choose a major defined as other.
   C) Girl, because 10% of girls choose a major defined as other.
   D) It is equally likely that they will be a boy or a girl, because 50% of students majoring in something defined as other are boys and 50% are girls.

8. What is the expected probability that a student chosen from Jessica's class at random would plan on studying engineering?
   A) 12%
   B) 24%
   C) 26%
   D) 32%

9. If Jessica is one of 500 students in her class, 80% of whom will attend college, approximately how many students in her class are expected to be planning to major in medicine?
   A) 120
   B) 144
   C) 180
   D) 204

Education Level	Men	Women	Total
No education	4,215	6,379	10,594
Primary level	3,332	4,514	7,846
Secondary level	4,330	4,464	8,794
Higher level	1,886	880	2,766
Total	13,763	16,237	30,000

Use the table above for questions 10 through 12. The table summarizes a study on education levels among a population of 30,000.

10. Which of the following is the greatest within this group?
    A) The percentage of women with no education
    B) The percentage of people with secondary education who are female
    C) The percentage of men with no education
    D) The percentage of people with no education who are men

11. If two people from the population were randomly selected, which of the following combinations would be most probable?
    A) One man with no education and one woman with primary education
    B) One man with higher education and one woman with no education
    C) One man with secondary education and one woman with secondary education
    D) One woman with no education and one woman with higher education

12. If one person from the population was randomly selected, which of the following situations would be most probable?
    A) One man with no education or one woman with higher education
    B) One man with primary education or one man with secondary education
    C) One woman with primary education or one woman with secondary education
    D) One man with higher education or one woman with no education

	Team Sport	No Team Sport	Total
Musical Instrument	0.13	0.20	a
No Musical Instrument	b	c	0.67
Total	0.56	d	1.00

Use the above chart for questions 13 through 15. The information is drawn from a high school survey on extracurricular activities. Approximately 4,800 students attend the high school at which the survey was given, and the survey was a representative sample of the entire school.

13. Which series of percentages correctly fills in the rest of the chart?
    A) $a = 0.33, b = 0.69, c = 0.02, d = 0.44$
    B) $a = 0.07, b = 0.43, c = 0.64, d = 0.56$
    C) $a = 0.07, b = 0.43, c = 0.80, d = 0.44$
    D) $a = 0.33, b = 0.43, c = 0.24, d = 0.44$

14. When picking two students at random, which situation is most likely based on the data from the survey?
    A) One student plays a musical instrument and a team sport; one student plays a musical instrument but no team sport
    B) One student plays a musical instrument and a team sport; one student plays a team sport but no musical instrument
    C) One student plays no team sport and no musical instrument; one student plays a musical instrument but no team sport
    D) One student plays a team sport but no musical instrument; one student plays no team sport and no musical instrument

15. If 30% of the students at that school are freshmen, approximately how many freshmen are expected to not play a team sport? Assume there is no correlation between grade level and whether or not a student plays a sport.
    A) 634
    B) 806
    C) 1478
    D) 1880

	Plan to Try Out for Basketball Team	Does Not Plan to Try Out for Basketball Team	Total
below 5'4"	1	3	4
5'5" – 5'9"	2	4	6
5'10" – 6'1"	3	6	9
6'1" and up	6	2	8
Total	12	15	27

Use the above chart for questions 16 through 17. A random sample of freshmen boys at Breckenridge High School were grouped by height and surveyed as to whether or not they plan to try out for this year's basketball team. The results are shown the table above.

16. The basketball coach plans to extrapolate the data of this survey to all of the boys in the school to determine how many people to expect at try-outs this year. Is this a good idea, and why or why not?
    A) Yes, the heights of the members of the freshmen class should be representative of the heights of the members of all of the school.
    B) Yes, the willingness to play basketball of the members of the freshmen class should be representative of the willingness to play basketball of the members of the entire school.
    C) No, the heights and willingness to try out for the basketball team of freshmen boys are not necessarily representative of the boys of the school as a whole.
    D) No, there are more boys in the other three classes than there are in the freshman class.

17. Of the 270 members of the freshman class, approximately half are boys. If the sample above is representative of all of the boys in the class, approximately how many boys who are between 70 and 73 inches tall would be expected to try out for the basketball team?

SAT Red Math
Lesson 9B: Two-Way Tables – Probabilities and Frequencies

	Candidate A	Candidate B	Candidate C	Did Not Vote	Total
18- to 30-year-olds	86	54	21	58	219
31- to 50-year-olds	340	115	100	23	578
51- to 70-year-olds	300	113	77	17	507
71 years old and over	93	63	36	4	196
Total	819	345	234	102	1500

Questions 18 through 20 refer to the table above. A stratified survey was conducted among a randomly chosen sample of Texas voters from four different age groups in the 2012 presidential elections. The results are considered representative of the 13.6 million registered voters in the state of Texas.

18. To the nearest percent, what percent of the Texas voters above the age of 50 voted for either Candidate B or C?

19. Approximately 51.3 percent of the 26.5 million Texas citizens are registered to vote. In millions, how many Texans were expected to not vote in the election?

20. Given that a registered Texas voter did not vote, what is the expected probability that that voter is under the age of 50? Round to the nearest whole percent.

RED MATH LESSON 10A: PRACTICE SECTIONS
Learning to Swim

Directions: Answer each question below.

PRACTICE SET 1 (NO CALCULATOR)

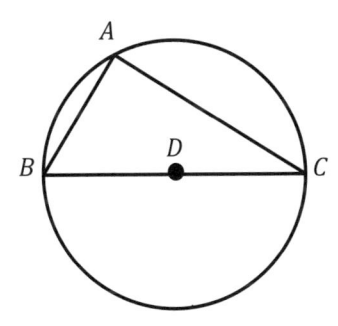

1. In the diagram above, $\overline{BC}$ is a diameter of Circle D. If the radius of Circle D is 5, the length of $\overline{AC}$ is 8, what percent of the area of the circle falls outside of $\triangle ABC$?

2. If $\sin\theta = \frac{4}{5}$ and $\frac{\pi}{2} \leq \theta \leq \frac{3\pi}{2}$, what is $\cos\theta$?

3. The "loudness" of a sound, dB, is measured in decibels. The formula for loudness is $dB = 10\log I$, where I measures how many times more intense a sound is than the threshold for hearing. For example, the decibel level of a sound which is 10 times the threshold of sound would be given as $dB = 10\log 10$. If the average loudness of a library is 40 decibels, how many times louder than the threshold of sound is that library?

$$y^2 - x + 7 = 2$$
$$x - 3y = 3$$

4. What is the sum of the x-values of the solutions to the above system of equations?

$$f(x) = \frac{2x^3 - x^2 - 8x + 4}{x^2 - x - 6}?$$

5. What are the horizontal and vertical asymptotes of the above function?

Red Math Lesson 10A: Practice Sections
Diving into the Deep End

Directions: Answer each question below.

Practice Set 2 (Calculator)

6. An election poll is estimated by statisticians to have a 2.6 percentage-point *margin of error*; that is, the actual percent of votes received by a given candidate is expected to be within 2.6 percentage points of the percent of polled voters who indicate they plan to vote for that candidate. If the poll predicts the candidate will receive 48.3% of the vote, and a total of 20,000 votes are cast in the actual election, the number of votes V received by the candidate is predicted to satisfy which of the following inequalities?
    A) $|V - 0.483| \leq 0.026$
    B) $|V - 0.483(20,000)| \leq 0.026(20,000)$
    C) $\left|\frac{V - 0.483}{20000}\right| \leq 0.026$
    D) $|V - 0.026(20,000)| \leq 0.483(20,000)$

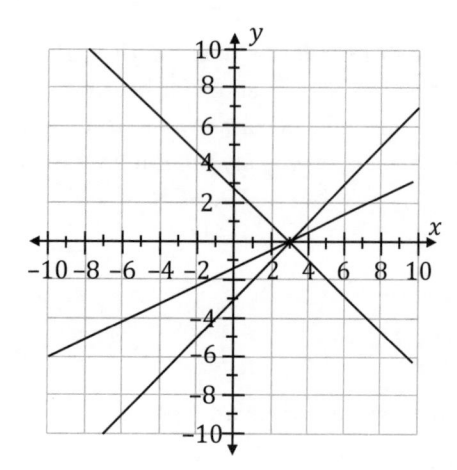

7. Three lines intersect at (3,0) in the coordinate plane above. If each of their equations is written in the form $Ax + By = C$, which of the following quantities must be equal for all three lines?
    A) A
    B) C
    C) $\frac{C}{A}$
    D) $\frac{C}{B}$

8. How many mL of a solution that is 5% hydrochloric acid (HCl) and 95% water must be combined with 45 mL of a solution that is 1% HCl and 99% water to produce a solution that is 2% HCl and 98% water?
    A) 9
    B) 15
    C) 18
    D) 60

9. A printer takes 10 seconds to print one page. How many such printers, all of them working simultaneously, are needed to print 140 copies of a 144-page book in 8 hours?
    A) 7
    B) 42
    C) 56
    D) 70

$$x = \frac{x^2 - 9}{7 - x} + 3$$

10. If the equation above is true, what is a possible value of x?
    A) 2
    B) 4
    C) 5
    D) 10

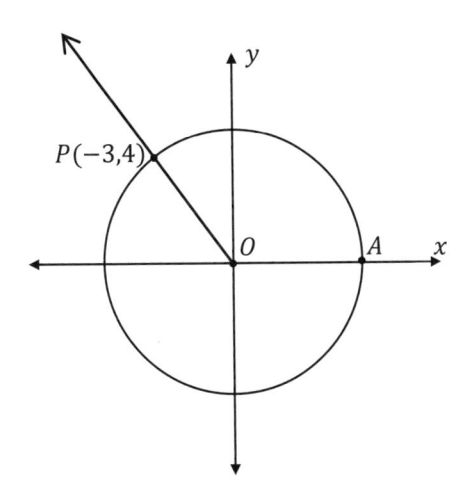

SAT Red Math | 275
Lesson 10A: Practice Sections

11. Circle O depicted above is centered at the origin, and ray $\overrightarrow{OP}$ passes through the point $P(-3,4)$ such that $m\angle AOP = \theta$, where θ is measured in radians. What is the value of $\sin(2\pi - \theta)$?
   A) -0.8
   B) -0.75
   C) -0.6
   D) 0.8

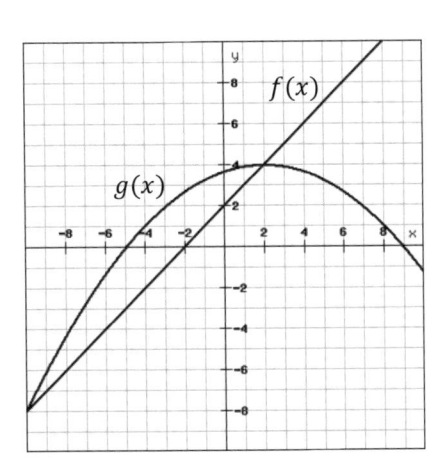

Use the above graph for questions 12 and 13.

12. If $f(k) = g(-4)$, what is the value of k?
   A) -8
   B) -6
   C) -1
   D) 1

13. Which of the following is $y = g(f(x))$?
   A) 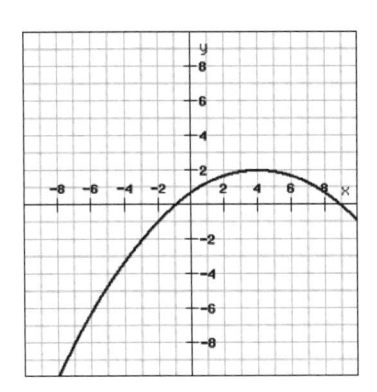
   B) 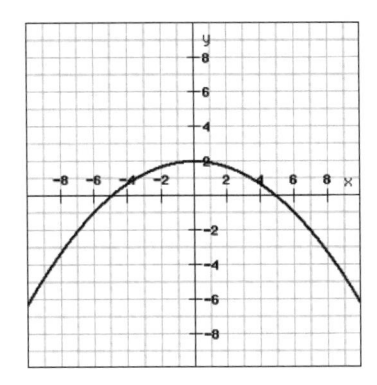
   C) 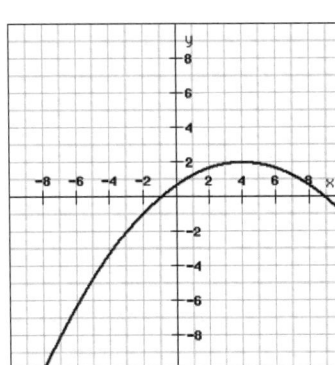
   D)

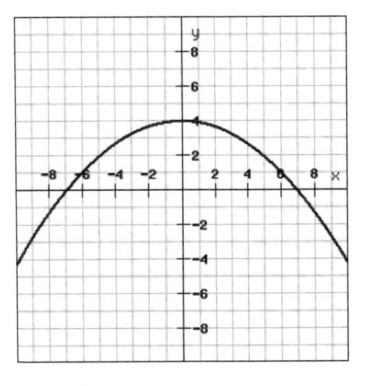

14. A cylindrical hole 1 cm wide and 3 cm deep is drilled into a face of a wooden block of length 11 cm, width 9 cm, and height 7 cm. If the density of the wood is 0.85 g/cm³, what is the mass of the block to the nearest gram? (Density = mass ÷ volume)

15. If $(2x + c)^2 = (3x + 2)^2 - 5x^2 + 5$ for all real values of x, what is the value of c?

Practice Set 3 (Calculator)

16. Sarah received a payment of $2250 today. After taking a finance course, she deposits her $2250 in an account that pays an annual interest rate of 6.54% compounded monthly. What will be its value in 30 years?
    A) $2294.99
    B) $2648.48
    C) $15050.93
    D) $15920.43

17. The typical graph of $f(x) = x^2$ is transformed by a reflection over the x-axis, a vertical shift upwards 4 units, a horizontal shift to the right 3 units, a vertical stretch by a factor of 5, and a horizontal compression by a factor of 2. Which of the following functions most accurately describes this transformation?
    A) $f(x) = -\frac{1}{5}\left(\frac{x-3}{2}\right)^2 + 4$
    B) $f(x) = -5(2x - 6)^2 + 4$
    C) $f(x) = -\frac{1}{5}(2x + 3)^2 + 4$
    D) $f(x) = -5\left(\frac{x+3}{2}\right)^2 + 4$

18. A circle is placed on the coordinate plane such that it passes through the points $(4, 1)$ and $(6, 5)$. Provided that the center of the circle lies on the line $4x + y = 16$, what is the circle's radius?
    A) $\sqrt{6}$
    B) $2\sqrt{2}$
    C) $\sqrt{10}$
    D) $\sqrt{12}$

19. Suppose that the circle in question 18 contains a minor arc with arc length 8. What angle does the arc create inside the circle?
    A) 2.31 radians
    B) 144.9°
    C) 2.83 radians
    D) 187.1°

$$y - 6x + 1 = 3x^2$$
$$x + y = 9$$

20. What is a possible product of the x- and y-coordinates of a solution to the system of equations above?
    A) $-\frac{370}{9}$
    B) $-\frac{109}{3}$
    C) $\frac{37}{9}$
    D) $\frac{61}{3}$

$$f(x) = x^7 + 3x^6 - 2x^3 - 6x^2$$

21. Which of the following statements is true about the above function?
    A) The roots of $f(x)$ are $x = -3, -\sqrt{2}, 0, \sqrt{2}$.
    B) $f(x)$ will have 7 real roots, since the highest power contained in it is 7.
    C) The function's end behavior rises on the right side and falls on the left side.
    D) There is not enough information given to verify any of the above statements.

$$x = \frac{-b \pm \sqrt{b^2 - 4ac}}{2a}$$

22. The quadratic formula is listed above, which of the following expresses c in terms of a, b, and x?
    A) $-(ax^2 - bx)$
    B) $-(ax^2 + bx)$
    C) $\frac{(2ax+b)^2}{-4a}$
    D) $\frac{(2ax+b)^2}{4a}$

23. If $\tan \theta = \frac{3x}{\sqrt{27x^2 - 72x + 36}}$, what is the value of $\sin \theta$?
    A) $\frac{x}{2(x-1)}$
    B) $\frac{x}{3x-1}$
    C) $\frac{x}{3(3x-2)}$
    D) $\frac{3x}{x+6}$

24. A cake decorator wants to cover the side of a circular cake that is 8 inches across and 5 inches high with frosting. The recipe requires 1 part butter to 9 parts sugar. One batch covers an area of 20 square inches. To the nearest tenth of a cup, how many cups of sugar will the decorator need?

$$1 + \sqrt{4x + 13} = 2x$$

25. What is the product of the solution(s) to the above equation?

RED MATH LESSON 10A: PRACTICE SECTIONS
Race to the Finish

Directions: Answer each question below.

HOMEWORK SET (CALCULATOR)

1. Jackie is receiving $2000 as part of an annuity payout. What will be the total value of this amount in 10 years if the annual interest rate is 7.44%?
   A) $2127.52
   B) $4099.11
   C) $4199.02
   D) $4208.67

	Density (in g/cm³)
Calcium	1.54
Beryllium	1.85
Magnesium	1.73

2. A group of chemists have uncovered a mysterious metal. They want to identify if the substance is a new metallic element or if they discovered an element that has already been found. The mass of the metal is 147 kg, and its volume is 3 ft³. Based on that, as well as the table above, what metallic element have the chemists uncovered?
   A) Calcium
   B) Beryllium
   C) Magnesium
   D) An unknown metallic element.

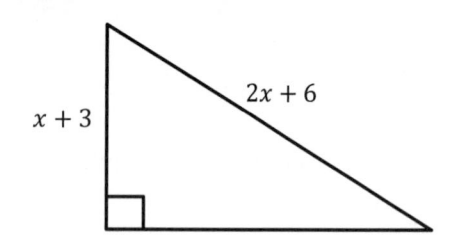

3. The perimeter of the triangle above is $24 + 8\sqrt{3}$. What is its area?
   A) 124
   B) $32\sqrt{3}$
   C) $72 + 16\sqrt{3}$
   D) It cannot be determined from the given information.

4. In 1990, the population of New Jersey was approximately 7.8 million people, and by 2013, the population increased by approximately 1.1 million people. If the formula for population growth is $P = P_o e^{rt}$ where P_o is the initial population at a chosen starting year, r is the growth rate of that population, and t is the number of years since the starting year, and if the growth rate of New Jersey's population does not change, what will the population of New Jersey be in 2016?
   A) Approximately 8,901,600
   B) Approximately 9,054,000
   C) Approximately 9,073,000
   D) Approximately 9,160,000

5. If a and b are positive integers and $(a + bi)(a - bi) = 25$, then $a + b = ?$
   A) 4
   B) 5
   C) 7
   D) 25

$$\frac{-4}{y-3} + 1 = \frac{-10}{y^2+y-12}$$

6. Solve the above equation.
   A) $y = -3$ or $y = -6$
   B) $y = -3$ or $y = 6$
   C) $y = 3$ or $y = -6$
   D) $y = 3$ or $y = 6$

	Livia	Penny	Yunjin
Median	10	10	10
Mean	12	10	8
Mode	0	8	10
Standard Deviation	8.0	4.0	2.7

Questions 7 and 8 use the above table. Livia, Penny, and Yunjin are on the same basketball team. They keep track of the points they have scored in each of the team's 20 games. The results are shown above.

7. Based on the information above, which of the following statements is most likely true?
   A) Livia scored more points in her 3 highest-scoring games than either of the others did in their 3 highest-scoring games.
   B) Livia scored 10 or more points more times than either of the other players.
   C) Penny scored between 10 and 12 points, inclusive, more often than the other players.
   D) Yunjin scored the most total points of the three players.

8. The team's coach gives out an award to the "most consistent player," which she defines as the player who scores roughly the same number of points in each game. Which of the players would be the best candidate for this award, and why?
   A) Livia, because her scores have the highest standard deviation.
   B) Penny, because her mean score is the same as her median score.
   C) Yunjin, because her scores have the lowest standard deviation.
   D) Yunjin, because her mode score is the same as her median score.

9. If $1 + \frac{1}{d} + \frac{1}{d^2} + \frac{1}{d^3} = 1$, what is the value of $d^2 + d + 1$?
   A) -1
   B) 0
   C) 1
   D) 2

$$10e^{3x+7} = 4e^{-x+5}$$

10. Which of the following expressions is a solution to the above equation?
    A) $x = \frac{1}{4}\ln\left(\frac{4}{10}\right) - \frac{1}{2}$
    B) $x = -\frac{50}{34}$
    C) $x = \frac{1}{2}\ln\left(\frac{4}{10}\right) - 6$
    D) $x = \frac{\ln(4)}{\ln(10)} + 12$

11. If $e^{i\theta} = \cos\theta + i\sin\theta$ for all θ expressed in radians, what is the value of $4e^{i\frac{\pi}{6}} \cdot 6e^{i\frac{11\pi}{6}}$?
    A) -24
    B) 8
    C) 12
    D) 24

12. If $2 - \frac{1}{4}x^2 > mx + b$ implies $-2 < x < 4$, what is the value of m?
    A) -2
    B) $-\frac{1}{2}$
    C) $\frac{1}{2}$
    D) Cannot be determined from the information provided.

Carsten, who lives in Bruges, Belgium, and Leila, who lives in Sluis, Netherlands, x feet away, decide to ride their bikes along the canal towpath to meet each other somewhere in the middle. Carsten travels at a constant rate of r_1 feet per minute and Leila travels at a rate of r_2 feet per minute.

13. Which of the following expressions gives their distance from Bruges when they meet?
    A) $x - \frac{r_1 x}{r_2}$
    B) $\frac{xr_1}{r_1+r_2}$
    C) $\frac{xr_2}{r_1+r_2}$
    D) $\frac{(r_1+r_2)x}{r_1}$

Use the following information for questions 14 and 15:

223	273
174	201
285	126
237	299
250	263
117	223
192	254
258	298

14. Jesse makes a histogram of the temperature data above by breaking the temperatures into 25 degree intervals over a range of 100 degrees to 300 degrees Fahrenheit. What does he notice when he plots his data?
    A) The temperatures are evenly spread over the entire range.
    B) The temperatures are concentrated both at the high and low extremes of the temperature ranges.
    C) The temperatures seem to skew left.
    D) The temperatures seem to skew right.

15. If the engine in Jesse's truck requires a temperature under 300 degrees Fahrenheit to operate safely, which of the following will guarantee safe operation of the truck?
    A) No additional steps are required, as the truck did not exceed the limit during testing, and 300 degrees falls outside the standard deviation range of the mean.
    B) Installing a thermal dampener that will lower the standard deviation of the engine temperature by 10 degrees, and thus make the truck's performance more consistent.
    C) Using an oil additive that will lower the average temperature of the engine by 10 degrees.
    D) Installing an engine cutoff switch that will prevent the engine from going more than 50 degrees over the median temperature from the data.

Use the following information for questions 16 through 18:

State	Players	Goals
Minnesota	173	1310
Michigan	121	872
Massachusetts	75	604
Other	31	290
Total	400	3076

The above table shows the distribution of states that are represented in the fictitious American Hockey Association (AHA), a hockey league that only allows players from America. The number of players from each state and goals scored by those players are recorded. Assume that the AHA's overall distribution is representative of each AHA team's distribution, and that there is a correlation between the number of goals a player scores and his home state.

16. If 40 players played for the AHA's Denver Punishers, then which of the following is the least likely combination of players by home state?
    A) 18 from Minnesota, 12 from Michigan, 8 from Massachusetts, and 2 from Other
    B) 20 from Minnesota, 10 from Michigan, 6 from Massachusetts, and 4 from Other
    C) 15 from Minnesota, 9 from Michigan, 8 from Massachusetts, and 8 from Other
    D) 16 from Minnesota, 13 from Michigan, 8 from Massachusetts, and 3 from Other

17. The AHA's Memphis Icemen has 20 players from Minnesota, 10 from Michigan, 8 from Massachusetts, and 2 from other states. What is the expected number of total goals scored by the Memphis Icemen, to the nearest goal?

18. For the AHA All-Star Game, the home team is comprised of players only from Minnesota, and the road team is comprised of players from the rest of America. If each team has 25 players, then what is the expected number of players from Michigan playing for the road team to the nearest whole player?

19. If $a^2 - 14a = 15$ and $a < 0$, what is the value of $7 - a$?

20. The solutions to the equation $x^2 + 4x + 29 = 0$ are in the form $a \pm bi$, where $i = \sqrt{-1}$ and a and b are integers. What is the value of $a + b$?

RED MATH LESSON 10B: PRACTICE SECTIONS
Learning to Swim

Directions: Answer each question below.

PRACTICE SET 1 (NO CALCULATOR)

1. Nana drives to work in 45 minutes. On his way home, he takes the same route but chooses to drive at a more leisurely pace. If his average speed home is $\frac{5}{6}$ as fast as his average speed driving to work, how many seconds longer does it take him to return home?

$$\frac{x^4 - 2x^3 - 7x^2 + 8x + 12}{x^3 - x^2 - 6x} = 0$$

2. How many solutions does the above equation have?

3. Can H and can J are both right circular cylinders. The radius of can H is 2.5 times the radius of can J, while the height of can H is $\frac{2}{5}$ the height of can J. If it costs $9 to fill half of can J with the premium extra virgin olive oil, *olio nuovo*, how many dollars would it cost to fill can H completely with the same *olio nuovo*?

4. Line l is tangent to a circle which has a center at $(4, -5)$. If the point of tangency between line l and the circle is $(9, -8)$, what is the equation of line l?

5. If the sum of the interior angles of a regular polygon is $1080°$, how many sides does the polygon have?

Red Math Lesson 10B: Practice Sections
Diving into the Deep End

Directions: Answer each question below.

Practice Set 2 (Calculator)

6. The volume of a spherical weather balloon is 120,000 cubic feet. The balloon is completely covered with a special heat-reflecting polymer that costs $42.00 per square meter. What is the total cost, in dollars, of the entire polymer cover? Assume 1 inch =2.54 cm and round to the nearest thousand dollars. (The volume of a sphere is $\frac{4}{3}\pi r^3$, and the surface area of a sphere is $4\pi r^2$.)
   A) $46,000
   B) $117,000
   C) $121,000
   D) $245,000

7. A hemispherical bowl with inner radius 10 cm is filled with 15 grams of cereal with density 0.25 grams per milliliter. If 1 mL = 1 cm³, how many milliliters of milk can the bowl now hold?
   A) $\frac{200\pi}{3} - 60$
   B) $\frac{2000\pi}{3} - 60$
   C) $\frac{2000\pi}{3} - 3.25$
   D) $\frac{4000\pi}{3} - 60$

8. A cubical building is redesigned to increase its size. When the side of the cube was increased by 4 meters, the exposed surface area of the building (the four walls plus the roof) increased by 1000 square meters. What was the volume of the original building before the expansion?
   A) 225
   B) 576
   C) 1000
   D) 12,167

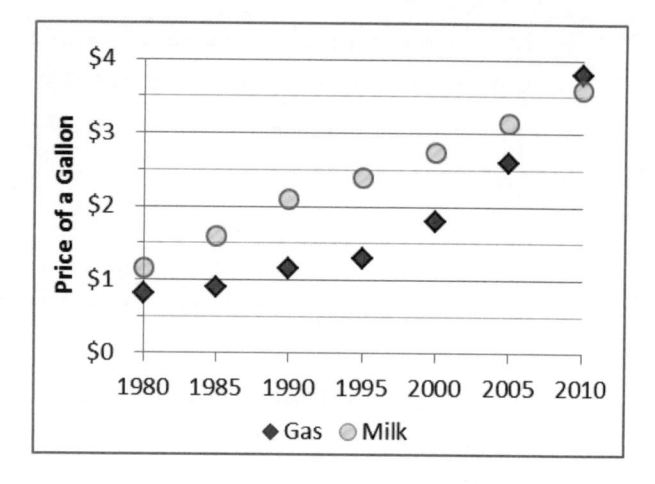

Questions 8 and 9 use the scatterplot above.

9. Which of the following accurately describes the curves of best fit for the two data sets?
   A) The curves of best fit for both data sets are linear.
   B) The curve of best fit for the price of gas is linear, and the curve of best fit for the price of milk is exponential.
   C) The curve of best fit for the price of gas is exponential, and the curve of best fit for the price of milk is linear.
   D) The curves of best fit for both data sets are exponential.

10. Assuming the trends in the above graph continue into the future, what is the best prediction for the price of a gallon of milk in the year 2020?
    A) Under $5 per gallon
    B) Between $5 and $6 per gallon
    C) Between $6 and $7 per gallon
    D) Over $7 per gallon

11. If X, Y, and Z are positive numbers and $Y < 100$, then the number obtained by increasing Z by X% and decreasing the result by Y% exceeds Z only if:
   A) $X > Y$
   B) $X > \dfrac{Y}{100-Y}$
   C) $X > \dfrac{Y}{1-Y}$
   D) $X > \dfrac{100Y}{100-Y}$

12. At how many points does the graph of $3x + y = 7$ intersect that of $x^2 + y^2 + 6x + 10y = 2$?
   A) 0
   B) 1
   C) 2
   D) 3

13. The function Z is the inverse of $f(x) = \dfrac{2x-3}{x+5}$. What is the value of $Z(x)$ at $x = 0$?
   A) $\dfrac{1}{4}$
   B) $\dfrac{2}{3}$
   C) $\dfrac{3}{2}$
   D) 2

14. Livia has borrowed $5,000 for her post-graduation trip to Europe. She will repay the entire amount of the loan by making one payment in 3 years, then another payment in 6 years. The second payment will be exactly double the amount of the first payment. How much is the first payment if the interest rate of the loan is 8.5%, compounded annually? Round to the nearest dollar.

15. Athena is training for a marathon race, and she must be able to complete a full marathon in 3 hours and 35 minutes before she can sign up. If she completed her last half-marathon in 2 hours, by what percent does her average speed need to increase to finish a full marathon at the same rate? Round your answer to the nearest tenth of a percent. (Note: 1 marathon = 26.2 mi.)

PRACTICE SET 3 (CALCULATOR)

16. What is the sum of all real values of x that satisfy the equation $|x + 2| = 2|x - 2|$?
    A) $\frac{1}{3}$
    B) $\frac{5}{3}$
    C) $\frac{20}{3}$
    D) $\frac{21}{5}$

17. A cup is 6 inches tall with an inner diameter of 3.5 inches at the top and 2.5 inches at the bottom with straight sides. If a fluid ounce is equal to 1.804 cubic inches, how many fluid ounces of soft drink can the cup hold (to the nearest hundredth)? (The volume of a cone is $\frac{1}{3}$ the volume of a cylinder with the same base and height.)
    A) 15.14 fl. oz.
    B) 18.04 fl. oz.
    C) 23.73 fl. oz.
    D) 95.67 fl. oz.

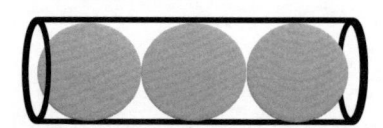

18. A cylindrical can contains three spherical tennis balls. The tennis balls are tangent to each other and to the walls of the container as indicated in the figure above. If the radius of each ball is 2 inches, what is the total volume of the space inside the cylinder not occupied by the tennis balls?
    A) $\frac{3\pi}{2}$
    B) 8π
    C) 16π
    D) $\frac{32\pi}{3}$

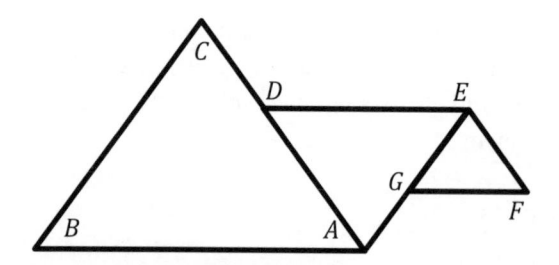

19. The ground floor of Gauss University's new mathematics department building consists of triangles ABC, ADE, EFG above, all of which are equilateral. Points D and G are midpoints of $\overline{AC}$ and $\overline{AE}$, respectively. The side of the largest triangle is 16 meters. The floor will be covered with equilateral triangle floor tiles which cost \$36 per tile. The tiles have sides of one meter. How much will it cost to cover the entire floor of the mathematics building?
    A) \$6,048
    B) \$12,096
    C) \$24,192
    D) \$96,768

20. Three constants $A, B,$ and C satisfy the equation $\frac{3x-2}{x^3+2x^2+x} = \frac{A}{x} + \frac{B}{x+1} + \frac{C}{(x+1)^2}$. What is the value of the product ABC?
    A) -36
    B) -20
    C) 20
    D) 36

21. Jung Uk buys a painting for \$700, and sells it to Sarah for a 30% profit. If Sarah sells it to Sanjeevi for \$700, what was the percentage of Sarah's loss?
    A) 23%
    B) 30%
    C) 60%
    D) 90%

	Chocolate	Vanilla	Strawberry
Democrat	26	43	13
Republican	45	12	8
Independent	9	13	4

22. The above table shows the results of a study that asked 173 people for their political affiliation and their favorite ice cream flavor. If another study was done of 300 Republicans, how many would be expected to prefer chocolate ice cream?
   A) 45
   B) 135
   C) 208
   D) 255

23. For which of the following would $f(g(x)) = x$?
   A) $f(x) = 2x - 3, g(x) = \frac{1}{2}x + 3$
   B) $f(x) = 2x - 3, g(x) = 2x + 3$
   C) $f(x) = 2x - 3, g(x) = \frac{x+3}{2}$
   D) $f(x) = 2x - 3, g(x) = \frac{x-3}{2}$

$$y = x^2 - 3x - 18$$
$$y = -2x + 2$$

24. If (x_1, y_1) and (x_2, y_2) are ordered pairs that satisfy the system of equations above, what is the sum of y_1 and y_2?

Salary	300	400	450	800	940	1050
Frequency	6	2	2	1	1	1

25. The frequency table above shows weekly salaries for employees at a consulting firm, including senior analysts, junior analysts, and office clerks. What is the positive difference between the mean and the median of the dataset? Round your answer to the nearest dollar.

SAT Red Math
Lesson 10B: Practice Sections

RED MATH LESSON 10B: PRACTICE SECTIONS
Race to the Finish

Directions: Answer each question below.

HOMEWORK SET (CALCULATOR)

$$N = N_0 \left(\frac{1}{2}\right)^{\frac{t}{t_{1/2}}}$$

1. A substance decays according to the half-life equation above, where N_0 is the initial amount of substance, in g, N is the amount of substance left after t days, and $t_{\frac{1}{2}}$ is the half-life of the substance in days. If there is a mass of 2 g left after 5 days, and 1.8 g left after 18 days, what is the length of the half-life?
   A) 13 days
   B) 85.5 days
   C) 130.7 days
   D) 258.3 days

2. A 60° sector is cut out of a circular piece of paper with radius 5 cm, and the remaining paper is formed into a cone by taping together the cut edges with no overlap. What is the volume of the resulting cone?
   A) 38.72 cm³
   B) 50.25 cm³
   C) 54.54 cm³
   D) 150.74 cm³

$$f(x) = \frac{x^2 - 5x + 6}{x^2 + 4x - 21}$$
$$g(x) = \frac{x^2 + x - 6}{x^2 + 7x + 12}$$

3. Given $f(x)$ and $g(x)$ above, what is the domain of $\frac{f(x)}{g(x)}$?
   A) All real numbers except -7
   B) All real numbers except -7 and -4
   C) All real numbers except $-7, -3, 2,$ and 3
   D) All real numbers except $-7, -4, -3, 2,$ and 3

4. A sector of a circle with a radius of 4 has a central angle of $\frac{\pi}{3}$. What is the arc length of the sector?
   A) $\frac{\pi}{3}$
   B) 4
   C) $\frac{4\pi}{3}$
   D) 3

5. What is the equation of a circle if the endpoints of a diameter of the circle are $(2, 8)$ and $(5, 4)$?
   A) $(x - 3.5)^2 + (y - 6)^2 = 6.25$
   B) $(x - 3.5)^2 + (y - 6)^2 = 25$
   C) $(x + 4)^2 + (y - 2)^2 = 16$
   D) $(x + 4)^2 + (y - 2)^2 = 8$

6. If $I = \frac{PN}{RN + A}$, what does N equal?
   A) $\frac{IR + IA}{P}$
   B) $\frac{IA}{P - IR}$
   C) $PR + IA$
   D) $\frac{PR}{IA}$

7. Which of the following is NOT a true statement regarding the function $y = 2\sin(x - 2) + 2$?
   A) The amplitude is 2.
   B) The vertical shift is 2 units in the positive y direction.
   C) The horizontal shift is 2 units in the negative x direction.
   D) The period is 2π.

SAT Red Math
Lesson 10B: Practice Sections

8. Determine the period (P), amplitude (A), and horizontal shift (h) of $y = \frac{3}{2}\sin(x+2)$.
   A) $P = \pi$, $A = 3$, $h = 2$ units to the left
   B) $P = \pi$, $A = 3$, $h = 2$ units to the right
   C) $P = 2\pi$, $A = \frac{3}{2}$, $h = 2$ units to the left
   D) $P = 2\pi$, $A = \frac{3}{2}$, $h = 2$ units to the right

	Rose	Tulip	Carnation	Total
Yellow/Orange	15	18	6	39
Pink/Red	48	21	18	87
Violet/Purple	24	30	18	72
Total	87	69	42	168

Questions 11 and 12 use the above information. A gardener counts the number of flowers of three types that are currently blooming in his garden and sorts them by color.

9. The electrostatic force between two charged particles is given by the equation $F = k\frac{q_1 q_2}{r^2}$, where F is the electrostatic force, k is the electrostatic constant, q_1 is the charge of particle 1, q_2 is the charge of particle 2, and r is the distance between the two particles. Which of the following changes would cause the electrostatic force to quadruple?
   A) Increasing q_1 by a factor of 2
   B) Decreasing r by a factor of 4
   C) Increasing q_1 by a factor of 2 and decreasing q_2 by a factor of 2
   D) Decreasing r by a factor of 2

11. Which of the following has the highest probability?
    A) A randomly chosen rose is violet or purple.
    B) A randomly chosen tulip is pink or red.
    C) A randomly chosen yellow or orange flower is a tulip.
    D) A randomly chosen pink or red flower is a carnation.

12. The gardener takes a random sample of 20 pink or red flowers. Of these, 11 are red and 9 are pink. What is the expected probability that a randomly selected rose will be red?
    A) 13%
    B) 19%
    C) 25%
    D) 30%

10. Tina's phone company currently charges a $40.00 monthly fee and allows 500 minutes of talking plus 1000 text messages. Additional minutes cost $0.05 per minute, and additional texts cost $0.02 per text. She is considering switching to another company to save money. This alternative company charges a $50.00 monthly fee and allows unlimited talking minutes and text messages. For which of the following usage rates would it be advisable for Tina to switch to the second company? Assume she wants to minimize her monthly fee.
    A) 630 minutes, 1000 texts
    B) 660 minutes, 900 texts
    C) 690 minutes, 800 texts
    D) 720 minutes, 700 texts

13. A car is currently stopped at a red light. When the light turns green, the car begins to accelerate at a constant rate while moving along the road. The car's speed with respect to time can be modeled using the equation $v = 10t$, where v represents the car's current speed and t represents the time elapsed since the light turned green. Which of the following statements regarding this situation is true?
    A) Graphing the car's position vs. time would exhibit a linear relationship.
    B) Graphing the car's speed vs. time would exhibit an exponential relationship.
    C) After the light turns green, the car moves along the road at a constant speed.
    D) During the period of acceleration, the car's speed increases by 10 units per unit time.

14. A bank offers 2% annual interest on certificates of deposit (CDs). This means that 2% of the initially deposited amount is added to the CD for each year that passes. Customers can choose an integer number of years at the beginning of the process, and the initial amount plus the accumulated interest will be available to them after the allotted time has passed. Which function type and equation would most appropriately model the accumulated interest from a CD? Assume I is interest, P is initially deposited amount, and t is time (years).
    A) Linear; $I = P(0.02t)$
    B) Quadratic; $I = P(0.02t^2)$
    C) Exponential; $I = Pe^{0.02t}$
    D) Sinusoidal; $I = P\sin(0.02t)$

15. It is widely accepted in the tech industry that the memory capacity of a computer chip doubles every 2 years. Which of the following functions most appropriately models this phenomenon? Assume M is memory capacity, M_0 is initial memory capacity, and t is time elapsed between M_0 and M (years).
    A) $M = M_0(2t)$
    B) $M = M_0(t^2)$
    C) $M = M_0\left(2^{\frac{t}{2}}\right)$
    D) $M = M_0(2^t)$

16. A bank offers 5% interest compounded semi-annually (twice a year). This can be quantified using the equation $Y = P\left(1 + \frac{r}{n}\right)^{nt}$, where Y is the final amount, P is the initial amount invested, r is the interest rate, n is the number of times per year the interest is compounded, and t is time in years. Which of the following expressions represents the number of years necessary to double one's initially deposited amount of money?
    A) $t = \frac{\ln(2)}{\ln(1.05)}$
    B) $t = \frac{1}{2}\left(\frac{\ln(2)}{\ln(1.05)}\right)$
    C) $t = \frac{1}{2}\left(\frac{\ln(2)}{\ln(1.025)}\right)$
    D) $t = \frac{1}{2}(\log_2 1.025)$

17. Jim wants to know what he needs to score on his last biology test to receive an A in the course. To receive an A, a student's average test score, rounded to the nearest integer, must be 90%. His first 4 test scores were 88, 94, 89, and 92. If each test is weighted equally, what is the lowest he can score on the last exam to receive an A in the course? Assume all test scores must be integer values.

18. What is the product of the solutions to the equation $(\log_2 x)^2 + \log_2(x^{-2}) = 8$?

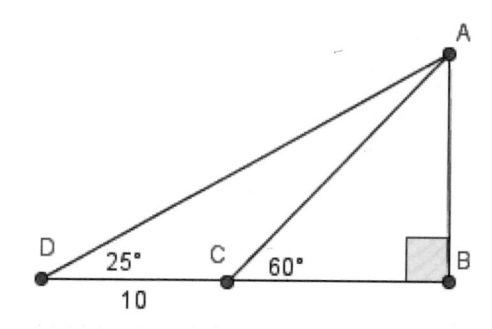

19. For the figure above, the length of line segment DC is 10. What is the area of triangle ABD, to the nearest whole number?

20. A cylinder with a height of 10 is inscribed in a sphere with a diameter of 14. What is the volume of the space outside the cylinder but inside the sphere (to the nearest whole number)?

RED MATH LESSON 11A: REVIEW OF ARITHMETIC AND ALGEBRAIC CONCEPTS
Learning to Swim

Directions: Answer each question below.

PRACTICE SET 1 (NO CALCULATOR)

$$v_f^2 = v_0^2 + 2a(\Delta x)$$

1. A test driver is overviewing the mechanics of a new car by driving it at a constant acceleration. His velocity at the end of the drive can be found by the equation above, where v_f is the driver's final velocity, v_0 is his initial velocity, a is his acceleration, and Δx is the distance of the track he is testing the car on. The driver wants to test the car on a straight track two times, and he also wants his velocity at the end of the second test to be double that of the first test. Assuming he starts initially at a velocity of 0 both times, what factor should he increase the acceleration by for the second test?

2. Using information from the previous question, for the first test, the driver achieves a final velocity of 30 m/s. If the track is 1200 meters, what is the difference between the driver's acceleration during the second test and that during the first test, in m/s²?

3. If $f(x) = 3x^2$ and $g(x) = \frac{3}{x^6}$, what is $f(g(x))$?

4. If $\frac{p}{2}$ is a solution to the equation $x^2 + 2x + 1 = 0$, what is the value of $-p^2 - 2p$?

5. If $a^2 - 3ab - 130b^2 = -120$ and $a + 10b = 15$, what is the value of $13b - a$?

Red Math Lesson 11A: Review of Arithmetic and Algebraic Concepts
Diving into the Deep End

Directions: Answer each question below.

Practice Set 2 (No Calculator)

6. If x laborers can dig d ditches in m minutes, how many ditches can y laborers dig in h hours?
   A) $\frac{xdm}{60yh}$
   B) $\frac{60ydm}{xh}$
   C) $\frac{ydh}{60xm}$
   D) $\frac{60ydh}{xm}$

$$\frac{1}{x} = \frac{y}{x-3}$$

7. Given the above equation, which of the following expressions is equivalent to x for all values of y?
   A) $\frac{y-1}{3}$
   B) $-\frac{3}{y}$
   C) $\frac{3}{1-y}$
   D) $1 - \frac{3}{y}$

8. A parking meter accepts only quarters. The first 20 minutes are free; after that, each quarter purchases an additional 12 minutes of parking time. Which of the following equations could be used to find h, the number of hours one can park at this meter for d dollars?
   A) $h = \frac{1}{3} + \frac{4}{5}d$
   B) $h = \frac{20+3d}{60}$
   C) $h = 20 + 12\left(\frac{d}{5}\right)$
   D) $h = \frac{1}{3} + \frac{d}{5}$

9. A speed of f feet per second is equal to a speed of i inches per minute. Which of the following equations correctly relates f and i?
   A) $i = \frac{f}{720}$
   B) $i = \frac{f}{5}$
   C) $i = 5f$
   D) $i = 720f$

10. A furniture shop buys defective pieces of furniture directly from their manufacturers at a discount of 34% off the normal wholesale price. The shop then repairs and refurbishes the furniture, and sells it at a 50% markup from what the shop paid for it. This price is still only 90% of the normal new retail price for undamaged pieces, which itself represents a 10% markup over the normal wholesale price. The shop that sells refurbished furniture sells furniture at a retail price that is what percent of the normal wholesale price?
    A) 51%
    B) 99%
    C) 100%
    D) 110%

11. If $\frac{a}{b} = \frac{3}{4}, \frac{d}{c} = \frac{4}{7}$, and $a = 3d$, which of the following is equal to $\frac{c}{b}$?
    A) 0.4375
    B) 0.5625
    C) 1.3125
    D) 3.9375

Lesson 11A: Review of Arithmetic and Algebraic Concepts

12. If $-\frac{1}{3} \leq c \leq -\frac{1}{4}$ and $-\frac{1}{5} \leq d \leq -\frac{1}{6}$, what is the minimum value of $c^2 d$?

    A) $-\frac{1}{96}$
    B) $-\frac{1}{54}$
    C) $-\frac{1}{45}$
    D) $-\frac{1}{36}$

13. In a mayoral election, the winner received $\frac{5}{6}$ of the ballots cast. The runner-up received $\frac{7}{8}$ of the remaining ballots, and Steve Hauza, a Green Party candidate, received the rest of the votes. If Hauza received 480 votes in the election, how many votes did the winner receive?

    A) 4,608 votes
    B) 12,000 votes
    C) 19,200 votes
    D) 23,040 votes

14. If $a^2 - 2a = 15$ and $a < 0$, what is the value of $5 - a$?

15. If $(x+3)(x+c)^2 = x^3 - 7x^2 + cx + 75$ for all x, what is the value of $-2c - 3$?

Practice Set 3 (Calculator)

16. On each shift she works, a barista earns d dollars per hour for the first 8 hours worked in each day and $1.75d$ dollars for each hour over 8 hours in the same day. If the barista earns \$595 for one week in which she worked 6 shifts, what is the value of d?

    A) 8.5
    B) 9
    C) 9.5
    D) It cannot be determined from the information given.

17. $3^4 + \frac{1}{3^4} = ?$

    A) $\frac{3^8 + 1}{3^4}$
    B) $\frac{3^{16}}{3^4 + 1}$
    C) $\frac{3^5 - 1}{3^4}$
    D) 1

18. A certain paint shade can be created by mixing r gallons of blue paint, costing \$15 per gallon, with s gallons of yellow paint, costing \$13 per gallon. Which of the following expresses the cost, in dollars per gallon, of the resulting mixture?

    A) $\frac{15r + 13s}{r + s}$
    B) $\frac{28(r+s)}{15r + 13s}$
    C) $28(15r + 13s)$
    D) $\frac{15r + 13s}{28}$

19. $\frac{\sqrt{2{,}525}}{\sqrt{0.2525}} = ?$

    A) 0.0001
    B) 0.01
    C) 100
    D) 10,000

SAT Red Math
Lesson 11A: Review of Arithmetic and Algebraic Concepts

20. Working independently, Asafu can paint an entire conference room in 5 hours, and Neil can perform the same task on his own in 6 hours. If Asafu and Neil work together in painting the conference room for 2 hours, at which point Neil leaves, how many minutes will it take Asafu to finish painting alone?
    A) $\frac{4}{15}$
    B) 16
    C) 44
    D) 80

21. A farmer gets more motivated after each harvest day so that on three consecutive harvest days, he picks exactly 20% more peaches each day than on the previous day. If, in the course of the three days, he picks a total of 10,920 peaches, how many peaches does he pick on the second day?
    A) 2,400 peaches
    B) 3,000 peaches
    C) 3,600 peaches
    D) 3,800 peaches

22. $\frac{1}{2^6} + \frac{1}{2^7} + \frac{1}{2^7} + \frac{1}{2^7} + \frac{1}{2^7} = ?$
    A) $\frac{1}{2^{34}}$
    B) $\frac{5}{2^{34}}$
    C) $\frac{5}{2^6}$
    D) $\frac{3}{2^6}$

23. A square has the same area as a circle with radius 2. What is the perimeter of the square?
    A) $2\sqrt{\pi}$
    B) π^2
    C) 4π
    D) $8\sqrt{\pi}$

24. If $10m - 5n = 31$ and $3m - 12n = -4$, what is the value of $m + n$?

25. If $(x + y)^2 = (x - y)^2$ and $y > 0$, what is the value of x?

Red Math Lesson 11A: Review of Arithmetic and Algebraic Concepts
Race to the Finish

Directions: Answer each question below.

Homework Set (No Calculator)

1. Marcia and Chang can construct a geodesic dome in 6 days. Anna and Chang can do the same job in 3 days. Anna and Marcia can build the dome in 5 days. How many days does it take for all three of them to construct the dome, working together, if Marcia gets injured at the end of the first day and can't come back?

   A) $\frac{7}{20}$
   B) $\frac{7}{10}$
   C) $\frac{39}{20}$
   D) $\frac{59}{20}$

$$a + 2b = 1$$
$$2c - b = 2$$
$$d - c = 5$$

2. What is the value of $a + b + c + d$ if a, b, c and d satisfy the above system of equations?

   A) -8
   B) 4
   C) 8
   D) Cannot be determined from the given information.

3. Kali's retail store had a $1000 surplus last quarter, so she awarded employee bonuses. She divided the entire surplus among her sales team, which includes a sales manager, five full-time sales associates and four junior associates. Each junior associate received the same amount of money. Each full-time sales associate received twice as much as each junior associate. The sales manager received three times as much as each full-time sales associate. What was the amount of the sales manager's bonus?

   A) $50
   B) $100
   C) $150
   D) $300

4. Last year, Bernardo earned money by performing repair jobs for his neighbors. He had no other source of income. The combined amount Bernardo earned during January, February and March was one-twelfth of his yearly income. During April, May and June, combined, he earned one-sixth of his yearly income. Bernardo earned one-half of his yearly income during July, August and September. If the combined amount he earned during October, November and December was $2,000, what was his total income last year?

   A) $8,000
   B) $9,600
   C) $12,500
   D) $18,750

SAT Red Math
Lesson 11A: Review of Arithmetic and Algebraic Concepts

5. Cynthia and Andrea were both competing in long-distance bike races. Cynthia's race was 150 km long, and Andrea's race was 180 km long. They completed their races in the same amount of time. If Andrea's average rate was 2 km/h faster than Cynthia's, what was Cynthia's average rate, in km/h?

    A) $2\frac{5}{8}$
    B) $6\frac{2}{3}$
    C) $8\frac{1}{2}$
    D) 10

6. The original price for a pair of Everest Hiking boots was increased by 150% because of increased demand, and then this new price was reduced by three-fourths when the boot was no longer popular. By what percent must the last price of the boots be increased to equal the original price?

    A) $57\frac{2}{7}$
    B) 60
    C) 160
    D) $166\frac{2}{3}$

7. Kaleigh began painting a room at 9:00 a.m. Aarav, who can paint twice as fast as Kaleigh, started helping Kaleigh at 9:20 a.m., and they worked together until the room was fully painted at 10:00 a.m. What fraction of the room had been painted by 9:30 a.m.? Express your answer as a common fraction.

    A) $\frac{2}{14}$
    B) $\frac{2}{7}$
    C) $\frac{5}{14}$
    D) $\frac{11}{16}$

8. To develop ideal soil conditions in a large field, an organic farmer must rotate his crops. In the first two years, he can grow 120 acres of wheat, which earns w dollars per acre per year. After two years, he must grow alfalfa, brussel sprouts, lima beans, and tomatoes for one year, which earn $a, b, l,$ and t dollars per acre per year, respectively. Each of these crops grows in a 30 acre sector of the field where the wheat used to be cultivated. After these crops are grown and harvested at the end of one year, the farmer can immediately begin growing wheat again. Given this information, what expression models how much the field will earn in 10 years, starting with the first year of wheat, assuming the farmer maintains ideal soil conditions?

    A) $3[280w + 30(a+b+l+t)]$
    B) $480w + 3(a+b+l+t)$
    C) $540w + 3(a+b+l+t)$
    D) $4[280 + \frac{3}{4}(a+b+l+t)]$

9. If $f(x) = 2x - 3$, find $\frac{f(x+h) - f(x)}{h}$.

    A) 2
    B) -3
    C) $2x + 2h - 3$
    D) $\frac{2x-3}{h}$

10. The electric force between two charged particles is given by the equation $F = k\frac{q_1 q_2}{r^2}$, where F is the force, k is a constant, q_1 and q_2 are the charges of the two particles, and r is the distance between the particles. If the distance between the particles is multiplied by 3, what has to be done to keep the force the same?

    A) Divide the each of the charges by 3.
    B) Divide one of the charges by 3.
    C) Multiply each of the charges by 3.
    D) Multiply one of the charges by 3.

11. The distance traveled by an object experiencing uniform acceleration is found by using the equation $d = \frac{1}{2}at^2$, where d is the distance, a is the acceleration, and t is the time. Which of the following would have the effect of doubling the distance?
A) Multiplying both t and a by 2
B) Multiplying t by 2 and dividing a by 2.
C) Dividing t by 2 and multiplying a by 2.
D) Dividing both t and a by 2.

12. The period of a spring is represented by the equation $T = 2\pi\sqrt{\frac{m}{k}}$, where T is the period, m is the the mass attached to the spring, and k is the spring constant. If k is multiplied by 2, what effect will that have on the period?
A) The period will be doubled.
B) The period will be multiplied by $\sqrt{2}$.
C) The period will be divided by 2.
D) The period will be divided by $\sqrt{2}$.

13. The formula for finding the distance between an image and a mirror is $\frac{1}{f} = \frac{1}{d_o} + \frac{1}{d_i}$, where f is the focal length, d_o is the distance between the object and the mirror, and d_i is the distance between the image and the mirror. Solve this equation for d_i.
A) $\frac{1}{f} - \frac{1}{d_o}$
B) $f - d_o$
C) $\frac{f d_o}{d_o - f}$
D) $f d_i - f d_o$

14. One motion equation is $v_f^2 = v_i^2 + 2ad$, where v_f is the final velocity in m/s, v_i is the initial velocity in m/s, a is the acceleration in m/s², and d is the distance traveled in meters. If Marina throws a ball straight up with a velocity of 3 m/s, how high does it go before it comes to a very brief stop prior to turning around? The acceleration of an object in free fall is −9.8 m/s².
A) −0.46 m
B) 0.46 m
C) 0.92 m
D) 4.9 m

15. For a particular right triangle, the lengths of the sides are x, $3x + 6$, and $3x + 8$. How long is the hypotenuse?
A) 14
B) 42
C) 48
D) 50

16. For a particular cone, the height is equal to twice the circumference. What is the equation for the volume of the cone in terms of r?
A) $4\pi^2 r^3$
B) $\frac{4}{3}\pi^2 r^3$
C) $\frac{1}{3}\pi r^3$
D) $4\pi r^3$

SAT Red Math
Lesson 11A: Review of Arithmetic and Algebraic Concepts

17. If $\frac{3\sqrt{x-1}}{x-1} = 1$, what is the value of x?

18. If $\frac{3}{x} = \frac{-2}{y}$ and $\frac{3}{p} = \frac{-2q}{y}$ and $q = \frac{3}{p}$, what is the value of x?

19. If $|x + 3| = y - 3$ and $x > 0$, what is the value of $y - x$?

20. If $a^2 + 11a = -10$ and $a + 5 = b$ and $a + 6 = c$, what is the value of bc?

Red Math Lesson 11B: Advanced Multi-Step Unit Conversions

Metric Conversions:

Prefix	Symbol	Factor
Giga	G	10^9
Mega	M	10^6
Kilo	k	10^3
Hecto	h	100
Deca	da	10
Deci	d	0.1
Centi	c	0.01
Milli	m	0.001

Distance Conversions:

Inch (in)		2.540 cm
Foot (ft)	12 in	0.305 m
Yard (yd)	3 ft	0.914 m
Mile (mi)	5280 ft	1.609 km

Area Conversions:

Acre	43,560 ft^2	4046.9 m^2

Weight Conversions:

Ounce (oz)		28.349 g
Pound (lb)	16 oz	453.59 g
Ton	2000 lb	907.185 kg

Volume Conversions:

Teaspoon (tsp)		4.927 mL
Tablespoon (tbsp)	3 tsp	14.781 mL
Fluid Ounce (fl oz)	2 tbsp	29.563 mL
Cup (cp)	8 fl oz	0.237 L
Pint (pt)	2 cup	0.473 L
Quart (qt)	2 pint	0.946 L
Gallon (gal)	4 quart	3.784 L
	1 cm^3	1 mL

Temperature Conversions:

$$F = \frac{9}{5}C + 32$$

Time Conversions:

Second (sec)	
Minute (min)	60 secs
Hour (hr)	60 mins
Day	24 hrs
Week	7 days
Year	52 weeks

RED MATH LESSON 11B: ADVANCED MULTI-STEP UNIT CONVERSIONS
Learning to Swim

Directions: Answer each question below.

PRACTICE SET 1 (CALCULATOR)

1. Christy wants to install a fence around her home. The base of her house has a width of 20 feet and a length of 11 yards. She wants the fence to be placed 183 centimeters away from the house on all sides. How many inches of fencing material does Christy need to purchase to complete this project? Round to the nearest inch.

2. A recipe calls for 1 liter of liquefied apples, which can be obtained by blending solid apples whose total volume amounts to 1 liter. If the density of apples is 0.65 grams per cubic centimeter, and apples are sold at $1.30 per pound, what is the total cost of the apples used in the recipe? Assume that 1 cubic centimeter is equivalent to 1 milliliter and that a decimal amount of pounds can be purchased. Round to the nearest cent.

3. Bill wants to catch a train that is scheduled to depart from the train station at 4:00 PM. The station is 3 miles from Bill's house, and the fastest average speed that he can manage to run over a length of 3 miles is 4.4 meters per second. If Bill runs in a straight path to the train station, to the nearest minute, what is the latest time that he can leave his house in order to arrive at the station by the train's departure time?

4. A cyclist is biking along a straight racing track, beginning at the starting line. After 2 seconds, she has travelled 14 feet from the starting line. After 3 minutes, she crosses the finish line. If the track has a total length of 1 mile, what was her average speed between these two time points (2 seconds after starting and 3 minutes after starting) in yards per second? Round to the nearest yard per second.

5. A lab researcher needs to use a water bath to catalyze a chemical reaction. The temperature of the water bath is currently 40°C, and the reaction requires a 37°C environment. To achieve the necessary temperature level, the researcher plans to dump an appropriate amount of ice into the water bath. Every 20 grams of ice decreases the temperature in the water bath by 0.1°F. How many pounds of ice must be added to decrease the temperature inside the water bath from 40°C to 37°C? Assume any amount of ice can be added, i.e. decimal amounts are allowed. Round to the nearest tenth of a pound.

Red Math Lesson 11B: Advanced Multi-Step Unit Conversions
Diving into the Deep End

Directions: Answer each question below.

Practice Set 2 (Calculator)

6. Electric utilities charge customers a certain rate per kilowatt-hour (kWh), a measure of energy used. For example, a 2 kW appliance running for 3 hours would use 6 kWh of energy. Debbie's apartment has incandescent 60 W light bulbs. She knows that her average monthly lighting use is equivalent to having all 12 bulbs in the apartment on for 176 hours, and the average cost for her lighting each month is $20.87. What will be her average yearly savings if she replaces all of the 60 W bulbs with compact fluorescent 13 W bulbs? Round your answer to the nearest cent.
   A) $4.52
   B) $16.35
   C) $54.26
   D) $196.18

7. A store sells a 100 oz. bottle of Laundry Detergent A for $8, and advertises that the bottle has enough detergent for 66 loads. A concentrated version of the same detergent (Laundry Detergent B) costs $5 for a 32 oz. bottle and has enough detergent for 32 loads. Which is the more cost-effective option, and why?
   A) Laundry Detergent A, because it requires fewer ounces per load.
   B) Laundry Detergent B, because it requires fewer ounces per load.
   C) Laundry Detergent A, because it has a lower cost per load.
   D) Laundry Detergent B, because it has a lower cost per load.

8. A car commercial advertises that its car accelerates from 0 miles per hour to 60 miles per hour in 5 seconds. What is the acceleration of the car in meters per second per second?
   A) 0.2 m/s^2
   B) 5.4 m/s^2
   C) 26.8 m/s^2
   D) 321.9 m/s^2

$$1 \text{ N} = \frac{\text{kg} \cdot \text{m}}{\text{s}^2}$$
$$1 \text{ J} = \text{N} \cdot \text{m}$$

9. In the International System of Units, all units can be defined using seven base units: A, cd, K, kg, m, mol, and s. The sievert (Sv) measures ionizing radiation in J/kg. Using the equivalencies above, what is 1 Sv using only the base units?
   A) $1 \frac{\text{N} \cdot \text{m}}{\text{kg}}$
   B) $1 \frac{\text{m}}{\text{s}}$
   C) $1 \frac{\text{m}^2}{\text{s}^2}$
   D) $1 \text{ m}^2 \text{s}^2$

10. Hot air balloons work because the density of air decreases as temperature rises. Under average conditions, it takes 3.91 m³ of envelope volume to lift 1 kg. If a certain balloon has 2800 m³ envelope volume with a mass of 113.4 kg, how much additional mass can be lifted? Round your answer to the nearest tenth of a kg.
    A) 602.7 kg
    B) 716.1 kg
    C) 10,834.6 kg
    D) 10,948 kg

SAT Red Math
Lesson 11B: Advanced Multi-Step Unit Conversions

$$PV = nRT$$

11. The equation above, the ideal gas law, can be used to predict the behaviors of gasses under many conditions. Pressure, P, is measured in $\frac{N}{m^2}$; volume, V, is measured in m^3; the amount of gas, n, is measured in mol; and temperature, T, is measured in K. R is a constant. What must the units of R be to correctly balance the above equation?

   A) $\frac{mol \cdot K}{N \cdot m}$
   B) $\frac{N \cdot m}{mol \cdot K}$
   C) $\frac{N}{m \cdot mol \cdot K}$
   D) $N \cdot m \cdot mol \cdot K$

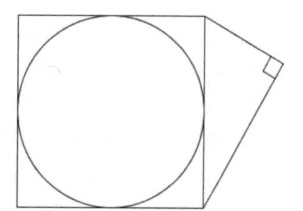

12. The figure above represents the layout of a city with a total population of 140,000. The area of the square is 16 mi². The inscribed circle includes both residential and commercial zones, with an average population density of 10,030 people per mi². The remaining area between the circle and square is zoned for industrial use and has no residents. The east side of the square is also the hypotenuse of a 30°-60°-90° triangle representing farmland and forest. What is the positive difference in space per person for those living in the circle and those living in the triangle? Round your answer to the nearest ft²/person.

   A) 2086
   B) 4139
   C) 4646
   D) 6000

Warm-up:	4 mph, 2 minutes
Main:	6.5 mph, 10 miles
Cool-down:	3 mph, 5 minutes

13. The table above shows Laura's workout plan. If she follows the plan, what will be her average speed, in mph, over the course of the run? Round your answer to the nearest hundredth.

   A) 4.50
   B) 4.59
   C) 5.18
   D) 6.27

14. Stevie wants to mix equal volumes of ice and tea to make iced tea. Water is different from most substances because the density of its most common solid form (0.917 kg/L) is lower than that of its liquid form (1 kg/L). If the iced tea pitcher is cylindrical with a diameter of 15 cm and height of 25 cm, what volume of liquid water is needed to make the ice cubes? Round your answer to the nearest hundredth of a liter.

15. Rachel is taking a trip to Chile. Her credit card is based in the United States, and uses an exchange rate of 578.35 Chilean pesos per dollar. After the foreign price is converted to dollars, a 6% fee is added to the bill. How many Chilean pesos can she actually spend for each dollar charged by the credit card company? Round your answer to the nearest peso.

Practice Set 3 (Calculator)

16. William is trying to decide how many machines he should upgrade in his chocolate factory. He has to invest $1000 to upgrade the first machine and $500 for each additional one. However, he predicts that his monthly profits will increase by $375 for each machine upgraded. William will upgrade at least one machine. If n is the number of machines he chooses to upgrade and t is the number of months since the upgrade, which expression can be used to model the time it takes to earn back his investment?

   A) $-1000 - \frac{500}{n-1} + \frac{375}{nt}$
   B) $-1000 - \frac{500}{n-1} + \frac{375}{n}t$
   C) $-1000 - 500n + 375nt$
   D) $-500 - 500n + 375nt$

17. According to the U.S. National Institute of Standards and Technology, there are 1024 bytes (B) in a kibibyte (KiB), 1024 KiB in a mibibyte (MiB), and 1024 MiB in a gibibyte (GiB). This is the system used to measure memory capacity of RAM. On the other hand, there are 1000 bytes in a kilobyte (kB), 1000 kB in a megabyte (MB), and 1000 MB in a gigabyte (GB). This is the system used to measure storage on a hard drive. How many more bytes fit in a gibibyte of RAM than in a gigabyte of hard drive space?

   A) 72
   B) 13,824
   C) 48,576
   D) 73,741,824

18. Water in Boston costs $55.45 per 1000 cubic feet for the first 1300 cubic feet per day, and $58.40 per 1000 cubic feet above that amount. A Boston swimming pool is a rectangle measuring 50 yards × 30 yards, with a uniform depth of 6 feet. If this pool is filled within a single day, what will the water cost?

   A) $521.77
   B) $1572.97
   C) $1575.52
   D) $4726.57

Cupcakes: yields 24
3 cups flour
½ teaspoon salt
2 teaspoons baking powder
½ cup butter
¾ cup sugar
2 eggs
1 cup milk
1 teaspoon vanilla

Use the above information for questions 19 and 20.

19. To make baking powder, 2 parts cream of tartar and 1 part baking soda are combined. How much cream of tartar is required to make 90 cupcakes?

   A) 2.5 teaspoons
   B) 3.75 teaspoons
   C) 5 teaspoons
   D) 7.5 teaspoons

20. In order to make this recipe gluten-free, the flour is made from a combination of rice flour, potato flour, and tapioca flour, in the ratio 1:2:4. Approximately how many ounces of rice flour are needed to make 60 cupcakes? (1 cup of rice flour weighs 5.64 ounces)

   A) 3.02
   B) 4.29
   C) 6.04
   D) 8.57

21. Ellen has a leaky faucet. She places a measuring cup underneath it for the 9 hours she is at work, and finds that 39 ounces of water accumulate in that time. If her water costs 0.7 cents per gallon, approximately how much does the leak cost her over the span of one week?

   A) 4¢
   B) 36¢
   C) $3.98
   D) $652.28

SAT Red Math
Lesson 11B: Advanced Multi-Step Unit Conversions

22. A single text character stored in a computer file takes up one byte of data. A file contains the hourly readings from a large set of air pollution monitoring devices. Each reading is a three-digit number precise to the tenths place. There are three readings per line, separated by commas. A line break (represented below by "n") also counts as a character and consumes one byte of space. Thus, a single line of this file might look like:

    104.3,221.2,301.4n

    The file contains 1.5 million lines of data. Approximately how large will this file be in megabytes? (Note: 1 mibibyte (MiB) = 1024 kibibytes (KiB), and 1 kibibyte = 1024 bytes.)
    A) 25.75 MiB
    B) 26.37 MiB
    C) 27.00 MiB
    D) 28.31 MiB

23. In the United States, when gasoline is priced at $3.30 per gallon, a certain car's gas tank can be filled for $46.20. How much would it cost to fill the same tank in France at a price of €1.25 per liter? (Assume an exchange rate of $1.00 = €0.75)
    A) €30.21
    B) €42.97
    C) €66.22
    D) €88.32

24. Residential housing densities are often expressed in terms of dwelling units per acre (du/acre) where a "dwelling unit" refers to a house, apartment, or condominium. A new suburban subdivision, occupying a square of land ½-mile on a side, is permitted to have up to 8 du/acre. If the average household size in this community is 3.5 people, what is the expected number of people that live in this area?

25. A *render farm*, used in computer graphics studios, is a set of networked computers that produce the professional-quality 3D images seen in movies and video games. Multiple computers linked together in a farm are able to combine their processing power toward rendering a set of images.

    A certain feature film is 84 minutes long and (like most movies) has a *frame rate* of 24 frames per second. Each frame, or still image, would take a single computer 7 minutes and 30 seconds to render. To the nearest day, how many days will it take a render farm consisting of 42 identical computers to render the entire film?

Red Math Lesson 11B: Advanced Multi-Step Unit Conversions
Race to the Finish

Directions: Answer each question below.

Homework Set (Calculator)

	Styrofoam	Cork	Oak	Sugar	Salt	Aluminum	Tin	Nickel	Copper	Lead	Gold
Density (g/cm³)	0.005	0.24	0.70	1.59	2.16	2.70	7.30	8.90	8.92	11.34	19.32

Use the table above for questions 1 through 5.

1. It is recommended that a person eat less than 1500 mg of salt in a day. What is the volume of this amount in cubic centimeters?
   A) 0.694 cm³
   B) 0.943 cm³
   C) 694 cm³
   D) 943 cm³

2. A soda can is made up of a metallic mixture including 97% aluminum. When the can is empty, its mass is 0.45 ounces. How much aluminum is needed for 100 cans?
   A) 458 cm³
   B) 472 cm³
   C) 2263 cm³
   D) 17536 cm³

3. A cork board has a mass of 1 kg. What is the volume of the cork board in cubic inches?
   A) 254 in³
   B) 283 in³
   C) 646 in³
   D) 1640 in³

4. In preparation of making a statue, an artist bought a block of bronze measuring 2 meters by 3 meters by 5 meters. Bronze is comprised of 88% copper and 12% tin, by volume. What is the total mass of the block of bronze?
   A) 2.35×10^4 g
   B) 2.62×10^4 g
   C) 2.35×10^8 g
   D) 2.62×10^8 g

5. Copper has a market price of $6.75/kg. Copper electrical wire is solid and cylindrical in shape with a diameter of 0.5 mm. A school under construction is to require a total of 8.5 kilometers of wiring. If this wire is made of pure copper, which of the following is closest to the value of the metal contained in it?
   A) $10.09
   B) $100.49
   C) $229.15
   D) $403.76

SAT Red Math
Lesson 11B: Advanced Multi-Step Unit Conversions

6. A wooden board is 2 inches by 4 inches in rectangular cross-section and 6 feet long. The density of cedar is 23 pounds per cubic foot. If a wagon can carry a maximum of 250 pounds, what is the maximum number of these boards it can carry at once?
   A) 7
   B) 11
   C) 23
   D) 32

7. Iron has a density of 7.84 $\frac{g}{cm^3}$, and aluminum has a density of 2.70 $\frac{g}{cm^3}$. If a block of iron and a block of aluminum have masses of 1120 kilograms and 540 kilograms, respectively, what is the total volume of the two blocks, in cubic meters?
   A) 0.157 m³
   B) 0.2 m³
   C) 0.343 m³
   D) 12.1 m³

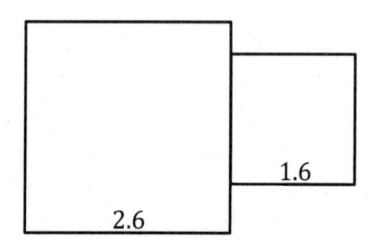

8. A thousand acres is equal to 4.05 square kilometers. If a farm is made up of two square-shaped plots with side lengths of 2.6 kilometers and 1.6 kilometers as shown above, what is the farm's area rounded to the nearest 100 acres?
   A) 1000 acres
   B) 2300 acres
   C) 4400 acres
   D) 9300 acres

9. A parsec is a unit of distance equal to 3.26 light-years. The Oort Cloud, a spherical collection of comets and other objects, has a diameter of 0.6 parsecs. What is the approximate volume of the space contained inside the Oort Cloud, in cubic light-years? (The volume within a sphere is $\frac{4}{3}\pi$ times the cube of its radius.)
   A) 3.9 light-years³
   B) 10.0 light-years³
   C) 15.6 light-years³
   D) 31.3 light-years³

1 U.S. dollar = 3.3 Malaysian ringgits
1 U.S. dollar = 33 Thai baht

10. A family takes a trip to Malaysia, converting a total of $2,000 into Malaysian ringgits. After paying a 5% exchange fee, the family spends 2,000 ringgits. Then, the family travels to Thailand, converting the remaining money into Thai baht (and paying another 5% exchange fee). Using the exchange rates below, how many baht does the family have (rounded to the nearest hundred baht)?
    A) 40,600 baht
    B) 41,500 baht
    C) 43,700 baht
    D) 46,000 baht

11. One bullet travels at a constant speed of 2,000 feet per second. Another bullet travels at a constant speed of 2,000 miles per hour. If the two bullets are fired simultaneously at a target 1,000 feet away, approximately how much time would elapse between the two bullets hitting the target?
    A) 0.16 seconds
    B) 0.23 seconds
    C) 0.34 seconds
    D) 0.39 seconds

Lesson 11B: Advanced Multi-Step Unit Conversions

12. The density of wet sand is 1920 kilograms per cubic meter. The density of dry sand is 1600 kilograms per cubic meter. A rectangular sandbox with an area of 3 square meters is filled to a depth of 0.5 meters with dry sand. Enough water is then added to make all the sand wet. What is the weight of the water added?
    A) 320 kilograms
    B) 480 kilograms
    C) 960 kilograms
    D) 1440 kilograms

	1 Dollar =	1 Euro =	1 Yuan =	1 Real =
Dollars	---	1.25	0.16	0.40
Euros	0.80	---	0.13	0.30
Yuan	6.25	7.70	---	2.50
Reals	2.50	3.33	0.40	---

Use the table above for questions 13 through 15. A currency exchange charges a fee equal to 2% of the amount exchanged.

13. A traveler exchanges 1000 euros into reals. After spending r reals, he exchanges the remaining amount into euros, receiving 863 euros. What is r?
    A) 99
    B) 263
    C) 331
    D) 393

14. Another traveler has 500 yuan and 500 dollars. She converts both into euros. How many euros does she receive, to the nearest euro?
    A) 456
    B) 705
    C) 3525
    D) 3750

15. A French diplomat is about to leave Brazil to go to China and he currently has 20,000 euro and 10,000 real. He converts all of his real and 30% of his euro into yuan, spends all of it, then converts 60% of his remaining euros into yuan, half of which he spends. When he returns to France he converts all of his currency back into euros; how many euros does he have to the nearest euro?
    A) 9638
    B) 12,434
    C) 13,667
    D) 13,861

16. Building fire codes set the maximum occupancy of buildings such that a building can be evacuated in a fixed window of time. If r people can leave each exit every second, and there are n exits, what should the maximum occupancy be in order to ensure all occupants can be evacuated in x minutes?
    A) rnx
    B) $60rnx$
    C) $\frac{60nx}{r}$
    D) $\frac{60n}{rx}$

17. Electricity is priced in *kilowatt hours* (kWh), or the amount of energy required to supply one kilowatt (1000 watts) of power for 1 hour. Sara's apartment contains 5 lamps, each with a 60-watt lightbulb. The 5 lamps are on for an average of 6 hours per day. Sara's monthly electricity bill comes to $80.00. Assuming 30 days to the month, and an electricity rate of 18.5¢/kWh, what percent of the electricity she uses is devoted to keeping her lights on? Round to the nearest tenth of a percent.

SAT Red Math
Lesson 11B: Advanced Multi-Step Unit Conversions

Cars on the highway typically maintain a *following distance* equivalent to 2 seconds' drive time from one another; that is, if you are driving and count 2 seconds, you should be at the point where the car in front of you was when you began counting.

18. Using the information above, at a speed of 60 miles per hour, what is a 2-second following distance, measured in feet?

19. A football field is 120 yards by 160 feet. To the nearest square meter, what is the area of the field in m²?

20. The largest diamond ever found was 3106.75 carats. If a carat is equal to 0.2 grams, then what is the weight of the largest diamond in pounds? Round to the nearest hundredth of a pound.

Red Math Lesson 12A: Understanding and Analyzing Systems of Equations
Learning to Swim

Directions: Answer each question below.

Practice Set 1 (No Calculator)

$$\frac{4}{x} + \frac{3}{y} + \frac{1}{z} = 15$$
$$4y = -15x$$
$$5x = 14z$$

1. Using the system above, what is the value of $\frac{xy}{z}$?

$$3x - 5y + 6z = 3$$
$$2x + 4y - 3z = 23$$
$$-2x + 3y - 5z = 1$$

2. Using the system above, what is the value of $\frac{z}{x} + y$?

$$x^2 + y^2 - 6x + 2y = -6$$

3. The equation above represents a circle. If the radius of the circle were doubled, and the center of the circle shifted up two units, then what is the point of intersection of these two circles?

$$-0.1x - 0.15y + 0.2z = -0.45$$
$$\frac{5}{3}x - \frac{2}{3}y - z = 4$$
$$\frac{x}{6} + \frac{y}{4} - \frac{z}{3} = \frac{-3}{4}$$

4. Using the system above, what is the value of x?

$$(x - 6)^2 + (y - 4)^2 = 16$$
$$y = x$$

5. For the system of equations above, a is the sum of possible x values and b is the sum of possible y values of the solutions of the system. What is the value of $a + b$?

RED MATH LESSON 12A: UNDERSTANDING AND ANALYZING SYSTEMS OF EQUATIONS
Diving into the Deep End

Directions: Answer each question below.

PRACTICE SET 2 (NO CALCULATOR)

$$x = \sin z$$
$$y = \sqrt{1 - x^2}$$
$$y = 2xy$$

6. Using the system above, what is NOT a possible value of z?
   A) $\frac{\pi}{3}$
   B) $\frac{\pi}{2}$
   C) $\frac{5\pi}{6}$
   D) $\frac{3\pi}{2}$

$$ab = 15$$
$$bc = 6$$
$$ac = 10$$

7. Given the above system of equations, what is the value of abc?
   A) 30
   B) 31
   C) 300
   D) 900

	Test 1	Test 2	Final	Grade
Amy	60	80	90	82
Brian	50	100	80	78
Cody	40	60	100	80
Dan	25	75	70	62

8. The table above shows the scores that four students received on two exams and the final exam; each of the three exams is out of 100 points. The final grade is calculated by taking $x\%$ of the average of the two tests and adding the result to $y\%$ of the final. What are $x\%$ and $y\%$, the respective weights of the exams and final exam?
   A) 40% for tests, 60% for final exam
   B) 60% for tests, 40% for final exam
   C) 70% for tests, 90% for final exam
   D) 75% for tests, 80% for final exam

$$x^2 + y^2 = 100$$
$$x^2 + y^2 - 2y = 24$$

9. If the equations above were graphed in the real coordinate plane, what would be the y-value of their point of intersection?
   A) -38
   B) 0
   C) 38
   D) No solution

$$y = x^2 + x + 20$$
$$y = 3x^2 + 5x - 28$$

10. What is the midpoint of the line segment connecting the two points of intersection of the system of equations above?
    A) $(-5, 5)$
    B) $(-2, 90)$
    C) $(-1, 45)$
    D) $(45, -1)$

$$2x - 6 = 4y$$
$$x = 2y + a$$

11. If the system of equations above has an infinite number of solutions, then $a =$
    A) -6
    B) -3
    C) 3
    D) 12

SAT Red Math
Lesson 12A: Understanding and Analyzing Systems of Equations

12. A café sells sandwiches for $5.50 each, bowls of soup for $4.00, and a soup/sandwich combo for $7.50. On Tuesday, a total of 165 lunches were sold, each of them a sandwich, soup, or combo. The total revenue was $995. The staff also knows that two thirds of all bowls of soup sold that day were sold as part of the combo meal. How many soup/sandwich combos were sold?
    A) 35
    B) 60
    C) 70
    D) 100

$$\sqrt{2x-1} = x$$
$$-2y = \sqrt{4x+12}$$

13. Using the system of equations above, which of the following is a possible value of $\frac{x^2}{y}$?
    A) $\frac{-1}{2}$
    B) $\frac{-1}{3}$
    C) $\frac{1}{2}$
    D) 4

$$x = 0$$
$$3x + y = 39$$
$$5x - 12y = 24$$

14. The three equations above, when graphed, enclose a triangle in the coordinate plane. What is the area of the triangle?

$$y - 4 = \frac{1}{2}(x-2)^2$$
$$2x - y + 6 = 0$$

15. What is the sum of the x-coordinates of all ordered pairs (x, y) that satisfy the system of equations above?

Practice Set 3 (Calculator)

$$3|x+2y| - 6|x+2y| + 10 = -2$$
$$5|2x+y| = 3|2x+y| + 2$$

16. Using the system of equations above, which of the following is NOT a possible value of $3(x+y)$?
    A) -5
    B) 1
    C) 3
    D) 5

17. A plumbing service is deciding between two possible pricing models. In Option A, customers would be charged a flat fee of $100 per visit, and an additional $3 per minute after the first 30 minutes. In Option B, customers would pay a flat fee of only $40 per visit, but the per-minute charge would be $3.75 per minute beginning after 20 minutes. Option B will result in a higher fee than Option A for all visits, and only for visits, lasting
    A) less than 60 minutes.
    B) less than 70 minutes.
    C) more than 60 minutes.
    D) more than 70 minutes.

18. Ann and Blake open up a bakery that sells only cookies and brownies. Ann proposes selling each cookie for $1.80 and each brownie for $2.22. Blake proposes selling each cookie for $2.10 and each brownie for $1.90. They use Ann's pricing for the first day and earn $351.00. Blake calculates that had they used his pricing, they would have instead earned $347.40. How many more brownies than cookies did the bakery sell?
    A) 6
    B) 13
    C) 25
    D) 31

SAT Red Math
Lesson 12A: Understanding and Analyzing Systems of Equations

$$(x-5)^2 + y^2 = 25$$

19. If $y = ax + b$ is a line that is tangent to the circle above at the point $(2, 4)$, then what are the values of a and b?
    A) $a = -4, b = 20$
    B) $a = -\frac{4}{3}, b = \frac{20}{3}$
    C) $a = \frac{3}{4}, b = \frac{5}{2}$
    D) $a = 6, b = 20$

20. If another line is tangent to the circle from the previous problem at the point $(1, -3)$, then what is the point of intersection of this and the previous tangent line?
    A) $(-2, 1)$
    B) $(0, 5)$
    C) $(1, -2)$
    D) $(5, 0)$

21. Cirque de la Lune came to town. On day one, it sold $2a$ child tickets and b adult tickets, earning a revenue of 11600. On the second day, it tripled its sales in child tickets and doubled its sales in adult tickets, earning a revenue of 24800. If a child admission costs $8 and an adult costs $20, then how many tickets were sold in the two days?
    A) 600
    B) 700
    C) 1600
    D) 2300

$$3x^3 - 3y = 21$$
$$6x^3 + 4y = 12$$

22. Using the system of equations above, what is the value of x^2?
    A) 2
    B) 4
    C) $\sqrt[3]{4}$
    D) $2\sqrt[3]{2}$

$$(x+3)^2 + (y-2)(y+2) = 12$$
$$x^2 - 5x = y^2 - 4$$

23. In the system of equations above, what is a possible value of xy?
    A) 0
    B) $\frac{5}{2}$
    C) 4
    D) No solution

24. Joanne is planting a garden. She has decided which vegetables she wants to plant and knows that she will need an area of exactly 360 square feet. She has 78 feet worth of chicken-wire fencing with which to enclose the garden to keep out rabbits; thus, she wishes the perimeter to be 78 feet. What should the length of the longer side of the garden be in feet?

25. If the circle with equation $x^2 + (y-5)^2 = 32$ intersects the x-axis at exactly one point, (x, y), at which x is positive, what is the value of x^2?

RED MATH LESSON 12A: UNDERSTANDING AND ANALYZING SYSTEMS OF EQUATIONS
Race to the Finish

Directions: Answer each question below.

HOMEWORK SET (CALCULATOR)

$$2x - 3y + 4z = 2$$
$$4x + 2y - z = -1$$
$$3x - \frac{1}{2}y + 3z = -\frac{7}{2}$$

1. Using the system of equations above, what is the value of z?
   A) $-\frac{8}{3}$
   B) 0
   C) $\frac{13}{18}$
   D) No solution

2. Cassandra is planning production for 2 of her products: purses and wallets. Wallets cost $5 each to produce, require 1 yard of fabric, and are sold for $10. Purses cost $10 each to produce, require 3 yards of fabric, and are sold for $30. Cassandra has a maximum of $10,000 to spend on production costs. The minimum factory order for wallets is 500 units and 250 units for purses. How many yards of fabric should Cassandra order if she is going to produce a quantity of purses and wallets that will maximize her profits?
   A) 1500
   B) 2500
   C) 2750
   D) 3250

$$3x + 4y = 9$$
$$4x^2 + 20x + 10 = -6$$
$$y - 19 = -y^2 - 7$$

3. Using the system of equations above, what is the value of $x + 4$?
   A) -4
   B) -1
   C) 0
   D) 3

$$ax + by + cz = 2$$
$$cx + ay + bz = -5$$
$$bx + cy + az = -3$$

4. The solution to the system of equations above is the point (1, 2, 3) in the xyz-coordinate plane. What is the value of $a + b + c$?
   A) -6
   B) -1
   C) 3
   D) 4

$$y^2 = 3(2 - x)$$
$$y^2 = x + 4$$

5. How many solutions to the above system of equations exist?
   A) 0
   B) 1
   C) 2
   D) Infinitely many

$$y = -|x - 2| + 1$$
$$y = \left|\frac{x}{2}\right|$$

6. The solution to the system of equations above is the coordinate pair (a, b). What is the product of a and b?
   A) -2
   B) 1
   C) 2
   D) 8

SAT Red Math
Lesson 12A: Understanding and Analyzing Systems of Equations

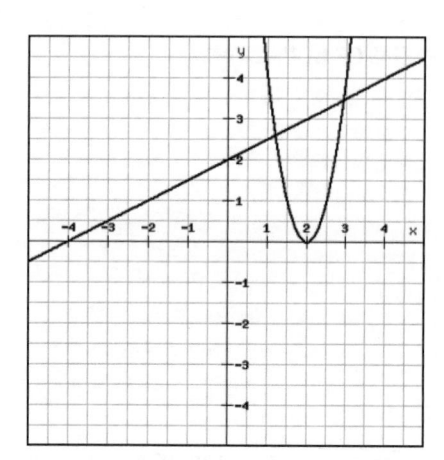

7. Above is the graph of the linear equation $g(x)$ and the quadratic equation $h(x)$. If the system of equations composed of $g(x)$ and $h(x+c)$ has exactly one solution, what is the value of c?
   A) -6
   B) -4
   C) 4
   D) 6

$$x + 2y + 4z = 0$$
$$3x - y + 2z = -5$$
$$2x - 2y + z = -9$$

8. In the system of equations above, what is the value of y?
   A) -3
   B) -2
   C) 2
   D) 5

$$(x-2)^2 = (y+6)^2$$
$$2y - 2x = -6$$

9. Using the system of equations above, what is the value of $x - y$?
   A) $\frac{-5}{2}$
   B) -3
   C) 3
   D) $\frac{5}{2}$

10. Anurati is putting together fruit baskets of pears and mangos to sell at her gift shop. The baskets must have between 8 and 16 pieces of fruit each. The price of each basket is calculated as follows: $1 for each pear it contains, plus $2 for each mango. Anurati's costs are $0.50 per pear, $1.25 per mango, and $3.00 for the other materials necessary for 1 basket. There must be at least 2 pears and 2 mangos in each basket. How many pears should Anurati put in each basket in order to maximize her profits?
    A) 2
    B) 8
    C) 14
    D) 16

$$x^2 + y^2 = 4$$
$$xy = -2$$

11. What is the distance between the two points that are solutions to the system above?
    A) $\sqrt{2}$
    B) 4
    C) $2\sqrt{2}$
    D) 8

$$x + 2y + uz = 1$$
$$2x + 4y + 10z = 3$$

12. If the above system has no simultaneous solutions (x, y, z), what is the value of u?
    A) -5
    B) 2
    C) 5
    D) 10

$$(x+1)^2 = y - 2$$
$$x + y = 5$$

13. What is the sum of the possible x-values to the system of equations above?
    A) -6
    B) -3
    C) 3
    D) 6

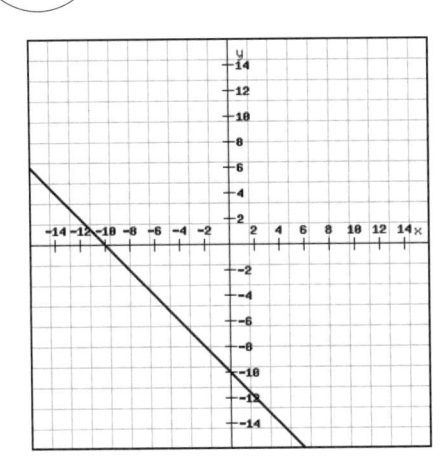

14. When $f(x)$ is the function graphed above and $g(x) = -2x^2$, (x_1, y_1) is the point in Quadrant III of the xy-plane such that $y_1 = f(x_1) = g(x_1)$. What is $x_1 + y_1$?
   A) -16
   B) -10
   C) -8
   D) -6

15. If $x = \frac{a}{b}$ and $y = \frac{b-a}{b+a}$, what is $x + y + xy$?
   A) $\frac{b^2 - 2ab + a^2}{b^2 + ab}$
   B) $\frac{b+a}{b}$
   C) $\frac{b^2 + 2ab - a^2}{b^2 + ab}$
   D) 1

16. Toby is considering 3 membership options for his local art museum. Plan 1 is a lifelong membership for a one-time payment of $200. Plan 2 costs $50 upfront, and $5 for each visit. Plan 3 is to pay the non-member ticket price of $10 per visit. Which of the following statements is true?

   I. If he is going to visit the museum 31 times, Plan 1 is the least expensive choice.
   II. If he only has $150 to spend, Plan 2 will buy him the most visits.
   III. If he is going to visit the museum 13 times, Plan 2 is the least expensive choice.

   A) I only
   B) I and III
   C) II and III
   D) I, II, and III

17. Sebastian deposited a total of $3000 in two savings accounts, one earning a 3% and the other a 5% interest rate, compounded annually. Two years later, he had a total of $3224.30. How much money did he initially deposit into the 3% account in dollars?

HW

$$\frac{y}{2}+\frac{x}{3}=\frac{1}{2}$$
$$\frac{y}{5}+\frac{x}{2}=\frac{1}{5}$$
$$ay-8x=2$$

18. If the equations above all intersect at one point, then what is the value of a?

$$3ax+8by=7$$
$$5ax+4by=7$$

19. If $(x,y)=\left(\frac{1}{3},\frac{1}{4}\right)$ represents a unique solution to the system above, then what is the value of $\sqrt[a]{b^3}$?

20. A soap store packages its products in bundles to provide a more attractive gift option. A small bundle of two shampoos, three lotions, and five hand sanitizers costs \$50. A premium bundle of four shampoos, seven lotions, and ten hand sanitizers costs \$105. If the average of the three different prices of the products is \$6, then how much would a bundle of two shampoos, one lotion, and four hand sanitizers cost in dollars? (Assume no tax.)

RED MATH LESSON 12B: FUNCTIONS
Learning to Swim

Directions: Answer each question below.

PRACTICE SET 1 (NO CALCULATOR)

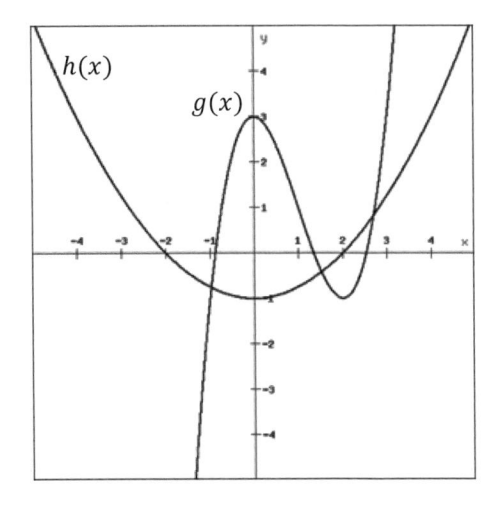

1. The cubic function $g(x)$ and quadratic function $h(x)$ are shown above. If $f(x) = h(x) - g(x)$, then the most number of zeroes that $f(x)$ can have is what?

$$f(x) = \frac{10x^2 - 13x - 3}{12x^2 - 5x - 2}$$

2. For what real values of x does the function above have a positive value?

$$f(x) = \frac{x^3 - 18x^2 + 77x}{x^2 - 2x - 35}$$

3. Find any vertical asymptotes of the function above.

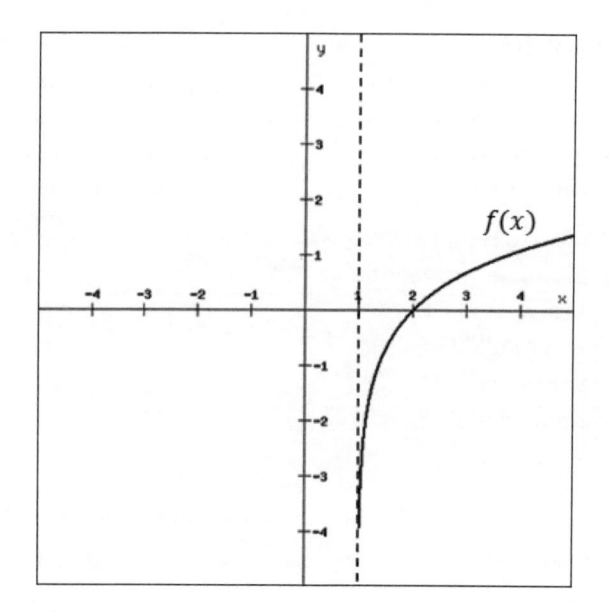

4. The graph of $f(x)$ is given above. If $g(x) = f^{-1}(x+1) - 1$, then what is the range of $g(x)$?

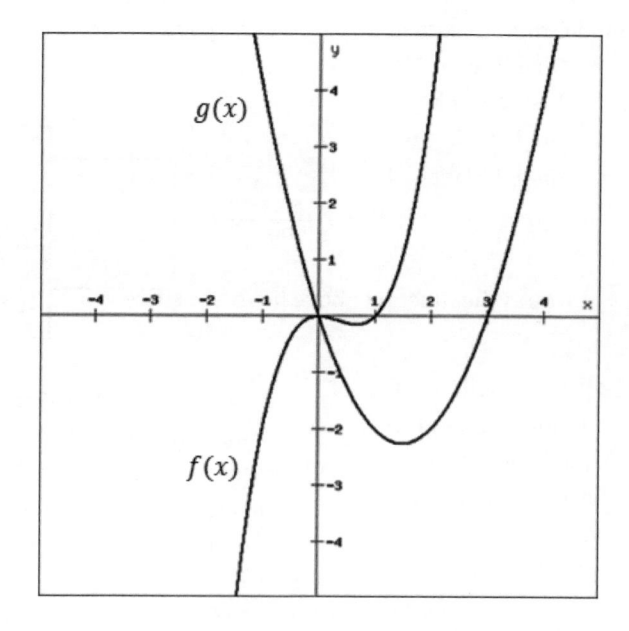

5. The functions $f(x) = x^3 - x^2$ and $g(x) = (x-1)^2 - x - 1$ are shown above. What is the value of $(g \circ f)(2)$?

Red Math Lesson 12B: Functions
Diving into the Deep End

Directions: Answer each question below.

Practice Set 2 (No Calculator)

6. Allen, an avid tennis player, develops a rating system to rank tennis players based on skill. This system gives everyone a rating and then adjusts it upwards or downwards based on whether the player wins or loses. The formula that calculates the rating for a player is as follows: the sum of all of player's opponent's ratings (T) is tabulated and added to the product of 400 and the cubed difference of a player's wins (W) and losses (L). Next, this total is then divided by total matches played (M) to give a rating, R. Which of the following functions represents Allen's formula?

   A) $R = \dfrac{400T(W-L)^3}{M}$
   B) $R = \dfrac{400T(L-W)^3}{M}$
   C) $R = \dfrac{T+400(W^3-L^3)}{M}$
   D) $R = \dfrac{T+400(W-L)^3}{M}$

7. Which of the following relationships is modeled by a quadratic function?
   A) The relationship between the cost of a car and the profit earned, where demand changes based on the cost.
   B) The relationship between area of a trapezoidal door frame and the length of its lower base, where the base is six meters longer than the height.
   C) The relationship between the angle of a catapult launch and the distance its projectile travels.
   D) The relationship between the principle amount invested and interest earned in a bank account that compounds continuously.

x	-2	-1	0	1	2	3
y	1	4	3	-1	-5	2

8. The data above represents a polynomial function. Based on the data, there must be roots of the function in which intervals?
   A) $[0, 1]$ only
   B) $[3, 4]$ only
   C) $[0, 1]$ and $[2, 3]$
   D) $[0, 1]$, $[2, 3]$, and $[3, 4]$

9. The city of Calabasas's population increases at an annual rate of 3.45%. Which of the following represents the time, t, in years, it takes for the population to increase from 100,000 people to a population of p people?
   A) $t = \dfrac{\ln(100{,}000p)}{0.0345}$
   B) $t = 3.45 \times \ln\left(\dfrac{p}{100{,}000}\right)$
   C) $t = \dfrac{\ln(100{,}000-p)}{\ln(1.0345)}$
   D) $t = \dfrac{\ln(p)-\ln(100{,}000)}{\ln(1.0345)}$

10. If $f(x) = \log_{10}(x^2 + 3x - 18)$ and $g(x) = 2x - 5$, then what are the x values that are excluded from the domain of $f(g(x))$?
    A) All real numbers
    B) $\left[-\dfrac{1}{2}, 4\right]$
    C) $\left(-\dfrac{1}{2}, 4\right)$
    D) $\left(-\infty, -\dfrac{1}{2}\right)$ and $(4, \infty)$

328 | SAT Red Math
Lesson 12B: Functions

11. Which of the following graphs corresponds to $y = \cot\left(\frac{x}{2}\right)$?

    A)

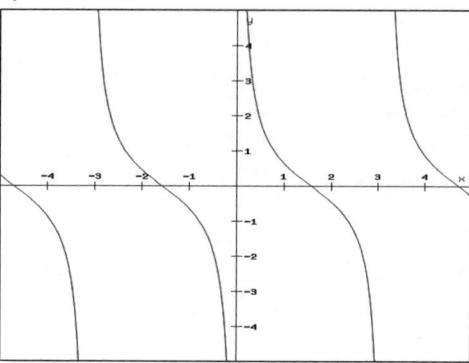

    B)

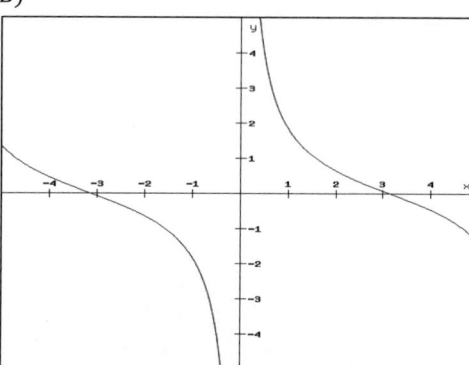

    C)

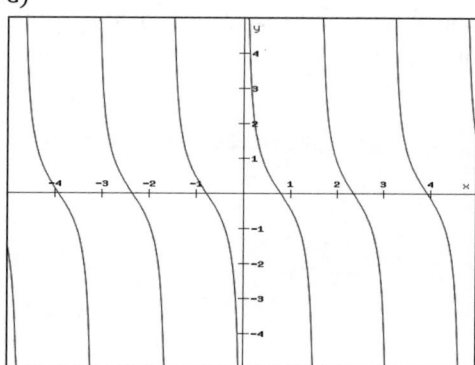

    D)

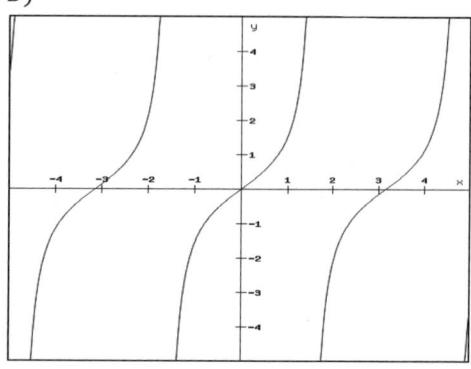

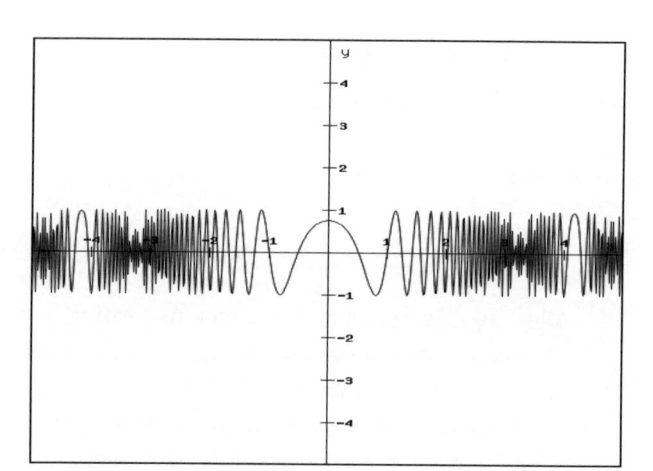

12. In the function graphed above, the sum of the roots is 0 for the domain $[-4, 4]$. Based on that information and the graphical representation above, which of the following is most likely to be true?

    A) $f(x) = f(-x)$
    B) $f(x) = -f(x)$
    C) $f(-x) = -f(x)$
    D) $-f(-x) = f(-x)$

13. Let $L(y) = 2 + \frac{2}{y}$. If $L(M(y)) = y$, which of the following functions could be $M(y)$?

    A) $M(y) = -\frac{2}{y}$
    B) $M(y) = \frac{2}{y-2}$
    C) $M(y) = \frac{2-y}{2}$
    D) $M(y) = \frac{y+2}{2}$

14. If $1 + \frac{1}{n-6} = \frac{2}{n^2-10n+24}$ what is the value of n?

$$\frac{21n^2-7n-15}{(n-3)(7n-4)} = \frac{3n}{n-3} + \frac{T}{7n-4}$$

15. If the identity above holds for all values of n for which both sides are defined, what is the value of T?

SAT Red Math — Lesson 12B: Functions

PRACTICE SET 3 (NO CALCULATOR)

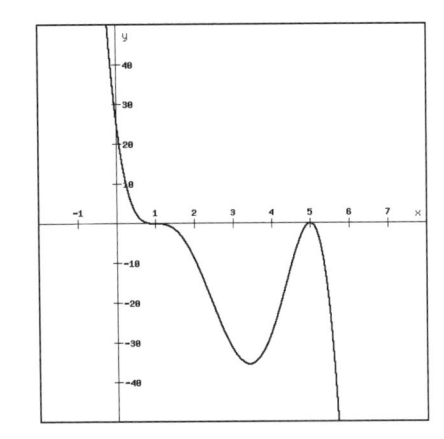

16. Which of the following equations could represent the above function?
    A) $f(x) = -(x+1)^3(x+5)^2$
    B) $f(x) = -(x-1)(x-5)$
    C) $f(x) = (x-1)^3(x-5)^2$
    D) $f(x) = -(x-1)^3(x-5)^2$

$$f(x) = x^3 - 8$$
$$g(x) = x^2 - 25$$

17. Using the equations above, $h(x)$ is equal to $g(f(x))$. If $h(x)$ is reflected across the x-axis and vertically compressed by a factor of $\frac{5}{2}$, what is the resulting function?
    A) $h(x) = \frac{2}{5}(x^3 + 13)(x^3 + 3)$
    B) $h(x) = \frac{2}{5}(-x^3 + 13)(x^3 - 3)$
    C) $h(x) = \frac{5}{2}(-x^3 + 13)(-x^3 + 3)$
    D) $h(x) = \frac{5}{2}(x^3 + 13)(x^3 + 3)$

$$f(x) = \begin{cases} \frac{1}{3}(3)^x & \text{if } x \geq c \\ 18 \log_9 x & \text{if } x < c \end{cases}$$

18. What value of c makes this function continuous?
    A) $\frac{1}{3}$
    B) 1
    C) 3
    D) 9

19. Which of the following best represents the graph of $y = \sin|2x|$?

    A)

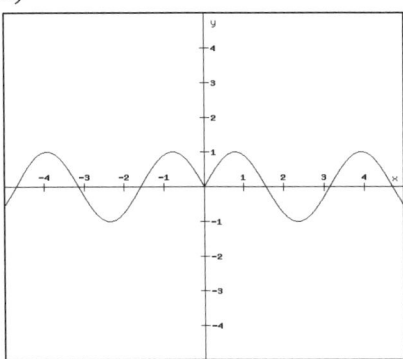

    B)

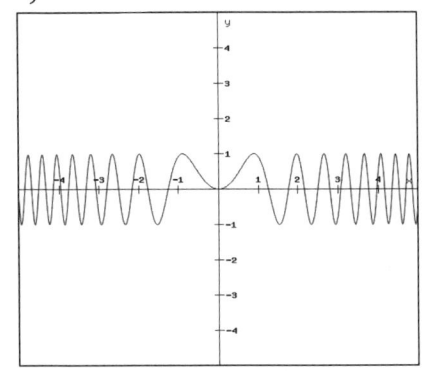

    C)

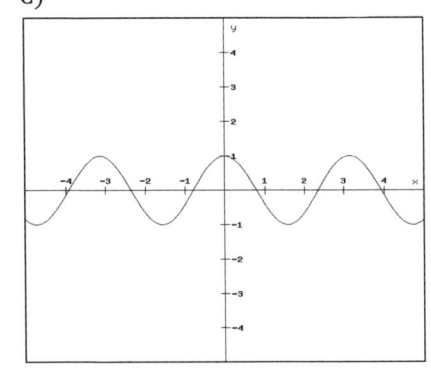

    D)

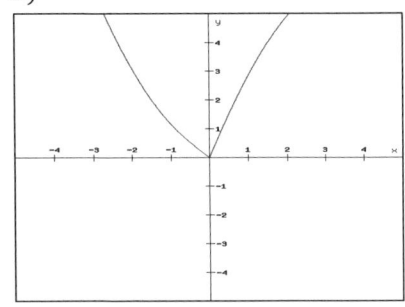

SAT Red Math
Lesson 12B: Functions

$$f(x) = x^5 - 3x^4 - 6x^3 + 10x^2 + 21x + 9$$

20. Which of the following is a graph of the above function?

    A)

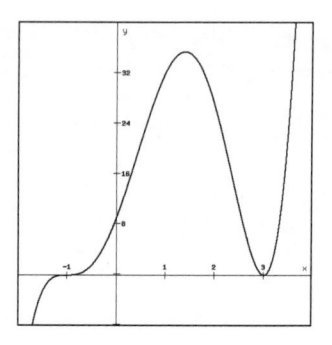

    B)

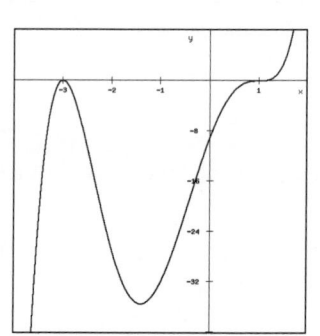

    C)

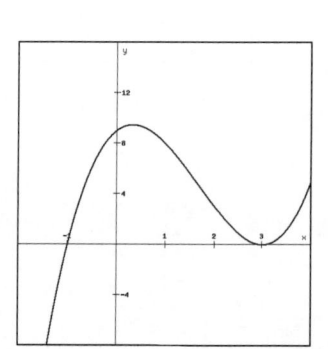

    D)

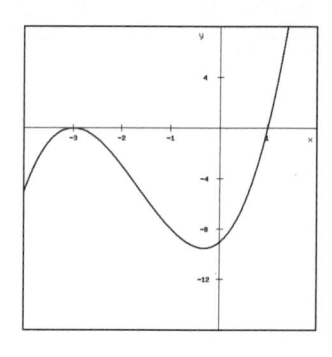

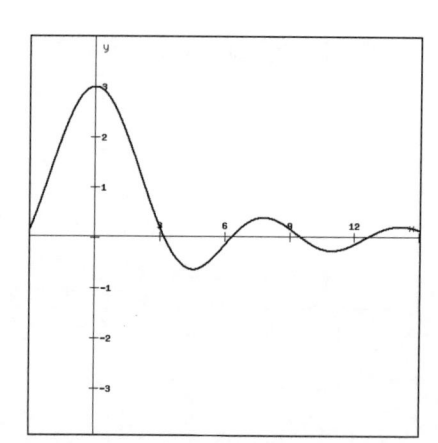

21. A damped spring can be considered to have a general equation in the form $f(x) = A\sin(x)$. For the damped spring represented by the graph above, which of the following could be A?

    A) $-3x$
    B) $\ln x$
    C) $-\dfrac{3}{x}$
    D) $\dfrac{3}{x}$

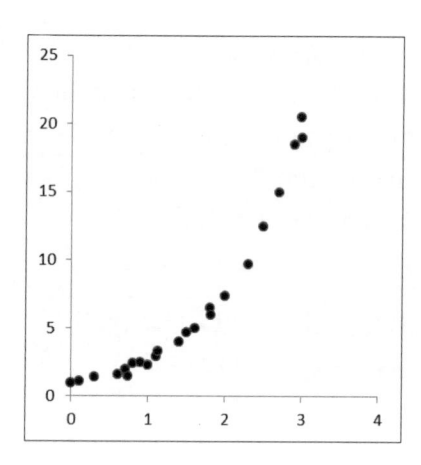

22. Which type of function correctly describes the above data?

    A) $f(x) = ax$
    B) $f(x) = ax^3$
    C) $f(x) = ae^x$
    D) $f(x) = a\ln x$

x	0	1	3
$f(x)$	$\frac{1}{4}$	$\frac{1}{2}$	2

23. Which of the following equations could match the data above?

    A) $f(x) = \frac{x+1}{4}$
    B) $f(x) = \frac{3x+1}{4}$
    C) $f(x) = \frac{2^x}{4}$
    D) $f(x) = \frac{2(2)^x}{4}$

24. A Frisbee is thrown up in the air from a height of 36 inches. The height of the Frisbee in inches is defined as $h(t) = -2t^2 + 36t + 36$, where t is time in seconds. How long, in seconds, is the Frisbee at or above a height of 100 inches? Round to the nearest tenth of a second.

25. If $\frac{3}{n+7} - \frac{2n}{n-4} = \frac{-2n^2 - Bn - 12}{n^2 + 3n - 28}$ for all values of n except -7 and 4, what is the value of B?

SAT Red Math
Lesson 12B: Functions

RED MATH LESSON 12B: FUNCTIONS
Race to the Finish

Directions: Answer each question below.

HOMEWORK SET (CALCULATOR)

1. The volume of a sphere is given by the equation $V = \frac{4}{3}\pi r^3$, where r is the sphere's radius. The surface area of a sphere is given by the equation $A = 4\pi r^2$. A particular single-celled bacterium has a spherical shape, and its surface area-to-volume ratio in nanometers is 3:2. What is the volume of this bacterium (in cubic nanometers)?

   A) $\frac{8\pi}{3}$
   B) $\frac{16\pi}{3}$
   C) $\frac{32\pi}{3}$
   D) $\frac{64\pi}{3}$

$$a(x) = \begin{cases} x^2 - 4x + 7, & x < 0; \\ 3x^2 + 8, & x \geq 0 \end{cases}$$
$$b(x) = 4(x + 7)$$

2. The functions $a(x)$ and $b(x)$ are defined above. If $2a(x) = b(-x^2)$, which of the following could be the value of x?

   A) -1
   B) $-\frac{3}{4}$
   C) 1
   D) $\frac{7}{3}$

3. A business's total cost for x months of operation is given by the equation $c(x) = e^x x^4 - 4e^x x^2$, where $x = 0$ corresponds to January 1, 2013. Its revenue over x months is given by $r(x) = 13e^x x^2 - 16e^x$. For how many months during 2013 was this business profitable?

   A) 1
   B) 3
   C) 4
   D) 6

x	0	2	4	6	8	10
$f(x)$	3	1	-1	-8	8	-2

4. A function $f(x)$ is continuous on the interval $0 \leq x \leq 10$. Some of its values are given by the tables above. What is the minimum number of zeroes that f has on the interval $2 \leq x \leq 8$?

   A) 1
   B) 2
   C) 3
   D) 4

5. An odd function follows the identity $f(-x) = -f(x)$. Which of the following functions is odd?

   I. $s(t) = t^4 - t^2$
   II. $p(\theta) = -\sin(4\theta)$
   III. $v(x) = |1 - e^x|$

   A) I only
   B) II only
   C) I and II
   D) II and III

6. Let $g(x) = 3x^2 - 1$. If $g(x)$ and $h(x)$ both have the domain $[0, \infty)$, for which of the following functions does $(g \circ h)(x) = (h \circ g)(x)$?

   A) $h(x) = 3\sqrt{x + 1}$
   B) $h(x) = 3\sqrt{x - 1}$
   C) $h(x) = \sqrt{\frac{x+1}{3}}$
   D) $h(x) = \sqrt{\frac{x-1}{3}}$

HW

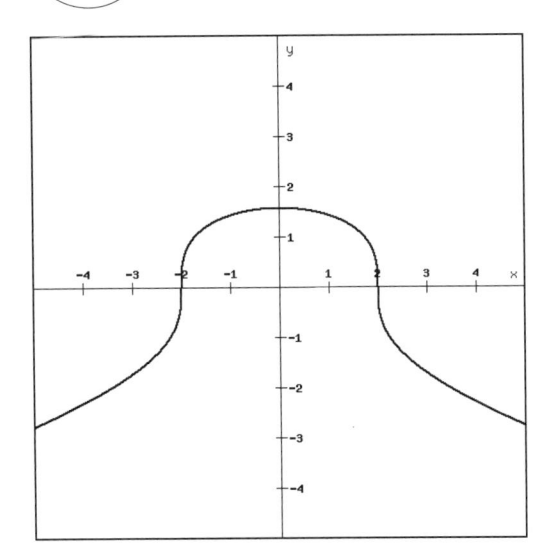

SAT Red Math | 333
Lesson 12B: Functions

7. The graph of $f(x)$ is shown above. If $g(x) = x^{3/2}$, what is the domain over which $g(f(x))$ is real-valued?
   A) $(-\infty, \infty)$
   B) $(-\infty, 1.5)$
   C) $[0, \infty)$
   D) $[-2, 2]$

8. A polynomial has the general form $g(x) = x^2 + bx + c$. If one of its roots is $x = 1 - \frac{\sqrt{2}}{2}i$, what is the value of $g(2)$?
   A) -4.5
   B) 0.5
   C) 1.5
   D) 9.5

9. For the function $f(x) = 2x^2 - ax + a - 34$, a is a constant. If the function has a zero at $x = 5$, what is the other zero of the function?
   A) -1
   B) -2
   C) -3
   D) -4

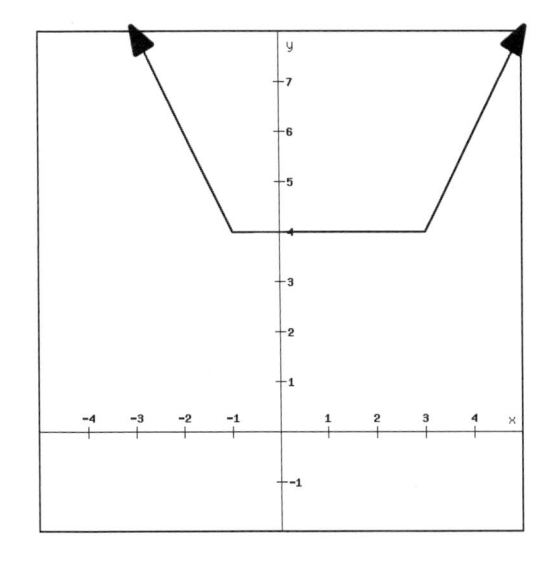

10. The graph of $p(x)$ is shown above. What is the range of the function $q(x) = -2[p(2-x) + 2]$?
    A) $(-\infty, -12]$
    B) $(-\infty, -6]$
    C) $(-\infty, 0]$
    D) $(-\infty, 2]$

11. For the function $f(x) = 8x^3$, $f^{-1}(x)$ is the inverse of $f(x)$. What is the value of $f^{-1}\left(f(f^{-1}(27))\right)$?
    A) $\frac{3}{2}$
    B) $\frac{8}{3}$
    C) $\frac{27}{4}$
    D) $\frac{27}{8}$

12. The function $f(x) = |x - 2| + 7$ is first reflected about the y-axis, then translated 3 units left and finally translated 4 units down. The function as a result of this transformation is $g(x)$. What is $g(0)$?
    A) 2
    B) 5
    C) 8
    D) 9

334 | SAT Red Math
Lesson 12B: Functions

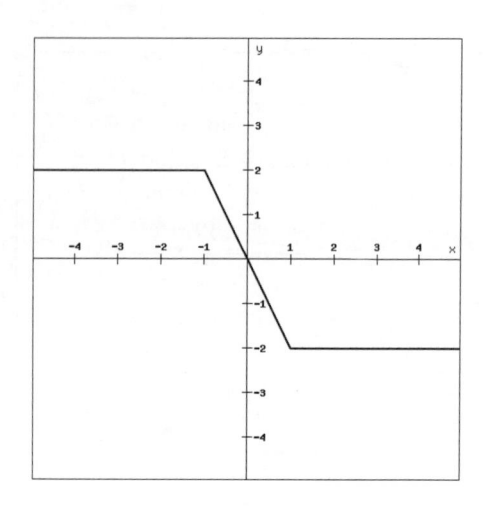

13. Which of the following could be the equation of the function shown above?

A) $|x| - |x+1|$
B) $|x+1| - |x|$
C) $|x+1| - |x-1|$
D) $|x-1| - |x+1|$

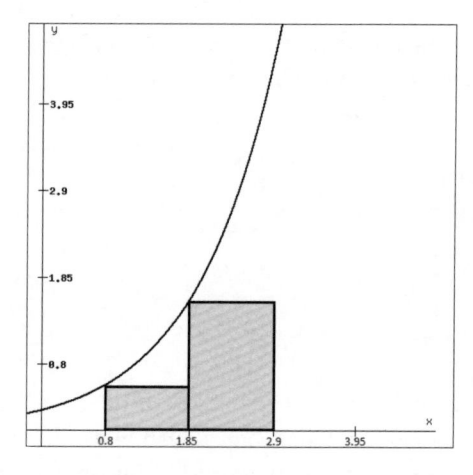

14. The function shown above has the equation $f(x) = \dfrac{e^x}{4}$. What is the sum of the area of the two rectangles shown?

A) 1.75
B) 2.25
C) 3.00
D) 3.75

$$\frac{8x+24}{x+2} - \frac{1}{x^2+10x+16} = \frac{Q}{x+8}$$

15. If the equation above has a solution at $x = -3$, which of the following could be a value of Q?

A) -1
B) 1
C) 2
D) 4

16. Which of the following functions is symmetric with respect to the origin?

A) $f(x) = 2x^2 + 5x$
B) $f(x) = 3x + 4$
C) $f(x) = x^7 + x^3 + 2$
D) $f(x) = x^5 + 3x^3 + 5x$

$$\frac{n+8}{60n^3+32n^2+4n} + \frac{4n}{2n} = \frac{An^3+Bn^2+Cn+D}{4n(3n+1)(5n+1)}$$

17. If the identity above holds for all values of n for which both sides are defined, what is the value of $A - B - C - D$?

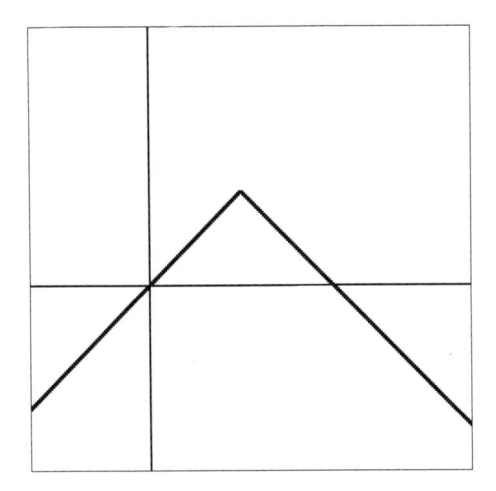

18. The function above has the equation $f(x) = -|x - 4| + a$, where a is a constant. What is the area of the triangle formed by the function and the x-axis?

19. After an explosion, the amount of dust particles in the air increases at a rate of 15% every 30 seconds. If there are now 3 times as many dust particles in the air as there were to begin with, how many minutes have elapsed? Round your answer to the nearest minute.

20. If $125^{2x+3} = 5^{-x^2}$, what is the value of $-x$?

RED MATH LESSON 13A: PRACTICE SECTIONS
Learning to Swim

Directions: Answer each question below.

PRACTICE SET 1 (CALCULATOR)

1. The population of lions is increasing by 1.5% every year and the population of gazelles is decreasing by 0.5% every year. If there were originally 520 lions, write an equation that represents the number of lions as a function of time, in years.

2. Using information from question 1, lions require a ratio of at least 320 gazelles for every 1 lion. If there were originally 382,000 gazelles, for how many more years will this ratio be satisfied?

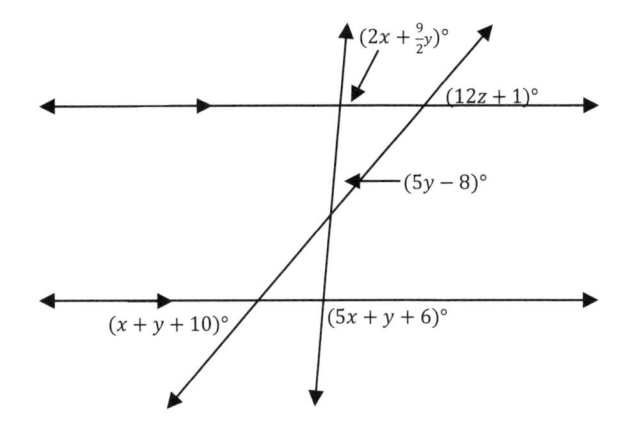

[Figure: Two horizontal parallel lines crossed by two transversals, with angles labeled $(2x + \frac{9}{2}y)°$, $(12z + 1)°$, $(5y - 8)°$, $(x + y + 10)°$, and $(5x + y + 6)°$]

3. What is the value of $x + y + z$ in the image above?

4. A prism has a height of b. If both bases of the prism are represented by the equation $x^2 + y^2 = a^2$ where $x \geq 0$ and $y \geq x$, what is an expression for its volume?

	Less than 4	4 − 12	12 − 26	Greater than 26	Total
200-350	18	17	7	1	43
350-500	29	84	82	28	223
500-650	19	82	61	45	207
650-800	4	14	14	19	51
Total	70	197	164	93	

5. The table above contains data about a random sample of graduating seniors. Each row groups students whose SAT Math score falls into the indicated range according to the number of weeks for which they prepared. What is the probability that a randomly selected student did not study for more than 12 weeks and got above a 650?

RED MATH LESSON 13A: PRACTICE SECTIONS
Diving into the Deep End

Directions: Answer each question below.

PRACTICE SET 2 (CALCULATOR)

6. If $f(x) = a\ln(bx + c)$, what is the function's domain?
   A) $x \neq -\frac{c}{b}$
   B) $x > -\frac{c}{b}$
   C) $x \neq 0$
   D) $x > 0$

$$f(x) = ax^3 + bx^2 + cx + d$$

7. In the polynomial $f(x)$ above, $a \neq 0$. Which of the following is NOT a possible number of distinct, real zeroes for this function?
   A) 0
   B) 1
   C) 2
   D) 3

$$0 = \frac{2-x}{x-2} + \frac{5}{2x+6}$$

8. What are all of the real solutions to the equation above?
   A) -0.5
   B) $-0.5, -2$
   C) $\frac{3+\sqrt{57}}{4}, \frac{3-\sqrt{57}}{4}$
   D) $-0.5, -2, -3, 2$

9. A figure is made by circumscribing a square about a circle and then circumscribing another circle about that square. If the diameter of the outer circle is d, what is the area between the two circles, in terms of d?
   A) $\frac{\pi d^2}{2}$
   B) $\frac{\pi d^2}{4}$
   C) $\frac{\pi d^2}{8}$
   D) $\frac{\pi(\sqrt{2}-1)^2 d^2}{8}$

Questions 10 and 11 use the following information:
A poll of 1,000 likely voters in a gubernatorial election has a margin of error of at most $\pm 4\%$ on all measurements. The poll shows that 38% of voters support Candidate A, 36% support Candidate B, and 26% support Candidate C.

10. Which statement is most accurate based on the information above?
    A) There is a reasonable chance that Candidate A could be leading Candidate B by 8 or more percentage points.
    B) There is a reasonable chance that Candidate A will receive more votes than Candidate B.
    C) There is a reasonable chance that Candidate B could be leading Candidate A by 8 or more percentage points.
    D) There is a reasonable chance that Candidate C could be leading Candidate A.

11. Candidate C drops out of the race before the election. Assuming that Candidate C's supporters split evenly between the other two candidates, if 400,000 people vote in the election, which of the following is most likely to be the number of votes that Candidate A receives?
    A) 144,000
    B) 170,000
    C) 216,000
    D) 260,000

12. If the function $f(x) = \frac{x^3 + ax^2 + bx + c}{x(x+2)}$ is to have no vertical asymptotes, which of the following statements must be true?
    A) $a = 2b$
    B) $c = 0$
    C) $b = c$
    D) $a < cb$

Lesson 13A: Practice Sections

13. To determine the proper size for a heating and air conditioning unit, Emily must first calculate the volume of air in her home. The rectangular base of the house has dimensions 25' by 60', and the height from the base of the house to the base of the roof is 10'. The roof is a triangular prism with an isosceles triangle cross-section: it has a 25' base and 3:12 pitch (every 12" along the base the roof's height increases by 3"). What is the total volume of air that can be contained between the base of the house and the top of the roof? Round your answer to the nearest cubic foot. (Note: area of a prism = base area × height.)
    A) 2,344
    B) 15,000
    C) 17,344
    D) 19,688

14. The daily production cost of a luxury goods company is modeled by the function $C(x) = 0.1x^2 - 100x + 60,000, x \geq 0$, where C is the cost in dollars and x is the amount of products made that day. What is the minimum production cost each day of operation in thousands of dollars? Round to the nearest integer.

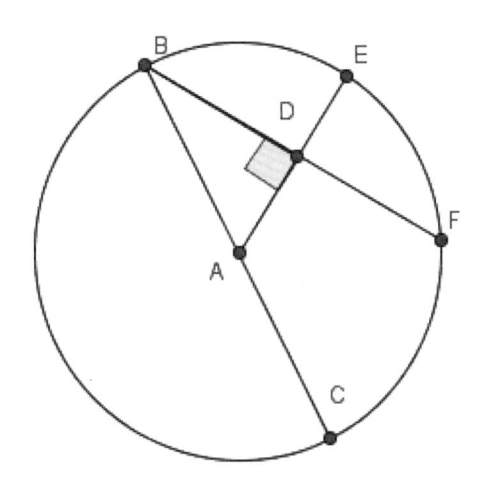

15. For Circle A above, the diameter of the circle is 42.2. If the length of segment $\overline{DF}$ is 19.6, what is the length of segment $\overline{DE}$?

Practice Set 3 (Calculator)

	Tennis	Track & Field	Golf	Total
Freshman	1	4	1	6
Sophomore	4	8	3	15
Junior	5	4	3	12
Senior	3	2	2	7
Total	13	18	9	40

Questions 16 and 17 use the table above.

16. A high school athletics department polled students to gauge popularity of the school's individual sports. Students were asked which competitions they attended most (either as a competitor or a spectator) among Tennis, Track & Field, and Golf. Which of the following statements is most likely correct, based on the results summarized in the table above?
    A) A survey of 45 sophomores would reveal that 9 of them are on the Golf team.
    B) A survey of 60 juniors would reveal that 25 attend Track & Field competitions the most.
    C) Freshmen are more likely to attend Track & Field meets than the students of any other grade.
    D) Juniors are more likely to attend Track & Field meets than any other competition.

17. If there are between 375 and 425 students in each grade at this school, does it seem likely that these results could be extrapolated to the whole school?
    A) Yes, because all grades are represented.
    B) Yes, because the results represent 40% of the students.
    C) No, because the students polled are not evenly distributed among the three sports.
    D) No, because the students polled are not evenly distributed among the four grades.

18. What is the tangent of the angle formed between the line $y = 4x$ and the positive x-axis?
A) $-\frac{1}{4}$
B) $\frac{\sqrt{17}}{17}$
C) $\frac{4\sqrt{17}}{17}$
D) 4

19. A student tries to figure out the height of a nearby tower by using trigonometry. He calculates that the tower is 5 miles away, and its tip is at an angle of inclination of 4°. He calculates that it is 6.6 miles tall. The student recognizes that this is obviously wrong. What mistake might he have made to obtain this result?

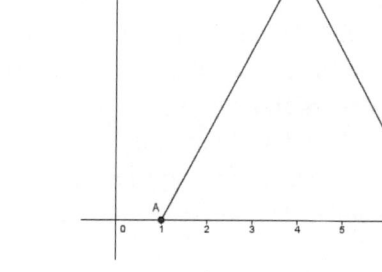

A) Used an angle of inclination of 20 degrees by accident.
B) Treated 10 degrees as an angle of depression rather than an angle of inclination.
C) Hit the inverse tangent button instead of the tangent button on his calculator.
D) Switched the values for the degrees and the miles away.

20. A merchant sells an item at a 20% discount, but still makes a gross profit of 20% of the cost. After reducing the discount to only 10% off, sales drop to 90% of what they were. What was the percent change in gross profit as a result of the price adjustment?
A) Down 19%
B) Up 50%
C) Up 57.5%
D) Up 75%

21. For the figure above, $\triangle ABC$ is equilateral. What is the y-intercept of the line that contains points B and C?
A) $\sqrt{3}$
B) $2\sqrt{3}$
C) $7\sqrt{3}$
D) $12\sqrt{3}$

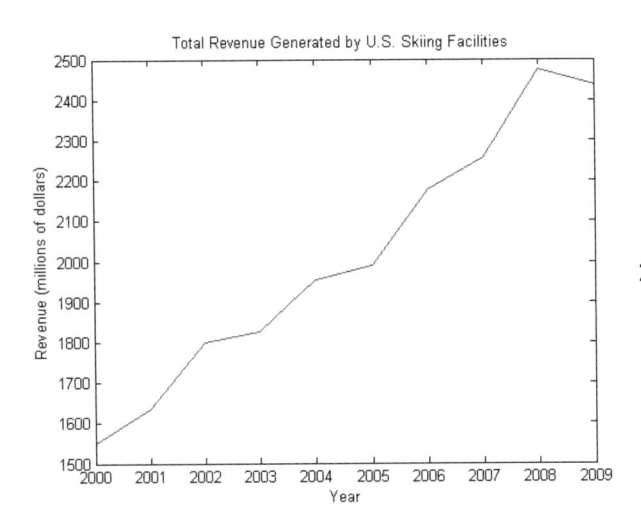

Questions 22 and 23 use the figure above.

22. The above graph demonstrates the growth of the U.S. skiing tourism industry between 2000 and 2009. Based on the trend, what is the best prediction of the total revenue generated in 2014?
    A) 2.1 billion dollars
    B) 2.5 billion dollars
    C) 2.9 billion dollars
    D) 4.2 billion dollars

23. In 2005, a market analyst used the 2000-2004 revenue data shown in the graph to predict the total revenue that would be earned in 2009. By how much did the actual revenue fall short of this projection?
    A) 17 million
    B) 109 million
    C) 224 million
    D) The projection actually underestimated the revenue.

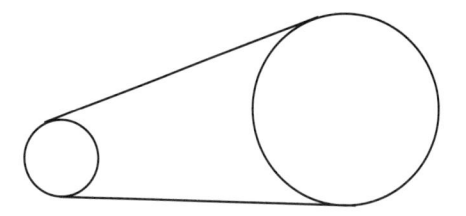

24. The chain of a bicycle goes around a gear attached to the pedals and around a gear attached to the rear wheel, as shown above. In the second-highest gear on a particular brand of mountain bike, the front gear has a radius of 3.8 inches, while the gear on the wheel has a radius of 0.95 inches. When the rider is pedaling at 36 revolutions per minute, what is the wheel's speed in revolutions per minute?

25. A hot-air balloon is 2 miles due west of Old Faithful when the passengers look down and see that landmark with a 21° angle of depression. At the same time, tourists at Old Faithful see an airplane cruising at 10,000 feet elevation, also due west of them, with an angle of elevation of 65°. What is the straight-line distance between the balloon and the airplane? Round to the nearest foot.

RED MATH LESSON 13A: PRACTICE SECTIONS
Race to the Finish

Directions: Answer each question below.

HOMEWORK SET (CALCULATOR)

1. Two circles are symmetric with respect to the line $y = x$. If the equation of one circle is $x^2 + y^2 + 22x - 4y + 76 = 0$, what is the equation of the other circle?
   A) $(x - 2)^2 + (y + 11)^2 = 49$
   B) $(x + 4)^2 + (y - 13)^2 = 49$
   C) $(x + 11)^2 + (y - 2)^2 = 49$
   D) $(x - 13)^2 + (y + 4)^2 = 49$

Section A		Section B
5	0	0,0,0
	1	0,0,5
	2	
9	3	
7,3,1	4	
9,8,6,6,4	5	7,8
5,5,5,5,3	6	1,3,5,8
9,2	7	2,4,4,4,4,6
9,8,6,5,3,2,1	8	3,6,6,8
8	9	1,7,8

2. Two physics classes with 25 students each take a midterm exam, with the resulting grades shown on the above stem-and-leaf plot. (The center column shows the tens digit of each grade with the ones digits listed to either side.) Which of the following statements about this data is false?
   A) Section B had a higher median score than Section A.
   B) Section B had a higher mean score than Section A.
   C) Section B had a higher mode score than Section A.
   D) Section B had a wider range of scores than Section A.

Richter Scale Magnitude	Joule Equivalent
0.0	6.3×10^4 J
0.5	3.6×10^5 J
1.0	2.0×10^6 J
1.5	1.1×10^7 J

3. Each increase by one unit of magnitude on the Richter Scale corresponds to a multiplication by a constant factor in the amount of energy output. A magnitude 19 earthquake would completely shatter and explode the Earth. Approximately how many Joules is this?
   A) 3×10^{28} J
   B) 2×10^{29} J
   C) 7×10^{31} J
   D) 2×10^{33} J

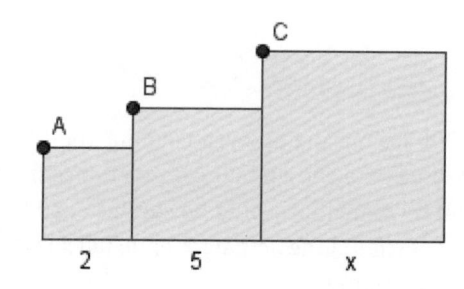

Note: Figure not drawn to scale.

4. Points $A, B,$ and C are vertices of squares. If $A, B,$ and C are collinear, what is the sum of the area of the three squares?
   A) 90.75
   B) 102.50
   C) 130.00
   D) 185.25

5. A transformer is a device that changes voltage in an electrical circuit; each side consists of a coil of wire, and the voltage in each side varies directly as the number of turns of wire in the coil. One side of a small transformer has 1430 turns of wire to take standard European wall current, which is supplied at 220 volts. What is the difference between the number of turns of wire required on the other side to produce standard Japanese voltage, 100 V and the number required to produce standard U.S. voltage, 110 V?
   A) The U.S. version has 715 more turns.
   B) The Japanese version has 650 more turns.
   C) The U.S. version has 65 more turns.
   D) The Japanese version has 286 more turns.

6. Mrs. Anderson made a mistake while grading her student's test scores. She forgot to multiply each student's score by two. After adjusting the test scores, she should expect the standard deviation of the scores to:
   A) Remain the same
   B) Half in Value
   C) Double in value
   D) Quadruple in value

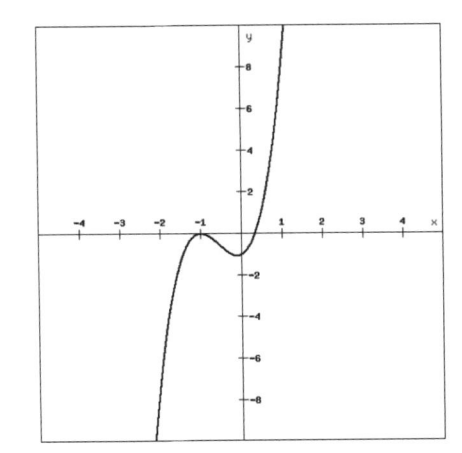

7. The graph of the function above passes through the point (1, 8). Which of the following states its equation?
   A) $f(x) = (x+1)\left(x - \frac{1}{3}\right)$
   B) $f(x) = (x+1)\left(x - \frac{1}{3}\right)^2$
   C) $f(x) = (x+1)^2(3x-1)$
   D) $f(x) = -(x+1)^2(3x-1)$

Use the following information for questions 8 and 9:

A startup game designer is marketing games for a popular console, and finds that if the games are priced at $8 each, they will only be able to supply 5700 copies per month. If the unit price goes up, however, they will be able to hire enough staff to produce an additional 30 copies each month for every dollar price increase. Market research indicates that at $8, there would be a demand for 10,560 copies per month, but monthly sales would go down 150 copies for each dollar of price increase.

8. At what price will supply match demand?
   A) $35
   B) $52.50
   C) $98
   D) $14,750

Total Revenue = Price × Sales

9. What is the maximum revenue for the game designers?
   A) $188,256
   B) $230,496
   C) $272,736
   D) $314,976

10. If $x = \frac{a}{b+a}$ and $y = \frac{b-a}{a}$, what is $x + y$?
    A) $\frac{a^2}{a^2+ab}$
    B) $\frac{b^2}{a^2+ab}$
    C) $\frac{a}{a^2+ab}$
    D) $\frac{b}{a^2+ab}$

11. If 2 is a solution to $x^3 - 6.5x^2 + 11x - 4 = 0$, what is the difference between the other two solutions?
    A) 2
    B) 3.5
    C) 4.5
    D) 6

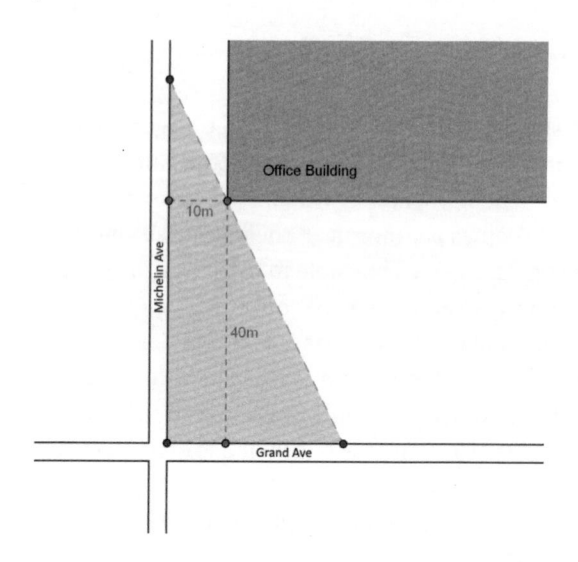

12. Miri is assigned to survey a 900 m² property on the above street corner. The owner has specified that the property should be a triangle bounded by the streets and a line passing through the corner of his office building, and the property will be deeded to the city to create a park. What is a possible length of the park's boundary with Grand Avenue?
    A) 10 m
    B) 20 m
    C) 30 m
    D) 60 m

13. The population of the world in billions of people t years since 1975 can be approximated by the expression $4e^{0.019t}$. On average, the population grew by how many millions of people per year between 2000 and 2010?
    A) 1.4
    B) 837
    C) 1,346
    D) 2,666,300,000

14. Putnam County has 1.5 million residents. The wealthiest 20% of residents have an average income of $56,000 per year, while the average income of the remainder is $15,000 per year. When a mining operation moves to the county, the lower 80% see a 10% increase in earnings, while the income of the upper 20% increases by only 5% on average. By what amount does the total income of the county increase?
    A) $2.64 billion
    B) $15.45 billion
    C) $17.64 billion
    D) $19.8 billion

15. If $2^{\sqrt{\frac{16}{x^2} - 2y - 13}} = \frac{2}{\sqrt{\left(\frac{1}{4}\right)^{y+5}}}$, what is a possible value of $x(y + 7)$?
    A) -4
    B) 0
    C) 6
    D) The equation has no real solutions.

$$(x - 1)^2 + (y - 2)^2 = 9$$
$$(x + 2)^2 + (y - 2)^2 = r^2$$

16. If the above system has exactly one solution pair (x, y) and $r > 0$, what is the value of r?
    A) 3
    B) 6
    C) 9
    D) It is not possible to have exactly one solution to this system.

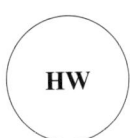

People Living Below the Poverty Line in the United States
Source: U.S. Census Bureau

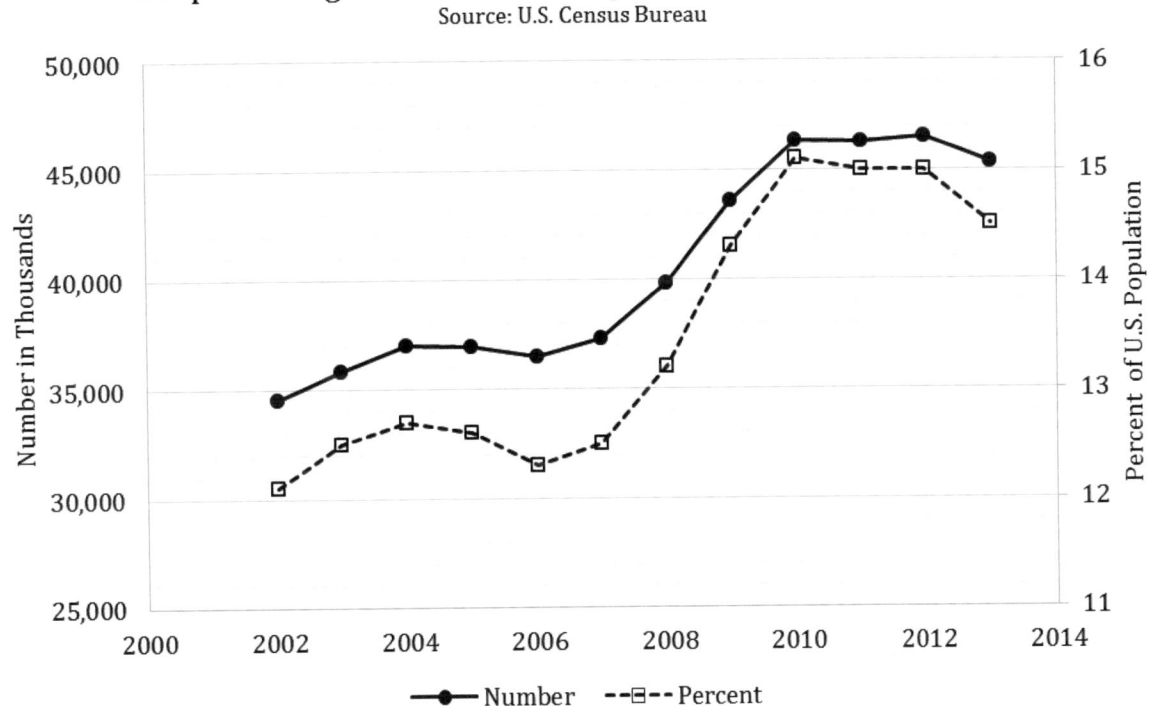

17. By what percent did the number of people living below the poverty line increase from 2002 to 2004? Round to the nearest tenth of a percent.

18. If the trend observed during 2007 to 2010 had continued, the number of people living below the poverty line would have been approximately what percent greater in 2013 than actually happened? Round to the nearest percent.

19. By approximately how many people did the U.S. population increase from 2002 to 2013, in millions?

Mineral powder	Calcium (mg/g)	Iron (mg/g)	Zinc (mg/g)
A	580	0	0.5
B	0	18	4
C	80	6	4

20. A manufacturer of dietary supplements is using the mineral powders above to create a pill to meet the recommended dietary allowance of these minerals for girls aged 14 to 18: 1300 mg of calcium, 15 mg of iron, and 9 mg of zinc. If each pill has exactly these quantities, what will its total mass be? Round to the nearest tenth of a gram.

SAT Red Math | 347
Lesson 13B: Exponential Functions

RED MATH LESSON 13B: EXPONENTIAL FUNCTIONS
Learning to Swim

Directions: Answer each question below.

PRACTICE SET 1 (NO CALCULATOR)

1. What is the domain of the function $q(x) = \log_5(-2x - 5)$?

2. Give the coordinates of all the intercepts of the graph of $h(x) = 2\log_3(x + 9)$.

3. At what point do the graphs of $y = 3^x$ and $y = 9(2^{x-2})$ intersect?

Month	Population density (lemmings per hectare)
0	2
12	29
24	424

4. Lemmings are small rodents that live in the Arctic; they can produce 3 to 6 litters of young per year. Given the information in the table above, by what percentage does the lemming population increase each month?

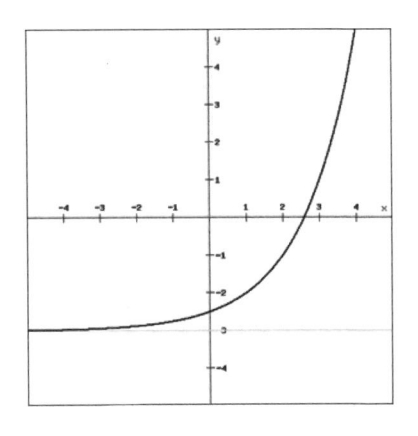

5. The graph above is a transformation of $g(x) = 2^x$ that passes through the points $(1, -2)$ and $(3, 1)$. What is its equation?

Version 3.0

RED MATH LESSON 13B: EXPONENTIAL FUNCTIONS
Diving into the Deep End

Directions: Answer each question below.

PRACTICE SET 2 (CALCULATOR)

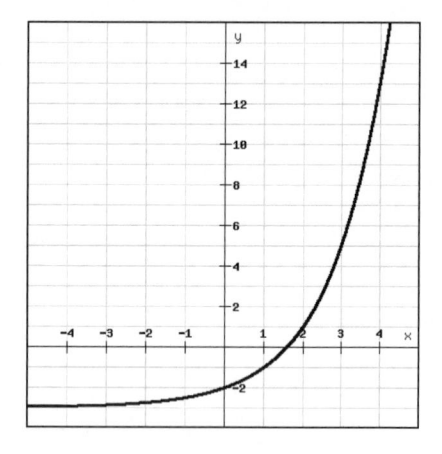

6. Which of the following exponential equations matches the graph in the xy-coordinate plane shown above?
   A) $f(x) = 2^x - 2$
   B) $f(x) = 2^x - 3$
   C) $f(x) = 2^{x-2}$
   D) $f(x) = 2^{x-3}$

7. For all positive real numbers a and b, what is the domain of the function $g(x) = e^{x-a} + b$?
   A) All real values of x
   B) All real values of x greater than a
   C) All real values of x greater than b
   D) All real values of x except a

8. An exponential function passes through the points (2,1) and (3,10). Which of the following could be that function?
   A) $f(x) = 10^{x-2}$
   B) $f(x) = 10^{x+2}$
   C) $f(x) = 3^{x-1} - 2$
   D) $f(x) = 3^{x-1} + 1$

9. A study of the effectiveness of anti-smoking campaigns surveyed the habits of 500 people, all of whom were regular smokers in the year 2000. The study found that each year, 6% of the participants who still smoked opted to quit smoking. Which of the following functions models the number of people who have not stopped smoking in year y?
   A) $A = 500(1 - 0.06)^{\frac{y}{2000}}$
   B) $A = 500 - (1 - 0.06)^{y-2000}$
   C) $A = 500(1 - 0.06^{y-2000})$
   D) $A = 500(1 - 0.06)^{y-2000}$

10. What is the range of $f(x) = -e^{x-3} + 2$?
    A) All real values of y less than 3
    B) All real values of y greater than 3
    C) All real values of y less than 2
    D) All real values of y greater than 2

11. The population of monarch butterflies in a colony under study by ecologists has been decreasing exponentially due to predation and loss of habitat. The scientists measured the butterfly population every other year from 2004 to 2014 and then estimated that, if observed trends continue, the population in year y will be given by the formula:

    $$P_y = 340 \cdot 0.955^{\frac{y-2014}{2}}$$

    Which of the following is an accurate statement?
    A) The butterfly population is expected to be greater than 340 in the year 2020.
    B) The butterfly population is expected to decrease by 4.5% every 2 years.
    C) The butterfly population is expected to decrease by 9% every year.
    D) The butterfly population is expected to decrease by 95.5% every 2 years.

SAT Red Math
Lesson 13B: Exponential Functions

12. In the function $h(x) = a^x - b$, a and b are positive real numbers. Which of the following is a solution to the function?
    A) $(0, -b)$
    B) $(0, 1 - b)$
    C) $(a - b, 1)$
    D) $(a, 1 - b)$

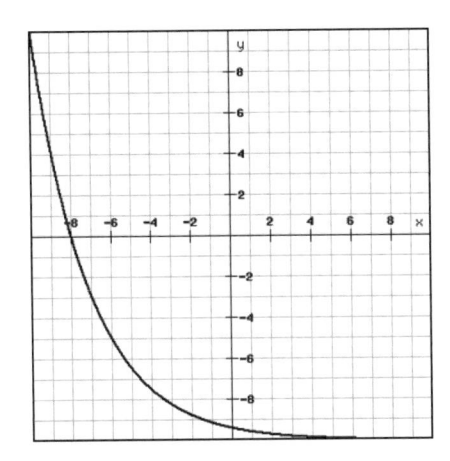

13. Which of the following equations describes the graph depicted above?
    A) $y = \left(\frac{5}{8}\right) 2^{-\frac{x}{2}} - 10$
    B) $y = \left(\frac{5}{8}\right) 2^{-x} - 10$
    C) $y = \left(\frac{5}{8}\right) \left(\frac{1}{2}\right)^x - 10$
    D) $y = 10 \cdot (-2)^{\frac{x}{10}}$

14. In an experiment, a population of viruses is exposed to a new anti-viral drug. The number of individual viruses decays at a continuous rate of 10% per day. If there are 303 viruses at the end of the fifth day, approximately how many are there at the end of the tenth day?

15. After hiring a new chef in January, the number of customers at a restaurant has been decreasing by 2% every week. How many weeks, to the nearest integer, will it take for the restaurant to have half the customers it did in January?

PRACTICE SET 3 (CALCULATOR)

16. What is the domain of $g(x) = \log(2x)$?
    A) All real values of x
    B) All real values of x greater than 0
    C) All real values of x greater than 1
    D) All real values of x except 0

Year	Subscribers (Millions)
2006	11
2007	25
2008	58
2009	134
2010	310

17. The data table above shows the approximate number of *Social Media Weekly* subscribers, in millions, in February of each of five years early in the site's growth. If the membership in millions, M, in year y can be approximated by the function
    $$M = 11 \cdot a^{y-2006}$$
    for some constant a, which of the following is closest to the value of a?
    A) 2.3
    B) 2.5
    C) 4.0
    D) 14.0

18. If $\log x = a$, what is $\log(100x)$ in terms of a?
    A) $a + 1$
    B) $a + 2$
    C) a^2
    D) $a^2 + 1$

350 | SAT Red Math
Lesson 13B: Exponential Functions

19. $$2^{3x+2} - 2^{6x+2}$$
    Which of the following expressions is equivalent to the above expression?
    A) 8^{-x}
    B) $-4 - 3 \cdot 2^x$
    C) $4 \cdot 8^{-x}$
    D) $4(8^x - 8^{2x})$

20. Which function matches the graph in the xy-coordinate plane shown above?
    A) $f(x) = \ln(x+1) + 1$
    B) $f(x) = \ln(x-1) + 1$
    C) $f(x) = 2 \cdot \ln(x-1)$
    D) $f(x) = 2 \cdot \ln(x)$

21. The graph of $y = \frac{2^{x+2}}{8}$ can be obtained by doing any of the following to the graph of $y = 2^x$ EXCEPT:
    A) dividing the y-coordinate of each point by 2.
    B) shifting each point 1 unit to the right.
    C) shifting each point 1 unit down.
    D) All of the above will produce the correct graph.

22. In the xy-coordinate plane, the graph of the function $f(x) = 2^x + 1$ is reflected across the line $y = x$ to form the function $g(x)$. What is $g(x)$?
    A) $g(x) = \log_2(x) - 1$
    B) $g(x) = \log_2(x-1)$
    C) $g(x) = \log_2(x) + 1$
    D) $g(x) = \log_2(x+1)$

23. $$4^{x+1} + \frac{8^{x+2}}{2^{x+1}} = 9$$
    What value of x satisfies the equation above?
    A) -4
    B) -2
    C) -1
    D) 2

24. The equation for continuously compounded interest is $A = Pe^{rt}$, where A is the ending amount, P is the starting amount (the principal), r is the interest rate, and t is the time. If the interest rate is 5% per year, how long will it take an investment to double in value? Round your answer to the nearest tenth of a year.

25. If $\log \frac{3x}{8} = \log(2x - 1)$, then $x =$

RED MATH LESSON 13B: EXPONENTIAL FUNCTIONS
Race to the Finish

Directions: Answer each question below.

HOMEWORK SET (CALCULATOR)

1. If $y = 16x^3$, then $\log_2 y = ?$
   A) $4 \cdot \log_2 x + 3$
   B) $3 \cdot \log_2 x + 4$
   C) $12 \cdot \log_2 x$
   D) $\log_8 x + 4$

Years since Purchase	Resale Value
0	$16,000
1	$14,400
2	$12,960
4	$10,500
8	$6,890

2. The data table above shows the average resale value of a car, originally sold new for $16,000, at various times after its purchase. If this depreciation (decline in value) can be modeled by the equation $V = 16000 \cdot \left(1 - \frac{r}{100}\right)^t$, where t is the number of years since purchase, which of the following values of r most closely fits the data shown in the table?
   A) 0.1
   B) 10
   C) 11.1
   D) 88.9

$$P = N_0 e^{rt}$$

3. Given the equation above, which of the following is an expression for r in terms of P, N_0, and t?
   A) $r = \frac{\ln P - \ln N_0}{\ln T}$
   B) $r = \ln P - \ln N_0 - t$
   C) $r = \frac{\ln(P - N_0)}{t}$
   D) $r = \frac{\ln P - \ln N_0}{t}$

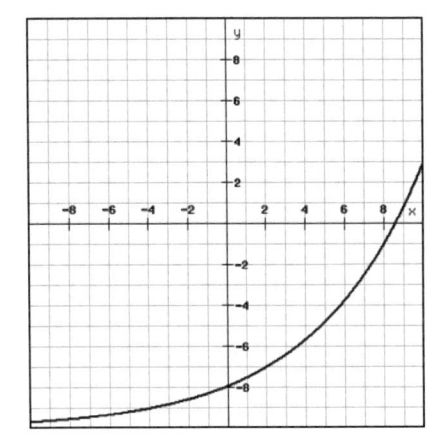

4. The above graph is described by which of the following equations?
   A) $y = 3^{\frac{x+4}{6}} - 10$
   B) $y = 3^{\frac{x+4}{6}} - 8$
   C) $y = 3^{\frac{x}{6}} - 10$
   D) $y = 3^{\frac{x}{6}} - 8$

5. A game show host offers a contestant a choice: if she can remain in the game without losing for x minutes, she can win either x^3 dollars or 2^x dollars. The catch is that she must decide in advance which formula to use. To win the maximum number of dollars, she should choose the exponential formula if she expects to stay in the game for at least how many minutes?
   A) 8
   B) 10
   C) The exponential formula is always the better choice.
   D) The cubic formula is always the better choice.

SAT Red Math
Lesson 13B: Exponential Functions

6. Which of the following is the graph of $y = 27 - 3^{\left(\frac{x}{3}+1\right)}$?

   A)

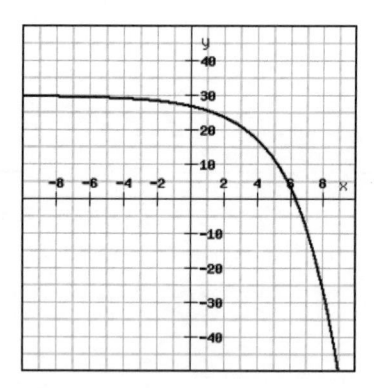

   B)

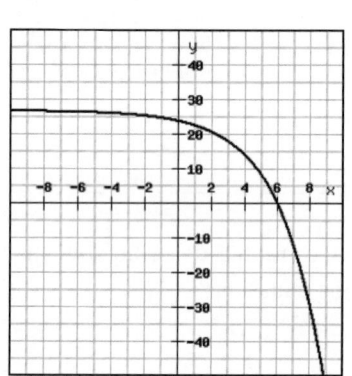

   C)

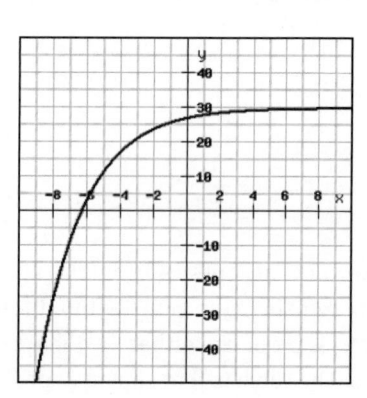

   D)

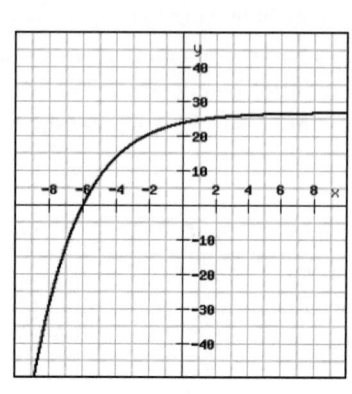

7. Which of the following is the graph of $y = 3\log(x + 20)$?

   A)

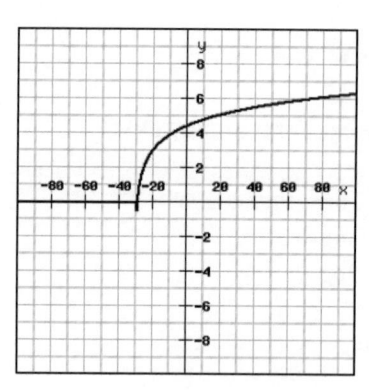

   B)

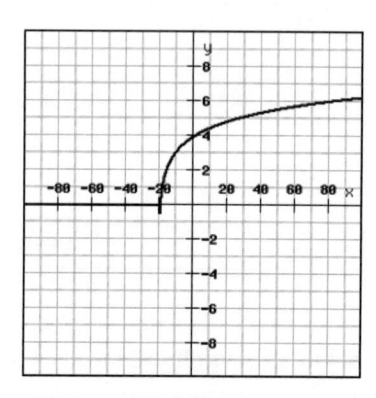

   C)

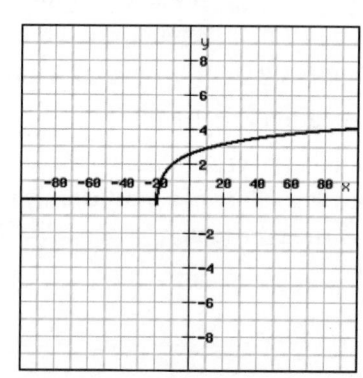

   D)

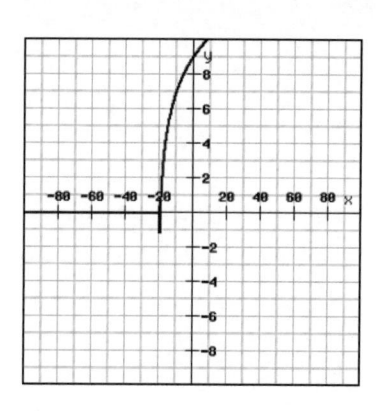

SAT Red Math
Lesson 13B: Exponential Functions

8. Which of the following graphs matches the function $f(x) = \ln(-x)$?

   A)

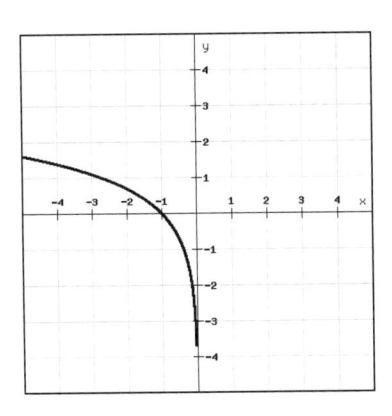

   B)

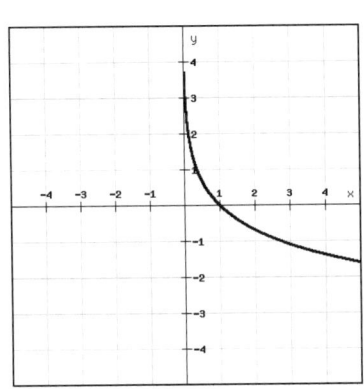

   C)

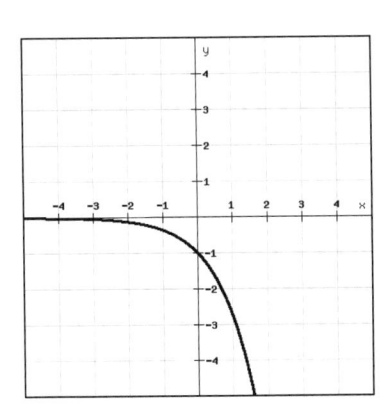

   D)

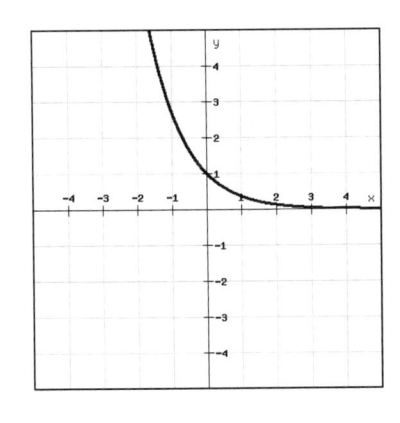

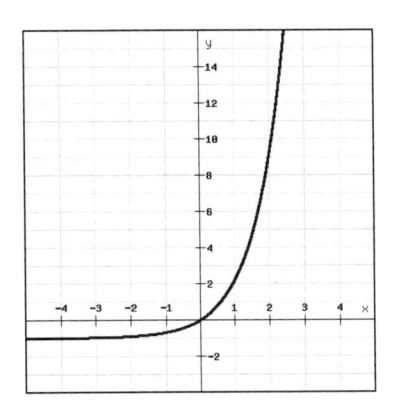

9. Which of the following exponential functions is graphed above?
   A) $f(x) = 10^{0.5x} - 1$
   B) $f(x) = 10^{0.5x}$
   C) $f(x) = 0.5 \cdot 10^x - 1$
   D) $f(x) = 0.5 \cdot 10^x$

10. If an exponential function passes through the points $(-1, 2)$ and $(1, 5)$, that function could be which of the following?
    A) $f(x) = 2^{x+1}$
    B) $f(x) = 2^{x-1} + 1$
    C) $f(x) = 2^x + 1$
    D) $f(x) = 2^{x+1} + 1$

11. The population of a certain bacteria doubles every 10 hours. If there are 50 bacteria in the sample initially, which equation could be used to determine how many bacteria are in the sample after h hours?
    A) $B = 5 \cdot 2^h$
    B) $B = 5 \cdot 2^{10h}$
    C) $B = 50 \cdot 2^{h/10}$
    D) $B = 50 \cdot 2^{h-10}$

SAT Red Math
Lesson 13B: Exponential Functions

12. The graph of an exponential function in the xy-coordinate plane passes through the point $(1 - b, a)$. Which of the following could be that function?
    A) $h(x) = a^{x-b}$
    B) $h(x) = a^{x+b}$
    C) $h(x) = b^{x-a}$
    D) $h(x) = b^{x+a}$

13. If a and b are integers greater than 1, what is the domain of the function $f(x) = \log_a(x) + b$?
    A) All real values of x greater than 0
    B) All real values of x greater than a
    C) All real values of x greater than b
    D) All real values of x

14. A function has a domain of all real values of x and a range of all real values of y less than 0. Which of the following could be the function?
    A) $f(x) = \log x$
    B) $f(x) = -\log x$
    C) $f(x) = e^x$
    D) $f(x) = -e^x$

15. In chemistry, a substance's pH is defined as follows: $\text{pH} = -\log a_{H+}$, where a_{H+} is the hydrogen ion activity of the substance. If Sample A has a pH of 4 and Sample B has a pH of 8, what is the ratio of Sample A's hydrogen ion activity to that of Sample B?
    A) 1:10,000
    B) 1:40
    C) 40:1
    D) 10,000:1

For questions 16 and 17 an investment account pays $r\%$ annual interest, compounded monthly.

16. Terrence deposits $1,500 in this account and leaves it there for 12 years, neither putting any more money in nor taking any money out. Which of the following equations represents this situation?
    A) $A = 1500 \cdot \left(1 + \frac{r}{12}\right)^{144}$
    B) $A = 1500 \cdot \left(1 + \frac{r}{100}\right)^{12}$
    C) $A = 1500 \cdot \left(1 + \frac{r}{1200}\right)^{144}$
    D) $A = 1500 \cdot \left(1 + \frac{r}{1200}\right)^{12}$

17. What is the minimum integer value of the annual interest rate r at which Terrence could quadruple his original investment in less than or equal to 30 years? Round to the nearest whole percent.

18. The graph of the function $f(x) = \log(x+3)$ is translated 1 unit to the right and 2 units up. Where does the resulting graph cross the y-axis? Round to the nearest hundredth.

19. Jeff's restaurant has a customer increase of 2% every year and Sal's restaurant has a customer decrease of 2% every year. If both Jeff and Sal served 12,000 customers in 2010, how many more customers, to the nearest integer, will Jeff serve in 2014 when compared to Sal?

Investment Plan A: 5% annual interest, compounded annually.
Investment Plan B: No interest for 10 years, then 8% annual interest, compounded annually.

20. A money management firm offers the above two investment plans to its clients. Plan B is designed to reward long-term investors, as its interest rate is higher than that of Plan A once the 10-year threshold passes and the customer's account begins to earn interest. What is the least integer number of years that a client's money must remain invested with this firm for Plan B to result in greater total financial gains than Plan A?

Red Math Lesson 14A: Rational Functions
Learning to Swim

Directions: Answer each question below.

Practice Set 1 (No Calculator)

1. Simplify $\dfrac{x^5+3x^4-7x^3-27x^2-18x}{x+3}$.

2. How many distinct real solutions exist for the equation $\dfrac{2x^2+x-6}{x^2-2x-8} \cdot \dfrac{x^2+5x+4}{2x+3} = 0$?

3. What is the remainder when $3x^3 - x + 11$ is divided by $x - 2$?

4. What is the domain of the function $y = \dfrac{3x^2-x-4}{2x^2+7x-15}$?

5. Simplify $\dfrac{y-5}{y+1} + \dfrac{3-y}{y+2}$

SAT Red Math
Lesson 14A: Rational Functions

RED MATH LESSON 14A: RATIONAL FUNCTIONS
Diving into the Deep End

Directions: Answer each question below.

PRACTICE SET 2 (NO CALCULATOR)

6. Assuming $x \neq 3$ or -3, $\frac{x^2-5x+6}{x^2-9} \cdot \frac{x^2+x-6}{x-3} =$
   A) $\frac{(x-2)^2}{(x-3)^2}$
   B) $\frac{(x-2)^2}{x-3}$
   C) $\frac{x-2}{(x-3)^2}$
   D) $\frac{(x-2)^2}{x+3}$

7. Assuming $y \neq 1$ or -4, $\frac{y^2+8y+16}{y^2+3y-4} \div \frac{y^2-2y+1}{y+4} =$
   A) $y - 1$
   B) $\frac{(y+4)^3}{(y-1)^2}$
   C) $\frac{(y+4)^2}{(y-1)^3}$
   D) $\frac{(y+4)^3}{(y-1)^3}$

8. What is $\frac{z-2}{z+2} + \frac{z-4}{z+4}$?
   A) $\frac{z-4}{z+2}$
   B) $\frac{2z^2-16}{z^2+6z+8}$
   C) $\frac{2z^2-16}{z^2-6z-8}$
   D) $\frac{2z^2-4z-16}{z^2+6z+8}$

9. If $\frac{2x}{x-3} = \frac{1}{x+4} + C$, what is C in terms of x?
   A) $\frac{2x+1}{x+4}$
   B) $\frac{2x^2+9x+3}{x^2-x-12}$
   C) $\frac{2x^2+9x+3}{x^2+x-12}$
   D) $\frac{2x^2+7x+3}{x^2+x-12}$

10. Which of the following is *NOT* a solution for $\frac{y^3-2y^2-16y+32}{y^2+5y+4} = 0$ despite being a zero of $y^3 - 2y^2 - 16y + 32$?
    A) $y = -4$
    B) $y = -1$
    C) $y = 2$
    D) $y = 4$

11. Simplify the above expression $\dfrac{\frac{x}{x+1} + \frac{13}{x-1} - \frac{58}{x^2-1}}{\frac{46}{x^2-1} + \frac{16}{x+1} + \frac{x}{x-1}}$ for $x \neq -15, -1,$ or 1:
    A) $\frac{x-3}{x+2}$
    B) $\frac{x-3}{x+8}$
    C) $\frac{x+5}{x+2}$
    D) $\frac{x+5}{x+8}$

12. At the International Institute of Food Research, Franklin is studying the viscosity of tomato-based condiments. A sample of Abe's Ketchup requires m minutes to travel c centimeters. It takes the same amount of George's Catsup 3 minutes longer to travel $c + 2$ centimeters. How much faster, in meters per second, does Abe's Ketchup flow?
    A) $\frac{3c-2m}{6000m(m+3)}$
    B) $\frac{10(3c+2m)}{6m(m+3)}$
    C) $\frac{2m-3c}{m(m+3)}$
    D) $\frac{6(3c+cm+2m)}{10m(m+3)}$

SAT Red Math — Lesson 14A: Rational Functions

$(3x^3 + 12x^2 - 75x - 300) \div (x + 5)$

13. Simplify the above expression for $x \neq -5$.
    A) $3(x + 4)(x - 5)$
    B) $3(x - 4)(x + 5)$
    C) $3(x + 5)(x - 6)$
    D) $3(x - 5)(x + 6)$

14. How many distinct real solutions exist for the equation $\dfrac{x^2 - 3x - 10}{x + 2} \cdot \dfrac{x^2 + 4x + 4}{x - 5} = 0$?

15. What is the remainder when $4x^3 - 2x^2 - 15x + 15$ is divided by $x + 2$?

Practice Set 3 (No Calculator)

$f(x) = \dfrac{(x+2)(x-4)}{x-1}$

16. Given the function f above, let the function g be defined such that $g(x) = f(x + 1)$ for all values of x in the domain of g. Which of the following is a formula for x?
    A) $g(x) = \dfrac{x^2 - 2x - 7}{x}$
    B) $g(x) = \dfrac{x^2 - 9}{x}$
    C) $g(x) = \dfrac{x^2 + 6x + 9}{x}$
    D) $g(x) = \dfrac{x^2 - x - 9}{x - 1}$

$\dfrac{10}{x(x-2)} + \dfrac{4}{x} = \dfrac{5}{x-2}$

17. Which of the following values of x satisfies the equation above?
    A) -2
    B) 2
    C) -2 and 2
    D) None of the above

$p(x) = \dfrac{x^2 + 3x - 4}{x^3 + 3x^2 - 4x}$

18. Given the function p defined above, the graph of $y = p(x)$ has a vertical asymptote at $x =$
    A) -4
    B) 0
    C) 1
    D) All of the above

Version 3.0

Lesson 14A: Rational Functions

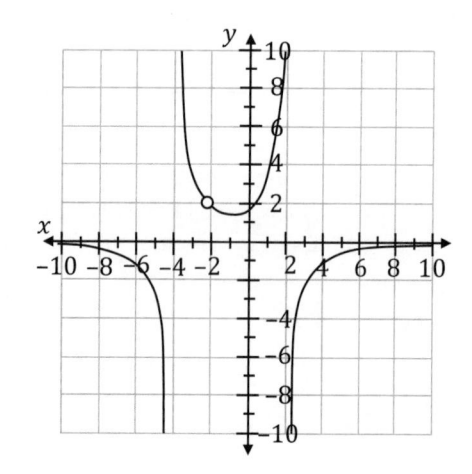

19. The above graph could be described by which of the following equations, for some positive constant a?

    A) $y = \frac{a(x-2)}{(x^2-4)(x+4)}$

    B) $y = \frac{a(2+x)}{(4-x^2)(x+4)}$

    C) $y = \frac{a(x^2-4)(x+4)}{x-2}$

    D) $y = \frac{a(4-x^2)(x+4)}{2+x}$

$$f(x) = \frac{x}{x^2-25}$$

20. Which of the following values of x is in the domain of the function f defined above?

    A) -5
    B) 0
    C) 5
    D) None of the above

$$f(x) = \frac{x}{x-1}$$
$$g(x) = x - \frac{1}{x}$$

21. Given the functions f and g defined above, which of the following is a valid formula for $g(f(x))$ for all x not equal to 0 or 1?

    A) $g(f(x)) = x+1$

    B) $g(f(x)) = \frac{(x+1)(x-1)}{x^2-x-1}$

    C) $g(f(x)) = \frac{2x-1}{x(x-1)}$

    D) $g(f(x)) = \frac{x^2-x+1}{x(x-1)}$

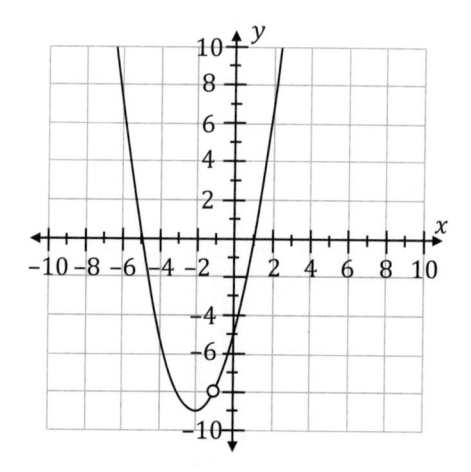

22. The above graph could be described by which of the following equations?

    A) $y = \frac{x^3+5x^2-x-5}{x-1}$

    B) $y = \frac{x^3+5x^2-x-5}{x+1}$

    C) $y = x^2 + 4x - 5$

    D) $y = \frac{x^2+4x-5}{x+1}$

$$f(x) = \frac{(x^2-a^2)(x^2-2bx+b^2)(x+c)(x-d)}{x(x-a)(x-b)(x-c)}$$

Use the above function for questions 23 and 24. Assume $a \neq b \neq c \neq d$.

23. Which of the following is not a solution to $f(x) = 0$?

    A) $x = -a$
    B) $x = b$
    C) $x = -c$
    D) $x = d$

24. How many vertical asymptotes does $f(x)$ have?

$$f(x) = \frac{x^2-x+6}{2x^2-12x+18}$$

25. What is an excluded value of the domain of the above function?

Red Math Lesson 14A: Rational Functions
Race to the Finish

Directions: Answer each question below.

Homework Set (Calculator)

$$\frac{a}{a+1} - \frac{a+1}{a+2} = \frac{k}{(a+1)(a+2)}$$

1. Given that the equation above is true for all values of a other than -1 and -2, what is the value of k?
   A) -1
   B) 1
   C) 2
   D) 3

   I. $x^2 - 5x - 6 = 4x + 4$

   II. $\frac{x^2-5x-6}{x+1} = 4$

2. Which of the following values of x is a solution to equation I above but NOT to equation II?
   A) -1
   B) 10
   C) -1 and 10
   D) None of the above

$$f(x) = \frac{x^2-1}{x^2}$$

3. Which of the following values of $f(x)$ is NOT in the range of the function f defined above?
   A) -1
   B) 0
   C) 1
   D) All of the above

$$g(x) = \frac{x+3}{x^3+4x^2-9x-36}$$

4. Given the function g defined above, the graph of $y = g(x)$ has a vertical asymptote at $x =$
   A) -3
   B) 3
   C) 4
   D) all of the above.

$$x + \frac{12}{x} = 7$$

5. What is the sum of all values of x that satisfy the equation above?
   A) -7
   B) -1
   C) 7
   D) 12

$$f(x) = \frac{5-x}{x^2-25}$$

6. Given the function f defined above, which of the following is a true statement?
   A) The graph of f has a vertical asymptote at $x = 5$.
   B) -5 is in the domain of f.
   C) All real numbers other than -5 are in the domain of f.
   D) All real numbers other than 0 and $-\frac{1}{10}$ are in the range of f.

Version 3.0

SAT Red Math
Lesson 14A: Rational Functions

7. Which of the following is the domain of $y = \dfrac{x^2+4x-12}{2x-4}$?

    A) $(-\infty, 2), (2, \infty)$
    B) $(-\infty, -2), (-2, \infty)$
    C) $(-\infty, -2), (2, \infty)$
    D) $(-\infty, 2), (-2, \infty)$

$$\dfrac{9x+23}{(x+4)(x+5)} = \dfrac{A}{x+4} + \dfrac{B}{x+5}$$

9. For certain constants A and B, the above equation is true for all x not equal to -4 or -5. Which of the following systems of equations could be used to find A and B?

    A) $A + B = 9$
       $4A + 5B = 23$
    B) $A + B = 9$
       $5A + 4B = 23$
    C) $4A + 5B = 9$
       $A + B = 23$
    D) $5A + 4B = 9$
       $A + B = 23$

$$P(x) = \dfrac{x^3+2x^2-5x-4}{x-3}$$

8. The function $P(x)$ above is equivalent to $x^2 + bx + c + \dfrac{d}{x-3}$ for certain integer constants b, c, and d. What is the value of d?

    A) -4
    B) -1
    C) 26
    D) 30

10. If $y \neq -2, -3$ or -6, $\dfrac{y^2+9y+18}{y^2+5y+6} \div \dfrac{y^2+8y+12}{y+3} =$

    A) $\dfrac{1}{y+3}$
    B) $\dfrac{y+3}{(y+2)^2}$
    C) $\dfrac{(y+3)^2}{(y+2)^2}$
    D) $\dfrac{(y+6)^2}{y+3}$

SAT Red Math
Lesson 14A: Rational Functions
363

11. Which of the following is the graph of $y = \frac{4x+12}{x+2}$?

A)

B)

C)

D)

12. Assuming $x \neq -5$ or -2, $\frac{x^2+3x-10}{x^2+7x+10} \cdot \frac{x^2-4}{x+5} =$

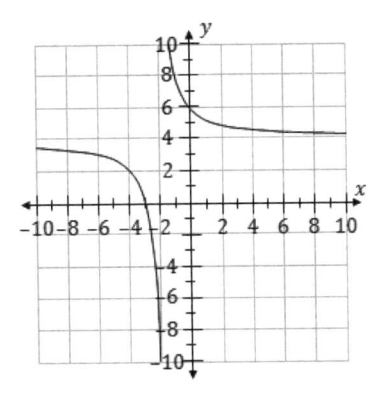

A) $\frac{x-2}{(x+5)^2}$

B) $\frac{x-2}{x+5}$

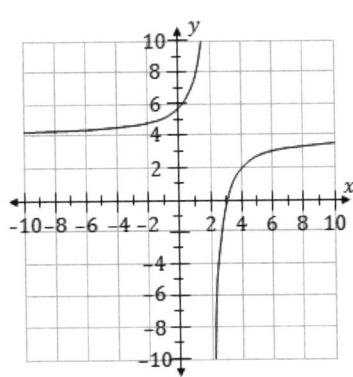

C) $\frac{(x-2)^2}{(x+5)^2}$

D) $\frac{(x-2)^2}{x+5}$

13. If $\frac{3}{x+2} = \frac{x}{x-1} + C$, what is C in terms of x?

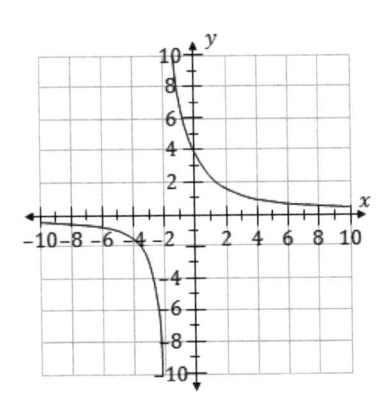

A) $\frac{3-x}{x+2}$

B) $\frac{-x^2+x-3}{x^2+x-2}$

C) $\frac{x^2-x+3}{x^2+x-2}$

D) $\frac{x^2+5x-3}{x^2+x-2}$

14. Assuming $x \neq 5$, $\frac{x^5-2x^4-19x^3+8x^2+60x}{x-5} =$

A) $x^3 + 3x^2 - 4x - 12$

B) $x^4 + 3x^2 - 4x - 12$

C) $x^4 + 3x^3 - 4x^2 - 12x$

D) $x^4 + 3x^3 - 4x^2 - 12x + 60$

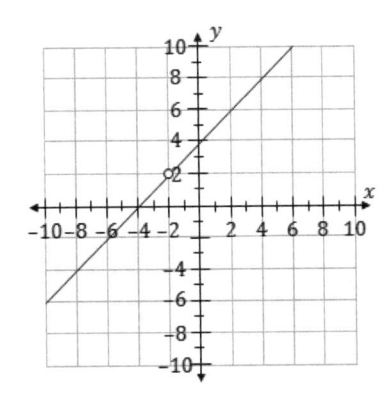

15. If $f(x) = \sqrt{x+2}$, $g(x) = (x-3)$, and $h(x) = (x+2)$, then which of the following is in the domain of $i(x) = \frac{f(x)}{g(x)h(x)}$?

A) -3

B) -2

C) 0

D) 3

SAT Red Math
Lesson 14A: Rational Functions

Use the following information for questions 16 and 17: In baseball, a batter's on-base percentage (OBP) is calculated by dividing the sum of his hits, walks, and times hit by a pitch by the sum of his at-bats, walks, times hit by a pitch, and sacrifice flies.

A batter's slugging percentage (SLG) is calculated by dividing his total bases by his number of at-bats.

A batter's on-base plus slugging percentage (OPS) is calculated by adding his OBP with his SLG.

Let the variables be defined as follows:

- H ~ hits
- W ~ walks
- HBP ~ times hit by a pitch
- SF ~ sacrifice flies
- AB ~ at-bats
- TB ~ total bases

16. During the first month of the baseball season, a batter had 10 walks, had been hit by a pitch twice, and had no sacrifice flies. If he had half as many hits as total bases and 4 times as many at-bats as hits, then which of the following represents his on-base plus slugging percentage (OPS) as a function of hits?

    A) $\dfrac{H+12}{4H+12}$
    B) $\dfrac{3H+18}{4H+12}$
    C) $\dfrac{4H+21}{4H+12}$
    D) $\dfrac{5H+24}{4H+12}$

17. The same batter in Question 17 actually had 25 hits during that first month of the baseball season. He would like to improve his OPS to 0.900 by the end of the season. Over the final 5 months of the season, he gets 500 more at-bats, 33 more walks, and 5 sacrifice flies. He doesn't get hit by another pitch, and still gets half as many hits as total bases. To achieve his goal, what is the minimum number of hits he needs over the final 5 months?

$$\dfrac{x^3+3x^2-x}{x+2} = x^2 + x + A + \dfrac{B}{x+2}$$

18. If the above equation is true for all $x \neq -2$, what is the value of $A + B$?

$$h(x) = \dfrac{1}{x^3-7x+6}$$

19. The graph of the function h described above has a vertical asymptote at $x = 1$. What is the sum of all values of x, including 1, at which the graph has a vertical asymptote?

$$\dfrac{5x+4}{x^2+x-2} = \dfrac{A}{x+2} + \dfrac{B}{x-1}$$

20. Given that the equation above is true for all x not equal to -2 or 1, what is the value of $A + B$?

RED MATH LESSON 14B: LINEAR, QUADRATIC, AND EXPONENTIAL MODELS
Learning to Swim

Directions: Answer each question below.

PRACTICE SET 1 (CALCULATOR)

1. The population of City A is projected to increase each year by 4% of the previous year's population. The population of City B is projected to decrease each year by 1% of the previous year's population. If the projections are accurate and each city currently has a population of 10,000, what will be the difference in population between the two cities in six years? (Round to the nearest whole number.)

2. A quadratic function $f(x)$ is modeled by the equation $y = \frac{1}{2}x^2 - 2x + 6$. A linear function $g(x)$ is modeled by the equation $y = 5x - 18$. For what values of x is $g(x) > f(x)$?

3. The average value of a home in Neighborhood A, which is currently $390,000, is expected to increase at a constant rate of $15,000 per year. In Neighborhood B, where the current average value of a home is $520,000, the value is expected to increase by one-third of the rate of Neighborhood A. In how many years will the average home values of the two neighborhoods be the same?

4. Five years ago, Angelo invested $1000 in the stock market. For the first three years, the investment decreased by 3% of the previous year's value. In the next two years, the value increased by 5% of the previous year's value. How much is Angelo's investment currently worth? (Round to the nearest whole dollar.)

5. A group of biologists tracked the population size of an endangered species of fish in a lake. They observed that the population decreased each year by 2% of the previous year's population. How many full years will it take for the population size to drop to less than half of its original amount?

RED MATH LESSON 14B: LINEAR, QUADRATIC, AND EXPONENTIAL MODELS
Diving into the Deep End

Directions: Answer each question below.

PRACTICE SET 2 (CALCULATOR)

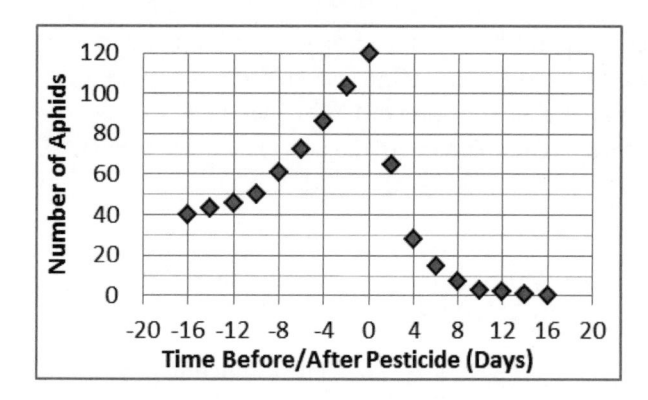

6. A biologist measures the number of aphids present on a group of plants before and after applying a pesticide (at time $t = 0$), as shown in the scatterplot above. Which of the following best describes the data?
   A) Linear growth followed by exponential decay
   B) Linear growth followed by quadratic decay
   C) Quadratic growth followed by exponential decay
   D) Quadratic growth followed by linear decay

7. Which of the following relationships could be modeled with a linear function?
   A) A town's population, which increases by 3% per year, relative to time
   B) The area of a square window relative to its side length
   C) The number of ways a group of people can be ordered relative to the number of people
   D) The number of oranges you can buy (at a constant price per orange) relative to the amount of money you have

8. If $g(x)$ is a quadratic function and $g(2x) - g(x) = 9x^2$, which of the following could be $g(x)$?
   A) $x^2 - 3x + 5$
   B) $3x^2 + 5$
   C) $3x^2 - 3x$
   D) $9x^2$

x	-2	-1	0	1
y	-2	-1	1	5

9. Which of the following functions produces the table of values shown above?
   A) $2^{x+2} - 3$
   B) $2^{x+3} - 2$
   C) $(x + 2)^2 - 3$
   D) $(x + 3)^2 - 2$

$$f(x) = 2x$$
$$g(x) = x^2$$
$$h(x) = 2^x$$

10. Given the functions defined above, which of the following is true?
    A) $g(x)$ is the largest of the 3 functions for $0 < x < 1$.
    B) $f(x)$ is the largest of the 3 functions for $1 < x < 2$.
    C) $h(x)$ is the largest of the 3 functions for $2 < x < 4$.
    D) $g(x)$ is the largest of the 3 functions for $x > 4$.

Lesson 14B: Linear, Quadratic, and Exponential Models

11. Which of the following functions is an example of decay for $0 < x < 10$?
    A) $f(x) = -x^2 + 5$
    B) $f(x) = (x-5)^2$
    C) $f(x) = (-x)^2 + 5$
    D) $f(x) = -(x-5)^2$

12. A bank offers a savings account that pays 2% yearly interest, compounded quarterly. Which equation can be used to find how much an initial $1000 investment is worth after y years?
    A) $A = 1000 \cdot 1.005^{(y/4)}$
    B) $A = 1000 \cdot 1.005^{(4y)}$
    C) $A = 1000 \cdot 1.02^{(4y)}$
    D) $A = 1000 \cdot 1.08^{(y/4)}$

13. Which of the following describes the function $f(x) = e^{-x+1} - 2$?
    A) Exponential growth with an asymptote at $y = -1$
    B) Exponential growth with an asymptote at $y = -2$
    C) Exponential decay with an asymptote at $y = -1$
    D) Exponential decay with an asymptote at $y = -2$

14. You acquired 430 g of an unknown substance. After 15 days in your possession, you have 230 mg left. What is the half-life of this substance? Round to the nearest tenth of a day.

15. A car's depreciation can be modeled as: $V = C(1-r)^t$, where V is the final value of the car after t years, C is the initial cost, and r is the annual depreciation rate. What is the rate of depreciation if a car's value drops from $25,000 to $14,500 in 3 years? Round to the nearest tenth of a percent.

Practice Set 3 (Calculator)

16. Bacterial growth can be modeled with: $N(t) = N_0 \times 2^t$, where $N(t)$ is the number of bacteria present after an amount of time, t, and N_0 is the initial number of bacteria in the culture. Which of the following would be the correct way to find the amount of time it takes for a culture to increase its population from N_0 to $N(t)$?
    A) $t = \left(\frac{N(t)}{N_0}\right)\left(\frac{1}{2}\right)$
    B) $t = \frac{\log N(t) - \log N_0}{\log 2}$
    C) $t = \frac{\log N(t)}{\log N_0} \times \log 2$
    D) $t = \frac{N(t)}{N_0} 2$

17. You have designed a new mobile device and have found its profit function to be
    $\text{Profit} = -350P^2 + 105{,}000P - 7{,}175{,}000$,
    where P is the sale price of the device. At what sale price points, P, will you break even?
    A) $50.00, $105.28
    B) $105.00, $123.00
    C) $105.28, $194.72
    D) $150.00, $204.72

18. $3500 is placed in a fund that continuously compounds. If the annual interest rate is 1.35%, how long would it take the fund to have $8500?
    A) $t = \frac{\ln\left(\frac{8500}{3500}\right)}{0.0135}$
    B) $t = \frac{8500}{3500^{0.035}}$
    C) $t = \frac{8500}{3500 e^{0.0135}}$
    D) $t = \frac{\ln(8500)}{\ln(3500)} \times 0.0135$

SAT Red Math
Lesson 14B: Linear, Quadratic, and Exponential Models

19. Thomas purchased a tractor worth $154,000. Assume the tractor depreciates according to the straight line depreciation model: $depreciation = \frac{Cost - Salvage\ Value}{Lifespan}$, where Salvage Value is the value of the truck after depreciation. If the tractor is estimated to have a salvage value of $27,000 at the end of 15 years, which of the following models most accurately represents the truck's value over time?
    A) $V(t) = 154,000e^{0.18t}$
    B) $V(t) = 154,000(1 - 0.15)^t$
    C) $V(t) = 154,000 - \frac{27,000}{t}$
    D) $V(t) = 154,000 - 8466.67t$

20. The population of a popular town increases by 8% every year. If there are 300,000 people in the town today, how many people will there be t weeks from now?
    A) $300,000(0.08)^t$
    B) $300,000(1.08)^t$
    C) $300,000(0.08)^{\frac{t}{52}}$
    D) $300,000(1.08)^{\frac{t}{52}}$

Use the information from question 21 for questions 22 and 23.

21. The loudness of sound is measured in units called decibels (dB). They are measured as follows: $d = 10 \log \frac{I}{I_0}$, where I is the intensity of the desired sound and I_0 is the intensity of a base "soft sound," known as the threshold. Normal conversations occur at 60 dB. How much more intense is this than the threshold sound?
    A) 3.98
    B) 1000
    C) 1.0×10^6
    D) 1.0×10^{60}

Source	Decibels (dB)
Whisper	$d = 30$
Vacuum Cleaner	$d = 75$
Lawn Mower	$d = 90$
Rock Concert	$d = 110$
Firecracker	$d = 145$
Shotgun	$d = 165$

22. If one wants to add a third column to the table above that indicates the sound intensity I from a source, then which equation should be used to populate that information?
    A) $I = I_0 10^{\frac{d}{10}}$
    B) $I = I_0 10^{-d}$
    C) $I = I_0 10^d$
    D) $I = I_0 10^{-10d}$

23. If the sound intensity of a source quadruples, then how does the decibel level change?
    A) Decibel level increases by 4 dB.
    B) Decibel level increases by 6 dB.
    C) Decibel level scales by a factor of 4.
    D) Decibel level scales by a factor of 6.

24. Iodine-131 has a half-life of 8 days. If we started with 545 g on November 1, how much would we have left 30 days later? Round to the nearest tenth of a gram.

25. Height, in meters, can be modeled as a function of time with the following equation $s(t) = -4.9t^2 + v_0 t + s$, where s is the initial height of the object, in meters, and v_0 is the initial vertical velocity of the object, in meters per second. If an object is launched at 20.5 m/s from a height of 300 meters, what is the maximum height this object can reach? Round to the nearest meter.

RED MATH LESSON 14B: LINEAR, QUADRATIC, AND EXPONENTIAL MODELS
Race to the Finish

Directions: Answer each question below.

HOMEWORK SET (CALCULATOR)

1. A logging company owns two areas of forested land. The number of trees in Area A decays by 500 per year. The number of trees in Area B decays by 5% per year. If both areas have 12,000 trees this year, which system of equations represents this scenario?
   A) $y = 12,000 + 500x$
      $y = 12,000 \cdot 0.95^x$
   B) $y = 12,000 - 500x$
      $y = 12,000 \cdot 0.95^x$
   C) $y = 12,000 + 500x$
      $y = 12,000 \cdot x^{0.95}$
   D) $y = 12,000 - 500x$
      $y = 12,000 \cdot x^{0.95}$

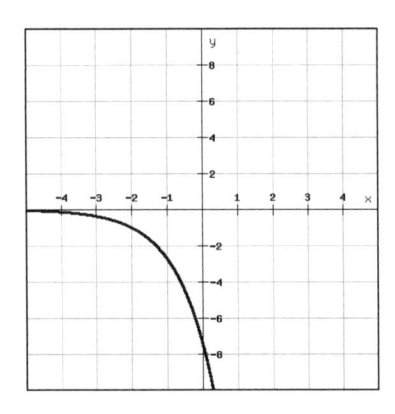

2. Which of the following matches the graph above?
   A) $e^{-x} - 7$
   B) $-e^x - 7$
   C) $-e^{x-2}$
   D) $-e^{x+2}$

3. If $\left(\frac{1}{7}\right)^{x+2} = (343)^{x-y}$, what is x in terms of y?
   A) $2y - 1$
   B) $y + 4$
   C) $\frac{3y+2}{2}$
   D) $\frac{3y-2}{4}$

4. pH can be calculated as follows: $\text{pH} = -\log[H^+]$, where $[H^+]$ is the concentration of H^+ ions in moles per liter. pOH is calculated as: $\text{pOH} = -\log[OH^-]$ where $[OH^-]$ is the concentration of OH^- ions in moles per liter. The sum of pH and pOH is always 14. The lower the pH, the more acidic a solution is. Which of the following is the most acidic?
   A) A solution with $[OH^-] = 7.3 \times 10^{-7} \frac{\text{moles}}{\text{liter}}$
   B) A solution with a pOH = 6.97
   C) A solution with $[H^+] = 1.0 \times 10^{-7} \frac{\text{moles}}{\text{liter}}$
   D) A solution with $[H^+] = 5.7 \times 10^{-6} \frac{\text{moles}}{\text{liter}}$

$$C(t) = C_0 e^{rt}$$

5. The equation above gives the amount of Carbon-14, $C(t)$, that remains in a sample initially containing C_0 kilograms of Carbon-14 after time t for some constant decay rate r. At a construction site near Vancouver, WA, a forensic detective wants to determine if recently discovered remains are that of a notorious criminal. Forty-three years ago, he jumped from a commercial airliner near the Washington-Oregon border with $200,000 in ransomed cash; his whereabouts since have been a mystery. The forensics lab's results indicate that 99.48% of the original Carbon-14 remains. If a separate 10 kg sample of Carbon-14 decays to 9.999 kg over a period of 302 days, then what conclusion can the detective most reliably make?
   A) The remains are about 4.3 years old; they cannot belong to the criminal.
   B) The remains are about 43 years old; they could belong to the criminal.
   C) The remains are about 431 years old; they cannot belong to the criminal.
   D) The remains are about 15,744 years old; they cannot belong to the criminal.

SAT Red Math
Lesson 14B: Linear, Quadratic, and Exponential Models

Use the following information for Questions 6 through 8:

Joe, 35 years old, wants to invest $10,000. He is presented with three investment options:

- Option 1 – Investment grows by continuous compounding at annual interest rate $r = 0.05$ according to the following formula:
$$I_1(t) = 10{,}000e^{rt}$$

- Option 2 – Investment grows according to following formula:
$$I_2(t) = 13{,}000 + 35t^2$$

- Option 3 – Bank provides extra $5,000 in initial investment, and investment then grows at $1,000 per year.

6. Which of the following is an appropriate model for Option 3?
   A) $I_3(t) = 10{,}000 + 1{,}000t$
   B) $I_3(t) = 10{,}000 + 5{,}000t$
   C) $I_3(t) = 15{,}000 + 1{,}000t$
   D) $I_3(t) = 15{,}000 + 5{,}000t$

7. If Joe plans to redeem his investment at 55 years old, then which investment should he select?
   A) Option 1
   B) Option 2
   C) Option 3
   D) Option 1 or 2

8. For what values of t, in years, would Option 2 be the best option?
   A) $0 < t < 10.1$
   B) $10.1 < t < 30.4$
   C) $t > 30.4$
   D) Option 2 is never the best option.

	Firm A	Firm B	Others	Total
Year 1	25	0	25	50
Year 2	100	25	50	175
Year 3	125	50	75	250
Year 4	100	100	100	300
Year 5	25	200	125	350
Year 6	0	400	150	550
Year 7	0	800	175	975
Year 8	0	1600	200	1800

Use the table above for questions 9 and 10. Doug, a technology market researcher, is studying the history of the smartphone industry. The following table shows the annual revenues of Firm A, Firm B, and other firms over the first 8 years of the smartphone industry.

9. As a function of time, which of the following best represents the behavior of the annual smartphone revenues for Firm A, Firm B, and other firms?
   A) Firm A – linear, Firm B – quadratic, and Others – quadratic
   B) Firm A – linear, Firm B – exponential, and Others – quadratic
   C) Firm A – quadratic, Firm B – quadratic, and Others – linear
   D) Firm A – quadratic, Firm B – exponential, and Others – linear

10. A firm's market share is defined as its revenues as a percentage of the industry's combined revenues. If trends continue, then during which year does Firm B achieve 95% market share of the smartphone industry?
    A) Year 8
    B) Year 9
    C) Year 10
    D) Year 11

Lesson 14B: Linear, Quadratic, and Exponential Models

11. A theater company is attempting to find a reasonable price for tickets to its shows. First, a $30 price for a ticket is tested, and this results in 2,124 sales. Then, for $35, a turnout of 1,898 people occurs. Lastly, a $20 price is implemented, which has an outcome of 2,576 sales. If the company will not sell its tickets for more than $75, which of the following models would best fits the relation between ticket sales s and prices p?

   A) $s = 3480 - \left(\frac{226p}{5}\right)$
   B) $s = (p - 75)^2 + 279$
   C) $s = 3480 \cdot 2.26^{-p}$
   D) None of the models above are a good fit for the specified relation.

12. Smallpox is running rampant in a densely populated city. The model that shows how many people will be infected is given by $P(t) = P_0 e^{\frac{t}{3}}$, where P_0 is the population that is initially infected, and $P(t)$ is the population with smallpox after t days of the initial infection. Which of the following would NOT be useful in determining which value of t yields an infected population $P(t)$?

   A) $3 \log_5 \frac{P(t)}{P_0} \cdot \frac{1}{\log_5 e}$
   B) $3 \log \frac{P(t)}{P_0} \cdot \frac{1}{\log e}$
   C) $3 \ln \frac{P(t)}{P_0}$
   D) $3 \log \frac{P(t)}{P_0}$

13. If $\left(\frac{1}{64}\right)^x = 32(8^{x+1})$, what is x?

   A) $\frac{-9}{8}$
   B) $\frac{-8}{9}$
   C) $\frac{8}{9}$
   D) $\frac{9}{8}$

14. A certain computer algorithm has an exponential asymptotic time complexity. This means that the amount of time the algorithm takes to solve a problem is an exponential function of the size of the problem. If this algorithm solves a problem of size 10, it takes 10 seconds to compute the answer. Likewise, it will take 20 seconds to solve a problem of size 11 and 40 seconds for a problem of size 12. Which of the following best models the relationship between computation time $f(x)$ and problem size x?

   A) $f(x) = \frac{5}{512}(2^x)$
   B) $f(x) = \frac{5}{256}(2^x)$
   C) $f(x) = \frac{5}{64}(2^x)$
   D) $f(x) = \frac{35}{256}(2^x)$

Questions 15 and 16 use the following information: Continuously compounded interest is calculated by the formula $A(t) = Pe^{rt}$, where $A(t)$ is the accumulated amount after t years, P is the principal amount, and r is the rate of interest.

15. $300 is invested at a rate of 3% compounded continuously. How many years, to the nearest integer, will it take the amount invested to quadruple in value?

   A) 1 year
   B) 14 years
   C) 37 years
   D) 46 years

16. Amy invests $1000 in the bank with an interest rate of 1.5% and Emily invests $900 in a different bank with a rate of 2%. After how many years, to the nearest integer, will Amy and Emily have the same amount of money in the bank?

   A) 21 years
   B) 14 years
   C) 7 years
   D) 5 years

17. Bill is doing an experiment on heat transfer, which measures how heat dissipates over time. He does this by heating water under a polystyrene container so that the temperature of the water when he stops heating it is 80°C. The function that can model heat transfer is given as $\Delta T(t) = \Delta T_0 e^{-\frac{t}{\tau}}$, where ΔT_0 is the initial temperature, $\Delta T(t)$ is the temperature after t minutes, and τ is a time constant (which, for polystyrene, is 65). After how much time, rounded to the nearest minute, should Bill expect the temperature of the container to be half of what it initially was? Round to the nearest whole minute.

18. Using the information from the previous question, suppose Bill tries the same experiment in a glass container, whose time constant τ is 49. If Bill heats the water to 80°C again, how many fewer minutes will it take the water to cool down to half of that temperature inside the glass container than it would inside the polystyrene container? Round to the nearest whole minute.

19. Caffeine is a drug that experiences exponential decay in the liver. The equation for the amount of caffeine inside an individual is $N(t) = N_0 e^{\frac{-t \ln(2)}{T}}$, where $N(t)$ is the amount of caffeine, in mg, after time t, N_0 is the initial amount consumed at $t = 0$, and T is the half-life of caffeine. If Chris consumes 150 mg of caffeine, and, 3.51 hours later, 100 mg is still left in his body, what is T, to the nearest whole hour?

20. Using the correct value of T from the previous question, how long would it take for the body to contain $\frac{1}{3}$ of the caffeine it initially had? Round to the nearest hundredth of an hour.

C2 education
be smarter.

RED MATH LESSON 15A: ADVANCED RIGHT TRIANGLES AND TRIGONOMETRY
Learning to Swim

Directions: Answer each question below.

PRACTICE SET 1 (CALCULATOR)

1. Suppose $\cos\theta = \frac{\sqrt{12(x+3)}}{x+6}$ and $x > 0$. If $\tan\theta$ takes on a negative value, what is $\csc\theta$ in terms of x?

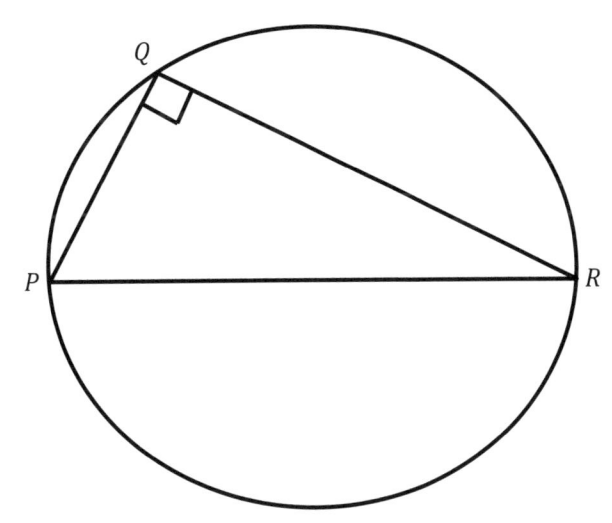

2. In the figure above, $\overline{PQ} = 6$ and $\overline{PR}$ is the diameter of the circle. If the area of the circle is 64π, then what is the measure of $\angle PRQ$ to the nearest degree?

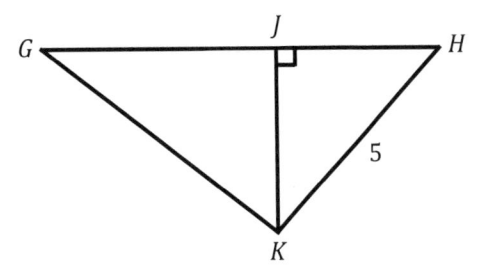

3. In the figure above, $\angle G$ and $\angle H$ are complementary angles, and $\angle HKJ = 39°$. What is the length of $\overline{GJ}$?

4. If $\cot\theta = \frac{8}{15}$, and $\frac{\pi}{2} < \theta < \frac{3\pi}{2}$, what is $\cos\theta$?

5. A unit circle contains the points $A(-1, 0)$, $B\left(\frac{\sqrt{2}}{2}, \frac{\sqrt{2}}{2}\right)$, and $C\left(-\frac{1}{2}, -\frac{\sqrt{3}}{2}\right)$. How much greater, in radians, is the length of the minor arc $\widehat{AB}$ than the length of the minor arc $\widehat{AC}$?

SAT Red Math
Lesson 15A: Advanced Right Triangles and Trigonometry

RED MATH LESSON 15A: ADVANCED RIGHT TRIANGLES AND TRIGONOMETRY
Diving into the Deep End

Directions: Answer each question below.

PRACTICE SET 2 (CALCULATOR)

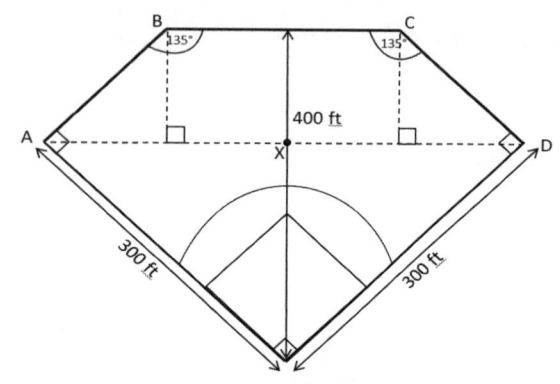

6. A baseball field is designed according to the figure above. The distance from home plate to the foul poles is 300 ft, while the distance from home plate to the center field wall is 400 ft. How much outfield fencing (length of $\overline{AB} + \overline{BC} + \overline{CD}$), in feet, is needed?

   A) $1000(\sqrt{2} - 1)$
   B) $300\sqrt{2}$
   C) $400\sqrt{2}$
   D) $1400(\sqrt{2} - 1)$

$$\tan\theta \sin\theta - \frac{1}{2}\tan\theta = 0$$

7. If $0 \leq \theta \leq 2\pi$, then for which value of θ is the above equation NOT true?

   A) $\frac{\pi}{6}$
   B) $\frac{5\pi}{6}$
   C) $\frac{7\pi}{6}$
   D) π

8. For what values of θ is the function $f(\theta) = \tan\left(\frac{\theta}{3}\right) + 1$ negative? Let $-2\pi \leq \theta \leq 0$.

   A) $-\frac{7\pi}{4} < \theta < -\frac{3\pi}{2}$
   B) $-\frac{3\pi}{2} < \theta < -\frac{3\pi}{4}$
   C) $-\frac{3\pi}{4} < \theta < -\frac{\pi}{2}$
   D) $-\frac{\pi}{2} < \theta < -\frac{\pi}{4}$

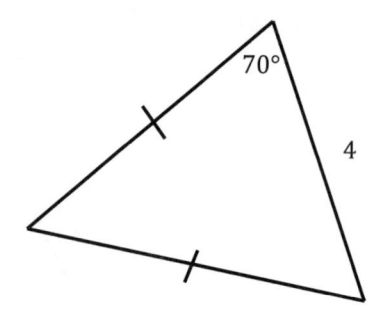

9. The area of a triangle can be found via the formula $A = \frac{1}{2}xy \sin Z$, where x and y are side lengths of the triangle and Z is the angle between those two sides. What is the area of the triangle above?

   A) $\frac{1}{2}(4)(4) \sin 70°$
   B) $\frac{1}{2}(4)(4) \sin 40°$
   C) $\frac{1}{2}(5.85)(5.85) \sin 40°$
   D) Cannot be determined.

10. In the domain $-2\pi \leq x \leq 2\pi$, the function $f(x) = \cos(x)$ has relative minimum values at $x = \pm\pi$. How many relative minima does $g(x) = \cos(20x)$ have in the domain $-\frac{2\pi}{10} \leq x \leq \frac{2\pi}{10}$?

    A) 1
    B) 2
    C) 4
    D) 8

11. If $\cos\theta = \frac{\sqrt{2}}{2}$, then which of the following is NOT a possible value of θ?

    A) $\frac{\pi}{4}$
    B) $\frac{3\pi}{4}$
    C) $\frac{7\pi}{4}$
    D) $\frac{9\pi}{4}$

SAT Red Math
Lesson 15A: Advanced Right Triangles and Trigonometry

$a = \cos[10° + (\sin^{-1}\cos 80°) + (\cos^{-1}\sin 80°)]$
$b = \sin[10° + (\sin^{-1}\cos 80°) + (\cos^{-1}\sin 80°)]$

12. Using the above expressions what is the value of $a - b$? (Note that $\sin^{-1} x$ and $\cos^{-1} x$ in these expressions return angle measures in degrees.)
    A) $\frac{-1-\sqrt{3}}{2}$
    B) $\frac{-1+\sqrt{3}}{2}$
    C) $\frac{1-\sqrt{3}}{2}$
    D) $\frac{1+\sqrt{3}}{2}$

13. Solve $\tan\left(x - \frac{\pi}{2}\right) = \sqrt{3}$ over the interval $0 \leq x \leq 2\pi$.
    A) $\frac{\pi}{3}$ and $\frac{4\pi}{3}$
    B) $\frac{5\pi}{6}$ and $\frac{11\pi}{6}$
    C) $\frac{\pi}{3}$ only
    D) $\frac{5\pi}{6}$ only

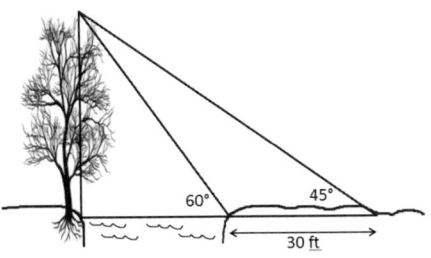

14. As seen above, Sam stands at the bank of a river and observes that the angle of elevation of the top of a tree on the opposite bank is 60°. When standing 30 ft from the bank, he observes an angle of elevation of 45°. To the closest foot, what is the height of the tree?

15. Helen is standing on the bank of a river that runs straight east to west. A straight path heads off at an angle of 23° to the north of the river. Helen hurries along the path for 2 hours at a speed of 4 miles per hour. She then cuts straight south through the jungle at a speed of ½ mile per hour until she reaches the river again. How long does she spend trekking through the jungle? Round to the nearest hundredth of an hour.

PRACTICE SET 3 (CALCULATOR)

16. Which of the following is equal to $\cot 75°$?
    A) $\tan 75°$
    B) $\sin 75°$
    C) $\cos 15°$
    D) $\tan 15°$

17. What is $\csc\left(\frac{-37\pi}{3}\right)$?
    A) $-\frac{2\sqrt{3}}{3}$
    B) $-\frac{\sqrt{3}}{2}$
    C) $\frac{2}{\sqrt{3}}$
    D) 2

18. If $\tan x = \frac{-15}{8}$, and $\frac{\pi}{2} < x < \pi$, what is $\csc x$?
    A) $-\frac{17}{15}$
    B) $-\frac{15}{17}$
    C) $\frac{17}{15}$
    D) $\frac{8}{17}$

19. What is the horizontal shift of the graph $y = 2\cos(3x - \pi) + 7$?
    A) π
    B) 7
    C) $\frac{\pi}{3}$
    D) $-\pi$

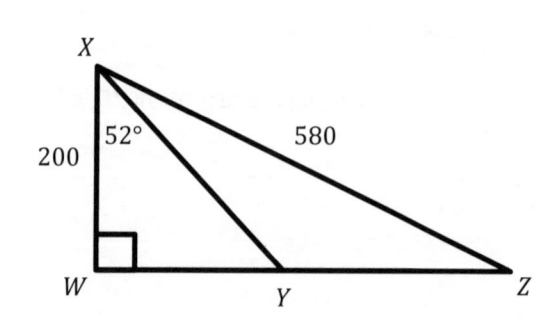

20. In the figure above a person is standing on a beach at point X and watching a boat at a constant distance of 200 meters. What is the distance from point Y to point Z?
A) 256
B) 288
C) 480
D) 535

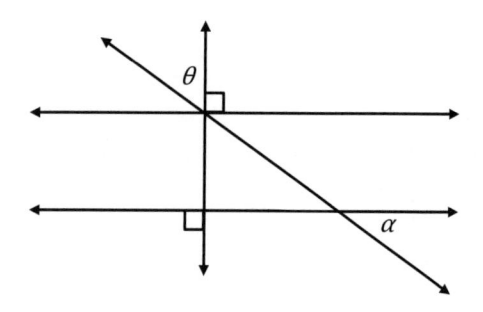

21. If, in the figure above, $\tan\theta = \frac{7}{10}$, what is $\tan\alpha$?
A) $\frac{7}{10}$
B) $\frac{\sqrt{149}}{10}$
C) $\frac{10}{7}$
D) $\frac{\sqrt{149}}{7}$

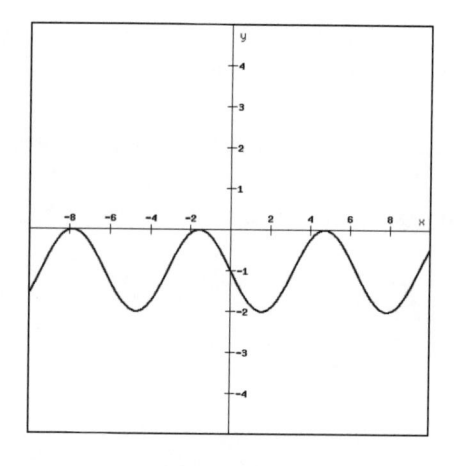

22. If $\sin\theta = -\cos\theta$, and $\pi < \theta < 2\pi$, what is $\sec\theta$?
A) $-\sqrt{2}$
B) $\frac{2\sqrt{3}}{3}$
C) $\sqrt{2}$
D) 2

23. The graph above shows the function $f(x) = -\sin\theta - 1$. Which of the following functions is equivalent to $-f(x)$?
A) $g(x) = \cos\left(\theta - \frac{\pi}{2}\right) + 1$
B) $g(x) = \cos(\theta + \pi) + 1$
C) $g(x) = -\sin\theta + 1$
D) $g(x) = \cos\left(\theta + \frac{\pi}{2}\right) + 1$

24. Gary's angle of elevation to a 50 meter tall building is 40°. He moves toward the building until his angle of elevation is 50°. How far did he walk? Round to the nearest meter.

25. If $0° < x < 90°$, solve $\cot(x) - 2 = 1$. Round to the nearest tenth of a degree.

RED MATH LESSON 15A: ADVANCED RIGHT TRIANGLES AND TRIGONOMETRY
Race to the Finish

Directions: Answer each question below.

HOMEWORK SET (CALCULATOR)

1. If $\tan \alpha = \frac{\sqrt{3}}{3}$ and $\frac{\pi}{2} \leq \alpha \leq \frac{3\pi}{2}$, what is α?
   A) $\frac{5\pi}{6}$
   B) $\frac{7\pi}{6}$
   C) $\frac{5\pi}{4}$
   D) $\frac{4\pi}{3}$

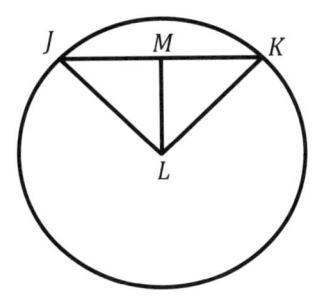

2. In the figure above, the length of the chord $\overline{JK} = 8$, and $\angle JLM = \angle KLM = 35°$. What is the area of circle L?
   A) 32.63π
   B) 48.63π
   C) 89.58π
   D) 194.53π

3. If $\pi < \alpha < 2\pi$, which of the following must be true?
   A) $\sin \alpha < 0$
   B) $\cos \alpha < 0$
   C) $\tan \alpha < 0$
   D) $\cos \alpha > 0$

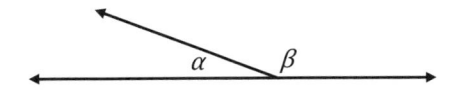

4. In the figure above, which of the following must be true?
   A) $\sin \alpha = \sin \beta$
   B) $\sin \alpha = \cos \beta$
   C) $\cos \alpha = \sin \beta$
   D) $\cos \alpha = \cos \beta$

5. If $\sin \theta = \frac{2}{3}$ and $\tan \theta = -\frac{2\sqrt{5}}{5}$, what is $\cos \theta$?
   A) $-\frac{3\sqrt{5}}{5}$
   B) $-\frac{\sqrt{5}}{3}$
   C) $\frac{\sqrt{5}}{3}$
   D) $\frac{3\sqrt{5}}{5}$

6. If $\sin \theta = \frac{1}{2}$, $\sin \alpha = \frac{1}{2}$, and $\cos \theta = -\cos \alpha$, what is a possible value of $\theta + \alpha$?
   A) 0
   B) $\frac{\pi}{2}$
   C) π
   D) $\frac{3\pi}{2}$

7. Which of the following represents the graph of $g(x) = 2\cos x + 2$?

   A)

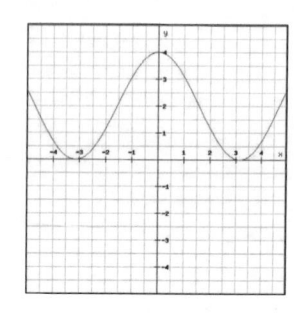

   B)

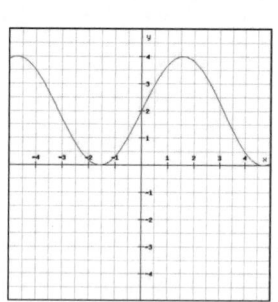

   C)

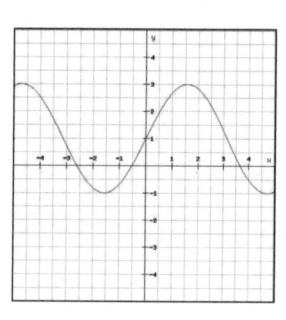

   D)

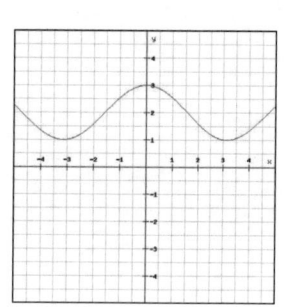

8. For which value of α is $\tan\alpha = \cot(\alpha + \pi)$?

   A) $\frac{\pi}{4}$

   B) $\frac{\pi}{3}$

   C) $\frac{2\pi}{3}$

   D) $\frac{4\pi}{3}$

9. If $\sec\theta = a$ and $\sin\theta = b$, what is $\tan\theta$?

   A) $\frac{1}{ab}$

   B) $\frac{a}{b}$

   C) $\frac{b}{a}$

   D) ab

10. If $\tan\beta < 0$ and $0 < \beta < 2\pi$, which of the following must be true?

    A) $\frac{\pi}{2} < \beta < \pi$ or $\frac{3\pi}{2} < \beta < 2\pi$

    B) $0 < \beta < \frac{\pi}{2}$ or $\pi < \beta < \frac{3\pi}{2}$

    C) $\pi < \beta < 2\pi$

    D) $\frac{\pi}{2} < \beta < \frac{3\pi}{2}$

11. If $\cos\alpha = a$ and $\cot\alpha = b$, which of the following is equivalent to $\csc\alpha$ wherever it is defined?

    A) $\frac{1}{ab}$

    B) $\frac{a}{b}$

    C) $\frac{b}{a}$

    D) ab

SAT Red Math — Lesson 15A: Advanced Right Triangles and Trigonometry

12. For which value of θ is $\cos\theta = \cos\left(\theta + \frac{\pi}{2}\right)$?
    A) $\frac{\pi}{4}$
    B) $\frac{\pi}{3}$
    C) $\frac{2\pi}{3}$
    D) $\frac{3\pi}{4}$

13. If $\cos\theta = -\frac{12}{13}$ and $\tan\theta$ is positive, what is $\sin\theta$?
    A) $-\frac{5}{12}$
    B) $-\frac{5}{13}$
    C) $\frac{5}{13}$
    D) $\frac{12}{13}$

14. If $\tan\theta = -\sqrt{3}$ and $\pi \leq \theta \leq 2\pi$, what is θ?
    A) $\frac{5\pi}{4}$
    B) $\frac{4\pi}{3}$
    C) $\frac{5\pi}{3}$
    D) $\frac{7\pi}{4}$

15. If $\sin\theta = \frac{\sqrt{3}}{2}$, $\sin\alpha = \frac{\sqrt{2}}{2}$, and both θ and α are between 0 and $\frac{\pi}{2}$, what is $\theta + \alpha$?
    A) $\frac{\pi}{2}$
    B) $\frac{7\pi}{12}$
    C) $\frac{2\pi}{3}$
    D) $\frac{5\pi}{6}$

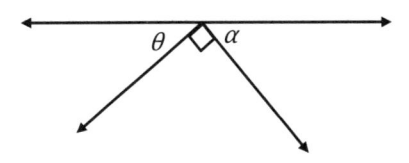

16. In the figure above, which of the following must be true?
    A) $\sin\theta = \sin\alpha$
    B) $\sin\theta = \cos\alpha$
    C) $\tan\theta = \cos\theta$
    D) $\cos\theta = \cos\alpha$

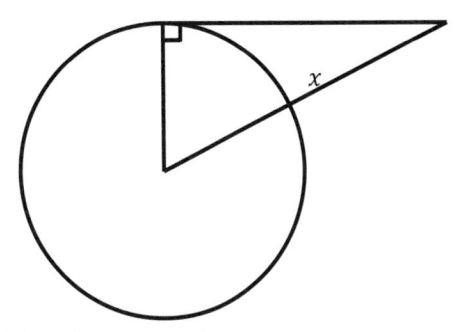

Note: Figure not drawn to scale.

17. If the area of the circle above is 36π and the area of the sector is 5π, what is x? Round to the nearest tenth.

18. Lisa is looking at a 93-meter tall radio tower from 47 meters away. She wants to calculate the angle a tension line tied to the top of the tower makes with the ground where she stands in order to ensure the tower is safe during an earthquake. What angle should the line form with the ground? Round to the nearest tenth of a degree.

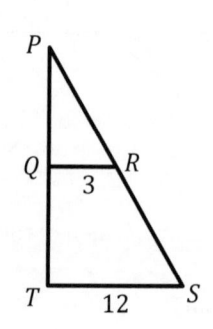

19. In the figure above, $\overline{QR}$ and $\overline{TS}$ are parallel, and the measure of ∠RST is 71°. What is the area of the trapezoid QRST, to the nearest integer?

20. The following points are plotted on a graph: $L(-3,-7)$, $M(-7,-7)$, and $N(-3, 1)$. What is the measure of ∠LMN to the nearest tenth of a degree?

RED MATH LESSON 15B: PRACTICE SECTIONS
Learning to Swim

Directions: Answer each question below.

PRACTICE SET 1 (CALCULATOR)

1. A survey was conducted to examine the exercise habits of college students. A sample of 15 students was randomly chosen, and each student was asked to estimate how many hours per week that he or she spends exercising. The following data represent the survey results, in hours: 0, 0, 0, 2, 3, 4, 4, 5, 5, 6, 6, 7, 7, 8, 12. What is the difference, in minutes, between the median and the mean of this dataset?

2. A paint can with a height of 5 inches and a radius of 4 centimeters weighs 21 ounces when empty and 3 pounds when it is filled with paint. What is the density of the paint, in grams per cubic centimeter? Round to the nearest tenth. (Density is mass divided by volume.)

3. An equilateral triangle lies within a circle such that the triangle's vertices perfectly coincide with three points on the circle. The three legs of the triangle are thus three chords of the circle. What is the ratio of the sum of the three chord lengths to the circumference of the circle?

4. If the cosine of an angle is $\frac{4}{5}$, what are two possible values for the cosecant of the same angle?

5. In populations of bacterial cells, the growth pattern is such that the number of cells in each population doubles after each replication cycle. However, populations differ in the initial amount of cells present and how often the replication cycles occur. Consider two populations of bacterial cells. Population A replicates 3 times per hour and initially contains 20,000 cells, while population B replicates 5 times per hour and initially contains 100 cells. If the initial populations begin growing at the same time, how much time will pass before the two populations momentarily have the same number of cells? Give your answer as a time range in the form of $C \leq t \leq D$, where C and D are consecutive integers and represent hours.

Red Math Lesson 15B: Practice Sections
Diving into the Deep End

Directions: Answer each question below.

Practice Set 2 (Calculator)

6. Consider two rational functions $f(x)$ and $g(x)$. The equations of the two functions are as follows: $f(x) = \frac{2x^2+x-6}{x^2+x-2}$ and $g(x) = \frac{3x^2+12x+12}{2x^2+2x-4}$. Which of the following is an accurate statement regarding these functions?
   A) The two functions have the same horizontal asymptote.
   B) The two functions have different domains.
   C) One function has a positive zero, while the other function has no zeros.
   D) At least one of the functions crosses the origin.

Year	Revenue (thousands of dollars)
2010	464
2011	490
2012	516
2013	542

7. A shop owner wishes to model the revenue of her shop as a function of time. The table above displays the annual revenue that her shop generates. Which of the following types of functions would most appropriately model this trend?
   A) Linear function
   B) Quadratic function
   C) Exponential function
   D) None of the above

8. Consider the function $f(x) = \sin^{-1}(\cos x)$. Which of the following values of x is NOT a zero of this function?
   A) $-\frac{3\pi}{2}$
   B) $-\frac{\pi}{2}$
   C) $\frac{\pi}{2}$
   D) 2π

9. According to Coulomb's law, the electrostatic force between two charged particles can be computed using the equation $|F| = k\frac{|q_1 q_2|}{r^2}$, where F is the electrostatic force, k is the electrostatic constant, q_1 is the charge of particle 1, q_2 is the charge of particle 2, and r is the distance between the two particles. A student working in a physics lab is measuring electrostatic forces between particles. If the student doubles the mass of one particle and moves the particles such that the distance between them is halved, what will happen to the force measured?
   A) F will decrease by a factor of 8.
   B) F will decrease by a factor of 4.
   C) F will increase by a factor of 4.
   D) F will increase by a factor of 8.

10. Consider a sector of a circle. What is the ratio of the sector's area to its arc length in terms of the circle's radius, r, and the angle spanned by the sector, θ?
    A) $\frac{2}{r}$
    B) $2r\frac{\theta}{360°}$
    C) $\frac{r}{2}$
    D) $\frac{\pi r}{2}\frac{\theta}{360°}$

SAT Red Math
Lesson 15B: Practice Sections

11. Certain elements undergo radioactive decay over time. This decay is exponential for every radioactive element, but the elements differ with respect to decay rate and starting amount. Which of the following equations is the least appropriate model for such exponential decay? C is current amount, C_0 is starting amount, and t is time.
    A) $C = C_0 e^{-20t}$
    B) $C = C_0 e^{-1000t}$
    C) $C = C_0 2^{-5t}$
    D) $C = C_0 e^{30t}$

12. If $\cos(-\theta) = -\frac{7}{25}$ and $0 \leq \theta < \pi$, what is $\tan \theta$?
    A) $-\frac{7}{24}$
    B) $-\frac{24}{7}$
    C) $\frac{7}{24}$
    D) $\frac{24}{7}$

13. If $f(x) = x^2 - 16$ and $g(x) = \frac{x+4}{x-4}$, which of the following functions has a domain that does NOT include $x = -4$?
    A) $g(x)$
    B) $\frac{f(x)}{g(x)}$
    C) $f(g(x))$
    D) $g(f(x))$

14. A couple is planning their wedding, and they would like lasagna to be the main dish at the reception. The only ingredient that they do not currently possess is cheese. Cheese blocks have a density of 118.6 pounds per cubic foot. Each block has a mass of 16 grams, and it takes 5 blocks to produce 70 ounces of lasagna. Which of the following most closely approximates the volume of cheese blocks, in cubic inches, that the couple needs to acquire to produce 200 pounds of lasagna? Round to the nearest cubic inch. (Density is mass divided by volume.)

15. The vertical position of an object in free fall is given by the function $y = y_0 + v_0 t - \frac{1}{2} g t^2$, where y is current vertical position (meters), y_0 is initial vertical position (meters), v_0 is initial vertical speed (meters per second), g is $9.8 \frac{m}{s^2}$, and t is time (seconds). If a ball is thrown upward with an initial velocity of 4 meters per second, approximately how long does it take for the ball to fall back to the ground? Assume the initial position of the ball is 0 meters. Round to the nearest hundredth.

Practice Set 3 (No Calculator)

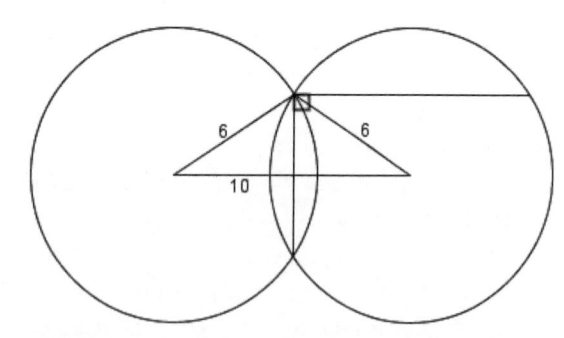

16. Two identical circles with radii measuring 6 centimeters are overlapped such that their centers are 10 centimeters apart. A chord is drawn to connect the two points that form the boundaries for this overlap. Finally, a second chord is drawn beginning at one of these points such that this second chord is perpendicular to the first chord. The second chord is thus a chord in only one of the circles. What is the shortest distance between the second chord and the center of the circle in which it lies?

   A) $6 - \sqrt{11}$
   B) $\sqrt{11}$
   C) 5
   D) $4 + \sqrt{11}$

17. A regular hexagon is inscribed in a circle of radius r. Which of the following expressions best models the area of the hexagon in terms of r?

   A) $\frac{2\sqrt{3}}{3}r^2$
   B) $\frac{3\sqrt{3}}{2}r^2$
   C) $\frac{3\sqrt{3}}{4}r^2$
   D) $3\sqrt{3}r^2$

$$|F| = k_e \frac{|q_1 q_2|}{r^2}$$

18. The equation above, Coulomb's Law, gives the magnitude of the electrostatic force, F, between two point charges, q_1 and q_2, that are a distance, r, apart. The term k_e is the electrostatic constant. Which of the following would result in the largest percent increase in $|F|$?

   A) Increase q_1 by 100%
   B) Increase q_1 by a factor of 10
   C) Increase r by a factor of 9
   D) Decrease r by a factor of 8

19. A researcher is studying the effectiveness of four different antibiotic treatments on a new strain of bacteria. After conducting her experiments, she graphs her population data over time on scatterplots and uses a line of best fit to model the population under each treatment. Of the four models given below, which decreases the population, y, to half of the initial population, y_0, in the shortest time, t?

   A) $y = y_0 1.2^{-t}$
   B) $y = y_0 0.8^{-t}$
   C) $y = y_0 0.8^{t}$
   D) $y = y_0 (2) 0.8^{t}$

$$9y + 2(x-3)^2 = 108$$
$$4y - x = 7$$

20. If (x, y) is a solution to the system of equations above and $xy > 0$, what is xy? Round your answer to the nearest whole number.

   A) 3
   B) 15
   C) 36
   D) 45

$$E = (6.3)(10^4)(10^{3M/2})$$

21. The equation above gives the approximate energy release E, measured in joules, for an earthquake of magnitude M, measured on the Richter scale. What is the positive difference in magnitude for two earthquakes if one releases 100 times more energy than the other?

    A) $\frac{1}{6}\log\frac{E}{6.3}$
    B) $\frac{1}{12}\log\frac{E}{6.3}$
    C) $\frac{4}{3}$
    D) 2

22. A ray r is drawn from the origin to $(-15, 8)$. If θ is the counterclockwise angle from the positive x-axis to r, which of the following is correctly ordered from least to greatest?

    A) $\sin\theta, \tan\theta, \cos\theta$
    B) $\sec\theta, \cos\theta, \tan\theta$
    C) $\tan\theta, \cos\theta, \cot\theta$
    D) $\cos\theta, \sin\theta, \tan\theta$

$$x = y^2 - 6y + 11$$
$$y = \frac{1}{3}x + 1$$

23. If (x, y) is a solution to the system of equations above, what is a possible value of x^2?

    A) 3
    B) 4
    C) 9
    D) 49

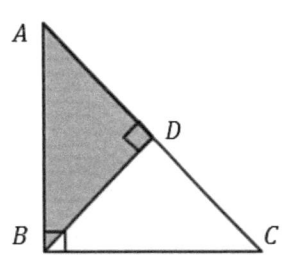

24. In the figure above, $\overline{AB} = 6$ and $\overline{BC} = 8$. What percentage of the entire triangle, $\triangle ABC$, is shaded?

$$f(x) = \frac{12x-3}{2x-1} + k$$

25. If $y = 10$ is an asymptote of the graph of the above rational function, what is k?

SAT Red Math
Lesson 15B: Practice Sections

RED MATH LESSON 15B: PRACTICE SECTIONS
Race to the Finish

Directions: Answer each question below.

HOMEWORK SET (CALCULATOR)

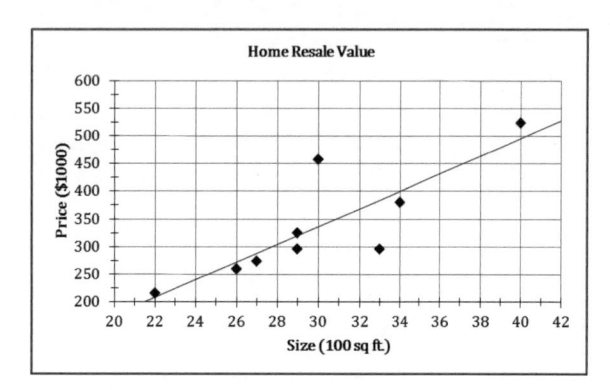

Use the scatterplot above for questions 1 and 2. It shows the size and sale price for 9 randomly selected homes in a community. Prices are measured in thousands of dollars and sizes are measured in hundreds of square feet.

1. Based on the data above and the line of best fit shown, which of the following models is most likely to predict the price y, in dollars, for a home of size x, in square feet, in this community?

   A) $y = \frac{2}{3}x + 200$
   B) $y = \frac{2}{3}x + 377$
   C) $y = 15x - 110$
   D) $y = 150x - 110,000$

2. Based on the data above, which of the following statements is most likely to be true?
   A) 3000 sq. ft. houses cost $450,000 in this community.
   B) Neither dataset has a mode.
   C) The mean is the best measure of center for the price data, because the range is large.
   D) The median of the size data is 2900 sq ft.

$$2x^2 - 7x = -6$$
$$x = |y - 3|$$

3. If (x, y) is the solution to the system above, what is NOT a possible value of $\frac{x}{y}$?

   A) 0.4
   B) 1
   C) 2
   D) 3

x	$f(x)$	$g(x)$
-2	0	-1
-1	2	0
0	1	1
1	0	2
2	-1	3

4. Given the values in the chart above, which of the following is not true?
   A) $-f(g(1)) = f(g(-1))$
   B) $f(g(0)) = g(f(0))$
   C) $f(f(1)) = g(g(-1))$
   D) $g(f(0)) = g(0) + f(0)$

5. If the circle represented by the equation $x^2 + y^2 - 4x + 2y = 11$ is shifted down 2 units and to the right 5 units, where is the center of the resulting circle?
   A) $(0, 4)$
   B) $(2, -1)$
   C) $(5, -2)$
   D) $(7, -3)$

6. In the function $f(x) = 3x^2 + 8x - 3$, what value of x makes $f(x-2) = f(x) - 2$ true?
   A) -6
   B) $-\frac{1}{6}$
   C) $\frac{1}{6}$
   D) 6

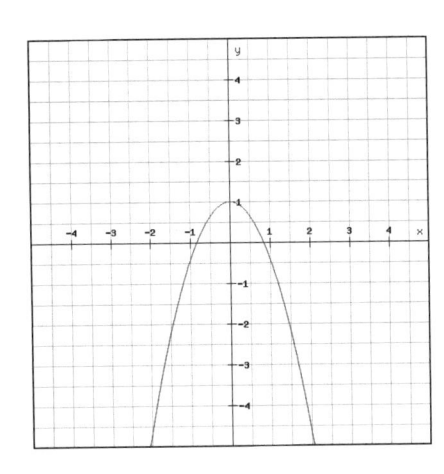

7. Which of the following could be the equation for the graph above?
   A) $1 - \sqrt{2x}$
   B) $1 - \sqrt{2x^2}$
   C) $1 - \sqrt{2x^3}$
   D) $1 - \sqrt{2x^4}$

$$2x - 5y + 3z = -20$$
$$4x + 3y - z = 13$$
$$3x + 2y + \frac{z}{2} = \frac{13}{2}$$

8. Using the system above what is the value of xyz?
   A) -9.3
   B) -6.2
   C) -3
   D) No solution

9. A poll was conducted asking 100 college students what source of media they use to keep up to date with news: TV, radio, or Internet. 92 said they use the Internet, 35 said they use TV, and 14 said they use radio. 8 said they use Internet and radio, 27 said they use TV and Internet, 11 said they use TV and radio, and 5 said they use all three. How many students use only internet to keep up to date with news?
   A) 52
   B) 57
   C) 62
   D) 73

10. In the function $f(x) = 2x^3 - x^2 - 25x - 12$ one of the zeroes is $x = -3$. What is the product of all zeroes of this function?
    A) -6
    B) -2
    C) 2
    D) 6

11. What is $\cot \frac{25\pi}{6}$?
    A) $\sqrt{3}$
    B) $\frac{\sqrt{3}}{3}$
    C) $\frac{2\sqrt{3}}{3}$
    D) 2

394 | SAT Red Math
Lesson 15B: Practice Sections

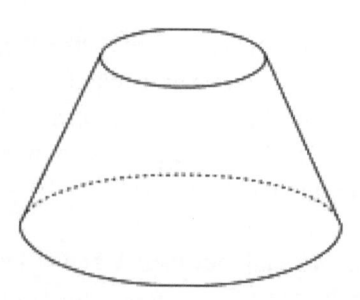

Use the diagram above for questions 12 and 13. The diagram above shows a frustum. A frustum is formed when part of a cone is cut off creating two parallel bases. The part that is removed is a cone that is proportional to the original cone.

12. A frustrum with a height of 6 has two circular bases with radii of 4 and 8. What is its volume?
    A) 96π
    B) 224π
    C) 256π
    D) 672π

13. A cone has a height of 8 and a base radius of 6. Part of the cone is removed to form a frustum. What should the radius of the smaller base of the frustum be so that the frustum has half the volume of the original cone?
    A) $\sqrt[3]{108}$
    B) $\sqrt[3]{256}$
    C) $8 - \sqrt[3]{108}$
    D) $8 - \sqrt[3]{256}$

14. An ice cream cone has a radius of 2 cm and a slant height of 6 cm. What should be the maximum radius of the spherical scoop of ice cream such that, if allowed to melt, the ice cream would all fit within the cone? Assume that the volumes of the liquid and solid forms of the ice cream are equivalent.
    A) 1.78 cm
    B) 2.83 cm
    C) 2.88 cm
    D) 3.02 cm

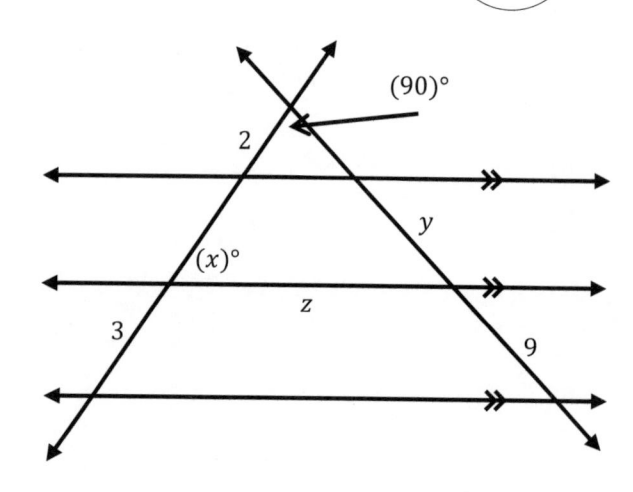

Use the diagram above for questions 15 and 16.

15. What is the value of x?
    A) 18°
    B) 35°
    C) 58°
    D) 72°

16. If $y = 12$, what is the approximate value of z?
    A) 19
    B) 25
    C) 32
    D) 50

	Car	Truck	Total
Under 6	46.2	27.8	74.0
6-8	26.9		40.0
9-11	23.3	10.7	
12 & over	26.8	18.6	45.4
Total	123.2		

Use the table above for questions 17 and 18. The incomplete contingency table above shows the number of cars and trucks in use in the United States by age. Frequencies are reported in millions of cars.

17. What percentage of vehicles in use are 12 years old or older? Round your answer to the nearest whole percent.

18. If 80 vehicles that are 6-8 years old are randomly selected, what is the expected number of trucks, to the nearest integer, in the group?

Tier	Electricity cost ($/kWh)
Each kWh used below the Baseline	0.16474
Each kWh used between 101% and 130% of Baseline	0.18856
Each kWh used between 131% and 200% of Baseline	0.36896
Each kWh used above 200% of Baseline	0.38896

19. The above table shows the electricity rate schedule for a region. If the Baseline is 300 kWh per month and a household used a total of 700 kWh in the last month, what percentage of the bill is due to electricity use above the baseline? Round your answer to the nearest percent.

20. What is the average electricity rate, in $/kWh, for a household that used 600 kWh of electricity in a month? Round your answer to two decimal places. (Note: Baseline use is 300 kWh per month.)

RED MATH LESSON 16A: ADVANCED CIRCLES
Learning to Swim

Directions: Answer each question below.

PRACTICE SET 1 (CALCULATOR)

1. The London Eye is a giant Ferris wheel with a diameter of 120 meters. The wheel completes one revolution every thirty minutes, making the linear speed of each car on the edge of the wheel slow enough to allow passengers to hop on and off without the wheel stopping. One city plans to build its own version of the London Eye that will have a diameter that is 20% bigger. If the cars on the bigger Ferris wheel have the same linear speed as the London Eye, how many minutes would it take for the wheel to make one revolution?

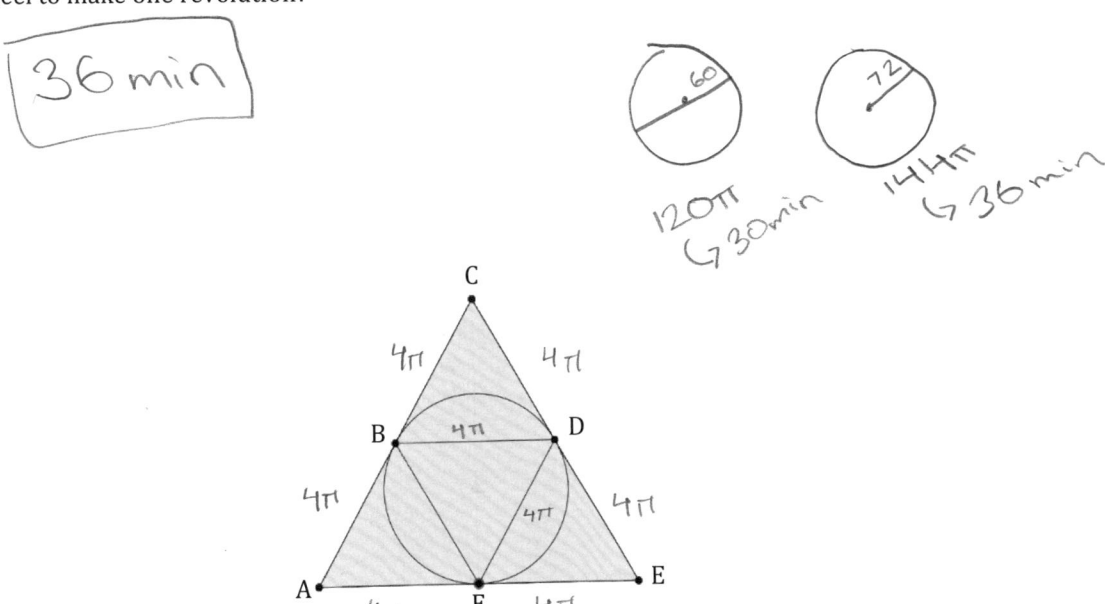

2. If $\triangle ACE$ and $\triangle BDF$ are both equilateral triangles and minor arc BD has a length of 4π, then what is the perimeter of $\triangle ACE$?

3. A carousel, or merry-go-round, that is 40 feet in diameter has two rings of seats for riders. The seats in the inner and outer rings are placed 8 and 2 feet from the circumference, respectively. If the carousel makes one complete revolution in 15 minutes, how much faster are the outer seats compared to the inner seats in terms of linear speed? Express the difference in feet per minute.

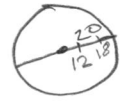

4. A circle is centered at the origin. If a line is tangent to the circle at (5,12), then what is the x-intercept of the tangent line?

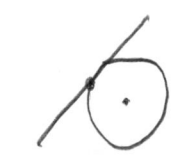

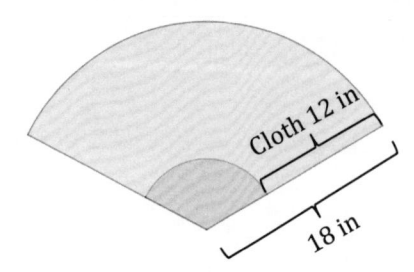

5. A Chinese hand fan company receives an order of 1000 fans with the specifications shown above. When folded, the fan will be 18 inches long with the cloth portion being 12 inches long. When fully spread out, the central angle will measure 120°. When cutting the cloth for the fans, 1 square inch is wasted for every 9 square inch of useable cloth. To complete the order, approximately how much cloth, in square feet, will be needed?

RED MATH LESSON 16A: ADVANCED CIRCLES
Diving into the Deep End

Directions: Answer each question below.

PRACTICE SET 2 (CALCULATOR)

6. If a circle has an area of 882 and the diameter is one side of an equilateral triangle, what is the area of the triangle?
   A) 220.5
   B) $\frac{882}{\pi}$
   C) 441
   D) $\frac{882\sqrt{3}}{\pi}$

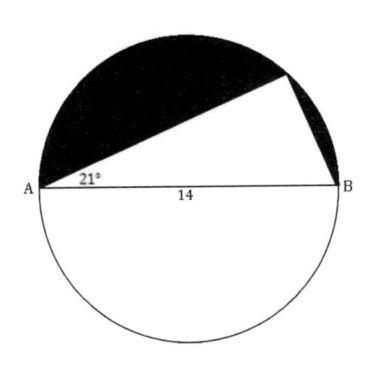

7. If $\overline{AB}$ is the diameter of the circle, what is the area of the shaded region?
   A) 39.4
   B) 44.2
   C) 270.3
   D) 275.1

8. A square is inscribed in a circle. If the area of the square is 392, then what is the area of the circle?
   A) 98π
   B) 196π
   C) 392π
   D) 784π

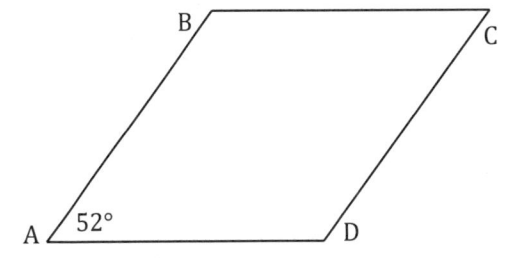

9. A circle is drawn around the rhombus $ABCD$ such that $\overline{AC}$ is a diameter of the circle. If $AB = 3$, what is the length of arc $\widehat{AC}$?
   A) 3.7
   B) 8.5
   C) 11.6
   D) 16.9

10. A circular pizza is cut in half. One half is cut into five slices, while the other half is cut into 8 slices. If the area of one of the smaller slices is 4π, what is the shortest arc length that borders four entire slices, where at least one slice is included from both halves of the pizza?
    A) $\frac{16\pi}{5}$
    B) 4π
    C) $\frac{23\pi}{5}$
    D) $\frac{26\pi}{5}$

11. If a circle with a diameter of 12 is inscribed in a regular octagon, what is the area of the region outside the circle but inside the octagon?
    A) 34.6
    B) 11.3
    C) 8.6
    D) 6.2

Version 3.0

SAT Red Math
Lesson 16A: Advanced Circles

12. A circle is inscribed in a square and the square is then inscribed in another circle. If the radius of the small circle is 8, what is the area of one of the different congruent regions within the large circle but outside the square?
    A) $32\pi - 64$
    B) $64\pi - 64$
    C) $128\pi - 256$
    D) $256\pi - 256$

13. Four cylindrical soda cans, each having diameter d, will be placed into a cylindrical bucket that is exactly as tall as one soda can. In terms of d, what is the inner circumference of the smallest such bucket that will contain them?
    A) $(2d)\pi$
    B) $(\sqrt{2}d + d)\pi$
    C) $(2\sqrt{2}d)\pi$
    D) $(\sqrt{2}d + 2d)\pi$

14. Chloe buys some pie from Parsa's Pie Shop. She pays $3.50 for two pieces of pie. He informs her that she could have bought the entire, circular 9-piece pie for $15. Chloe measures one of her pieces of pie as having an arc length of 3π cm. If the pie is divided evenly, how much more money did Chloe spend per square centimeter of pie (to the nearest tenth of a cent) than she would have had she bought the whole pie?

15. If the area of a circle is 169π, what is the perimeter of a quarter of that circle, to the nearest tenth?

Practice Set 3 (Calculator)

16. A chord is drawn in a circle such that the shortest distance between the chord and the center of the circle is 1 centimeter. If the length of this chord is 4 centimeters, which of the following is the correct value for the area of the circle?
    A) 3π square centimeters
    B) 5π square centimeters
    C) 9π square centimeters
    D) 17π square centimeters

17. A circle is inscribed in an equilateral triangle. If the circumference of the circle is 9π, what is the perimeter of the triangle?
    A) $13.5\sqrt{3}$
    B) $18\sqrt{3}$
    C) $27\sqrt{3}$
    D) 54

18. Derek has a circular rug with a radius of 6 feet. He wants to cut this rug with a sharp object that is shaped like an equilateral triangle. When he places the object on top of the rug to remove a triangular portion, the three vertices of the object coincide with three points on the rug. After he removes the inner triangular portion of the rug that was cut out, three pieces of the rug remain. What is the area of one of these pieces?
    A) 6π square feet
    B) $12\pi - 9\sqrt{3}$ square feet
    C) 12π square feet
    D) $36\pi - 27\sqrt{3}$ square feet

SAT Red Math
Lesson 16A: Advanced Circles

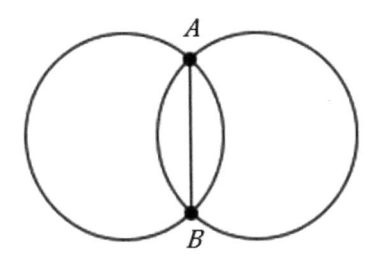

19. The figure above shows two congruent circles, each with a 13-cm diameter. If chord $\overline{AB}$ is 5 cm, what is the area of the region where the circles overlap? Round your answer to the nearest tenth of a cm².
    A) 3.4
    B) 16.7
    C) 36.4
    D) 44.2

Note: Figure not to scale.

20. A circle with a radius of 5 and a line with a slope of −1 are tangent to each other and coincide at the origin. Which of the following could represent the point at which the center of the circle lies?
    A) $\left(\frac{5\sqrt{2}}{2}, -\frac{5\sqrt{2}}{2}\right)$
    B) $\left(-\frac{5\sqrt{2}}{2}, \frac{5\sqrt{2}}{2}\right)$
    C) $\left(-\frac{5\sqrt{2}}{2}, -\frac{5\sqrt{2}}{2}\right)$
    D) $(5\sqrt{2}, 5\sqrt{2})$

21. A chord is drawn parallel to the diameter of a circle, which has an area of 25π cm². If the distance between the diameter and the chord is 2.5 cm, what is the ratio of the diameter length to the chord length?
    A) $\sqrt{3} : 2$
    B) $2 : \sqrt{3}$
    C) $\sqrt{3} : 1$
    D) $1 : \sqrt{3}$

22. Two diameters are drawn in a circle such that the smaller angle between them is 15 degrees. These two diameters split the circle into 4 arcs, 2 long ones and 2 short ones. What is the ratio of the sum of the two long arcs to the sum of the two short arcs?
    A) 1:22
    B) 1:11
    C) 11:1
    D) 22:1

23. A square is inscribed in a circle. If the square has an area of 2048 cm², what is the circumference of the circle?
    A) $32\pi\sqrt{2}$ cm
    B) 64π cm
    C) $64\pi\sqrt{2}$ cm
    D) 1024π cm

24. Consider a circle with a radius of 5 feet. A chord is drawn inside the circle such that the chord and two radii form a triangle whose vertices are the ends of the chord and the center of the circle. If the length of the chord is 6 feet, what is the area of this triangle in square feet?

25. A circle is inscribed in a square which is in turn inscribed in another circle. What is the ratio of the area of the big circle to the area of the small circle?

SAT Red Math
Lesson 16A: Advanced Circles

RED MATH LESSON 16A: ADVANCED CIRCLES
Race to the Finish

Directions: Answer each question below.

HOMEWORK SET (CALCULATOR)

1. Three friends would like to split a circular pizza. The amount, in terms of area, that will be distributed to each person corresponds to a ratio of 4:2:1. If the pizza they bought has a diameter of 14 inches, what is the total area of the biggest portion, in square inches?
   A) 7π square inches
   B) 28π square inches
   C) 49π square inches
   D) 112π square inches

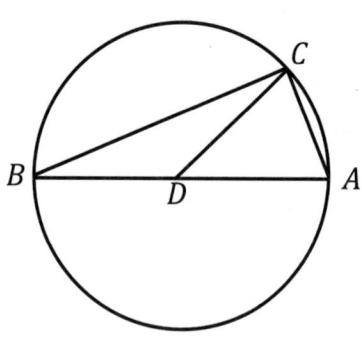

2. If $\sin \angle CBA = \frac{2}{7}$ and the length of radius CD is 14, what is the length of chord BC?
   A) 8
   B) $2\sqrt{33}$
   C) $12\sqrt{5}$
   D) 28

3. A circle is inscribed in an equilateral triangle such that the circle is tangent to each side of the triangle. What is the area of the triangle in terms of the radius, r, of the circle?
   A) $2\sqrt{2} \times r^2$
   B) $2\pi \times r^2$
   C) $3\sqrt{3} \times r^2$
   D) $6\sqrt{3} \times r^2$

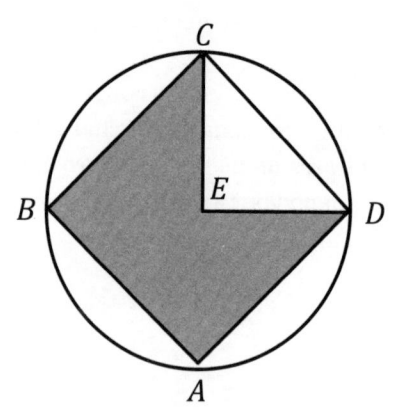

4. Square $ABCD$ is inscribed in Circle E above. If the length of ED is 12, what is the area of the shaded portion of the figure above?
   A) $108\sqrt{2}$
   B) 216
   C) $216\sqrt{2}$
   D) 432

5. A square is placed inside a circle such that a radius of the circle is also a diagonal of the square. If the circumference of the circle is 50π inches, what is the area of the portion of the circle that lies outside of the square?
   A) $\frac{625}{2}$ square inches
   B) $\frac{3}{4} \times 625$ square inches
   C) $\frac{625}{2}\pi$ square inches
   D) $625\left(\pi - \frac{1}{2}\right)$ square inches

6. How many different circles exist that are tangent to both the lines $y = 3 - x$ and $y = 2x - 6$ and have centers which lie on the y-axis?
   A) 1
   B) 2
   C) 3
   D) 4

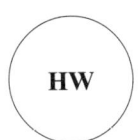

7. Five friends decide to evenly split a circular cake by making 5 radial slices from its center. If each piece has a perimeter of 52 centimeters, which of the following most closely approximates the diameter of the cake?
   A) 20 centimeters
   B) 25 centimeters
   C) 30 centimeters
   D) 40 centimeters

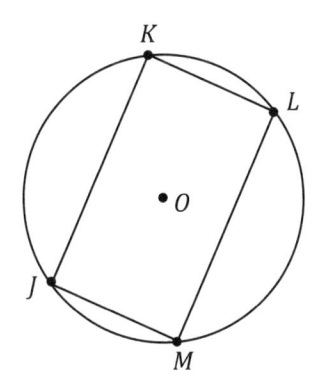

8. Circle O depicted above has radius $4\sqrt{5}$. Rectangle $JKLM$ is inscribed in circle O and has perimeter 48. What is the length of chord $\overline{JK}$?
   A) 8
   B) 12
   C) 15
   D) 16

9. A large pizza of diameter 16" is cut into eight identical slices. A smaller pizza of diameter 12" is cut into six identical slices. The slices of the large pizza are what percent greater in area than the slices of the small pizza, to the nearest whole percentage point?
   A) 25%
   B) 33%
   C) 75%
   D) 78%

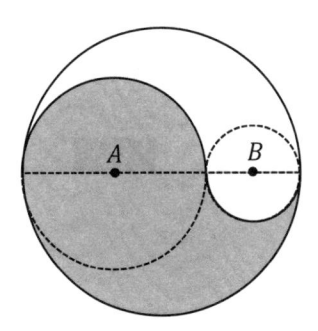

10. The figure above consists of two tangent circles centered at points A and B, and of radii 6 and 3, respectively, both internally tangent to a larger circle of radius 9. What is the area of the shaded region?
    A) 27π
    B) 54π
    C) 72π
    D) 81π

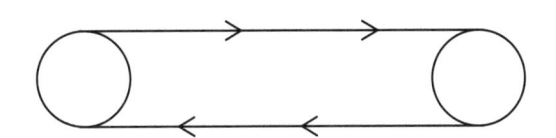

11. A pulley system contains a closed loop of rope wrapped around two identical circular axles, as shown in the figure above. If the distance between the centers of the axles is equal to six times the diameter of each axle, and the total length of rope is 200 cm, what is the diameter of each axle to the nearest tenth of a centimeter?
    A) 6.6 cm
    B) 10.9 cm
    C) 13.2 cm
    D) 21.9 cm

12. A bicycle wheel has a diameter of 26 inches. A cyclist pedaling forward on level ground such that the wheels complete 2 revolutions each second is traveling how many miles per hour, to the nearest tenth?
    A) 3.0
    B) 9.3
    C) 18.6
    D) 19.2

SAT Red Math
Lesson 16A: Advanced Circles

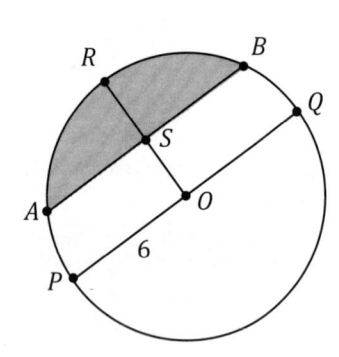

Use the figure above for questions 13 and 14. In circle O above with radius 6 and diameter $\overline{PQ}$, chord $\overline{AB}$ and segment $\overline{OR}$ bisect each other.

13. What is the length of $\overline{AB}$?
    A) $3\sqrt{3}$
    B) 6
    C) $6\sqrt{2}$
    D) $6\sqrt{3}$

14. What is the area of the shaded region?
    A) $4\pi - 9\sqrt{3}$
    B) $9\pi - 9\sqrt{2}$
    C) $12\pi - 9\sqrt{3}$
    D) $12\pi - 18\sqrt{3}$

15. An arc of a given circle whose central angle measures 20° has arc length π. What is the area of the circle?
    A) 9π
    B) 18π
    C) 81π
    D) 324π

16. What could be the equation of a circle whose graph is tangent to the line $y = \frac{3}{4}x$ at the point (12,9)?
    A) $(x-15)^2 + (y-5)^2 = 25$
    B) $(x-16)^2 + (y-6)^2 = 36$
    C) $(x-12)^2 + (y-9)^2 = 25$
    D) $(x-12)^2 + (y-9)^2 = 81$

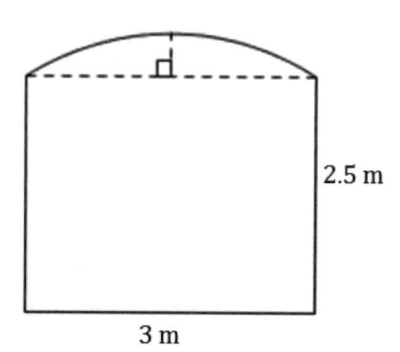

17. An architect is designing an archway between two rooms. The width of the opening is 3 m and the straight height along the wall is 2.5 m. If the arch is part of a circle with center midway between the walls at the base of the opening, what is the vertical distance between the top of the wall and the top of the arch? Round your answer to the nearest hundredth of a meter.

HW

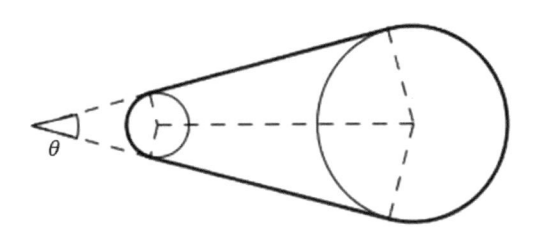

SAT Red Math | 405
Lesson 16A: Advanced Circles

18. The figure above shows a fan belt drive system. The smaller circle (2" diameter) represents a motor, which turns the larger circle (6" diameter) via the belt that connects the two. If the tangent lines representing the belt are extended to the point where they intersect, a 40° angle is formed (denoted by θ). What is the total length of the belt? Round your answer to the nearest tenth of an inch.

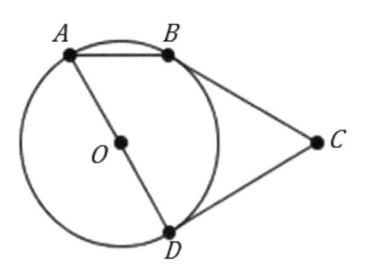

Note: Figure not drawn to scale.

20. In the figure above, $\overline{BC}$ and $\overline{CD}$ are tangent to Circle O. If $m\angle C = 20°$, what is $m\angle OAB$?

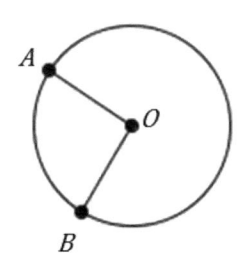

19. The circle above represents a piece of paper with a radius of 6 cm. A sector is cut out from the circle such that the area of the remaining sector is 21π cm². If the remaining sector is used to form a cone (i.e., segments $\overline{OA}$ and $\overline{OB}$ are joined), what volume can it hold? Round your answer to the nearest whole cm³.

Version 3.0

RED MATH LESSON 16B: GRAPHS OF CIRCLES AND PARABOLAS
Learning to Swim

Directions: Answer each question below.

PRACTICE SET 1 (NO CALCULATOR)

1. A circle centered at the point $(2a, -a)$ crosses the x-axis at $x = 5$ and passes through the point $(12, -7)$. What is the value of a?

$$x^2 + y^2 + 2\sqrt{2}x - y = \frac{3}{4}$$

2. What is the center and radius of the circle given by the above equation?

3. Circle A is given by the equation $(x - 4)^2 + (y - 6)^2 = 20$. The line $y = mx + b$, where m and b are constants, passes through the point $(7, 10)$ on Circle A as well as through its center. What is $m + b$?

$$y = (x+3)^2 - 2$$
$$y = 3 - x^2$$
$$y + x = 1$$

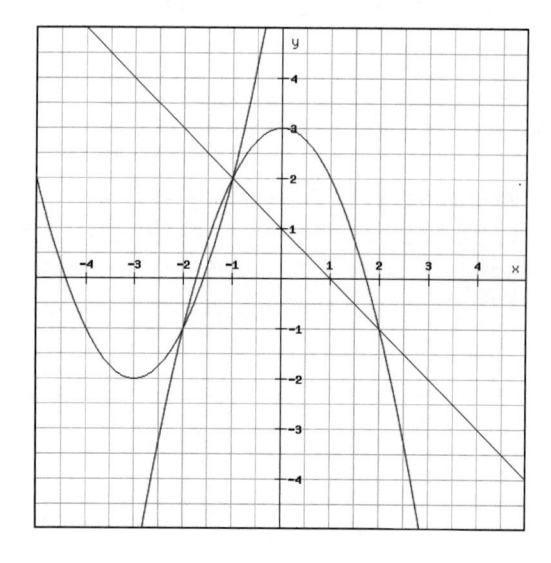

4. A system of three equations and their graphs in the xy-plane are shown above. How many solutions does the system have?

$$(x-2)^2 + (y+3)^2 < 144$$
$$y > -x - 1$$
$$y < x - 5$$

5. What is the area of the figure bounded by the inequalities above?

RED MATH LESSON 16B: GRAPHS OF CIRCLES AND PARABOLAS
Diving into the Deep End

Directions: Answer each question below.

PRACTICE SET 2 (NO CALCULATOR)

6. A circle with equation
   $x^2 + 26x + y^2 - 28y + 340 = 0$ is tangent to which of the following lines?
   A) $y = 10$
   B) $y = 18$
   C) $x = -20$
   D) $x = -8$

7. An equilateral triangle in the first quadrant has two endpoints on the x-axis at $(0, 0)$ and $(6, 0)$. A circle with the equation $(x - h)^2 + (y - k)^2 = r^2$ is inscribed in the triangle. What is the product of h and k?
   A) $3\sqrt{3}$
   B) 6
   C) $6\sqrt{3}$
   D) 12

8. A circle with the equation
   $x^2 + y^2 - 12x - 12y + 36 = 0$ is translated to the left 4 units and up 5 units. What is the equation of the circle after the transformation?
   A) $x^2 + y^2 + 20x - 2y + 65 = 0$
   B) $x^2 + y^2 - 4x - 22y + 89 = 0$
   C) $x^2 + y^2 - 22x - 4y + 89 = 0$
   D) $x^2 + y^2 - 2x - 20y + 65 = 0$

9. What is the diameter of a circle that has the points $(3,9), (-15,11),$ and $(-5,1)$ on the circumference?
   A) $\sqrt{41}$
   B) $\sqrt{82}$
   C) $2\sqrt{41}$
   D) $2\sqrt{82}$

10. A parabola with the equation
    $4p(y - k) = (x - h)^2$ passes through the points $(0,4), (4,12), (1,3)$, what is the x-coordinate of the vertex?
    A) $x = 0$
    B) $x = 1$
    C) $x = 2$
    D) $x = 4$

11. A parabola with the equation
    $4p(x - k) = (y - h)^2$ passes through the points $(9, 5), (2, 6), (2, 12)$, what is the value of p?
    A) $\frac{1}{4}$
    B) $\frac{1}{2}$
    C) 1
    D) $\frac{3}{2}$

12. Which of the following is the equation of a parabola that passes through $(-3, -4)$ and has its vertex at $(-2, -6)$?
    A) $y = -2x^2 + 8x - 14$
    B) $y = 2x^2 + 8x + 2$
    C) $y = \frac{4}{29}(x + 2)^2 - 6$
    D) $y = 2x^2 - 8x + 2$

SAT Red Math
Lesson 16B: Graphs of Circles and Parabolas

13. The endpoints of a diameter of a circle are $(2, -1)$ and $(-6, 5)$. What is the equation of the circle?
    A) $x^2 + y^2 + 4x - 4y = 17$
    B) $x^2 + y^2 + 4x - 4y = 92$
    C) $x^2 + y^2 - 8x - 6y = 0$
    D) $x^2 + y^2 - 4x + 4y = 33$

14. A circle with equation $(x - h)^2 + (y - k)^2 = r^2$ has a center that lies on the y-axis and is inscribed in a square. If the circle is tangent to the lines $x = 3$ and $y = 14$ what is the area of the square?

15. The graphs of $y = 3x^2 - 6x + 1$ and $(x - 1)^2 + (y - 4)^2 = 9$ intersect at how many points?

PRACTICE SET 3 (NO CALCULATOR)

16. The circle described by $x^2 + y^2 + 4x - 2y = 11$ is tangent to:
    A) $x = 2$ and $y = -1$
    B) $x = 14$ and $y = 17$
    C) $x = -6$ and $y = 3$
    D) $x = 2$ and $y = -3$

17. The equation of the parabola graphed above is best described by:
    A) $y = 4x^2 + 40x + 21$
    B) $y = x^2 - 10x + 21$
    C) $y = x^2 + 10x + 24$
    D) $y = \frac{1}{4}x^2 - \frac{5}{2}x + \frac{21}{4}$

18. How has the graph of $y = \frac{1}{3}x^2 + 6x + 36$ been altered from the graph of the parent function $y = x^2$?
    A) Shift left 1; shift up 35; compress vertically
    B) Shift left 3; shift up 33; stretch vertically
    C) Shift left 9; shift up 36; compress vertically
    D) Shift left 9; shift up 9; compress vertically

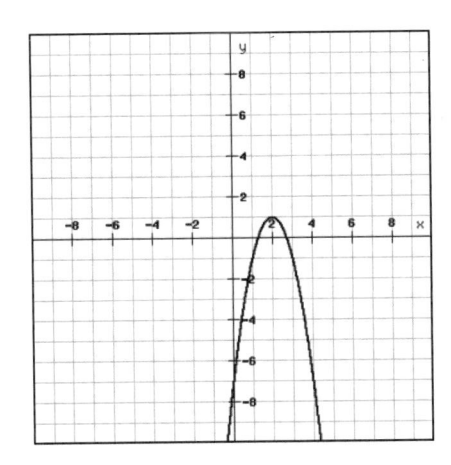

SAT Red Math
Lesson 16B: Graphs of Circles and Parabolas
411

19. The parabola graphed above intersects with the line $y = 4x - 23$ at what point?
    A) $(-2, 1)$
    B) $(4, -7)$
    C) $(2\sqrt{5}, 8\sqrt{5} - 23)$
    D) There is no real solution.

20. Circle A is given by the equation $4x^2 + 4y^2 - 4x + 16y + 9 = 0$. Circle B has the same center as circle A, but its radius is the square of circle A's. Which of the following is an x-intercept of circle B?
    A) $(0.25, 0)$
    B) $(0.5, 0)$
    C) $(1, 0)$
    D) The circle does not cross the x-axis.

21. Which of the following is the equation of the vertical parabola with vertex $(2, -6)$ and passes through the point $(0, 2)$?
    A) $y = -2x^2 + 2$
    B) $y = -x^2 - 4x + 2$
    C) $y = x^2 - 4x - 2$
    D) $y = 2x^2 - 8x + 2$

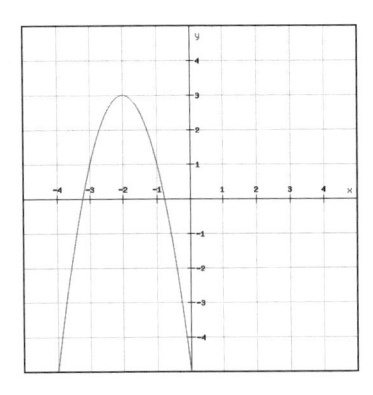

22. What is the equation to the graph above?
    A) $y = -2x^2 - 8x - 5$
    B) $y = -2x^2 + 8x - 5$
    C) $y = -x^2 - 4x - 1$
    D) $y = 2x^2 + 8x + 11$

23. If the parabola represented by $y = \frac{1}{2}x^2 + 4x + 10$ is reflected over the x-axis and reflected over the y-axis, in which quadrant is the vertex of the resulting parabola?
    A) Quadrant I
    B) Quadrant II
    C) Quadrant III
    D) Quadrant IV

24. The diameter of a circle with equation $(x - h)^2 + (y - k)^2 = r^2$ has endpoints with the coordinates $(7, -8)$ and $(-1, 10)$. What is the product of r^2 and h?

Circle Q: $2x^2 + 24x + 2y^2 + 8y + 72 = 0$
Circle R: $x^2 - 4x + y^2 + 8y = -11$

25. What is the ratio of the area of Q to the area of R?

RED MATH LESSON 16B: GRAPHS OF CIRCLES AND PARABOLAS
Race to the Finish

Directions: Answer each question below.

HOMEWORK SET (NO CALCULATOR)

1. If the parabola represented by $x - 3 = \frac{y^2}{3} - 2y$ is translated down 1 unit and to the left 2 units, where is the vertex of the resulting parabola?
   A) $(-2, -2)$
   B) $(-2, 2)$
   C) $(2, -2)$
   D) $(2, 2)$

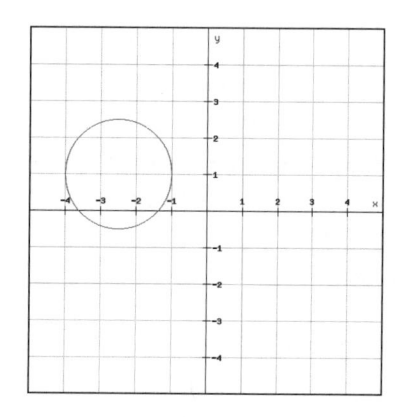

2. What is the equation of the graph above?
   A) $x^2 + y^2 + 5x - 2y + 5.75 = 0$
   B) $x^2 + y^2 - 5x + 2y + 5.75 = 0$
   C) $x^2 + y^2 + 5x - 2y + 5 = 0$
   D) $x^2 + y^2 - 5x + 2y + 5 = 0$

3. Which of the following is the equation of the circle with center $(-4, 2)$ and that goes through the point $(1, -8)$?
   A) $x^2 + y^2 + 8x - 4y = 105$
   B) $x^2 + y^2 + 2x - 16y = 60$
   C) $x^2 + y^2 - 8x + 4y = 105$
   D) $x^2 + y^2 - 2x + 16y = 60$

4. What is the sum of the y-intercepts for the parabola $x = -y^2 - \frac{4}{3}y - \frac{13}{9}$?
   A) $-\frac{13}{9}$
   B) -1
   C) $\frac{1}{3}$
   D) This parabola doesn't cross the y-axis

5. A circle is defined by starting with the circle represented by the equation $x^2 - 6x + y^2 + 10y = -25$ and translating it left 4 units and up 6 units. Which point on the resulting circle has the largest y value?
   A) $(-1, 1)$
   B) $(-1, 4)$
   C) $(7, -11)$
   D) $(7, -8)$

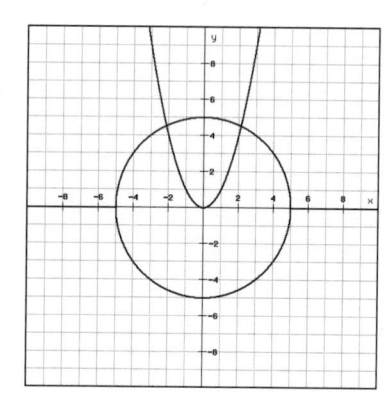

6. If the parabola above is vertically compressed by a factor of 3, reflected over the x-axis, and shifted down by 1 unit, then what would be the new points of intersection of the two graphs?
   A) $(-3, -4), (3, -4)$
   B) $(-3, 4), (3, 4)$
   C) $(-4, 3), (4, 3)$
   D) $(-4, -3), (4, 3)$

SAT Red Math | 413
Lesson 16B: Graphs of Circles and Parabolas

7. Which of the following graphs depicts a circle that is concentric with the circle given by $(x-2)^2 + (y-3)^2 = 4$ but has half the radius?

   A)

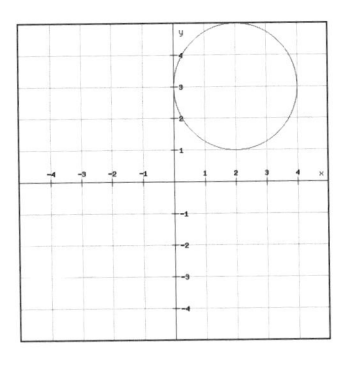

   B)

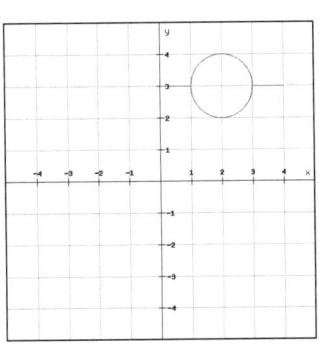

   C)

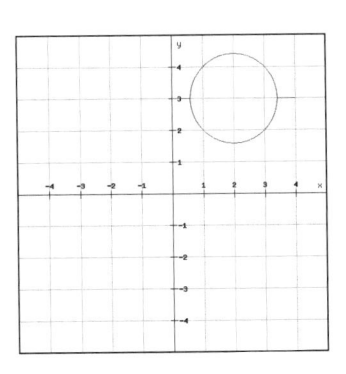

   D)

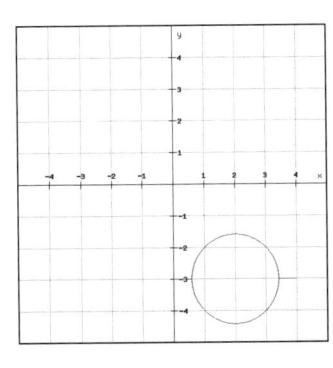

8. Which of the following is the graph of $y = -2x^2 - 12x - 19$ reflected over the y-axis?

   A)

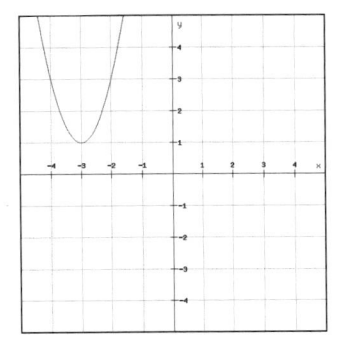

   B)

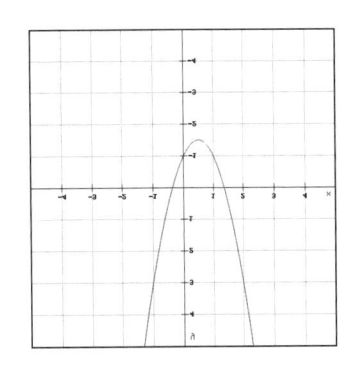

   C)

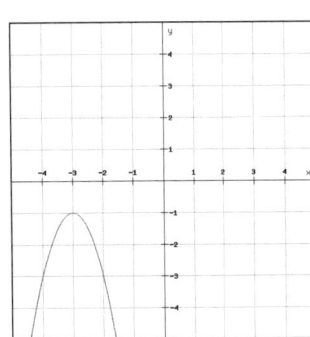

   D)

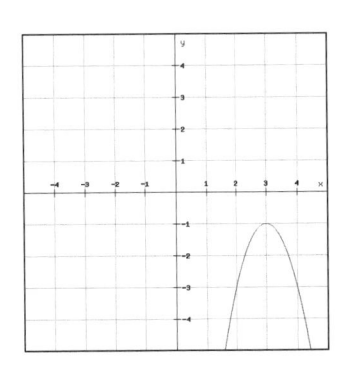

414 | SAT Red Math
Lesson 16B: Graphs of Circles and Parabolas

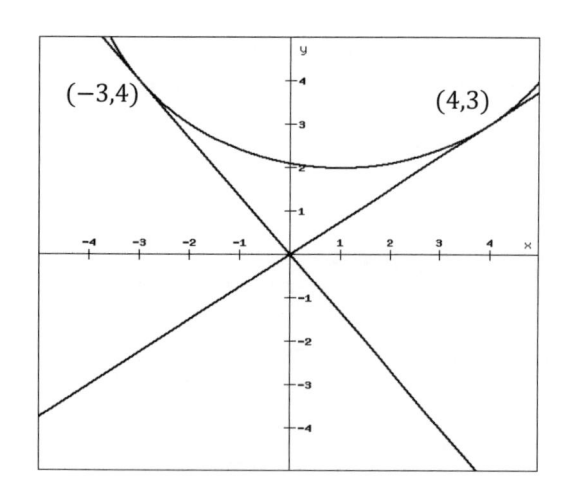

HW

9. In the figure above, two lines are tangent to a circle that is partially shown at the points $(4,3)$ and $(-3,4)$. What is the center of the circle?
   A) $(1, 7)$
   B) $(2, 8)$
   C) $(2, 6)$
   D) $(7, 1)$

10. The radius of the circle in the previous problem is 5. What is the area of the region bounded by the two lines and the circle?
    A) 5
    B) $25 - \frac{25}{4}\pi$
    C) $\frac{25\pi}{4}$
    D) 25

11. The function $g(x) = 2x^2 - 12x + 19$ is obtained from its parent function $f(x) = x^2$ by which of the following transformations?
    A) Shifted right three units, up one unit, stretched vertically by a factor of 2
    B) Shifted left three units, up one unit, stretched vertically by a factor of 2
    C) Shifted right three units, up one unit, shrank vertically by a factor of 2
    D) Shifted up 19 units, stretched vertically by a factor of 2

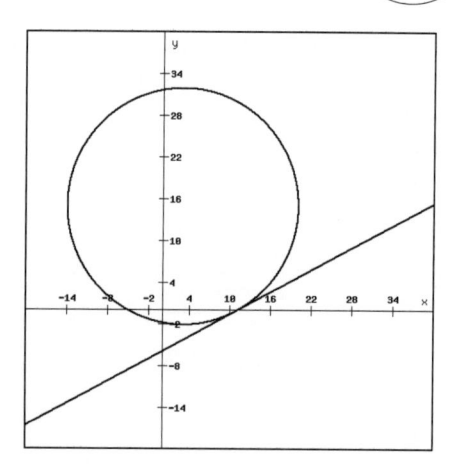

12. The circle above is represented by the equation $(x - 3)^2 + (y - 15)^2 = 289$. The line shown is tangent to the circle at point $(11, 0)$. If $y = C$ is another line that is tangent to the circle and $C > 0$, then what is the point of intersection of the two tangent lines?
    A) $\left(\frac{29}{4}, -2\right)$
    B) $\left(\frac{29}{4}, 32\right)$
    C) $(71, -2)$
    D) $(71, 32)$

13. Which of the following is the equation of a circle whose center lies in Quadrant IV and which passes through the points $(0,5)$ and $(0, -19)$?
    A) $(x + 5)^2 + (y + 7)^2 = 169$
    B) $(x - 5)^2 + (y + 7)^2 = 169$
    C) $(x - 7)^2 + (y + 5)^2 = 169$
    D) $(x + 7)^2 + (y - 5)^2 = 169$

$$x^2 + y^2 - 6x + 4y = -4$$

14. The vertex of which of the following parabolas lies on the same point as the center of the above circle?
    A) $3 - x = (y + 2)^2$
    B) $2 - x = (y + 3)^2$
    C) $3 - y = (x + 2)^2$
    D) $2 - y = (x + 3)^2$

Version 3.0

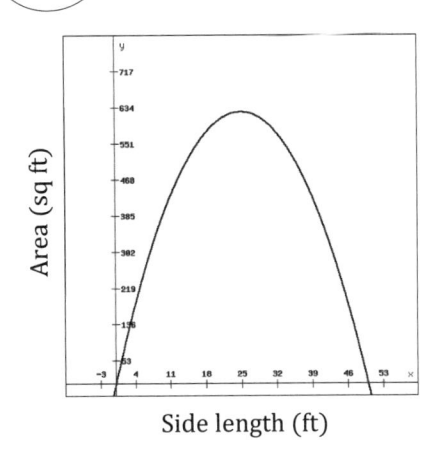

SAT Red Math
Lesson 16B: Graphs of Circles and Parabolas

15. Michael plans to build a rectangular garden with a fixed perimeter. The graph above shows the possible area of such a garden as a function of the length of one side. Which of the following functions correctly describes A, the area, as a function of s, the side length in feet.
   A) $A = -s^2 + 50s$
   B) $A = -s^2 + 50s + 625$
   C) $A = -(s - 25)^2 - 625$
   D) $A = -(s + 25)^2 + 625$

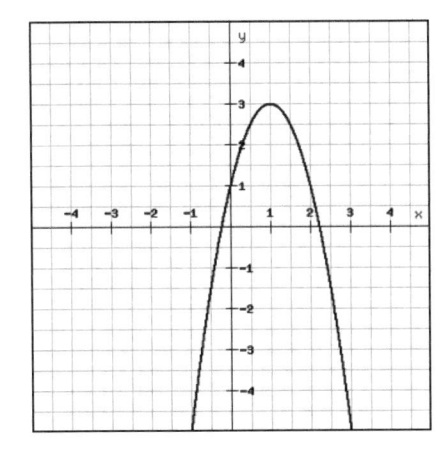

16. If the graph above is shifted to the left by 5 units and down by 4 units, then the resulting graph is best represented by which of the following equations?
   A) $y = -2(x - 1)^2 + 3$
   B) $y = -2(x + 4)^2 - 1$
   C) $y = -2(x - 5)^2 - 2$
   D) $y = -2(x - 6)^2 - 1$

17. The graphs of $x = (y + 1)^2 - 4$ and $x^2 + y^2 + 16x + 2y = -56$ intersect at how many points?

Questions 18 and 19 use the equation of the circle below:

$$2x^2 - \frac{1}{2}x + 2y^2 - \frac{1}{3}y = 8$$

18. What is the x-coordinate of the center of the circle whose equation is shown above?

19. What is the y-coordinate of the center of the circle whose equation is shown above?

$$2x^2 + 4x + 2y^2 + 8y = 8$$

20. If the area enclosed by the circle represented by the equation above is equal to $k\pi$ for some integer k, what is the value of k?

RED MATH LESSON 17A: ADVANCED GEOMETRY
Learning to Swim

Directions: Answer each question below.

PRACTICE SET 1 (CALCULATOR)

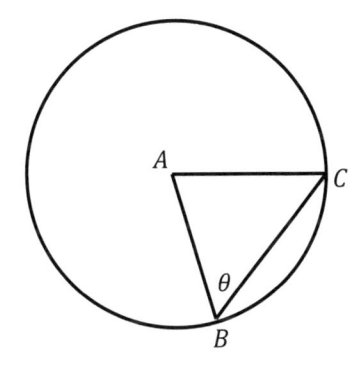

1. Circle A shown above has a radius of r. If the value of θ is $\frac{\pi}{3}$ what is the area of triangle ABC in terms of r?

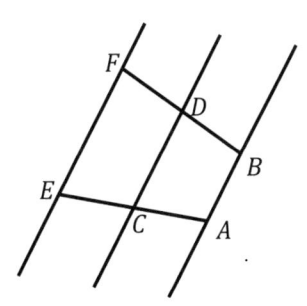

2. In the figure above, lines AB, CD, and EF are all parallel. If the length of EC is 4, the length of EA is 11, the length of DB is 14, and the length of FD is $x + 1$, what is the value of x?

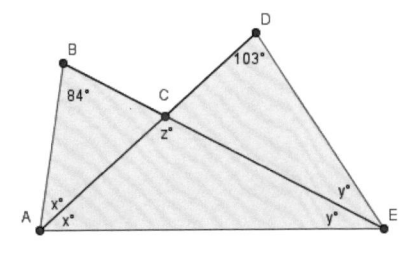

3. In the figure above, what is the value of z?

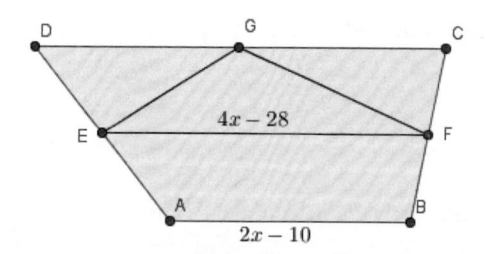

4. For the trapezoid above, line $\overline{DC}$ is parallel to line $\overline{AB}$. Line $\overline{EF}$ is the midsegment of the trapezoid. If the altitude of the trapezoid is 6 and the length of line $\overline{DC}$ is 14, what is the area of triangle EFG?

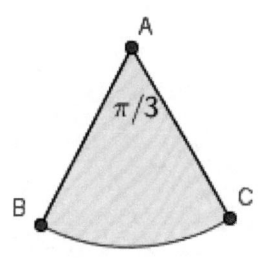

5. The figure shown above is part of a circle with center at A. The measure of angle $\angle BAC$ is $\frac{\pi}{3}$ radians. If the length of line segment $\overline{BC}$ (not shown) is 5. What is the perimeter of the figure?

Red Math Lesson 17A: Advanced Geometry
Diving into the Deep End

Directions: Answer each question below.

Practice Set 2 (Calculator)

6. A cake has the shape of a right circular cylinder with height 5 inches and diameter 8 inches. Each slice is a wedge cut from the center of the cake to its edge. If each slice has volume 10π cubic inches, what is the central angle (in radians) of each slice?
   A) $\frac{\pi}{8}$
   B) $\frac{\pi}{6}$
   C) $\frac{\pi}{4}$
   D) $\frac{\pi}{3}$

7. Megan makes a cake identical to the cake in the previous question. She cuts it into 6 congruent wedge-shaped slices. She needs to frost each slice on all sides except the bottom and package each slice separately. In order to prepare the correct amount of frosting, she must know the surface area of the cake slices. What is the combined surface area of the 6 slices, excluding their bases?
   A) $28\pi + 120$
   B) $56\pi + 120$
   C) $28\pi + 240$
   D) $56\pi + 240$

8. An equilateral triangle is inscribed in a circle of radius 1. What is the shortest arc length, in radians, between any two adjacent vertices of the triangle?
   A) $\frac{\pi}{3}$
   B) $\frac{2\pi}{3}$
   C) $\frac{4\pi}{3}$
   D) 2π

9. In a circle of radius 5, a sector is chosen with central angle θ such that $\sec\theta$ is undefined. What is a possible arc length for the sector?
   A) 2.5π
   B) 3.75π
   C) 15π
   D) 22.5π

10. If the figure above is a rectangle and $\sin\theta = \frac{1}{2}$, what is the perimeter of the entire figure?
    A) $\frac{1}{2} + \frac{\sqrt{3}}{2}$
    B) $2 + 2\sqrt{3}$
    C) $\frac{r}{2}(1+\sqrt{3})$
    D) $r(1+\sqrt{3})$

11. An equilateral triangle with side length t, a square with side length s, and a circle with radius r all have the same area. Which of the following puts $t, s,$ and r in ascending order of length?
    A) r, s, t
    B) s, r, t
    C) t, s, r
    D) t, r, s

420 | SAT Red Math
Lesson 17A: Advanced Geometry

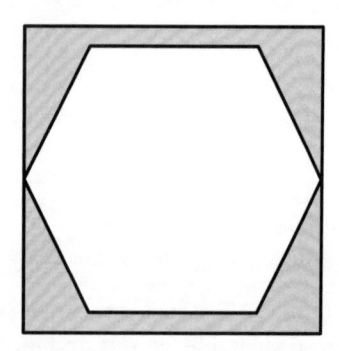

12. In the figure above, a regular hexagon is drawn inside a square so that two of the vertices are on the square and the diagonal connecting those vertices is parallel to the top and bottom edges of the square. What is the ratio of the area of the shaded region to the area of the unshaded region?

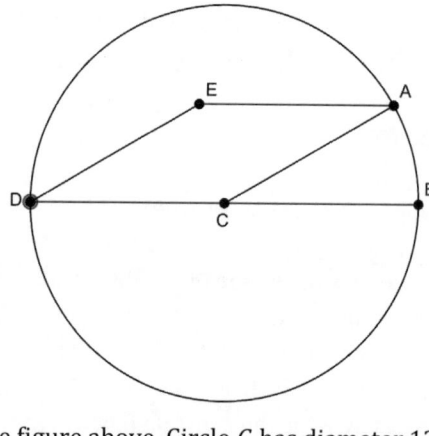

A) $\frac{2-\sqrt{3}}{3}$

B) $\frac{2\sqrt{3}-3}{2}$

C) $\frac{3\sqrt{3}}{10}$

D) $\frac{8\sqrt{3}-9}{9}$

14. In the figure above, Circle C has diameter 12 and the measure of minor arc $\widehat{AB}$ is π. What is the area of parallelogram $ACDE$?

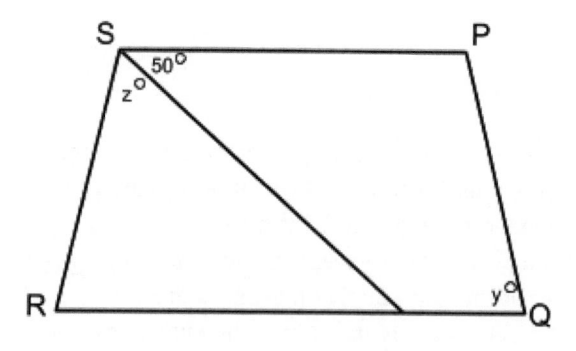

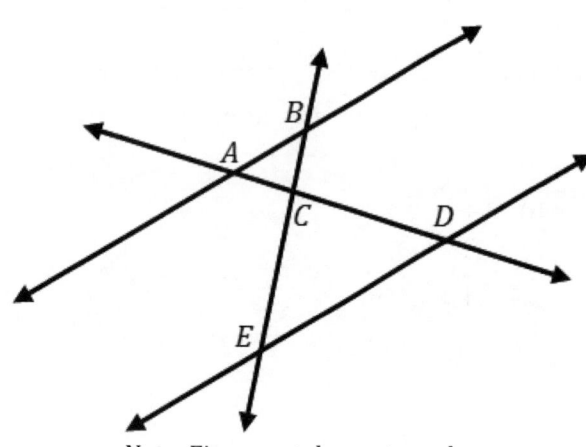

15. In trapezoid $PQRS$ above, $\overline{PQ} = \overline{RS}$. What is the value of $y + z$?

Note: Figure not drawn to scale.

13. In the figure above, $\triangle ABC$ is similar to $\triangle EDC$. Which of the following statements must be true?

A) $\overleftrightarrow{AB} \parallel \overleftrightarrow{ED}$

B) $\angle BAC \cong \angle CDE$

C) $\sin \angle ACB = \cos \angle DCE$

D) None of the above statements are true.

Practice Set 3 (Calculator)

Use the following image for questions 16 and 17.

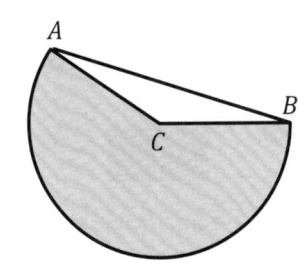

16. The shaded portion of the figure above is a sector of a circle. If the area of the shaded portion is 42π and the radius of the circle is $6\sqrt{2}$, what is the measure of $\overline{AB}$, to the nearest tenth?
    A) 4.4
    B) 8.2
    C) 14.7
    D) 16.4

17. What is the area of the unshaded portion of the image above, to the nearest tenth?
    A) 9.0
    B) 13.5
    C) 18.0
    D) 22.6

18. What is the area of the largest triangle that can fit within a square of perimeter 100?
    A) 50
    B) 100
    C) 312.5
    D) 625

Use the following information for questions 19 and 20.

$180(n-2)°$ = Sum of the angle measures of the interior angles of a polygon

$360°$ = Sum of the angle measures of the exterior angles of a polygon

19. A regular polygon has congruent interior and exterior angles. How many sides does that polygon have?
    A) 4
    B) 6
    C) 8
    D) 12

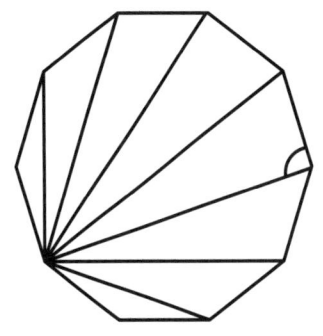

20. A regular 10-sided polygon is drawn, and one of its vertices is connected by a diagonal to each of its non-adjacent vertices, as shown above. What is the measure of the marked angle?
    A) 72
    B) 90
    C) 108
    D) 126

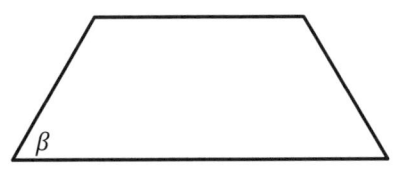

21. The isosceles trapezoid above has a leg of length 15 and its shorter base has a length of 24. If $\tan\beta = \frac{4}{3}$, what is the area of the trapezoid?
    A) 396
    B) 432
    C) 450
    D) 495

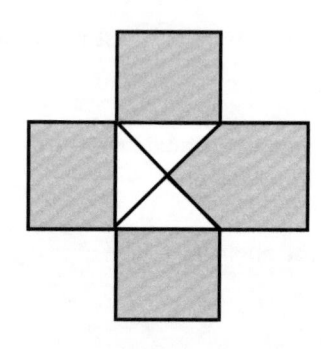

22. In the diagram above, there are five congruent squares each of area 24, four of them sharing a side with the central square, which is divided into four triangles by its two diagonals. One of these triangles is merged with one of the squares to form a pentagon. What is the total perimeter of the four shaded regions?

A) $30\sqrt{6} + 2\sqrt{3}$
B) $30\sqrt{6} + 4\sqrt{3}$
C) $30\sqrt{6} + 2\sqrt{3}$
D) $32\sqrt{6} + 4\sqrt{3}$

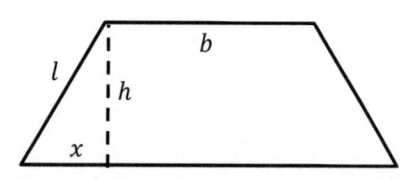

23. An isosceles trapezoid with leg length l, height h, and shorter base length b is shown above. x represents half the difference between the lengths of both bases. Which of the following equations can be used to find the area of the trapezoid above?

A) $\frac{h}{2}(b + \sqrt{l^2 - h^2})$
B) $h(b + \sqrt{l^2 - h^2})$
C) $\frac{h}{2}(b + \sqrt{l^2 + h^2})$
D) $h(b + \sqrt{l^2 + h^2})$

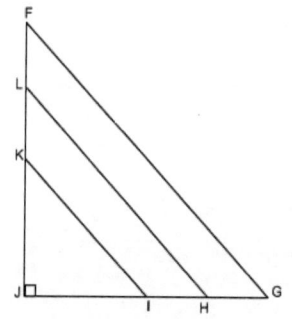

Note: Figure not drawn to scale.

24. In the figure above, $FG \parallel LH \parallel KI$. $\overline{FG} = 15$, $\overline{GH} = 3$, $\overline{JF} = 12$, and $\overline{KL} = 4$. What is the area of trapezoid $LHIK$?

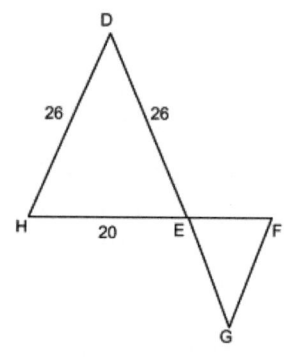

25. Triangle EFG is similar to triangle EHD. If triangle EFG has perimeter 36, what is its area?

RED MATH LESSON 17A: ADVANCED GEOMETRY
Race to the Finish

Directions: Answer each question below.

HOMEWORK SET (CALCULATOR)

1. An orange has a volume of 288π cubic centimeters. After the 2 mm thick peel is removed, what is the volume of the remaining fruit, to the nearest cubic centimeter?
   A) 268
   B) 524
   C) 817
   D) 896

2. The two acute angles of a right triangle have degree measures of x and y. If $\tan x = \frac{5}{12}$, what is the value of $\cos y$?
   A) $\frac{5}{13}$
   B) $\frac{5}{12}$
   C) $\frac{12}{13}$
   D) $\frac{12}{5}$

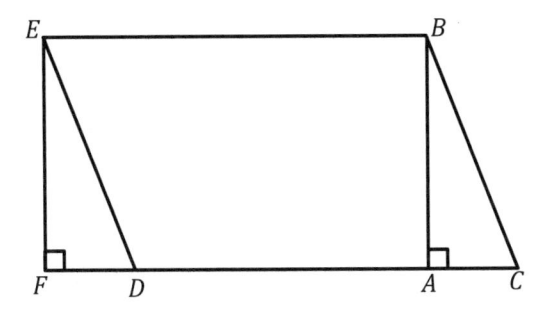

3. In the figure above, AC is equal to 13, DE is equal to 26, and $EF \cong BA$. If $\angle BCA \cong \angle EDF$, what is the measure of $\angle FED$?
   A) 30°
   B) 45°
   C) 60°
   D) 75°

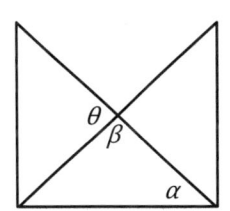

4. Which equation must be true based on the information in the diagram above?
   A) $\cos \alpha = -\cos \beta$
   B) $\cos \alpha = -\cos \theta$
   C) $\cos \beta = -\cos \theta$
   D) $\cos \beta = -\sin \beta$

5. A construction company is repaving a four-way intersection. The two roads of the intersection meet perpendicularly and consist of two lanes each. If each lane is 12 feet wide, and the asphalt must be 2 inches thick, what volume of asphalt, in cubic feet, is needed to cover both the intersection and the area 2 feet beyond the intersection (within each lane) on each road?
   A) 128
   B) 768
   C) 1152
   D) 1536

6. A batch of 128 spherical grapes is placed in the sun to dehydrate, a process by which water is removed from the grapes. If each grape initially measures 3 cm across, and the final volume of the dried grapes is 900 cubic cm, how much water did the grapes lose, rounded to the nearest mL (1mL = 1 cm³)?
   A) 118
   B) 910
   C) 1810
   D) 13577

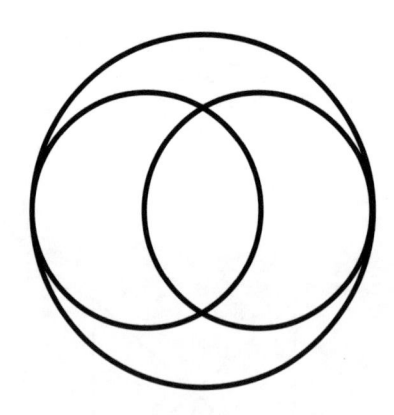

424 | SAT Red Math
Lesson 17A: Advanced Geometry

HW

9. What is the area of triangle ABC?
   A) $6\sqrt{3}$
   B) 12
   C) $9\sqrt{3}$
   D) $12\sqrt{3}$

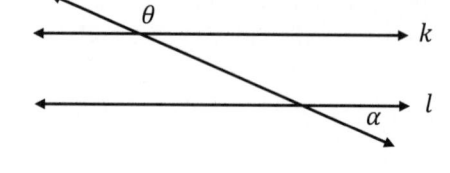

7. In the figure above, each of the two smaller circles passes through the other circle's center and also touches the larger circle tangentially. The larger circle has a diameter of 54. What is the area of a circle formed with radius equivalent to the difference between the radius of the larger circle and one of the smaller circles?
   A) 9π
   B) 18π
   C) 81π
   D) 324π

10. If, in the figure above, lines k and l are parallel and $\tan \alpha = \frac{5}{12}$, what is $\tan \theta$?
    A) $-\frac{12}{5}$
    B) $-\frac{5}{12}$
    C) $\frac{5}{12}$
    D) $\frac{12}{5}$

Use the image below for Questions 8 and 9.
In the figure below, $\sin \gamma = \frac{1}{2}$, and the area of Circle B is 36π.

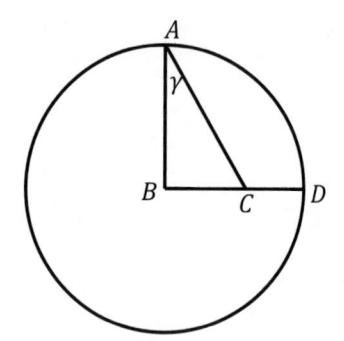

8. What is the length of CD?
   A) $6 - 2\sqrt{3}$
   B) 3
   C) $2\sqrt{3}$
   D) 6

11. A diagonal is a line segment drawn from one vertex of a polygon to another, non-adjacent vertex of the polygon. Which of the following expressions can be used to find the total number of diagonals that can be drawn for an n-sided polygon, where $n > 2$?
    A) $\frac{n(n-3)}{2}$
    B) $\frac{n(n-2)}{2}$
    C) $n(n-3)$
    D) $n(n-2)$

Version 3.0

Use the image and information below for Questions 12 and 13.

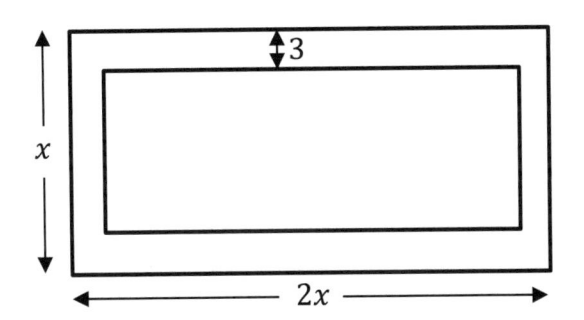

The figure above represents a rectangular painting with a frame that is 3 inches wide. The expression $2x^2 - (x-6)(2x-6)$ represents the area of the frame, in square inches.

12. What does the quantity $(x-6)(2x-6)$ in the expression above represent?
    A) The width of the painting, in inches.
    B) The length of the painting, in inches.
    C) The area, in square inches, of the inner rectangle.
    D) The combined area, in square inches, of the frame and painting.

13. If the area of the frame shown above is 144 square inches, what is the perimeter of the painting in inches?
    A) 10
    B) 36
    C) 56
    D) 60

Use the image below for Questions 14 and 15.

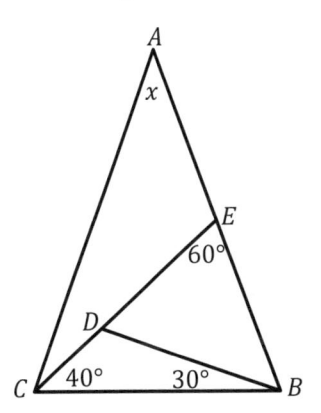

14. In isosceles triangle ABC above, $\overline{AB} \cong \overline{AC}$. What is the value of x?
    A) 20°
    B) 30°
    C) 50°
    D) 80°

15. Which of the following side lengths is longest?
    A) $\overline{DE}$
    B) $\overline{EB}$
    C) $\overline{BD}$
    D) $\overline{CB}$

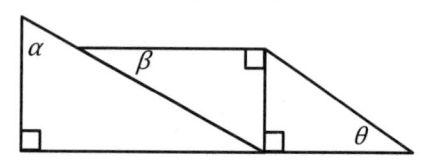

16. Which equation must be true for the information in the diagram above?
   A) $\sin \alpha = \cos \beta$
   B) $\sin \alpha = \cos \theta$
   C) $\sin \beta = \cos \theta$
   D) $\sin \alpha = \sin \beta$

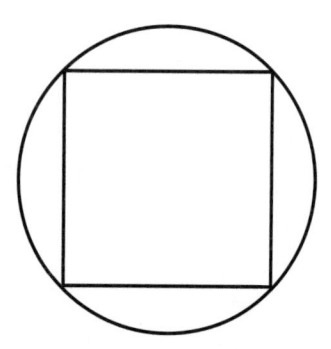

17. Every morning Clara runs along a running trail that consists of a large circular path and an inscribed square path, as shown in the image above. Jogging at a constant 5 miles per hour, she completes the square path in 48 minutes. If during her timed run today she maintains a rate of 8 mph, how long will it take her, to the nearest minute, to complete both the circular path and the square path?

18. Amy and Rory are constructing and installing a stained glass window for an art gallery. The window will fill a space of 48 square feet and consist of 3 identically sized square panels. The pattern for each of the panels is identical, and one of the panels is shown above. The window is composed of blue and white glass, which costs 50 cents per square inch and 25 cents per square inch respectively. The large square of the middle panel is made of blue glass and is surrounded by white triangles, while the side panels have a large white square surrounded by blue triangles. If installation costs $235, how much did the stained glass window cost the art gallery, to the nearest dollar?

19. A restaurant wishes to commemorate its grand opening by baking a giant soufflé, which will have a volume equal to 100 of its regular soufflés. Each regular soufflé is approximately cylindrical and has a diameter of 3 inches and a height of 2 inches. What is the volume of the large celebration soufflé, to the nearest tenth of a cubic foot?

20. An architectural model of a new building is set up to have a scale factor of 1:12. If the building is intended to house a library with a floor that spans 216 square feet and 96 inch bookcases that stretch from the floor to the ceiling, what is the volume of the architectural model of the library, in cubic inches?

C2 education
be smarter.

RED MATH LESSON 17B: ADVANCED VOLUME
Learning to Swim

Directions: Answer each question below.

PRACTICE SET 1 (CALCULATOR)

1. A sphere is inscribed within a cube with volume 125 in³. What is the volume of the sphere, to the nearest in³?

2. A rectangular fish tank of length 20 cm, width 10 cm, and height 14 cm is being filled with water. The tank already contains two decorative objects: a 10-cm-tall square pyramid, with a base of side length 7 cm; and an igloo in the shape of a half-sphere, with radius 4 cm. What volume of water (to the nearest mL) is required to fill the tank to 2 cm below the top of the tank? (1 mL = 1 cm³)

3. Amin is ordering boxes for his doughnut shop. His donuts have a diameter of 4 inches and a height of 1.5 inches. What is the minimum volume of a box that could hold a dozen donuts, laid out side-by-side in a single layer? Answer to the nearest in³.

4. Sean is stacking barrels of maple syrup onto a forklift that has a weight capacity of 1800 lbs. Each barrel weighs 10 lbs. when empty and has a volume of 20 gallons. The barrels are completely full of syrup, which has a density of 5 lbs./gallon. What is the maximum number of barrels that Sean can stack on the forklift without exceeding its weight capacity? (Density = mass ÷ volume)

5. A regular hexagonal prism with a side length of 3 cm and depth of 5 cm has a density of 3.5 grams per cubic cm. Three cylindrical bores are removed from the hexagonal prism, parallel to its depth. Each bore is 5 cm in length, and the radii of the bores are 1 cm, 1.5 cm, and 2 cm. Calculate the final mass of the object to the nearest tenth of a gram.

SAT Red Math
Lesson 17B: Advanced Volume

RED MATH LESSON 17B: ADVANCED VOLUME
Diving into the Deep End

Directions: Answer each question below.

PRACTICE SET 2 (CALCULATOR)

6. A skyscraper is cylindrical for its lowest 100 meters of height. On top of the cylindrical portion, the building is shaped like a hemisphere. If both parts of the building have a radius of 15 meters, what is its volume?
   A) $24{,}750\pi$ m^3
   B) $27{,}000\pi$ m^3
   C) $45{,}000\pi$ m^3
   D) $48{,}750\pi$ m^3

7. Chicken broth comes in two types of containers. One container is a can, a cylinder with radius 4 cm and height 10 cm. The other is a box, a rectangular prism with length 10 cm, width 6 cm, and height 20 cm. If a recipe calls for 6 liters of broth (1 liter = 1000 cubic centimeters), the recipe requires either
   A) 5 cans or 12 boxes of broth.
   B) 6 cans or 6 boxes of broth.
   C) 8 cans or 4 boxes of broth.
   D) 12 cans or 5 boxes of broth.

8. The megaphone shown in the figure above is formed by cutting off the top 8 inches from the height of a cone. If the radii of the top and bottom of the remaining figure are 4 inches and 10 inches, respectively, what is the volume of the remaining figure?
   A) 357π in^3
   B) 539π in^3
   C) 603π in^3
   D) 624π in^3

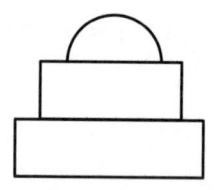

9. A wedding cake has two cylindrical layers and a hemispherical layer, as shown in the side view above. Each layer is 6 inches tall. The layers have radii of 6, 8, and 10 inches. What is the total volume of the cake?
   A) 1056π in^3
   B) 1128π in^3
   C) 1200π in^3
   D) 1272π in^3

10. A sphere has a radius of x cm. Another sphere has a radius that is 3 cm larger. What is the positive difference in the volumes of the two spheres, in terms of x?
    A) $(9x^2 + 27x + 27)\pi$
    B) $(x^3 + 9x^2 + 27x + 27)\pi$
    C) $(12x^2 + 36x + 36)\pi$
    D) $(x^3 + 12x^2 + 36x + 36)\pi$

11. A cylindrical water tank is to be constructed, and it must be capable of holding 7 days' water supply for a town of 2,000 people. Data collected by the local water utility indicate residents use an average of 12 cubic feet of water per person per day. If the tank's diameter is 20 yards, what is its minimum possible height, to the nearest whole yard?
    A) 5 yards
    B) 20 yards
    C) 45 yards
    D) 60 yards

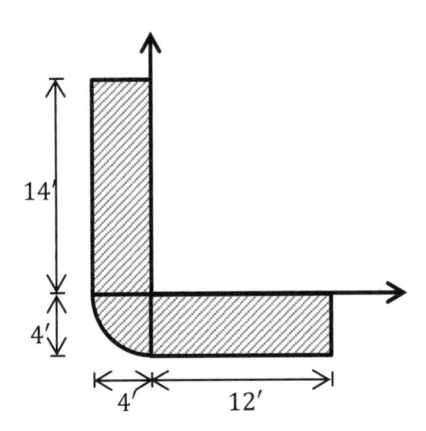

SAT Red Math
Lesson 17B: Advanced Volume
431

14. A cubic block of wood has a side length of 18 inches. If the block is carved into the largest possible pyramid, and the remaining wood is discarded, what is the volume of the discarded wood? Round to the nearest whole cubic inch.

12. A garden consists of rectangular raised beds along the side and front wall of a house, with a rounded corner, as shown in the figure above. Potting soil costs $3.00 per 40 lb. bag, and has a density of 25 lb/ft³. What is the cost of the potting soil necessary to fill the whole raised garden bed to a depth of 18 inches?
    A) $93.00
    B) $111.00
    C) $330.00
    D) $840.00

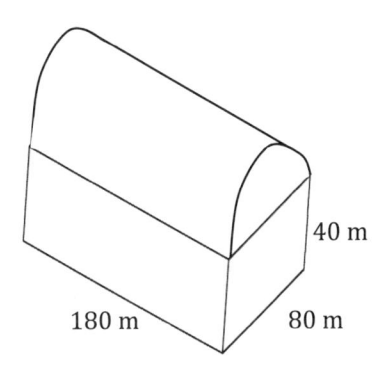

15. A cylindrical hole is drilled through the center of a rectangular prism made of stone for the prism's entire height. The prism has a base that is 6 centimeters by 10 centimeters, and the hole's radius is 2 centimeters. If the volume of the remaining figure is $480 - 32\pi$ cm³, what is the figure's height? Round to the nearest whole centimeter.

13. Air has a density of 1.225 kg/m³ at normal atmospheric pressure and in temperate weather conditions. A stadium under construction is rectangular in shape with dimensions 180 m × 80 m, and a rounded roof that comprises half a cylinder. The vertical portions of the walls are 40 m high. What is the mass, to the nearest metric ton (1000 kg), of the air in this stadium if its interior is a completely empty space?
    A) 840 metric tons
    B) 844 metric tons
    C) 1260 metric tons
    D) 1814 metric tons

Version 3.0

Lesson 17B: Advanced Volume

PRACTICE SET 3 (CALCULATOR)

16. Which of the following, if done to a cylinder, will have the effect of doubling the lateral surface area (not including the top and bottom) and quadrupling the volume?
    A) Double the radius of the cylinder and do not change the height
    B) Double the height of the cylinder and do not change the radius
    C) Double the height of the cylinder and multiply the radius by 4
    D) Multiply the cylinder's radius by 4 and divide its height by 4

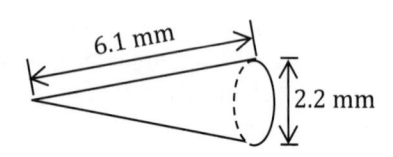

17. A drill bit is in the shape of a cone with slant height 6.1 mm and diameter 2.2 mm, as shown above. It is made of high-speed steel, a type of steel specially designed for tools, which has a density of 8.0 g/cm³. What mass of steel, to the nearest thousandth of a gram, is required to make this drill bit?
    A) 0.061 g
    B) 0.062 g
    C) 0.182 g
    D) 0.186 g

18. Iron ore has a density of 11,340 kg/m³. A cylindrical glass of radius 6 cm is filled with water to a level of 8 cm. When a solid iron sphere is dropped into the water, the water level rises to 8.037 cm. What is the mass of this sphere, to the nearest tenth of a gram?
    A) 3.5 g
    B) 4.8 g
    C) 34.7 g
    D) 47.5 g

19. A triangular prism has two equilateral triangle bases and a length (from base to base) of 20 cm. If its volume is $180\sqrt{3}$ cm³, what is the length of a side of its base?
    A) 3 cm
    B) 6 cm
    C) 9 cm
    D) $6\sqrt{6}$ cm

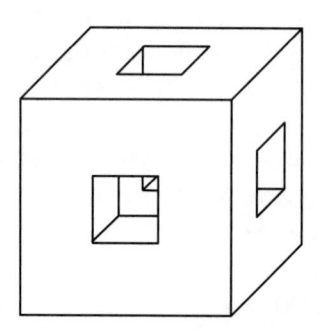

20. A cube has side length 3 inches. In the center of each of its six faces, a square of side length 1 inch is cut out, and a hollow shaft perpendicular to that face is bored through to the opposite face. (Thus there are 3 such shafts, which meet in the center of the cube.) What volume of solid material remains in this cube?
    A) 9 cm³
    B) 18 cm³
    C) 20 cm³
    D) 21 cm³

21. What is the volume, in cubic yards, of a pyramid of height 120 ft. whose base is a square of side length 144 ft.?
    A) 30,720
    B) 92,160
    C) 276,480
    D) 829,440

SAT Red Math | 433
Lesson 17B: Advanced Volume

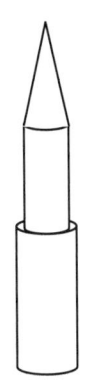

24. A pencil has a regular hexagonal cross-section. Each side of this hexagon has a length of 6 mm. The pencil's original height is 10 cm. Then, the top 3 cm of the pencil are sharpened into a hexagonal pyramid. What is the volume of the pencil, to the nearest tenth of a cubic centimeter?

22. A skyscraper is built in three distinct segments: a cylinder of diameter 180 feet and height 420 feet, a smaller cylinder of diameter 100 feet and height 180 feet, and a cone of diameter 100 feet and height 240 feet. Which of the following is closest to the volume of the entire building?
    A) 470,000 cubic yards
    B) 1.41 million cubic yards
    C) 12.73 million cubic yards
    D) 38.19 million cubic yards

25. A block of stone is carved into three pyramids with 8 cm-square bases. If the pyramids are 3 cm, 6 cm, and 9 cm high, what is the combined volume of the pyramids? Round to the nearest whole cubic centimeter squared.

23. A miner wants to test an irregularly shaped metallic nugget to see if it its density matches that of gold. He weighs the nugget and finds that it weighs 99 grams. He then submerges it in a cylindrical bucket of water of radius 5 cm. This causes the water level to rise by 0.2 cm. What is the density of the nugget?
    A) 6.3 g/cm^3
    B) 19.8 g/cm^3
    C) 25.2 g/cm^3
    D) 31.5 g/cm^3

Version 3.0

RED MATH LESSON 17B: ADVANCED VOLUME
Race to the Finish

Directions: Answer each question below.

HOMEWORK SET (CALCULATOR)

1. What is the volume of the largest sphere that can be fit inside a cylinder of height 12 inches and diameter 6 inches?
   A) 36π in³
   B) 108π in³
   C) 144π in³
   D) 576π in³

2. At its mouth, a large river is flowing at a rate of 3 feet per second and has an average depth of 7.5 feet. It is ¼ mile wide. What volume of water is discharged by this river every minute, in cubic yards?
   A) 1,100 yd³
   B) 3,300 yd³
   C) 66,000 yd³
   D) 198,000 yd³

3. A cylinder of height y and radius x has the same volume as a cone of height h and what radius, in terms of h, x, and y?
   A) $\frac{3h}{x^2 y}$
   B) $\sqrt{\frac{3x^2 h}{y}}$
   C) $\sqrt{\frac{x^2 y}{3h}}$
   D) $\sqrt{\frac{3x^2 y}{h}}$

4. Which of the following has the same effect on a cylinder's volume as dividing the circumference by 4 and multiplying the height by 8?
   A) Multiplying the height by 2 and leaving the circumference unchanged
   B) Dividing the height by 2 and leaving the circumference unchanged
   C) Multiplying the diameter by 2 and dividing the height by 32
   D) Multiplying the radius by 4 and dividing the height by 16

5. An isosceles triangle with legs 5 units long and base 8 units long is the base of a triangular prism with height 4 units. What is the volume of the prism in cubic units?
   A) 24
   B) 48
   C) 80
   D) 160

6. A kitchen step stool is in the form of a frustum of a cone, i.e. the solid that remains when a cone is sliced parallel to its base and the tip is removed. The step stool is 14 inches high; the diameter at the base is 16 inches and the diameter of the top surface is 12 inches. What is its volume?
   A) $\frac{196}{3}\pi$ in³
   B) $\frac{518}{3}\pi$ in³
   C) $\frac{896}{3}\pi$ in³
   D) $\frac{2072}{3}\pi$ in³

SAT Red Math — Lesson 17B: Advanced Volume

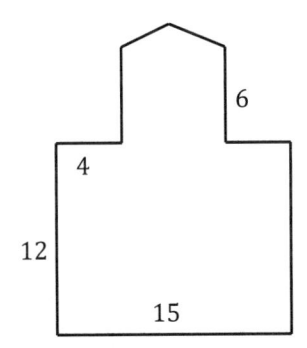

7. A common design for a barn uses a raised roof down the center aisle, with windows on the upper walls to let light into the interior. A shed based on this design is 20 feet long, and the roof peak rises 2 feet above the top of the upper walls; other dimensions are as shown in the cross-section above. What volume does the shed enclose? (Assume all lines that connect in the above diagram are perpendicular and that the figure is symmetric.)
   A) 229 ft³
   B) 4580 ft³
   C) 4720 ft³
   D) 5140 ft³

8. A compactor crushes aluminum cans for recycling; it exerts enough force to reduce their volume until they have a density of 23 pounds per cubic foot. The rectangular floor of the compactor is 1 foot wide and 1.5 feet long; a particular load is 0.75 feet high after crushing. If the amount of aluminum in this block is melted down and made into a sphere, what will be the sphere's radius? (Aluminum has a density of 2.7 g/cm³, and there are 453.59 grams in 1 pound.)
   A) 10.1 cm
   B) 19.7 cm
   C) 1039 cm
   D) 4351 cm

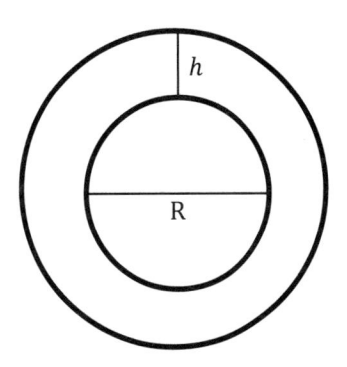

9. Tires are sized using three numbers: The number following the "P" indicates the width of the tread in millimeters; the number following the slash gives the percentage of that width that equals the tire height h, and the number following the "R" indicates the diameter in inches of the wheel on which the tire is to be installed. To the nearest cubic inch, what volume of air is contained in a tire marked P245/65R17?
   A) 998 in³
   B) 1191 in³
   C) 4423 in³
   D) 7655 in³

10. A cylindrical castle turret 40 meters tall and 6 meters across is capped by a conical roof 6 meters high. If the base of the cone extends horizontally 2 meters further out than the wall of the turret, what is the volume of the space enclosed?
    A) 378π m³
    B) 410π m³
    C) 1490π m³
    D) 1564π m³

436 SAT Red Math
Lesson 17B: Advanced Volume

HW

11. A cylindrical mug with a radius of 5 cm and a height of 10 cm is filled with 1200 grams of liquid broth. What is the density of the broth, to the nearest tenth of a gram per cubic cm? (Density is mass divided by volume.)
    A) 0.8
    B) 1.5
    C) 6.1
    D) 7.6

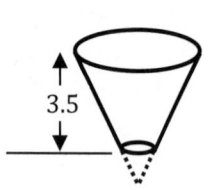

12. A funnel is designed in the shape of a cone with a smaller cone chopped off its tip, as illustrated above. If the large opening of the funnel has a radius of 2 inches and the small opening has a radius of ¼ inch, and the height of the funnel is 3.5 inches, what is its volume in cubic inches?
    A) 11.2 in³
    B) 14.7 in³
    C) 16.7 in³
    D) 17.2 in³

13. A chef at a diner wishes to prepare enough batter for 200 pancakes. For the purpose of this problem, assume a pancake is a cylinder with height 0.25 in and diameter 6 in, and each pancake weighs 8 ounces (half a pound). The liquid batter has a density equal to 4.5 times that of the solid pancakes, because they rise and develop air bubbles while cooking. What volume of batter should be produced, to the nearest cup (1 cup = 14.432 in³)?
    A) 22 c.
    B) 87 c.
    C) 125 c.
    D) 392 c.

14. Sugar dissolves in water at a rate that is directly proportional to its exposed surface area. In a science experiment, a sugar cube 1 cm on each side is placed in a glass of warm water and observed to begin dissolving at a rate of 18 milligrams per second. In another identical glass of water, the same total mass and volume of sugar is placed, but in the form of eight identical smaller cubes. At what rate will that sugar initially dissolve?
    A) 18 mg/s
    B) 36 mg/s
    C) 108 mg/s
    D) 144 mg/s

15. A steel plate used in the assembly of a car has a thickness of 2.5 mm, and takes the form of a 24 cm × 18 cm rectangle whose corners are rounded off with a radius of 1 cm. The density of steel is 8 grams / cm³. What is the mass of this plate to the nearest gram? (Density is equal to mass divided by volume.)
    A) 710 g
    B) 862 g
    C) 864 g
    D) 870 g

16. A machine is stacking dice in a cardboard box to ship to a casino. The box is 18 inches tall with a square base of area 64 in². Each cube-shaped die is ⅔ of an inch wide. How many dice will fit in the box?
    A) 341
    B) 1728
    C) 2592
    D) 3888

17. A new video game is shipping out to stores. Each copy comes in a plastic box measuring 0.5 in × 6 in × 8 in. These boxes are shipped in crates measuring 2 ft. × 2.5 ft. × 1.5 ft. If the games can be packed in with no room to spare, how many such crates are necessary to hold 81,000 copies of this game?

Use the following information for questions 19 and 20:

A swimming pool is a rectangle 30 meters long with a uniformly sloping floor so that its depth changes along its length. It is 1 meter deep at its shallow end and 4 meters deep at its deep end. The pool is 20 meters wide.

19. What is the volume of the pool in cubic meters?

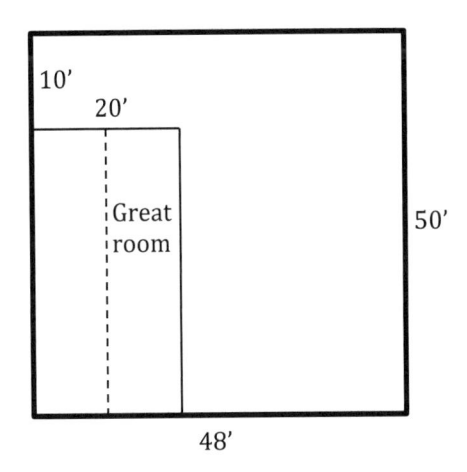

18. The Jones family is planning to install a cathedral ceiling over their great room. The walls are currently 9 feet high throughout the house, but the ceiling will be raised to 17 feet along the dashed line in the floor plan above. The new ceiling will slope evenly from that line to the tops of the two walls parallel to it. By what percent does the volume of the house increase? Round to the nearest tenth of a percent.

20. This pool needs to be treated with chlorine at a concentration of 2 mg/kg; that is, 2 milligrams of chlorine for every kilogram of water. To accomplish this, what mass of a liquid chlorine solution that is 15% chlorine by mass should be added to the pool? Round to the nearest whole kilogram. (Note: the density of water is 1 g/cm^3.)

SAT Red Math
Lesson 18A: Practice Sections

RED MATH LESSON 18A: PRACTICE SECTIONS
Learning to Swim

Directions: Answer each question below.

PRACTICE SET 1 (CALCULATOR)

1. The Richter scale measures the magnitude of earthquakes using a base-10 logarithmic scale. A 6.0 magnitude earthquake is 10 times as strong as a 5.0 magnitude earthquake. The Richter scale can be represented by the equation $R = \log_{10} A$, where R and A are the Richter scale measurement and seismic wave amplitude, respectively. In 1906, San Francisco experienced a devastating earthquake of magnitude 7.8. In 1989, the area experienced another large earthquake of magnitude 6.9. How many times larger was the seismic wave amplitude of the 1906 earthquake than that of the 1989 earthquake?

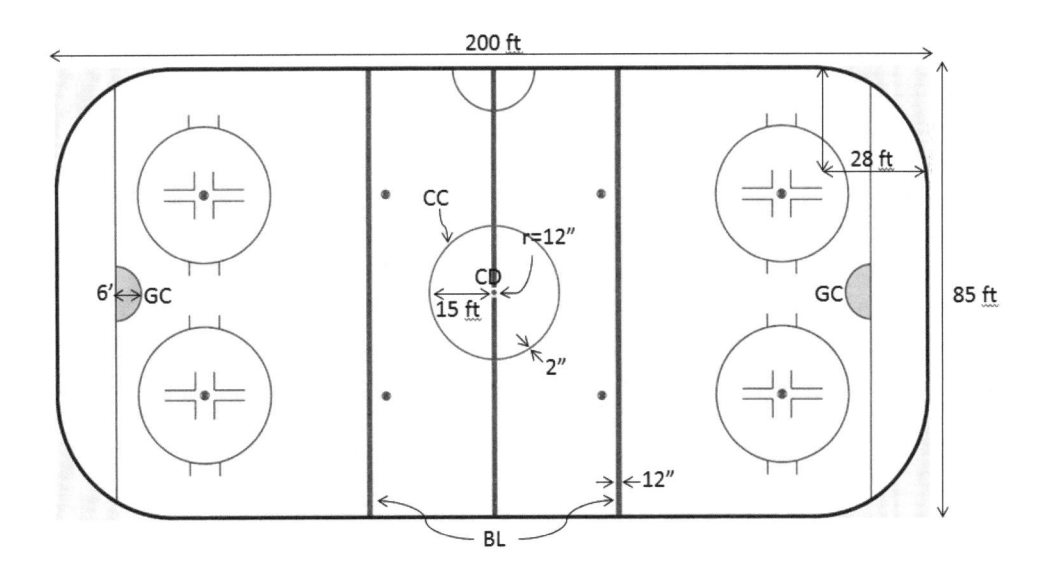

2. As the upcoming hockey season arrives, Henry, the arena manager, must prepare the ice surface. To prepare for the painting step, Henry wants to know how the ice surface is distributed among its colors. A hockey rink is 200' long, 85' wide, and its corners are rounded with quarter circles of radius 28'. (Refer to the figure above.) Blue paint is required in 4 areas:

   2 Blue lines (BL) – each 12" thick across width of rink
   1 Center dot (CD) – 12" diameter
   1 Center circle (CC) – 15' radius with 2" line thickness (radius goes to center of line)
   2 Goal creases (GC) – each a semicircle with radius 6'

   To the nearest tenth of a percent, what percent of the ice surface requires blue paint?

3. An observation tower sits directly under the flight path of a jet cruising 11 km above the tower. When the jet is first spotted, the angle of elevation from the tower to the jet is 5°. If the jet is cruising at 900 km/hr, what is the angle of depression from the plane to the tower after five minutes? Round your answer to the nearest degree.

4. A circle has the equation $(x - h)^2 + (y - k)^2 = 6.25$ and intersects the line $3x + 4y = 12$ at the line's x- and y-intercepts. What is the value of hk?

5. Melissa wants to find the density of an oddly-shaped object. When the object is submerged in a cylindrical tank of water with a diameter of 20 cm, the water level in the tank rises by 6 cm. If the object has a mass of 3.6 kg, what is its density, in g/cm³? Round your answer to the nearest tenth. (Note: $1 \text{ kg} = 10^3$ g.)

Red Math Lesson 18A: Practice Sections
Diving into the Deep End

Directions: Answer each question below.

Practice Set 2 (Calculator)

6. Which of the following is not true for all values of x?
   A) $\frac{1}{x} - \frac{1}{x-1} = \frac{-1}{x(x-1)}$
   B) $(x+3)^2(x-3)^2 = x^4 - 3^4$
   C) $3 \cdot 2^{x+4} = 48 \cdot 2^x$
   D) 20% of $\frac{300}{x^2} = 60\%$ of $\left(\frac{x}{10}\right)^{-2}$

7. What is the area of the region defined by $y < -|x+3| + 6$ and $y > |x+3| - 1$?
   A) $-\frac{49}{4}$
   B) $\frac{49}{2}$
   C) 49
   D) The region is unbounded.

$$y = 3x^2 - 30x + 73$$

8. Which of the following equations is equivalent to the above equation?
   A) $y + 2 = 3(x-5)^2$
   B) $y - 73 = 3(x-5)^2$
   C) $y - 73 = 3(x-15)^2$
   D) $y - 152 = 3(x-15)^2$

$$f(x) = \frac{x^3 + x^2 - 12x}{x^3 + 8x^2 - 5x - 84}$$

9. Find all vertical asymptotes of the function above.
   A) $x = -7$
   B) $x = 0$
   C) $x = \{-7, -4, 3\}$
   D) $x = \{-3, 4, 7\}$

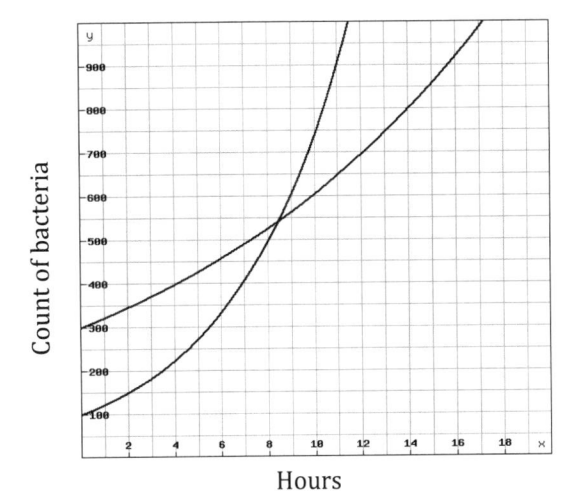

10. A microbiologist places 100 bacteria A and 300 bacteria B in two separate petri dishes and records the number of each species every hour. The result is shown in the two curves above. If she started each experiment with 400 bacteria of each species instead, then approximately what percentage of the total bacteria present after 3 hours would be bacteria B?
    A) 0.40
    B) 0.49
    C) 0.60
    D) 0.68

11. Given that -2 is a zero of the equation $y = x^3 + 5x^2 - 34x - 80$, what is the domain of $f(x) = \sqrt{x^3 + 5x^2 - 34x - 80}$?
    A) $[-\infty, -2], [5, \infty)$
    B) $[-8, -2], [5, \infty)$
    C) $(-8, -2), (5, \infty)$
    D) $(-\infty, -8], [-2, -5]$

PRACTICE SET 3 (CALCULATOR)

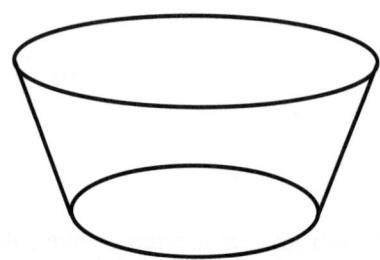

12. The diameters of the pail above are 20 and 16 inches. If the pail is 12 inches tall, what is the volume of liquid that it can hold?
    A) 976π in^3
    B) 1008π in^3
    C) 1200π in^3
    D) 3904π in^3

13. *Antipodes* are two points on the Earth's surface that are exactly opposite each other; i.e. they are at either end of a diameter of the Earth. Two of the largest cities to be antipodes of each other are Santiago, Chile, and Xi'an, China. Given that Earth is a sphere and its radius is 3,959 miles, a direct flight from Santiago to Xi'an averaging a speed of 580 miles per hour would take how long, to the nearest minute?
    A) 13 hours and 39 minutes
    B) 21 hours and 27 minutes
    C) 21 hours and 44 minutes
    D) 42 hours and 53 minutes

14. At a restaurant where the sales tax rate is 7.0%, a customer leaves an 18% tip on the total bill including tax. What percent of the pre-tax bill is the quantity of money that customer left as tip? Round to the nearest tenth of a percent.

$$N - 230 = -9(y - 1996)$$

15. The number of sightings of a rare species of parrot at an ecological monitoring station in the rainforest has been found to be decreasing linearly. If the number of parrots N seen annually in year y is given by the above equation, what is the first year in which, if the current trend continues, there will be no more parrots sighted?

$$A = 500 \cdot \left(\frac{1}{2}\right)^{\frac{d}{80}}$$

The *half-life* of a decaying substance is the time required for the amount of the substance remaining to fall to half of its value at the start of the measurement period. Radioactive waste from a cancer treatment lab normally has a half-life of 80 days. The decay of 500 grams of this waste is modeled by the equation above, where A is the amount, in grams, remaining after d days.

16. A chemical treatment is discovered which accelerates the decay of the radioactive waste, reducing its half-life to 20 days. Let A_t represent the amount of waste, in grams, remaining after d days under this treatment. Which of the following formulas correctly gives A_t in terms of A and d for the decay of 500 grams of the substance using the newly accelerated decay rate?
    A) $A_t = \frac{1}{4}A \cdot \left(\frac{1}{2}\right)^{\frac{d}{80}}$
    B) $A_t = A \cdot \left(\frac{1}{2}\right)^{\frac{d}{4}}$
    C) $A_t = A \cdot \left(\frac{1}{2}\right)^{\frac{3d}{80}}$
    D) $A_t = A^{\frac{1}{4}}$

17. Which of the following is the correct equation for a parabola that passes through the points $(1, 6)$, $(4, 75)$, and $(6, 161)$?
    A) $y = 3x^2 + 10x - 7$
    B) $y = 3x^2 + 13x - 25$
    C) $y = 4x^2 + 3x - 1$
    D) $y = 6x^2 - 7x + 7$

18. A square and a circle are arranged such that two perpendicular radii of the circle are two sides of the square. If the diagonal of the square measures 4 centimeters, what is the area of the portion of the square that does not lie within the circle?
   A) $8 - 2\pi$ square centimeters
   B) 2 square centimeters
   C) $8 - \pi$ square centimeters
   D) 2π square centimeters

$$\text{Total cost} = 125g + 2f + C$$

19. Laura is planning a wedding and uses the function above to estimate her total cost (in dollars) as a function of g, the number of guests, and f, the square footage of the venue. C is a constant representing the other costs. Her initial estimates were 200 guests and a venue with 4000 square feet. After being told that the number of guests has declined by 25%, she relocates the wedding to another venue which is 30% smaller. If the other costs remain unaffected, what was the reduction in total cost due to these two adjustments?
   A) $2400
   B) $6250
   C) $8650
   D) $24350

20. Laura from the previous problem has to work within a $40,000 budget and there must be at least 15 square feet per person in venue space. If other costs are $8000 regardless of the number of attendees and venue space, then which of the following inequalities correctly describes the constraints on venue space in relation to the number of guests?
   A) $\frac{40000-8000-125g}{2} \leq f \leq 15g$
   B) $15g \leq f \leq \frac{40000-125g}{2}$
   C) $15g \leq f \leq \frac{40000-8000-125g}{2}$
   D) $15g \leq f \leq \frac{40000-8000}{2} - 125g$

21. Consider the function $f(x) = \frac{2x^2+7x+3}{x^2-9}$. Which of the following statements is true regarding this function?
   A) The graph of this function has a vertical asymptote of $x = -3$.
   B) The graph of this function has a horizontal asymptote of $y = -2$.
   C) The graph of this function has a vertical asymptote of $x = 3$.
   D) The domain of this function includes $x = 3$.

22. If $0 \leq 7x \leq \frac{\pi}{2}$, and $\cos(7x) = \sin(5x)$, what is the value of x?
   A) $-\frac{\pi}{24}$
   B) $\frac{\pi}{24}$
   C) $\frac{\pi}{12}$
   D) $\frac{\pi}{6}$

Lesson 18A: Practice Sections

Item	Price / Package	Servings / Package	Cal. / Serving
Rice	$6.53	101	150
Potatoes	$2.97	5	354
Whole Milk	$2.59	8	146
Banana	$1.34	4	100
Eggs	$2.48	18	78
Chicken	$1.99	1	499
Green Grapes	$1.78	5	62

Use the above table for questions 23 and 24.

23. Which of the following four foods is the least expensive, as measured in calories per dollar?
    A) Eggs
    B) Potatoes
    C) Whole Milk
    D) Chicken

24. If a person were to buy one package of each item in the table, what is the average number of calories received for each dollar spent on this purchase, to the nearest calorie?

25. The pressure of a gas in a closed container varies inversely as its volume and directly as its temperature. 20 grams of this gas is in a cylindrical tank with a pressure of 1.0 atm (standard atmospheric pressure). If the gas is transferred to another evacuated tank with the same height but twice the radius, and it is heated to twice the temperature, what will its pressure be, in atm? Round to the nearest tenth of an atm.

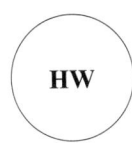

RED MATH LESSON 18A: PRACTICE SECTIONS
Race to the Finish

Directions: Answer each question below.

HOMEWORK SET (CALCULATOR)

Age	Scary	Heroic	Funny	Other
10 to 13	0.05	0.06	0.09	0.06
14 to 17	0.04	0.06	0.09	0.05
18 to 21	0.05	0.06	0.03	0.04
22+	0.08	0.09	0.06	0.09

Use the above information for questions 1 and 2.

1. A survey asked people of different ages what categories of costumes they'll wear this Halloween. The results are recorded above as a percentage of the total number of people who answered the survey. For which age group did the greatest fraction of people report that they'll wear a scary costume?
   A) 10 to 13
   B) 14 to 17
   C) 18 to 21
   D) 22+

2. Which of the following is most likely of someone who is wearing a costume?
   A) Someone wearing a heroic costume is 10-17.
   B) Someone age 14-21 is wearing a scary or heroic costume.
   C) Someone wearing a funny costume is over the age of 18.
   D) Someone wearing a costume is not wearing a heroic, funny, or scary costume.

$$(x + 3)^2 + (y - 2)^2 = 25$$
$$3y = 21x - 6$$

3. If the solutions to the systems of equations above are expressed as coordinate points on a plane, what is the distance between them?
   A) $\sqrt{10}$
   B) 5
   C) $5\sqrt{2}$
   D) $25\sqrt{2}$

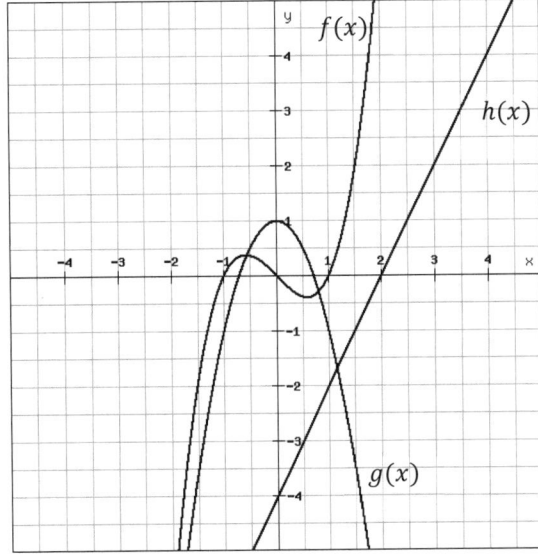

4. In the graph above, $f(x)$ is a cubic polynomial, $g(x)$ is a quadratic polynomial, and $h(x)$ is a line. If $h\big(f(g(x))\big) = -4$, then which of the following could not be the value of x?
   A) -1
   B) 0
   C) 0.5
   D) 1

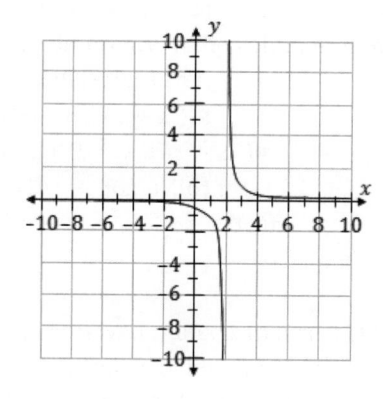

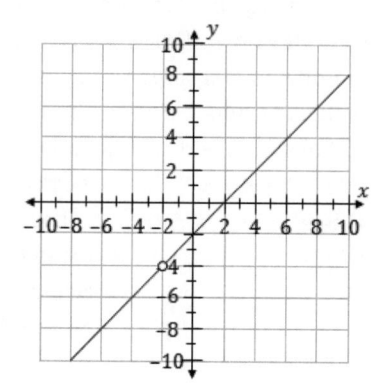

SAT Red Math
Lesson 18A: Practice Sections

5. Using the graph from the previous problem, which of the following equations best represents $g(x) - h(x)$?
   A) $-2x^2 - 2x + 5$
   B) $2x^2 + 2x + 5$
   C) $2x^2 + 2x - 5$
   D) $x^3 - 3x + 4$

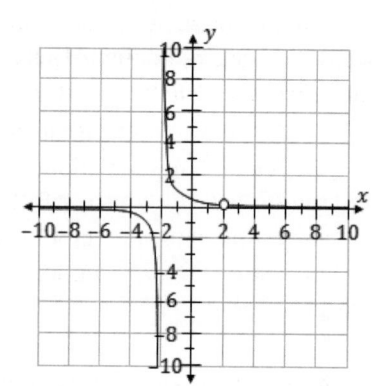

$$x^2 + y^2 = 196$$
$$f(x) = \begin{cases} x, x \geq 0 \\ 0, x < 0 \end{cases}$$

6. What is the area of the graph of the region containing all solutions to the above system of inequalities?
   A) 24.5π
   B) 63.375π
   C) 73.5π
   D) 122.5π

7. Which of the following is the graph of $f(x) = \frac{x^2-4}{x+2}$?

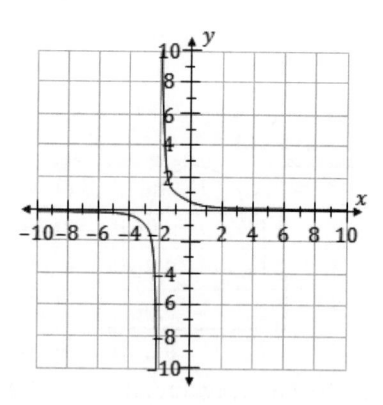

A)

B)

C)

D)

8. Patricia bought a large pizza for dinner, and is considering ways to cut it into slices so that she can save some leftovers. She decides to split the pizza in half and further split the two halves separately. She splits one of the halves into radial slices whose central angles measure $\frac{\pi}{3}$ radians each, and the other half into radial slices whose central angles measure $\frac{\pi}{6}$ radians each. For dinner tonight, Patricia wants to eat 6 slices in total, and she wants to eat more small slices than large ones. If the length of the crust for one of the large slices is 3π inches, what is the maximum amount of pizza, in terms of area, that she can eat for dinner tonight?

A) 12π square inches
B) 54π square inches
C) 60.75π square inches
D) 216π square inches

9. Eugene is standing on the side of the street and notices two cars that are stopped at a traffic light. After two seconds at rest, the light turns green, and the cars begin to accelerate. Car A accelerates uniformly for 9 seconds, after which it continues moving at a constant speed. Similarly, car B accelerates uniformly for 7 seconds, after which it continues moving at a constant speed. If the two cars have the same speed after both have finished accelerating, which of the following statements must be true?

A) When the light turns green, the two cars accelerate at an equivalent rate.
B) Car A's position 1 second after the light turns green is further along the road than car B's position.
C) One minute after the light turns green, the distance that car A and car B have traveled is equivalent.
D) The average speed of car B's motion during the first 6 seconds is higher than that of car A.

10. Consider two rational functions $f(x)$ and $g(x)$. The equations of the two functions are as follows: $f(x) = \frac{2x^2 - 4x - 6}{x+5}$ and $g(x) = \frac{x^2 + 2x - 35}{x^2 - 25}$. Consider also a third function $h(x)$ that is defined as $h(x) = f(x) + g(x)$. Which of the following statements is true?

A) The function $h(x)$ has a vertical asymptote of $x = 5$.
B) The functions $f(x)$, $g(x)$, and $h(x)$ have one common zero.
C) Of the three functions, two have a horizontal asymptote of $y = 2$.
D) Of the three functions, two have the same domain.

11. A psychologist studying the effect of monetary incentives on task performance conducts an experiment in which test subjects are paid different amounts of money to solve a problem. On average, the results show that for every $5 increase in payment, the time it took to complete the task was shortened by 30 seconds. Which of the following equations cannot be used to model this relationship?
(t: seconds to completion, d: dollars)

A) $t = -6d + 200$
B) $t = 6d + 600$
C) $5t = -30d + 750$
D) $-\frac{5t}{30} = d - 20$

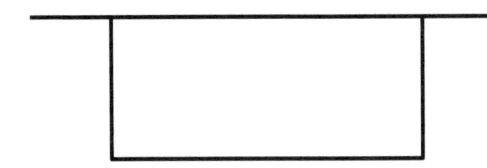

12. Farmer Johnson wants to fence off a rectangular area where he'll keep his 45 chickens. He has 60 feet of fencing and decides to locate the area adjacent to a wall to economize on fencing. If he encloses the largest area possible, how many square feet on average does each chicken have?

A) 5
B) 9
C) 10
D) 20

448 | SAT Red Math
Lesson 18A: Practice Sections

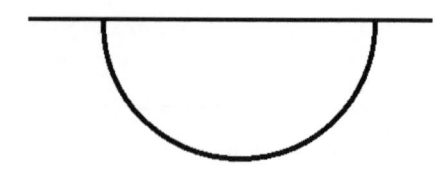

13. Farmer Johnson from the previous problem realizes that a semicircle would be more efficient. If he encloses an area that will allow 4 square feet of space per chicken, how much fencing will not be needed?
    A) 5 ft
    B) 12.4 ft
    C) 26.4 ft
    D) 36.2 ft

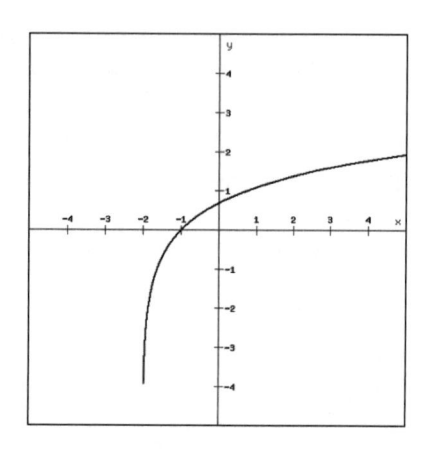

14. If the function $f(x)$, graphed above, is undefined for $x \leq -2$ and $g(x) = f^{-1}(x+3) - 4$, which of the following might be the range of $g(x)$?
    A) $(-6, \infty)$
    B) $(-5, \infty)$
    C) $(-2, \infty)$
    D) $(2, \infty)$

15. Which of the following is equivalent to $\ln(x+2) + \ln(x-2) - \ln(2x+5)$ when $x > 2$?
    A) $\ln(-5)$
    B) $\ln(2x^3 + 5x^2 - 8x - 20)$
    C) $\ln\left(\frac{2x+5}{x^2-4}\right)$
    D) $\ln\left(\frac{x^2-4}{2x+5}\right)$

Age	16-25	26-35	36-45	46+	Total
Texting	260	40	60	75	435
Calling	25	130	120	225	500
Internet	120	240	220	15	595
Apps	40	75	30	30	175
None	35	15	20	55	125
Total	480	500	450	400	1830

A company that makes cellphone operating systems ran a focus group letting a random sample of its customers try out its newest version. Each customer was asked to name which feature he or she was most dissatisfied by, if any, and the results of this questionnaire were categorized by the customer's age and summarized in the table above.

Questions 16 through 18 refer to the above information.

16. Which of the following has the lowest likelihood?
    A) A respondent in the 26-35 age group being dissatisfied with the apps function of the phone
    B) A respondent who is dissatisfied with the texting function being in the 36-45 age group
    C) A respondent who is perfectly content with the phone being 35 years old or younger
    D) A respondent in the 16-25 age group being either dissatisfied with calling or perfectly content

17. What is the probability that someone who is perfectly satisfied with this company's product is in the age range of 26-35? Round to the nearest whole percent.

18. How many more people between the ages of 16 and 35 are dissatisfied with a function of the phone as compared to people in the same age range that are perfectly satisfied with the phone?

Version 3.0

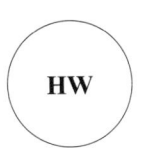

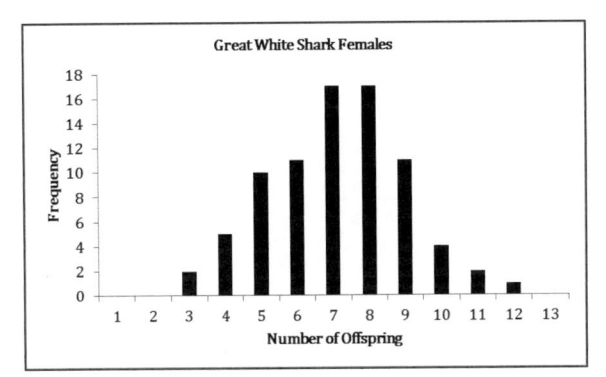

19. The histogram above shows the number of offspring produced in a lifetime by each of 80 female great white sharks. What is the mean number of offspring produced? Round your answer to the nearest tenth.

20. On January 1, 2001, Larry won $100,000 from a lottery, which was disbursed in equal payments each year for four consecutive years starting with 2001. As he received them, Larry deposited all of the payments in a savings account that earns a 2% interest rate, compounded annually. Had he received the entire sum in 2001 and invested it in the same account, how much more money would Larry have had in 2014, 13 compounding periods later? Round to the nearest whole dollar.

Red Math Lesson 18B: Advanced Statistics
Learning to Swim

Directions: Answer each question below.

Practice Set 1 (Calculator)

1. Come up with a data set, of at least 10 points, in which its mean is larger than its median.

2. Come up with a data set, of at least 10 points, in which its median is larger than its mean.

3. Analyze the difference between the two data sets.

SAT Red Math
Lesson 18B: Advanced Statistics

	Age ≥ 35	Age < 35
Percent of people who save ≥ $10,000 per year	60	20
Mean annual health spending	$10,000	$2,000

For questions 4 and 5 use the above table. It contains information about a random sample taken among the population of employed adults in Indianapolis, Indiana.

4. The population of working adults in Indianapolis is 600,000, 45% of which are 35 or older. How many people can be expected to save more than $10,000 a year in Indianapolis?

5. The working population of the state of Indiana is 4 million. Assuming 50% of the working population is over 35 and the mean annual health spending in Indianapolis is representative of Indiana as a whole, what is the expected annual health spending of working adults in Indiana? Round to the nearest million dollars.

Red Math Lesson 18B: Advanced Statistics
Diving into the Deep End

Directions: Answer each question below.

Practice Set 3 (Calculator)

6. Which of the following data collection methods would be most appropriate for determining how many people prefer each of four different brands of coffee in a particular state?
   A) Send surveys to random addresses.
   B) Ask people to fill out a survey upon being seen in public with coffee.
   C) Analyze the coffee sales data for the region.
   D) Call random people out of a phone book and ask about their coffee preferences.

Questions 7 and 8 refer to the following information. A survey was conducted about brand preference among a randomly chosen sample of coffee drinkers of four different counties. The table below displays a summary of the results.

County	1	2	3	4
Brand A	101	802	244	536
Brand B	246	1080	200	371
Brand C	591	1312	490	467
Brand D	235	909	239	203

7. What is the percent chance that a coffee drinker chosen at random from County 2 or County 4 prefers Brand A coffee?
   A) 21.7%
   B) 23.6%
   C) 25.5%
   D) Not enough information to determine.

8. County Z is formed when the above counties are redistricted; the county is made up of 30% of the citizens of County 1 and 70% of the citizens of County 3. Provided that those citizens are representative of their original home counties as a whole, which brand of coffee do the citizens of County Z prefer least?
   A) Brand A
   B) Brand B
   C) Brand C
   D) Brand D

9. Which of the following would decrease confidence interval ranges?
   A) Increasing the sample size.
   B) Increasing the standard deviation.
   C) Increasing measurement error.
   D) Increasing observational bias.

10. Which of the following is NOT true about standard deviation?
    A) Standard deviations exist in the units of the data itself.
    B) Standard deviations positively correlate with the width of a data set's range.
    C) Standard deviations correlate positively with the data set's mean.
    D) Standard deviations correlate positively with the ranges of confidence intervals.

11. Which of the following would most likely result from a decrease in observer bias?
    A) A decrease in confidence interval ranges.
    B) A decrease in measurement error.
    C) A decrease in standard deviation.
    D) A decrease in the number of outliers.

SAT Red Math
Lesson 18B: Advanced Statistics

12. If two different sets of observations on the same behavior were taken and indicated very different conclusions, what is the least likely cause of the discrepancy?
    A) One or both sets was influenced by observer bias.
    B) One or both sets used incorrect measurement instruments.
    C) One or both sets have outliers that should be removed before analysis.
    D) The two sets of data were measured by different people.

Questions 13 through 15 refer to the following information.

Biologists recorded the number of chipmunks in 11 different 10 acre plots of land in two different forests. The table below displays a summary of the survey results.

	Median	Sample Size	Mean
Forest A	6	11	124
Forest B	7	11	1082

13. Which of the following is most likely true?
    A) Forest A has a larger range of chipmunks sighted than Forest B.
    B) Forest A has larger confidence interval ranges of chipmunks sighted than Forest B.
    C) Forest A has less potential measurement error of chipmunks sighted than Forest B.
    D) Forest A has a larger mode number of chipmunks than Forest B.

14. The biologists noticed that, within each forest, no two plots they sampled had the same number of chipmunks. If the data for Forests A and B were combined, what would be the median of the new data set?

15. Using the combined data set from the previous problem, what would be the mean of the new data set?

PRACTICE SET 3 (CALCULATOR)

Questions 16 through 18 refer to the following information.

A survey was conducted among a randomly chosen sample of shoppers in Dallas, Texas. The shoppers were placed into three different income brackets and asked which of three department stores they preferred to shop at.

Annual Income	Greater than $100,000	Between $40,000 and $100,000	Less than $40,000
Store A	76	250	42
Store B	16	379	311
Store C	9	404	590

16. If the working population of Dallas is 800,000 how many people can be expected to shop at Store B?
    A) 265,768
    B) 271,931
    C) 411,962
    D) Not enough information to determine.

17. If the working population of Texas is 18 million how many people can be expected to have an income over $100,000 per year?
    A) 830,561
    B) 875,301
    C) 920,041
    D) Not enough information to determine.

18. Based on the above information, which of the following is the most valid conclusion?
    A) Department Store C is the most popular department Store in Texas.
    B) Department Store B is the least popular department store in Dallas.
    C) Department Store B is the cheapest of the three.
    D) Department Store A is preferred by people who make more than $100,000 a year.

SAT Red Math
Lesson 18B: Advanced Statistics

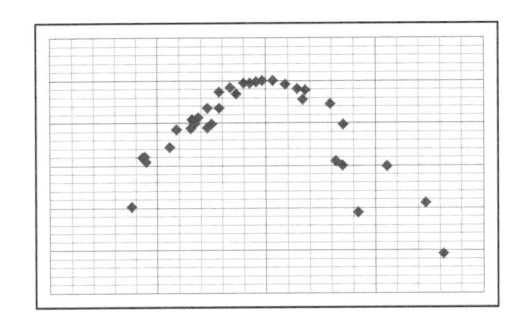

Use the graph above for questions 19 through 21.

19. Which of the following best models the data above?
    A) A linear model
    B) A quadratic model
    C) A positive exponential model
    D) A negative exponential model

20. Which of the following is the best measure of center for the data above?
    A) Mean
    B) Median
    C) Mode
    D) Range

21. Which of the following most likely represents the data graphed above?
    A) The amount of bacteria in a developing culture.
    B) The amount of profit at different price points.
    C) The amount of money in a savings account accruing compound interest.
    D) The volume of a cube as the side length increases.

22. Which of the following is the best method of determining the preferred style of mailbox of San Diego homeowners?
    A) Ask random San Diego residents what styles of mail boxes they prefer.
    B) Send random surveys to homeowners in San Diego asking about their preferred style.
    C) Stand outside a hardware store and ask people about their preferred mailbox style.
    D) Count the mailboxes on two streets.

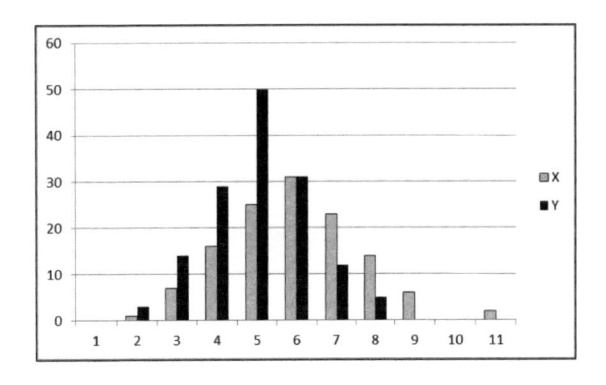

Use the chart above for questions 23 and 24.

23. Which of the following is most likely true about the graph above?
    A) Sample X has a greater standard deviation.
    B) Sample Y has a greater mode.
    C) Sample Y has a greater measurement error.
    D) Sample Y has greater confidence interval ranges.

24. Which of the samples above is likely to have greater measurement error?
    A) Sample X
    B) Sample Y
    C) Both samples have identical measurement error
    D) Not enough information to determine

$$\{1, 7, 13, 25, 41, 45, 50\}$$

25. A statistician recorded the age of Ley's Whitebeam specimens in the Westonbirt Arboretum. Seven of the ten measurements are recorded in the the dataset above. Three of the data points he recorded are illegible, but he had written down that the range of the data set was 52, the mode was 25 and the median was 28.5. What is the mean of the data set?

Red Math Lesson 18B: Advanced Statistics
Race to the Finish

Directions: Answer each question below.

Homework Set (Calculator)

	Data Set X	Data Set Y
Mean	100	110
Median	99	103
Range	59	61
Standard Deviation	$\sigma = 10.1$	$\sigma = 7.4$

In the general population, intelligence quotient (IQ) is typically normally (symmetrically) distributed with mean 100. The above table summarizes the results of IQ tests issued to the first-grade students at two elementary schools.

Use the above information for questions 1 and 2.

1. Which of the following conclusions is best supported?
   A) Data Set X has a higher mode.
   B) Data Set Y has a higher mode.
   C) Data Set X has higher measurement error.
   D) Data Set Y has higher measurement error.

2. If these two sets of data were collected analyzing the same variables, which of the following conclusions is NOT supported?
   A) Data Set X is more likely to be flawed because it has a higher standard deviation.
   B) More observations need to be recorded to clarify why the analysis is so different.
   C) Data Set X is less likely to make accurate predictions because it has a higher standard deviation.
   D) Data Set X is less likely to be flawed because it has a smaller range.

3. Which of the following is NOT necessary to maximize accuracy in data collection?
   A) An unbiased data collector.
   B) Calibrated, appropriate instruments.
   C) A sufficient sample size.
   D) A hypothesis about the results.

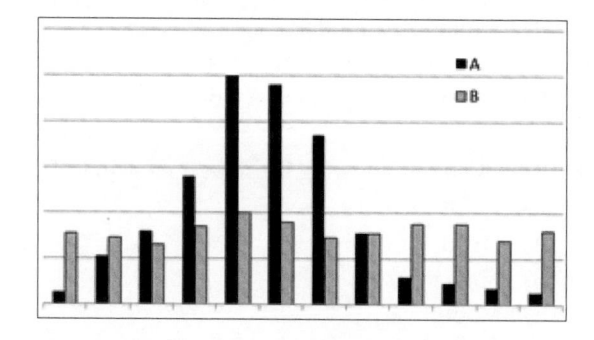

Questions 4 and 5 refer to the graph above.

4. Which of the following is the best measure of center for Data Set A?
   A) Mean
   B) Median
   C) Mode
   D) Range

5. Which of the following is most supported by the graph above?
   A) The standard deviation of Data Set A is higher.
   B) The median of Data Set A is higher.
   C) The mode of Data Set A is higher.
   D) The measurement error of Data Set B is higher.

6. If there is a 95% confidence interval of x between values a and b with $a < b$, which of the following is true?
   A) There is a 95% chance that $a \leq x \leq b$.
   B) There is a 95% probability that $a \leq x \leq b$.
   C) There is 95% confidence that $a \leq x \leq b$.
   D) None of the above.

5, 5, 5, 5, 5, 5, 5, 6, 6, 6, 6, 6, 6, 6, 7, 7, 7, 7, 7, 7, 7, 7, 7, 7, 8, 8, 8, 8, 8, 9, 9, 9, 9, 10, 10, 10, 23, 24, 31

Use the data above for questions 7 through 10.

7. If the above data were graphed, which of the following would be true?
   A) The graph would be left-skewed.
   B) The graph would be right-skewed.
   C) The graph would not be skewed.
   D) Not enough information to determine.

8. What would likely happen to this data set if the observations {5, 6, 6, 21, 44, 56} were added?
   A) Predictions would be able to be made with greater confidence.
   B) Measurement error would increase.
   C) Standard deviation would decrease.
   D) The median would increase.

9. What would most likely happen to this data set if the sample size was increased without changing the standard deviation?
   A) Confidence interval ranges would decrease.
   B) Measurement error would increase.
   C) The mode would change.
   D) Observer bias would decrease.

10. If the data represents the ages of people on a playground in an elementary school, which of the following conclusions is best supported?
    A) There are more children in first grade (Ages 5 and 6) than fifth grade (Ages 10 and 11) in this school.
    B) More first graders (Ages 5 and 6) are likely to go to recess than fifth graders (Ages 10 and 11) at this school.
    C) The student-teacher ratio is approximately 12:1 at this school.
    D) The third grade (Ages 7 and 8) has the smallest population of students at this school.

	Data Set A	Data Set B
Median	6	7
μ	5.4	5.4
σ	3.1	2.1

The above table summarizes the ages in equally-sized random samples of children chosen from two day care centers. None of the children are more than 9 years old.

Use the information above for questions 11 and 12.

11. If the data from Data Set B were added to Data Set A, which of the following would be most likely to happen?
    A) The confidence interval ranges would decrease.
    B) The mean would decrease.
    C) The median would decrease.
    D) The number of outliers would decrease.

12. Which of the following is most likely true about the graphs of Data Sets A and B?
    A) The center of Data Set A would be to the right of Data Set B.
    B) The measurement error of Data Set A would be less than Data Set B.
    C) The range of Data Set A would be more than Data Set B.
    D) The confidence interval ranges of Data Set A would be less than Data Set B.

458 | SAT Red Math
Lesson 18B: Advanced Statistics

HW

Annual Income	Less than $30,000	Between $30,000 and $100,000	Greater than $100,000
Actuarial Science	3%	77%	20%
Nursing	7%	81%	12%
Psychology	21%	75%	4%

Use the table above for questions 15 through 17. The table shows data about the incomes of Seattle residents with various majors five years after graduation. The highest level of education each individual received was a bachelor's degree.

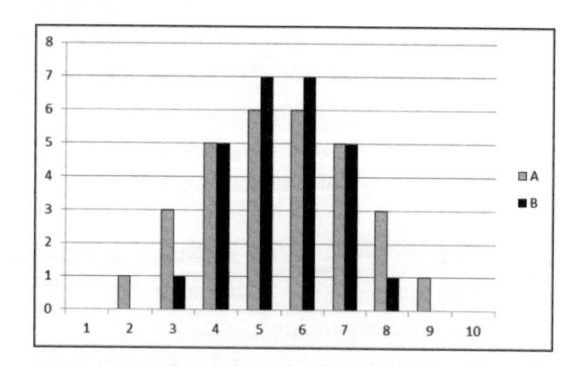

13. Which of the following is most likely true about data sets A and B above?
    A) Data Set A has a higher mean than Data Set B.
    B) Data Set A has a lower standard deviation than Data Set B.
    C) Data Set A has higher standard deviation than Data Set B.
    D) Data Set A has narrower confidence interval ranges than Data Set B.

15. A sample of Seattle residents contains 15% people who majored in actuarial science, 35% who majored in nursing and 50% who majored in psychology. If all of these people graduated five years ago, what percentage of the sample currently makes more than $100,000 a year?
    A) 9.0%
    B) 9.2%
    C) 9.4%
    D) Not enough information to determine.

14. Which of the following is NOT likely to increase measurement error in data collection?
    A) The presence of outliers
    B) Uncalibrated instruments
    C) A biased data collector
    D) Increased sample size

16. Seattle contains 20,500 actuaries, nurses, or psychologists who make more than $100,000 a year. If the professions exist in the proportion 1:3:3, how many nurses work in Seattle?
    A) 36,765
    B) 110,294
    C) 183,823
    D) Not enough information to determine.

17. The previous sample is representative of the incomes of the Seattle suburb of Renton. Among Renton residents who graduated five years ago are 100 actuarial science majors, 200 nursing majors, and 400 psychology majors. What percentage of these people make less than $30,000 per year? Round to the nearest tenth of a percent.

Version 3.0

SAT Red Math
Lesson 18B: Advanced Statistics

18. A statistician has collected data on 15,671 people and determined that the median weight is 177 pounds. Eight people are added to the sample size with weights of 110, 180, 175, 201, 164, 177, 142, and 199 pounds. What is the new median weight in pounds?

	Sample Size	Mean Weight (pounds)
Aladdin	301	3.0
Hooligan	137	6.9
Neon	60	8.4

Use the above chart for questions 19 and 20. A random sample of pumpkin species were measured in a particular garden and their average weight was recorded.

19. What is the average weight of pumpkins in the garden? Round to the nearest hundredth of a pound.

20. Assume the above sample is representative of pumpkins in the entire city. Two neighboring gardens have 448 and 158 Aladdin pumpkins, 200 and 6 Hooligan pumpkins, and 100 and 10 Neon pumpkins respectively. If 15% of a pumpkin's weight is lost while preparing them to be turned into puree, how much pumpkin puree can the two gardens make with their combined pumpkins? Round to the nearest whole pound.

Red Math Lesson 19A: Advanced Scatterplots
Learning to Swim

Directions: Answer each question below.

Practice Set 1 (Calculator)

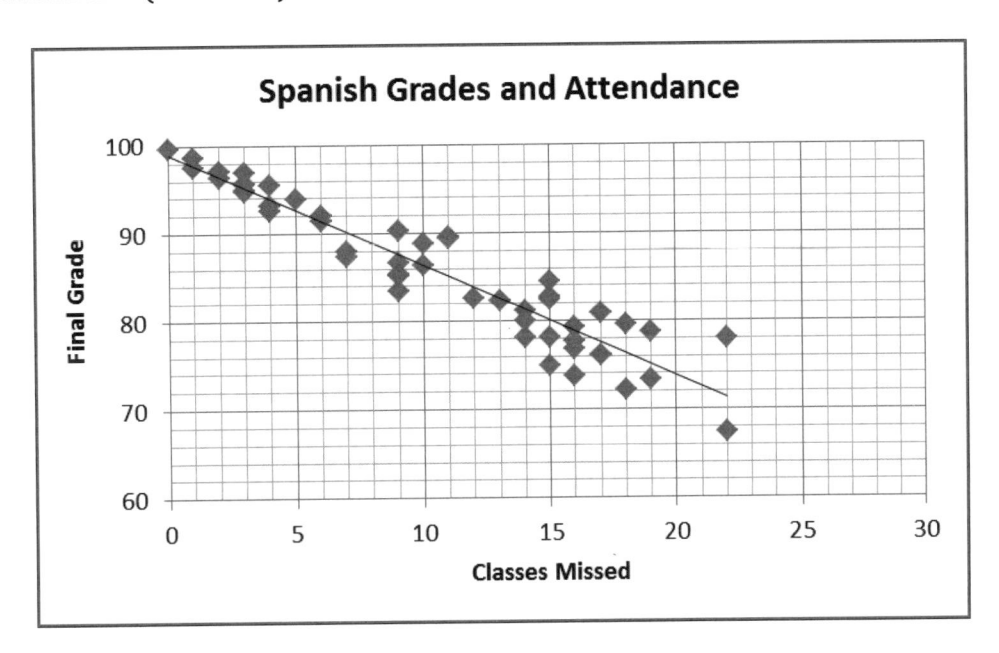

Spanish Grades and Attendance

For questions 1 through 3 use the scatterplot above. The scatterplot above represents the grades and absences of a high school Spanish class.

1. Approximate the line of best fit for the scatterplot above.

2. According to the line of best fit, how many absences would be expected from a student with a grade of 86%? Round to the nearest integer.

3. How many absences would reduce a student's expected grade from 90 to 80? Round to the nearest integer.

Lesson 19A: Advanced Scatterplots

Capture Probability of Caddisfly

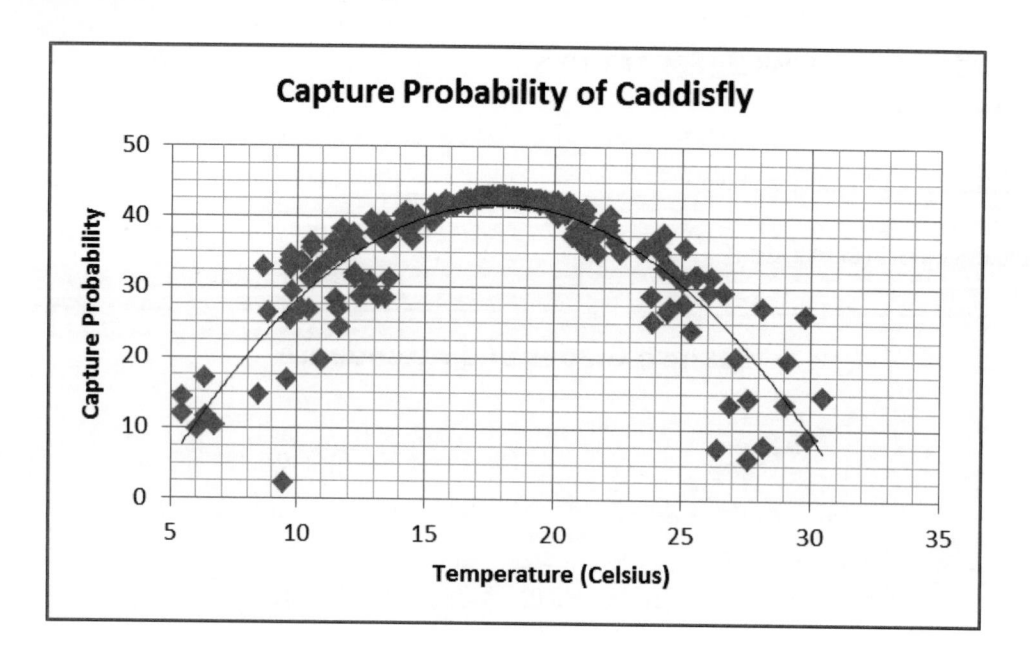

For questions 4 and 5 use the scatterplot above. A trap is designed to catch caddisflies, and it records whether or not the attempt was successful based on the average temperature outside. The results from many different days over the course of a year are shown above. The curve of best fit of the data shown above is $y = -0.22x^2 + 7.87x - 28.66$.

4. According to the curve of best fit, what is the expected probability of the trap catching a caddisfly when the temperature is 41 degrees Celsius? Round to the nearest tenth of a percent.

5. What is the difference in probabilities of the trap catching a caddisfly at 20 degrees Celsius and the trap catching a caddisfly at 13 degrees Celsius? Round to the nearest tenth of a percent.

RED MATH LESSON 19A: ADVANCED SCATTERPLOTS
Diving into the Deep End

Directions: Answer each question below.

PRACTICE SET 2 (CALCULATOR)

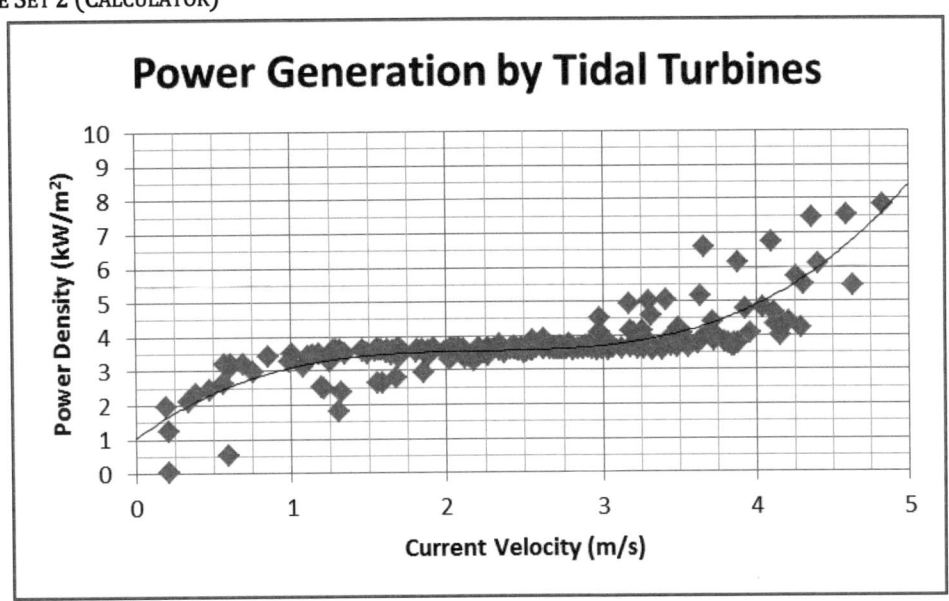

Power Generation by Tidal Turbines

For questions 6 through 8 use the scatterplot above. The data from numerous copies of the same model of tidal turbine yielded the above data about their power densities and velocities over the course of two years.

6. What is the curve of best fit for the scatterplot above?
    A) $y = 0.22x^3 - 1.46x^2 + 3.29x + 1.04$
    B) $y = 0.22x^3 - 1.46x^2 + 5.16x + 1.04$
    C) $y = 0.33x^3 - 2.21x^2 + 3.29x + 1.04$
    D) $y = 0.33x^3 - 2.21x^2 + 5.16x + 1.04$

7. According to the curve of best fit, how much power density is generated while the current is $14.4 \frac{km}{hour}$?
    A) $3.41 \frac{kW}{m^2}$
    B) $3.91 \frac{kW}{m^2}$
    C) $4.42 \frac{kW}{m^2}$
    D) $4.92 \frac{kW}{m^2}$

8. What is expected to happen to the power density in $\frac{kW}{m^2}$ if the current velocity increases from 1.9 to 2.8 $\frac{m}{s}$?
    A) It decreases by 0.15
    B) It decreases by 0.11
    C) It increases by 0.11
    D) It increases by 0.15

SAT Red Math
Lesson 19A: Advanced Scatterplots

Bacterial Growth

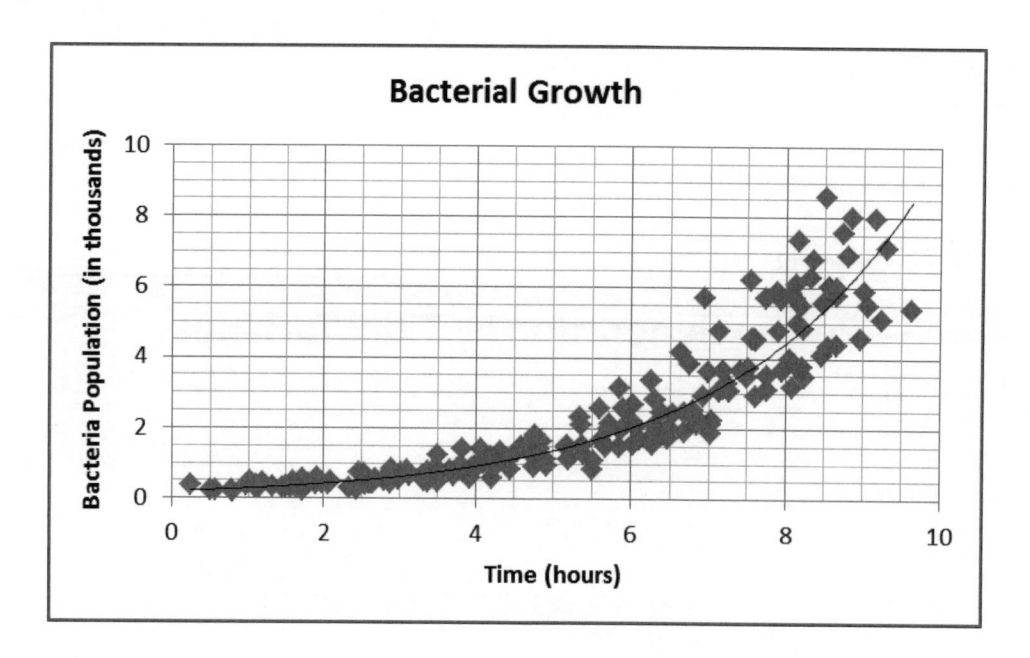

For questions 9 through 11 use the scatterplot above. Scientists separated out many different cultures of the same bacteria in slightly different conditions and recorded the population at various times to try and figure out the bacteria's average growth rate in controlled conditions. Their data is recorded above.

9. What is the curve of best fit for the scatterplot above?
   A) $y = 0.14e^{0.22x}$
   B) $y = 0.14e^{0.39x}$
   C) $y = 0.19e^{0.22x}$
   D) $y = 0.19e^{0.39x}$

10. According to the curve of best fit, how many thousands of bacteria would be present after twelve hours?
    A) 10.22
    B) 13.86
    C) 15.09
    D) 20.48

11. By what percentage is the bacterial population expected to grow over the course of 6.5 hours?
    A) 650%
    B) 854%
    C) 958%
    D) 1,162%

Measurements of Long-Tailed Hawks

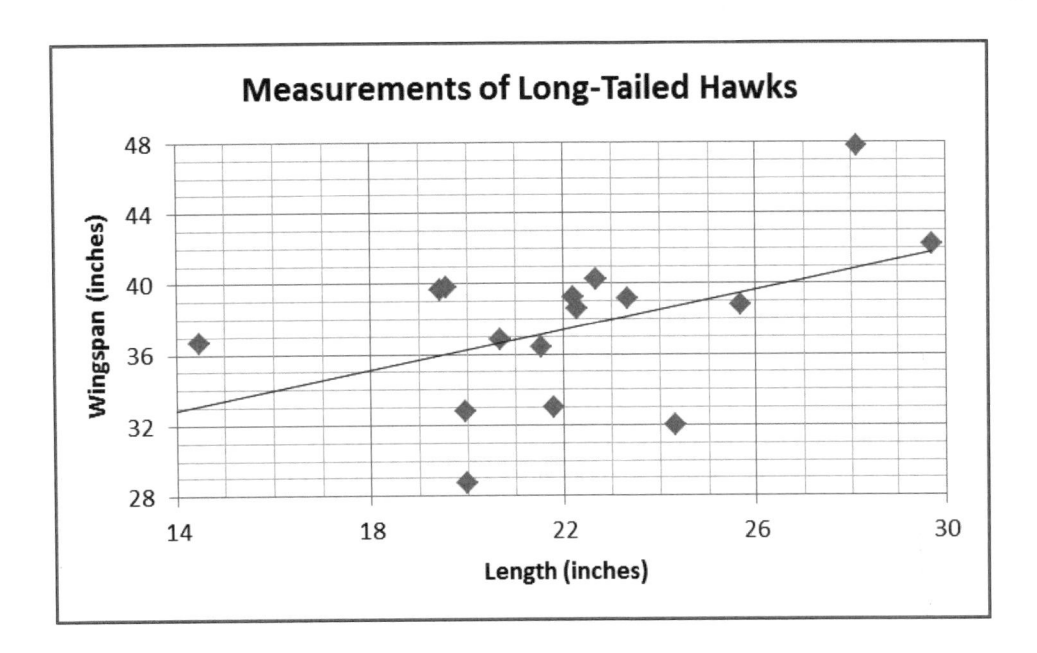

For questions 12 through 15 use the scatterplot above. Biologists examined the specimens of long-tailed hawks at the Cincinnati Zoo to try and determine the relationship between their length and wingspan. Their results are recorded above.

12. What is the line of best fit for the scatterplot above?
    A) $y = 0.41x + 18.77$
    B) $y = 0.57x + 18.77$
    C) $y = 0.41x + 24.92$
    D) $y = 0.57x + 24.92$

13. The scatterplot above has a relatively weak line of best fit because the data set contains many outliers. What would be most likely to improve the line of best fit?
    A) Switching to an exponential curve of best fit.
    B) Switching to a polynomial curve of best fit.
    C) Recording the data on more long-tailed hawks.
    D) Omitting the data that does not match the intended line of best fit.

14. According to the line of best fit, how many inches long would you expect a long-tailed hawk with a 7-foot wingspan to be? Round to the nearest inch.

15. How much would you expect the length of a long-tailed hawk to increase if its wingspan increased by 6.2 inches? Round to the nearest tenth of an inch.

PRACTICE SET 3 (CALCULATOR)

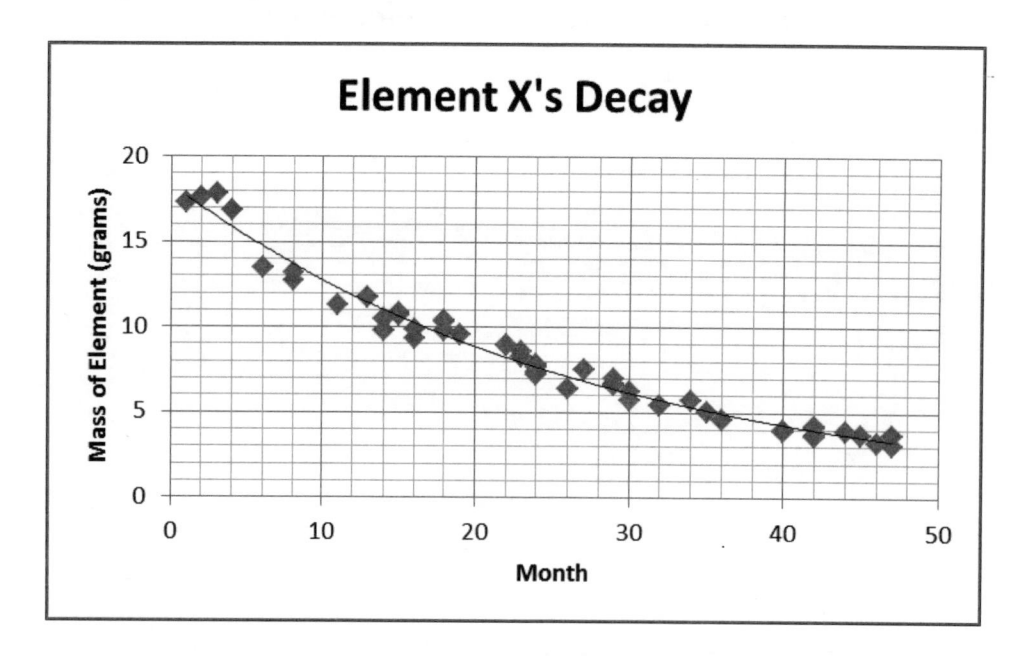

Element X's Decay

For questions 16 through 18, use the scatterplot above. Scientists find a mysterious element, but don't have the proper equipment to identify its composition, so they separate several different samples of similar mass and observe their radioactive decay over time. The results are recorded above.

16. What is the curve of best fit for the scatterplot above?
    A) $14.194e^{-0.036x}$
    B) $14.194e^{-0.054x}$
    C) $18.355e^{-0.036x}$
    D) $18.355e^{-0.054x}$

17. According to the curve of best fit, how long would a sample of Element X have been sitting if it had a mass of 1 gram?
    A) 79.8 months
    B) 80.8 months
    C) 81.8 months
    D) 82.8 months

18. What is the half-life (the amount of time it takes for half of a substance's mass to decay) of Element X?
    A) 19 months
    B) 19.25 months
    C) 19.5 months
    D) 19.75 months

Lake Cultures After Treatment

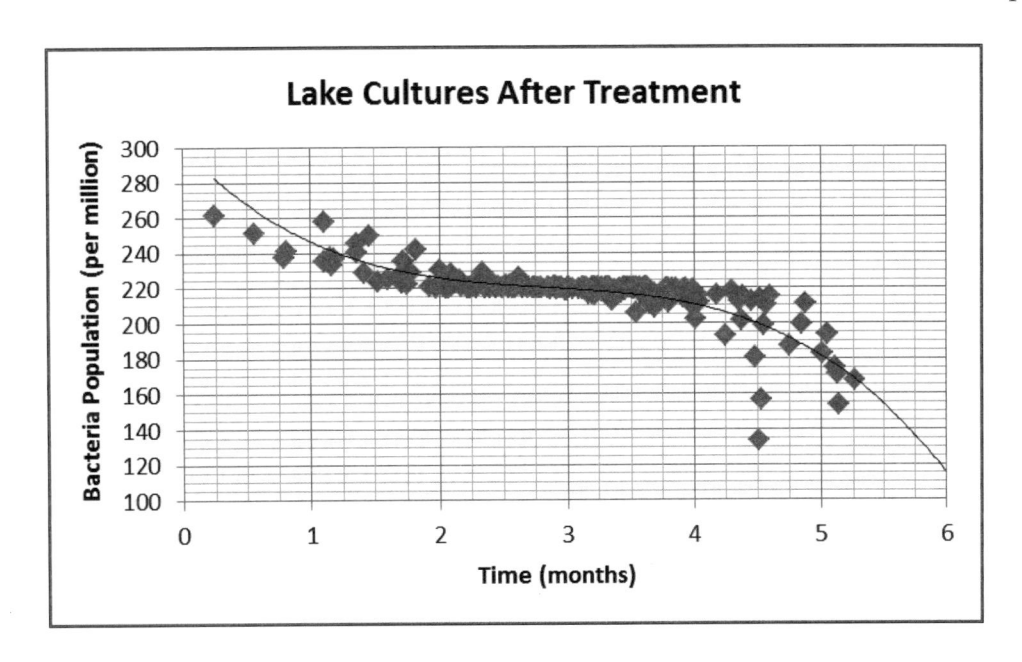

For questions 19 through 21 use the scatterplot above. An invasive bacterium has invaded several local lakes with similar lake chemistries and has caused problems for the local ecosystem. A group of biologists apply a treatment to these lakes and then record the results to see the effectiveness of the treatment over time. Their results from several different lakes are recorded above.

19. What is the curve of best fit for the scatterplot above?
    A) $y = -2.87x^3 + 19.81x^2 - 74.08x + 299.18$
    B) $y = -2.87x^3 + 24.48x^2 - 74.08x + 299.18$
    C) $y = -4.02x^3 + 19.81x^2 - 88.11x + 299.18$
    D) $y = -4.02x^3 + 24.48x^2 - 88.11x + 299.18$

20. How many bacteria per million are expected to be present after 6.5 months?
    A) 0.0
    B) 1.90
    C) 63.8
    D) 68.9

21. According to the curve of best fit, how many fewer bacteria per million are expected to be around 2.3 months later for a lake currently 1.8 months into its treatment?
    A) 11.70
    B) 14.21
    C) 16.74
    D) 19.26

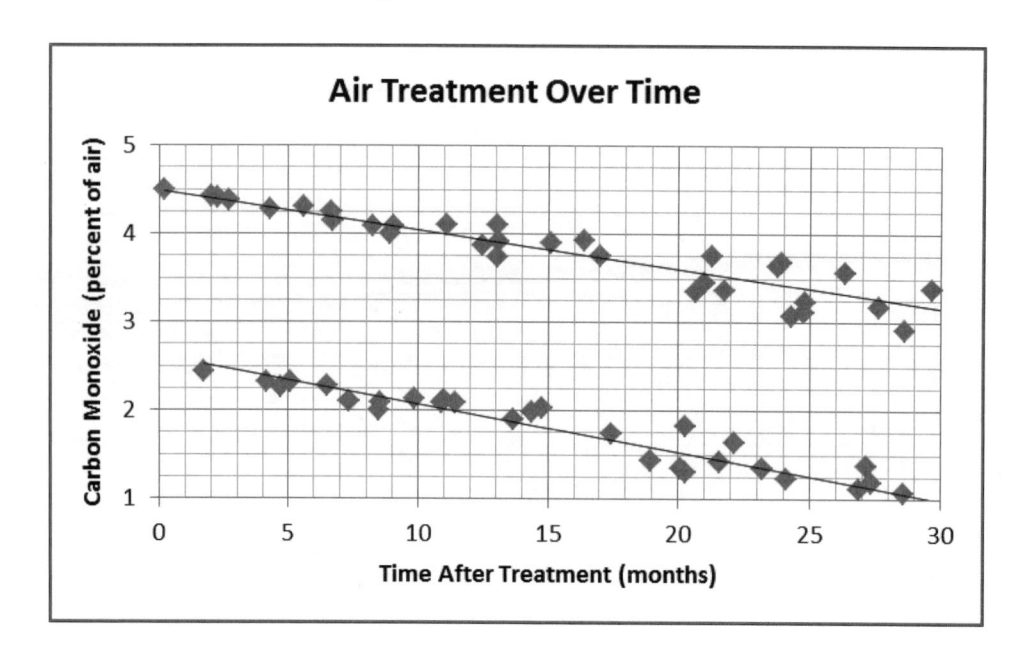

SAT Red Math
Lesson 19A: Advanced Scatterplots

Air Treatment Over Time

(Scatterplot: Carbon Monoxide (percent of air) vs. Time After Treatment (months), showing two downward-sloping lines of best fit through two clusters of data points.)

For questions 22 through 25 use the scatterplot above. This data represents the carbon monoxide percentage of the air of two different cities that have undergone treatment for air pollution. The cities have roughly the same volume of air, and the results of the treatment are recorded above.

22. What are the lines of best fit for the scatterplot above?
   A) $y = -0.032x + 2.619$, $y = -0.044x + 4.487$
   B) $y = -0.032x + 4.487$, $y = -0.044x + 2.619$
   C) $y = -0.044x + 2.619$, $y = -0.054x + 4.487$
   D) $y = -0.044x + 4.487$, $y = -0.054x + 2.619$

23. What is the best explanation for this data set having two separate lines of best fit?
   A) Different locations within a city have different conditions, which lead to different measurements.
   B) The air treatment has a different impact on different environments.
   C) The two cities had different initial levels of carbon monoxide, but the treatment acts on them roughly equally.
   D) The data was collected incorrectly and the extra line is a result of measurement error.

24. According to the top line of best fit, what percentage of a city's air will be carbon monoxide after 45 months if the air initially has 4.5% carbon monoxide? Round to the nearest tenth of a percent.

25. If a treated city has seen improvement at the same rate as indicated by the top line of best fit, achieving to date a carbon monoxide level of 1.5% of the air volume, what was the carbon monoxide level six months ago? Round to the nearest tenth of a percent.

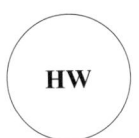

RED MATH LESSON 19A: ADVANCED SCATTERPLOTS
Race to the Finish

Directions: Answer each question below.

HOMEWORK SET (CALCULATOR)

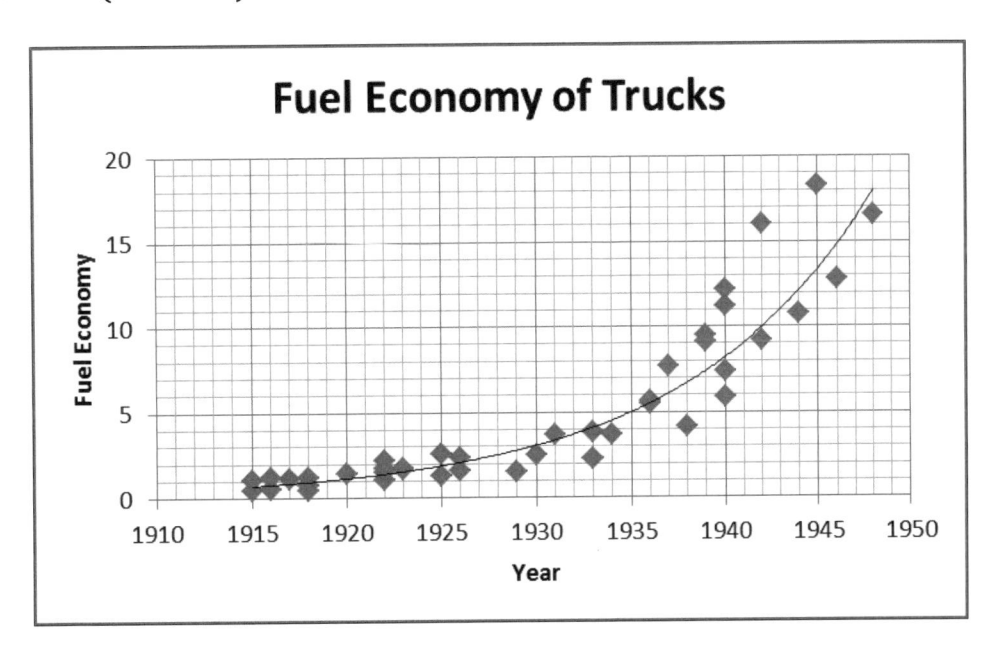

Fuel Economy of Trucks

For questions 1 through 3 use the scatterplot above which records the historic fuel economy, in miles per gallon, of truck engines during their early development.

1. What is the curve of best fit for the scatterplot above?
    A) $y = 0.42e^{0.099(x-1910)}$
    B) $y = 0.42e^{0.099(x-1920)}$
    C) $y = 0.67e^{0.099(x-1910)}$
    D) $y = 0.67e^{0.099(x-1920)}$

2. According to the curve of best fit what was the expected fuel economy of a truck in 1926?
    A) 2.00 miles per gallon
    B) 2.05 miles per gallon
    C) 2.10 miles per gallon
    D) 2.15 miles per gallon

3. How much did the average fuel economy of trucks improve between the years of 1931 and 1947?
    A) 4.84 miles per gallon
    B) 8.93 miles per gallon
    C) 13.01 miles per gallon
    D) 20.76 miles per gallon

SAT Red Math
Lesson 19A: Advanced Scatterplots

Fuel Efficiency of Automobiles

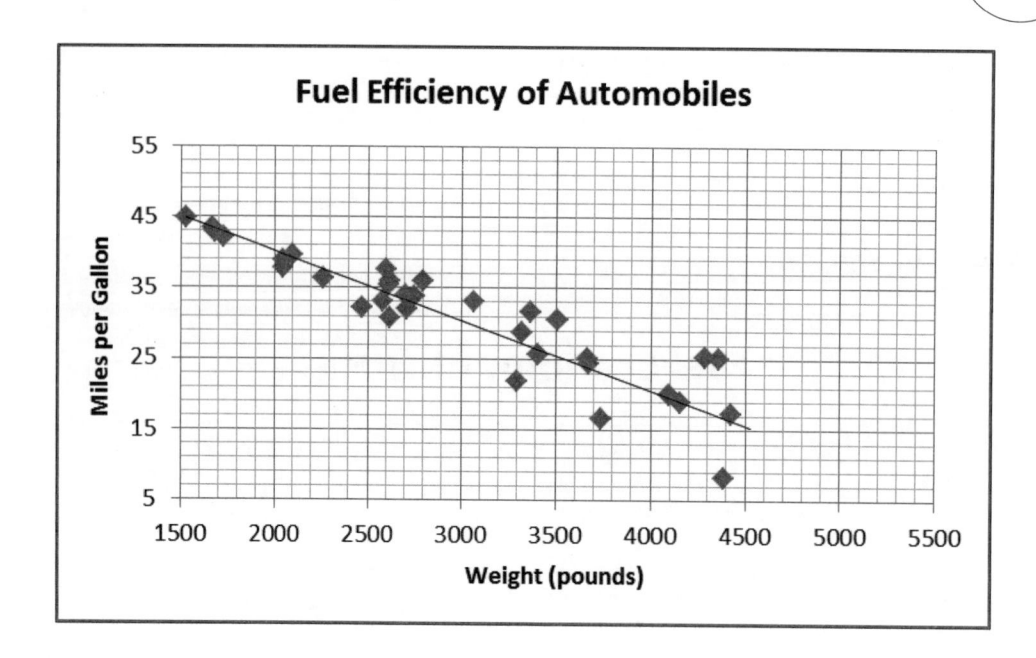

For questions 4 through 6 use the scatterplot above, which contains information about the fuel efficiency of various modern vehicles compared to their weight.

4. What is the line of best fit for the scatterplot above?
   A) $y = -0.0099x + 54.94$
   B) $y = -0.0099x + 59.94$
   C) $y = -0.099x + 54.94$
   D) $y = -0.099x + 59.94$

5. According to the line of best fit what is the expected weight in pounds of a car that gets 10 miles per gallon?
   A) 4539
   B) 4707
   C) 4876
   D) 5044

6. If a car were redesigned to weigh 260 pounds less, what would be the expected change in its mileage per gallon?
   A) Decreases by 25.74
   B) Decreases by 2.57
   C) Increases by 2.57
   D) Increases by 25.74

SAT Red Math
Lesson 19A: Advanced Scatterplots

CAT Math and Reading Scores

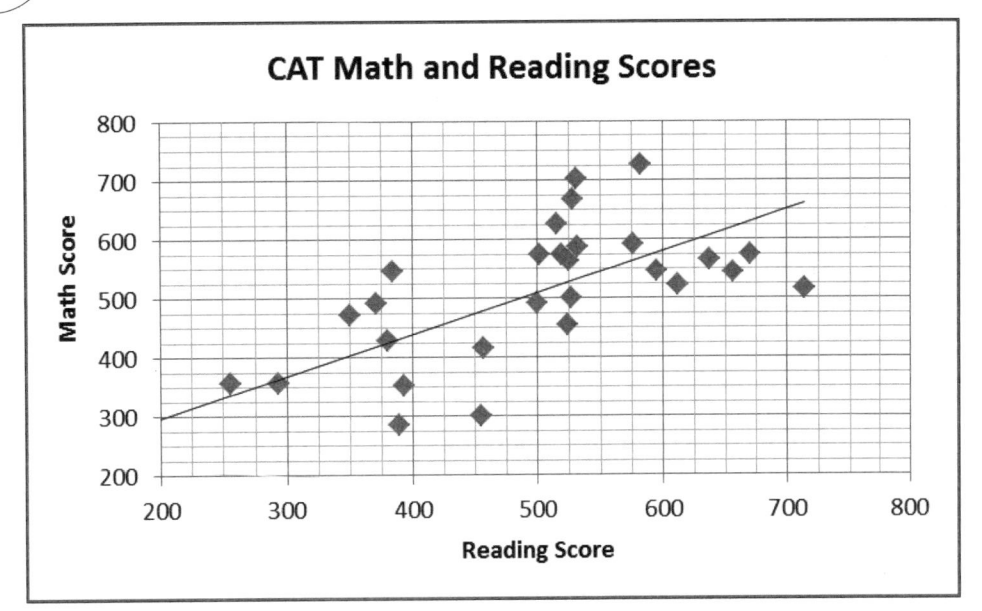

For questions 7 through 9 use the scatterplot above which shows information about numerous student's grades on the math and reading portion of the CAT (College Assessment Test). The line of best fit is $y = 0.71x + 154.57$.

7. According to the line of best fit, what is a student with a CAT Math score of 622 expected to get in CAT Reading?
   A) 658
   B) 660
   C) 662
   D) 664

8. If Jim has a CAT reading score 90 points higher than Dave, how much higher than Dave's is Jim's CAT math score expected to be?
   A) 63.6
   B) 63.7
   C) 63.8
   D) 63.9

9. Which of the following conclusions is most supported by the scatterplot above?
   A) A student with a high score on CAT Math will have a high score on CAT Reading.
   B) A student with a high score on CAT Reading will have a high score on CAT Math.
   C) There is a strong but not absolute correlation between CAT Math and Reading scores.
   D) There is an absolute correlation between CAT Math and Reading scores.

Gas Station Profitability

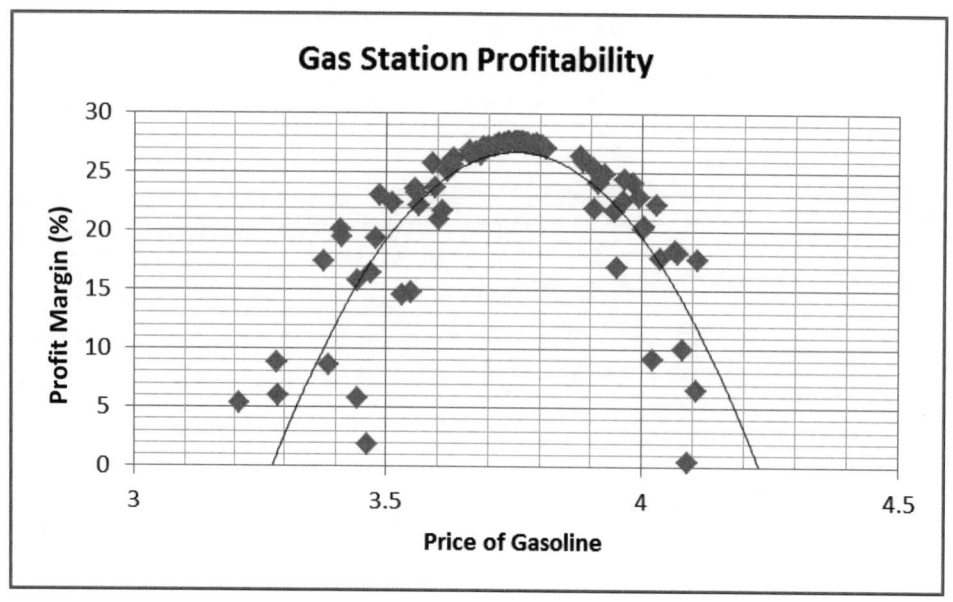

For questions 10 through 12 use the scatterplot above, which contains information about the profitability of gas stations at different suggested prices of a gallon of gasoline, in dollars.

10. What is the curve of best fit for the scatterplot above?
    A) $y = -93.02x^2 + 884.82x - 1633.8$
    B) $y = -93.02x^2 + 716.99x - 1633.8$
    C) $y = -117.87x^2 + 884.82x - 1633.8$
    D) $y = -117.87x^2 + 716.99x - 1633.8$

11. According to the curve of best fit, what is the profit margin of a gas station selling gas for $4.5/gallon?
    A) −39.0%
    B) −4.5%
    C) 0%
    D) 4.5%

12. If a gas station changed its price from $3.7/gallon to $4.0/gallon, what would be the expected change in profit margin?
    A) −65.4%
    B) −6.8%
    C) +6.8%
    D) +65.4%

Urban Transportation

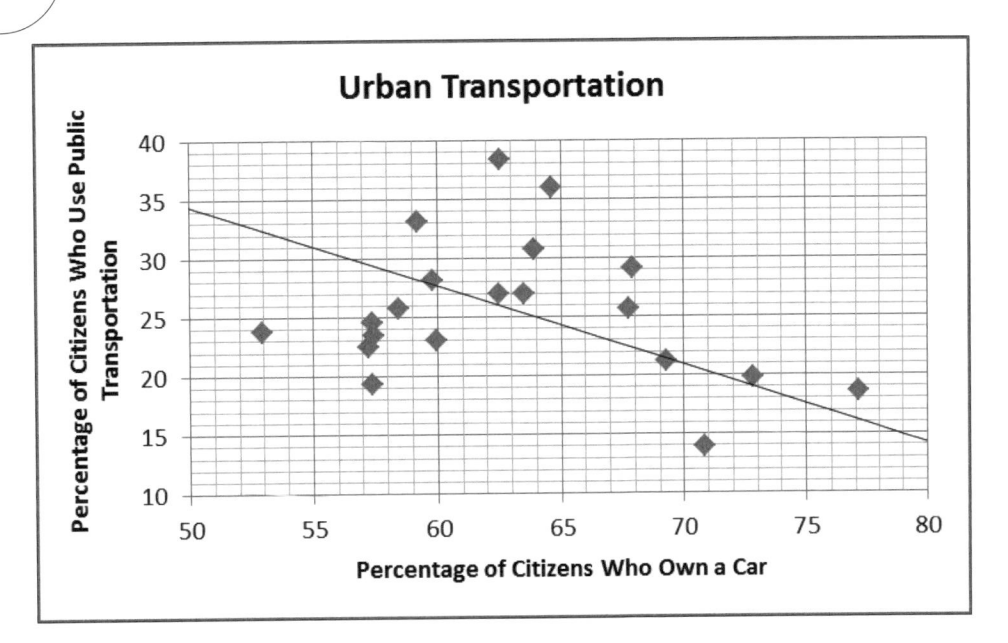

For questions 13 through 16 use the scatterplot above with information about various cities and which forms of transportation its citizens choose to use on a daily basis.

13. What is the line of best fit for the scatterplot above?
    A) $y = -0.67x + 34.81$
    B) $y = -0.67x + 68.12$
    C) $y = -0.73x + 34.81$
    D) $y = -0.73x + 68.12$

14. Which of the following inferences is most supported by the scatterplot above?
    A) There is an absolute correlation between how many of a city's residents use public transportation and how many own a car.
    B) All residents of cities either use public transportation or own a car, but never both.
    C) A city with more public transportation will tend to have a population where less people own a car.
    D) There are only two cities where people who own cars use public transportation.

15. According to the line of best fit what percentage of people are expected to own a car if 5.3% of the population uses public transportation? Round to the nearest tenth of a percent.

16. If a city's percentage car ownership goes from 75.4% to 63.0% over four years, what is the expected increase in the percentage of residents who use public transportation? Round to the nearest tenth of a percent.

Crane Population Decline

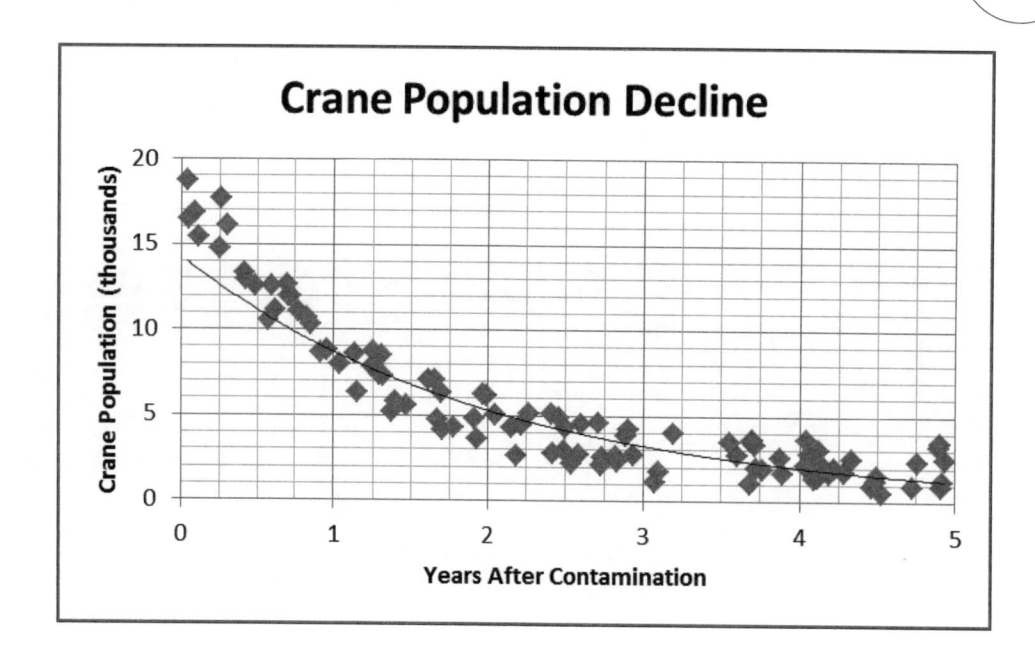

For questions 17 through 20 use the scatterplot above about the decline of crane populations in several equally sized sections of nature preserves following a breakout of parasites.

17. What is the curve of best fit for the scatterplot above?
    A) $y = 12.31e^{-0.5x}$
    B) $y = 12.31e^{-0.6x}$
    C) $y = 14.26e^{-0.5x}$
    D) $y = 14.26e^{-0.6x}$

18. Which of the following conclusions is most supported by the scatterplot above?
    A) The crane population has decreased exponentially in the presence of the parasite.
    B) The parasites exponentially killed more and more cranes.
    C) Ten years after the parasite breakout all cranes are expected to be dead.
    D) Before the parasite breakout, the crane's population was exponentially decreasing.

19. According to the curve of best fit, how long in years after the parasite contamination has a sample population been exposed if half the initial population has died? Round to the nearest hundredth of a year.

20. What percentage of the initial crane population is expected to die between 1.7 and 4.0 years after the parasite outbreak? Round to the nearest tenth of a percent.

Red Math Lesson 19B: Two-Way Tables – Probabilities and Frequencies
Learning to Swim

Directions: Answer each question below.

Practice Set 1 (Calculator)

	Guitar	Cello	Mandolin	Violin	Total
Under 18	195	10	3	1	209
18 – 35	56	14	6	3	79
35 – 50	39	36	7	20	102
Over 50	26	11	5	34	76
Total	316	71	21	58	466

Use the above chart for questions 1 through 3. The chart lists the primary instrument that a randomly selected group of musicians play by their age.

1. What is the probability that a randomly selected person from this sample between the ages of 18 and 50 plays the mandolin as their primary instrument? Round to the nearest hundredth of a percent.

2. Given that a randomly selected person from this sample does not play the guitar, what is the probability that this person knows how to play the violin? Round to the nearest hundredth of a percent.

3. If the number of people aged 18-35 in each instrument category in this sample were doubled, the proportions of musicians in each category of the new table would be representative of another group of 1,090 musicians in a nearby area. How many musicians in this second group are expected to play either the cello or the guitar as their primary instrument?

SAT Red Math
Lesson 19B: Two-Way Tables – Probabilities and Frequencies

	Homeowner	Renter	Other	Percent of Adult Population
Married	35%	62%	3%	47%
Engaged	27%	68%	5%	4%
Single	14%	78%	8%	49%

Use the above table for questions 4 and 5. The table shows information about the city of Jacksonville. Jacksonville has an adult population of 650,000.

4. How many adults in Jacksonville are homeowners?

5. Given that an adult resident of Jacksonville is neither a homeowner nor a renter, what is the probability that he or she is engaged? Round to the nearest hundredth of a percent.

SAT Red Math — Lesson 19B: Two-Way Tables – Probabilities and Frequencies

RED MATH LESSON 19B: TWO-WAY TABLES – PROBABILITIES AND FREQUENCIES
Diving into the Deep End

Directions: Answer each question below.

PRACTICE SET 2 (CALCULATOR)

	State A	State B	State C
Taiga	38%	21%	0%
Forest	46%	36%	0%
Grasslands	16%	28%	29%
Desert	0%	15%	71%

Use the table above for questions 6 through 8. State A has an area of 665,384 mi², State B has an area of 71,298 mi² and State C has an area of 110,572 mi².

6. Given that a point of land is desert, what is the probability that the point of land is in State C?
   A) 86%
   B) 87%
   C) 88%
   D) Not enough information to determine.

7. Which of the following is most probable?
   A) A randomly selected point of taiga among these three states is in State B.
   B) A randomly selected point from States B and C is grassland.
   C) A randomly selected point amongst these three states is in a desert.
   D) A randomly selected point of grassland among these three states is in State A.

8. Among these three states, which is the correct order of area by biome?
   A) Taiga > Grasslands > Forest > Desert
   B) Forest > Taiga > Grasslands > Desert
   C) Grasslands > Taiga > Forest > Desert
   D) Grasslands > Forest > Taiga > Desert

	High School	Bachelor's Degree	Graduate Degree
<$30,000	230	217	12
$30,000 – $70,000	401	616	180
>$70,000	32	73	102

Use the above table for questions 9 through 11. The table shows the results of a random sample asking those working in Detroit, Michigan about their annual income and highest level of education.

9. If the working population of Detroit is 450,000, how many Detroit residents are expected to have a graduate degree and make between $30,000 and $70,000 a year?
   A) 35,331
   B) 43,478
   C) 51,625
   D) Not enough information to determine.

10. Which of the following is least probable, assuming all people are residents of Detroit?
    A) Someone makes more than $70,000 a year given that he or she possesses no more than a bachelor's degree.
    B) Someone possesses no more than a high school diploma given that he or she makes more than $70,000 a year
    C) Someone makes more than $70,000 a year given that he or she has only a high school education.
    D) Someone makes less than $30,000 a year given that he or she possesses a graduate degree.

Lesson 19B: Two-Way Tables – Probabilities and Frequencies

11. How much more likely is it for someone with only a bachelor's degree to earn over $70,000 a year than someone with only a high school diploma?
    A) 3.23%
    B) 5.35%
    C) 7.50%
    D) Not enough information to determine.

	A. Dent	F. Prefect	P. Jeltz
City X	31	102	26
City Y	64	156	100
City Z	71	81	69

Use the above table for questions 12 through 15. Above are the early poll results for an upcoming county election in the county's three biggest cities. The poll is believed to be a representative sample of all three cities.

12. Which of the candidates is most likely to win the election?
    A) A. Dent
    B) F. Prefect
    C) P. Jeltz
    D) Not enough information to determine.

13. Which of the following is most probable for people amongst these three cities?
    A) An A. Dent voter is from City X.
    B) A City Y voter voted for P. Jeltz.
    C) An F. Prefect voter is from City Z.
    D) A City X voter voted for A. Dent.

14. If the sample is representative of the voters of the entire county, and the county has a population of 220,000, how many thousands of people are expected to vote for F. Prefect? Round to the nearest thousand.

15. Given that a voter didn't vote for P. Jeltz, what is the probability that he or she is not from City Y? Round to the nearest tenth of a percent.

SAT Red Math
Lesson 19B: Two-Way Tables – Probabilities and Frequencies

PRACTICE SET 3 (CALCULATOR)

	Track & Field	Band	Debate Club
Grade 9	7	6	4
Grade 10	8	11	6
Grade 11	6	18	8
Grade 12	9	25	12

Use the table above for questions 16 through 18. The table contains information about the breakdown of three clubs at Dartmouth High School. Assume students are in a maximum of one club.

16. What is the probability that a ninth-grader chosen at random from all of the students in the school is in the band?
    A) 35%
    B) 44%
    C) 55%
    D) Not enough information to determine.

17. Which of the following is most likely about someone in one of these three clubs?
    A) A ninth-grader is in the debate club.
    B) A debate club member is in the twelfth grade.
    C) An eleventh-grader is in the band.
    D) A band member is in the twelfth grade.

18. Of the students in these three clubs that are not in the grade 12 or in debate club, what percent are in the band?
    A) 37.5%
    B) 47.3%
    C) 62.5%
    D) Not enough information to determine.

Annual Income	City Q	City O	City P
< $35,000	70	153	40
$35,000 – $85,000	132	216	201
> $85,000	47	109	114

Use the table above for questions 19 through 21. A random sample of people from the working population of three cities was collected and sorted by their incomes.

19. Which of the following has the highest probability for someone who lives in one of these three cities?
    A) Someone with an annual income under $35,000 lives in City P.
    B) Someone who lives in City P has an annual income under $35,000.
    C) Someone with an annual income over $85,000 lives in City Q.
    D) Someone who lives in City Q has an annual income over $85,000.

20. Which of the following has the lowest probability for someone who lives in one of these three cities?
    A) Someone with an annual income under $35,000 lives in City O
    B) Someone who lives in City Q has an annual income between $35,000 and $85,000
    C) Someone who lives in City P has an annual income between $35,000 and $85,000
    D) Someone who lives in City O has an annual income between $35,000 and $85,000

21. If the combined working population of the three cities is 600,000, how many people are expected neither to live in City P nor have an annual income over $85,000?
    A) 253,420
    B) 285,028
    C) 316,636
    D) 348,244

Version 3.0

SAT Red Math
Lesson 19B: Two-Way Tables – Probabilities and Frequencies

	Humanities	Math	Science	Other
Humanities	64%	6%	8%	22%
Mathematics	3%	51%	32%	14%
Science	8%	33%	50%	9%
Other	25%	10%	10%	55%

Use the table above for questions 22 through 25. Data was collected amongst a group of students currently working on a Master's degree. The rows represent the students Bachelor's major while the columns represent the students Master's major.

22. What is the probability someone with a Bachelor's in mathematics chooses Science or Other as their major for a Master's degree?
    A) 32%
    B) 46%
    C) 65%
    D) 83%

23. Which of the following is the most popular choice for a Master's degree?
    A) Science
    B) Mathematics
    C) Other
    D) Not enough information to determine.

24. If these results are representative of a group of 10,000 students, 30% of whom got a Bachelor's degree in Humanities, how many of these students are expected to get a Bachelor's in Humanities and a Master's in Mathematics?

25. Given that this sample is representative of a group of graduate students with an equal mix of majors in all four areas for their Bachelor's, what percentage of these students majored in science for their Master's degree? Round to the nearest tenth of a percent.

RED MATH LESSON 19B: TWO-WAY TABLES – PROBABILITIES AND FREQUENCIES
Race to the Finish

Directions: Answer each question below.

HOMEWORK SET (CALCULATOR)

	Country A	Country B	Country C
Desert	31%	1%	0%
Grasslands	67%	51%	2%
Forest	2%	43%	37%
Tundra	0%	5%	61%

	High School	Bachelor's	Master's
< $40,000	146	127	37
$40,000 – $70,000	290	409	155
> $70,000	67	145	89

Use the table above, which gives the percentage of the land area of each of three countries that is in each of four biomes, for questions 1 through 3.

1. Which of the following is the least likely to occur if a point is chosen randomly from a single country?
   A) A point in Country A is desert or tundra.
   B) A point in Country B is desert or forest.
   C) A point in Country C is not tundra.
   D) Not enough information to determine.

2. Which of the following is most likely to occur if a point is chosen randomly from a single country?
   A) A point in tundra or forest is in Country B.
   B) A point not in tundra is in Country A.
   C) A point in grasslands or forest is in either Country A or B.
   D) Not enough information to determine.

3. If Country A is 1.5 times as large as Country B, and Country B is 4 times as large as Country C, what percentage of all three countries is covered in forest?
   A) 19%
   B) 20%
   C) 21%
   D) 22%

Use the table above for questions 4 through 6. The table summarizes a survey of random working adults in the city of Milwaukee, Wisconsin and their annual incomes and highest level of education.

4. Which of the following is most likely for a working adult in Milwaukee?
   A) Someone with an annual income under $40,000 having a Master's degree
   B) Someone with only a high-school education making more than $70,000 a year
   C) Someone who makes between $40,000 and $70,000 a year having a Bachelor's degree but not a Master's
   D) Someone with a Master's degree making less than $40,000 a year

5. Which of the following is least likely for a working adult in Milwaukee?
   A) Someone with a Bachelor's but not a Master's degree making $40,000-$70,000 annually
   B) Someone with a Master's degree making $40,000-$70,000 annually
   C) Someone with only a high school education making $40,000-$70,000 annually
   D) Someone who makes over $70,000 a year having only a Bachelor's

484 — SAT Red Math
Lesson 19B: Two-Way Tables – Probabilities and Frequencies

6. If the working population of Milwaukee is 400,000, what percentage of people in Milwaukee can be expected to either have an annual income over $70,000 or a Master's degree?
   A) 27.7%
   B) 33.7%
   C) 39.7%
   D) Not enough information to determine.

	Spanish	French	Mandarin	Latin
Grade 9	104	56	12	13
Grade 10	109	48	13	19
Grade 11	91	51	12	26
Grade 12	98	46	15	41

Use the table above for questions 7 through 9. A high school offers four foreign languages and students are only allowed to enroll in one at a time. The data above represents all students at the school.

7. What is the probability of an eleventh-grader taking Spanish minus the probability of a twelfth-grader taking Mandarin?
   A) 7.5%
   B) 35.6%
   C) 43.1%
   D) 50.6%

8. Which of the following is most likely of a student in the school who is enrolled in a language?
   A) A tenth-grader taking Latin.
   B) A Latin student being in the ninth grade.
   C) An eleventh-grader taking Latin.
   D) A Latin student being in the tenth grade.

9. The school stopped offering French and all current French students joined another language class. If the proportions of Spanish, Mandarin and Latin didn't change in each individual grade, what is the probability that a tenth-grader enrolled in a language is not enrolled in Mandarin?
   A) 88.4%
   B) 89.2%
   C) 90.0%
   D) 90.8%

Age	Homeowner	Renter	Other
Under 25	4	61	6
25 – 40	15	170	10
40 – 55	31	157	14
Over 55	40	148	18

Use the table above for questions 10 through 12. The data comes from a random sample of adult residents of Denver, Colorado.

10. Which of the following is least likely about an adult resident of Denver?
    A) Someone aged 25-40 is not a homeowner or a renter.
    B) Someone aged 40-55 is not a homeowner or a renter.
    C) A homeowner is under 25.
    D) Someone under 25 is a homeowner.

11. Which of the following is most likely about an adult resident of Denver?
    A) Someone aged 40-55 is a homeowner.
    B) A homeowner is aged 25-40.
    C) A renter is under 25.
    D) Someone who is not a homeowner or renter is under 25.

12. If Denver has an adult population of 420,000, how many adults are expected to be in the "Other" category or between the ages of 40 and 55?
    A) 20,634
    B) 21,187
    C) 86,364
    D) 147,062

SAT Red Math
Lesson 19B: Two-Way Tables – Probabilities and Frequencies

Annual Income	Married	Engaged	Single
< $25,000	21%	26%	28%
$25,000 − $45,000	34%	39%	41%
$45,000 − $75,000	39%	30%	27%
> $75,000	6%	5%	4%

Use the table above for questions 13 - 16. The entries are the percentages of people in each relationship category that are in each income bracket. This data is representative of the adults in the city of Portland, which has a population of 210,000 married adults, 15,000 engaged adults, and 260,000 single adults.

13. Which of the following is most likely about an adult resident of Portland?
    A) Someone with an annual income under $25,000 is married
    B) Someone with an annual income between $25,000 and $45,000 is married
    C) Someone with an annual income over $75,000 is single
    D) Not enough information to determine.

14. Which of the following is least likely about an adult resident of Oregon?
    A) Someone with an annual income under $25,000 is single
    B) Someone with an annual income between $25,000 and $45,000 is single
    C) Someone with an annual income between $45,000 and $75,000 is single
    D) Not enough information to determine.

15. How many thousands of people in Portland, Oregon are expected to have an annual income over $75,000 in five years if the adult population increases by ten percent but stays proportional to the sample above? Round to the nearest thousand people.

16. The sample above is representative of the adult residents of Seattle. If Seattle has a married population of 300,000, an engaged population of 20,000 and an adult single population of 450,000, how many thousands of people in Seattle have an annual income above $45,000? Round to the nearest thousand people.

	M. David	K. Greene	U. Danson	S. Lewis
Georgia	202	309	280	622
Alabama	120	201	137	390
Florida	571	710	414	1015
South Carolina	126	196	130	577

Use the table above for questions 17 through 20. An exit poll was conducted on 6,000 random people from the four states above in a primary election with only four candidates.

17. What is the probability that a voter from Alabama or Florida didn't vote for U. Danson?
    A) 84.0%
    B) 84.5%
    C) 84.9%
    D) Not enough information to determine.

18. Which of the following is most likely, given the person voted within the four states above?
    A) Someone from South Carolina voted for U. Danson.
    B) Someone who voted for M. David is from Alabama.
    C) Someone from South Carolina voted for M. David.
    D) Someone who voted for M. David is from South Carolina.

19. How much more likely is it that a voter from Florida didn't vote for M. David than a voter from Alabama didn't vote for S. Lewis? Round your answer to the nearest tenth of a percent.

20. If there are 1 million voters from the four states above, how many votes is U. Danson expected to get in thousands? Round to the nearest thousand voters.

Red Math Lesson 20A: Practice Sections
Learning to Swim

Directions: Answer each question below.

Practice Set 1 (Calculator)

1. If $\left(\frac{1}{3}\right)^{3x} = 27^{x+4}$, what is the value of x?

2. The points $(3, -1)$ and $(-3, 7)$ are both on the diameter of a circle in the xy-coordinate plane. What is the equation of that circle?

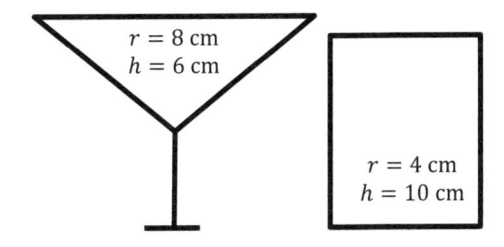

   $r = 8$ cm
   $h = 6$ cm

   $r = 4$ cm
   $h = 10$ cm

3. Amy has a choice between a conical glass and a cylindrical glass, as shown in the side-view above. What is the difference between the volumes of the two glasses in cm³?

4. A logarithmic function has a domain of all real values of x greater than -2. It passes through the point $(-1, 3)$. Which of the following could be this function?
   A) $f(x) = \ln(x - 2) + 2$
   B) $f(x) = \ln(x - 2) + 3$
   C) $f(x) = \ln(x + 2) + 2$
   D) $f(x) = \ln(x + 2) + 3$

5. Esmil purchases a cube-shaped block of clay with a side length of 60 cm. Which of the following solids CANNOT be constructed with this amount of clay? (The volume of a cone or pyramid is one-third of its base area times its height)
   A) A cone with base radius of 45 cm and height of 100 cm
   B) A pyramid with a square base of side length 75 cm and height of 120 cm
   C) A cylinder with base radius of 30 cm and height of 75 cm
   D) A rectangular prism with side lengths of 30 cm, 100 cm, and 70 cm

Red Math Lesson 20A: Practice Sections
Diving into the Deep End

Directions: Answer each question below.

Practice Set 2 (Calculator)

6. A cone of clay (with the base on the ground) has a height of 24 inches and a radius of 9 inches. The top one-third of the cone's height is cut off to form a new cone. What is the ratio of the volume of the small cone to the volume of the original cone?
   A) 1:27
   B) 1:18
   C) 1:9
   D) 1:3

7. A circle in the xy-coordinate plane has the equation $(x-2)^2 + y^2 = 25$. If this circle is shifted 3 units to the left and 4 units down, what is the resulting equation?
   A) $(x-5)^2 + (y-4)^2 = 25$
   B) $(x-5)^2 + (y+4)^2 = 25$
   C) $(x+1)^2 + (y-4)^2 = 25$
   D) $(x+1)^2 + (y+4)^2 = 25$

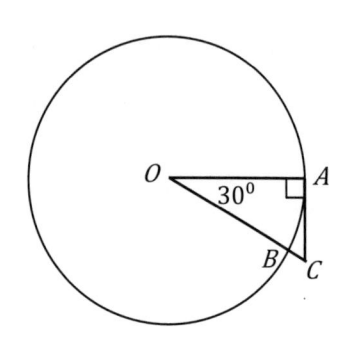

8. In the figure above, the length of arc $\widehat{AB}$ is $\frac{2}{3}\pi$. What is the length of $\overline{AC}$?
   A) $\sqrt{2}$
   B) $\frac{4\sqrt{3}}{3}$
   C) $2\sqrt{2}$
   D) $\frac{8\sqrt{3}}{3}$

9. The combined volume of a tree's roots, trunk, branches, and leaves increases by 7% each year. If the tree has a volume of 2 cubic meters today, which function could be used to find its volume y years ago?
   A) $V(y) = 2 \cdot 0.93^{(-y)}$
   B) $V(y) = (2 \cdot 0.93)^y$
   C) $V(y) = 2 \cdot 1.07^{(-y)}$
   D) $V(y) = 1.07^{(-2y)}$

10. What are all of the real solutions to the equation $\frac{x^2-5x+4}{x^2+4x+4} \cdot \frac{x^2+7x+10}{x-4} = 0$?
    A) $x = -2$ and 4
    B) $x = -5$ and 1
    C) $x = -5, -2,$ and 1
    D) $x = -5, -2, 1,$ and 4

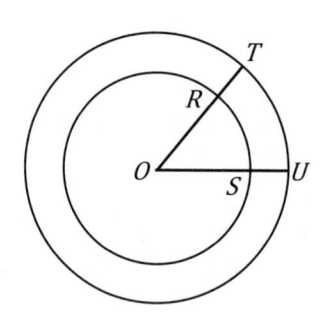

11. In the figure above, the area of sector OTU is 10π and the area of the smaller circle is 18π. If the ratio of $\overline{OT}$ to $\overline{OR}$ is $\sqrt{2}:1$, what is $m\angle O$ in radians?
    A) $\frac{2\pi}{9}$
    B) $\frac{5\pi}{18}$
    C) $\frac{\pi}{3}$
    D) $\frac{5\pi}{9}$

SAT Red Math
Lesson 20A: Practice Sections

12. If the cosine of an angle is negative and the sine of the same angle is positive, which of the following could NOT be the measure of that angle?
    A) $\frac{\pi}{2}$
    B) $\frac{4\pi}{7}$
    C) $\frac{7\pi}{10}$
    D) $\frac{5\pi}{6}$

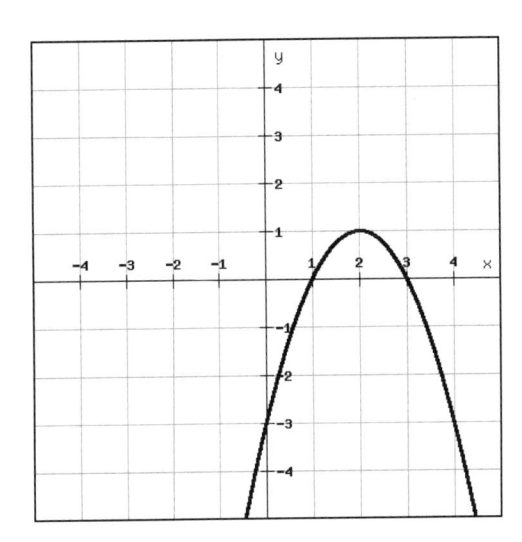

13. What is the equation of the parabola graphed in the figure above?
    A) $y = -x^2 - 4x - 5$
    B) $y = -x^2 - 4x - 3$
    C) $y = -x^2 + 4x - 5$
    D) $y = -x^2 + 4x - 3$

14. A box 4 cm wide, 10 cm long, and 16 cm high is filled with sugar. The sugar is then poured into 4-cm-high cylinders, each with a radius of 2 cm. How many of the cylinders will be completely filled with the sugar from the box?

15. Two spheres each have a radius of 6 cm. One is made of concrete (density: 1.5 $\frac{g}{cm^3}$) and the other is made of steel (density: 7.9 $\frac{g}{cm^3}$). How much greater, to the nearest hundred grams, is the mass of the steel sphere?

PRACTICE SET 3 (CALCULATOR)

16. What is the domain of $f(x) = \log(x + 5) - 3$?
    A) All real values of x
    B) All real values of x except -5
    C) All real values of x greater than -5
    D) All real values of x greater than -3

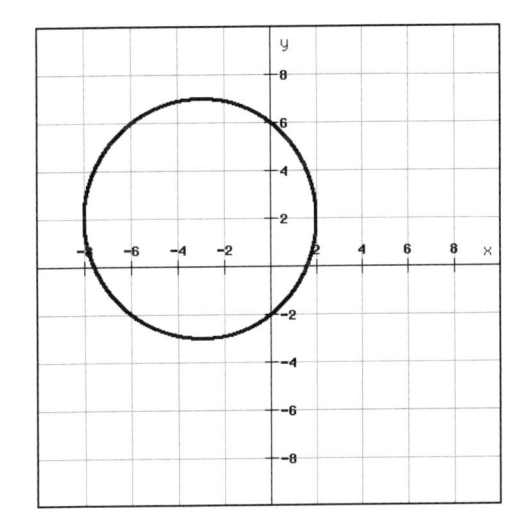

17. What is the equation of the circle shown in the xy-coordinate plane in the figure above?
    A) $(x + 3)^2 + (y + 2)^2 = 25$
    B) $(x + 3)^2 + (y - 2)^2 = 25$
    C) $(x + 6)^2 + (y - 4)^2 = 100$
    D) $(x + 6)^2 + (y + 4)^2 = 100$

18. The average price of a gallon of gasoline y years after 1990 is given by $P = \frac{1}{100}(-y^2 + 38y + 80)$. The average price of a gallon of milk is given by $P = \frac{1}{100}(15y + 140)$. In what two years are the gallon prices of gasoline and milk the same?
    A) 1993 and 2010
    B) 1994 and 2005
    C) 1996 and 2000
    D) 1998 and 2005

19. What is the tangent of one of the interior angles of an equilateral triangle?
    A) $\frac{\sqrt{3}}{3}$
    B) $\frac{\sqrt{3}}{2}$
    C) 1
    D) $\sqrt{3}$

Day	1	2	3	4	5	6
Lava Flow (L/s)	0.4	0.9	2.1	5.0	11.7	27.5

20. Scientists recorded data on the rate of lava flowing from a volcano, as shown in the table above. This data is an example of:
    A) exponential growth.
    B) exponential decay.
    C) linear growth.
    D) linear decay.

21. What are all of the real solutions to the equation $\frac{2}{x-3} - \frac{x+1}{x^2-6x+9} = 0$?
    A) $x = 3$ only
    B) $x = 7$ only
    C) $x = -1$ and $x = 3$
    D) $x = -1$, and $x = 7$

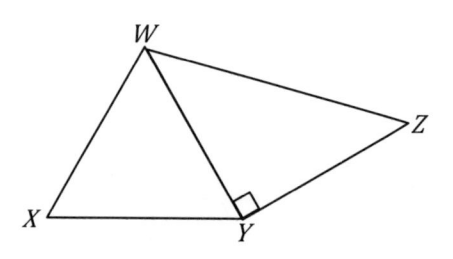

22. In the figure above, triangle WXY is equilateral and triangle WYZ is isosceles. What is the cosine of angle XYZ?
    A) $-\frac{\sqrt{3}}{2}$
    B) $\frac{1}{2}$
    C) $\frac{\sqrt{3}}{2}$
    D) $1 + \frac{\sqrt{3}}{2}$

$$(x - h)^2 + (y - k)^2 = r^2$$

23. A circle with the equation above passes through three points: $(2, 9), (-2, -3), (-10, 13)$. What is the sum of h and k?
    A) -1
    B) 1
    C) 4
    D) 11

24. Two pyramids each have a height of 30 meters and a square base. If one has a side length of 30 meters and the other has a side length of 40 meters, what is the difference in their volumes? Round to the nearest cubic meter.

25. A new car was purchased for $35,000. If a car is estimated to lose x% of its value every year, what is the value of x when, after 6 years, the car is worth $15,000? Round to the nearest tenth.

RED MATH LESSON 20A: PRACTICE SECTIONS
Race to the Finish

Directions: Answer each question below.

HOMEWORK SET (CALCULATOR)

1. A projectile is shot at a 45° angle with respect to the ground. The height of the projectile can be modeled as $d(t) = -4.9t^2 + 30t + 5$. The velocity of the projectile can be modeled as $v(t) = -9.8t + 30$. What is the velocity of the projectile when it is 8.6 meters off the ground on its descent?
   A) -28.8
   B) -19
   C) 5
   D) 28.8

$$\sin(A + B) = 0.30$$
$$\sin(A) = \frac{1}{2}$$
$$90° < A + B < 180°$$

2. Using the system above, what is a possible value of B?
   A) 12.5
   B) 30
   C) 42.5
   D) 55

$$4a + 2b + c = 1$$
$$c = -3a + 3b$$
$$-2a + 4b = -2$$

3. For the system of equations above, what is the value of $b + c$?
   A) -7
   B) -3
   C) 1
   D) 4

4. If $f(x) = 4\ln(x - 5)$ and $g(x) = e^{\frac{x}{2}}$, which expression is equivalent to $g(f(x))$ when $x > 5$?
   A) e^{2x-10}
   B) e^{x-5}
   C) $(2x - 10)^2$
   D) $x^2 - 10x + 25$

5. What is the area of a circle with the equation $x^2 + y^2 - 32x - 2y + 248 = 0$?
   A) 3π
   B) 9π
   C) 18π
   D) 81π

6. Which of the following functions is symmetric with respect to the origin?
   A) $f(x) = 7x^2 + 3x$
   B) $f(x) = 2x + 6$
   C) $f(x) = 4x^7 + 12x^5 + x$
   D) $f(x) = 9x^9 + 5x^5 + 3x^3 + 1$

7. In the xy-coordinate plane, what shape is formed by the set of points whose distances from the origin are three times their distances from the point $(3, 4)$?
   A) A line
   B) A parabola
   C) A circle
   D) None of the above

8. Which of the following graphs matches the graph of the function $f(x) = -2^{(x+2)}$ in the xy-coordinate plane?

A)

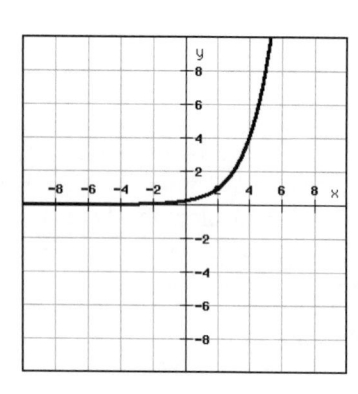

B)

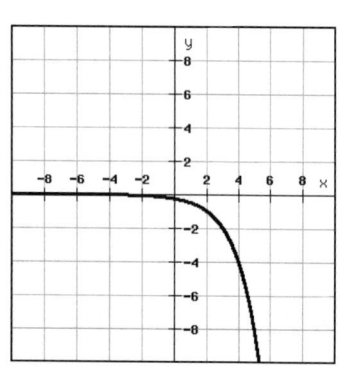

C)

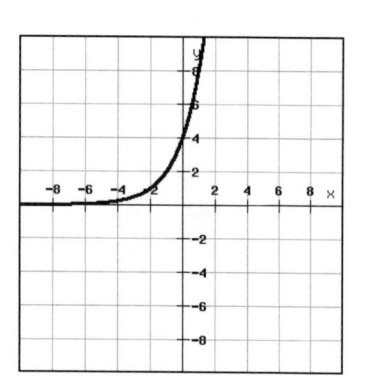

D)

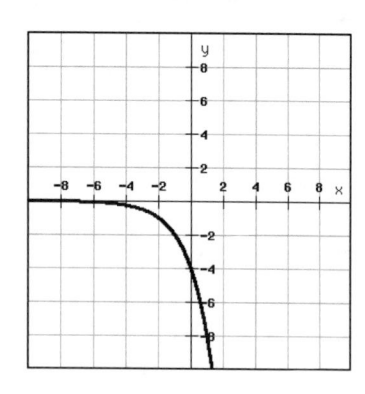

9. A circle with center in the second quadrant is tangent to the lines $x = -11, y = 4,$ and $x = 1$. What is the equation of the circle?
   A) $(x + 5)^2 + (y + 2)^2 = 36$
   B) $(x - 5)^2 + (y + 2)^2 = 144$
   C) $(x + 5)^2 + (y - 10)^2 = 36$
   D) $(x + 5)^2 + (y - 10)^2 = 144$

10. The concentration of sulfuric acid in a solution prepared for use in a chemistry lab must be equal to 0.2 mL/L, and at least 30 liters of this solution are required. Which of the following inequalities describes the constraint on the amount A of pure sulfuric acid, in mL, required to prepare this solution?
    A) $A \geq 0.2(30)$
    B) $A \geq 0.02(30)$
    C) $A \geq 0.002(30)$
    D) $A \geq 0.0002(30)$

$$\frac{1}{a} + \frac{1}{2a} = \frac{500{,}000}{s}$$

11. A water tank with capacity 500,000 gallons is filled in s seconds by two faucets, one of which discharges twice as much water per minute into the tank as the other. If this situation is modeled by the above equation, what does a represent?
    A) The number of seconds it takes the faster faucet to discharge one gallon of water.
    B) The number of seconds it takes the slower faucet to discharge one gallon of water.
    C) The number of seconds it would take the faster faucet alone to fill the tank.
    D) The number of seconds it would take the slower faucet alone to fill the tank.

Lesson 20A: Practice Sections

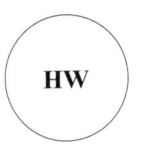

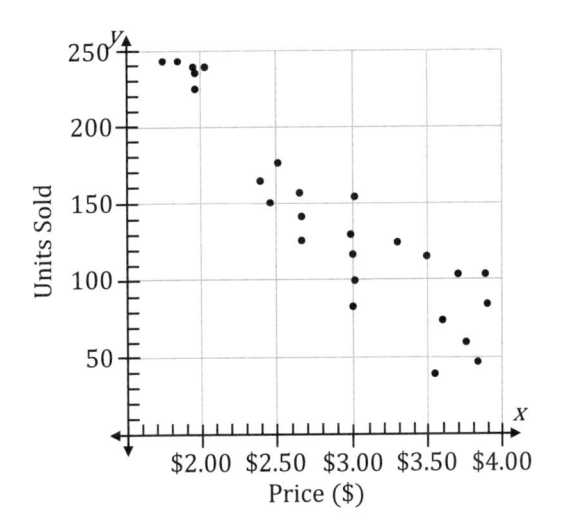

12. Each week for a period of 26 weeks, a grocery store recorded the price of a half-gallon of milk and the number of half-gallons sold that week. The results are shown in the scatterplot above. Which of the following could be the equation of a best-fit line to the above data?
    A) $y = 275 - 90x$
    B) $y = 275 - 0.8x$
    C) $y = 410 - 90x$
    D) $y = 410 - 0.8x$

13. An equilateral triangle is inscribed in a circle. If the circle has radius 4, what is the area of the triangle?
    A) 12
    B) $12\sqrt{3}$
    C) 24
    D) $24\sqrt{3}$

14. The graph of a quadratic equation has a y-intercept of 0 and vertex $(4, 12)$. What is the equation?
    A) $y = -x^2 + 8x - 28$
    B) $y - 12 = -\frac{3}{4}(x - 4)^2$
    C) $y - 4 = -\frac{4}{3}(x - 12)^2$
    D) $y = -\frac{3}{4}(x + 4)^2 + 12$

$$\sqrt{9-x} = 3 + \sqrt{8+x}$$

15. What is the sum of all values of x that satisfy the above equation?
    A) -7
    B) 1
    C) 8
    D) 1

16. A *board foot* is a measure of volume commonly used for lumber. It is equal to 1 ft. × 1 ft. × 1 in. How many board feet comprise 54 cubic yards?
    A) 1,458
    B) 1,944
    C) 5,832
    D) 17,496

$$-7x + 4y + 2z = -24$$
$$x - 3y - 5z = 6$$
$$5x - 6y + 7z = 35$$

17. Using the system of equations above, what is the value of $-xyz$?

18. What is the smallest angle in the triangle made by the intersection of the x-axis, y-axis, and the line with equation $5y - 2x - 10 = 0$? Round to the nearest tenth of a degree.

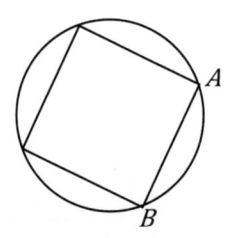

20. In the figure above, a square is inscribed in a circle, and the length of arc $\widehat{AB}$ is 8π. What is the length of chord $\overline{AB}$? Round to the nearest tenth.

19. If angle θ is positive and obtuse and $\tan(\theta) = -1$, what is the value of $\sin\left(\frac{\theta}{2}\right)$? Round to the nearest hundredth.

RED MATH LESSON 20B: PRACTICE SECTIONS
Learning to Swim

Directions: Answer each question below.

PRACTICE SET 1 (NO CALCULATOR)

1. The fraction of a body infected with virus cells, v, detected t hours after administering an antiviral drug, is estimated by $v(t) = 10t^{-3}$ for all $t > 1$. If $\frac{5}{256}$ of the body is infected, how many hours has it been since the drug was administered?

	Age Range				
Candidate	18-30	31-45	46-60	61-80	Total
Smith	50	71	85	34	240
McKee	122	131	104	53	410
Nuñez	48	78	131	93	350
Total	220	280	320	180	1000

Questions 2 and 3 use the table above. A newspaper conducts a poll using a random sample that is stratified to ensure that the ages of the respondents reflect the ages of the general population of Atlanta. The poll asks respondents to choose between three candidates for mayor.

2. Based on the information above, if there are 510,000 adults age 18-80 in Atlanta, approximately how many adults age 60 or younger prefer Nuñez to the other candidates?

3. When the mayoral election occurs, the voters in the 18-30 age range vote at a much lower rate than voters in the other age ranges. Based on this information, which statement is most likely true?
   A) Smith is less likely to win the election than the data in the table implies.
   B) McKee is less likely to win the election than the data in the table implies.
   C) Nuñez is less likely to win the election than the data in the table implies.
   D) The data in the table remains an accurate predictor of the election's outcome.

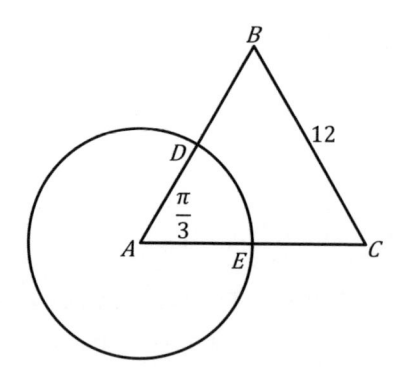

4. In the figure above, circle A bisects two sides of triangle ABC. If $\overline{BC} = 2 \cdot \overline{DB}$, what is the area of sector ADE?

5. A scientist measures the size of lobsters caught in two locations. Lobsters caught near shore had a mean size of 5 pounds, with a standard deviation of 0.4 pounds. Lobsters caught off-shore had a mean size of 4.3 pounds, with a standard deviation of 1.1 pounds. Weights in both populations are normally distributed. Which statement is true?
   A) A lobster caught off-shore is more likely to weigh more than 5 pounds than one caught near shore.
   B) A lobster caught off-shore is more likely to weigh more than 6.5 pounds than one caught near shore.
   C) More than half of the lobsters caught near shore weigh less than 4.5 pounds.
   D) More than half of the lobsters caught off-shore weigh more than 4.5 pounds.

RED MATH LESSON 20B: PRACTICE SECTIONS
Diving into the Deep End

Directions: Answer each question below.

PRACTICE SET 2 (CALCULATOR)

6. If $a = \log_b c$, then $b^{2a+1} =$?
   A) b^{c+1}
   B) bc^2
   C) $b^2 c$
   D) $c + 1$

$$y(3x + 5y) = 7xy$$

7. Given the above equation, what is the value of $\frac{x}{y}$?
   A) $\frac{2}{3}$
   B) $\frac{4}{5}$
   C) $\frac{5}{4}$
   D) It cannot be determined from the given information.

$$\frac{3x+4}{x+3} - 2$$

8. Which of the following expressions is equivalent to the above expression?
   A) $2x - 1$
   B) $\frac{2x-1}{x+3}$
   C) $\frac{x-2}{x+3}$
   D) $\frac{5x+7}{x+3}$

$$D = 500 \cdot 1.004^{12t}$$

9. The number of dollars D in a savings account earning compound interest t years after the initial deposit of $500 is given by the equation above. What is this account's annual interest rate, to the nearest tenth of a percent?
   A) 0.4%
   B) 4.0%
   C) 4.8%
   D) 8.4%

$$P(x) = x^3 - 15x^2 + 71x - 89$$

10. For the polynomial function $P(x)$ defined above, $\frac{P(x)}{x-5} = (x^2 - 10x + 21) + \frac{R}{x-5}$. What is the value of R?
    A) -194
    B) -84
    C) -16
    D) 16

11. For $i = \sqrt{-1}$, if $i^k = i$, what is the value of i^{2k+1}?
    A) -1
    B) 1
    C) $-i$
    D) i

$$\frac{|2-3x|}{5} = 7$$

12. In the above equation, what is the sum of all possible values of x?
    A) -11
    B) $\frac{4}{3}$
    C) 4
    D) $\frac{37}{3}$

13. One machine in a car assembly plant takes 35 seconds to put a piece in place on the radiator. Another machine takes 50 seconds to tighten the screws that hold it. As these machines operate, a backlog develops of radiators that have the piece but have not yet had the screws tightened. How many such radiators will there be after 70 minutes?
    A) 18
    B) 35
    C) 36
    D) 280

14. A company that produces cylindrical cans of soda wants to increase the volume of the cans by 20%. If the height of the can is increased by 15%, what is the percent increase of the can's radius? Round to the nearest tenth of a percent.

15. The tip of a clock's pendulum travels a path of length 30. If the angle through which it swings is 2.5 radians, what is the length of the pendulum? Round to the nearest tenth.

PRACTICE SET 3 (CALCULATOR)

$$\frac{x}{3} - \frac{y}{4} = 17$$
$$ax - 12y = 816$$

16. For what value of a will the above system of equations have no solution?
    A) -9
    B) 9
    C) 16
    D) No such value exists.

$$\frac{-2x-15}{x^2+x-12} = \frac{A}{x-3} + \frac{B}{x+4}$$

17. In the above equation, A and B are constants. If the equation is true for all x except 3 or -4, what is the value of $A + B$?
    A) -15
    B) -4
    C) -2
    D) 1

18. If $f(x) = \frac{x^4}{5} + x^3 + 5x^2$, what is $f(10)$?
    A) 3,500
    B) 7,100
    C) 11,500
    D) 21,500

19. The graph above is described by which of the following equations?

A) $y = 5 \cdot 2^{\frac{x}{2}} - 95$
B) $y = 5 \cdot 2^{\frac{x}{2}} - 100$
C) $y = 5 \cdot 2^{2x} - 100$
D) $y = 2^{\frac{2x}{5}} - 100$

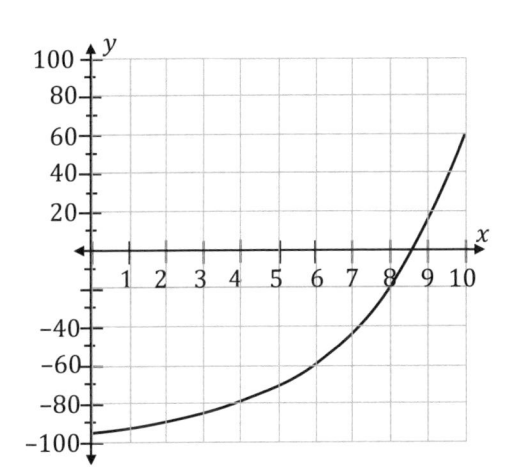

$$x^3 - y^2 = x^2 + 2$$
$$x + 1 = y$$

22. Using the system of equations above what is a possible value of $\sqrt{y}$?

A) -1
B) 0
C) 1
D) 2

23. If $g(x) = 120x^{-3}$ and $h(x) = \frac{x^2}{240}$, for which of these values of x is $h(x)$ greater than $g(x)$?

A) 2
B) 4
C) 6
D) 8

$$2x + 5y - z = 6$$
$$x = 6z + 5y$$
$$z - 3y = 18$$

20. Given the system of equations above, what is z?

A) -6
B) -4
C) 6
D) 16

24. From 2000 to 2010, the annual number of homicides committed in a certain city dropped from 95 to 76. In the same city during the same time period, the population increased by 28%. By what percent did the per capita homicide rate decrease during this time? Round to the nearest tenth of a percent.

21. How many distinct real solutions exist for the equation $\frac{x^2+5x+6}{x^2+6x+5} \cdot \frac{x^2+4x+3}{x+2} = 0$?

A) 0
B) 1
C) 2
D) 3

25. It costs Caleb $8 in materials to make a hat and $40 in materials to make a sweater. Caleb anticipates he can sell twice as many hats as sweaters. If he has $448 to spend on materials, how many hats should he make?

SAT Red Math
Lesson 20B: Practice Sections

RED MATH LESSON 20B: PRACTICE SECTIONS
Race to the Finish

Directions: Answer each question below.

HOMEWORK SET (CALCULATOR)

1. The temperature at which water boils decreases with altitude. At sea level, this temperature is 100°C, and at an elevation of 3,000 meters, it is 90°C. Lake Tahoe, in California, has a surface elevation of 1,897 meters above sea level. Assuming the boiling point-altitude relationship is linear, which of the following is closest to the boiling point of water on the shore of Lake Tahoe?
   A) 63.2°C
   B) 93.7°C
   C) 96.3°C
   D) 106.3°C

Hospital	30-day Death Rate (Heart Attack)	Number of Patients (Heart Attack)	30-day Death Rate (Pneumonia)	Number of Patients (Pneumonia)
Southeast Alabama Medical Center	14.3%	666	10.9%	371
Marshall Medical Center South	18.5%	44	13.9%	372
Helen Keller Memorial Hospital	19.6%	85	15.0%	324
South Baldwin Regional Medical Center	15.8%	66	9.8%	199

Use the above table for questions 2 and 3. The above data is from a study of U.S. hospitals that attempted to assess quality of care by tracking the 30-day mortality rates among Medicare patients from various common causes of death.

2. Which hospital had the highest overall 30-day death rate for heart attack and pneumonia patients combined?
   A) Southeast Alabama Medical Center
   B) Marshall Medical Center South
   C) Helen Keller Memorial Hospital
   D) South Baldwin Regional Medical Center

3. Among these four hospitals, what was the lowest overall 30-day death rate for heart attack and pneumonia patients combined, to the nearest tenth of a percent?
   A) 11.3%
   B) 12.6%
   C) 12.8%
   D) 13.1%

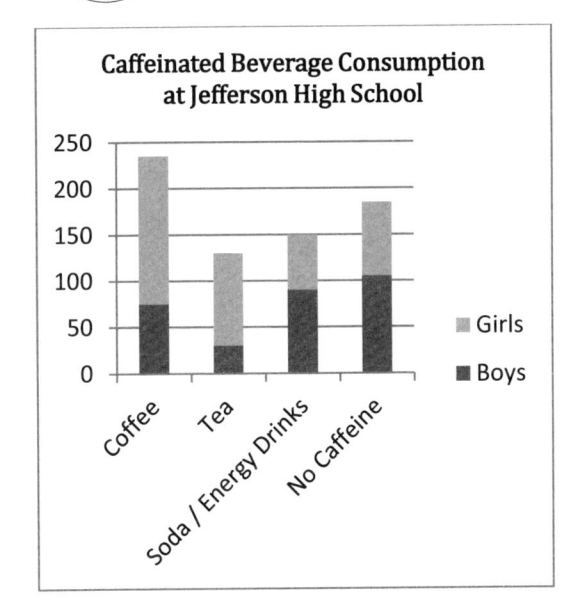

SAT Red Math
Lesson 20B: Practice Sections

Caffeinated Beverage Consumption at Jefferson High School

Use the above graph for questions 4 and 5. Students at a high school were asked whether they primarily prefer to drink coffee, tea, soda or energy drinks, or no caffeinated beverages at all. Each student chose only one answer.

4. Approximately what percent of boys in the survey preferred to drink coffee?
   A) 10%
   B) 25%
   C) 40%
   D) 70%

5. Approximately how many more girls than boys participated in the survey?
   A) 100
   B) 200
   C) 300
   D) 400

$$x^3 - 2x^2 + x - 2$$

6. Which of the following expressions is equivalent to the above expression?
   A) $(x^2 + 1)(x - 2)$
   B) $(x - 1)(x + 1)(x - 2)$
   C) $(x + 1)^2(x - 2)$
   D) $(x - 1)(x + 1)(x + 2)$

$$(x - 3)^2 + (y + 2)^2 = 16$$
$$x = \frac{y}{2}$$

7. Using the system of equations above what is a possible value of y?
   A) -2
   B) 0
   C) 2
   D) 4

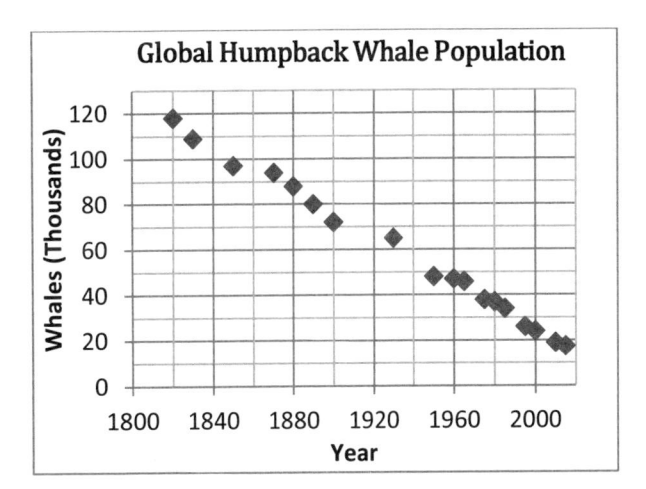

Global Humpback Whale Population

Use the scatterplot above for questions 8 and 9. It shows various estimates for the historical population of humpback whales.

8. If the line of best fit for the scatterplot above is graphed in the xy-coordinate plane, where x is the years since 1800 and y is the number of whales divided by 1,000, what would that line's equation be?
   A) $y = 15 + 0.5x$
   B) $y = 125 - x$
   C) $y = 125 - 0.5x$
   D) $y = 125 + 0.5x$

9. If the trend in the above data continues, in approximately what year would humpback whales become extinct?
   A) 2020
   B) 2030
   C) 2040
   D) 2050

Grade	Books Read This Year				Total
	5 or fewer	6-10	11-15	16+	
1-5	64	219	108	25	416
6-8	59	182	88	14	343
9-12	117	222	55	15	409
Total	240	623	251	54	1168

Use the table above for questions 10 and 11. A school district performed a random poll of its students at the elementary (grades 1-5), middle (grades 6-8), and high school (grades 9-12) levels. It asked each student how many books he or she had read during the year.

10. If a student is picked at random from each level (elementary, middle, and high school), which would be most likely?
    A) The elementary school student will have read at least 11 books.
    B) The middle school student will have read at least 11 books.
    C) The high school student will have read at least 11 books.
    D) The high school student will have read 5 or fewer books.

11. Which conclusion can be most reasonably drawn about this school district from the data above?
    A) Over half of the students who have read 11 or more books are in elementary school.
    B) The percentage of students who've read between 6 and 10 books this year varies greatly among the age groups.
    C) High school students read somewhat fewer books than younger students.
    D) The student who has read the most books is in grades 1-5.

12. If the secant of an angle is $\sqrt{2}$ and the sine of the same angle is $-\frac{\sqrt{2}}{2}$, which of the following could be the angle's measure?
    A) $\frac{\pi}{4}$
    B) $\frac{3\pi}{4}$
    C) $\frac{5\pi}{4}$
    D) $\frac{7\pi}{4}$

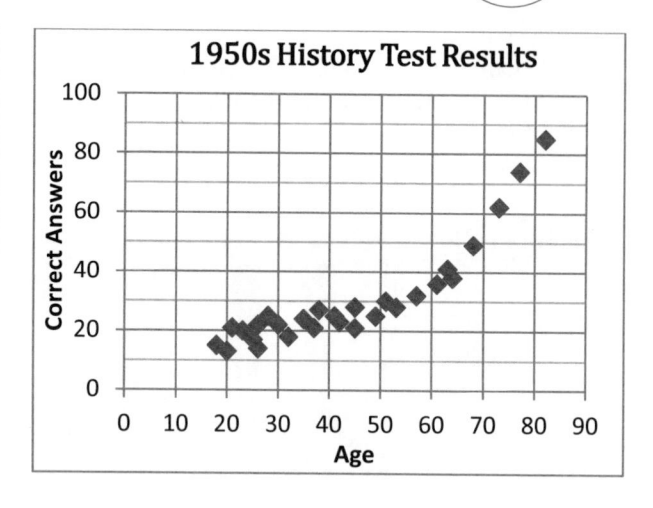

Use the above scatterplot for questions 13 and 14. It shows the results when various adults took a 100-question test about historical events from the 1950s.

13. Which statement is accurate based on this data?
    A) A person's age has no relationship to his or her test score.
    B) A person's test score increases logarithmically with age.
    C) A person's test score increases linearly with age.
    D) A person's test score increases exponentially with age.

14. It can be reasonably inferred from the data in the scatterplot that a 15-year-old taking the same test would likely get about how many questions correct?
    A) 3
    B) 13
    C) 23
    D) 33

SAT Red Math
Lesson 20B: Practice Sections

15. The mass of a sample of nuclear material experiences exponential decay. Its initial mass is 1 kilogram; after one year, its mass has been reduced by 40 grams. Which equation could be used to determine the sample's mass (in grams) after t years?
   A) $m = 1000 - 40t$
   B) $m = 1000 + 40t$
   C) $m = 1000 \cdot 0.96^t$
   D) $m = 1000 \cdot 1.04^t$

$$x^3 = 3y^2 + 4y - 12$$
$$x = y$$

16. Which of the following is not a possible value of $x + y$, where (x, y) is a solution to the system of equations above?
   A) -4
   B) 4
   C) 5
   D) 6

17. A line through the point $(4, 3)$ makes an acute angle measuring θ with the positive x-axis at the origin. What is the value of $\sin \theta$?

18. What is the area of a triangle whose three interior angles have measures $\theta°$, $(90 - \theta)°$, and $90°$, given that $\cos \theta = 0.8$ and the triangle's perimeter is 144?

19. What is the remainder when $x^4 + 3x^2 + 8$ is divided by $x + 1$?

20. A cycling track is circular, with a radius of 100 meters. If a cyclist rides around the track's circumference 6-and-a-half times in 15 minutes, what is that rider's average speed, to the nearest tenth of a kilometer per hour?

Contributors

A very special thank you to the following contributors:

Abigail Burns *(Johns Creek, GA)*
Alicyn Henkhaus *(Palos Verdes, CA)*
Ankit Rawtani *(Bridgewater, NJ)*
Anne Hellerman *(Coppell, TX)*
Ashley Zahn *(ESC)*
Benjamin Yu *(Bridgewater, NJ)*
Brent Cash *(Germantown, MD)*
Brett Vigil *(Johns Creek, GA)*
Brian Cabana *(Paramus, NJ)*
Brian Hester *(Roswell, GA)*
Brian MacNeel *(ESC)*
Caitlin Pancarician *(Middletown, NJ)*
Casey Lynch *(Livingston, NJ)*
Christopher Muyo *(New York)*
Christopher Thomas *(ESC)*
Christopher Woodside *(Edison, NJ)*
Danielle McMullin *(Clifton, NJ)*
Darbi Maddux *(ESC)*
David Rutter *(Snellville, GA)*
Drew McKelvy *(Olney, MD)*
Edward Helmsteter *(Westfield, NJ)*
Eli Aghassi *(Northridge, CA)*
Elizabeth Peterson *(Centreville, VA)*
Erica Schimmel *(West Portal, CA)*
Erin Lynch *(Coppell, TX)*
Erin Short *(Palo Alto, CA)*
Greg Hernandez *(Rancho Cucamonga, CA)*
Heather Kelly *(Issaquah, WA)*
Ivan Dietrich-Neto *(Roswell, GA)*
James Kyrsiak *(Old Alabama, GA)*
James Wagner *(Los Angeles, CA)*

Jeffrey Pereira *(Scarsdale, NY)*
Jessica Loud *(Palos Verdes, CA)*
Jin Park *(Frisco, TX)*
John F. Callahan *(Parsippany, NY)*
Jonathan Smith *(Medlock Bridge, GA)*
Kaleab Tessema *(Coppell, TX)*
Katharine Galic *(Palo Alto, CA)*
Kyla Bye-Nagel *(Sterling, MD)*
Kyle Hurford *(Johns Creek, GA)*
Kyle Mesce *(Chatham, NJ)*
Lane D'Alessandro *(King of Prussia, PA)*
May-Lieng Karageorge *(Lorton, MD)*
Micah Medders *(ESC)*
Michael Fienburg *(Calabasas, CA)*
Michael Lupi *(Paramus, NJ)*
Monica Huynh *(Johns Creek, GA)*
Morgan McLoughlin *(Brentwood, CA)*
Nicole Lampl *(Calabasas, CA)*
Peter Lee *(Hamilton Mill, GA)*
Qi-lu Lin *(Parsippany, NY)*
Rachel Becker *(Burke, VA)*
Rachel Tucker *(Naperville, IL)*
Richard Faulk *(Fremont, CA)*
Robert Jedrzejewski *(Timonium, MD)*
Sam Anderson *(Paramus, NJ)*
Sarah Plunkett *(Cumming, GA)*
Sean Llewellyn *(Lynnwood, WA)*
Thach Do *(Monrovia, CA)*
Tina-Anne Mulligan *(Paramus, NJ)*
Zack Arenstein *(Livingston, NJ)*
Zafar Tejani *(Little Neck, NY)*

Version 3.0